# Gay Seattle

# Gay Seattle

## Stories of Exile and Belonging

### GARY L. ATKINS

UNIVERSITY OF WASHINGTON PRESS

Seattle and London

Copyright © 2003 by the University of Washington Press
Printed in the United States of America
Designed by Pamela Canell

Library of Congress Cataloging-in-Publication Data
Atkins, Gary, 1949–
Gay Seattle : stories of exile and belonging/Gary L. Atkins.
p.   cm.
Includes bibliographical references and index.
ISBN 0-295-98298-5 (alk. paper)
1. Gays—Washington (State)—Seattle—Social conditions.
2. Gay rights—Washington (State)—Seattle—History.
3. Gay liberation movement—Washington (State)—Seattle—History
4. AIDS (Disease)—Washington (State)—Seattle—History.
I. Title.
HQ76.3.U52 S433  2002     305.9'0664'09797772—dc21     2002014517

The paper used in this publication meets the minimum
requirements of American National Standard for Information Sciences—
Permanence of Paper for Printed Library Materials, ANSI Z39.48-1984.♾ⓔ

# CONTENTS

# ILLUSTRATIONS

# ACKNOWLEDGMENTS

Since *Gay Seattle* is an account of individuals who struggled for decades to make of the city a community where gay men and women could feel a greater sense of belonging, acknowledgment must first go to those who lived the stories told here.

At several critical points, Seattle University provided support in the form of sabbaticals or releases from classes. I am particularly grateful to Dr. Jeffrey Philpott for arrangements made to help complete the manuscript. Also, over a period of three years, students at Seattle University videotaped oral history interviews with members of Seattle's gay and lesbian community. I have drawn upon several of these tapes for insights and quotations. I have also used oral history interviews gathered by volunteers for the Alice B. Theatre and the Northwest Lesbian and Gay History Museum Project. Without these community efforts, much of the city's gay history would have been lost. The efforts of Mikala Woodward and Ruth Pettis are especially noteworthy. Also, without the assistance of many reference librarians, I would never have found the few records of gay and lesbian life in the city that do exist. Especially helpful were Karyl Winn of the University of Washington, Ed Nolan and Joy Werlink of the Washington State History Society, and Carolyn Marr at the Museum of History and Industry, Seattle.

At a more personal level, I thank my partner, Anthony Krebs, and my son, Nathan Atkins, as well as my parents, Roy and Adele Atkins, for years of encouragement and tolerance as the research and writing moved through numerous frustrations. I know that the kitchen conversations about this or that detail of history must have grown tiring. My close friend Larry Poon provided a sharp eye for word choices and the organization of the book. Finally, several fine reviewers and editors at the University of Washington Press, particularly Michael Duckworth and Jacqueline Ettinger, challenged and honed the manuscript so it could make sense to a variety of audiences, gay and heterosexual, academic and lay. To all of them, and to many not named here, I am very grateful.

# Part One

## IMAGINING AN EXILE

# *Prologue*

## From Exile to Belonging

*J*ohn Collins arrived at the street corner in downtown Seattle on a Monday night, November 25, when the sun had already been settled for almost three hours even though it was only about 7 P.M. The electric lights in the red brick buildings were pinpoints in an otherwise dark, cold evening. It was 1895, and Collins was on shore leave from the naval ship *Philadelphia,* where he worked as a fireman, having joined the crew at Mare Island in San Francisco. Seattle at the time was less than fifty years old. Collins was a youthful eighteen, and every year hundreds of men like him arrived aboard the ships that docked at what had once been just a short strip of tidal mudflat fronting steep hills, a spot native tribes called "the little crossing-over place." Thousands of other young men found their way to the flat from the logging camps set up near town to clear the greenly upholstered Northwest. Still others arrived from railroad camps where they maintained new links between Seattle's protected port and the grain fields of the Midwest.

For these young men, the mudflat offered relief from the drudgery of rain and the casualties of work. There were saloons and halls for poker, steam baths to wash away the grime. And there was sex: the first brothel had been built in 1861, just a few years after the city's founding. By the 1890s, when Collins arrived, Madame Lou Graham had opened the Northwest's most famous bordello. It was located on Washington Street, which had already become legendary as a center of action, a nineteenth-century equivalent of the Strip in Las Vegas—or at least the best available along the thousands of miles of coastline and woodlands between San Francisco and Alaska.

Collins was just a block away from Madame Lou's when he met two men slightly younger than himself selling crabs at the corner of Washington Street and Second Avenue. He stopped to banter with them. Whether Collins had aimed for that particular corner or was simply wandering, we do not know for certain. He might have heard of the People's Theater, which was located in a basement on that corner and had developed a reputation as one of Seattle's best bawdy theaters, offering women who danced and sang on stage and then strolled among the playing tables trolling for drinks. Couch-like box seats were deep enough for the men to draw the women inside and then pull curtains for whatever sexual pleasures could be had. But the People's had temporarily closed. As Collins chatted on the corner near the stairway, a third young man joined the two who were selling crabs. His name was Benjamin Layton. The night was about to take a distinctly sexual turn.

What, if anything, Collins might have been hunting for that night, we also do not know for certain. From county court records we do know what Collins found: an urban conflict over the future of Seattle that he probably knew nothing about.[1]

Not everyone in the city liked what Washington Street and the mudflat symbolized, as Collins would soon discover. Different impulses had lured different kinds of settlers to the Northwest. There were those like the pragmatic Arthur Denny, who brought his family and wanted to recreate the kind of Midwestern town he had left behind, endowing it with commercial success. There were also those like David "Doc" Maynard, who escaped from a worn marriage by moving west and then acquired a reputation for drinking. The story of the city's creation goes that when the two men surveyed the half-mile or so of mudflat, Denny set off north toward a small knoll, planting his stakes parallel to the beach, while Maynard walked in the opposite direction, following a compass heading rather than the beach line. When the two men rejoined at the end of the day, they had platted survey lines that did not match. The Northwest was a big territory, and some arguments between its few inhabitants were best passed over. Rather than redraw the lines to make the downtown grid consistent, they simply etched a diagonal line across their plats and connected the angled north-south lines, leaving later generations to cope with the sudden skew in the city's streets. In keeping with the compromise, the connecting diagonal was eventually named after a third settler, Henry Yesler, who ran the local sawmill, but for many decades it was better known as the "Deadline" and then as Skid Road. It came to symbolize the divide between two approaches to city life: Would Seattle, this frontier post, be "open" or "closed" to gambling, drinking, and sex?

The Denny knoll would house the institutions of the respectable elites: the City Hall, the courts, the police station, and the first campus of a state university, which in 1863 would instruct its students to stay out of the saloons and theaters and go to chapel instead. Below the Deadline, on Maynard's plat, saloons, cheap hotels, gambling halls, and brothels prospered, refuges for thousands of working-class single men and hundreds of single women.

As the city's sexual history began to unfold in this urban geography, the "respectables" of the knoll often locked in bitter combat with the riffraff below the Deadline, trying to control their behaviors. Sometimes, of course, the "respectables" also fought among themselves over whether the city should actually be "closed," since the prospect of making money from the mudflat's gambling, drinking, and sex was a more powerful incentive than their professed morality. Two years before Collins arrived, the national panic of 1893 had so wracked the local economy that the mudflat was now booming more with unemployment than profits, and, in that climate, the "respectables" in favor of a closed city had won two important battles. In 1894 they seized control of enough city council seats to prohibit women from being present in places where liquor was sold, such as the combination saloon/theaters like the People's at Washington and Second. If Collins had walked down the stairs into the underground theater, he would have found that its manager had fled to Spokane to open another theater out of the reach of moralists and that men like himself had turned the box seats previously used for sex into sleeping quarters.

It was the other moralist victory, won early in 1893 just as the economic panic was starting, that was about to become more pertinent to the young sailor.

According to court records, Benjamin Layton, the young man who had joined Collins and the two others on the corner, lived with his mother just a few blocks away, at Sixth and Main. His father was gone, working for the Great Northern Railroad, which had arrived in Seattle the same year as the great panic. Layton himself washed dishes at a nearby restaurant called the KP, where he usually took his meals. As the four men talked, Layton apparently told none of this to Collins. There is also no indication in the records that he mentioned his age, fifteen. Layton seems typical of the restless male teenagers who gathered at night on the mudflat. They were not really "boys" as we might call them now. Rather, they were more experienced and mature, the sons of fathers who had also gone to the camps. The young men foraged for meals where they could, took jobs to help the family income, and either cared for their mothers or else declared their separation in whatever ways they could find. On the mudflat, they presumably discovered initiation and independence, particularly after dark and particularly on Washington Street with its appeal to that free-floating male audience of whatever age, whatever marital status—and whatever sexual desire.

According to Collins's later testimony, Layton quickly made it clear that he wanted the two other young men to leave him alone with the sailor. The two left. Collins then told Layton he needed to return to his room in one of the cheap hotels a short distance away. Layton supposedly asked, "Would you please give me enough money to eat on and get a bed?" Collins said he replied, "I got no money, but you can go up and sleep with me." Layton agreed, even though he would later testify that he normally slept at his mother's home.

It was an innocent enough pick-up. In the bed-starved West, it was not uncommon for two men or two women to sleep together—although the speed of the suggestion between the two strangers might have signaled something out of the ordinary.

At the Canal Saloon on Washington, Collins first checked with the manager to get a key. Although he told Layton that he had previously rented the room, it is not certain whether he actually had or whether he was just now renting it for the two of them—in a hotel apparently known for its upstairs brothel, according to the court records. Layton waited on a nearby staircase. He must have been an attractive young man, because in the few minutes he stood there he immediately ignited the attention of a woman named Fay Carlson, who had been chatting with several other women a short way down the hall. She later tried to convince an attorney she was just a housekeeper who cleaned rooms, but under questioning she would admit that by living above the saloon, she knew she was rooming in a brothel. The implication of the attorney's questioning was clear, although Carlson denied she was a prostitute. When the two men headed down the hall to the sailor's room, Carlson excused herself from the other women and drifted slowly after them.

The two men went into Collins's room and closed the door, leaving the electric light burning. Outside in the hallway, Carlson listened. "I heard them pulling off their shoes," she would later tell the court. "I said something wrong is going on there. . . . I heard the boy making a groaning noise and from that I took a stand and went around in the hallway, put the stand against the door, and got up on the stand and looked over the transom, and I saw the boy lying on his face." Neither man had underwear on, she would testify, only their shirts, and Collins was on top of Layton.

A moment or two passed. Then Layton turned his head. To his shock, he saw Carlson peering through the window. From the look on Layton's face, Collins must have known instantly that something had gone wrong.

"Who's there?" the sailor called out. Carlson forced the transom window wider and shouted at the men, "Come out of there!"

Layton pulled on his pants, opened the door, and dashed from the room with Carlson in pursuit. She caught him and, with help from another woman in the hotel, she summoned a police officer. Meanwhile, Collins made no attempt to leave or even to dress. By the time the policeman arrived, Collins had shut off his light and fallen asleep. He would later testify, "I didn't know what I was arrested for 'til we got up to the station house."

The charge would not have anything to do with the two being teenagers, because in the nineteenth century adolescent sex was not as scandalous as today, and neither man was a "minor" in the present legal sense. Instead, the charge was a new one for Seattle.

Sodomy.

It was a moral transgression that churches had long condemned, but until just two years before Collins arrived, it had not been a crime in frontier Washington. Legislators had changed that in 1893, and now Collins faced a sentence of ten to fourteen years in the state penitentiary. A new legal weapon had suddenly publicly penetrated what had been two young men's private search for companionship on the mudflat. Collins stood accused of being among Seattle's earliest sodomites.

The story of Seattle's present gay and lesbian community can be said to start with Collins and Layton, and with others whose individual stories of same-sex affection began to be recorded at the turn of the century because of legal prosecutions arising from the 1893 law.

To be sure, there are a few earlier stories. Anthropologists have studied indicators of same-sex desire and cross-dressing among several of the Northwest's native tribes. It also appears that Chinook, the sparse trade language used by the tribes, absorbed the word that French-speaking Catholic missionaries used to denounce the practice of men loving men—*burdash,* as dictionaries of Chinook spelled the French word for sodomite, *berdache.* Additionally, there are stories of sexual freedom among early pioneers in the Northwest. For example, Sarah Yesler, the wife of the same Henry Yesler for whom the Deadline was named, is said by some historians to have had a love affair with Eliza Hurd, who once ran a dressmaking shop and who wrote passionate letters about the two of them sleeping and bathing together.[2]

However, it was with the passage of the Washington sodomy law in 1893 and with the almost simultaneous rise of a new psychiatric definition of "homosexuality" that certain of Seattle's citizens began to be singled out as a group of criminals and psychotics based on their same-sex desire. Northwest historian Norman Clark has pointed out that even though the bonds between church and state were dissolved after the American Revolution, citizens still demanded moral leadership from government and, I would add, from other social institutions such as medicine. It was not enough to have laws against actual crimes such as murder or theft. "People wanted protection also from slavery, dueling, gambling, adultery, prostitution, and drunkenness," Clark argues.[3] Add certain sexual desires, even if consensual and between adults, and the list is complete.

At the end of the nineteenth and beginning of the twentieth century, the desire for moral order in America became even more acute, as the panic of 1893 leveled the economy, as waves of immigrants from non-Anglo countries challenged virtually every social structure, and as capitalism's abuses began to be steadily revealed by muckraking reformers. Clark and other historians have explored the responses by moralists: the drives to prohibit alcohol, to eliminate saloons, and to control certain kinds of entertainment through strict licensing; the launching of campaigns both for and against sexual education; and the creation of tools like the initiative, referendum, and recall processes so that if legislators did not act, majorities could impose their own morality directly rather than balancing it against values held by a minority.

All those factors influenced, even fueled, the rise of a new community in Seattle that coalesced in reaction to the moral response. The pages that follow look at what happened in Seattle when a small and quite diverse band of its citizens became defined as legal and psychological outcasts. These outcasts, like their counterparts throughout America, faced the challenge of recreating a sense of belonging—belonging with each other and belonging within the city's own civic conversation about who constituted citizens worth hearing.

Often, the manner in which they chose to respond seemed a direct counterpoise to what was considered to be morally correct. If moralists considered the saloons to be evil, then for this emergent minority the saloons would become the first and the most basic of their community institutions. If certain kinds of theater offended the moralists, then the outcasts would make their cult heroes out of the most outrageous and theatrical of the entertainers on the mudflat—the men lipsticked and dressed in drag. If sexually expressive dancing offended the moral enforcers, then a dance of sweat and exhibitionism would be a way of constructing a new bond with one another. If moralists wanted the talk about certain kinds of sex to be carefully hedged, then being suggestive or bluntly graphic could be used to sift members of the new minority from outsiders. If the respectables did not like the People's Theater, then the People's space would become the place where the new outcasts found their first community of belonging. And if the citizens who thought they were moral wanted to use the initiative or the referendum to control homosexual behavior, then there would be recurring electoral contests to determine whether the majority would ever respect the minority.

What is most fascinating is that those who became homosexual outcasts in Seattle at the beginning of the twentieth century did actually succeed. By the end of the century, the group not only had defined a new identity for itself but had established its own public role in the city's conversations about law, health care, business, theater, church, and family. After a one-hundred-year struggle—concentrated especially in the final forty years of the twentieth century—homosexuals, who had been so in conflict with notions of progress at the beginning of the 1900s, by the end were part of the civic and moral landscape.

In the mid-1990s, I sought to learn how that had been done in Seattle. The gradual acceptance of homosexuals has often been told as a national story, but I believe it is the local stories that are more compelling. It is at the local level that neighbor confronts neighbor—or, to use a metaphor, that Denny and Maynard look each other in the eye and then decide what to do with the sudden angle that disturbs both of their visions of public order. I wanted to learn how several generations of Seattle citizens, whose sexual desire was considered a sign of mental illness and whose expression of that desire was criminal at the start of the century, had eventually claimed a public role in the discourse about who matters in a city.

Three elements were important in the research. First, most obviously, were the historical stories about individuals and important events that had played a role in the evolution of the gay community—such as the story of Collins and Layton, the passage of the sodomy law, and, more recently, the arrival of AIDS. Second, less obviously, were the challenges of communication faced by each generation—the ways in which gay men and women, coming from diverse backgrounds, learned to talk among themselves as a group, and the way they spoke publicly to the rest of the city. Finally, there was the journey the group had taken as it wove itself into the city's geography, first looking for refuge and then claiming new space.

Easily visible racial and ethnic minorities often find their identities symbolized by particular pieces of geography. In Seattle, African Americans were quickly identified with the city's Central District; Scandinavian immigrants with a village to the north called Ballard; Asian Americans with an International District east of the mudflat. In Seattle, the story of homosexuals differs in that theirs has been a "moveable" community that has relocated its symbolic center as its visibility in the city has changed. First, during its least visible stage, it became a part of the city's ongoing and very divided discourse about the Deadline area of Pioneer Square. Then, lesbians in particular claimed a role in the city's intellectual center around the University of Washington. Gay men moved into a previously established mental and physical "healing zone" on the southern edge of the city's Capitol Hill. Finally, with their visibility in the city's discourse assured, gays and lesbians claimed as their symbolic center Capitol Hill itself. There, they encountered an already existing social geography, the symbolic center of the city's Catholic community. In each "zone," the gay and lesbian story has been shaped by the story that was already present in the geography—and, in turn, has helped reshape it.

Examining this movement from exile to belonging thus incorporates history, communication, and the geographic creation of a sense of place. This is true whether it is the story of an individual that is told—the story of a gay or lesbian teenager, for example—or, as here, the story of an entire group of individuals. As the theologian Walter Bruggemann once said when writing of those whose common experience is not race, class, or religion, but living emotionally as outcasts, "the central problem is not emancipation but rootage, not separation from community but location within it, not isolation from others but placement deliberately between the generation of promise and fulfillment."[4]

The book is divided into three parts. Most of its focus—in parts 2 and 3— examines the way in which gays and lesbians first created refuges and then organized to claim a visible civic role in Seattle. Practically speaking, that effort to "come out" began in 1958 when two gay bar owners sued the city to fight police harassment of their customers and won—sort of. The most fervent political period occurred from 1958 until 1978, when gays and lesbians forged a new public identity, fought against the legal and psychiatric designations inherited from earlier in the century, and ultimately won a major political battle to protect their civil rights in the city. The following two decades marked a period of maturation, as gays and lesbians became more visible in other areas of the city's life.

Part 1 of the book serves a different function. It represents a scan of the earlier period of gay invisibility in the city. This is not a detailed review of the history of this period—Northwest researchers still have much work to do to uncover more information about early gay and lesbian history. However, part 1 aims to give a flavor of the imaginations, rhetoric, and stories of prosecution that later generations of gays and lesbians had to overcome. Without such a scan, it would be difficult to understand, for example, why a police payoff system that stemmed from the 1890s became important to gays in the 1950s and 1960s. Or why it was important in the 1970s for homosexuals to secure the repeal of the state's sodomy law from the turn of the century. Or why gays and lesbians so distrusted the local mental health system that they felt motivated to set up their own counseling structures even when psychiatry stopped viewing homosexuals as "sick." I also hope that part 1 helps those interested in Seattle's general history see connections between battles waged in the early twentieth century and those later fought by the gay and lesbian community.

As a writer trained in communication and journalism, I have tried to keep the focus on the narrative as it unfolds through time, rather than on an academic analysis of demographics or of social development theories, which would be an approach more suitable for a historian or social scientist. My hope has been that by offering people's individual voices through oral histories and public records, and by adding a few reflections for context, I could construct what might be called a "community narrative," told as much as possible from the perspective of the community itself—the gay and lesbian voices and the public accounts in the news media that were registering a steadily increasing visibility. Embedded in this overall "community story" are individual stories that have been particularly important in the oral history of Seattle's gay and lesbian community and that this book retells and documents by using archival, published, and interview sources.

By no means does this book cover all of the stories that have shaped or intertwined with a gay and lesbian presence in Seattle, nor does it attempt to address the urban history of other sexual minorities such as bisexuals or transgendered persons. I am especially aware that a great deal more historical research needs to be done to surface the voices of those in the city who were members not only of its homosexual minority, but also of its racial and ethnic minorities. Also, many of Seattle's underground stories overlap, for example among its alternative music communities, its sexual communities, its political activist communities, and its art communities. There is still a great deal of story-weaving to be done: this book is at best a thread, not a quilt.

The philosopher Martin Heidegger once asked, "What is it to dwell?" What is it to feel a sense of belonging rather than alienation? In his answer, he suggested that it is a process of communication. Each generation leaves symbols and stories, rooted in time and place.[5] Those of us in subsequent generations learn to belong by receiving and reinterpreting those stories, as well as by adding our own. My hope is that this book makes a small contribution to that effort in Seattle, not only for gays and lesbians, but for all of the city's members.

To return, then, to the story. The existing King County court record of the prosecution of John Collins is rare in that it contains an actual transcript of the testimony. This affords a brief glimpse into the legal issues that were important in such early cases: the motivation of the men involved, whether the act was consensual, and whether there had been any actual sex. More importantly, though, it tells us what happened when two young men sought affection from each other.

By the time his preliminary hearing was called, John Collins had languished in jail for almost two weeks. To get any details at all, the prosecutor had decided not to charge Benjamin Layton with participating in sodomy, but rather to use the younger man as a state witness. The prosecutor wanted the court to believe that Layton had been an unwilling victim and that Collins had forced himself on the younger boy. So Layton at first testified that Collins had grabbed him and virtually carried him down Washington Street, and that the sailor had then locked him in the bedroom and demanded that the younger boy "get down and suck me off." Then, Layton said, "he took me and turned me over on my belly and got on top of me." But Collins's defense attorney tore through that testimony. First, Layton admitted that he had voluntarily waited for Collins while the sailor got the hotel key—hardly the action of someone being forced to have sex.

"Did you try to get out [of the hotel room]?" the defense attorney asked.

"No sir," Layton replied.

"Make any noise?"

"No sir."

"Make an outcry?"

"No sir."

Later, the defense attorney questioned Layton about the actual sex between the two men. Referring to Collins's penis, he asked, "Was it hard?"

"Yes sir."

"You say his private parts didn't enter your rectum at all?"

"Well, a little."

"How much?"

"Well, I didn't measure it."

"Did you feel it?"

"Yes, I felt it."

"You had that thing done to you before, didn't you?"

"No sir."

"Were your legs spreaded [*sic*] out?"

"A little bit."

"About how much?"

"Well, I guess my feet were about a foot and a half apart."

"Didn't you wiggle and close your feet up again?"

"Yes, I wiggled around but he was on top of me and I didn't do much."

For his part, Collins denied anything at all had happened. He had simply gotten into bed, he said, "and pulled up the blankets when I saw a lady looking over the transom. . . . The boy went out and I turned the light out, took off my pants, and went to bed."

Reluctant to continue as a state witness against the sailor he had picked up, Layton was jailed after the preliminary hearing and his bail set at three hundred dollars to ensure that he would show up for the trial. Despite the size of the sum, somehow Layton found the money, posted bail, and promptly skipped town. An entire month passed, with Collins still sitting in jail since he had been unable to post his substantially higher bail of five thousand dollars. Finally, on January 7, 1896, the case ended anticlimactically—but perhaps predictably. The prosecutor reported to the court that the state's key witness, Benjamin Layton, had last been seen in North Bend, a logging town thirty miles east of Seattle. He was on a train headed east.

With no witness, the prosecutor dropped the charge against Collins. Finally, the sailor went free. But for men in Seattle who wanted affection with men, the legal exile had just begun.

# *1*

# *The Law*

## Sodomy on the Mudflat

*I*n Seattle, as elsewhere, the legal exile of homosexuals would take many forms. Men holding hands in public could be threatened with disorderly conduct. Those waiting too long at a particular corner on the mudflat known for pickups could be accused of loitering. Anyone who publicly wore clothing presumed to belong to the opposite gender could be subjected to harassment. Those in darkened theaters who kissed or touched too sensually might be prosecuted for indecent behavior.

The most extreme legal weapon, however, was the one applied to Collins and Layton: the 1893 sodomy law that made it a crime to engage in certain sexual behaviors regardless of the age of the individuals, the level of consent, or the privacy of the circumstances.

Presumably, the police never detected most sodomy since it occurred between consenting adults in closed bedrooms. In fact, the number of prosecutions in Seattle in the two decades after 1893 seems relatively small (about sixty), and those cases included a range of circumstances. Because the single legal term "sodomy" described a variety of sexual crimes, it lumped all homosexual sex together with such widely varying acts as adults molesting children, adults having sex with animals, and heterosexuals engaging in disapproved behaviors such as oral or anal intercourse. However, even if the police only infrequently used the law, an accusation of sodomy provided the cornerstone of the sexual imagination that defined all homosexuals as criminals, either because they desired forbidden sex or because they had already had it. As such, the law was the foundation for an expansive list of discriminations—for who would want a sexual lawbreaker as a police officer, a teacher, a mother, or a legislator?

It is difficult to learn much from King County's court records about the individual histories of those in Seattle who were arrested once the sodomy law began to be deployed. The existing files retain descriptions only erratically. Partly, that is an effect of the routine purging of information, but it may also be the result of a squeamishness about describing, for the record, what types of sex happened. There is, however, a detectable thread of a story, and one of the elements is that those who were prosecuted and about whom there are details most often seemed to be working-class and somehow associated with the mudflat. Presumably, sexual touch and romance between men and between women also sometimes occurred in Seattle's respectable middle and upper classes, as it may have with Sarah Yesler and Eliza Hurd. Those, apparently, were not discovered, or at least not prosecuted.

For the four decades from the 1850s until the 1890s, the territorial and then state legislatures seem to have been content to limit morals legislation to regulating marriage, adultery, fornication, and the male seduction of women—in other words, those areas that most directly relate to the management of procreation. It was not until March 1893 that the regulation expanded, when the state's third legislative session suddenly, with what appears to have been very little if any debate, made sodomy a crime. The new law was evasive about what, exactly, constituted the prohibited behavior. "Every person," it said, "who shall commit the infamous and detestable crime against nature, either with mankind or with any beast, shall be deemed guilty of sodomy." The most it explained was that "any sexual penetration, however slight, is sufficient to complete the crime against nature."

What was very clear was the severity of the punishment—"hard labor in the state penitentiary for not less than ten nor more than fourteen years"—and the urgency of state legislators in putting the law into effect: "Whereas, there is not now any statute of this state providing for the punishment of the crime against nature, an emergency is declared to exist, and this act shall take effect and be in force from and after its passage."

The codifiers placed the new law at the top of the list of crimes against morality and decency, its punishment far stiffer than for those other sex offenses. Bigamists, for example, could be sentenced to only three years in prison; adulterers, to two.

What exactly was the "crime against nature" that could not be defined? Two legal scholars, Karl Bowman and Bernice Engle, have written that "of the body of sex laws, sodomy laws are the most confused and vague." Among Christians, they pointed out, the crime was "peccatum illud horribile"—too horrible to be mentioned—and so, in the law, it simply was not. Wayne and Alice Bartee note in *Litigating Morality* that "courts and legislators agreed that the crime of sodomy was of such a 'disgusting nature' that a description of it in detail in either a law, in a criminal indictment, or in a court opinion would constitute obscenity."[1] That may be one reason the surviving King County court records are so spartan in their descriptions.

Sir Edward Coke, who presented a legal treatment of the subject in his essay "Of Buggery, or Sodomy" in 1628, had focused on defining the word as meaning sex with animals or anal intercourse. However, since nineteenth-century religion and medicine (and thus law) tended to assume that the only natural sexual instinct was a desire for procreation, to pursue any other sexual desires—for pleasure, intimacy, or just physical release—was also considered perverse. Broadly speaking, then, the "detestable crime against nature" could include almost any form of nonprocreative sex, be it bestiality, anal sex, or ordinary oral sex. Turn-of-the-century courts in America adopted what the Bartees call a "decorous language" approach that allowed them to expand the definition as they wished, without having to graphically describe specific behaviors.

Washington's first law could have been applied equally to oral and to anal sex, although the law was sufficiently unclear that this may have been a matter for local prosecutors to decide. It also did not make any distinctions about the sexual orientation of the offenders. It applied to heterosexuals as well as to homosexuals. However, at least in Seattle, a survey of court records indicates that the early arrests and prosecutions were overwhelmingly of males having or attempting anal sex with males.

Exactly why Washington State legislators decided to add the law in 1893 is not at all clear. Neither the legislative journal for the state house of representatives nor that for the state senate describes any debate. Nor do any legislative committee records survive at the state archives. The Seattle newspapers do not appear to have printed any stories about the new law or why it might have been needed.

What is known is that the house Judiciary Committee initiated the bill under the chairmanship of Albert E. Mead, then a youthful thirty-one-year-old from rural Whatcom County next to the Canadian border. Mead, who represented an area of logging camps and small farms, would later become governor and a significant figure among the moralists who wanted to eliminate the state's saloons. The full house passed the main clause on February 28, by a vote of seventy to one, the sole dissenter being a representative from tiny Garfield County in southeastern Washington. His "nay" was not explained, and, defeated on the main vote, even he joined to make the passage of the emergency clause unanimous. The bill was then adopted by the state senate at the last minute on the final evening of the session, March 9, 1893. Twenty-five senators voted for it; nine others either abstained or were absent.[2]

The unanimity underscores just how powerful the religious heritage against non-reproductive sexual behaviors was at the time, even in what had been a remote hinterland. The religious proscriptions passed easily into law.

But why 1893, and not earlier?

Perhaps the legislature simply noticed a criminal code oversight already addressed by Eastern states and decided to play catch-up. The Northwest was undergoing a transformation from its frontier nature toward a more urban and industrial society by then, and as historian Carlos Schwantes observed, "the last thing many a northwestern urbanite wanted was to be viewed as an uncouth country bumpkin by easterners."[3] Schwantes was not referring to the sodomy law specifically, but the control of sexual behaviors could certainly be considered part of becoming a more settled and "civilized" society.

Perhaps, too, the arrival of the state's second transcontinental railroad—the Great Northern in Seattle on March 2, 1893—prompted nervousness about how a railroad moves not only products but immigrants and, with them, passions. Historian Norman Clark, in *The Dry Years*, notes that the coming of the transcontinental railroads transformed Washington's population and industry enormously: In Seattle alone, the population would almost double between 1890 and 1900, from about 42,000 to 80,000. That pattern would accelerate in the following decade; by 1910, the city held almost 240,000.

Certainly, in 1893 the sexual and emotional climate in the Northwest was tightening as medical doctors began making more warnings about how the new urban middle class should properly raise children. In mid-February 1893, for example, the *Seattle Press-Times* carried a caution against two persons habitually sleeping in the same bed "no matter who they are." That had been customary on the frontier. The article specifically pointed to two sisters, ages fifteen and seventeen, who had usually fallen asleep in each other's arms. A medical doctor had put an end to that, and the article noted approvingly that "two pretty brass bedsteads side by side offered propinquity . . . but prevented contact" between the two girls. Another article helpfully warned that holding and rocking babies could lead to liver and kidney disease and quoted a doctor as saying that "thousands of people are being rocked to death, slowly but surely." Friendly touching, sexual or not, was being constrained in accord with Victorian concepts more established in the East (though already being challenged there by the emergence of those popular urban leisure pastimes of going to the movies and climbing on roller coasters).[4]

Finally, perhaps the early indicators were clear enough that later in the year the United States would suffer its greatest economic collapse thus far, the panic of 1893, and that the Northwest and Seattle would be especially hard hit. Just three weeks before the senate passage of the sodomy bill, the *Press-Times* had carried a story about panic on Wall Street and a rush to sell railroad securities. Soon enough, thousands of men who went to the mudflat in search of entertainment would have no jobs. It was a world, in other words, where everything seemed to be shifting, and order appeared to be in short supply.

Six months after the state legislature adopted the law, Seattle saw what was apparently its first sodomy prosecution—or at least the first where records have survived.[5] These particular records are sparse in their details, noting only that a man named Charles Wesley was accused of the "intent to know" Eddie Kalberg, "a male person." Convicted on October 25, 1893, Wesley was sentenced to seven years "at hard labor" at the new state penitentiary in eastern Washington. The punishment was actually less than the ten-year minimum specified in the law, so, based on comparisons to issues that arose in later sodomy trials, it is possible to speculate that Wesley and Kalberg had engaged in an act of consensual sex and possibly one or both had been drinking. Juries in later cases would sometimes express uncertainty about how responsible they should hold drunk defendants. The sodomy may have only been attempted, but not completed. There might have been a dispute about what actually constituted "penetration, however slight." Later court debates centered on whether a penis lying between buttocks, or touching an anus but not actually inside, or touching lips but not actually in a mouth, constituted penetration. Perhaps, as was common in that day, the two men had shared a bed in a cheap boardinghouse and one had mistaken the other's intent in a groggy hug. Or, since the boardinghouses offered little privacy, Wesley and Kalberg may have actually been enjoying themselves when they were discovered by one of the two witnesses who testified before the grand jury (the defendants' testimony is not in the record).

In 1895, two months before the sailor Collins and young Layton ever met each other, the problem of defining a "good" sodomy case became apparent in a charge against Oscar Brunson, described in the court records as a "deep sea sailor in this port," and a friend of his named J. P. MacKendray. The two met on the mudflat and, according to a prosecution memo, "together they went about from one saloon to another, indulging in social drinks." That night, they returned to MacKendray's shack on the mudflat, and Brunson drank another beer. For the court, Brunson would later claim that the final drink was the one that "occasioned a state of stupefaction that grew upon him after retiring," a stupefaction that made him unable to resist MacKendray who "during the night had carnal knowledge of [Brunson] against the order of nature." The type of "knowledge"—oral, anal, or simply masturbatory—is not specified in the record.

Three days later, again drunk and having second thoughts about what had happened, Brunson visited the prosecutor, who was not impressed by his story. But rather than stop there, Brunson then forced the issue by filing a complaint in justice court. The prosecutor still lacked enthusiasm for the case, even though here there was a willing complainant, something that would be missing two months later with Collins and Layton. The problem as the prosecutor saw it: Brunson was six feet tall and weighed more than two hundred pounds. MacKendray, on the other hand, was "undersized," according to a memo asking that the case be dismissed. Brunson, the prosecutor reasoned, was well able to defend himself against whatever had happened. Although the state law technically allowed no exceptions, in this case, the prosecutor seems to have reasoned that no judge or jury would convict since the sex could be construed as consensual, even if Brunson now felt guilty about it.

MacKendray spent a month in jail waiting for the prosecutor to decide.[6]

As well as attracting pragmatic businessmen and transient male laborers, Seattle from the start of its history also tended to draw a third type of immigrant: idealists who saw in the remote beauty of the Northwest the potential for utopia. One of the earliest proponents of the idea that the Northwest could be a new city on a hill was Theodore Winthrop, the great-great-great grandson of the first Puritan governor of Massachusetts. In 1853, twenty-five years old and with a Yale degree in hand, he traveled through the region, rhapsodizing in his book *Canoe and Saddle* that with "great mountains as companions of daily life," those who lived in the

Northwest would carry "to a newer and grander New England of the West a full growth of the American Idea." That new western utopia, he believed, would one day "crystallize" and then would "elaborate new systems of thought and life." Toward those voices already in the land—the Native Americans, for example, or sailors and loggers wandering about as a male fringe group driven by testosterone—Winthrop held a kind of anthropological bemusement at best and, more commonly, derision. The Klallam guide who helped him navigate Puget Sound and who later became the tribe's chief, Winthrop caustically dubbed a drunk and a scoundrel. The Klallams themselves were "bow-legged" and "a sad-colored Caravaggio brown, through which salmon-juices exude." In general, the actual people of the Northwest smelled of too much smoke from too many campfires and were permanently grunged from the rain. After a journey that lasted all of eleven days, Winthrop left the task of cleaning up utopia to others.[7]

Some of those who later followed Winthrop's trek to the Northwest practiced separatism, withdrawing into their own communal retreats in the forests or the cities to create different sorts of relationships or economics. That was a theme that would be important a century later to the city's separatist lesbians and radical gay men. They also would set up either farm communes or urban collectives based on analyses that rejected capitalism and evaluated monogamous heterosexual marriage as a capitalistic institution.

Other idealists turned into fervent crusaders, seeking to ensure that Seattle would be a New Jerusalem rather than a Babylon. Norman Clark and other historians have pointed out that as one century ended and another began, these moral crusaders were able to capitalize on the growing middle-class angst about order in Seattle. The public talk was not focused directly on sodomy, of course—since it was a crime not discussed publicly. Rather, the talk focused more on who was and was not to be considered a desirable citizen. In the campaigns, the symbolic target—the metaphor for all evil, whether gambling, drinking, or sex—became the very institution that would one day provide the foundation for a public gay community in Seattle: the saloon. And among the most fervent of the anti-saloon crusaders would be a young man who arrived in Seattle in 1884, George Cotterill.

Cotterill had emigrated from England, and as a youth in a New Jersey high school had watched the skyline of New York City take shape. He was particularly impressed by two pieces of architecture, the Trinity Church spire and the Tribune Tower. They were symbolic of the religion and public politics that would characterize his life. Cotterill was bright, articulate, and well educated. He had been valedictorian of his high school class and had trained as a surveyor. He would eventually write a book called *Climax of a World Quest,* in which, like Winthrop three decades earlier, he would portray the Northwest's waters and mountains as a kind of ultimate moment of divine creation. Historian Roger Sale notes that Cotterill's writing "is redolent with the conviction that this area [the Northwest] was created by God to be the best that Europeanized white people . . . would ever know." At first, Cotterill sought to create order in the Northwest through civil engineering, but when that was not enough, he turned to politics as a way to engineer social behavior.[8]

An entry in Cotterill's personal papers chronicles his journey west and his arrival in the Northwest: "With Horace Greeley's urge—'Go West Young Man'—armed with three years surveyor's training and a high school diploma, I followed the new 'Iron Trail' of the Northern Pacific to the 'jumping off place.'" That happened to be the town of Tacoma, thirty miles south of Seattle. There, he helped lay out the town cemetery, but, he sniffed, "Unfortunately my employer in that enterprise collected the entire compensation and deposited it in all the saloons of Tacoma and vicinity." Even as a teenager, Cotterill disliked saloons.

On December 31, 1884, when he was just eighteen and one of those young men drifting around the Northwest, Cotterill climbed aboard a tugboat for the three-hour ride north from Tacoma to Seattle. As he rounded a point into Elliott Bay and saw the city, he would later write, "Seattle seemed indeed a queenly crown of brilliancy, suddenly revealing a thousand gems against the background of fir-clad hills."

Utopia. Except for one thing.

"The south side of the wharf was a motley array of waterfront 'hotels,' lodging houses, saloons, etc., a line of shacks perched on piles, forming a gauntlet from the wharf to the shore, to be run by all going or coming from the steamers."[9] As Winthrop had before him, Cotterill felt he was beholding a paradise—except for that sullied geography below the Deadline and the gauntlet that ran up Washington Street.

At first he became an assistant city engineer, designing more than twenty-five miles of bike paths that, with the advent of the car, would eventually become the basis of Seattle's boulevards. But he longed to have even more impact, and so in 1900 Cotterill ran for mayor. One of his cards from a later campaign shows how he liked to promote himself: "Every good citizen movement," it said, "every contest for the people's rights against the abuse of special interests, every struggle for law and order against vice and crime, every election where moral issues were at stake—in all these . . . George F. Cotterill has tried to do a man's work wherever duty called for service or sacrifice."

A few years earlier, Cotterill might have won, but by 1900 the ever-shifting battle over morality in Seattle—which had produced the earlier victories for the more respectable classes—had dramatically shifted toward a new embrace of the saloon and all the evils it represented.

Enter a second settler, of a very different type.

John Considine was born in Chicago in 1868 and drifted into Seattle in 1889, just five years after Cotterill had arrived. Historian Murray Morgan notes that at the time, Considine was like the city: "young, tough, promising, and nearly broke." He was a Catholic, schooled by nuns and priests, a graduate of St. Mary's College in Kansas. He had wanted to be an actor.[10]

First and foremost, John Considine was about style and show, quite a contrast

Four men's actions set the stage for Seattle's homosexual citizens. Clockwise from upper left: State Rep. Albert E. Mead chaired the house Judiciary Committee that wrote the first Washington sodomy law in 1893; State Sen. George Cotterill revised it in 1909; the Rev. Mark Matthews crusaded against sex and drink in Pioneer Square; John Considine operated the raucous People's Theater. *(MSCUA, University of Washington Libraries, UW 18857; Museum of History and Industry, Seattle; MSCUA, University of Washington Libraries, UW 18856; Museum of History and Industry, Seattle)*

to his now twenty-something peer in town, Cotterill. A later photograph published in a copy of *Washington Magazine,* after he had become successful, shows Considine looking like a round-faced altar boy with slicked hair and a babyish soft jaw. For the photographer, he dressed conservatively in a dark bow tie and pin-striped suit, but when he walked the streets, according to Morgan, Considine knew the value of accessories: sparkling ties, white gloves, brown derbies, gray rain capes, and, to top it all off, a brindle bulldog attached to a silver chain. He was, Morgan wrote, "a show-man," "a good talker," "a hard man to forget." Even though he would run saloons, he shied from gambling himself and preferred ice water and chewing gum to liquor.

By 1891, Considine had started managing the People's Theater, underground at the corner of Washington and Second. When, in 1894, the Seattle City Council passed its barmaid ordinance declaring that women could not be employed where intoxicating drinks were sold, Considine fled to Spokane to continue to run the combined saloon/theaters. After the legislature followed with a similar statewide law, Considine challenged its constitutionality. He lost. But then one of those quirks of history made the loss—as well as the enforcement of the barmaid laws and George Cotterill's hopes of reforming Seattle—temporarily irrelevant.

Gold.

As quickly as the panic of 1893 had destroyed the Northwest's economy and encouraged the moralist crackdown on the mudflat, the Klondike gold rush of 1897 restored wealth and exploded prohibitions, especially in Seattle, which would become the major embarkation point for the miners headed north. Suddenly, the mudflat boomed again. Young men crammed into the hotels until there were no more beds. They thronged the saloons. Morgan described John Considine's return from his Spokane exile to the People's Theater, now run by Mose Goldsmith, in late December 1897:

> He paused for a moment . . . to watch the men going down the steps into the People's Theater. Even on a miserable midwinter night, the place was drawing well: young sports out on the town, loggers in for the holidays, businessmen, and most of all, lonesome Easterners waiting for ships bound for Alaska. . . . He went down the steps, paid fifty cents for a seat near the stage, ordered a glass of "water, plain unadorned water," from an amazed waitress, and turned his attention to the crowd. The place was full. The bar, which stretched along one wall, was crowded; three bartenders were kept busy. Nearly every table was occupied. Women with painted cheeks and skirts nearly up to their knees roamed the room, smiling at the patrons; from time to time the girls went to the stage and sang a loud song or danced an awkward dance. From the curtained box seats in the low balcony came laughter and shouts and giggles and, most impor-tant, a steady ringing of bells as the box-hustlers summoned waiters with drinks.[11]

Forty years later, it would be the city's gays and lesbians who would be cram-ming that basement and crowding the bar, and a hundred years later it would be the city's "goths" and industrial music rockers. Drink, show, and sexual challenge—everything that settlers such as Cotterill disliked—were what that underground basement would come to represent in the city's history. For the moment, Considine wanted the People's back. Morgan notes that Goldsmith, who had reopened the theater, had spent about three thousand dollars cleaning it up, and had already netted that amount in two weeks of catering to the gold rushers. But Goldsmith held only a verbal contract with the building's owners. Considine instead negotiated a written contract and was back in business by February 1898. By July 1899, the *Post-Intelligencer* observed of the corner at Washington and Second that business had boomed and "every evening, week in and week out, the beauties of the drama are unfolding to the admiring gaze of audiences." Admittance cost ten cents.[12]

According to Morgan, Considine's secret for success was to separate the tasks of acting and of serving drinks, rather than having the same waitresses do it all. In his darkened underground, he staged shows that sometimes featured national attractions, like the famous "coochee-coochee" dancer and stripper Little Egypt, who had perfected the art of the shimmy dance, wriggling her body to slinky music.

Considine also created another not-so-secret reason for success. The barmaid ordinance was still on the books. To ensure that it would not be enforced against the People's, he started paying the police patrol officers for their "tolerance."

As far as is known, Considine was heterosexual—he married and began a theatrical lineage that continued right down to his grandson Tim Considine, an actor in Walt Disney's *Spin and Marty* series in the 1950s as well as television's *My Three Sons*. Yet John Considine became important to the story of Seattle's homosexuals, for four reasons: First, historically, he believed that there was an imaginative role for sex and theater on the mudflat far different from the one propounded by moralists like George Cotterill. Second, geographically, Considine more than anyone else launched the corner at Washington and Second into its role as a sexual and social meeting place. Third, Considine mothered in Seattle the particular type of entertainment laced with sexuality that the city's gay men and women would eventually use to move from their individual feelings of exile toward more public networks of belonging—the communication called vaudeville. Finally, he helped initiate the police payoff schemes that, decades later, would at first protect the emergent gay underground on the mudflat and then actively attempt to manage it.

As the century turned, John Considine, at age thirty-two, represented one imagination about the role of sex in Seattle; George Cotterill, at age thirty-four, another.

Gold had made too much of a difference for Cotterill to win his bid for mayor. Too few wanted to risk the city's new prosperity, which was based not only on the sales of outfitting equipment to the miners but on their entertainment while they waited for ships. The impact on law enforcement, including sodomy enforcement, was immediate. Richard Berner observed in *Seattle 1900–1920* that "after the gold rush . . . mechanisms for maintaining law and order broke down. Political leaders hesitated to exercise their public responsibility. The police department, when not directly in league with the 'vice lords' simply found itself outnumbered."[13]

During this period, the nature of the sodomy charges prosecuted in the city's courts seems to have changed. For two years, 1897 and 1898, for example, there is no record of any sodomy prosecution whatsoever in King County, even as thousands of young men jammed the mudflat's hotels, gambling halls, theaters, and brothels. That the Seattle police could not find a single case of oral or anal sex to prosecute, whether consensual or nonconsensual, homosexual or heterosexual, begs for incredulity.

From 1899 until 1904, once the initial rush had passed, nineteen cases of sodomy or attempted sodomy were docketed, but most of those involve specific statements that a child, often a preadolescent child, was the victim. Typical, for example, was a prosecution against a man named Andrew Cleary who was said to have "with a nickel enticed a six year old girl" into an alleyway behind a saloon in an apparently unsuccessful attempt to get her "to suck his penis." That was a great distance from the sex that had happened between Collins and Layton, Wesley and Kalberg, or MacKendray and Brunson—an indication of just how flexible the charge of sodomy could be and just how adaptable it was to the ever-changing social and economic climate.

Although Cotterill was not elected mayor in 1900, the moralist forces did succeed in provoking the city council into an investigation of the city's tolerance of the gold rush vices. A new Seattle police chief, William Meredith, who had once been John Considine's friend but had fallen out with him, had begun enforcing the barmaid ordinance—but, according to Morgan, only on John Considine's side of Washington Street. Incensed, Considine told the council committee that he had paid one of Meredith's officers five hundred dollars and then had followed the man and seen him give the money to the police chief. Meredith counterattacked by testifying that Considine was a bad influence on young women. When the council eventually dismissed Meredith for overseeing a department where officers accepted bribes, he bought a sawed-off shotgun, stalked Considine to a drugstore just north of the People's Theater, and tried to kill him. Considine's brother, Tom, instead killed Meredith first.

After that brief and violent emergence of the payoff scheme into public view, it went back underground. For his part, Considine began to diversify and buy more respectable properties north of the Deadline.

In 1902, George Cotterill tried for a congressional seat, campaigning again on an anti-saloon platform. Again, he lost. For the moment, Cotterill and others who stood against the saloons and the denizens south of the Deadline needed help in Seattle's seesaw battle with morality. They were about to get it.

Style could be met with style.

He was six-foot-five and some say never weighed much more than about 160 pounds. He dressed in long black waistcoats, more like a preacher of the eighteenth century. He left his curly hair long beneath his black hat. As one of his biographers noted, Mark Matthews knew how to use both his body and his voice. Even before the members of Seattle's First Presbyterian Church met him in 1901, Matthews had cut a reputation as a southern preacher through Georgia and Tennessee. He was called a "prince of platform speakers," a man whose sermons fairly bubbled with denunciations, humor, and rebuke. The church, as he was fond of saying, was his "force" and not his "field," by which he meant that parishioners were not in church simply to be an audience. They were his army; he was the general.[14]

He arrived in the Northwest in 1902. Seattle, Matthews fervently believed, had the most important spiritual role of any city. "Ours is the greatest field for Christian work on the continent," he would say in a sermon in 1906. "This is the gateway and through our gates thousands are marching to and fro. . . . More good things could be successfully launched in this city without opposition than in any other city in the world."

His target was clear: "Regarding the saloon, the gambling den . . . and the house of prostitution . . . they are sin's coffin houses where souls, bodies and minds are consigned to an everlasting and horrible death. . . . Victims fill niches in the chambers of death. . . . So it is without question the duty of upright citizens to exterminate these dens of vice."

Again: "The liquor traffic is the most fiendish, corrupt, and hell-soaked institution that ever crawled out of the slime of the eternal pit."

To anyone who opposed his vision of a moral Seattle, Matthews thundered: "We have a great city and we are going to build a much greater one. . . . No one dare raise his hand or voice in opposition to our future work or to the city's progress. Should a croaker be found or a pessimist discovered, let him be taken without the walls of the city and there executed. He has no right to live among such progressive people." Quiet compromise in the style of Denny and Maynard was not Matthews's "progressive" approach.

Under Matthews's guidance and his command, the First Presbyterian Church in what was still a remote northwestern corner would become the largest in the world. Those who wanted a more respectable city had found their voice, and the results would soon show.

In May 1902, just a few months after Matthews arrived in the city, the *Seattle Times* published a full-page article on the necessity of the "removal of the Tenderloin," which it identified as an area of the mudflat south of Yesler Way, north of Jackson Street, and between First and Third Avenues. That included places like the People's, Madame Lou's brothel, and the old Canal Saloon where Collins and Layton had found a respite. "Within that district," the newspaper noted, "are located all the larger public gambling houses and kindred resorts of the city of the more notorious character, and within it has gathered for the past six years that motley class of men and women who are attracted by the glamour, the fascination or vicious- ness of such surroundings."

By 1905, encouraged by Matthews, evangelists such as the Reverend Wilbur Chapman were organizing tent revivals on the northern edge of the Deadline and sending waves of marchers into the red-light district. The *Times* reported in April that "thousands of pure-minded men and women from homes on the hills viewed for the first time in their lives the haunts of the low and the depraved." "The preach- ers," the *Times* said, "with uncovered heads and uplifted eyes led their followers right into the very core and heart of the vicious and depraved part of Seattle."[15]

By 1906, Cotterill was running for election again, and this time he won, voted the state senator for a Republican-heavy district on Queen Anne Hill even though he ran as a Democrat. The area was then just developing as a middle-class neigh- borhood peering down on the raucous waterfront from a safe distance to the north. To the city's middle class, the *Seattle Mail and Herald* proclaimed, Cotterill was "a ray of light," one of the "friends of reform and purity."

Indeed, city historians have usually referred to Cotterill and Matthews as part of the Northwest's version of the nationwide "Progressive Movement." The two men urged and engineered the state's adoption of the tools of direct democracy, the initiative and referendum processes by which majorities of citizens could directly write or overturn legislation. Cotterill supported women's suffrage. Matthews pro- moted programs to help the poor. But sometimes their zeal for regulating behav- ior through law could become embarrassing, with Matthews hiring private detectives to spy on government officials or, in his later years, going so far as to twice ask J. Edgar Hoover, the director of the Federal Bureau of Investigation, for an FBI badge that he could use to "assist" the bureau, presumably in making his own arrests. Hoover tactfully declined.

Opponents of the two men had a different view of them. The *Seattle Patriarch* denounced Cotterill as a "demagogue" and a "tool of degeneracy," a fanatic bent only on seizing power over individual lives. "Pretensions for purity," the paper sniffed in November 1907. By 1909 and 1910 it was attacking Cotterill for his "squeaky voice," which, it suggested, meant "a sneaky character." Even Cotterill's facial hair came under attack, as the paper printed satirizations referring to him as a "bearded effeminate." For those on the mudflat, Cotterill and Matthews rep- resented trouble because so many of the reforms they sought—whether women's suffrage or letting majorities of voters ban liquor—pointed in only one direction: creating a majority vote that would eliminate alcohol and the saloons.[16]

Public pronouncements from Cotterill and Matthews presumed that vice in Seattle was heterosexual. For example, Matthews's sermons—although full of warnings about how drink, smoke, and sex in general could lead one astray—do not explic- itly target homosexual sodomy in the way that conservative ministers in the city would by the 1960s. The silence is not surprising, of course, since to have been explicit about sodomy would have required describing a crime that was "peccatum illud horribile."

Slowly, though, after 1904, Seattle's prosecutors seem to have turned more vigilantly against men having sex with men. At the very least, they learned two lessons about prosecuting sodomy cases where both parties had consented. First, they began collecting physical evidence. The court records indicate that the Seattle police scavenged in bedrooms, gathering circumstantial evidence such as sheets and jars of lubricant that might serve as corroborative physical evidence of male sex.[17] They also started putting the "innocent victims" in jail right alongside the alleged criminals to keep the future Benjamin Laytons from hopping the next freight out of town. That jailing of both men became a strong incentive to turn consenting participants into stool pigeons, willing to provide state's evidence against bed partners.

The change coincides with the election of Kenneth Mackintosh as prosecutor in 1904 and his selection of George Vanderveer as his deputy prosecutor. Mackintosh and Vanderveer had attended Stanford Law School together, and Vanderveer would develop a reputation for prowling below the Deadline. His biographers Lowell Hawley and Ralph Potts note in *Counsel for the Damned* that Vanderveer was fascinated by what Mark Matthews had taken to calling the Skid Road district of Seattle. "He studied its people," they wrote, "and tried to understand them: how they lived and how they operated and how they looked upon life." But this was not an attempt to truly understand their perspectives. Instead, Hawley and Potts add, it was to understand "how they planned and executed crimes." The authors also suggest that even Vanderveer "never could have told just how much of his interest was inspired by his desire to gather knowledge for the better execution of his job, and how much of it was inspired by personal fascination and morbid curiosity."[18]

Mostly, Vanderveer waged a public crusade against political graft and illegal gambling, but, along the way, he seemed to come across more sodomy cases than his predecessors had. In November 1904, for example, a man named Pat Morrow was arrested for having what was called "a venereal affair" with seventeen-year-old Alfred Franseen. The fact that Franseen was not a preadolescent child may in itself indicate a shift in prosecution focus, as do the details of what was clearly a consensual affair—if it was an affair at all. Vanderveer told the court in an affidavit that he had a witness who would testify that he had found Morrow and Franseen in a bed in the downtown Phoenix Hotel. The witness "examined the sheet on the bed where Franseen was lying and found a damp stain of Vaseline and semen, and he found Vaseline on said Franseen's rectum." (The court records do not explain how the witness came to examine Franseen's rectum.) The witness had the sheet and the bottle of Vaseline, Vanderveer said, and would produce them for the court. Clothes had also been seized as evidence.

Both Morrow and Franseen were held in jail for three months. Then, in February 1905, Vanderveer's boss, Mackintosh, reluctantly reported to the court that Franseen "has always persistently stated that no crime was committed and that his prior contradictory statements to the police officers were extorted from him by threats and duress." The prosecutor's office had "tried in every legitimate manner to persuade said Alfred Franseen to confirm the story which he heretofore told the police officers, but has been unable to do so." Even the sheets and clothes did not help. "Extensive analytic and microscopic examination" had been made, but the sodomy charge was impossible to prove.

The court dismissed the case, noting that Franseen should be paid $150 for the ninety-six days he had been locked up as a so-called "witness."[19]

Later, the police and prosecutors had better luck. First, in 1906, they arrested and successfully convicted a man from Portland, Philip McGuire. He had sodomized a "male child" named Herbert Carpenter—his age is not given, but he may have been a teen from the mudflat since the two were found in a downtown hotel about 1 A.M.[20]

A few months later, in 1907, police arrested Thomas Longbottom, a worker for the Great Northern Railroad. From the testimony on his behalf, Longbottom appears to have been a rather pleasant worker at the freight yards. The court records do not tell his age, but they do say that he often paid social calls to a single mother by the name of Jenner who was raising several sons and daughters and living in a working-class neighborhood north of downtown Seattle. One of the woman's children, a fourteen-year-old named Albert, often visited Longbottom at the freight yards, sometimes skipping school to do so.

On a Monday afternoon, February 25, 1907, young Albert was there when two police officers suddenly appeared and forced Longbottom to jail. Curious, Albert followed along. Longbottom would later say that in the jail, he was subjected to curses from the police officers who ordered him to plead guilty to sodomy. According to the somewhat redundant charges, Longbottom did "wickedly, diabolically, and against the order of nature . . . commit and perpetrate feloniously, wickedly and diabolically the detestable crime of nature" with a teen named Leroy Spink. While the descriptions of the criminal behavior were not getting any more specific, the condemnatory rhetoric surrounding them had definitely grown more Matthews-like.

Spink was described in the court papers as a "thoroughly incorrigible, dishonest, and bad boy" who had been convicted of breaking and entering a store and sentenced to a reform school. But he was being presented as a credible witness anyway.

"You'd better plead guilty or we'll make it hot for you," Longbottom claimed one of the officers told him. When he asked what would happen if he confessed, the officer supposedly answered, "I'll fix it so you'll only get a short sentence."

At first, Longbottom refused to plead guilty. In an affidavit sworn later, he said that one of the officers then struck him across the side of the face with his fist and continued to curse him. Eventually, under the pressure, Longbottom relented and agreed to plead guilty. He was never allowed to contact an attorney during the initial questioning.

Outside the jail, young Albert Jenner had made the mistake of trying to see what was happening to his friend. A police officer named Corbett saw the opportunity to corner him and demand that he testify against Longbottom or else be sent to reform school. The potential charge: Albert had skipped school both when he played at the freight yards and when he followed his friend Longbottom to the jail.

Frightened, Albert quickly agreed to testify that Longbottom had also had sex with him. The testimony from the two young men, Jenner and Spink, was recorded at the arraignment and in affidavits. At the trial, a judge sentenced Longbottom to twelve years in the state penitentiary.

A few days afterward, now free from police detainment, Albert recanted his testimony. He swore another affidavit in which he said that Longbottom had "never committed any indecent assault upon me or any assault anytime . . . [and] never used any bad words to me or in my presence." In fact, Albert said, Longbottom had always been a "kind" man.

It was too late. There is no indication in the court records that Longbottom's sentence was ever reconsidered.[21]

By 1908, significant political control had returned to those urging more respectable morality in Seattle and in the state. George Vanderveer would replace Kenneth Mackintosh as chief prosecutor. Mark Matthews had established himself as Seattle's most powerful crusader. George Cotterill was one of the leaders of the state senate. Albert Mead, who had chaired the judiciary committee that had written the state's first sodomy law, was governor. And an organization called the Anti-Saloon League, supported by all of them, was about to engineer the defeat of many of its legislative opponents who had been resisting the idea that local communities should be allowed to go dry.

Meanwhile, the upper floors of the building that housed the People's Theater had been gutted by fire, and John Considine, perhaps wisely sensing that his future lay elsewhere, had already made a deal with New York politico Tim Sullivan to create a national chain of vaudeville theaters.

The corner at Washington and Second was quieting down.

When the 1909 state legislature convened, two issues dominated the agenda: the Anti-Saloon League's plan to give each county the right to vote dry and thereby eliminate saloons, and a proposed revision of the state's criminal code. The successful anti-saloon effort has drawn the most attention from regional historians, since it was one more step toward statewide and then national Prohibition. Cotterill helped craft that new law. Less commented on has been Cotterill's other effort: a new criminal code that contained many provisions putting the state in firm control of sexual expression. Vanderveer had chaired a commission to propose changes; Cotterill took charge of pushing the changes through the legislature.[22]

The new code Cotterill proposed in 1909 was remarkable for its scope of sexual and moral prohibitions. It outlawed all forms of abortion and made anyone assisting or participating, including doctors, midwives, or the pregnant women themselves, subject to five years in the state penitentiary. It instructed saloon owners to keep their interiors visible from the street so the police could watch the activities of those inside. It made boisterous sports games on Sundays a crime. It defined "lewdness" as a felony and redefined all public nudity, whatever the context, as lewd and indecent—a break with custom and privacy in a wilderness society where it had always been permissible to at least swim naked at an isolated lake or river. It declared common-law heterosexual marriages "lewd and vicious," even though they were rather customary in a frontier society. The code revisions also punished any male seduction of an unmarried female, even if she was an adult and even if she consented. The offending male in the relationship could be sentenced to five years in the state prison unless he agreed to properly marry the woman and stay with her at least three years. If he left her sooner, he could still be sent to prison.

Cotterill did not neglect the definition of sodomy either. New wording was added to the law, going into much greater detail than the 1893 legislation that had simply banned the "crime against nature." Section 204 of the new code read: "Every person who shall carnally know in any manner any animal or bird or who shall carnally know any male or female person by the anus, or with the mouth or tongue; or who shall voluntarily submit to such carnal knowledge; or who shall attempt sexual intercourse with a dead body, shall be guilty of sodomy and shall be punished by imprisonment in the state penitentiary for not more than 10 years."

In one respect, Cotterill's provision was progressive. It now spelled out exactly what the crime of sodomy was. That specificity would make Washington one of only three states that, even as late as 1956, detailed the previously unspeakable crime.

On the other hand, Cotterill and his allies precluded the possibility that judges and juries of the future might gradually narrow the vague definition as sexual customs and tolerance changed. And, just in case there had been any doubt about whether the original sodomy law meant to criminalize oral as well as anal sex, Cotterill and his allies specified that both were illegal. They also removed the need to prove penetration, a requirement that had bedeviled prosecutors. It was enough, now, if the partners simply "knew" one another "by the anus, or with the mouth or tongue." A wrongly placed kiss or positioning of an erection was all that was technically needed.

Although the punishment for sodomy, at a maximum of ten years, was slightly reduced from that allowed by the 1893 law, it was still greater than the punishment for forcibly raping a woman, which earned only half as much time in jail.

Finally, as if banning the acts themselves was not enough, Cotterill's new code also prohibited any printed discourse on them. Section 209 warned that those who published "any detailed account" of "the commission or attempted commission" of sodomy, or other sex crimes like adultery or seduction, were guilty of a misdemeanor. That included any publication about "evidence of indecent, obscene or immoral acts" offered during a trial or prosecution.

If the surviving records about Seattle's early homosexuals are slender, then, that could be because no one could legally write about the subject—at least, not about the sexual behaviors themselves.

In the moral heat of the day, the new criminal code containing the sodomy law— initiated in the state senate this time—passed thirty-two to seven on March 1, 1909. The state house of representatives passed the bill three days later by a vote of seventy-four to five. The discussions and dissents focused on other sections of the omnibus bill. No one in either the house or senate seems to have questioned the section on sodomy or the prohibition on published accounts of disapproved sexual behaviors. As with the 1893 law, each chamber's journal is silent about sections 204 and 209, and there are no surviving committee reports at the state archive.[23]

Ironically, George Cotterill—ever the idealist—would vote against the criminal code bill because he had lost the battle over one other section that still permitted private gambling in homes and apartments. He indignantly puffed that that single section was a "blot upon the statute books of the state of Washington."

Still, he and his allies had now won a more precisely engineered intrusion into state control of sexual expression.

It did not take long for the effect to show. For 1910, the year following the new code's enactment, the docket for King County's superior courts is filled with charges related to Sabbath breaking, obscured views of saloons, seduction of females, adultery, and "lewd and vicious cohabitation" of men and women— charges that simply do not appear on the earlier dockets. These were not misdemeanors either; they were felonies requiring a new array of defense attorneys and court trials.

In May 1910, the Reverend Matthews dispatched members of his church on a fact-finding mission below the Deadline. In their report, the vice committee said that "one respectable man" saw conditions so disgusting "that we had to dispense with his company during the latter part of the evening." Except for one pointed reference to San Francisco as the "sodem [sic] of the Pacific Coast," most of the descriptions were of scantily clad women and carefully skirted any too specific wording about sex acts, since that would have been criminal. But the report contained what may have been a veiled reference to the oral sodomy Cotterill's new law now specifically outlawed. "[Girls] are all in their little $1 cribs," the committee said, "and any of them will do anything the depraved nature of the most depraved creature on earth might suggest. They not only are on to the French ways of doing things terrible with all that word means but they will simply do anything for $1 with anybody no matter what his condition as to sobriety or sanity might be."[24]

Among the first men in Seattle to feel the sting of Cotterill's new code was a man known in the court records as "Antone Mor," or, intriguingly, "A. Mor" for short. According to a memo from prosecutor Vanderveer, Mor and Robert Timmons checked into the Peerless Hotel in Pioneer Square in March 1910, intending sodomy. Timmons claimed the two had sex, while Mor consistently denied that any sex had occurred. For whatever reason—the court records are silent—the jury chose to believe Mor instead of Timmons.[25]

A month later, the Seattle police arrested another man, Frederick Evans, who may have been the target of a relationship gone sour. Evans was charged with "knowing" a man named Dan Paxman "in the anus" two years earlier, in 1908. Evans had lived for a considerable time at a downtown boarding room run by the Young Men's Christian Association, and the two men supposedly met and had sex there. The records indicate that their relationship lasted for some time, and when the two men quarreled Paxman threatened to reveal to the prosecutor that they had had sex. When he did so, Evans vehemently denied sex had occurred.

The judge told the jurors they could take into account the two men's "manner of consorting," certain photographs, and "medical testimony . . . as to the present condition of the anus" of Paxman. Apparently whatever condition Paxman's anus was in was not sufficiently convincing. Also, Paxman's "manner of consorting," according to Evans's attorney, included appearing as a female impersonator in the "vicious theaters" of Pioneer Square. Evans's attorney also argued that Paxman had engaged in the same "degenerate practices" he had accused Evans of, and that he "had been degenerate from his youth." "The habits of his life and immoral practices of said Paxman have so broken down his moral character that he is unable to make any elections in favor of the truth," the defense argued. Given those factors, the jury decided to acquit Evans, but the police soon arrested him again. This time Vanderveer charged him with sodomy that had supposedly occurred with Paxman three years earlier, in 1907, at a cabin on nearby Mercer Island. Eventually Vanderveer dropped the second charge against Evans, but only after five months of harassing him.[26]

In November 1910, as Vanderveer ended his term, the prosecutor's office would win two other sodomy cases, including one against a youth named Harry Douglass. Douglass was probably a teenager, since according to a handwritten memo in the court file the jury recommended that both Douglass and his "victim," Russell Spitler, be treated as "boys" who should be "instructed in right ways and not left at large to contaminate other poor boys."[27]

The prosecutor's office would lose a different kind of sodomy case—this one the first in the court records against two consenting heterosexuals, Charles

Morrhauser and Ora May Spriggs. The sodomy that occurred was described as "the touching of the female sexual organs with the mouth or tongue." "Any touching," the prosecutor's office insisted, "however slight, is sufficient to complete the crime." Morrhauser was found not guilty.[28]

In 1912, Cotterill decided to run for mayor of Seattle once again. His friend Reverend Matthews provided more than a ringing endorsement from the pulpit. "Save the city's reputation," he urged. "Prove to the world that this community will never become an asylum nor the home of the lawless." A vote against Cotterill, Matthews said, would be "an enemy's bullet fired directly at the heart of the city." The moralists still intended to clean out those they considered undesirable citizens and the acts they believed immoral. The saloon was still the most public symbol of moral corruption.

Finally, fourteen years after his first attempt, Cotterill won the mayoralty of the city. Two years later, in 1914, the Anti-Saloon League also triumphed, using the initiative process Cotterill and Matthews had promoted to force a statewide vote on Prohibition. The League won, with farmers and anti-drinking forces in the cities overwhelming those who wanted to keep the saloons. At least ostensibly, Washington State would go dry.

Two seesaw decades after their first major triumphs in 1893 and 1894, the moralists had finally won the victory they had aimed for all along.

Cotterill congratulated his police chief, Claude Bannick, for his crusade against the evil that seemed to be everywhere and for bringing moral order to Seattle. "It is to your lasting credit," Cotterill wrote to Bannick, "that you have steadily faced and trodden your path of duty, paying no heed to the yelps of the hurt horde of vice coyotes haunting in the shadows. . . . Human life has been safe and peace and good order have been preserved in Seattle."[29]

Then, of course, as the gold rush before had done, a world war and a Great Depression changed everything again.

Historians still have work to do to discover how many, if any, homosexuals from Seattle actually ended up in Walla Walla or other jails simply for making love to one another, particularly after 1914. However, for homosexuals themselves, it was never the actual number of prosecutions that was important. Rather it was the particular imagination about sex criminalized by the law that turned the city's homosexuals into outcasts. It was the threat of prosecution, not the actual enforcement, that sealed one's sexual desires outside the bounds of acceptable citizenry. The state prison at Walla Walla was well known as a warren for the state's worst armed robbers, drug addicts, and murderers, a place where the state pressed 1,300 inmates into cells intended for 750, where a riot over bad food in 1934 led guards to machine-gun the inmates, and where a judge in 1953 called the living conditions "intolerable and impossible."[30] Even the possibility of that vivid nightmare coming true because of a playful or loving act of mutually agreed upon sex built a closet that, in turn, was reinforced by the additional criminal prohibition for even describing those acts. Federal constitutional protection for descriptions of disapproved sex was still five decades in the future.

The climax of Cotterill's quest thus limited the only legal sex to vaginal intercourse between a husband and wife who had been duly married and issued a license by the state. All other desires, all other relationships, needed to be kept silent. In that silence rested the first method of exile, and both the silence and the sodomy law that grounded it would need to be removed before Seattle's homosexuals could ever really feel they belonged again as respectable citizens.

# 2

# *Mental Health*

## The Psychiatric Pick

*A* few blocks from the corner of Washington and Second, east up a steep hill, sits Harborview Medical Center, a brown fortress-like complex that is King County's hospital for those considered mentally ill. It seems to loom over the mudflat and, from the 1930s through the 1960s, it loomed in the imagination of the city's homosexuals. Frances Farmer arrived there on March 21, 1944, but not willingly. Earlier in the morning, she had been grabbed by three hospital attendants, straitjacketed, and thrown screaming into a van.

Born thirty years earlier while her parents were living on Seattle's Capitol Hill, Farmer had grown up a tomboy in West Seattle, across the Duwamish River from the mudflat, and as a child she had enjoyed playing kick-the-can into the late evening hours. She liked hiking in the Olympic Mountains and once, in 1941 after she had moved to Hollywood, she even drove by herself from California to hike alone near Sol Duc Hot Springs, out of sight of the movie cameras and the news cameras that by then had become her life. Many of those who met her, both as a teen and as an adult, would almost invariably comment about how little she seemed to care for the traditionally feminine clothing people expected her to wear, especially since she could appear so beautifully feminine in the publicity photos that had accompanied her rise to Hollywood stardom. Given the chance, she ignored her dresses and opted for blue jeans and work shirts. One famous wire-service photograph of her, taken at a time when she was running from her mother and from the psychiatrists, shows her looking especially hardened and masculine, clad in overalls and an army shirt and grasping a cigarette in her left hand. The news story about her that time quoted her as saying, "I want to be strong enough to fight for myself."

Throughout her years at West Seattle High School, she had showed little interest in boys. No one seems to remember her dating when she attended the University of Washington, either. An autobiography ghostwritten years later by her closest friend, a woman, said, "I accepted dates only when I needed someone to take me to a special event. They soon learned not to paw, and any adolescent attempt at lovemaking resulted in a tongue-lashing that sent them scampering." A movie magazine reported that she had once written a letter in 1935 about her experience with men in Hollywood in which she said, "I prefer my own company to that of most of the men in this town. If they want to pass me by, that's all right with me." She added, "If I couldn't stand my own company, I'd be the unhappiest girl in the world, because I'm alone, morning, noon, and night."

Farmer waited for two days at Harborview. Under Washington law, family members were allowed to file complaints that could lead to involuntary commitment for mental observation. Psychiatrists could then determine whether those detained needed treatment for any of a wide variety of symptoms, with the treatments ranging from simple counseling to drug therapies to those designed to physically shock the body, through either electricity or plunges into cold water. The treatments could be done at Harborview or, if it seemed that a longer period of therapy was required, at a state mental asylum about thirty miles south of Seattle. There, the treatments could be even more extreme.

In Farmer's case, her mother, Lillian, had filed the complaint. She claimed the actress had refused to work anymore in Hollywood, that she was depressed, and that she was becoming violent. On March 23, Farmer was taken to her hearing before two psychiatrists, Drs. Don Nicholson and George Price. According to a *Seattle Times* story, Lillian Farmer told the two that her daughter had "turned the radio up loudly, which I knew would annoy the neighbors. I asked her to turn it down and she became quite angry, grabbed my wrists and pushed me into a chair."

"I realize," Lillian Farmer continued, "that she needs institutional care, as I am entirely unable to control her at home."

Nicholson and Price asked Frances Farmer a series of questions. According to the *Times* story, the doctors said that she was "voluble and at times rambling." They also noted that while at home with her mother, Farmer had "started drinking [and had become] agitated and delusional." The two psychiatrists thought the delusions indicated that she was "paranoid" and concluded that she was suffering from schizophrenia.

For the cause, they looked to her previous emotional and sexual life. While in Hollywood, Farmer had eloped with an actor named William Anderson—his better-known stage name was Leif Erikson—but the marriage, while pleasing to Hollywood publicists, had lasted only about three years. In her autobiography, *Will There Really Be a Morning*, Farmer would call the marriage a mistake. "I neither loved him, nor was in love with him," the book said. "He was simply an attractive childlike man who seemed to want to understand me. . . . I considered him totally dull. In my mind he had become the youngest pup in a crowded litter, and I could find no place for him to fit. I was miserably unhappy and deeply discontented."

Nicholson and Price concluded that "marital difficulty is said to be a pre-disposing cause of the insanity." The next day, a King County superior court judge committed Frances Farmer to Western State Hospital, the state mental asylum.[1]

If the first method of constructing Seattle's sexual minorities as a group of outcasts was the use of law, the second was a mental health rhetoric founded on psychiatry. As members of a young medical profession that emerged during the nineteenth century, psychiatrists quickly set up classifications determining which behaviors and passions could be considered normal and which were abnormal. Although the classifications might have been well intentioned, sometimes they simply reinforced nonmedical moral choices, so that those who veered from the expected norms for sex or for acting in an appropriately masculine or feminine way might find themselves declared sick. The American Psychiatric Association, in its *Diagnostic and Statistical Manual,* would eventually define homosexuality as a sociopathic personality disturbance, but psychiatric patients also included women who wore men's clothing or vice versa, those who masturbated too much, or those who felt guilty or angry because they engaged in any behavior that somehow did not live up to the expectations of respectability.

Just as the legal rhetoric against homosexuality had its most extreme weapon—prosecution for sodomy—psychiatry also developed its most extreme cure, the lobotomy, used primarily during the 1940s and 1950s. As with the sodomy law, it was the force of rhetoric and imagination, in this case about homosexuals being "sick," that created an exile disproportionate to the number of attempted "cures."[2]

Tracking exactly what happened to specific individuals in Seattle as the medical definitions were deployed remains a future task for the city's historians. It is a difficult one for two reasons: First, personal medical records are confidential, and second, the diagnostic terms used in what few records are public mostly seem to refer to the symptoms that were to be treated rather than mentioning homosexuality itself. "Sodomy" initially defined an expansive range of sexual behaviors with little in common other than society's disapproval, and psychiatric terms such as "dementia praecox" and "involutional melancholia," referring to schizophrenia and depression, were applied to the emotional behaviors of widely varying individuals. Sometimes the only hint of a cause, rather than a symptom, is a phrase like "failed to make heterosexual adjustment" or, as in the Farmer case, "marital difficulties"—but of course those could refer not only to homosexuals but also to heterosexuals.

One early example of the medical rhetoric in Seattle occurred indirectly in the sodomy case that George Vanderveer pursued against Frederick Evans in 1910. In attempting to discredit Evans's accuser, the defense attorney pointed out that medical personnel believed that "persons addicted to the habits, practices and courses of the complaining witnesses are of unsound mind and incompetent to testify." The defense attorney was referring to accuser Dan Paxman's homosexuality and his "habits" of dressing as a female impersonator in the mudflat's vaudeville theaters. The medical personnel the attorney referred to are not named, so he may simply have been referring to general beliefs already accepted in Seattle. Apparently, the jury agreed with his argument about Paxman's credibility.[3]

As for those committed to Western State Hospital, located at Steilacoom, the admission entries for the inmates registered there between 1916 and the late 1940s suggest a link between unacceptable morality in sex and the diagnoses for mental illness, even if the sexual orientation of the patient is not clear. There was George Kincaid, for example, committed in 1916 at the age of seventeen for masturbating. And Fred Schlig, admitted at age twenty-two in 1916 and kept for more than two years, also for masturbating. Carl Sundling, a twenty-one-year-old delivery boy from King County, was deemed schizophrenic in 1917 because of masturbation and died at the asylum twelve years later. Albert Kohlmorgan, a twenty-six-year-old painter, was diagnosed as paranoid because of his masturbation. Annie Walton, a twenty-three-year-old art designer, was admitted in 1918 for four months because of her masturbation, which had caused her to become depressed. In later records, only the new psychiatric identities are listed next to names—catatonia, paranoia, schizophrenia, involutional melancholia—making it impossible to determine what the psychiatrists thought were the causes. Sexual minorities were invisibly scattered among a variety of individuals who showed similar symptoms.[4]

The young men committed to Western in the earlier years of the century almost inevitably listed their occupations as something at the lower end of the economic scale—as painters or delivery boys for example. Perhaps those better off would have been sent to private psychiatrists. Not surprisingly, the admissions record also notes several escape attempts by inmates who had been committed as insane because of masturbation.

The story of Frances Farmer's involuntary commitment to Western State in 1944 has become something of an underground urban legend in Seattle, appealing in particular to those who feel the city itself has remained seriously schizophrenic in its utopian dream of creating a "city beautiful" to match the natural environment by controlling citizens who do not fit the vision. Every decade since her death in 1970, Farmer's story has resurfaced. In the 1970s came Farmer's autobiography, an investigative book titled *Shadowland* by *Post-Intelligencer* reporter William Arnold, and a rebuttal by Farmer's sister, Edith Farmer Elliott, *Look Back in Love*. In the 1980s, the films and stage productions arrived: a Hollywood biography called *Frances* that starred Jessica Lange, a television miniseries, a documentary, and two New York plays. In the 1990s, Seattle's famous grunge rock group Nirvana enshrined the actress in a song titled "Frances Farmer Will Have Her Revenge on Seattle." In it, the band's lead singer, Kurt Cobain, referred to Farmer as "our favorite patient" who had shown a "display of patience" for "disease-covered Puget Sound." The actress, the band warned, would "come back as fire, to burn all the liars, and leave a blanket of ash on the ground."

Like any good Hollywood movie, Farmer's story has lent itself to multiple layers of interpretation by vastly different audiences. For gays and lesbians in Seattle, the story became emblematic of their own struggle against the city's mental health system, particularly as it intertwined with a story about a psychiatrist named Walter Freeman, who became one of the leading proponents of lobotomies and made repeated visits to the state mental asylum while Farmer was incarcerated there. In 1979, for example, the lesbian newspaper in the city, *Out and About,* recounted Farmer's story with pages of details, matching it with a story about another woman who had been involuntarily committed to Western State, as if to remind gay women in the city of the threat they had faced if they were found dressing inappropriately, speaking inappropriately, or entering into inappropriate relationships.

Farmer's story went like this:

She was strong-willed and strongly opinionated, particularly for a woman of the 1930s. She served as president of the debate club at West Seattle High, not surprising since her father was an attorney. As a high school student, she read essays by Nietzsche and then wrote an essay of her own telling how, as a child, she prayed to God to help her find a misplaced hat. God had helped, but then an accident killed a classmate's parents. In the essay, Farmer wondered why a god would respond to trivia like lost hats but allow tragedy. She concluded that God was really quite a "useless thing," someone who "stayed in heaven and pretended not to notice." "God," she wrote, "was gone." Her teacher thought the essay so well written that she submitted it to a national contest, and when it won a first prize of one hundred dollars, Seattle newspapers published headlines like "Seattle girl denies God and wins prize." Furious Christians in the city denounced the sixteen-year-old as an example of atheism and paganism and wondered why the city's school system would encourage such rebellious thinking.

In 1931, Farmer enrolled as a student at the University of Washington. One magazine article written about her a quarter-century later noted that while at the university she had sometimes dressed in a plaid boy's shirt, with a rolled collar open at the neck and her tightly cut hair "slicked back, masculine style." Initially she studied journalism, but soon became intrigued by a fellow student described in her autobiography as "the girl reporter from the Drama Department." The woman, according to the autobiography, clothed herself "with a special flair" and cropped her hair in a boy's bob. "She moved like a stalking lioness," the autobiography says, and she was "involved with" another female drama student that Farmer thought "strikingly feminine."

Although lesbians were not highly visible on the university campus in the 1930s, they were beginning to have certain safe places where they could meet. Historian Lillian Faderman, in her study of lesbian life in twentieth-century America, quoted one woman as saying that she and other lesbians regularly gathered at a certain table in the university commons each day. They were discreet. As the woman Faderman interviewed said, "You didn't belong if you were the blabbermouth type."[5]

One night, Farmer accompanied the two lesbian lovers from the drama department to a local "black and tan," one of the African American bars that nourished Seattle's blues and jazz musicians and drew audiences of young blacks and whites either into the city's Central District or down to the mudflat. There, Farmer met a powerful woman who would change her life, a U.W. drama instructor named Sophie Rosenstein who just then was in her mid-twenties. Although married to a businessman who sold women's hats, Rosenstein was in no way hobbled to him; her ideas about a woman's role encompassed much more than the home. At a later meeting between the two women, Rosenstein decided to convince Farmer to go on stage. She reached across the table, picked up Farmer's hand, pressed it against her cheek, and then said, "You've got everything you'll ever need. Look at you. You're beautiful."

When Farmer objected that she knew nothing about acting, Rosenstein supposedly replied with passion, "I'll teach you. You've got a voice, a fabulous instrument. Use it. Make it come alive. Capture with it. Love with it. Live with it."

Finally, Farmer felt she belonged somewhere. "I was alive for the first time in my life, functioning in a world that was young and intent on experimentation"— and then the book adds suggestively, "whether in a scene on stage or in a bed."

Rosenstein promoted a realistic approach to acting that was inspired by Konstantin Stanislavsky of the Moscow Art Theater, called simply "the method." In a 1936 book she coauthored, Rosenstein explained that acting meant re-creating "the inner life of the character" and bringing all of the character's "thoughts, sensations, perceptions and emotions" to bear.[6] Farmer's autobiography intriguingly describes the training this way: "If our characters were sleeping together, we slept together. If homosexuality was involved in a characterization, we were likewise involved, for how could you act what you had not experienced?"

Farmer's most memorable success at U.W. came in a play called *Alien Corn,* produced in December 1934. She played a music instructor at an all-women's college who wanted desperately to achieve her ambition of going to Vienna, but was thwarted by male interference. Preparing for the play, she seemed to discover something about herself. "I had a great deal of difficulty separating my own personality from that of the character," the autobiography says. "I was as much Elsa Brandt as I was Frances Farmer."

"I began to sense a dual faculty within me. The prospect of this schizoid condition was fascinating, but it also left me uneasy and frightened."

If the critics in the audience noticed, it only heightened their appreciation. One review was in the *Seattle Times,* written by Virginia Boren, a descendant of one of Seattle's original pioneer families that had become part of the city's elite. Boren exuded confidence about Farmer's future, using the royal "we" to convey her blessings. "Miss Frances Farmer, we predict, will go a long way. We are not clairvoyant, but we do feel that her name will be in electric lights. . . . She has a something, that divine intangible something, without which an actress is a hack."[7]

While Farmer studied, the 1929 depression crumpled the Northwest even more severely than the panic of 1893 had. Seattle turned into a hotbed for both the labor movement and, as had occurred after the panic, a moral backlash, this time embodied in a group called the American Vigilantes of Washington. The vigilantes charged that Communists had penetrated the Northwest's unions and schools. They provoked arrests of anyone they considered agitators, they destroyed bookstores, they burned books with which they disagreed. Soon enough, university students were speaking out against them and distributing leaflets in favor of union workers.

In the midst of this turmoil, Farmer's friends decided to help send her to New York City to meet with members of what was then one of the most influential organizations in American drama, the Group Theater.[8] The drama students entered a subscription contest run by Seattle's activist newspaper, the *Voice of Action*, which was operated by dissident U.W. students. Farmer's friends sold subscriptions in her name, winning for her the first prize of a ten-day trip to Russia via New York City. The headlines began again. Seattle's YMCA refused to allow the newspaper to hold its awards banquet at the downtown building. Farmer's mother publicly protested her daughter's decision, but Frances was twenty-one by then and could not be stopped. Frances kept repeating that she was not a Communist and just wanted to visit the Group Theater, as well as the famed Moscow Art Theater. A photograph in the *Seattle Times* even showed her typing out a story entitled "Why I am Going to Russia."[9]

Her explanations did little to appease her critics. Among them was a conservative Seattle lawyer named John Frater, who repeatedly denounced her in several speeches. But Farmer went to Russia anyway. The moral vigilantes, according to Arnold's *Shadowland*, warned they would never forget her, and Frater in particular would take a crucial role in her story.

After the Moscow trip, in October 1935, Farmer was invited to join Paramount Studios in Hollywood. The *Seattle Times* on October 29 printed two pictures of her. One, described as being taken "as Seattle knew her" just before she left for Russia, showed a rather sullen Farmer, her hair tightly cropped in a masculine style and her eyes looking seriously across her left shoulder. The other, taken "as Hollywood knows her," showed a face-front, smiling Frances Farmer, her hair curled and brightly springy, her eyes radiantly youthful, her lips deeply lipsticked. The *Times* called it a "study of contrasts," and the newspaper seemed clearly delighted by the makeover. "What a difference Hollywood makes!" the caption exclaimed. Farmer, it explained, was now "one of the seven girls who are most likely to become the star of tomorrow." Another *Times* headline, in early 1936, praised her as the "U.W. girl" who had won an "ingénue lead."[10]

Frances Farmer was already a created character who could embody all of the city's schizophrenic visions of itself.

In 1936, just after Farmer went to Hollywood, the psychiatric profession acquired a new tool, a form of psychosurgery called the prefrontal lobotomy, introduced in the United States by two East Coast doctors, James Watt and Walter Freeman.

Watt was a neurosurgeon; Freeman was a psychiatrist who until then had been using the older methods of counseling, straitjackets, and drugs.

The problem with mental patients, Freeman often said, was that their fantasies became too charged by powerful, shifting emotions. The cure was to disconnect the two, since a fantasy unfueled by emotion would be harmless. In his writings Freeman called it "smashing the fantasy life."[11] At first, the separation was made by drilling burr holes through the scalp and using a blunt knife to slice apart the neural connections between the brain cells that controlled emotions and those that created the imagination. The successfully lobotomized patient ended up with flattened emotions and typically lacked either creativity or the passion to pursue goals. At least any schizophrenia, paranoia, melancholy, or tension was relieved. For Freeman, success was measured by whether patients could leave the asylum and hold jobs—usually as something like sales clerks or receptionists—and whether they could get married and raise families. As for the failures who had to remain at the asylums, they were at least easier to control.

Initially, the operation was extreme enough to be used only as a possible cure for the most intransigent of mental patients, such as those who were prone to violence or who had been through every other form of treatment psychiatrists had to offer. Eventually, it began to be considered as a way to cure nonviolent mental patients, including those whose symptoms stemmed from problems with sexual adjustment.

In the mid-1940s, Freeman initiated a new, easier technique called a transorbital lobotomy. He included a sketch of the operation with an article he published in the *American Journal of Psychiatry* in April 1949. In it, a hand grasps the bridge of a patient's nose to hold the head steady. A slender ice pick with a looped handle extends from below the patient's chin past the tip of the nose into the bony top of the eye socket and on into the brain, almost reaching the top of the skull. No drilling was necessary. Freeman described the procedure to a *Seattle Post-Intelligencer* reporter in 1949: "I lift the upper eyelid and insert a sharp instrument. The instrument is driven through the roof of the eye socket to a depth of about two inches. Then, I move the instrument so as to cut across the nerve connections between the centers for imagination in the front part of the brain and the centers for emotions in the center of the brain, thereby divorcing the imagination from the emotions as they concern self. The operation does not disturb emotion and imagination as regards other things."[12]

The only visual result was a temporary black eye. To hide it, Freeman provided dark sunglasses. The ease of the technique made it possible, he argued, for the ordinary psychiatrist to administer lobotomies without the attending services of a neurosurgeon. His own neurosurgeon colleague, Watts, parted with him at that point, feeling that any poking in the brain required surgical training, but Freeman was not to be stopped. During the 1940s and 1950s, he became an evangelist for transorbital lobotomies, enthusiastically proclaiming in his book that "psychosurgery has come of age."[13] At least twenty thousand transorbital lobotomies would be performed in the late 1940s and early 1950s.

Freeman found his converts particularly among the harried administrators of overcrowded insane asylums. In 1947, he arrived at one of the most pressured of those institutions—Western State Hospital at Steilacoom. Even though Freeman's own home asylum on the East Coast was beginning to have reservations about the doctor's zeal for his new transorbital technique, the psychiatrists at Western State agreed to let him introduce the practice on the West Coast. By that time the institution had acquired a reputation, with the *Tacoma Times,* for example, blasting its often overcrowded conditions as a "naked idol of barbarity" even as early as the 1920s. Every decade brought an unsettling litany of newspaper clips, all with interchangeable headlines about promises of reform that never came. In the asylum's own annual reports during the 1940s, the only consistently cheery note was not about the hospital itself but about the two-hundred-acre farm next door where Western maintained a herd of Holstein dairy cattle. In 1948, when the hospital was perhaps in its very worst years, a state investigator boasted that one of the cows was the world's greatest milk producer. That, he said, was an example of the asylum's "efficiency and zeal." Less an example, apparently, was the fact that the medical staff was quitting at a rate of thirty-three a month, which meant a 100 percent turnover each year.[14]

In his writings, Freeman did not explicitly say that lobotomies could cure an individual's underlying sexual orientation, but he did recognize that lobotomy emasculated the passion to be homosexual. In the 1942 edition of *Psychosurgery,* for example, he wrote that he had not yet "knowingly undertaken the operation on any overt homosexual" and so could not "report upon the possible alteration brought about in this type of case." But in the second edition, published in 1950, he noted that many schizophrenics exhibited latent homosexuality. (He does not seem to have wondered about the possibility that homosexuals had been driven to mental illness by the need to appear heterosexual.) Freeman urged doctors to use lobotomies to cure the schizophrenia and consequently eliminate homosexual inclinations. By 1973, he was writing that "many instances of latent homosexuality have been relieved of their preoccupations and ideas of reference so that the patients regained equanimity."

"It would appear," he added in an incredible understatement, "that homosexuality is of little practical importance after frontal lobotomy."[15]

One specific operation that he performed on a homosexual involved a patient known in his studies as Case 465, a male physician whom Freeman described as "brilliant." Because of the guilt and shame the physician felt about his homosexuality, he was suicidal, Freeman said. Using the suicidal tendencies as his rationale, Freeman operated rather than trying to help the patient see that the guilt and shame were caused by society's feelings about homosexuality. The lobotomy effectively separated the patient's thoughts about suicide from the emotional will

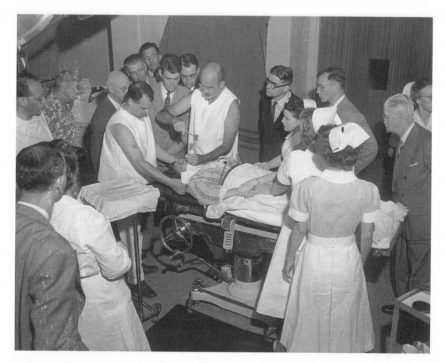

In the 1940s, lobotomies became the extreme cure for those judged to be mentally ill, including homosexuals. One of the country's leading lobotomists, Dr. Walter Freeman, performs a transorbital lobotomy at Western State Hospital in Steilacoom, July 1949. *(Seattle Post-Intelligencer Collection, Museum of History and Industry, Seattle)*

to implement them. It also, Freeman reported, turned sex into something that "as a whole meant little to him."

Interestingly, in the follow-up interviews, Case 465 did not remember the lobotomy ever having occurred. That loss of memory was a side effect, Freeman noted.

One final reference to Case 465, in an article published in 1973, makes it clear that not all turned out well in the psychiatrist's opinion. The lobotomy pick had gone too far into 465's brain and had "trespassed on posterior regions and probably the temporal lobe." Freeman cryptically noted that 465 "failed to make a good adjustment," perhaps meaning that he still desired men. Freeman also conceded that one other homosexual whom he had lobotomized had appeared to meet the criteria for success—he married and fathered five children—but throughout his life he continued to feel that his only real loves had been three other men.[16]

At first Frances Farmer was a stunning success in Hollywood. She completed fourteen movies before she turned twenty-nine in 1942. Hollywood columnist Louella Parsons wrote that Farmer would be "as great, and probably greater, than Garbo."

Her most successful film came quickly, a 1936 Samuel Goldwyn production called *Come and Get It* in which—appropriately for her Northwest roots—Farmer played a saloon girl courted by a lumber baron and his son. She had a beautiful voice, and critics relished her rendition of an old romantic song called "Aura Lea."

In 1937 she starred with Cary Grant in *The Toast of New York*, and it was in that film that she seems to have begun to feel the most pain of the divided life she was leading. Describing the film in her autobiography, Farmer wrote that the original story for the movie excited her because it told about Jim Fisk and his mistress Josie Mansfield, who had dominated Wall Street in the 1860s. Mansfield, metaphorically, was like Seattle. She had been, the autobiography says, a "designing harlot" but "also a woman of pathos in her desire for respectability." Farmer wanted to play the conflict in the character, but "instead of a cheap vixen" the studio wanted "an ingénue fresh from Sunnybrook." Farmer rebelled, arguing, getting into what the book called "verbal knockdown battles with the writers." She even publicly belittled the film. Ultimately she lost, and "Josie Mansfield was safely tucked into a chastity belt."

Always an individualist, Farmer kept rebelling, refusing to trade her old jalopy for a fancy car, to keep her eyebrows plucked, or to wear glittering dresses instead of the boyish sweaters and jeans she preferred. A 1937 *Movie Mirror* story noted that Frances was "a beauty who isn't a devotee of the makeup table." "Away from cameras, she wears no makeup, and so she could gaily go along and haul in fish without any furtive qualms."

By 1942, Farmer could not stand the emotional strain any longer. She and Anderson had separated. In October, she was arrested for drunk driving in a wartime blackout zone and put on probation. In January 1943, police arrested her for violating the probation and took her to the Los Angeles County jail, where she angrily hit one policeman and yelled at matrons before being strapped into a straitjacket. "Have you ever had a broken heart?" she screamed as she was taken. News reports at the time interpreted that as a comment about the separation from her husband, but given the later statements in the autobiography, it is more likely that something else had broken her heart. When a judge asked whether she had been drinking, Farmer defiantly replied, "Yes, I drank everything I could get, including Benzedrine . . . I get liquor in my orange juice—in my coffee. Must I starve to death to obey your laws?"

Farmer was jailed, but not before yelling at the judge, "I haven't any lawyer. What I want to know is do I have any civil rights?"

That night, Farmer slept in her cell, exhausted. The next morning, according to another wire-service story, she was quite calm. She drank a cup of jail coffee, which, the story said, "she eyed with distinct disdain," and she asked the jailer, "Well, where are the instruments? When are you going to torture me? I thought you would brand me with a hot iron." The same day, her sister-in-law, Ruth, employed a psychiatrist and filed a complaint asking for a sanity hearing. Farmer was quickly shipped to the psychopathic ward at the L.A. General Hospital. Once again, news reports said she remained calm at the hospital. Ruth Farmer helpfully volunteered to the press that she thought Frances knew "she was ill, but did not have the courage to ask for help."

The courts eventually assigned her mother as guardian, and Farmer first spent several months at a psychiatric hospital in California. Judging from news reports, she had already calmed even before she was transferred, but she was now drugged and given insulin shock treatments, according to Arnold's account. When her mother finally pulled her from the hospital to return to Seattle in April 1943, a psychiatrist declared success. "She now is the same Frances Farmer you knew when she first came to Hollywood," he told a reporter for the Hearst news service.

But, of course, she wasn't.

One of the debates about Frances Farmer has been whether she should be considered heterosexual or lesbian. Farmer herself never claimed to be a lesbian, and as a Hollywood film star, she played decidedly heterosexual roles. *Frances,* the 1982 Hollywood film about Farmer, went to great lengths to portray her as heterosexual, including the creation of a fictional male character who supposedly loved her, and she him. Yet her autobiography disdained all the heterosexual relations in which she was involved. She eventually married three times, but each marriage lasted only a few years. Arnold speculated in *Shadowland* that the energetic creativity that drove the talented, often rebellious actress was "a latent homosexuality that never quite made it to the surface." After her death in 1970, at a time when gay activism was fervent, some claimed Farmer had been a closeted lesbian and pointed to the fact that her autobiography, for example, appeared to have been written mostly by her close female friend Jean Ratcliffe. The book describes the deep love she shared with Ratcliffe, of whom Farmer supposedly said, "I was given a friend and finally a family." Ratcliffe was "my most cherished friend," and in Farmer's final years the two shared a country house with thirteen cats, a dog, and a set of visiting nieces. As presented in the book, it was the only truly joyful relationship in Farmer's whole life. However, as critics of the book have pointed out, it seems to have been written mostly by Ratcliffe after Farmer died, and so it is difficult to determine how much of the characterization is Farmer's and how much is Ratcliffe's.

After Farmer died, her sister, Edith Elliott, denounced the Ratcliffe book in a letter to the *Indianapolis News* as "lesbian pornography fiction [full of] filthy lies."

Farmer's sexual relations may have been so distorted by the stresses of her life that it is probably impossible at this point to know her actual orientation. Part of the difficulty of naming it lies with how the definition of "lesbian" evolved over the decades. Arnold wrote his book in the 1970s, a decade influenced by the notion of "coming out" and of lesbians having genital sex with each other. Farmer, though, was a product of the attitudes of the 1920s and 1930s, when, as historian Lillian Faderman has pointed out, it was more common for women who loved other women to frame their relationships as a type of romantic friendship that did not necessarily include sexual affection and did not call itself "lesbian." There was Sarah Yesler, for example, and Eliza Hurd, with Hurd writing passionate letters about sleeping and bathing together, although both women remained in marriages and never publicly used words like "homosexual" to refer to themselves.

At the very least, as indicated by *Out and About*'s decision to retell the story in so much detail in 1979, Farmer became for many lesbian women a symbol of resistance.

When she died, the only pallbearers would be six women who had become her family.

After Farmer left the hospital in California, she convalesced for a while in Nevada and then, by early 1944, returned to Seattle. That was when she had the fateful encounter with her mother that led to the March 23, 1944, hearing at Harborview.

The morning after Drs. Nicholson and Price gave their report, it went to a King County Superior Court judge, the same one who had signed the initial complaint that Lillian Farmer had filed against her daughter and that had resulted in the forced trip to Harborview. His name was John A. Frater—the same man, Arnold points out, who had once been a member of Seattle's American Vigilantes, the same one who had denounced Farmer for going to Russia. Frater had also selected for the hearing the psychiatrist Nicholson, about whom Arnold wrote that "there seemed to be endless questionable aspects of his practice." Arnold's investigation of Nicholson revealed that after coming to Seattle in 1906, the psychiatrist had committed thousands of people to the state's insane asylum. He had become a pillar of the local psychiatric community, honored as president of the King County Medical Society, the Washington State Medical Association, and the Washington Society for Mental Hygiene. But, according to Arnold, Nicholson apparently thought he could judge sanity on the basis of a few short questions. Once he said he thought Communists were at least "suspect" of being insane. Among those he committed, Arnold suggested, were individuals who were not psychotic at all but rather those whom Nicholson considered politically or socially undesirable in Seattle.

On March 24, after receiving the report from Dr. Nicholson that Frances Farmer was suffering from schizophrenia, it was Judge John Frater who signed the order sending "Mrs. F. E. Anderson"—Frances's married name—to Western State Hospital.

At the Washington State Archives in Olympia, two small gray ledgers make tangible the landscape of fear that once shadowed the lives of homosexuals in Seattle. There are ink stains on the outside covers and seemingly nonsensical scribbles written at random in red ink on the inside of the covers. The individual pages of the ledgers are more carefully inscribed and hold the record of surgeries conducted at

Seattle actress Frances Farmer, whose sexual orientation became a matter of speculation and denial, was Western State Hospital's most famous patient in the 1940s. She reads fan mail while on a temporary release from the hospital in 1944. *(Seattle Post-Intelligencer Collection, Museum of History and Industry, Seattle)*

Western State Hospital from 1942 until 1954. There is the usual list: appendectomies, hemorrhoid treatments, and so forth. But also on the pages—and, chillingly, on almost every page—are the listings of lobotomies performed during those twelve years. There were 252 in all. It is an eerie read through this ledger, with its dates of operations, names of surgeons and assistants, and types of anesthetic used. Almost inevitably the anesthetic of choice was an electric shock to induce a coma prior to the work of disassembling part of the emotional center of the brain. The instructions to the staff nurses giving the "Preparatory Orders for Lobotomy" are handwritten. On the day before, shampoo the head. Then, grant a light supper and give an enema. At 8 P.M. on the night before, administer one and one-half grams of a sedative, Nembutal. At 6 A.M. on the day of the operation, more Nembutal. Then, a morphine compound.

When Walter Freeman arrived at Western State for his first visit in August 1947, beds needed to be cleared, and the doctor from the East offered hope. On August 19, in a display of just how quick and simple his new transorbital technique was, Freeman lobotomized thirteen different patients at Western State Hospital. Eleven of the patients had been diagnosed as schizophrenic; two were considered manic-depressive. First they were given electroshock as an anesthetic. Then Freeman slid in the ice pick. The ledgers give the patients' names. Five were men: Oren Brown, John Dillaway, Peter Ireland, Henry Robinson, and George Stranger. The other eight were women: Gladys Rodgers, Patricia Hawley, Gloria Alex, Jessie Lancaster, and three named Frances with the last names of DeSellum, Lawder, and Peterson. The final woman was named Ethel Anderson.[17]

After the lobotomies, eleven of Freeman's thirteen demonstration cases were paroled within a month. In a report to the Seattle Neurological Society in February 1948, two Western State doctors, Charles Jones and James Shanklin, detailed the successes on a chart, although they did not list specific names. Among the comments about the individuals lobotomized on August 19 were these: "worked Christmas rush as salesgirl in a department store," "steady worker on family farm," and "makes own living as a cosmetic saleswoman." Of the two patients who did not receive parole, one was a woman in her early thirties who had been diagnosed as schizophrenic. The chart noted that even though she still remained in the hospital, her "vicious behavior [has] disappeared [and she] now quietly embroiders."[18]

Freeman returned in October 1948 to perform three more transorbital lobotomies, and then in July 1949 he joined in another lobotomy day when nine patients had their brains incised, three of them by the famous doctor himself. That time, Freeman invited journalists for the mass demonstration. Photographs from the *Seattle Post-Intelligencer* show him in a sleeveless white surgical gown assisted by one of the asylum's own psychiatrists. In the first picture, the Western State physician, Dr. Shanklin, is clamping a horseshoe-like device over a patient's head to deliver the electric shock that would induce a coma. In the second, the bald-headed and goateed Freeman taps his ice pick into a patient's eye socket while several men look on. Doctors from two other Washington State asylums had come there that day and they enthusiastically promised to adopt the ice pick method at their hospitals.

In 1951, Freeman was back to complete seven more transorbitals.

In between Freeman's visits, Western's own doctors busily practiced the techniques he had taught them. For example, between Freeman's visit in August 1947 and Christmas of that year, thirteen additional transorbital lobotomies were performed, along with nineteen of the regular prefrontal lobotomies.

Each transorbital lobotomy averaged only about seven minutes.

At first Frances Farmer stayed only three months at Western State, and then the psychiatrists pronounced her cured and released her in July 1944. The *Post-Intelligencer* announced that she was "in glowing health" and published a photograph of her at her mother's home, curled on a couch reading fan letters. Once again, though, she was under her mother's control and her mother's insistence that she return to Hollywood to play a role that never fit. She instead ran, was caught in California, and then stayed at an aunt's house in Nevada. She returned to Seattle in April 1945. By May, her mother had her recommitted to the asylum. There she would stay for most of the next five years, from 1945 until 1950, the same period during which Freeman was visiting.

Her autobiography describes days when she was stripped naked or tied to a toilet and forced into it. Other days, it says, attendants connected electrodes to her temples, gagged her, and then switched on the electricity and watched her convulse and bounce on the table until she passed out. She was cast into tubs of frigid water day after day—the infamous hydrotherapy used to level a patient's emotions and resistance. Her autobiography claims she was left in the water for ten hours sometimes rather than the prescribed three. Once, it says, she chewed her lower lip off because she was in so much pain.

In her autobiography, she also claimed to have been "gnawed on by rats and poisoned by tainted food." By 1947, she was being fed experimental drugs that would later become commonly used tranquilizers in psychiatric hospitals across the country—Prolixin, Thorazine, Stelazine.

She claimed she knew all along that she was not insane. It was her own schizoid abilities, her talent at detaching and watching herself play a role that she said saved her. Arnold noted in *Shadowland* that a student nurse once visited Farmer several times and sent a report saying the actress was not insane at all. The student was quickly transferred.

Then quite suddenly, after 1949, Farmer's mental condition improved, and according to a medical record quoted in the autobiography and in *Shadowland* she suddenly turned "cooperative." The report said, "She sits in a corner with a blanket covering her head, but she has learned to answer pleasantly." By spring 1950, Farmer was paroled. Even Farmer herself professed bafflement at the change. In her autobiography, she suggests the turnabout was due to a letter from her parents asking that she be released to care for them in their old age. In 1953, the psychiatrists declared her completely cured and approved the removal of her mother as her guardian, finally restoring Farmer's civil rights.

As with the question of Farmer's sexuality, the circumstances surrounding her "cure" have been a source of speculation and legend making. After Arnold finished his investigation, he concluded that Farmer had forgotten a key part of what happened to her at Steilacoom, perhaps the same thing that Walter Freeman's homosexual Case 465 had forgotten.

Perhaps the asylum's most famous visiting doctor had met its most famous and truculent inmate.

The gray ledger books at the state archives do not list a "Frances Farmer" as one of those who received the operation. Nor do they list any lobotomies of "Mrs. F. E. Anderson," the married name that was used when Frances was registered into Western State. Only that one name in the gray ledgers, the "Ethel Anderson" who was lobotomized during Freeman's first visit, comes suggestively close, since it is not clear what the "E" in "F. E. Anderson" represented. No legal middle name was ever designated on Farmer's Seattle birth certificate, and none was used on her tombstone. Her nephew David Farmer says the family called her Elena, which is also how her fans refer to her on a popular website established in the late 1990s. Elena was the name of a Russian spy character that Farmer played in a 1930s radio broadcast with Errol Flynn called "British Agent."[19]

On the chart of lobotomy successes that Jones and Shanklin produced for the Seattle Neurological Society, only the account of that one woman in her early thirties who had been diagnosed as schizophrenic and had not been paroled comes close to describing Frances Farmer's situation. But it could also describe one of the other women who had been lobotomized on that day of Freeman's first visit to Western State.

Farmer's sister, Edith Elliott, told a reporter for the *Indianapolis Star* in 1983 that doctors at Western State did indeed want her parents to let Frances be lobotomized, but they refused. According to the sister, they then pressured the hospital to release the actress, which is why she had suddenly been sent home. In a 1990s tabloid television program, however, Walter Freeman's son claimed that his father had told him that, indeed, he had operated on Farmer. The son set the date during Freeman's visit in 1949.[20]

In *Shadowland,* Arnold added to the legend by speculating that the doctor and the actress may have met several times. In all probability, Arnold wrote, Freeman took Farmer to a treatment room out of sight of the reporters and completely out of reach of the little gray ledgers now in the state archives. Freeman, Arnold suggests, sent the orderlies away. He then raised Frances Farmer's right eyelid and with a quick tap of a mallet forced the long slender ice pick into her brain.

It would have taken only about seven minutes.

For Frances Farmer, it may simply be a question of what is the least believable—not the most believable—scenario: that the country's most famous lobotomist passed through Steilacoom and did not try to cure Frances Farmer? Or that he did?

After she left the asylum, Frances Farmer worked sorting laundry and answering telephones as a hotel receptionist. She finished her life in Indianapolis, living with Jean Ratcliffe and for a while hosting a television movie series and even acting again in community plays. In 1970, she died of throat cancer. The autobiography says she found peace and a sense of belonging in her final years. A 1964 *Indianapolis Star* photo showed her sitting casually in a living room chair, flanked by Jean Ratcliffe and another friend, Betty Whitaker. Frances was smiling and Ratcliffe was holding a cat. The caption noted that Frances and Jean had begun a home decorating business.

While the tale of Frances Farmer may be the most emblematic and most remembered among the stories of psychiatric treatment in Seattle, there is another less glamorous story that may be more representative. The same year Seattle's lesbian newsletter *Out and About* was detailing the Frances Farmer case, 1979, it also recorded a long interview with Jackie Cachero, who like Farmer had been involuntarily committed to Western State. Cachero even referred to Farmer's experience. "You ever read that book by Frances Farmer?" she asked her interviewers. "What she tells you about what went on at Western State Hospital, she's not lying. I'll testify to it. Everything that happened when she was there was still happening while I was there."[21]

Born in 1943 in Bellingham, Cachero spent her first years with a father who beat her mother. Taken away because of her father's violence, Cachero spent the next several years in foster homes separated from her brother and sister as well as from her mother. At one foster home in Seattle, she discovered that "I liked girls." She and the other girls would play and touch while hiding in bushes.

Cachero was told that her mother had died, only to find out it was not true. Once she knew that, Cachero repeatedly ran away from the foster homes to try to find her, finally succeeding in her early teens. By then, though, rebelliousness had set too deeply as a trait.

"Never having spent any time with my mother," Cachero said, "I really didn't have any respect for anybody. So I started going out and drinking and having wild parties . . . getting into fights and stealing cars."

Frustrated, her mother sent her to a reform school, and that was where Cachero figured out her sexual orientation.

"Figure it out? Hell, they told me," she said.

"When I got into the cottage I was assigned to, I happened to see these two [girls] sitting really close on the couch, and the one looked like a dude. I said, 'Oh god, I didn't know they had boys here,' and they all cracked up. . . . They really got off on me because I was really stupid. They had me go put on a pair of Levis and slick my hair back and said 'Yeah, you make a good butch.' That's when I found out that all this holding hands sounded good to me."

At first, she was delighted to have discovered herself.

"Jesus Christ, I was so excited about it, that it was like, god, I don't know. I felt free, and here I was locked up in reform school." One day, her mother visited. "I was happy as a lark. I sat down and told my mom all about it. God. My mom just blew up."

Infuriated, her mother threatened to tell the state authorities regulating the school that her daughter had been turned into a homosexual there. Promptly, the school and her mother committed Cachero to Western State Hospital.

It was 1958 and Cachero was fifteen.

"They transferred me to what they call a 'shit ward,'" she said. "God, the building was so old, you know, the old wood floors, and they even swayed. . . . You walked down to the end of the hall, and there was a window that had big iron bars, painted black. You could reach through them and raise the window up a little bit—that was the fresh air. So I used to park this rocking chair down there, and I'd rock, and I'd just cry and wish my mom could find me and get me out."

The psychiatrists called her incorrigible.

Cachero did what she had done before. She found a way to escape. But she was caught in Tacoma and returned to a maximum-security ward. Still, she resisted. "I wasn't going to stay up there no longer," she said. She jumped a nurse, got the keys, ran and slid down a canyon, losing her shoes and slicing her legs and feet until they bled. A road crew spotted her and she was soon captured. Confined in the hospital again, she recalled, "They strapped me down in a little tiny room with nothing in it but a hospital bed, and they put these leather straps around my wrists, strung a belt through them, and they had me spread-eagled, my legs tied to the other end of the bed. They had a strap around my waist too. They'd come around and make me use a bedpan, and they'd come in with a tray to eat. . . . But I wouldn't eat . . . [then] they were giving me these goddamn pills, and all of a sudden, I couldn't resist."

Cachero could not recall how long she was strapped to the bed—perhaps two or three weeks, she thought. Once released, the nurses fitted her with leather hobbles that wrapped around her ankles and then hooked together with another belt. "They made it so small that I walked like a chinaman," Cachero said angrily. "And those motherfuckers would rub on my ankles, plus they had me doped up on this shit. . . . I looked just like one of the rest of these old ladies, taking these little tiny steps . . . I can remember being so doped up that I'd just come out of that room in the morning and shuffle over to one of them chairs by the window, and that's where I'd sit all day long."

Happiness about being homosexual had turned into a psychiatric insanity.

Cachero was seventeen by then. The hobbles, she said, wore her ankles raw until she bled.

Fortunately for Cachero, when she turned eighteen in 1961, the medical personnel told her that since she was now an adult, she could leave if she had a place to go.

By then, her mother had remarried and, according to Cachero, the new husband wanted nothing to do with a teenager labeled both incorrigible and homosexual. Nurses at the hospital pooled their money and bought her a bus ticket north.

Cachero made it as far as the mudflat in Seattle. There she did what other homosexual teens had begun to do as early as the 1930s. She went to the corner at Washington and Second and she walked down the stairway into the underground that had once been the People's Theater.

# Part Two

## CREATING REFUGES

# 3
# New Saloons
# and Vaudeville

Saloons had not always been metaphors for evil. As historian Norman Clark noted in his account of Washington's Prohibition movement, there had been a time, before George Cotterill and Mark Matthews, when American lawmakers thought saloons were "dedicated to the values of fellowship, equality, and euphoria" and had even mandated them in every town. Clark adds, "It was a warm and quiet retreat where men could explore the pleasures of friendship . . . a place where one could lift the burdens of caste, of status, and of the more restrictive social inhibitions, and thus freed, could grasp for the dim image of his own individuality." Even as late as the 1890s, a national committee of lawyers, clergy, and teachers concluded that saloons were "meeting the thirst for fellowship, for amusement, and for recreation."[1]

After 1916, saloons officially disappeared in Seattle when state voters banned the sale of liquor in them. Seattle's citizens still found plenty of ways to drink, but as a social institution the public saloon had to wait until 1933 for its return, after the repeal of national Prohibition. When that happened, the first traces of a public community of gay men and women in Seattle started to emerge. In the new saloons, the city's homosexuals would grasp for Clark's "dim image" of individuality, defining that in their terms—not in the rhetoric of law or psychiatry. For a quarter-century, from about 1933 until 1958, the community that was slowly forming found its center in saloons below the Deadline.

The end of Prohibition did not mean the end of restrictions, however. The new Washington Liquor Control Board had to approve all names, so it prevented any establishment from advertising itself as a "saloon," so powerfully negative were the connotations attached to the word itself. Instead, the replacements were restrictively licensed as taverns or, if they offered entertainment, as cabarets, or as after-hours clubs that operated once the taverns were forced to close by a curfew. The new regulators could dictate percentages of food to be sold in proportion to liquor. They could set restrictions on whether an establishment could sell beer, wine, or liquor, and whether it could be sold by the glass or the bottle. The inspectors and the city councils dictated how bright the new saloons had to be, how far inside pedestrians could see to ensure that behavior stayed respectable, whether there could be entertainment, what types of language the entertainers could use, how they had to dress. Sexual suggestiveness in particular could be controlled—the way entertainers or customers dressed. There were, in short, plenty of new rules that police and state inspectors could use to control the reemergence of the red-light district and the new homosexual subculture that gradually formed there. That meant there were also plenty of ways for the police to make money from tolerating violations of the rules, continuing the payoff tradition begun in John Considine's days.

Perhaps not surprisingly, among the first corners back in action was the one at Washington and Second. During the depression, the old People's underground had been converted into a dance hall called the Casino, possibly in association with the Casino Hotel located just across Washington. A marquee with the name "Casino Dancing" had been erected over the wide staircase that rose up to the avenue. Just a block away, according to city directories, a man named Joseph Bellotti was selling soft drinks and running billiard games at the Northwest Cigar Store. Once Prohibition ended, Bellotti appears to have seen an opportunity. The city directory indicates that by 1933 this man (who for several years listed his address simply as a hotel room) had taken charge of the renamed Casino Pool Room; by 1937, with the help of a bartender named John DelleVitti, he was also running a tavern upstairs.[2] Forsaking the old saloon names, he called it the Double Header, a clean-enough sports term to pass the liquor board's surveillance. Those who quickly filled both Bellotti's upstairs and downstairs could hardly have missed the either intended or unintended pun's reference to oral sodomy.

One gay man, going by the drag name of Vilma, remembered arriving at the Casino's staircase in the 1930s. "We could hardly wait to get down those stairs," he told local writers Don Paulson and Roger Simpson for their book *An Evening at the Garden of Allah*. Vilma had grown up in Minneapolis, enjoyed dressing in drag, and had heard about the Casino from two friends who had visited it. "That's all I heard," he said. "Seattle, Seattle, Seattle and this fabulous place called the Casino and all the neat kids there." On a whim, he hopped on a boxcar and headed west.[3]

The initial decorations in what seems to have been Seattle's first gay Shangri-la were spartan: a few Coca-Cola signs and a photo of Franklin Roosevelt. But it was the refuge and the people that mattered the most.

"John [DelleVitti] wouldn't let anyone mess with the queens," Vilma told Paulson and Simpson. "They protected us, and we loved them for that. They'd do anything for you if they liked you, even bail you out of jail. . . . The Casino was the only place on the West Coast that was so open and free for gay people." For the next three decades, one gay man or woman after another would find that all-important staircase on Washington Street, go down into the underground, and begin the process of both coming out and finding a new family.

Vilma remembered a gay man nicknamed Wilhelmina, who was still in high school. "She came down the stairs to the Casino," he said, "paused on the landing trying to look pretty and someone spoke to her and she fled up the stairs. Five

From the 1930s through the 1960s, gays and lesbians sought refuges and established social networks by meeting in rundown saloons or bathhouses, most often in Seattle's Pioneer Square. The oldest and two most famous bars were situated at the nondescript corner of Second Avenue South and South Washington Street, the location of John Considine's old underground People's Theater. The stairway to the underground (far left, behind pedestrian) led to the Casino, as did a smaller arched entrance (middle). The Double Header (right) provided aboveground drinking. *(MSCUA, University of Washington Libraries, UW18859)*

minutes later, she got nerve enough to come down the stairs only to fly up the stairs again. When she came down the stairs again, someone just grabbed her and said, 'It's okay, honey' and took her by the hand and introduced her to all the kids. Wilhelmina came out."

World War II provided a significant impetus for a more visible gay presence in Pioneer Square. As the conflict unfolded, the war first brought thousands of men to work in Seattle's airplane and shipbuilding industries, then packed the men away to military camps all around Puget Sound and replaced them with thousands of women. Women's roles in particular were altered. Boeing, for example, employed more than fourteen thousand women in its factories by 1943, and Miss Boeing of 1942 told her aerospace union's newsletter that she "liked men's work better because it doesn't seem so trivial and sissified."[4] After the war, many of the migrants stayed, and some found the mudflat. Pioneer Square began to take on a distinctly gay flavor—for those who knew where to look.

That was when Rose Bohanan made her way there. "Pioneer Square. That was the only place at the time," she recalled in a later interview. "It was full of gay people, walking from one place to another."

"Felt like a carnival."[5]

Bohanan was not a war worker; she was still a teenager from south Seattle when she hit the streets on the mudflat a few years after the war ended. "I walked past the Double Header once when I was around thirteen [in the early 1950s] and I saw this flaming drag queen standing on the tables, dancing, throwing toilet paper up into the air. I knew I was home."

Later, when she was fifteen, she turned the street corner and went down the stairway to the Casino. "You went down, and you didn't come out until the sun was coming up the next morning on Sunday. And the eighth step up from there was a different size than all the rest of the steps. Of course, you'd been drinking all night. And you hit that step and there's very few who did not bust their nose on that upper step.

"The place was huge. And there were all sorts of depravations going on in every damn corner of that place. It was great when you were fifteen, you know." She laughed. "Yeah, like fights. This woman here who's been married to this woman here for the past two years is looking at that woman over there, over her shoulder. The fight ensues. Or she gets her in the bathroom, in some dark corner for sex.

"The women were very sexual. Under the tables." She laughed again. "I think in a lot of ways they were much more outrageous than the men down there.

"But I didn't get to know the women very well, because they were kind of standoffish [with] a child of fifteen. They'd pat me on the head or something. That's as far as I could get with the women."

In these new saloons, Seattle's homosexuals began to take care of one another and teach one another the rules of relationships that were seen by the rest of the city as perverse. Drag queens who frequented the two bars sometimes took those who were just coming out under their care. Bohanan, for example, remembered a man named Dee as "one of them that raised me." The older lesbians also helped her, in particular one named Cat who worked as a supervisor for Boeing. "She was a beautiful older woman with white, bright hair, and she wore powder-blue suit jackets. I was mouthy and streetwise. [She told me] 'Sit on the floor. Keep your mouth shut and just listen.' It was good advice. I learned from the older ones by doing just that."

"I learned what was okay to treat a woman as, and what was not. You do open a car door. You do light that cigarette. You do treat her like a lady. You never hit a woman. That kind of stuff."

There were other rules peculiar to the need to hide. "You should not openly come on to each other," Bohanan said. "That's why all the gay bars had a mirror behind the bar, because you can make eye contact through a mirror and you could not do it face to face."

Also, very importantly, "I didn't even know anybody's last name, and they didn't know mine. Last names were a no-no. What did you do for a living was never spoken of, never in casual conversation. Your best friend might know, but that's it." What was discussed instead was "what kind of beer you liked, what kind of woman did you go for. That kind of stuff. But never any personal stuff. That just wasn't safe."

Harassment could be a problem. "Quite often," Bohanan recalled, "we had sailors come up from First Avenue [who] would try to crash a bar for women. . . . We had a bar full of lesbians and dykes. Toughies [and] real feminine girls, too, with high heels. [The sailors] came in and before the night was over the fight had begun. They [the women] weren't going to be pushed, they weren't going to be talked back to, they weren't going to do anything. And you couldn't call the cops. So, all the fixtures were torn off the walls. Women were dragging those men out on the sidewalk, just beating them to death."

Sometimes the harassment was directed at the different clothing homosexuals might wear. "[Heterosexual] men picked up some of the [drag] queens," Bohanan said, "the real small ones that are so effeminate—stabbing them, raping them, tearing them open. [The drag queens] couldn't go to the cops, they couldn't go to the hospital." If they did go to the hospital, they ran the risk of being harassed for not wearing the appropriate clothing—much as Bohanan and some of the more masculine-appearing women were for wearing male clothing. "Male impersonation, that was a cover-all [charge] for everything. They'd throw us in the men's tank, because we looked so manly they would say, [and they would] push you in there with the drunk men."

The Double Header and the Casino were pickup places too, both for the homosexuals in Seattle willing to be seen there and for those not willing—but who still knew about the corner at Washington and Second. When she first went to the Double Header, Bohanan said, eight women used to wait in the bar until "someone's chauffeur would come and pick one out and take them out to the lady's home." "Now, I hate to call them prostitutes. They're probably more like gigolos." Bohanan joined the group as its youngest member. "Off we would go in this chauffeured thing over to Bellevue. And usually there would be a note at the door as to what this lady [who had sent the driver] would want and what she would expect of you and what you were to be that evening . . . what kind of sex she liked, what kind of scene she wanted to play."

By the 1950s, then, John Considine's corner had become its own underground urban center for resisting the definitions of acceptability that had been created by Cotterill, Matthews, and the psychiatrists.

As homosexuals moved out of their individual isolation into loose social settings in Seattle, new forms of communicating became important in forging a sense of belonging.

Drag was most noticeable. Academics have written tomes trying to interpret

its use among homosexuals throughout the world, but perhaps the best explanation, at least of gay male drag, was offered by anthropologist Esther Newton in her
1970s book *Mother Camp*. She argued that "the drag queen symbolizes all that
homosexuals say they fear the most in themselves, all that they say they feel guilty
about: he symbolizes, in fact, the stigma" of not being masculine enough. Parodying
the stigma that gay men are not masculine is one way of directly challenging sex
roles that do not fit, Newton contended. Presumably her argument might also be
extended to lesbians, like Rose Bohanan, who enjoyed male clothing. Yet the symbol is complex. Depending on how a homosexual felt about himself, Newton noted,
the drag queen could easily be despised as embodying everything bad about homosexuality or, alternatively, be embraced as a powerful resistance to the expectation
that everyone behave and dress a certain way.[6]

Other academics have suggested that there is a psychological reward to assuming the different personalities adopted as part of wearing drag. There is also the
theatrical explanation: a mediocre performance given in gender-appropriate clothing may become a truly memorable extravaganza if acted in a spectacular gown.
There is also the sheer play and clubhouse sense of belonging with others who are
pursuing the same hobby of cross-dressing.

Whatever the explanation, two traditions in male drag quickly established themselves in Seattle, as elsewhere: that presented in respectable theaters, and that presented as part of vaudeville. In 1898, in the same month that John Considine was
reopening the People's after its temporary closure by anti-liquor crusaders, the
upscale Seattle Theater was staging *1492,* a dramatic as well as farcical reenactment
of the discovery of America. It featured one of the country's most noted female
impersonators. Both the *Seattle Times* and the *Post-Intelligencer* printed a sizable
sketch of him with coiffed hair, his "breasts" delicately concealed, and his arms
covered by a dress with puffed sleeves. His real name was Edward Stewart, but he
was called "Stuart, the Male Patti," a reference to Adelina Patti, a well-known col-
oratura soprano. Stuart sang in an operatic falsetto voice and sometimes traveled
to Europe to buy the latest Paris dresses for his act. In its review, the *Post-
Intelligencer* noted that *1492* had opened to a packed theater, and then assured its
readers that "Stuart, the central figure in '1492,' is inoffensively articulate in his
female impersonation."[7]

On the other hand, the tradition of drag in vaudeville can be detected in the
court records of that sodomy prosecution against Frederick Evans in 1910. Part
of Evans's defense strategy had been to hire a private detective to follow his accuser,
Dan Paxman, and to document what Evans probably already knew: that Paxman
worked as a drag queen at one of the vaudeville shows on the mudflat. The court
records do not say which theater Paxman acted in, but the detective reported that
he had observed Paxman "singing and dancing in the low dives and vicious theaters in the underworld district." Paxman, the detective said, would "assume the
garb of a female, greatly abbreviated at both ends, his face, neck and bosom rouged

and painted in the highest degree." Combined with the defense attorney's argument that doctors believed such persons were not credible as witnesses, the tactic of demeaning Paxman's reputation because he was an impersonator saved Evans from going to jail. No one believed the accusations of a drag queen.[8]

How extensive a role the early vaudeville theaters in Pioneer Square played in helping establish drag as a paying stage role in Seattle has not yet been well researched. For establishing vaudeville itself, though, John Considine played the protagonist, insisting on hiring real actresses and actors, leaving the drinks to be served by others, and employing an eventual stock company of twenty-five members. Considine touted it as "the grandest, greatest and best vaudeville and dramatic show ever seen in Seattle," and at one point, the People's even staged a presentation of *Damon and Pythias,* which its advertisement called "that soul-stirring four-act drama portraying brotherly love between man and man." Unfortunately, the advertisements the People's ran in city newspapers do not make clear how many of its acts may have included men or women dressed in drag, and so far the histories written about vaudeville in the city have focused on theaters more respectable than the People's.[9]

Vaudeville itself included two different types of drag queens: the glamorous prima donna who actually tried to look and even sing like an elegant woman, and the campy and often awkwardly costumed role of the "bitch." Unlike highbrow theater, vaudeville relied on improvisation, with both types of queens sometimes telling jokes, baiting audience members, and keeping control of hostile drunks or overly friendly admirers through the power of words alone.

Also unlike more formal theater, vaudeville audiences participated, creating their own role in the theatrical ritual, whether by catcalls, applause, or simply heading to the bar for a drink, something they could never do in a regular theater. In 1906, *Washington Magazine* portrayed why, by the 1940s and 1950s, vaudeville and drag could become an important method for constructing a new community among Seattle's homosexuals.

> The time is, say, 8:30 o'clock on any night of the year; the scene, one of the scores of playhouses scattered throughout the Northwest . . . where you hear the clapping of hands, the heavier stomping of feet, and the whole-souled laughter. . . . Inside the four walls of the ten-cent show, you may see the most democratic show on earth . . . rich and poor, old and young, looking only for pleasure, asking only to be amused, to forget for a while the strife and bitterness and pain of the outside world; to live for a while in a bright, painted, beautiful world of tinsel and brilliant lights and gaily dressed actors. . . . Long live vaudeville, democratic vaudeville, fascinating, cosmopolitan, generous, joyous vaudeville![10]

Similarly, historian Albert McLean argued that this particular form of theater helped assimilate waves of immigrants pouring into cities like Seattle at the end of the nineteenth century, wanting ways to spend their new leisure time after leaving work and wanting new urban myths that promoted a sense of belonging. Vaudeville was ultimately about aspiring to success. "That surge of magical power evoked by brassy rhythms, the staccato wise-cracks, the poised charm of the 'star' . . . were all more immediately assimilated by the mass audience than were the legends of Horatio Alger and his imitators."[11]

By the late 1940s, the type of vaudeville promoted by individuals such as John Considine was officially dead in the mainstream, and the immigrant needs for stories about romance and comedy could be moved to the movie screen instead. However, that was not possible for those whose language or romance had no access to the screen. For them, vaudeville was still king in the saloons.

In December 1946, two gay men, Fred Coleman and Frank Reid, opened a new venue. Coleman had already invested in a tavern called the Spinning Wheel, located a few blocks north of the Deadline near the corner of Second Avenue and Union Street. The bar attracted both heterosexuals and homosexuals and sometimes offered cabarets featuring drag queens. Coleman and Reid envisioned a new partnership that would create a full-time moneymaking vaudeville with singers, performers, comedians, and—most important—the drag queens.

They located their new club in the basement of an old Victorian-style hotel not far from the Spinning Wheel, where the club could attract a clientele that might have been reluctant to venture into the mudflat's red-light district. The hotel, the Arlington, had opened in 1894, and with its proudly advertised "electric lights, baths, elevators and steam heat," it was rated first class at the time. One end of its basement had been turned into the Arlington Cafe, with an arched entrance and a white marble staircase. When, after two decades, the hotel business declined, a billiards hall and then a speakeasy replaced the cafe. The speakeasy's owner christened the space the "Garden of Allah," likely a takeoff from a New York stage production that had become a movie. Even after Prohibition ended and the speakeasy became a honky-tonk, the name stuck.

Seattle's gay men and women began making their way through the arch and down that staircase into the underground. The acts were predictable—comedy skits, sentimental songs, one-line taunts, sexually suggestive lyrics, drag, even a snake dance or two. But for the gay men and lesbian women who went there, it felt, as one said, like "our secret place"—even though it was often packed.

The story of this particular saloon/theater has been well documented in Paulson and Simpson's *An Evening at the Garden of Allah,* as well as through additional published and unpublished interviews with gay customers and with one of Paulson's key sources, Skippy LaRue, a man who entertained at the Allah and later worked in one of the underground gay male bathhouses in Pioneer Square. All the accounts agree: It was the drag and vaudeville actors at the Allah that made it a special place in Seattle.[12]

There was Francis Blair, for example. He had been born just a year earlier than Frances Farmer, in the same West Seattle neighborhood. Like her, his tastes ran to performance, but he never made it to Broadway or Hollywood. Instead, during the depression he began sharpening his comic taunts and singing in Seattle's vaudeville halls. Even as a slender young teenager he enjoyed wearing dresses with a girl friend as they rode the city's streetcars. By the time the Garden opened, Blair was already a bit old at thirty-three to be considered truly sexy as a gay male actor, but as a woman he was stunning—an example of that magical ability of drag to transform the quality of a performance. According to Paulson and Simpson, the syndicated columnist Walter Winchell saw one of Blair's acts and called him "the boy with the million-dollar legs." Blair let his hair grow long and styled it into coquettish curls, and then accented his long slender body with tight white gowns and gloves. To contrast his glamorous prima donna performance with comedy, he pulled on black high-button shoes and ripped stockings to become one of "Two Old Bags from Tacoma."

Another star was Hotcha Hinton, who had gone on the vaudeville road when he was sixteen. His mother had been a circus aerialist, and Hinton had met most of the big circuit names such as Gypsy Rose Lee, Sally Rand, and Mae West. Heavyset, he perfected a campy and crude burlesque queen personality that included a snake act. One photo in *An Evening at the Garden of Allah* shows him at Christmas, wearing a wildly frilled dress with a tinsel star on his head and 168 light bulbs circling his ample body, the extension cord fully visible down his belly. He always insisted on being referred to as a woman. One Garden-goer told Paulson and Simpson, "When she came out on the stage, everyone said, 'Oh my God! What a hussy! What is this?' But by the end of her performance the audience loved her." Hinton once told an interviewer, "Honey, you got to love life and it'll love you back."

The biggest star at the Garden was appropriately named Jackie Starr. He had grown up in the Midwest, studied ballet, acting, and voice, and then began playing the burlesque circuit in the 1930s. For a while, he was with a traveling company called the Jewel Box Revue, which played throughout the United States and Canada. By the end of the war, Starr was aging, and his agent signed him into the Garden of Allah. He headlined for a decade, Seattle's best-known drag queen of the day. His personalities included both a prima donna role and a stripper.

Then there was Skippy LaRue himself, a Texan who migrated to Seattle during World War II to work for Boeing. He had started dressing in drag as a young boy of about nine. "I had to live, I had to survive," he said in an interview. "I'd be working in some places where people would grab my tits to see if I was a boy or a girl." He traveled the carnival circuit as a female stripper and, in states that had laws against female impersonation, was repeatedly arrested. He worked at Boeing for two months, then was hired on at the Garden, where he sang his own numbers in three shows a night and a finale.

With the mentoring of the more experienced vaudeville players like LaRue, Blair, Hinton, and Starr, some of those who came to the Garden were drawn into supporting roles in the cast. The Garden encouraged amateur nights, with the winners receiving small cash rewards or, if acting was an aspiration, the possibility of a job.

Robin Raye, for example, was twenty-two and had been in the navy. After the war, he pursued his interests in sewing and enrolled in costume design courses. In 1948, on a dare, he went to amateur night ready to do his first striptease. Tucking in his genitals, he stripped to a song called "In a Persian Market," winning first prize: cash and a week's booking at the Garden. That debut set him onto a new path that was to last for two decades. As he recollected in an interview for Paulson and Simpson's book, "Female impersonation was the farthest thing from my mind, but after one show it became my career."

Of course, most who walked down the staircase to the Garden and paid a dollar to enter stayed in the audience, but in a communication ritual like vaudeville, they were always more than just spectators. Every step, from the act of entering to the closing, triggered emotions. It meant joining a group of characters on the margins of civic life in Seattle. "You had no illusions about the Garden of Allah," one man who used to go, Bill Parkin, told Paulson and Simpson. "The Garden was very earthy, a real underground decadent cabaret straight out of Toulouse-Lautrec, and you loved it. . . . The finale of the show might be everyone on stage singing 'We don't care, we don't care, we don't care what happens to us. We're happy go lucky.'"

Pat Freeman was underage and still attending high school when she made her first visit in 1947. She told Simpson and Paulson about a Halloween party at the Garden when she and a male friend rented costumes: she went in top hat and tails, he wore a gown and heels. It was a way to practice a flowing sense of gender and to challenge the return to traditional sex roles then being encouraged at the end of World War II. Freeman said that at the Garden, "We met gay people, we got to know Jackie Starr, Francis Blair, and the other performers. We went to their parties, we were accepted, and they became our family."

"The Garden was our entree into the gay world; it was our support group."

Stephen Blair, a Seattle man who went there after World War II, told Paulson and Simpson that the Garden had helped him heal from the emotional wounds of the war. "It released some of the hurt," he said, "because you could laugh. It was one of the few places gays could laugh at themselves."

Like the Double Header and the Casino, the Garden was a point of arrival.

During this time, another form of drag also emerged as communication in Seattle, both for stage performance and for claiming gender identities within the group of homosexual women willing to be seen at the new public gathering places.

Rose Bohanan remembered that there were women who wore gabardine slacks, silk shirts, sweaters, and penny-loafers. The femmes, or as she called them, the "les-

The Garden of Allah became the most popular homosexual cabaret in Seattle in the late 1940s and 1950s. Regular vaudeville and drag shows gave a postwar generation its first sense of community. Stephen Blair (right) and an unidentified friend relax in 1948. *(Northwest Lesbian and Gay History Museum Project)*

bians." Then, there were the women in workers' uniforms and crew cuts. The butches.

Contrary to the heterosexual model, with the man supporting the woman, in the lesbian world of the 1950s it was often the femme who had to support the butch, according to Bohanan. "The dykes were pretty much unemployed," she said. "They couldn't get employment unless they were passing [dressing as women]. And that could only last a while before it knocked you in the head. . . . Mostly their femmes would have to support them because there was no work for them."[13]

Elaine Burnell, who grew up during the 1950s and arrived in Seattle in the 1960s from California, adopted the opposite role. "I liked to wear dresses and nail polish," she told an interviewer in 1995. "And I liked to cook. A butch wouldn't cook. You fit into one category or another."[14]

Some of the butches, like Shirley Maser, took to motorcycles; by the late 1940s she was riding with an all-women's group called "The Motor Maids of America" and had joined with five friends in their own small club, which they named "The Queen City Motorcycle Club." "We might have had the reputation of being gay— dykes on bikes—but it was more that we were 'tough women'. . . . We went to motorcycle races and to hill climbs."[15]

At the Garden of Allah, butch impersonators also claimed the stage, the best

Drag queen Paris Delair with two servicemen at the Garden in 1950. In the 1960s, the military would put most gay establishments in Seattle off-limits. *(Northwest Lesbian and Gay History Museum Project)*

known being one who used the name Nick Arthur and who became an emcee, singing in a tenor voice on weekends for four years.

In the decades before feminism would arrive, it was the butches who asserted that power belonged not only to heterosexual men but also to women, who could do things the same way heterosexual men could—violently when necessary. Pat Freeman remembered a butch named Big Bobbie, who always dressed in men's suits, leaving the Garden of Allah one night and drifting back to a gay bar in Pioneer Square. Freeman said, "She took exception to a straight male there and proceeded to knock his head against a wall."[16]

Rose Bohanan remembered the assertiveness this way: "I like to call it pissing in every corner. You go out and piss in every corner. Butch women do that. Mark your territory. I used to walk into the Double Header and, because I was single, I thought I looked tough. The butch women would grab their women and go, 'This one's mine!'"

"You'd know it was an exciting night when you'd see that."

By 1956 the drag queens and kings and vaudeville actors at the Garden of Allah ran into hard times, partly because—unlike the Casino and the Double Header—the Garden had tried to imitate Considine's approach of combining a theater and a saloon. The Double Header and the Casino had always remained neighborhood drinking taverns or, in later years for the Casino, an after-hours club. As had happened to the People's in 1894 with the barmaid ordinance, in the late 1950s the city moved against the saloons that combined drinking with live entertainment, this time by imposing a higher tax, according to Paulson and Simpson. The musicians' union then raised its price for hiring live instrumentalists—something that had also happened in Considine's day and had led him and other vaudeville owners to try to bust the union. This time, there were not enough vaudeville owners left to organize a response. Certainly, there were not enough gay vaudeville owners.

That was the end of the decade-long run of the Garden of Allah—although not of its impacts. Through the Casino and the Garden, gays and lesbians in Seattle had begun to form a public network and a sense of a new community.

It was not the end of drag or of drag's role in that new community either. "That's when lip synch started to come in," Paulson said, "because the girls couldn't afford musicians anymore." Phonographs became more portable, too. A good 45 rpm record could replace a live band, and, if anything, the portable phonographs would make drag performing even more accessible. Soon enough, drag and drag alone would be the act at a new set of downtown gay saloons in the 1960s and 1970s: the Mocambo, the Golden Horseshoe, the Golden Crown. By the 1970s, public drag clubs—called courts, with "emperors" and "empresses"—would be created in Seattle. Lip-synching would remove the need for singing talent and open the way to any man who could dance, quip, or even just costume. Performances would change, with ever-more flamboyant costuming, more energetic and choreographed dancing, and even laser shows.

For gays and lesbians in Seattle, the drag queen—and drag king—would be heroes, and the refuge provided by the saloons and by vaudeville would eventually embolden the next step in their journey. It was time to directly challenge the keepers of the city's morality.

# 4
# *Stirrings of Resistance*

*I*t was Boxing Day in Canada, when Christmas gifts are stored and alms passed
to the poor. In 1957, MacIver Wells and John Chadwick had other boxes to
worry about. They had just driven south from Vancouver, heading for Seattle
and a new life. It was time to unpack.

Mac, as he was always called, had been born in Quebec, that first name a reminder
of his mother's clan from the Scottish Highlands. John had grown up in Alberta.
In the early 1950s, the two had met in a beer parlor in Vancouver. When they met
again by chance on a city bus, they began a relationship that would last until
Chadwick died forty-four years later. Mac was in his thirties, working as a prison
guard, while Chadwick was in his twenties, selling retail goods for the Woodard
chain. Both dreamed of operating a business where they and their customers could
be openly gay.

In Vancouver they had tried managing a steam bath, catering to straight businessmen during the day but encouraging gays to come at night. Chadwick had eventually been disgusted by the hypocrisy of some of his closeted customers, the final
straw coming, he said, when he had admitted a closeted priest who paid with money
from his Sunday collections. Mac and Chadwick decided to head south to realize
their ambition of starting their own gay bar. In Canada it was too hard to secure
a license. "You had to be part of a hotel then, with a certain number of rooms,"
Mac explained during an interview in 1992.[1]

A real estate agent had already shown them possibilities in Seattle. The first four
or five they had disliked. Then they saw the Madison Tavern, located at the corner of Third Avenue and Madison Street, about six blocks north of the old Casino.
It was not that impressive—just a typical neighborhood bar—but the location in
downtown Seattle was compelling, in the middle of the knoll that Arthur Denny
had platted north of the mudflat. City hall and the police department sat a few
blocks south. Across the street, construction workers were building a new home
for City Light, the utilities department. The workers would make for good steady
lunch and after-work customers, and at night, the same strategy used for the steam
bath could work. "We figured we should run it straight until we got established,"
Mac recalled. "You don't want to make waves right away."

They preferred to serve gay men, but serendipity dictated a different choice.

"Two girls used to come in and drink after work," Mac said. "They were in a meat-packing place or something, and we got quite friendly with them." The women asked whether the two would mind if lesbians started coming to the Madison. Chadwick and Mac had envisioned a bar for gay men, but they decided homosexual women would be fine too. "Business was terrible running it as a straight place," Mac said. "God, it was awful."

"The girls must have spread the word," Mac said, "because they sure started coming in. From then on, it was a gold mine."

"Silver," Chadwick smiled.

"Yeah," Mac quickly agreed. "Silver, not gold."

Chadwick was the quieter of the two men, with a slight air of sophistication, comfortable at watching events unfold while tending the books in the back of the bar. By contrast, Mac was assertive and willing to hurl brusque epithets—although often with twinkling eyes. "I was a prison guard—that made you mean and rotten," he said, smiling all the while.

Even getting into the United States proved a problem since they were gay. "We went to a school to become American citizens and we got our call to go down to be interviewed [at the immigration office]. . . . We've been in gay business all of our lives, even in Canada, so I pretty well know who's gay most of the time by looking at them—and this little nelly faggot sitting behind the desk is the one that asks the questions. He asked us both to come in. He says, 'I'm going to close the window and I'm going to close the transom and [whispering] we're going to have a little talk. Just the three of us.' I say, 'That's fine.' And he says, 'I'm going to turn you two down.' I said, 'Why?' He says, 'Under code such and such, paragraph such and such.' I said, 'Let's start all over again, I don't know what the hell you're talking about.'"

"'Well,' he says, 'you and Chadwick have lived together many years. You own that house where you live and it's in your names, both of you. The businesses are in both of your names. Your bank accounts are joint bank accounts.' He says, 'What do you think?'"

At the time, the Immigration and Naturalization Act of 1952 specified that "aliens afflicted with psychopathic personality" should be excluded from the United States. With the American Psychiatric Association still listing homosexuality as a mental illness, the U.S. Public Health Service had determined that "psychopathic personality" included gay men, a determination that the Supreme Court would uphold in 1967.[2]

Wells looked at the immigration officer and said, "You're trying to tell me I'm a queer?"

"'Well,' he says, 'I'm trying to be friendly."

Chadwick remembered, "He made quite a procedure of it. He slapped the files together like that [snap]."

Mac: "I said, 'You're accusing me of being a queer? You must have a boss. Now I want to see the top supervisor over you right now.'"

"He said, 'Now you're getting all excited.'"

"'Excited! I'm not only excited, I'm mad.'"

"So he got on the phone and in came a guy, his supervisor. His supervisor said, 'What seems to be the trouble Mr. Wells?' I said, 'This guy just called me a queer!' He said, 'He called you a what?'"

"'I did NOT!'" Mac said the clerk responded. "'I told him he came under section so and so, paragraph such and such.'"

"I said, 'I didn't know what it was so I asked him and he said it was the homosexual one.' He said, 'Well you shouldn't get excited about that Mr. Wells. That's his opinion.'" But there was no real proof Mac and Chadwick had had sexual relations.

"We went through," Mac said. "We had no trouble after that. But see how that little fart could have scared me?" MacIver Wells was not one to be easily frightened.

When the women started to arrive, Chadwick redecorated the Madison. He decided it should look like a French sidewalk cafe. He and Mac placed awnings over the bar and hired one of the "girls"—their word—to paint wall murals of French street scenes. The tables sprouted red and white checkered cloths as well as a romantic touch with candles burning in glass containers. "It was different compared to the run-of-the-mill taverns [on the mudflat]," Chadwick said. "Picturesque, I guess you might say." Then a decidedly unromantic event occurred.

One day while Mac was working the bar, a Seattle police officer walked in. He chatted pleasantly for a few moments, then mentioned that he had noticed the Madison's clientele had changed. Mac listened. For thirty dollars a month, the beat cop said, the lesbians could be left alone, even given some "protection" against heterosexuals who might want to harass them in the bar. Neither partner had ever encountered such a suggestion in Canada. "In Canada," Mac said, "your business was your castle—a policeman didn't ever enter without your permission. Down here, it was a shock. A policeman could come into your tavern and do what he liked." Mac soon discovered that it was not uncommon for a Seattle police officer to make such suggestions.

The payoff system had begun at least by the late 1890s, when John Considine, faced with the barmaid ordinance that prohibited women from serving drinks, began enriching patrol officers for their tolerance. Once Prohibition ended in 1933 and new restrictions were put on saloons and gambling, police officers and inspectors had great leverage in deciding whether the lights inside a tavern seemed bright enough, whether views from sidewalks really were unobstructed enough, how often customers should be carded for age checks, and whether any singing or dancing by the clientele was impromptu or sufficiently a part of the bar business to require a different, more expensive cabaret or dance license.[3]

Later, in King County court records, it would be revealed that during the 1950s and 1960s the bar manager at the Double Header, John DelleVitti, had been required to pay the beat cop $60 per month. At his underground Casino, he had paid $100 every weekend it was open. By the 1960s the police were collecting almost $6,500 a year from the two gay gathering spots. At a nearby cocktail lounge at Second and Yesler, the Mocambo, the owner, Ivan Prather, would be approached by police officers in 1959. Prather paid $100 on the first of each month, according to the court records. He also started paying $50 per month to state liquor inspectors. Seattle police officers then demanded a raise, to $150 a month. Prather told prosecutors he eventually negotiated a different deal: $60 per month and two bottles of Old Hermitage. When Albert Romano opened the Submarine Room in the basement of the Smith Tower, a block north of the Double Header, he found his license application blocked until he agreed to pay $100 per month to beat officers. At one of the oldest steam baths on the mudflat frequented by homosexual men, the South End on First Avenue, the owner, Edwin McCleary, had been told to pay $75 a month. Eventually, according to court records, a patrol officer informed him that he had "too good of a thing" and the price would rise. McCleary was soon paying $200 per month, delivering the money in three separate envelopes, one for each police shift.[4]

Prosecutors would later allege that beat cops collected the cash and split the payoff with their shift sergeants, who in turn divided with captains. How far up the money went was a matter of speculation. Unlike John Considine, who in the 1890s claimed to have followed the police officer he had paid and seen him deliver the money to police chief William Meredith, gay bar owners could only speculate about where their cash went. The payoffs could also take different forms. Mac said he was once told it would be highly advisable for him to buy a couple of tickets to a fundraising party for the governor. Mac tried to reason his way out of the suggestion by saying that he and Chadwick were still Canadian citizens and could not even vote for the governor. The cop, unimpressed, dryly replied that a donation directly to the governor's campaign would still do. Other times, the payoff came in the guise of "voluntarily" hiring an off-duty policeman to be the bar bouncer and door checker. Although it was cheaper to assign a tavern employee to the door, the bars for homosexuals often were not allowed that choice.

Gay establishments were not the only ones hit. Taverns, card rooms, pinball arcades, and bingo parlors across the city had to pay, but, later investigations would show, the brunt of the extortion fell on the groups in Seattle that were stigmatized because of their color, their class, or their sexuality. Throughout the mudflat and in Seattle's Asian American and African American neighborhoods, those who ran social establishments for the city's outcasts paid the heaviest price. The First Precinct, covering Pioneer Square, became the most lucrative, according to the court records, generating from its largely run-down bars for transients and homosexuals up to ten thousand dollars per month for the police—enough in the late 1950s and 1960s to pay twelve officers' annual salaries.

Once the system was fully entrenched, it did not matter whether anything illegal was actually occurring at a particular bar. Just by making repeated entrances, the police could harass a business operator until the solution became obvious: pay off or close.

The system does appear to have worked for gay protection as well as extortion. For example, a heterosexual man once complained in an affidavit, filed in an unrelated 1960s criminal case, that he had been barred from the Madison. "At approximately midnight, accompanied by a female friend, a stewardess, I attempted to go into the Madison Tavern," he said. "We were stopped at the door by a uniformed policeman who said something to the effect that we really didn't want to come in there. 'Don't you know what kind of place this is?' [the policeman asked]. He then told us that after nine o'clock on Friday and Saturday nights, there was a cover charge of $3 per person, that [the cover charge] was awfully expensive and that we could get into other places for half that much. . . . It sounded as if he had been instructed to keep out 'straight couples.'"[5]

At the Madison, Mac had initially been taken aback by the demand for a payoff, but since he and Chadwick were new in town and not yet certified as citizens, they delivered. Then, in 1958, the rules changed. Mac recalled, "Up came a captain and wanted to see me in the back room. He says, we're going to stop accepting payments. I said, why, what's happening. He said, we've got a new mayor and he's really investigating all departments, so we won't accept money anymore. The captain called him Mickey Mouse—'While that Mickey Mouse bastard's in there, we can't take it [the payoffs].'"

Mac and Chadwick stopped making payments. More weeks passed, and then without warning police suddenly started raiding the Madison, entering unannounced and demanding to see everyone's identification, harassing homosexuals by threatening to report them to their employers. One Friday, October 3, 1958, was especially bad, according to Mac. Two police officers walked in and questioned the customers, ostensibly about their age. The officers walked out the door, then returned six minutes later with a sergeant and started the questioning all over again. Intimidated, every person in the bar left. Within a short period, the Madison went from making a profit to losing $350 a week.

Both Mac and Chadwick were confused. They had simply followed instructions. Yet suddenly, it seemed, the police had decided to make the Madison a target. Uncertain what to do, Mac relied on instinct—which for him meant fighting back.

That fall of 1958, the police had targeted not only the Madison but also a gay tavern called the Blue Note, which operated in Pioneer Square just a block from the Double Header and was run by a man named Jim Watson. The Blue Note had opened in August 1957, and even though Watson tried to get the raids stopped, he would say later that he had been told that the repeated visits were "a policy of the police department" even though the officers had never found any violations of the liquor laws. Instead, they just collected lists of names, addresses, and employers.

Watson had gone so far as to post a sign in the bar to encourage his customers to refuse to be intimidated. It said: "You do not have to answer any questions or give answers to any person when upon these premises." But most of his homosexual customers were not brave enough or out enough to withstand the police inquiries. They simply went elsewhere. Within a short while, according to statements Watson later made to the courts, he was losing more than a thousand dollars each week. He had already been told what he needed to do to stop the raids, but he was refusing. "Jim came up," Mac said, "because he didn't pay off, he wouldn't pay off—and they were really going to nail him. And I wasn't paying off because they wouldn't take it. And he said, 'I'm not going to lay down and take this, Mac. Are you willing to go in with me and fight this?' I said yes."

At the time, Watson apparently did not know that Mac had made previous payoffs. They found a lawyer, Gale Hilyer, and described both the raids and the payoff system. "Jim and I went down there," Mac recalled, "and that's when Jim found out I was making payments." The lawyer asked if either had made payments. "Jim says no. Then he asked me, and I didn't know what to say because I'd been telling Jim I didn't. And I say yes I do. Jim says, you phony son of a bitch. That's how Jim knew."

On October 9, 1958, Hilyer filed a lawsuit against the city on behalf of the Madison and the Blue Note. It appears to have been the first of its kind on behalf of Seattle's homosexuals, marking a new readiness to fight for a civil right—the right to peacefully gather in a public place without fear of government harassment. Even if only in a small way, it can be said to have signaled the beginning of the public struggle for gay civil rights in the city.[6]

The judge appointed to the case, Frank James, immediately granted a temporary restraining order against the police and set a trial date for November 25. In the meantime, the police were ordered not to question or intimidate any customers of the two bars unless there was "good cause" or the questioning was necessary for a "lawful arrest."

Judging from what can only be called a stumbling legal response, both the police and the city seem to have been unprepared for the possibility that homosexual bar owners would actually publicly challenge them. At first the city tried to defend the actions of its law enforcers. The city attorney claimed that the names being collected during the raids were necessary for an investigation of several felonies "which are believed to have involved homosexual persons." He argued that a list of such names would help in the investigation of "possible future felonies involving homosexual persons, the number and activities of which are believed to have undergone a rapid increase in recent months in Seattle." He did not cite any statistics.

It was a transparently unconstitutional logic. Had any attorney offered a similar rationale for raiding heterosexual taverns to gather the names of everyone there for the investigation of "future felonies," the lawyer would have been laughed from court.

The papers filed for the lawsuit had not mentioned the payoff system at all—just the raids. But putting police officers on the stand could mean that under cross-examination the payoff system would be revealed. Certainly the volatile MacIver Wells might talk about it.

Just a few days before the trial was to start, the city attorney and Hilyer conferred. Would Mac and Watson accept a settlement telling the police to stay out of the gay taverns unless they had legitimate reasons to enter? In return, would the two bar owners drop a request to be reimbursed for lost profits? The two owners also wanted the wholesale identification checks ended. If police came in to check, they should do so only if customers clearly looked underage.

The case ended almost as quickly as it had begun. On November 19, 1958, the deal was struck and the court order issued. It was rare for its time: an injunction instructing the city police not to question customers in gay bars unless there was "good cause" in connection with an actual investigation. In coming years, the order would save the emerging gay community in Seattle from the raids common in other cities—the kind that would eventually lead to the 1969 Stonewall riot in New York City that catalyzed later gay activists.

Mac's victory did not mean the end of the payoff system, though. No one thought that it would, and, possibly, few wanted it to. Even Mac quietly returned to paying off the police thirty dollars a month—although for reasons that would not become known for several more years.

Still, Mac and Watson had shown that homosexuals could resist the police officers, take them to court, and win. Hilyer had warned Mac that he would be "exposed" as a homosexual if he took the stand. Unafraid of being called a queer, Mac had scoffed and taken the risk.

# 5

# *Is Dance the Enemy?*

aving won his first battle against the Seattle police, MacIver Wells still faced a practical business problem at the Madison Tavern. He needed his customers back. Like any businessman, he decided that what he needed was a new gimmick. The one he chose happened to push the edge of homosexual acceptance in Seattle another step.

He leased a piano. It was time, he figured, to turn the Madison into a bar with live music; after all, the Garden of Allah had succeeded so well for a decade. Under city law, though, Mac's plan was illegal, because live music required a cabaret license.

Mac recalled that at first the city inspector looked the other way, aware of the bar owner's recent success in court and deciding the piano could be considered just another piece of decorative furniture. Then Mac added stools for singers. That went too far; the inspector insisted they be moved away from the piano. Mac responded by taking the stools away but sponsoring amateur nights during which anyone could stand next to the piano, either playing it or singing. They just could not sit. The inspector knew about the defiance, Mac said, but ignored it.

The bar was beginning to fill again, and the next step was obvious—at least from a business perspective, if not from a legal one. Mac remembered, "Then the girls wanted to know if they could dance. Dancing was allowed under that license, but you had to go and ask permission from the liquor inspector. But I let 'em dance anyway. Then the next thing I knew, the cabaret inspectors were up and they said, well if you're going to go ahead with this dancing, you'll have to have a policeman on the door on weekends. What the hell—on the weekends and not during the week—I don't know why. But we had to hire a policeman Friday and Saturday nights."

"That was the first gay tavern [in Seattle] that ever had dancing," he claimed. "From then on, it spread."

Margaret King, then a basketball coach teaching in Edmonds, remembered the impact Mac's decision had on her. "It was this little bar with a little dance floor. I thought I was in hog heaven," she recalled in 1992. The location and the clientele were better than what she had encountered in the bars on the mudflat. The women who went to the Madison, she said, "were all professionals. In fact, they were mostly all teachers. That's how I started living two lives—I had my life at school teaching PE. And then on weekends, I would come to Seattle to be a lesbian."[1]

Another woman, who preferred to remain unidentified during an interview in the 1990s, also remembered the effect Mac's decision had. The Madison became so popular, she said, "We had to have police at the door because the street people wanted to come in and see what the queers were doing!"

What they were doing was something new in Seattle. Mac's almost offhand decision made the Madison the first above-ground tavern that allowed Seattle's lesbians to dance—although many still chose to dance with gay men who came into the bar. It was a bar with windows, so the activities inside could easily be seen from the street.

The women who went to the Madison and the men who tagged along with them enjoyed a sense of camaraderie. One woman interviewed for the Alice B. Theatre Oral History Project (who asked to remain anonymous) remembered, "It seemed like [gay] people in Seattle in those years were very friendly toward one another. The girls liked having the fellas there. The guys probably didn't like it as much, but they put up with us." The guys did not dance with each other. That was a step not yet taken. If men danced in the Madison, according to Mac and others, they usually stayed in couples with women.

At about $150 per month, the cop on the door was part of the extra payoff demanded to allow lesbians to dance aboveground. It required a bit of adjustment in the local beat officers' attitude, what with homosexuals suddenly being aboveground and above the Deadline and dancing. The first two officers assigned did not even bother to show because, according to Mac, they said they could not stomach the notion of the lesbian celebration going on inside the Madison. But when the cops still insisted on collecting their money, Mac brusquely told their sergeant that if he had to pay extra to allow gay women to dance, then the cops had to at least show up. A different beat officer finally agreed.

One man in particular who would eventually take note of Mac's new success was his own young bartender, Joe McGonagle, hired in 1961. He had just arrived in Seattle, fresh from duty at Fairchild Air Force Base near Spokane, on the arid plain of eastern Washington. He had been eager to escape one frontier to discover another, one that had come to him by way of a party where he had danced with another airman's wife for so long that he had drawn what he thought were jealous glares from the husband. The next day the two men accidentally met, but to McGonagle's surprise, the other man was friendly and invited him for coffee at his bungalow. The wife had gone home to Seattle. A few weeks later, McGonagle stayed overnight and the two men shared a bed. Years later, in an interview, McGonagle would still remember how romantic that first experience had been, with French windows filtering the light and, outside, a lilac bush ready to bloom.[2]

As soon as he could, McGonagle sought a place where he could follow his yearnings more freely, and like a gold rusher, he went west to Seattle. Concealing his age with a fake ID—he was only nineteen—McGonagle took a job at the Madison. One night, off work at Seattle's curfew hour for bars, 2 A.M., he walked the half-mile south across the Deadline and to the corner at Washington and Second. He paused at the top of the same staircase that over the decades had been eyed by Collins, Considine, Vilma, Wilhelmina, Rose Bohanan, and hundreds of other gays and lesbians. Then he walked down into the old basement.

Like everyone before him, McGonagle was in awe. "There was this big barn of a room," he remembered. "As you came down the stairs, there was a little anteroom—they had a pool table there so that people could play pool if they wanted. You walked in and to your left, from the center of the dance floor, was where the men would hang out. To your right was a smaller area where the women would sit and drink. Then there was a huge long bar that went more than half of the room."

By the time of McGonagle's arrival, the Casino was beginning to change and add a new reputation. By then, it too had added dancing. In the 1960s, in fact, the club would come to be better known among gays and lesbians in the city as "Madame Peabody's School of Dance," a kind of English prep school reference to a dance school for children learning their first steps.

The focus, then, at both the Madison and the Casino was shifting from just drinking together or watching vaudeville together to actually moving together. While few on the new dance floors were likely to have contemplated the dramatic political impact their dancing would have in Seattle, in fact there would be a significant one. Some academics, like anthropologist Judith Hanna, have analyzed the impact of dance as a type of communication among repressed minorities and observed that dance often replaces an otherwise forbidden verbal expression. Dance historian Curt Sachs noted that in the flow of body and emotion, a dancer can "escape the sober facts of his existence" and go instead to a world where "imagination, fancy and vision waken and become creative." That which cannot yet be spoken publicly can instead be danced, and so, to dance together in any sort of public setting was both to enjoy a self-acceptance and to risk giving more offense to outsiders who happened to learn about it.[3] The heterosexual tourists who visited the Garden of Allah could still safely frame the events there as theater and entertainment—after all, vaudeville had always offered female impersonation. But the display of large numbers of men and women dancing with members of the same sex and sharing physical contact could provoke surprise, if not fear, as well. Descriptions of dancing at the Casino appeared in King County court records by the late 1960s.[4]

One witness, for example, attended a Halloween party:

> By 12:30 A.M., [the Casino] contained several hundred persons, mostly men and boys, ranging in age from the late teens to the thirties. A smaller number of women of these age groups entered also, and a smaller number of men past the late thirties and early forties. A coin-operated record-playing machine furnished dance music.

Generally, the women danced only with women; the men danced with men and boys. . . . The air in the hall was heavy, so foul that it became necessary for me to frequently seek out fresh air ducts around the sides of the room in order to avoid nausea and dizziness. Uniformed Seattle policemen were in attendance at the doorway of that establishment throughout the time I was present. At least twenty-five or thirty of the male attendees were obviously under the age of twenty years. . . . One boy, fifteen years of age, one who could not by any stretch of a knowledgeable person's mind be considered older than seventeen, entered the cafe, danced with older males, men past their middle twenties, and drank beer from a bottle which he carried around the floor. . . .

Conditions soon became dangerous to safety. Aisles between tables soon became slick with beer spilled from broken bottles on the floor. . . . When I took a paper sack and began picking up broken glass from one of the more obvious danger places, the act seemed singular enough to bring amused questions from one of the many scores of men who were dressed in women's gowns and party dresses. During the entire three hour-plus period that I remained . . . the scene was characterized by: men dancing with other men and with younger boys, women dancing with women, men and boys engaged in open-mouthed, hollow-jawed tongue kissing with one another, some while dancing, others while seated at tables; men and boys engaged in stroking one another's trousers directly over the buttocks, testicles and penises. . . . One far corner of the hall, off to the direct left of the entrance, was dimmer than any other area . . . and was far less frequented. . . . Occasionally, as the hours passed, isolated male couples would walk back into that area and situate themselves in the near-blind corners which parts of the wall structure afforded, and continue their kissing, embracing, and stroking while partially concealed from general view.

A public school teacher who went into the bar had this to report: "I observed young girls, some who may have been under twenty-one, dance together. Sometimes they would kiss and pet with passionate embraces. These girls would occasionally fondle their partners' buttocks in the area of the rectum and endeavor to rub their partner's genitals for the obvious purpose of sexual stimulation."

Another affidavit came from a man who went as a guest of two lesbians, seeking, as he said, "first hand knowledge of male and female homosexual activities." He was struck by the power of the dance and eventually agreed to be another man's partner.

To sit on the sidelines and observe from a distance does not compare with actually being in the midst of the crowd. I learned more in fifteen minutes of dancing than I had learned in ten hours. . . . The majority of those dancing were males, but how they were dancing is really something to be told. No self-respecting heterosexual couple would be caught dead dancing in the manner of the homosexuals. There were all kinds of poses used in dancing. All of the couples were holding each other very tight and close. Legs were intertwined, kissing was profuse and when you came near to the couple you could hear little moans and groans like you read about or hear being connected with sexual ecstasy. My partner, for one, was almost crushing me, sweat pouring off of him, until it was quite sickening.

The Reverend Mark Matthews, in one of his sermons in 1908, had posed a question addressed mostly to the city's mudflat. In "Is Dance the Enemy?" he had called the dances in Seattle's public halls and saloons a "whirling maze of physical attraction . . . beneath the respect of dignified, intelligent, refined people" and had warned that dancing was "only engaged in by the most vicious, the most depraved, the most vulgar and coarsest elements of society." But to the city's homosexuals in the early 1960s, it was this sexually tinged dance that was so empowering and freeing. The country's African Americans in the 1950s and 1960s used their traditional gathering spots in churches to launch a civil rights movement. Gays and lesbians used the dance floors.

"You could go in," Joe McGonagle remembered, "and dance your ass off all night long." Stephen Blair, who had healed some of his World War II traumas at the Garden of Allah, also went to the Casino in the 1960s. "I used to go there four nights in a row because I loved to dance, to do calypsos," he said. Madame Peabody's was a celebration of the physical, an invitation to the fun of belonging. "That goddamned place was loaded," Blair said, adding with what was both a degree of exaggeration and of fond impression, "It must have held about four thousand people."[5]

Some who arrived were scared—just as Wilhelmina had been three decades earlier when she paused at the top of the staircase that led to DelleVitti's underground Casino bar. The name, Madame Peabody's, served as a protective disguise. Tamara Turner had grown up during World War II in a house above Lake Union and by the late 1950s was studying history at the University of Washington. "Somebody at the U had said something about 'All the queers go to the Double Header,'" she would remember later. "So we went down there wearing blouses and straight skirts and flats and nylons and carrying our little purses. Some prostitutes there told us there was a gay club around the corner. We bought a six-pack, and at closing time, we walked around the corner to the place below Barney's Loans—on Second and Washington. Everybody referred to it as 'Miss Peabody's' or 'Aunt Peabody's' or 'Miss Peabody's School of the Dance.' And so you could say you were going to Miss Peabody's and gays would know what you were talking about, but straights wouldn't. In those days, everybody talked in code and it was the only way." Similarly, McGonagle recalled how "One Saturday night, somebody said, 'Let's go down to Madame Peabody's.' [And I said,] 'What the hell's Madame Peabody's?'"[6]

Some who went wanted still more secrecy than was guaranteed by the code name. Turner recalled seeing two women sitting at a table with brown paper bags over their heads. "They had drawn faces on the bags, and then cut out holes for eyes, nose, and mouth," she said. As it had in the 1940s and 1950s, the club still attracted a wide range of people. Turner remembered seeing "tough, working-class women" with short hair. "There'd usually be some really, really masculine women in white T-shirts with the sleeves rolled up to hold a pack of cigarettes, and then these other women in cocktail dresses and high heels."

By day, the Casino still drew neighborhood drinkers and pool shooters. Some were gay-friendly straight men, like one man who met Jackie Cachero, the eighteen-year-old lesbian who had been confined at Western State Hospital for three years. After her release from the asylum, Cachero had survived on the mudflat by turning tricks solely to earn money—"Ain't no way in hell I'd go to bed with some man for nothing," she said later in an interview with the lesbian newsletter *Out and About*. In the process Cachero had become pregnant, and, she said, the hospital authorities would not release her baby unless she married. "I met Mariano down at the Casino," she remembered. "They used to go down there and shoot pool all the time. . . . He kept asking me to marry him." So she did, but not in an attempt to pass as "normal." "I'm normal with women," she said.

"On our wedding night, I brought my old lady home; she slept in the middle. . . . And he said, 'Ooh, I don't care, I don't care.' So it's been him and me and my girl-friends ever since." By the time of the interview in 1979, they had been married for seventeen years. "I'm probably the only bull dagger in town that's got a hus-band, a wife, and seven kids," she said. She had found a place to belong.[7]

McGonagle, like many others, remembers dancing all night at Madame Peabody's and then staggering up the same staircase that Rose Bohanan had stum-bled up a decade earlier. He would emerge onto the corner of Washington and Second early in the mornings. "In summertime especially," he remembered, "the sun would be just coming up and you'd think, oh Jesus, I must look like the wrath of God."

"Get me home!"

# 6

## *Crossing Over*

## Challenging the Police

For a while, Joe McGonagle managed to deceive MacIver Wells and John Chadwick about his age. Neither knew that their bartender at the Madison was only nineteen. McGonagle fixed drinks for the lesbians who came in, watched them dance, and then, when he wanted to dance with men, carried his own beer over to Madame Peabody's. "I just loved it," McGonagle told me years later. "Here I was a nineteen-year-old and I'm getting into bars, having a great time." He managed the deception for a year.

Mac remembered what happened then: "A man and his wife came in from Spokane. They told me they owned a gay bar in Spokane, and they wanted to see Joe. Then the wife said, 'Is the law different here than in Spokane?' Her husband said, 'No, why?' She said, 'How can Joe work here when he's only twenty and we've got to have them twenty-one.'"

"'You goddamned stool pigeon!'" her husband cried.[1]

That was 1962, during the Seattle World's Fair, and McGonagle suddenly found himself remodeling the Madison instead of serving beer. The switch would have been unimportant, except for one thing. Now bored, McGonagle decided to pursue what until then had been just a daydream with another young man named Jake Heimbigner, who was managing a Belltown steam bath for homosexuals called Dave's. The two had fantasized about opening their own gay business, and since the only openly gay businesses were either bars or baths, they settled on the cheaper option: a bar. Before the year ended, the two found an old, failing saloon called the Majestic, located, not surprisingly, near the same corner as Madame Peabody's. Because he liked McGonagle, Mac agreed to loan them some money. The Majestic soon sported a new sign: the Golden Horseshoe.

From Mac, the younger men learned they needed a gimmick to attract gay business. The obvious choice was vaudeville, and so, within weeks, the two built a stage at the back of the Shoe, as it came to be called, and started drag shows, although with a change from the format used at the Garden of Allah. At the Horseshoe, the variety shows would not be elaborate, semiprofessional presentations, but amateur, grassroots drag. No headliners. No experience on the circuit necessary. McGonagle and Heimbigner encouraged the new lip-synching. "We'd take a Broadway musical and start at the beginning and go right through," McGonagle recalled. "Some turned out to be really good." Good enough to draw gay men. "The place was packed all the time."

It wasn't long before the beat cops in Pioneer Square showed up, demanding a payoff of a hundred dollars a month for permitting the drag shows. McGonagle and Heimbigner agreed.

Then they decided on a more lucrative gimmick. It was about 1963, McGonagle remembered. "About that time, Jake was approached by one of Seattle's finest, or Jake approached him, and said, 'What can we do about having men dance with men?' [The beat cop] said, 'Fine, for fifty dollars [extra] a week and a cop on the door Friday and Saturday night for fifteen dollars for three hours' work, we could arrange it."

"Shortly thereafter, boys started dancing with boys," McGonagle noted. Public dancing between men belowground and after hours had been common at Madame Peabody's. Now, in another small, symbolic change, it was aboveground.

Perhaps even more importantly, the dance was enough to fuel the business. McGonagle added, "We dispensed with the drag shows."

The police, he said, even "started letting us open up at six in the morning." So, on weekends, "we started having 'morning madness' or some silly name we put on it. Madame Peabody's would close at six A.M., so we would just open up." The Shoe was not as much a competitor for its cross-corner neighbor as it was a complement.

To the beat cops, it all meant more money. The new aboveground gay male dance generated an extra $320 a month, no small amount in 1963. Police shifts even began to compete for the revenue once those on the day shift realized that the night shift was collecting from the Shoe, while the graveyard shift was collecting from Peabody's.

McGonagle: "I went in one morning and I was standing at the bar when this big cop came in and took his night stick and banged it on the cigarette machine. [The sound] just ricocheted through the whole place. It sounded like a gunshot— scared the shit out of me. He says, 'What the hell's going on here?'"

"So I ran up to him. 'What do you mean what's going on?'"

"[The officer said] 'You're not supposed to be doing any of this stuff.'"

McGonagle explained that the arrangements had been cleared with another beat officer.

"'Well you haven't talked to me,'" the cop replied.

"'Well, who are you?'" McGonagle asked. "He told me his name, he was a prick, a real nasty bastard. Oh, he was mean. So anyway, I say I'll talk to Don [the other police officer] and I'll have Don get back to you. And out the door he went. He just wanted to make his point. He just wanted to let us know that he wanted in on the cut. It was a morning shift cop, not an afternoon or an evening shift."

The emergence of the gay male dance seems to have created a gradual shift in police attitudes over the next few months. At least some police officers must have realized that instead of just receiving money, they might actually be able to "grow" Seattle's gay marketplace as a kind of investment and even manage it for maximum return. Times were changing, and homosexual men and women in the city seemed to want their own bars.

For example, MacIver Wells was enviously eyeing the change his loan to McGonagle had helped make possible. In 1962, the same year the Horseshoe opened, Mac and Chadwick launched the first "chain" of gay bars in Seattle by purchasing a derelict tavern on Second Avenue a block north of Madame Peabody's, remodeling it and renaming it after its address, the 611. Chadwick cleaned crystal chandeliers and stretched red and gold drapes in the windows. Mac deliberately created an interior architecture to encourage male cruising and to complement the successful lesbian bar they had created at the Madison. Although the 611 was originally a long narrow room with a single-level floor, Mac redefined the space, building a narrow raised deck down one length and installing mirrors on both walls. That created a "line of sight" that let men stand on the raised floor in any part of the bar and, through the mirror, watch a man in any other part.

Business boomed; the 611 put Wells and Chadwick on the Pioneer Square gay map. Still, the 611 was just a social bar, not a dance bar. Wells wanted what McGonagle had, but when he asked the cops for permission to let men dance at the 611, they denied it. Wells remembered, "They said Jake's got the boys, and you've got the girls." The cops figured the city could handle only one gay male dance floor aboveground.

A year passed. Mac kept pestering the cops. Finally, he got permission—but only with the stipulation that he had to buy yet another bar. The police officers had their own agenda. The Shaggy Dog Night Club, located on First Avenue directly behind the 611, was going out of business. Instead of walking their beats on Sundays, the police usually skipped their jobs and used the tavern to play poker and pinochle, so they wanted the new buyer to be friendly. The offer: If Wells would buy the Shaggy Dog and continue to provide a friendly space there for police pinochle after hours, he could have a dance floor for men. Wells agreed; the renamed 614 Tavern would become the second male dance floor in Seattle.

The cops set the initial payoff at the same rate the Golden Horseshoe was paying. The state liquor control inspectors' charge was extra.

For a short while after that, stability seems to have reigned in Pioneer Square's new gay marketplace. The relationship with those who held power over the land—the police—was peaceful if not cozy. In the stability, the gay presence could become increasingly public. And it did. Just as Mac had expanded his holdings, so did Heimbigner, who began to build something of a small gay entertainment empire all within a one-block square. He acquired the Atlas Club Steam Baths around the corner from the Horseshoe as well as a part-interest in the Stage Door Tavern, next to the Casino. That way, if a gay man wanted to spend the afternoon at the baths, grab a dinner beer at the tavern, go to the Shoe for dancing, and then return to the baths for late-night sex—well, it was all Heimbigner's territory.

For agreeing to leave the men at the Atlas Club alone, according to King County court records, the cops charged two hundred dollars a month; from the Stage Door, they extracted sixty dollars per month.[2]

Other gay cocktail lounges, cafes, and bars also flourished, now overlapping with the older bars from the 1950s. The Grand Union at Yesler and Fourth. Cimbries on Occidental. Sappho's on Prefontaine. The Columbus, the 611, the 614, the Horseshoe, the Mocambo, the Submarine Room in the Smith Tower. For the first time, Seattle gained a recognizable gay district, one created not simply from gays and lesbians frequenting the streets and then disappearing underground, but one quite visibly aboveground. To promote sales and organize social events, the owners of the businesses even formed the first gay "chamber of commerce" in Seattle, the Queen City Business Guild, and began meeting at the Mocambo. McGonagle and Heimbigner made money, Mac and Chadwick made money, the police made money.

By the beginning of 1965, there was a flowering of tolerance on the mudflat, and gays and lesbians became publicly visible in a way never before seen in Seattle. As a group, however, they still did not have any political power, any civic purposes, or—beyond the business guild—any organized institutions.

Then one of those minor miscalculations with major consequences occurred.

In the winter of 1965, a beat cop summoned Mac to a meeting at the Golden Horseshoe with Heimbigner. Since the opening of the 614, the two men had become the major competitors for the gay dollar. Although Mac still felt close to McGonagle, he had never particularly liked Heimbigner, so he wondered why he was suddenly being told to meet with his business foe. Mac described what happened next:

"I asked the cop who told me, 'So what's it about?'"

"'Well, [to find out] if you're interested in opening up an after-hours spot.'"

"'I'll listen to it,'" Mac said.

"[The meeting] was held in the Horseshoe with Jake and I and a cop who's dead now and about four or five other cops. This one that's dead now did all the talking. He was gay, the cop was. He used to peddle his ass when he was fifteen or sixteen down around the Double Header. . . . He explained [the after-hours spot] was going to be in the Morrison Hotel. Jake and I would be partners if we wanted. They offered where it would be. There'd be no problem. I listened to all this and said, 'What do we have to pay you?'"

"He says, 'Fifty percent of the take.'"

"I say, 'And I split with Jake and I pay the help? Boy, that don't leave me much, does it?' I say, 'On top of that, I don't like Jake anyway. I wouldn't have nothing to do with him.'"

"[The cop] says, 'Well, you're a smart ass.'"

"And I say, 'Yes, and you're just a punk.'"

"He says, 'I'll club you into the floor, you ever call me a punk.'"

"[Another cop] was there, and he says, 'You're not going to club anybody. This is all bullshit as far as I'm concerned. C'mon Mac,' he says, 'let's go.'"

"And the other cop and I walked out and I never heard any more about that. Next thing I knew, Jake opened up."

The Caper Club, it was called. A police-initiated after-hours club for gay men. With Mac fuming, Heimbigner plunged into the venture alone. His application for a cabaret license had to be approved by the city council's license committee, but that posed no obstacle once the police investigators attached a note saying they did not object. The payoff for the new club was set at six hundred dollars a month, according to the later county court records. It was the highest extortion paid by any establishment in Seattle, gay or straight. But then the Caper Club was different. With elaborate ceilings, fancy curtains, and swank serving areas, the Caper Club strove for a far more elegant and upscale atmosphere than any of the old basements or remodeled taverns. For a change, customers walked upstairs into the Morrison Hotel for their capering.

"That was a beautiful bar," John Chadwick recalled.

Not only was it fashionable, it was safe. After all, it was located just across the street from police headquarters.

Probably nothing would have changed, and Mac would have quietly fumed about his competitor, if the miscalculation had not occurred. A new sergeant took command of the beats that included Mac's three bars. The sergeant walked into the 614 in September 1965. It is not clear whether the sergeant knew about the earlier meeting that had turned hostile at the Golden Horseshoe and decided to get even, or whether he simply wanted to cash in on what looked like a lucrative chain of gay bars. The cop was smoking a cigar.

He started complaining that Mac hadn't paid promptly on the first of the month. "'You're paying on the first if you know what's good for you,'" Mac remembered him saying.

Then the sergeant added, "You're going up in price too"—an extra fourteen hundred dollars per year. Mac's total annual payoff was going to be close to five thousand dollars.

The two men glared at each other.

"He was blowing smoke in my face, like a gangster," Mac said. "I hate cigar smoke."

"That's when I got mad."

Something else happened in 1965. While it did not seem directly connected to the behind-the-scenes disturbance that had begun on the mudflat, it involved a public arrest by the police and so seemed worrisome.

A young and charismatic heterosexual man named Keith Rhinehart had begun a new church called the Aquarian on Seattle's Capitol Hill, promoting the acceptance of a wide range of traditional and "New Age" beliefs. Eventually, he would open branches in Chicago, Spokane, and Honolulu, and the mother church in Seattle would claim more than six hundred members. As part of his ministry, Rhinehart called openly for tolerance and acceptance of homosexuals in the city. The church, according to documents that would eventually be filed with the King County court, took the "position that persons who by physical makeup or conscious desire are inclined toward sexual relationships with the same sex should be permitted to exercise these private sexual desires with the same anonymity that is granted to the heterosexual." In the early 1960s, that was a radical argument against the state sodomy law. The Aquarian Church in Seattle welcomed homosexuals, perhaps the first church in the city to publicly do so.

According to claims made in the later court records, the Seattle Police Department began investigating Rhinehart almost as soon as he started the Aquarian. In fall 1964, for example, a Seattle police sergeant supposedly questioned a man who had visited the Aquarian meetings and warned him to stay away from "that nut on the hill." The man said the sergeant told him, "We're going to put him [Rhinehart] behind bars one way or another, and if you are affiliated with him, we will put you in the penitentiary too." Police officers supposedly showed up at Rhinehart's apartment for visits, noting how he had decorated the interior.[3]

On April 6, 1965, Rhinehart began a series of hour-long local TV shows, interviewing others about morality and philosophy. Included in his first program was a lesbian. At the end of the program, Rhinehart pleaded with viewers to understand that each individual was a human being created by God and therefore was entitled to love and to privacy in their sexual relations.

Five days later, on Sunday morning, April 11, the Seattle police arrested a sixteen-year-old named James G. Miller, accusing him and two friends of trying to steal a car in downtown Seattle. Miller, as the officers knew, had a long record of burglary, theft, and larceny and was already on parole. He had been in and out of juvenile and foster homes since age six. Both Miller and the officers knew that the new charge could send him back to a jail for juveniles.

When the police officers found fifteen dollars in Miller's wallet the Sunday morning they arrested him, they asked him how he had gotten it. He claimed he had let another man fellate him. It is not clear whether that was actually true or just a teen's flippant answer. An officer fetched a week-old television guide, opened it, and showed Miller a photograph of Keith Rhinehart next to an announcement about Rhinehart's TV program on sexuality.

Yes, Miller quickly agreed, that was certainly the man who had fellated him.

Two days later, on April 13, without consulting an attorney, Miller signed a statement in which he claimed that at 1:15 A.M. on the same day he would later be arrested, April 11, he had been standing downtown on Pine Street, between Third and Fourth Avenues, when a young man in his mid-twenties pulled to the curb across the street from us and honked his horn. He was driving a lighter colored '61 or '62 Cadillac convertible. When he honked, I went over to see what he wanted. When I approached the car, he said, "Sorry, I thought you were a different person." Then he said, "Do you want to earn some money?" I said, "Yes." Then he said, "Do you want to come up to my apartment?" I agreed. . . . As he was driving, he asked me, "Have you ever had a blow job or, have you ever given anyone a blow job?" I replied "No." He then reached over and unbuttoned my jeans. After doing this, he reached over the top of my shorts and started playing with my penis. He did this for a minute or so. I told him to stop and I then buttoned my jeans back up. We arrived at his apartment a few moments later.

Miller's statement to the police was damning for its amount of detail.

When we were inside his apartment, he locked the door behind us. I then sat down and started looking at some pictures of nude men and women that was laying on the table. This was [a] one-roomed apartment with a bath. There were a lot of carvings in the room and a round bed. After we were in the room about five minutes, he said, "Why don't you take off your clothes?" We both then stripped nude. He then sat on the edge of the bed. . . . He offered me $15 if I would let him kiss me and blow me. I refused and then he said, "Well, I'll just blow you." I then walked over to where he was sitting. He started playing with my penis and privates until I got a "hard-on." He was masturbating himself at the same time. He then put his mouth over my penis. He continued this until I reached a climax in his mouth.

Miller noted that an officer had shown him the advertisement in the television guide. "I am positive," he asserted, "that the picture in this advertisement is the same man that had sex relations with me. The name on the advertisement lists this man as Keith Milton Rhinehart."

Quickly the police arrested Rhinehart and charged him with sodomy. Rhinehart agreed that he had honked at Miller, mistaking him for the son of a congregation member, and that the teen had then expressed an interest in riding in his car. He said Miller had then propositioned him, saying he would perform sex for a price, but Rhinehart had refused. Instead, Rhinehart said he had told Miller that he himself was not a homosexual but that he knew many homosexuals and they were welcome at his church. Rhinehart adamantly denied that the two had had sex or that Miller had gone to his apartment.

With Rhinehart charged, the authorities freed Miller a few days later. On April 22, a juvenile judge then formally dismissed the charge against Miller of attempted auto theft. Under the state's sodomy and prostitution laws, Miller had just confessed in his statement to two felonies. But he was never charged with either.

Within three weeks of being released by the police and courts, and before Keith Rhinehart's trial was to begin, James Miller recanted his accusation, signing a statement on May 17 that "there was no sexual act of any description between Rev. Rhinehart and myself." Much as the young Albert Jenner had done in the 1907 case against Thomas Longbottom, Miller now said the police had pressured him. He claimed the police had told him Rhinehart was "an atheist, a quack, and had put on a goofed-up TV show [with] a homosexual." Miller further said that the police had told him they were "really out to get Rhinehart and they needed a statement from me to help them."

Then, Miller fled. The police found him in California, returned him to Seattle, and then released him to await Rhinehart's trial. When he failed to show, the police found him again on June 11. While in custody, Miller signed a third statement reasserting that he and Rhinehart had had sex.

A parole report, written June 14, noted that Miller had been hiding at the Green Parrot Theater in downtown Seattle. The report described the theater as a "homosexual hangout" and noted that the police felt the teen had been "having more homosexual contact in the last two weeks for monetary reasons." The report added, "It is not believed that Jim is seriously homosexual, but it is felt that he has taken up this method to get spending money."

Miller was, in other words, hustling—which was what Rhinehart's defense attorney was contending had happened the night the two had met, except that Rhinehart had refused the offer.

At the trial during the summer of 1965, Miller repeated his accusation that the two had had sex and that Rhinehart had paid him. When Rhinehart's attorney attempted to impeach Miller's credibility by arguing that Miller had a reputation for hustling men, the investigating police officer testified he knew of no such reputation on Miller's part, despite the June 14 parole report that said the opposite.[4]

The jury chose to believe Miller and the police officer, convicting Rhinehart. Once again, Miller went free, still uncharged for his own supposed prostitution and participation in sodomy. Rhinehart, on the other hand, would be sentenced to spend ten years in the state penitentiary at Walla Walla.

Even amid a growing tolerance for gay bars on the mudflat, the trial was a reminder of just how vulnerable any gay man—or any heterosexual ally—could be to charges that he had engaged in homosexual sex of any kind.

But Rhinehart's case was not over yet.

One of the curious features of the police payoff system in Seattle is that it was such an open secret. Many knew about it, including (as it turned out) the Federal Bureau of Investigation. Yet the protection racket provided enough benefits for all of those involved that no one wanted to reveal it. Any bar owner who had paid a bribe, after all, could be prosecuted. Any police officer who had received one could be fired. And any disruption to the system meant that no one would make as much money anymore. If the system collapsed, everyone feared, the laws governing bar lighting, dancing, and socializing would end up having to be rigidly enforced—

and that would only play into the hands of Seattle's moralists who wanted to smash the activities on the mudflat.

But MacIver Wells was in a situation unique among those making payoffs. Almost as soon as he had settled his 1958 lawsuit against the city, an FBI agent had taken note of his resistance. Seeing a chance for a possibly disgruntled informant, the agent arrived at the Madison and demanded to know whether Mac was paying off. At first, Mac lied and said no. So the agent paid a visit to Jim Watson of the Blue Note. Watson, of course, had learned during the lawsuit that Mac had been making payments, and he told that to the FBI agent. The agent returned to the Madison and proposed a deal: Mac would resume his payments to the police but would keep a record of all the dates and times and people involved. Thus, during the seven years while he was expanding and adding dance floors, Mac had not only been making his payments to the Seattle police but had been reporting them all to the FBI.

To Mac, September 1965 seemed a good time to end the game. It was the cigar smoke from the cop who had told Mac to pay more. It really made him mad.

After the sergeant left, Mac angrily dialed the FBI agent. He wanted all the information he had been providing released—to a federal prosecutor, to a newspaper, to anybody. Anything to stop the police.

At first, the FBI agent was noncommittal. In reality, the federal agency could do little. No federal laws were actually being broken, since bribery was a matter for the state and county. The agent had been pouring Mac's information into his files, watching to see whether he could track any of the money to federal political candidates, but he had no case yet. Months passed. Then in May 1966, Mac was surprised by a call asking him to an appointment with the Seattle police chief, Frank Ramon. Word had already gotten out among the rank and file that someone was squealing.

Mac remembered:

The FBI had sent a memo to the police department about payoffs, that it was getting a little out of hand or something like that. They pieced together that it was me that had been giving the reports. They came around, one of the cops, and told me they wouldn't take any more payoffs. They thought I was the guy that was squealing. . . . That's when they started coming in and asking ID—didn't matter if you were seventy years old. My mother was there one night and they went over and they asked her, and she was eighty years old. One of the officers said, "Would you show me your ID ma'am?" She said, "I can assure you I'm over twenty-one." He said, "I'm asking you, show me the ID." She said, "I'm not going to show you anything son." So the sergeant called [the other officer] over. I heard the sergeant say, "That's Mac's mother, leave her alone."

I went down shortly after that to see Chief Ramon . . . and I told him about these cops in and out and that I made payoffs to his police department, and I would like to have it stopped. He said, "Just a moment." He went and opened up a door and he said, "Chief Cook [M. E. Cook, one of Ramon's assistants], would you come in. Now would you repeat all that you have told me in front of Deputy Cook here?"

I said, "You know, I'm not that stupid. You've got a witness, I don't. I'm not saying nothing."

Mac left. It looked like his plan for getting the FBI to act had backfired. But he wasn't about to surrender.

I went and I phoned the [Seattle] *Times* newspaper. They had a religious reporter at that time who was digging into harassment of the colored people and I phoned him. He said, "No I don't get involved in things like that but I will send down a reporter." So he sent down two—their names was Wilson and Wilson. John [Wilson] came down first. I told my story, and he listened and listened and he took notes. He said, "That's quite interesting, I didn't know this was going on." So I didn't hear from him for about two weeks. The police were still giving me a bad time.

Then he came down with Marshall Wilson. I had to tell my story all over again. I had to go up to the newspaper office and they made all these notes and then we both signed it, that what we were saying was honest. Then they told me, "We have dug around in the last two weeks and this is going on in quite a few places. But is there one way that you can prove that you've been reporting this? Can you prove that you did give a report to the FBI?"

I think it was Marshall who said, "We'll be down to your tavern next week, and we'll think up something." When they came down, he said, "You've got two telephones here, haven't you?" I said, "Yes, there's one in the back at the phone booth and there's one behind the bar." He said, "We'll listen in on the other phone." They went to the pay phone and I dialed the FBI and I asked for [the agent].

He came on. I said, "I don't know if you know of all the harassment I'm getting from the police, but it's pretty damn bad, and I have cooperated with you. Isn't there anything you can do to help me?"

And he said, "No, if it was political we could step in."

The newspapers [reporters] went like that [giving a high sign], they'd heard it. [The agent] says, "Mac, I'm awfully sorry I can't help you."

So then the Wilsons came back and said, "That's all we need. He admitted that you had made a report."

And that's when the shit hit the fan.

It was late summer 1966. By the return of autumn, a new tautness would emerge along the Deadline.

On Wednesday, September 21, 1966, John Wilson wrote the first article. But it was not the exposé Mac had expected. The reporters were apparently still investigating the specifics of his charges. Instead, under the headline, "Seattle Homosexual Problem Reported To Be 'Out of Hand,'" Wilson provided the first major public news about the city's homosexuals, doing so in a story that trumpeted the police side. It read:

"Police officials admitted today that Seattle's problem with homosexuals 'is out of hand.' *Times* reporters have learned that the city's homosexual population numbers in the thousands. An estimate of 12,000 was termed conservative by a Seattle–King County Health Department official. The official added that the total has been fairly stable the past few years. Police confirmed that Seattle has become known nationally as being tolerant toward homosexuals."

"'The word got out that Seattle is soft on homosexuals,' M. E. Cook, assistant police chief said."[5]

The story noted that Ramon was planning to move against the bars in the city that attracted homosexuals, partly by stripping them of the off-duty police who were working the doors on weekends. In a negative reference to Mac's 1958 lawsuit, Ramon said that the police could not do much more because of the court order, which, he implied, had allowed the number of gay bars in Seattle to double since it was issued. The court order, in other words, was the problem.

"Things just got out of hand," Cook told the newspaper. But Ramon promised, "We're not going to let this city get like San Francisco."

Although the *Times*' audience would have had no clue about what was happening behind the scenes, the police threat communicated through the story was hardly veiled. If Mac blew apart the payoff system publicly, the police could use the widespread disapproval of homosexuals to shut down the bars entirely. Chief Ramon himself did not necessarily know about the payoffs—a later grand-jury indictment against him would be dismissed for lack of evidence. But the timing of the threat seemed calculated.

The story also pointedly noted that the Armed Forces Disciplinary Control Board, which had been listing three bars and one steam bath as off-limits to military personnel, was now sending letters to a larger number of gay business owners and threatening them with an off-limits listing because "a significant percentage of sexual deviates among your regular patronage [creates] an undesirable atmosphere for service persons who frequent your establishment." Eventually, the list expanded to include fourteen gay bars, cafes, and bathhouses that were either off-limits or under observation.[6]

Although the initial *Times* article made no mention of coerced payoffs, John Wilson did signal that a bigger story was in the offing. First, he quoted health department officers who were concerned about the spread of sexual diseases in the gay steam baths in Pioneer Square. Then, he noted that Ramon was threatening to ask the city council to revoke bar licenses. But, Wilson added, "The Police Department as late as early this year voiced no objection in its report on a cabaret license being issued to one of the steam bath operators mentioned by the Health Department.

The man got the license and set up an operation that has become an after-hours place for dancing and drinking by homosexuals."

Wilson's story continued: "Although an establishment with a cabaret license and its customers must obey standards of morality and decency, Cook said he felt no police action could be taken where couples of the same sex dance or make physical contact in other ways in public. At least two of the gay bars refuse to admit anyone but 'members,' although they do not have private club liquor licenses."

That was the sole hint the initial story gave of a possible police policy of tolerating infractions. It did not name Jake Heimbigner as the operator of the Atlas and the new Caper Club, and it did not pursue the obvious question: Why were the police overlooking possible violations?

The next day, the Wilsons probed further. They asked the city licensing director what he thought of the police department's failure to prevent Heimbigner, who was still not named, from getting a cabaret license. After all, he was operating a steam bath that the health department thought problematic. The licensing director, Don Turnbull, bluntly said, "That's a mistake they made. They knew about him."[7]

The two reporters also talked to a city councilman, Charles M. Carroll, who headed the city council license committee. Although Carroll's committee had approved Heimbigner's license for the Caper Club, the councilman passed the blame to Ramon. He said that if the police department knew about the steam bath operator's background, it should have included the information in its report to the committee. "We would be guided by the recommendation of the Police Department in this area," Carroll added. "If there was any evidence of this fellow's background, the license wouldn't have been issued under any circumstances."

Then, the reporters noted that the new after-hours club allowed men to dance together, something that the city attorney doubted was a violation of the city's lewd conduct law, "the only laws used against homosexuals," he added. But, the attorney helpfully volunteered, if the city council wanted to pass such a law forbidding the gay dance, it could. "We could just say that members of the same sex can't dance together."

With the unexpected publicity, the grand plan for the Caper had come under sudden scrutiny. So had the gay dance. The two *Times* stories provided public notice—perhaps the first to the city's general populace—that homosexuals were dancing together in Seattle. Judging from the rhetoric in the story, not only was the dance a problem, but so was the police tolerance both of it and of Heimbigner's allegedly muddy reputation.

At first, Chief Ramon tried to deflect the criticism. In a long, confidential memo to Seattle mayor J. D. "Dorm" Braman on September 27, 1966, Chief Ramon referred to the "recent 'scare' publicity" about homosexuals in Seattle and wrote:

Every city, including Seattle, for many years has had a problem with homosexuals. Generally speaking, the problem is limited to a very few establishments where

Police Chief Frank Ramon (right) suggested new restrictions on homosexual bars, leading to the Seattle City Council's first hearing on lesbian/gay civil rights in 1966. *(Seattle Post-Intelligencer Collection, Museum of History and Industry, Seattle)*

Mayor "Dorm" Braman in 1966 urged the police to "discourage the inflow" of homosexuals to Seattle. *(Seattle Post-Intelligencer Collection, Museum of History and Industry, Seattle)*

homosexuals congregate. For more than fifteen years, the number of such places in Seattle was five or less. In recent years it has suddenly expanded to three times that number. The principle concern of the police with homosexuals is in three areas.

The first is that of homosexuals accosting or attempting to recruit persons who are not homosexuals. Secondly, there are the crimes that stem from homosexuality itself. There are at least five unsolved murders in Seattle, which are known to be the result of homosexual affairs and would appear to be destined to remain for a long time, if not forever, in the "unsolved" files. There are at least twenty cases of aggravated assault; the majority of them solved and some of them unsolved which stem from homosexual or lesbian activities. Thirdly, it is known to the police of every city that homosexuality causes many crimes, which are not reported to the police. One of the most continuing bunco actions is that of persons pretending to be policemen shaking down homosexuals for money under the guise of not prosecuting them for homosexual acts. This particular criminal activity is known throughout the United States.

Also in the shadow area, the police are convinced that hundreds of homosexuals are victimized by extortion or blackmail or robbery or assault and do not report these crimes to the police. There have been a few convictions for the so-called "degenerate shakedown" and a fairly recent one for extortion and robbery, but we are well aware that the percentage of these offenses known to police are minute. Another area of major police concern is the influx of homosexuals to any community when the information available is that the community is "soft" or "tolerant" of homosexuals.[8]

What the note failed to mention, of course, was that Seattle policemen themselves had managed much of the "white-collar" extortion of gay establishments. At the end of his lengthy memo, which reviewed developments in San Francisco and his request for military restrictions on gay bars, Ramon made an interesting recommendation. The problem, he said, was not violations of city ordinances, but violations of state regulations. No new city laws were needed, just more stringent inspections by inspectors from the state liquor control board. Indeed, he went so far as to write, "It is not recommended at this time that any new city ordinances be created to deal with this problem."

On the one hand, Ramon simply put the blame on state inspectors. But at the same time he seemed to suggest that city politicians not poke their noses too deeply by writing new ordinances.

The chief also proposed a substantial reduction in the safe territory gays and lesbians had been able to stake out. "I will recommend to your office for disapproval," he wrote, "the issuance, renewal, or transfer of any liquor license to any person who . . . will operate an establishment primarily oriented toward homosexual or lesbian patronage."

Mayor Braman responded the following day:

I have your complete report. . . . The picture you paint is a discouraging and sordid one, and I certainly have no suggestions to make to help resolve the situation. . . .

It would look like your department is doing everything possible to reach the hangouts of these people. But, as is well recognized, the incidence of this problem is far greater than generally understood; and in most instances, as I understand it, these people create no problem whatever for society or for anyone outside of perhaps their own family circles. Those few, however, who do either engage in illegal activities leading to serious crimes, or who gather in public places to the extent of becoming a nuisance, do create a problem and a real dilemma, as indicated by your report.

I am a little surprised, however, that any impression should be out that Seattle is soft on, or tolerates, these gathering places. If there is any basis for this and there is anything we could be doing to indicate that we are not tolerant or soft in this area, certainly we should be taking such steps. I would assume that a certain amount of close surveillance, even to the point almost of harassment of the most troublesome and noisome establishments, might have some effect to discourage the inflow of these people to Seattle.

By whatever means—this we must accomplish.[9]

While all of this was happening, there was also a new development in the police case against Keith Rhinehart. On September 26, 1966, just five days after the Wilsons began their string of stories, James Miller signed another statement—his fourth. In it, he swore: "The testimony I gave was false."

After being picked up for car prowling by some policemen, two other officers from the Seattle Police Department . . . questioned me about the time I spent with Mr. Rhinehart on the morning I was picked up. . . . [One] officer told me that if I did not "cooperate" I would get into trouble. My understanding was that if I didn't give them something which would permit them to arrest Mr. Rhinehart that I would undoubtedly continue to be confined and might be returned to Fort Worden where I had been previously detained. . . . The information in the statement about Mr. Rhinehart's home and what was in it and where it was located was all supplied to me by the police officer. He questioned me in such a way that I knew the answers that he wanted. He would say, "Did you see a round bed in his room?" and I would know from the way he asked the question that there must be one there so I would tell him that I did. I was not in Mr. Rhinehart's home and my testimony in this respect was not true.

Mr. Rhinehart did not commit sodomy on me or any sexual act of any kind. . . . I testified the way I did at the trial because I was under pressure. I felt that if I told the truth, the police officers who patrol First Avenue and the other areas that I would like to be in would be particularly watchful of me and my freedom would be substantially deprived.

Rhinehart's attorney filed an appeal to the state supreme court. The minister waited, his sentence to Walla Walla on hold for the moment.

Logically, the police might have picked MacIver Wells as their first target. They knew he had called the FBI; they probably suspected he was in touch with the *Seattle Times* reporters. But perhaps the heat from the *Times* stories determined the first public scapegoat. Or perhaps the police were simply wary of a man who had already taken them to court, started women dancing aboveground, stormed out of meetings, and reported the payoffs. Too, Mac himself had tried over the previous summer to reduce the amount of harassment. He had sold the Madison (to a man who had apparently promised to clean out its lesbian and gay clientele[10]) and then had converted the 614 into a tavern called the Gallery, which had begun catering to a heterosexual dance crowd as well as homosexuals.

For whatever reason, a few weeks after Ramon won his free hand from the mayor, the police department moved publicly against Jake Heimbigner, rather than MacIver Wells. Ramon urged the city council not to renew Heimbigner's cabaret licenses at both the Horseshoe and the Caper Club. He also asked that another gay cabaret, the Golden Goose, lose its license.

The recommendation posed a crucial challenge to the still fragile public life homosexuals had claimed in Seattle. Ramon's request specifically targeted gay dance floors. With Mac selling the Madison and converting the 614, those two dance floors for gays and lesbians were already vanishing. The allure of Madame Peabody's as an after-hours dance club had faded with the competition from the Caper Club, but now the Caper Club was targeted.

If the council followed the police suggestions, licensed gay or lesbian dance floors would no longer exist in Seattle.

November 29, 1966. Eight years had passed since Mac's initial, successful court suit against police harassment. Now the stage was set for the city's first legislative hearing over the place of homosexuals as citizens in Seattle. The specific issue before the city council's license committee was whether Jake Heimbigner, entrepreneur and owner of a gay bathhouse, deserved to hold a cabaret license and let men dance with men. The more general issue: Whether gays and lesbians in the city had a right to such public association.

For what normally would have been a routine bureaucratic decision about whether to revoke a bar owner's license, the *Seattle Times* reported a "near-capacity audience." The *Times* headlined the story "Standards Studied for Deviate Cabarets."[11]

The rhetoric the council heard that day would establish a pattern for the next several decades, ranging from debates about Holy Scripture to arguments about the First Amendment, from the psychology of what caused homosexuality to proposals for how a city should best respond.

Keith Rhinehart was there, temporarily free while awaiting the outcome of his appeal to the Washington State Supreme Court. So were other ministers. Rhinehart, the *Times* reported, "urged the Council to emulate the example of San Jose, Calif., which it was declared, has allocated more than $890,000 for a sex-education to begin in the fourth grade. Mr. Rhinehart urged Council members to ignore Chief Ramon's recommendations and renew the three licenses [saying] he could provide the Council with a list of more than 1,000 establishments in the United States which are gathering places for homosexuals."

The Reverend Thomas Miller, of the Calvary Bible Presbyterian Church, was not impressed. To give homosexuals "a place to meet," he responded, "is the worst thing you can do for them—it simply encourages them."

"Several speakers," the *Times* said, "asked councilmen to consider the existence of various physical aberrations and not to rule harshly against persons whose standards of behavior are different from normal standards."

The newspaper did not report any statements being made by the homosexuals who owned or used the bars. Publicly, at least, those voices were still silent. However, among those who testified for Seattle's gays and lesbians was a heterosexual minister from the United Church of Christ, the Reverend Mineo Katagiri, who countered the fundamentalist Miller. Katagiri would eventually become the first real organizer of and spokesman for the city's gay rights movement. In retrospect, his words take on a rhetorical importance since they reflect the first political strategy that politically minded gays and lesbians would use as they began trying to "talk to" heterosexuals in the city.

Katagiri's remarks were not reported in the *Times,* but he did later send a written copy to Mayor Braman. Here is some of what he had to say:

> The problem is twofold: society needs to learn to accept homosexuals as legitimate members of the community and homosexuals must learn to behave as responsible members of a larger community. . . . Any action which can be interpreted as persecution will make the task of integration more difficult. The proposed closing of the bars only says to the homosexuals that the official policy of Seattle is one of persecution. This makes our task of relating to homosexuals that much more difficult. . . .
>
> We are trying to get the homosexual communities to accept responsibility for setting their own standards of conduct. The lesbians I am meeting with have decided to organize with a set of officers so that they can begin to set standards which will be creative. For instance, I would like to see them say that sex should be between consenting adults and in the privacy of the bedroom. Hence, they would agree that they would not seduce minors nor show affection in public. Also, that the gay bars should be places of socialization, and not sexual gratification. But they will do so only if they are made to feel they are wanted in the larger community. If we make them feel as outcasts, they will behave as outcasts.
>
> This means we will need to help the responsible ones take over "power positions" in the gay community and set standards of conduct. It is their hand that we must

While Seattle government officials in the 1960s considered homosexuals to be a problem, others such as the Rev. Mineo Katagiri argued that lesbians and gays should be treated as respectable citizens. Katagiri provided help to those seeking to organize the Dorian Society. (*Seattle Post-Intelligencer Collection, Museum of History and Industry, Seattle*)

help strengthen. This is not easy because many have responsible jobs and can ill-afford exposure as homosexuals. Hence, the task before us is difficult but increasingly, if the stigma is taken away, they will come to the fore.[12]

Katagiri's proposed bargain with the city: Leave the bars open while encouraging a new class of respectable homosexual leaders to put a stop to all those sexual activities inside them.

Just in case the council members did not buy his long-range strategy, Katagiri had a few dire predictions if the bars were actually closed. He tied those to a visionary appeal:

Let me say a few words on the immediate possible results of closing "gay bars." One is that they will go "underground." Closing of bars does not mean homosexuals will leave Seattle. They will simply change the locale of activity to other "straight" bars, bus terminals, certain hotels, and so on. There are certain behavior patterns which can be called "signals" that enable a homosexual to communicate to another. It may well be that dispersion may bring greater embarrassment to some of our more respectable night spots and public gathering places. . . .

The vast majority of homosexuals do not depend on bars for their social life. They do not care about the fate of the bars as such. However, they feel deeply the fact that they cannot live openly and honestly as homosexuals. To live under a constant threat of exposure, loss of jobs, blackmail, ostracism is no life at all. What the vast majority of homosexuals basically desire is a chance at living honest and open lives. This, I think, they deserve to have.

Faced with intense argument from both sides, the city council's politicians did what politicians often do. They adjourned, saying they needed more study.

Three weeks later, with the publicity gone and the police apparently feeling their muscle over the mudflat sufficiently demonstrated, Jake Heimbigner's lawyers submitted a proposal to the license committee. Lights in the gay bars would be turned up slightly. Lewd and indecent conduct would be officially prohibited—although, of course, it always had been. The cabarets would stay on probation for four months and then be reviewed by the police before getting their full licenses returned. And the gay bar owners, some of whom had been accused of turning away heterosexuals at their doors, would promise to let anyone old enough in to join the gay dance.

Chief Ramon quietly okayed the proposal. It seemed as if the outbreak of tension could end, and the status quo could continue. Two problems remained, though. The police still managed the gay landscape in the city. And MacIver Wells was still mad.

Although he had escaped the direct police assault of autumn, Mac would no longer be ignored in the waning days of the year. The flurry before the city council had isolated him; other gay owners, he recalled, were furious that he had brought them so close to ruin.

Suddenly, inspectors started appearing from an entirely new direction—not from police headquarters but from the city comptroller's office. One visit to the Gallery occurred on December 2, 1966, just three days after Ramon had okayed the compromise with Heimbigner. Two comptroller inspectors arrived about 11 P.M. It was a Friday night. "The place was busy as hell," Mac remembered. One of the comptroller's men, E. L. McAllascer, would say that he and the other man, named Englen, had gone to discuss the payment of a delinquent admission tax. McAllascer's report, which he submitted not only to his bosses but also to the Seattle Police Department and to state liquor control inspectors, does not explain why such a visit would be made at a late hour on a weekend night.

From McAllascer's report:

Mr. MacIver Wells . . . was sitting drinking beer. I stopped to talk to the doorman regarding his tickets and Englen walked over to the bar to talk to Mr. MacIver Wells. Suddenly, Wells was on his feet screaming and hollering . . . Remarks such as "Don't call me an asshole, you son of a bitching asshole"; "If you call me an asshole again I'll throw you in the gutter."

I walked over and tried to calm him down but he acted like a maniac and wouldn't quit cursing and shouting. Wells claimed that Englen called him an asshole (a word with which he appeared to be obsessed) which Englen denies.

Englen says when he asked him about the delinquent tax, Wells says, "Don't worry, you'll get your fucking tax!" When Englen replied, "Don't swear at me," Wells apparently flipped. He was obviously drunk and impossible to talk with so we started out the door. He then stopped me and asked who I was. I told him and showed him my badge. He said "That don't mean nothing to me and beside[s] both you guys are drunk." I started out the door and he said, "Just a moment while I make a phone call." He went to the phone and called someone and told him to grab a cab and come down right away. He hung up the phone and told me to wait for someone. I asked him who I was to wait for and he told me "You wait here, you'll see!" I told him I wouldn't wait and started out the door. He followed us on the sidewalk, screaming that we were drunk chickens and cowards. The last we heard was the remark, "I sure out bluffed you guys."

It is my opinion that Wells is potentially dangerous and should not be permitted to operate an establishment of this type.[13]

Mac's version differs. He says the inspectors had been coming in on weekend nights demanding to see his liquor and cabaret licenses posted in plain view behind the bar.

"The band is playing and I'm busy as hell and so is John running the bar. [The inspector would say] I'd like to look at your license. I'd say, 'They're right over there. Go look.'

"'I'd like you to be with me,' the inspector would insist. The next weekend he'd come again. 'I'd like to check your licenses.'

"I said, 'Have they changed since last week?'

"I let him do this three Saturdays in a row. Next time he came in, he said, 'I want to see your licenses.' I was sitting on a stool and I got up and I said, 'You know, I'm about sick of you and I'm going to throw your ass out on the sidewalk.'

"I just pretended I was going to. They ran down the street, both of them out the door."[14]

McAllascer's report prompted an investigation by the state liquor board. An inspector showed up carrying the McAllascer letter with him, but "he wouldn't let me read it," Mac remembered. "He said this is a letter that says you're dangerous." Fortunately, the inspector was slightly more sympathetic. Mac remembers him saying, "I know you're not going to hurt anybody. Just cool it a little."

Even a police officer who had once staffed the Madison's door and who had then become friends with Mac cautioned him. "Mac, you're playing with dynamite. There's talk of cement boots," Mac said he was told. He answered, "You go back, and tell them don't bother with the cement boots because I can't swim anyway."

The harassment only made Mac more determined. He continued to try to persuade the Wilsons to publish the story about payoffs they had in the works, but they wanted something more convincing than just his statements. So in late December 1966, he set out to give it to them. Now that Mac was no longer paying off and no longer trusted by the police, he could not hide the two reporters in his bar to let them witness an actual payment. But there was another possibility. After Mac and John had bought the 614, on-duty cops had continued to freely use the tavern on Sundays, skipping their beat walks for pinochle and poker games, just as they had when the bar had been the Shaggy Dog. Once the friction with Mac developed, the beat officers had moved their games. Mac figured he could find out where by checking with other bar owners. It didn't take him long to find the cops playing cards at the Pacific Tavern, five blocks north of the 614. He phoned the reporters.

For the next three Sundays, the reporters, sometimes with Mac accompanying them, parked across the street. The pattern was the same each night and noted in the story the Wilsons eventually wrote:

"8 P.M.—Officer 'A' arrived in his private automobile, got out with his uniform coat unbuttoned and started across the street. . . . He used the [police] call-box on the corner, and then walked his beat for exactly three minutes, covering one-half block. . . . The officer unlocked the door of the Pacific Tavern . . . and went inside.

"9:15 P.M.—Uniformed officers 'B' and 'C' came around a corner into First Avenue and sauntered several doors past the tavern, swinging their night sticks. . . . They did an about-face, returned to the tavern, tapped on the door with their night sticks and were admitted by Officer 'A'."

And so on, through Officers D, E, F, and more. If the Wilsons were not yet comfortable exposing the payoff system, here was undeniable proof that Seattle's finest were not even bothering to do their regular jobs. One night, Mac said, the Wilsons told him to walk up to the tavern window and stare inside while they hid in the next doorway. Mac pressed his face against the tavern's glass window, eyeing the cops inside. As soon as they saw him, the cops began streaming out. "Did they get out fast!" Mac recalled. "They were coming out the door and the reporters were right there with their notebooks." The reporters told him to call off their names as they wrote down the badge numbers. "I couldn't name them all," Mac said, "but I got quite a few of them."

The final Sunday night of surveillance, January 8, 1967, marked the beginning of the end of police control of the gay territory in Seattle—as well as of the tolerance system that stemmed back to the gold rush era. The *Times* bannered the story of the card-playing cops on its front page. Emboldened, the paper then printed a story about the FBI investigation of the payoffs. While neither the FBI nor Chief Ramon would give any details, the Wilsons were able to state that a report had been passed. That they had confirmed through Mac's phone call.

Finally, on January 17, 1967, the *Times* published the details about payoffs that

Mac had been feeding the Wilsons. Mac was not named, but anyone familiar with the gay territory on the mudflat knew who was being quoted. The tone was different from the previous articles about the city's "homosexual problem." This time, the lead focused on the real problem: "'How much will it cost me to operate?' a Seattle night club operator said he asked a policeman in 1958. The operator quickly found out—$30 a month—and it grew by leaps and bounds until this past year he was paying a total of $370 a month for three establishments. . . . This is the account of the owner's role in the payoff operation from beginning to end." And, indeed, it was. Incident after incident was detailed, covering almost a decade from 1958 on, the same information Mac had passed to the FBI. "One of the beat men used to collect the payoff," Mac told the reporters. "He would take his hat off, put it on his lap, and wouldn't take the money in his hands. I had to toss it into his hat."[15]

It would be the 1970s before all the investigations by citizen commissions and grand juries could result in any trials—and in the end, only a very few patrol officers were ever convicted. But with that 1967 story, the payoff system began to collapse.

With it would go the foundation that for decades had permitted gays and lesbians to forge a few safe havens known mostly to them alone and to build a safe public territory of social networks on the mudflat. Now, there was an uncertain future to ponder.

Keith Rhinehart, meanwhile, was about to find more certainty—but not of the type for which he had hoped. Despite Miller's retraction the previous September, the Washington State Supreme Court ruled in March 1967 that Miller's new—and fourth—affidavit asserted no more new information than his second, similar withdrawal of the accusation. Since the second statement had been contradicted by his third—and the jury had considered both and then believed the third—there was no reason for a new trial, the justices said. It seemed an odd logic, the ping-ponging testimony of the state's only witness not being enough to undermine his credibility.

The court also dismissed Rhinehart's contention that the sodomy law itself was unconstitutional, ruling that this argument had "no merit" since the legislature had considered and adopted "the public interest served by" the law. The court also refused the argument that the Seattle police, through their tolerance scheme, had sometimes allowed homosexual acts to take place at bars like the underground Casino Club. The failure to prosecute others was no reason to order a new trial for Rhinehart.[16]

In trying unsuccessfully to prove that the police had violated Rhinehart's right to equal protection, his attorney Malcolm Edwards researched local sodomy prosecutions for the four years preceding Rhinehart's arrest. He found that from 1961 to 1965, King County prosecutors had charged some 105 people, almost all of them men, with sodomy. In more than half the cases, the sodomy charge was a way to prosecute an adult who had had sex, often heterosexual, with a child fifteen or younger. Of the remaining King County sodomy cases during that period, according to Edwards, seven accompanied arrests for murder, rape, or burglary. The other charges—about thirty in all—were for consensual acts with those aged sixteen and older, but some were arrests of gay prostitutes and others were for acts committed in public places. A sixteen-year-old like James Miller, while still not an adult, was presumed to have reached a greater degree of "biological maturity," according to the American Law Institute. Edwards argued that there was not a single other sodomy case in the study that resembled what had happened to Rhinehart—an arrest for an alleged homosexual act, consensually, with a person of "reasonable biological maturity" in private.[17]

It was to no avail. The state supreme court ruled that the minister would have to begin serving his ten-year sentence for sodomy. He was headed to Walla Walla.

It would be five years before a federal judge would finally overturn the conviction and free him.

# Part Three

## CLAIMING A CIVIC LIFE

# 7
# *Robert's Rules and Gay Liberation*

Shortly after MacIver Wells began his resistance against the police in late 1965, several gay men in Seattle received an invitation to the Roosevelt Hotel downtown. A gay activist from San Francisco, Hal Call, wondered if they would be interested in meeting; he had gotten their names from the subscription list of a national magazine for homosexuals called *One.*

By that time, gay men in most other cities on the West and East Coasts had already created social clubs to meet in homes, rather than bars, and to talk delicately about gaining civil rights protections. The Mattachine Society in Los Angeles was the most famous of the organizations, and, in other places like New York, Philadelphia, and San Francisco, similar groups had affiliated as chapters. They avoided the word "homosexual" in their titles for fear that no one would join otherwise.

The first attempt to start a chapter of Mattachine in Washington State appears to have been made in Tacoma, rather than Seattle. There, in 1959, a gay man named John Eccles began corresponding with Don Lucas, Mattachine's secretary-general in San Francisco, telling Lucas the organization was the "answer for my life's calling," which was to "show the reality of the homosexual problem in our society, to instigate a more understanding and sympathetic attitude in society."[1] Eccles, who was gay but had actually married and was blessed with both a supportive wife and parents, started a small discussion group in his home, with attendance ranging from three to ten. He also began corresponding with Dr. John Marks, the president of the Washington State Psychological Association (WSPA), eventually persuading Marks to let him and Lucas address the WSPA's convention in Tacoma in May 1960. "I make no plea for the homosexual to be honored as a special breed or a third sex," Eccles told the psychologists, "to be the repository of most of the world's artistic talent, or to be permitted any special moral licentiousness. There is . . . as wide a range of temperaments and character among homosexuals as in the population at large." He continued, "It is unfair and unfounded to assume that homosexuals as a whole are inclined to importune, initiate or seduce individuals." He urged the psychologists to support legal reforms and even began collecting names of those who would be helpful. "Our primary job," he concluded, "is not to glorify or apologize for homosexuality, but to understand it and to make it understood."

That would become the cry of gay activists in the 1960s. If homosexuality was a disease, as the American Psychiatric Association said, then homosexuals at least wanted to promote understanding of the disease.

Eccles's efforts in the Northwest ended shortly after 1960, though, when he moved to Los Angeles and became a vice president of Mattachine there.

In Seattle, the start of a civil rights organization languished, partly because the police tolerance system protected socializing in the bars. Thanks to the 1958 injunction MacIver Wells had won, harassment was minimal as long as the police were paid. There were no highly public bar raids such as routinely occurred in other cities, and so there simply did not seem to be as much need to organize.

Among the gay men who received Hal Call's invitation to come to the Roosevelt Hotel and discuss setting up a chapter of Mattachine was Nicholas Heer. He had just arrived in Seattle to assume a new teaching job at the University of Washington, coming from New York where he had already belonged to Mattachine. He had also been active in gay clubs in Philadelphia and Boston, and although new to Seattle, he felt strong enough in his own identity as a homosexual to help fill the obvious local gap. The Roosevelt meeting was held December 3, 1965, according to Heer, who decades later still kept his old appointment books. Three months after the introductory meeting, the men who were still interested gathered at the Reverend Mineo Katagiri's office at St. Mark's Cathedral on Capitol Hill, on March 8, 1966.[2]

That was to be the formal start of gay civil rights organizing in Seattle. It came just eight months before the city council would hold its hearing on whether Jake Heimbigner's license should be renewed.

For the first year, Heer and other gay men met informally in Katagiri's office and at homes on Capitol Hill. Heer's university connections gave the group a distinctly academic feeling. He invited another new U.W. teacher, Martin Gouterman, who in turn eventually called his friend Sheldon Daniels, whom he had known when both were chemistry students at the University of Chicago eight years earlier. By June 1966, both Gouterman and Daniels were teaching chemistry at U.W.

On January 22, 1967, just a few weeks after the story of the police scandal broke in the *Seattle Times,* the informal meetings became distinctly more serious. One member brought out a hardbound gray ledger and began to take minutes. The group voted to rent a post office box and decided to launch a newsletter. Within a week they were pondering how to incorporate, an issue that always led to the dilemma of what words homosexuals should use in public to describe their new organizations. Should the title include the word "homosexual"—since the purpose of the organization, after all, was to promote understanding and tolerance? Or should the name be deliberately vague so that homosexuals themselves would not feel as awkward about joining? They decided not to affiliate with Mattachine. Someone suggested the acronym "HIS," for "Homophiles in Seattle," but then another man pointed out that using "homophile" might be "prejudicial" and scare people away.

Gouterman proposed the eventual solution. He suggested they call themselves the Dorian Society. It was a coded reference, obscurely historical but symbolically pregnant. The Dorians had been Hellenic warriors who invaded Greece about 1100 B.C., eventually mingling with other Greeks but retaining their own rituals and dialect, moving within many different cultures—much as gay men and women did. One famous sex researcher, Havelock Ellis, had reported that the Dorians considered homosexuality a virtue. The word "Doric" also contained a popular image, its architectural meaning referring to a simple, straightforwardly phallic column, a contrast to the profligate, licentious, and frilly Corinthian style. Buried in the coded name, in other words, was a whole self-identity being offered in contrast to the stereotypes of the red-light district on the mudflat. The name was also dryly humorous. You had to think a bit in order to "get it," Gouterman said. Years later, he remembered why he had made the suggestion. "It had this kind of Greek flavor," he said, emphasizing the word "Greek," glancing down with an impish smile like a professor waiting for a student to get the joke. "And Doric columns were nice too," he added, putting particular emphasis on the word "columns."[3]

Although Nick Heer would be the Dorian Society's first president, he would not be the first public spokesman. Indicative of the state of homosexual men in Seattle at that time, none of the organizers were ready to risk a too-public face. Instead, the Reverend Katagiri would be the friendly heterosexual ally talking to newspapers and eventually, at the public hearing in fall 1966, to city officials. A Japanese American who had moved to Seattle from Honolulu in 1959, Katagiri had been asked by his denomination, the United Church of Christ, to launch a street ministry in Seattle. That had inevitably brought him into contact with the gay men who frequented Pioneer Square.

His defense of gay bars at the city council hearing in November 1966 reflected his meetings with Heer, Gouterman, Daniels, and others. It is easy to see whom he had in mind when he told the council members, "We will need to help the responsible [homosexuals] take over 'power positions' in the gay community and set standards of conduct. It is their hand we must help strengthen. This is not easy because many have responsible jobs and can ill-afford exposure as homosexuals. . . . They feel deeply the fact that they cannot live openly and honestly as homosexuals."

That became the Dorian Society's first "sound bite"—the core of the first rhetoric intended to persuade the city's heterosexuals to listen to its homosexuals. If gays in Seattle were to forge new public identities, heterosexuals needed to provide the space and support for undertaking the quest. The promised payoff: homosexuals who acted more respectably. The Dorians' constitution and bylaws echoed the message. While they proposed to reform the sodomy law and to promote the "legal, social, psychological, and medical welfare of homosexuals," they also promised "to encourage socially responsible conduct by all members of the homosexual community."

That could be a Faustian bargain—the kind of schizophrenic demand that seemed to have so invaded the image and perhaps even psyche of Frances Farmer thirty years earlier. It did, after all, leave the definition of respectability to hetero-sexuals. And what did vaudeville, drag, the underground bars, and the steam baths—not to mention homosexual sex itself—have to do with heterosexual respectability? The Dorian mission, forged by a minister and by academics at the University of Washington, seemed to call for an oddly sanitized image of the local homosexual, far removed from the experiences of mudflat survival.

Doug Wyman, another man who attended the original meeting with Hal Call and then others with Katagiri, remembered some of the first reactions to the for-mation of the Dorian Society. "The bars were really down on any kind of orga-nization because we were going to rock the boat," he said.[4]

The tension over respectability also appeared in the decision to start Seattle's first publication for homosexuals. Eventually named the *Dorian Columns,* the newsletter was to be "suitable for public reading," according to the minutes of January 22, 1967, but also to contain "news for local people." Since news might well address drag shows, bar events, dances, and even the sodomy arrests that were part of the homosexual experience in Seattle, there was an immediate conflict in the mission. Later minutes about the mimeographed newsletter note: "Decided to keep the tone high at first."

The Dorians also decided to beware of associating too closely with the anti-Vietnam and student movements then beginning in Seattle. When the editors of a new alternative newspaper called the *Helix* asked whether the homosexual organization might want a column, the Dorians pondered and then decided no. The July 1968 minutes noted: "Do we want [a] column in their paper? Dorian does not want to become associated with the 'hippie' movement."

Two other decisions were also critical. On May 5, 1967, Nick Heer raised a ques-tion about confidentiality and secrecy: "Should pseudonyms be used in letters and communications?" The proposition was adopted unanimously, and for the next year even the minutes carried only the members' initials. In their public commu-nications, each Dorian used a false name. Heer became "James Macalpine," using his mother's maiden name. Gouterman became "Paul Horton"; Daniels, "Gordon Stark." Although the founders believed the secrecy was necessary to avoid police harassment, the pseudonyms, combined with the rather academic reference to Hellenic Greeks, created an air of closeted elitism for the society.

The other crucial communication decision was about how to conduct the busi-ness of the new group. Socializing in bars and participating in vaudeville had pro-duced certain gay rituals of communication, but until the Dorians, homosexuals in Seattle had never really gathered with one another in task-oriented organiza-tions ruled through bylaws. It was really quite a new undertaking. Deciding how to organize internally for actions to be taken publicly would be an important build-ing block in exploring and then projecting a new identity.

The society settled on using *Robert's Rules of Order,* the guide to traditional parliamentary procedure for making decisions by presenting and seconding motions, calling the question, and then allowing the majority vote to rule. On the one hand, it was an obvious choice. To gain a respected face, one should mimic the conduct of business in respectable heterosexual organizations. But was it really an appropriate choice? Until then, the primary way homosexuals had communicated with one another had been within an informal oral culture. Rituals of gossip, of challenging the accepted order and accepted styles of dressing, of resisting—these were the communication strengths of those living on the margins of an urban society. Not surprisingly then, even this simple choice of how to conduct business would later become a very serious point of contention.

But, at first, the rules gave the Dorians their best public relations coup.

When the year 1967 opened with the *Seattle Times* story about MacIver Wells and his battle against the police, Wells was never identified by name and never photographed. The *Times* story lacked even the customary silhouette back shot of an anonymous source. Helping to end the payoffs was possibly the biggest civic contribution that homosexuals had yet made to the city, but they received no public credit at the time. And Katagiri was still the voice of the as yet unknown, fledgling Dorian Society.

It was time for a face.

Three months after the *Times* story, the *University of Washington Daily*, which had the third largest circulation of the city's newspapers, began publishing what appear to have been its first stories about homosexuals in Seattle. The five-part series in April and May 1967 broke new ground in two ways. First, the language the student writer Bob Hinz used spoke not of the "homosexual problem," as the earlier *Seattle Times* story had, but of the "problems of the homosexual." That was a small but important shift. Rather than quote health officials who saw the homosexual as some kind of syphilitic urban predator, the *Daily* articles tried to "explain" the homosexual, quoting psychiatrists, ministers, and lawyers. Of course, all the authoritative voices were heterosexual. Only in the very last article did a homosexual explain himself. Still, a local gay man was allowed to speak at length about his personal life.[5]

But he remained unnamed and was photographed only from the rear. Assigned the pseudonym "Jim," he responded only to questions that focused, rather Freudian-style, on his upbringing—presumably in keeping with the idea of the time that all homosexuality could be blamed on badly functioning families. The reporter did not ask questions that might have led "Jim" to criticize discrimination or attack hostile social attitudes toward homosexuals. A sample of the interview:

"Do you recall any single factor that might have caused you to become a homosexual?" the reporter asked. Jim responded, "According to a psychiatrist, it all goes back to my parents. I have a strong mother who's domineering. On the other hand, my father is a very successful businessman. He was never around and never cared much about me. . . . "

"What are your feelings toward your parents today?"

"I had to leave home last April because I had no freedom whatsoever. I had less freedom [than] when I was 14 years old. What started it was when my parents got phone calls from other parents complaining that I was molesting their children. I wasn't molesting their children, but they'd found out that I was having some sort of relations with some of them. That's when my parents began taking speedometer [*sic*] readings on my car. Wherever I went I had to leave a phone number and they'd call to check on me."

The reporter asked Jim what he did after he left home. "I went into the Marine Corps. . . . When I went down to fill in my draft card, I didn't tell them a thing about my homosexuality. . . . In two weeks I had a nervous breakdown. I told them everything and they put me in the base nut house."

Why had he joined the Marines? the reporter wondered.

"I felt that if I went to Vietnam, I could become a unique person. I wanted either to be killed or come back in a ticker-tape parade. I wanted to be an Audie Murphy [one of World War II's most decorated soldiers] in Vietnam. Then nobody would say that I was a queer."

That was the first homosexual man that any sizable portion of Seattle's newspaper audience met: troubled, confused, dishonest, and trapped within the belief that his homosexuality had been caused by a dysfunctional family.

Still, the *Daily* articles opened some sort of sluice gate of temporary media interest in the city's homosexuals.

A weekend later, in an article titled "It's a Gay, Gay World," the *Seattle Post-Intelligencer* pursued the same themes. Once again psychiatrists were called upon to explain the causes of sexual orientation, and once again the homosexuals remained anonymous and faceless. But at least the previously invisible child was beginning to be heard, if not seen. In the story, two homosexual men were able to discuss more than their psychosis. One quietly asserted, "What I do in my private life is my business and nobody else's. I just want to be left alone." And another argued, "The majority should not discriminate against a minority if that minority is quite helpless to be anything other than what it is. . . . We have not chosen to be outside, and the only crime we commit, as far as I am concerned, is that we fall in love with what the majority decrees is the 'wrong' sex."[6]

Several months later, in August 1967, the new media fascination with the city's homosexuals continued.

The police fight with the gay bars had revealed the U.S. military's policy of putting Seattle taverns off-limits. A *Seattle* magazine reporter realized that of all the West Coast cities, Seattle suddenly had the reputation for being the sexiest and the sleaziest.[7] Nineteen bars had been blacklisted by the military, supposedly more than in either San Francisco or Los Angeles. Of those nineteen, twelve catered to gays and lesbians. The magazine even published the list, effectively sending a double message. Heterosexuals could cluck disapprovingly; homosexuals suddenly had their first guide. Back over at the University of Washington, for example, one of the students who happened to read the article, Mike Ramey, remembered that it changed his life. Before, he said, he had been closeted and lonely. The article at least confirmed that there were other homosexuals in Seattle and told him exactly where he could go to meet other gay men. Once he started coming out, Ramey would later join the Dorian Society as well as numerous other gay civil rights groups as they formed.

So began a kind of cycle—the slow public coming out and binding together of a new group. Unlike the city's racial minorities, this community and its individual members had largely been invisible to themselves. Gays and lesbians in the city, especially those who disliked or had not found the red-light geography of Pioneer Square, relied significantly on the local media to announce the presence of homosexuals and to educate them about the group.

But still, no faces had been published in any of the initial wave of articles. And no real names.

In the Dorian Society meetings, people like Nick Heer and Martin Gouterman watched the new media coverage with interest. Maybe something was about to change. Maybe they could move the process along. Maybe *Seattle* magazine, with its lighthearted take on the perversities of sex life in Pioneer Square, would be interested in the more serious changes that were happening up on Capitol Hill. After all, the magazine, owned by the KING-TV Broadcasting Company and inspired and overseen by family scion Stimson Bullitt, was still looking for a niche as a smart urban publication that tackled stories the mainstream Seattle press overlooked.

As the summer ended, the Dorians decided to try.

"The meeting seemed remarkably ordinary."

So began Ruth Wolf's story in *Seattle* magazine in November 1967.[8]

Ordinary. Not since the passage of the sodomy law in 1893 had anyone considered anything about Seattle's homosexuals to be "ordinary." Even a plain choice of a word could be a rhetorical triumph. Wolf's article continued: "[The meeting] was being held in the oversize living room of one of those rambling houses which still dot Capitol Hill, and a total of fourteen members were present. The group's president, an associate professor at the U. of W., who is here called 'Ted,' apologized for the relatively poor turnout. 'It's hard,' he explained, 'to get people to a meeting like this when the weather is so nice.'

"The routine was like that at a gathering of Young Republicans. . . . Minutes of the last meeting were read and approved, new members were voted on, old business was discussed. Everything, in short, went according to *Robert's Rules of Order*.

"The men who gathered together on that warm evening were well-educated, bright and, in the main, articulate. . . . There were no limp wrists, no girlish giggles. Nevertheless, the entire group was composed of practicing homosexuals."

Again the choice of word was important: "nevertheless." Wolf had opened her story with the exact contrast the Dorians wanted to promote: the difference between the profligate, frilly "Corinthian" homosexuals of Pioneer Square and the Doric orderliness of *Robert's Rules*. Her article was full of the language of psychiatry: homosexuality was caused, Freudian-style, by "the family constellation [resulting] from an abnormal relationship with one or both parents." It was, according to "outstanding authorities in the field . . . a disease." However, it was the startling cover of the magazine that everyone would remember. A photograph showed a handsome and serious young man, looking not at all diseased, dressed conservatively in a blazer, vest, and creased pants. He sat in a leather swivel chair. By his side was an attaché case. He pressed his left hand thoughtfully against his chin. He had been photographed from the front so that his face was fully visible and in full light. He was even set against a plain white background; no shadows suggested any hiding. The headline read:

This is Peter Wichern.

He is a local businessman.

He is a homosexual.

For the first time, the Seattle public could see the actual face of an acknowledged homosexual and read his actual name. He looked respectable. Only two visual hints suggested that Wichern was any different from a heterosexual male. The most obvious was that beneath his otherwise ordinary blazer, he wore a bright red vest. The subtler hint was that the camera angled down at him, rather than being set at eye level or aimed upward. It was an angle more typically reserved at the time for photographing women rather than businessmen. It made Wichern seem boyishly unthreatening—another set of dual messages that moved the public conversation about homosexuals in Seattle forward while simultaneously assuring heterosexuals that they did not need to flee the parlor.

Not everyone in the Dorian Society was ready for the change. At a board meeting on October 3, a few weeks after Wolf's visit but still before her article had been published, one member identified only by the initials "PE" argued that since he was "known as a friend of Peter's," his own business would be endangered. Following *Robert's Rules,* he moved that the "Society ask Peter Wichern to remove his name and picture from the article." Stay in the closet, in other words, as "Jim" had. The motion failed, 3-1.

As the Seattle gay community's first poster boy, Wichern was almost too good to be true—almost too Doric. The son of a minister, he had been a Boy Scout and an assistant scoutmaster. He had worked in the United Christian Youth Movement, earned all A's in school, won a math contest, been a cadet commander in the Civil Air Patrol, and taken first place at the Tri-State Science Fair. At least initially, any problems he had about being gay had all come from heterosexual hostility, not from any feelings of self-hatred. For example, while he was in college, a psychiatrist "gave me a lecture on how wrong it was to mess around with boys, and how I should force myself to take an interest in girls," Wichern said. "He finally ended up warning that I had better stop what I was doing. Not only was it unhealthy, but it was against the law, and so I'd end up in jail if I didn't mend my ways."

The two fears: psychiatric treatment and the sodomy law.

The two forced Wichern into a marriage engagement while he was in college, but he ended it by telling his fiancée that he "was really a hopeless queer." She reported him to the college dean, who then expelled him. He moved to Seattle and, depressed, pondered suicide, but, after a breakdown that put him in the hospital for eight weeks, he decided to embrace being gay instead of punishing himself for his desires. He planned to start his own electronics firm and was settling into a relationship with another man. "I'm a reasonably happy, useful human being now," he said, "and I plan to go on being one. . . . I accept myself as I am and go on to other things. I want other people, too, to accept me as I am," he said, "and to understand that I, or any other homosexual, can be as decent as anyone else."

A path away from the images and restrictions of the mudflat was being cleared.

For *Seattle* magazine, the Dorian/Wichern issue helped signal its niche within a new national trend—urbane city magazines that were also brashly investigative and willing to examine under-reported topics. *Seattle* wanted to be a kind of local *New York,* or maybe even *New Yorker.* The Peter Wichern cover would become one of its four top sellers, pushing its newsstand sales toward the one hundred thousand mark. In future months the magazine would publish articles calling for the ouster of the county prosecutor and reporting on concerns of the city's other minority groups, particularly its African Americans. Such articles would also help seal the magazine's doom. Writing three years later, as he announced the magazine's end, editor Peter Bunzel revealed that the article about Seattle's homosexuals, along with subsequent stories about racism in the city, prompted an "intensive letter-writing campaign by right-wing militants" to the magazine's advertisers. "In short order," Bunzel wrote, "we lost a variety of prime accounts." By the end of 1970, the magazine was dead.[9] What would remain, though, would be a willingness in the more important Bullitt-owned medium—KING-TV—to eventually air documentaries about homosexuals in Seattle, particularly during the 1970s and 1980s.

Dorian Society members had to live a paradox. Could homosexuals as a group come out of the closet if individuals could not feel safe doing so?

And there was the problem of that Faustian bargain, too—living up to heterosexual Seattle's expectations of respectability.

The struggle was clearest when the Dorians began to speak in classrooms and churches while simultaneously trying to keep their identities private. Mike Ramey, who was able to join the society once he learned about it from reading the Wichern article, said: "I remember two occasions when we went to Bellevue Community

# SEATTLE

THE PACIFIC NORTHWEST MAGAZINE

60 CENTS · NOVEMBER 1967

This is Peter Wichern.
He is a local businessman.
He is a homosexual.
*(For his story, see page 35.)*

ALSO: NEW BLIGHT ON / WHERE TO GO FOR / AN ABOMINABLE
OUR SKYLINE / ITALIAN FOOD / SNOWMAN, *HERE?*

By the late 1960s, the Dorian Society had laid the groundwork for a new gay visibility in Seattle, first by cooperating with *Seattle* magazine to present the city's first media image of a professional and respectable homosexual, then by launching the *Dorian Columns* as the city's first newsletter devoted to covering lesbian and gay issues. *(Northwest Lesbian and Gay History Museum Project)*

In the late 1960s and early 1970s, the construction of a new image and identity for the homosexual was an important concern of the Dorian Society and other gay activists. Was a gay man to be "like" the respectable Peter Wichern, "like" a drag queen, or "like" a buffed outdoorsman? *(Personal collection, Nick Heer)*

College [in a Seattle suburb]. We insisted of the instructor that we have the class list in advance so we could go there as generic gays from Mars and be sure not to run into any neighbors we knew."

At one speaking engagement, Nick Heer encountered one of his own graduate students. Fortunately, Heer recalled, "He was very mature about it."[10]

Ken Hoole, who became Dorian president after Heer, panicked when he found his real name, rather than his pseudonym, listed in the syllabus for a class he was addressing at Portland State University. His letter to the professor reveals how carefully, and how futilely, Dorians tried to control their own individual disclosures while promoting more visibility for homosexuals as a group:

> I noted with some degree of alarm that the list of lecturers for your course again shows my real name rather than my pseudonym. This would not concern me except for two things: (1) although my mother knows everything, she is terribly uptight about anyone else who knows our family being aware; a family who lived almost next door to us at home in Montana for many years recently moved to Portland and their youngest child is now probably of college age. (2) I have recently learned that a Hoole family lives in Eugene, Oregon. The father is a fundamentalist-oriented minister and would possibly be upset at the connection of his family name with someone speaking on the topic of homosexuality. I am hoping to meet these people to see if we may be related but have not yet had a chance to do so.[11]

The threat of retaliation was, in fact, very real. James Gaylord, a high school teacher in Tacoma, joined the Dorian Society in 1970 just to socialize in private. He never participated as a public speaker or assumed any other public role, but when his principal discovered accidentally in 1972 that Gaylord was a Dorian member, the principal fired him. Although Gaylord had a record as an outstanding teacher, and there was no proof in the court record that he was actually a homosexual or had engaged in any homosexual acts, the Washington State Supreme Court would eventually uphold the dismissal. It was enough, the court said, that Gaylord simply associated with homosexuals. The U.S. Supreme Court refused to hear his appeal.[12]

It was often a strain to educate heterosexuals about homosexuality. At Portland State, students wrote seventeen pages of questions for the Dorian Society members, including these:

"Did you ever hear the old saying: 'Hey homo, take a bromo and wake up feeling yourself?'"

"Did you indulge in a lot of masturbation while growing up?"

"Are you sexually impotent with females?"

"Does your lover use a dildo on you?"[13]

Patiently, the Dorians steadily worked at their outreach. By 1969 they were receiving invitations to speak at high schools, the first being Seattle's Franklin High.

They ranged deep into the suburbs and rural areas. They addressed church congregations. They spoke at a coffeehouse in Tacoma with city council members. They collected toys for the children at a local hospital.

They also joined other community organizers in Seattle who were trying to increase racial harmony and avoid the riots occurring in Eastern cities. One such effort, called an "Urban Plunge," was sponsored by churches and took groups of middle-class whites into the city's minority subcultures for a weekend. A typical agenda, like one from April 1969, included "experiencing First Avenue" for forty-five minutes on a Friday night, then a "homosexual confrontation" for ninety minutes at the Mocambo, followed by two hours of visiting the gay hangouts at the Submarine Room in the basement of the Smith Tower, the Golden Horseshoe, and the Stage Door Tavern. The next day, it was off to the Central District to try to understand the black community.

Sheldon Daniels hired on as an Urban Plunge facilitator, in charge of showing groups of twenty or thirty people around. "The main event," he said, "was to split the group up and take them to various gay bars in the Pioneer Square area—the Golden Horseshoe and others—and let them experience what a gay bar was like. Most of it was positive. Women seemed to find it much easier to deal with than men. In fact, the women would dance with some of the people they met there."

Doug Wyman, another Dorian member who participated in the Plunges, said, "I was just fascinated by the idea of being able to expose straight people to someone who was gay." The Plunge organizers even went so far as to simulate gay bars for those Plungers who were under eighteen, taking them into the banquet room of the Mocambo cocktail lounge where they could safely be served soft drinks while gay men re-created the atmosphere of bars like the Horseshoe and the 614.

Not everyone in the Dorian Society liked the idea.

Marty Gouterman went to the Plunge twice but then stopped. "I was very uncomfortable," he said. "I felt like I was on exhibit, like I was an animal at the zoo."

Nick Heer refused to participate. "I didn't even like the idea."

Even Sheldon Daniels was tiring by 1969. "After a while I came to the conclusion that I had become so enamored of portraying myself as a regular guy to these straights that I was losing touch with myself. So I quit."[14]

The Dorians would eventually leave an impressive list of firsts. Most of them addressed communication processes that homosexuals in Seattle needed if they were to successfully speak in a new voice to themselves and to heterosexuals. From the Dorians, for example, came the first speakers' bureau, the first regularly published gay newsletter, and even the first drag balls to be held in very public locations, such as the Arena at Seattle Center, the site of the 1962 World's Fair.

The newsletter, begun as a mimeograph by 1968 and eventually named the *Dorian Columns,* reached not only members but also gays and lesbians who had not yet joined any public network. As the city's first newsletter for homosexuals, *Columns* reinforced the idea that gays were more than just a group of scattered individuals who talked to each other in bars. Through the medium of print, gay men and women could report their own news, create leaders who regularly spoke, and form a record of political concerns worthy of discussion—even if few of those concerns commanded the citywide agenda. The other decision, to begin sponsoring very public drag balls outside of the gay bars, at first seems unusual for a group seeking respectability. But it was a logical outgrowth of the Dorians' attempt to provide more acceptable alternatives to the bars, while still building on the traditional importance of drag and vaudeville within gay life.

The "political firsts" are easy to forget, though, in the face of another more lasting communication legacy: the creation of the city's first counseling service run by gays for gays. The need was obvious. As long as the professional psychology and psychiatry associations still considered homosexuality a disease, gay men and women wanted a safer place to talk about their identity, about coming out, about homosexual relationships, about surviving on the streets if they were kicked out by their parents, about sexual diseases, about depression and alienation. While work went on to change the designation, gays could begin to counsel one another.

The first indication of the Dorian interest in such a direct form of service came in the minutes of a meeting on December 19, 1967, just a few weeks after the article about Peter Wichern appeared. On that day, a health worker from the city's Crisis Clinic met with the Dorian members to talk about phone calls he was receiving from lonely people, who he suspected were homosexuals. He told the members he thought the clinic workers handling the calls "miss the homosexual aspects of the crisis." Another public health official attended the same meeting to ask advice on how to better educate homosexuals about venereal disease. He calculated that 25 percent of those visiting the city's public health clinics for treatment were homosexuals, many of whom did not want to visit their own personal doctors for illnesses such as gonorrhea.

Three weeks later, the discussion moved to helping gay teenagers. The Dorians wondered about setting up a coffeehouse, but, the minutes note, the group "dares not sponsor officially at this time." The risk of being accused of child molestation or corruption was too high.

In July 1968, a board member identified as "Larry" reported that he had just met with Dr. Robert Deisher, a physician and medical educator at the University of Washington. Deisher had worked at the university since 1949 and had already earned something akin to legendary status among Seattle's medical community. Elf-like, with a rounded kindly face, he was the perfect image of the consoling pediatrician. He had made his trademark the launching of innovative approaches to treating teenagers, creating a special adolescent clinic where he assembled teams of doctors, nutritionists, social workers, and nurses to solve problems that resisted treatment solely by medicine—problems like young gay boys catching venereal diseases while hustling on city streets because they had no emotional support at home and no other way to earn a living. To Deisher, it wasn't good enough to simply prescribe penicillin.[15]

Someone had told him he should talk to "Miss Dee" at the Double Header, a legendary bartender who dressed in drag, wore a bouffant, and had been caring for the street kids who showed up at the Casino and Madame Peabody's for years. Word got out that Deisher was interested; so many gay kids or their parents started calling his hospital office that finally one of his colleagues joked that he ought to start a counseling service. Another, a medical specialist in transsexual operations, sent over a brochure from a Louisiana organization, the Erickson Foundation, that was working specifically to help transsexuals.

"Larry" reported that Deisher wanted to ask for a grant to see how gay youth could be helped. Two weeks later, the Dorians discussed joining Deisher's effort. Some worried that outside funding could subject the group to unwelcome scrutiny, but they decided to risk it.

It was a significant turning point—choosing to engage in direct services to gay youth. Within two months, Deisher contacted the Erickson Foundation, and it agreed to provide thirty-six hundred dollars to fund Deisher's research and a space from which he could work. The Dorians raised one thousand dollars from an auction and promised to pay another hundred dollars a month in rent.

The question was where to locate. No one could expect gay teenagers living on the streets to feel comfortable traveling across town to the University of Washington. While a storefront on the mudflat was a possibility, it and the downtown streets represented the very aspects of gay life that the Dorians and Deisher wanted to help the youths escape.

Finally they settled on renting a place that would feel like a home. Deisher asked Pat Gandy, a research assistant who had been helping him with the gay teens, to find one, and the two eventually chose a battered old house located at 320 Malden Avenue East on Capitol Hill. The new program would be named the Dorian Counseling Service for Homosexuals, although quite quickly the name would evolve into the more inclusive Seattle Counseling Service for Sexual Minorities. The home would be known as the "Dorian House." It would be the first public gay institution on Capitol Hill, and the first in the city that was neither bar nor bathhouse.

By summer 1969, everything was in place. The Dorians now had a bricks-and-mortar expression of who they were and who they could be: homosexuals caring for homosexuals, including the next generation of gay youth. Also, an imaginative and public shift away from the mudflat had begun, and with it, the gay community's public rhetoric and its own image of itself. On Thursday night, June 26, 1969, the Dorians gathered at the house on Malden Avenue to celebrate. The minutes of the meeting note simply: "Champagne to celebrate our first meeting in Dorian House. Intermission to drink champagne. Urban Plunge tomorrow night." The Dorian members felt buoyed and successful.

Two days later, the end of the Dorian Society would be written in a New York City bar three thousand miles away.

"I don't think we had a sense of it being important," Nick Heer will tell you.

It took a while to even discover the details. Heer remembers learning the most from the New York Mattachine's newsletter, which did not arrive in the mail until weeks later. The budding national gay newspaper the *Advocate* did not report on the story unfolding in Greenwich Village that weekend of June 28 and 29 until its September issue.

Only gradually did the impact sink in. Homosexuals in New York had resisted a bar raid, locking the police inside, setting the Stonewall tavern on fire, blocking traffic, and hurling concrete blocks. "Gay power" would soon become a national slogan.

With the Stonewall riot, the rhetoric of "understand us" would be replaced by the rhetoric of resistance. As far as the new "gay liberationists" were concerned, any "problems of the homosexual" were not due to psychoses or malfunctioning families, but to heterosexual prejudice and discrimination. It was time for homosexuals to stop adapting to society, they believed, and start adapting society to homosexuals.

*Robert's Rules of Order* would no longer be the road to respectability. Instead, respectability would be seen as one of the obstacles.

The minutes of the Dorian meetings throughout that summer of 1969 say nothing about Stonewall. On July 17, immediately after the riots, the members were more concerned with spending an evening at the new Dorian House listening to LP recordings of the play *Boys in the Band*, a tale of gay men gathering for a party—at the time, a breakthrough in the presentation of gay friendships. "Much merriment was provoked by the first act," the minutes say, "while looks of stark self-analysis and abject anxiety could be seen among the members during the harrowing concluding act."

By fall, the impact of the Stonewall riots could not be ignored. Officially, the Dorian Society was focused on launching a Christmas Ball at the Seattle Center Arena, but the tensions over visibility and over a policy of education versus political action had heightened. These tensions were evident in the society's minutes:

November 13, 1969: Arthur is here to organize a political group. Aim to get [Brock] Adams or [Mayor Wes] Uhlman at a dinner. Purpose to bring us to attention of politicos so as to wield influence. [Sheldon Daniel resigns from the board]. His effort was for education and he is burned out.

December 11, 1969: Randy came to talk. He has been a member for a year and has done some speaking for us. He is working on the ball. He thinks we have not been active enough in keeping the gay people informed of what we do. We need to draw more on the membership for activities. He feels communication is poor. Randy feels that people do not join because they are afraid to declare themselves. Other people feel that we are rocking the boat and this may cause trouble and for this reason do not believe in our purpose. Randy feels we are very disorganized from his work on the ball. . . . Questions raised by Dave B: 1) "Who speaks for the Society?" 2) "We do not involve the members." 3) "We are very haphazard." Nick H gets very emotional. Marty says that we have institutionalized an active board and an inactive membership and should consider reorganizing if this is a problem.

December 23, 1969: Curtis D has resigned in a huff. Roger A says he resigned for personal reasons and because of his personal reaction to the board meetings. . . . It seems Dorian [would have] more direction with something like the chapter system. More reports and better communication. Discussion rages on—wow!

Suddenly, with calls for gay liberation spreading rapidly through the country, it seemed odd to have a passive membership that left most of the work to those few who could risk being more visible. Yet that was the way Dorian had been organized since its beginning.

The debates spread to conflict over the contents of the group's newsletter—where the editors, in the wake of Stonewall, began publishing more explicit pictures of partially and even completely nude men:

March 12, 1970: Mike H objected to cover for the "Our Love Needs Care" [issue]. Andy J was not pleased with cover either. Sales of the issue were up. Peter suggests equal time for girls on cover. A letter [arrived] calling the cover gross with three sets of initials. Dave B says that if it sells, it is good. The [male] figure [on the cover] did not appeal to Clark. Peter says it puts across a bad image. We are making efforts to get more girls involved in The Columns. Roger A feels sales should not be the only matter. Ken H feels we need to keep a respected image . . . Ken raises question as to whether cover should be reviewed by Executive Review Committee. Peter moves: entire magazine be reviewed before it appears. Roger A says that it is very difficult to be so hamstrung. MH and MG say we get a better magazine by giving the editorial board a free hand. . . . Dave B moves that the Executive Review Committee be abolished; Mike H wants to retain what [we] have. DB's proposal is defeated.

The lack of women in the Dorian Society also became a wound. One woman, Carol King, was trying to recruit others but having little success. Even the minutes reflect part of the problem, the constant reference to the "girls" rather than to women: "April 9, 1970: Carol feels we are not doing anything and this is a cause for resignations. She feels we talk about things but do not accomplish them. Carol feels she has been overlooked for the membership committee. Nick feels there just is not enough time for everyone to do everything because of other obligations.

Chuck T feels that one should ask what they can do for the society. Marty G argues that a voluntary organization has limitations. We are the only group to stand up for the gay community."

"May 14, 1970: Carol reported that more girls would join if there was a sub-group for girls. Marty suggested that we have a girls committee. We now have about 12 female members according to Ward. Marty suggests that Carol as membership chairman call together the girls and ask them if they would like a girls committee."

The old methods of screening members, which had required reviews and the assignment of fake names, suddenly was out of place:

"June 11, 1970: Ward thinks our system of accepting members is archaic. He thinks we do not have to screen members. He moves that we accept members automatically but that names of new members be reported to the board. Motion seconded and carried."

Even the counseling service and Dorian began to have difficulties being housemates. Closeted Dorian members did not like sharing the same parlor with openly gay teenagers. Closeted teenagers did not enjoy associating with older, openly gay Dorian members. The volunteer counselors, themselves often younger than the Dorian Society members, did not like answering questions about the society. Conflicts arose about who was in charge—Deisher, the society, or the counselors themselves.

Finally, the board members went on a retreat to try to settle some of the issues, particularly the thorny one embedded in the society's bylaws—that Dorian stood for encouraging only socially responsible behavior by gays.

"August 15–16, 1970: Roger questions phrase in Article 2 Sec 2 of bylaws: ' . . . encourage socially responsible conduct by members of the homosexual community.' This is a matter of subjective interpretation. Discussion pro and con, most feeling that Dorian cannot be the arbiter of values for individuals. Can we put down in writing when we might or might not want to defend or help a member in trouble with the law? How do we stand regarding offenses or arrests? . . .

"Do we need to re-word our goals? How can we implement the concept: 'Gay is Good'? [a favored slogan of the new, post-Stonewall gay activists who wanted to move beyond urging tolerance from heterosexuals]. Being gay is really an acceptable life style. This needs to be communicated to society."

By June 1970, a chapter of a new national organization, the Gay Liberation Front (GLF), had formed in Seattle. The GLF would urge confrontation instead of classroom visits, as well as the assembly of political coalitions with other minorities more accustomed to public demonstrations. Popular among GLFers at the time was an eighteen-point program developed in Philadelphia. Among other things, it called for the "right to be gay," "the right to change sex," the abolition of the nuclear family, "non-sexist child development," "the right to dress as one wishes," the release and payment of reparations to "gay prisoners," and the end of "domination of one by another." Since the GLF often drew young students as members, it could afford to be more open as homosexuals than could the employed Dorian members. They also used drugs more openly, and some GLFers even talked about bombing stores that were hostile to public displays of gay affection. The pressure on the Dorian Society to calculate a new course was building.

Paul Barwick was perhaps typical of the GLFers in his disdain for the Dorian members. He had served in the army's military police in Vietnam where he had learned to deflect attacks on his homosexuality by meeting hostility with direct confrontation. "I stood up for myself," he said years later in an interview. "If you stand up for yourself, people will back down, right? . . . I didn't get to be a faggot this old by being a sissy. . . . The more you stand up, the better off you are."

"We looked down on the Dorian Society as a bunch of closet cases who were afraid to push." In retrospect, he would add, "Pushy jerks is what we were. I was so much better because I was wearing a big Gay Power T-shirt, and they wouldn't be caught dead in anything but a three-piece suit."[16]

Barwick and two other men, Robert Perry and John Singer, rented their own house one block away from the Dorian House, at 422 Malden, and began to use it as the GLF base for launching their own in-your-face projects. Singer played an especially noteworthy role; later, he would become better known among Seattle gays as Faygele benMiriam, a name he chose to emphasize both his Jewish and his gay identity. Faygele, he would point out, was a woman's name in Yiddish as well as a derogatory term for "faggot." He had been born in a working-class family in New York and had inherited from his parents a passion for civil rights—serving, for example, as a VISTA volunteer in St. Louis in 1965. Growing up, he would later say in an interview, "life was political. The dinner table was always filled with all manner of political conversation."[17] A cousin was a political writer who would sometimes invite the likes of author Alex Haley to talk about racism. During the Vietnam War, Singer had been drafted into the army, even though he had already come out as gay in 1962 and even though he filed for conscientious objector status. After his discharge in 1969, the year of the Stonewall riot, he had enrolled in City College in New York. The excitement of the subsequent gay organizing "filled up my life," he once recalled. He brought that to Seattle when he moved to the city in early 1970.

"Ours was the group that would walk on Broadway holding hands," he recalled. "It just wasn't done. What was fun was to have two of us holding hands and someone else twenty feet behind just to listen to some of the comments, or occasionally react to some of the comments. That's where you're being open making it possible for others to be open."

Sometimes he dressed to outrage, not as a performing drag queen, but as what came to be known as "gender-fucking." "What was the thing about me being in a dress?" he said. "If I was that outrageous, it let other people be not quite as outrageous but to be much more expressive of who they were without crossing the line."

Singer tried going to meetings of the Dorian Society, "but I was radical," so he veered to helping set up the GLF instead. At one of the Dorian meetings, however, a seed was planted. A young lawyer and legislator named Peter Francis talked about the state's marriage law being rewritten. The new wording said only that marriage was a contract between two people eighteen years or older. There was no mention of gender. That gave Singer an idea.

The Dorian minutes again: "October 22, 1970: The GLF had an encounter with Dorian. We have a GLF confrontation committee of Lee, Ken, Jack, Mike. There were five GLF people and a fruitful meeting was held. They wanted to squelch rumors: they have banned pot at their meetings. They want to work with Dorian and bars. . . . They are holding a dance. They have been banned at Golden Horseshoe. So have we. They are thinking of picketing the Shoe. The spokesman for GLF was John T; also Randy was there. They have a ten-point manifesto. Graham attended ten meetings or so: GLF did talk of bombing stores that banned Gay people. They have [held a] love-in in Volunteer Park."

At one point, the Dorian board tried to incorporate some of the new gay liberation thinking, but the effort only increased the strain.

January 14, 1971: Sheldon spoke to nominate a GLFer to the board to improve communication. MG seconded move as did Jack A. Allen T was questioning. Ed D spoke against nomination suggesting we allow observer. Nick H suggests a conflict of interest. Allen T feels communication necessary but does not like Sheldon's plan. Allen favors a delegation. Nick H gets passionate about conflict of interest. Bob D feels observer is not enough. Roger A suggests we choose a Dorian member who goes to Gay Lib. Jack A suggests we-they is bad. . . . Sheldon's last word: We should be able to meet other gay people on equal terms if we want to be treated on equal terms by society.

February 11, 1971: [Bob Deisher reported on the formation of a student chapter of GLF that did not seem as leftist as the adult Seattle GLF]: Student group formed about three months ago. Association with Seattle GLF severed after about two meetings. Better structure than Seattle GLF. Should be close to them because they are a moving group and they approve of us. Bob D suggests a joint dance. . . . Harold: Their affiliation with radical left? Bob D: No ties with Seattle GLF. Jerry N: Anything with radical front is automatically associated with radicals. Church: Doesn't see where this will interfere with our image.

Meanwhile, projects began to spin away. The editors of *Columns* decided to make it independent. Deisher moved the counseling service toward its own incorporation as a separate group. The dances, including the one eventually held with the student GLF chapter, lost money. Dorian was even about to lose the sponsorship of the drag contests. By November 1971, the minutes were reporting with some weariness that the consensus of the board members was to allow a new group formed by gay bar owners, the Queen City Business Guild, to take the "whole she-bang." Drag contests would move back to the mudflat and back to the bars.

Two years after the Stonewall riots, the Dorians' turmoil came to an end. On June 24, 1971, the few remaining members voted to kill the society. Its time had passed.

Those Dorian Society members who still had a taste for gay organizing would eventually help create a new group called the Seattle Gay Alliance (SGA), the idea being to start an umbrella organization that included not only the old Dorians but the young GLFers and lesbians who had also begun to form their own political groups. During the summer of 1971, the new alliance endorsed its first action. It would not be a high school outreach, or a church meeting, or a collection of toys. Instead, the SGA voted to picket a coffee shop named the Last Exit on Brooklyn, a student hangout on Brooklyn Avenue near the University of Washington. The shop, according to the SGA, had been allowing "straight public displays of affection" while prohibiting embraces between gay men. It was time for promoting confrontation, not just promoting understanding.

A few months later, in September 1971, Singer acted on the idea Pete Francis had given him at the Dorian meeting. He and Barwick decided to get married. Well, not really. Singer was twenty-six at the time; Barwick, twenty-four. Unlike gays and lesbians in later decades, who would fight for the actual right to marry, neither Singer nor Barwick particularly believed in it. "We would just as soon abolish marriage," Singer said later. Barwick added, during an interview in 2000, that "in the 1970s, you weren't couples and lovers. We were collective. We weren't a pair. We weren't partners. [But] we were as close as anybody in that [GLF] house."

They wanted to make a point about having the same rights as heterosexuals. Singer enjoyed pointing out to the clerk at the marriage license office that the state law simply said that individuals had to be over the age of eighteen to marry, making no reference to the two needing to be a man and a woman. That was what he had learned from Francis.

Their friend Robert Perry, also a GLF member, alerted the media so that television cameras and newspaper reporters were on the scene when the clerk refused the license. Norm Maleng, a deputy prosecutor for civil cases who would later become the county's chief prosecutor, had given the order not to issue a license. Reporters took the incident lightly; one asked which was the bride. "We don't believe in role playing" Singer answered. "We're two people. We happen to be genital males, but two human beings who happen to be in love and want to get married." Then he launched into an explanation of how both he and Barwick could receive more

GI benefits and tax benefits if they were able to marry. Standing alongside, Barwick wore a T-shirt with the word "Gay" printed boldly on it so that, he said, "there wouldn't be any doubt."[18]

It was more than just a media stunt. Singer and Barwick pursued the case for almost three years, filing a lawsuit that was ultimately settled by the Washington State Court of Appeals in 1974, which ruled that the denial was neither discriminatory on the basis of gender nor unconstitutional. To do so, though, the court had to narrowly interpret the definition of "marriage" as an institution meant primarily to promote procreation.[19]

"If marriage is for procreation," Singer would said later, "if someone is beyond the point of procreation, how can you let them marry? Or if someone doesn't procreate after ten years, are you going to annul it?" He felt satisfied that the absurdity of the law's logic had been demonstrated: "We accomplished a lot of what we wanted to do."

Just a few months after Singer and Barwick's attempt to get a marriage license, it was Robert Perry's turn to make a statement—his and D. Carl Harder's, another GLF member. The two set off for Lynnwood, a suburb north of Seattle, aimed for the Rollaway Roller Rink. When the "couples only" skate time began, the two men casually skated onto the rink together, holding hands. Told to stop, they refused. According to news reports in the *Advocate,* the rink's management then called the police, who forced them from the floor, handcuffed them, and took them away to be booked for disorderly conduct. A judge later released them without bail and eventually the charges were dropped. But a week later, some twenty gay men were back at the rink for another protest. This time, several of them dressed in drag and joined other men to skate as "mixed" couples, challenging the rink's management to find a way to prove the "women" were not really women.[20]

The time for discretion had ended.

# 8
# Chautauquas of Feminism and Lesbianism

**B**ryher Herak came to Seattle in 1972 from Montana when she was twenty-five. "There's a lot of cowboy hats there," she would tell an interviewer two decades later. "Cowboy boots and big trucks." She was already used to women like her who preferred to dress in boots and denim jeans and jackets. "Bars are where people hung out," she added, "so that didn't change for me [when I moved]. I just had to find a lesbian bar."

Jane Meyerding arrived the same year, when she was twenty-two. She was from Chicago, college-trained and already soaked in political activism, the daughter of Quaker activists who had taken her to Vienna to work with Hungarian refugees, a protester against the Vietnam war, a volunteer for the Southern Christian Leadership Conference headed by Martin Luther King Jr. She had been arrested at age seventeen during a demonstration at the Pentagon, then arrested again in protests at the Democratic National Convention in Chicago in 1968. Before she moved to Seattle, she had been living with a man, but "I felt like I was a lesbian inside." She had not yet found a way to express that publicly. "I didn't think I could be a lesbian in any way that would interact with the world," she said in an interview. "It would just always be inside."

When each of them arrived, hers was the usual search to discover a place where she could belong. In a previous decade, they might have followed the footsteps of those women like Rose Bohanan or Jackie Cachero down the stairway into the underground at Washington and Second, but what is revealing about both of their journeys was reflected in something that Herak said in her interview.

"So what did I do? There was a bookstore, a women's bookstore, It's About Time, there in the U-district. So I went to It's About Time. I heard there was a lesbian party the first week I was in town. That's how you do it. You do it word of mouth. You call the women's bookstore, you call the YWCA. It's actually pretty easy."

For Meyerding, it was a similar story. "I cannot remember the first occasion on which I made contact with lesbians," she said, "but it must have been . . . on the Ave. in the University District, upstairs, over a typewriter repair place." That was the YWCA.[1]

By the time Meyerding and Herak arrived in Seattle, a geographic and political shift had begun to occur for the city's lesbians. Bars for women were still operating in Pioneer Square, particularly on South Jackson Street where a bar called the Silver Slipper had opened in 1969, but out in the University District a new place of arrival was forming, one that was going to have as historic an impact on the development of the city's homosexual community as the old underground had.

To some extent, gay women had always been more invisible in Seattle than gay men. When the *Seattle Times* published its 1966 story about the city's homosexual "problem," only gay men had been mentioned as the "problem," not lesbians. When the police threatened licenses and the city council held its first public hearing about homosexuals, the targets were men's bars. When the health department blamed homosexuals for spreading venereal disease, the doctors focused on men. And although it had been the women who had first danced aboveground at the Madison, that had happened at a bar owned by two men. Arguably, even the police had tacitly reinforced the lesser importance, or perhaps lesser offensiveness, of lesbians by their decision to extort fewer dollars from the Madison than they demanded at the men's bars. One of the women's bars had even adopted the name of the Annex, as if bars catering to women were some type of add-on to the gay male space in Pioneer Square.

Within the invisible homosexual culture in the city, then, there was a kind of doubled public invisibility for those homosexuals who were women.

Two who had met in Seattle in 1950 had already spent more than a decade trying to cope with that difficulty of creating a more visible presence for lesbians while sharing a spotlight that always focused, even if negatively, on homosexual men. Del Martin and Phyllis Lyon had fallen in love while working together at a Seattle publishing company in the post–World War II period. They moved to San Francisco in 1953, where they formed an organization called the Daughters of Bilitis. They gathered lesbians in private homes for meetings that were partly social but also political. Then, drawing on their publishing experience, they created what became the most noted lesbian newsletter of the 1950s and 1960s, the *Ladder*. They aimed it at women who were still in heterosexual marriages, who were unlikely to find any nearby lesbian bars in their cities, and who were unable to escape from their economic reliance on men.

The two clashed often with their early male activist counterparts. One tension was over sex. Historian John D'Emilio has noted that the Daughters of Bilitis "found gay male promiscuity and the police harassment that accompanied it an encumbrance that seemed to make lesbians guilty by association in the eyes of society." Martin and Lyon, he says, "resented the time taken in mixed gatherings on problems that had little to do with the lives of women." It was not surprising then that when a women's civil rights movement arose in the mid-1960s, Martin and Lyon quickly joined, writing in the *Ladder* that "the Lesbian is first of all a woman" and needed to ally herself with the incipient feminist movement.[2]

A few months after Herak and Meyerding arrived in Seattle, Martin and Lyon

The Ladder, published nationally by former Seattle residents Del Martin and Phyllis Lyon, became a forum for lesbians in the late 1960s and early 1970s. Lesbian self-imagery at the time was usually far less sexually oriented than that portraying gay men. *(Seattle Lesbian Resource Center, Northwest Lesbian and Gay History Museum Project)*

returned to the city to promote their book *Lesbian/Woman,* which had quickly become famous among gay women. Addressing a crowd at the University of Washington's student union building in April 1973, they reiterated the theme for which they had become best known, the *Seattle Post-Intelligencer* reporting Lyon as saying, "I think it's more important for us to work within the women's movement" than to work with gay male activists. "Even if we wiped out all discrimination against gay people, we'd still be women. The gay movement has been dominated by men, and the women in it find themselves in the same position as women in other movements, doing the typing and mailing the letters."

"Gay men are men and just as chauvinistic as any other men."[3]

Lesbian communication and identity were changing, and the saloons on the mudflat with their methods of dancing and butch-femme drag—however pleasurable, traditional, and valuable in previous decades—were simply not big enough to accommodate the new gay woman. The change in geography was part of the shift, and the selection of the University District had much to do with how that neighborhood had developed and what it, like the mudflat, had come to represent in the city's history.

The U.W. had first been housed on the downtown knoll platted by Arthur Denny, overlooking the mudflat that had been surveyed by Doc Maynard. Once it became apparent that the university's land was needed if the city's retail and office district was to expand, the professors relocated northward to a broad, forested slope overlooking Lake Washington on the east and Lake Union on the west. During Denny's time, most people considered the new site a long trolley ride to the boondocks, but the cheaper land gave the university freedom to expand, and the neighborhood that began to develop around the school assumed a character distinct from both the mudflat and the hills bordering downtown. If those living on Queen Anne Hill, like George Cotterill, were concerned with enforcing moral reforms, while those frequenting Pioneer Square aimed to flout them, those who eventually surrounded the university created something more like a tent chautauqua for unceasing argument and exploration.

In 1905, Professor Edward Meany hit on a clever way to secure more support for the still infant U.W. He proposed that the lightly developed campus serve as the site for a world's fair, knowing that Seattle would benefit from the international exposure, while the school would get new buildings and landscaping paid for by the fair's promoters. The theme would be the great gold rushes (which by then had already begun to fade) and the utopian prospect of a new Pacific century. If John Considine and others had found their money in the waves of actual miners and sailors passing over the mudflat, Meany could find profit in tourists who were fascinated by the same adventures but not ready to go beyond the comforts of Seattle in exploring them. In four years, Meany's idea was a reality. A university, and a neighborhood, were born on the back of passionate intellectualism combined with unembarrassed boosterism.

Among the exhibition buildings at what was called the Alaska-Yukon-Pacific Exposition was one representing the achievements of the Northwest's women. The city's Young Women's Christian Association sponsored a restaurant there, as well as a gallery of women's arts and a nursery for many of the fairgoers' weary children. Once the Expo closed, the women who had been volunteering decided to form a neighborhood YWCA, eventually nesting—in tidy auxiliary fashion—with their male counterpart, the YMCA, on the university's tree-lined fraternity row.[4] That neighborly arrangement lasted for several decades. By 1968, with the national feminist movement burgeoning, that locale among men—fraternity men at that— seemed at odds with the new identity many younger women hoped to forge. A new University YWCA director hired that year, Ann Schwiesow, took a single look at the men's landscaped building and the women's auxiliary office and saw a symbolism she wanted no part of.

"It was a traditional male-female relationship," she told a *Seattle Times* reporter in 1972. "Just what we're fighting against."

"We knew from the beginning we would be concerned first and foremost with women's liberation."[5]

In 1970, then, the YWCA left and located directly into a second-story office suite on busy University Way, the core of the retail district next to the university. The "Ave.," as it was called, bustled with pizza shops, real estate developers, used-book vendors, and tables of antiwar literature. Schwiesow moved the YWCA next to a fast-food shop called Sandwich a Go Go.

According to the *Seattle Times* story, she next issued a brochure describing the YWCA's mission in terms surprising to anyone with a traditional view of the organization. None of the usual swimming, cooking, and socializing. The YWCA women, the brochure asserted, were not just "volunteers" as they had been in past years, but "workers" who "describe their commitment as one of creating alternatives to those institutions which degrade or humiliate women, institutions which are inhuman, 'overprofessionalized' or unreasonably expensive."

Soon, the small cluster of otherwise nondescript offices embodied the new rhetoric physically, advertising a fount of possibilities. Notices about feminist events, women's services, jobs, and housing jammed bulletin boards. T-shirts flashed "Women are Changing the World." An abortion law reform group that had been ordered off the university campus was invited to set up a new office at the YWCA; soon its referral service was fielding about seven thousand calls a year. The Northwest Women's Law Center opened in the suite to pursue legal challenges. A local chapter of the National Organization for Women came. A rape counseling service began. Women formed a weekly co-op garage to learn how to repair their own cars. Women's artworks hung in a room devoted to a cultural center. Workers, not volunteers, remodeled a storeroom into a women's health clinic named Aradia. The Women's Divorce Co-operative started giving advice about inexpensive ends to unpleasant marriages. Women's studies classes burgeoned. A newspaper named *Pandora* was added, its name chosen deliberately to challenge male control of storytelling. Women, the newspaper asserted, had opened a box of blessings in mythic times, not the box of troubles that appeared in the male version of the story.

*Pandora* became one of the new media of communication among the city's women, including its lesbians. In 1976, it would be followed by *Out and About*, a newsletter published solely by lesbians.

In *Pandora*'s very first issue, in December 1970, a writer named Rachel daSilva described a historic gathering for gay women that had occurred in Seattle just a few weeks earlier, on November 19. Women from the Gay Liberation Front in Seattle had called a meeting "to allow us to meet other lesbians and get to know each other, [and to express] our feelings about GLF, the gay scene in general, sexual politics, the gay bars, and hopefully, what we wanted out of GLF or any other organization we might want to start." Forty-five women had shown up, "a surprisingly large turnout."

The idea of starting a separate lesbian group had been discussed. "The consensus was that at this point there is nothing bad about this kind of split. GLF is not on a 'power trip,' the majority of the men feel no antagonism toward women who want to work apart from the larger organization, and in fact they encourage women to do so if unable to relate to GLF as it now exists. It is hoped that, in the event a gay women's group does begin, there will be no hostility between it and GLF. In fact, something on the warm side of indifference might be more in line with our goals."[6]

The gay women wasted no time. Two weeks later, *Pandora* announced the start of the Gay Women's Alliance. In just a few hundred words, the announcement set the three-part mission for a new lesbian movement in Seattle.

First, it created a rationale: "For as long as women have been struggling against the male-domination prevalent in our society, lesbians have been the niggers of the women's movement. Women's liberation has been running scared in fear of the labels 'lesbian' and 'dyke' hurled by men trying to quell the rise of self-determination among women. And, for the most part, women have reacted defensively, and have put down their gay sisters in order to appear valid in men's eyes. But our common goal, as women, must be to write our own definition of woman and womanhood; in order to do this, all women, gay and straight, must work together without fear of one another. To rid ourselves of this fear, we must learn more about our various lives and life styles and by learning, come to accept each other as individuals."

Then it proposed a way for women to communicate: in small affinity groups "in which women can feel more at ease about discussing personal problems and where trust is built between women, a revolutionary idea in itself."

Finally, it laid out a strategy for achieving political changes: building coalitions. "As they begin to get themselves together to understand one another on a human, personal basis, gay women will want to establish contact with other women's groups in the Seattle area. Our goals as women may not be identical, but we have enough in common to warrant communication and common rallying points."[7]

Comparing the rhetorical differences between the GWA statement and the Dorian Society's mission is instructive. The GWA wanted to work as part of the larger women's civil rights movement, rather than independently, as the Dorians had. It wanted to write its own definition of "womanhood." It urged women to build trust and make decisions by discussing personal stories rather than by following *Robert's Rules of Order.*

Three months later, in March 1971, the GWA created a permanent organizing space within the YWCA's offices, using volunteers to staff a small Gay Women's Resource Center—the first in Seattle. They set about creating a survival file with the names of doctors, as well as of commercial businesses, friendly to gay women. The group also announced plans to create a speakers' bureau, much as the Dorian Society had done. Most important, though, as the GWA organizers told *Pandora,* was that "there will be a place, outside of the bar environment, where gay women can either come and talk or call and talk to other gay women." It would be open from noon until 10 P.M.—a daytime outpost away from the mudflat.

In October 1971—about the same time that Paul Barwick and Faygele benMiriam of the male-dominated Gay Liberation Front were confronting the city clerk with their demand to be married—the *Post-Intelligencer* discovered the gay women's center and printed a long article explaining why women thought the center was needed. A cautionary editor's note preceded the story: "Lesbianism, a fact of life that's been hidden from public discussion for centuries, has surfaced. Freer discussion of sex and the work of various homosexual activist groups have made this a current issue."[8]

Two lesbians, identified as Tudi Hassl and Carol Anna Strong, were shown in the accompanying photograph. In a parallel to *Seattle* magazine's decision to publish the photograph of Peter Wichern four years earlier, this may have been one of the earliest photos of "out" lesbians to appear in the city's press. Their youth was what was first noticeable—Hassl was twenty-six; Strong, twenty-three. Also noticeable was their choice of clothing. Hassl's long hair fell in front of what appears to be a flannel shirt, and Strong's striped T-shirt was matched by a bandanna wrapped around her hair. These were not stereotypical femmes in gabardine, but neither were they stereotypical butches in workers' uniforms.

Their words first focused on the pain that had brought them to the center.

"I knew I was gay when I was 12 or 13," Hassl said, "but I repressed it until I was in my 20s. I lived in a small town and felt all alone until I read something by a gay woman. For 13 years I went through hell. I went out with men. . . . I had sex

To:                                    Aug. 12, 1971
Gay Woman's Resource Center

To whom it may concern;

    I need help from somebody.
I have no contacts within your
society and I would like to meet
someone who would be willing to
help me. I am 21 years old, female,
shy and sensitive. I need someone
who would "show me the ropes" so
to speak. I am fairly inexperienced,
but have realized my tendencies.
    If you have any information
concerning this matter, or know
anyone interested, could you please
contact me. It is very lonely on this
side. Thank you.

      Very sincerely,
      Barbara ▓▓▓▓▓

BARBARA ▓▓▓▓
▓▓▓▓▓▓

BELLEVUE, WASH. 98004
▓▓▓▓▓

The new Gay Women's Resource Center, created in 1971 at the University YWCA, often drew pleas for help from isolated lesbians. *(Seattle Lesbian Resource Center, Northwest Lesbian and Gay History Museum Project)* with men and I could enjoy it. I had nothing to compare it to. But in retrospect, I didn't enjoy it as much as with women. I couldn't fall in love with men or get emotionally involved."

Strong added, "Before she can really 'come out,' a woman has to face how she feels and stop thinking she's sick just because society says she is. . . . There are two coming outs. One is personal. You face who you are and how you feel about it. You stop forcing yourself to laugh at 'queer' jokes and stop putting up with words like 'dyke.' The second is when you 'come out' politically, when you stand up publicly and say 'I'm a lesbian.'"

However, their words also revealed a growing divide with gay men in Seattle. Pointedly using a stereotype, Hassl argued that "Unlike much male homosexuality, gay women tend to form lasting relationships." Strong extended the generalization. "[Women] don't go in for a one night pick-up thing as much as men do. We may go to a gay women's bar to socialize and be together, but it's not a meat rack and it doesn't have the pick-up atmosphere of most heterosexual bars."

It was a conflict that was going to grow deeper and more public over the next five years. Quite quickly, for example, the Gay Women's Resource Center would instead become the Lesbian Resource Center, as women decided the word "gay" was too closely associated with male homosexuality.

Housing the city's first lesbian center in a YWCA caused controversy, but not as much as might have been expected. *Redbook,* for example, in an article written in 1975, said that most other YWCAs would rather have merged "with the D.A.R. than admit . . . that there might be a lesbian in their midst." But Schwiesow dismissed the differences. "Nobody knows who is gay and who is straight here," she told the *Seattle Times.* "The Gay Women's Resource Center is just a part of the University YW." Downtown, the better-known Seattle YWCA felt occasional criticism because the two branches were often confused, but its executive director, Dorothy Miller, papered over the differences. "I admire their dedication and commitment," she said. "I don't agree with everything they do, but I don't have to." Even the national executive director, ever respectful of a long tradition of independence among the different branches, publicly tempered any reservations she might have had. "They may be a little ahead of the rest of us," she said tactfully to the *Redbook* reporter, "but maybe we have a lot to learn from associations like theirs."[9]

"It wasn't easy walking in that door." Diane Winslow remembered her first visit to the Lesbian Resource Center about four years after it opened. Winslow wrote about her visit in *Pandora:*

I was a housewife and mother of teenagers, and some of these women were lesbians. I concentrated on being as inconspicuous as possible, but I soon began to peer out of my turtle's shell of aloofness at the other women in the small pillow-lined room. They looked like strong, independent women—delightful, real women. I was soon caught up in the discussions and expressed thoughts that had always raised eyebrows and frozen expressions with others, but these women simply nodded and smiled. I told them that I just wanted a woman friend to hold me. Every counselor I'd ever talked to—and there had been several—had told me that this was "inappropriate" behavior in our society and that I was just going to have to adjust. Short hugs were acceptable, but, in my fantasy of a hug, I was a shriveled, dry sponge, absorbing until I was full. One woman . . . commented, "That's what it's all about!"[10]

Something new began to happen in these "rap groups" at the Lesbian Center, something transformative simply as a result of talking. Winslow, who had been married for sixteen years, found that she "didn't want to be a useful appendage to someone else's life. I wanted to be a complete and productive person in my own right. I was troubled to see women with dynamic personalities compromising their individuality, entering into heterosexual relationships out of sexual need and little more."

Her attitude toward sex with women changed.

I came into the LRC rap group very much afraid of even the word "sex." I accepted my sensuality but believed I could forego passion if a woman would be my affectionate friend, entering into the giving and receiving of lovingness. . . . There was another inquirer in the group who had a history remarkably similar to mine. Between us, we had produced nine children, had spent a decade apiece in religious involvement and had emerged exhausted from long, unfulfilling marriages. . . . So one night, we got together at my house and talked freely, shared poetry, prose, and copies of letters—memoirs of our despair. As this woman and I parted, I reached out my arms and said, "Let's hug—it's obvious we've both been as hungry as hell." These words seemed to open both of our confined spirits and, like two entombed prisoners, we stumbled into the light. We knew through our womanness what the other felt.

The CR groups—consciousness-raising groups—that arose from the women's movement were a new outlet for discovery and communication. Part quilting bee, part therapy, part caucus meeting, they solidified a form of small-group communication for Seattle's lesbians different from that which occurred in bars or private homes. It was a structured way of talking about new ways of imagining themselves. Best understood as a kind of personalized chautauqua that could also serve as a base for political action, the CR groups were an exciting explosion of voices that suddenly began setting a course for lesbians joining the journey out. What happened was an exposition.

In such gatherings, perhaps five or ten individuals agreed to meet regularly to wonder through certain themes in their lives and then to make decisions about actions, either individual or collective. Importantly, the CR or "rap" group was not a club that passed motions according to *Robert's Rules* or undertook service work such as traditional women's auxiliaries did. Instead it was intended as a safe place to learn to support one another emotionally and then use personal experiences to analyze the causes of suffering and create change. *Robert's Rules* would come in for particular blasts from women who found the traditional and "respectable" styles of making decisions in organizations to be inappropriate for those whose voices had been so silent in the past. Betty Johanna, for example, an activist during much of the 1970s in Seattle, once wrote a letter to the lesbian newsletter *Out and About,* saying that she viewed "*Robert's Rules of Order* as oppressive and [I] do not wish to give them credibility via my participation. I want to resist the classism that requires one to know a specified terminology in order to participate in meetings. I do not want to be told that the only way I can relate to others is in a highly structured, non-flowing, non-human way."[11]

Lesbians were raising questions that the men in the Dorian Society, at least to judge from their minutes, had never considered.

In the CR groups, each woman would speak "her own truth." Indeed, the power of this particular form of group communication lay in its insistent demand that individuals speak from personal experience, as an "I." Yet from the individual stories arose a common narrative about what "we" shared together—the demands to conform to gender roles, the pain of hiding sexual attractions in high school, the early crushes not understood, the movement into marriages, the release when the obvious truth about sexual attraction became a revelation, the striving for a genuine life, even if others felt such a life was not respectable.

It encouraged something else too. In the democratic environment of the CR group, it was the willingness to tell and blend individual stories that was important, not the submission to any single leader. Insistence that any one person or group knew the truth about where gays and lesbians were headed, or what identity should be claimed, or what single path should be pursued, quickly became suspect. A new political value about leadership was emerging that would become a distinctive characteristic of the 1970s in Seattle. It would eventually be a serious point of political division within Seattle's gay and lesbian community.

Winslow again: "In our rap group, we share our fears . . . and the terror of every woman who contemplates stepping outside of tradition. We discuss the implications of keeping one's lesbian identity hidden or 'closeted.' We talk about radical lesbians, their political clout and their public image, and we realize we can place ourselves anywhere on the continuum from sexually independent to social anarchist according to our wishes.

"As we dare to be honest, the rap group I participate in is learning to laugh and cry together. . . . There is a world to be explored here and I am pleased with what I'm finding."

The fervor of the time reached in many directions, with lesbians becoming part of a web of collective undertakings that were intended to transform how people in Seattle thought, shopped, ate, read, sang, dressed, and lived together. Countless worker and living collectives formed, some only for women, some that included feminist-minded men. Sometimes they were based in the labor or socialist movements that dated back to Seattle's early years; sometimes they were brand new. The Seattle Workers' Brigade served as the umbrella for several of those that became better known to Seattle's public: Corner Green Grocery in Pike Place Market, Little Bread Company in Lake City, C. C. Grains, and Community Produce. Others were independent: Red and Black Books, formed by a women's collective to replace a well-known leftist bookstore in Seattle called Id, and Puget Consumers' Co-op, which headed up what eventually became a long list of neighborhood natural food buying collectives. All offered something that lesbians in the city seemed to be looking for: a receptive new place to work and to belong. A letter to *Out and About* from a woman who signed her name only as Gwen noted that she had been part of a milling team that worked at C. C. Grains. "I look at C. C. Grains," she wrote, "and I see something wonderful. A place where I could learn and grow non-oppressively. A place where I could dare to challenge my own socialization in a supportive atmosphere. The time, the energy, the tears and hurts, joys and laughter all rolled into a group of women committed to finding another way besides hierarchical, capitalistic, imperialistic ways."[12]

Some lesbians emphasized activism that reached many other political issues. Lois Thetford, for example, arrived in Seattle in 1970 at age twenty-four, having grown up in New Jersey and attended Cornell. She and fourteen friends came cross-country in three used mail trucks bought for one hundred dollars each; in Seattle, they used the trucks to help the Black Panther Party deliver breakfasts to children. Eventually, her collective became known as the People's Trucking Company. In 1970, Thetford helped found a women's health clinic in Fremont. By 1971, she was in Cuba with two members of her collective helping workers harvest sugarcane. Then she moved back to Tacoma, helping war resisters and organizing a lesbian rap group, and finally returned to Seattle, where she eventually began working with homeless families needing health care.[13]

Others, like Meyerding, focused on the lesbian community, in her case becoming one of the original members of the collective that published *Out and About*. Still others, like Herak, worked setting up women's coffeehouses so there would be alternatives to meeting in the bars. The best known was the Coffee Coven, located in Lake City next to the Little Bread Company, which was where another lesbian, Jan Denali, had decided to work on the granola team.

"We'd go up once a week," Denali recalled. "There'd be seven or eight lesbians [on the granola crew] and we would just like torque out with this quantity of granola that was unbelievable. Making it was just a riot . . . and it brought together different kinds of lesbians. The whole cooperative business scene—that was a place where lesbian culture had a place for growth and for struggle with a broader world."[14]

Denali, who was twenty-four when she settled in Seattle in 1973, also had a second entry point to belonging—the new feminist women's music that represented yet another piece of the growing web of change for Seattle's lesbians. She started a string band called LesBeFriends and eventually joined a street theater group called Shelly and Crustaceans that demonstrated against the construction of a Trident nuclear submarine base on the Hood Canal, west of Seattle. Then, in her enthusiasm, Denali joined another collective that produced the city's first lesbian radio show and aired it on a leftist-leaning public station, KRAB. "Amazon Media" covered stories ranging from city politics to lesbian poetry to women's writings on racism.

"It was just such an exciting time for lesbian women," Denali said. "There was so much happening."

Had you taken a hypothetical walk through the different feminist rhetorics present in the University District in 1973, you could have strolled into at least four imaginary chautauqua tents where women argued about how best to recreate their identities and roles. Lesbians were participating in each of the discussions.

In the first such "tent," women labeled "reform feminists" urged a focus on changing laws or business and health practices that discriminated against all women. The speakers argued that men could be allies, just as whites had been allies in the African American civil rights movement. On the subject of lesbians, though, the reformers spoke with mixed voices. Some were befuddled about why lesbian rights should be a concern and were embarrassed by the topic. Others were sympathetic, mostly because they knew that men had always derogated "uppity" women as lesbians as a way to put an end to their political demands. The way to overcome that male tactic was to embrace lesbians as full partners. This was the "tent" of the National Organization for Women (NOW), which, by 1973, had been struggling with the "lesbian question" for several years. Activists like Del Martin had pushed NOW to explicitly embrace lesbian concerns. NOW had passed a resolution recognizing that lesbian relationships were a feminist issue, but until the convening of a national conference in February 1973, the organization had dragged its feet for seventeen months on proposing specific actions. Even a task force appointed to study actions NOW could promote had been innocuously named the Task Force on Sexuality, and a heterosexual woman had been appointed to coordinate it. Only because of pressure the month before the 1973 conference was the name changed to the Task Force on Sexuality and Lesbianism, and a lesbian appointed as a co-coordinator.[15]

The second "tent" of rhetoric housed those labeled "radical feminists." Like reform feminists, they urged civil rights changes, but they also passionately argued to rout sexism from the entire culture, not just from the law or businesses. Art, relationships, language, religion, words—all were grist for change. It was just as important to establish a weekend mechanics course to teach women how to repair their own cars as to pass an Equal Rights Amendment. Radicalism meant dismantling male hierarchies and leaving behind those methods of decision making considered traditionally male—such as the parliamentary procedures dictated by *Robert's Rules of Order.* When it came to lesbians, this radical analysis encouraged women to accept the potential, if not the actual experience, of sexually bonding with one another. To be a lesbian was to make a political choice not to submit to traditional male-controlled relationships.

In the third tent, "socialist feminists" denounced capitalism as the real problem and focused on economic change as the arena for the most important revolution. Sexism and male domination were inherent in capitalism, so ending sexism meant ending capitalism. Their argument had a strong appeal in the overall tumult of the early 1970s—the time of student protests over the Vietnam War and the American invasion of Cambodia, the rise of the Black Panthers, and the economic crash of Boeing. It was especially appealing in Seattle, with its history of strong labor unions and socialism that dated to the days of George Cotterill. On gay and lesbian concerns, socialists veered, sometimes rejecting them as lacking political relevance to the class struggle and then sometimes embracing them as a new component of Marxist dialectic. For a while, the Socialist Workers Party (SWP) had endorsed an unwritten policy that gays be excluded, and its youth affiliate, the Young Socialist Alliance, had formally adopted such a rule. The policies were later reversed, but the SWP still emphasized that the primary struggle was that associated with the labor movement.

In Seattle, a Marxist feminist group called the Freedom Socialist Party (FSP) had emerged in 1966, asserting that oppressions could best be fought by forging coalitions among all the dispossessed, including sexual minorities. A group of socialist women called Radical Women had also formed—not to be confused with the nonaligned "radical feminists." By spring 1973, both the FSP and Radical Women had settled into an immense former factory renamed Freeway Hall at the bottom of the University hillside. Among the FSP and Radical Women members were several powerfully vocal gay and lesbian activists, among them Sam Deaderick, Doug Barnes, Patrick Haggerty (who had traveled with Lois Thetford to Cuba as part of the same workers' brigade), and Tamara Turner, who had enjoyed dancing at Madame Peabody's and then in 1972 had joined Radical Women. Three other women, Laurie Morton, Su Docekal, and Cindy Gipple, would also become well known for speaking out as representatives of Radical Women.

The relevance of socialism to lesbians was perhaps best explained in a speech that Morton gave in 1975 at a Washington, D.C., conference on the relationship between gays and the federal government. "Through socialist feminism," Morton said, "I have come to understand that we gays are not persecuted as social outcasts because we are sick, or perverse, or child molesters as our oppressors would have us believe. . . . No—the roots of our oppression go much, much deeper. The truth is that homosexuality challenges the most basic social institution in this system of private property and profit: the unit upon which capitalism is built—the hetero-sexual monogamous family. Two workers for the price of one is a key prerequisite for capitalist production and profit, whether it is free domestic labor in the home, or that kind of cozy slavery combined with low-paying wages in the industrial job market."

It was by understanding the homosexual challenge to the economy and to the patriarchal family structure, socialist feminists argued, that coalitions could be built with workers and other minorities to effect real change. Gays, lesbians, heterosexual women, blue-collar workers, and racial minorities had the same issues: A job and a home, the right to have and raise children, freedom from prejudice, and free-dom from police harassment. Socialism, Morton said, was "the connecting link between women, minorities, gays and workers."[16]

In this imaginary walk in 1973, there would have been one final chautauqua tent of feminist rhetoric, supported by lesbians who had sampled the other argu-ments and found all of them lacking. None of these approaches, they argued, really addressed the question of how lesbians should forge their own story and their own identity: What it meant to love another woman. How a lesbian community could be built. What political or social changes needed to be made for lesbians in par-ticular rather than for all women. All of the other stances simply annexed lesbian concerns to their own political agendas, turning them into a sideshow. Some of the women in this tent began to think about working for a separate lesbian nation—or at least for some lesbian farms out on a Puget Sound island, like Lopez up in the San Juans, or Vashon just a few miles from Seattle. In that regard, they fitted themselves within that long-standing utopian tradition in the Northwest of sep-arating from the cities to pursue a communal life among the trees.

In 1973, one such separatist group in Seattle, identified only as Alice, Gordon, Debbie, and Mary, began to circulate pamphlets entitled "Lesbian Separatism—An Amazon Analysis," and groups of lesbians in the city began to meet to discuss the paper. In it, the four argued that contrary to what reform, radical, and social-ist feminists thought, the key problem was male supremacy. Legal reform wasn't enough: "lesbians' basic oppression is NOT due to laws," they asserted, but to soci-ety viewing women as men's tools. The socialist approach was not acceptable either, because destroying capitalism would not destroy sexism and its devaluation of women. Alice, Gordon, Debbie, and Mary pointedly noted that even in socialist

Some feminists and lesbians in the early 1970s argued passionately that anti-gay prejudice needed to be seen as an out-growth of capitalism and that homosexuals needed to join in coalitions with the labor and socialist movements. Laurie Morton (above, left) and Tamara Turner speaking at a Radical Women's conference, 1976. (*Doug Barnes, Freedom Socialist Party*)

Cindy Gipple urged gay and lesbian support for labor workers. (*Freedom Socialist Party Archives*)

Cuba, men still reigned. Also, the four doubted whether the socialist emphasis on forming large groups such as unions would help, partly because large groups always produced hierarchies of leaders. Instead, they trusted the more democratic form of small base communities and CR groups.

Lesbians, the four argued, should work cautiously with other women. Heterosexual women were not the oppressors, they said, but "their interests are often opposite to ours, and, as the agents of men, their behavior is sometimes oppressive to us." Gordon commented in a *Pandora* interview: "I don't believe in working with straight women because they've proven that their interests are often opposite to mine. . . . They've flirted with lesbianism; they've flirted with lesbians; they've kept our attention focused on them while they made 'the decision' and diverted our attention from ourselves."

Working with men was out of the question. Even gay men, the four wrote, "are first and foremost men and have male privilege." They argued that unlike lesbians gay men were neither oppressed nor persecuted because they were, after all, still men.[17]

Besides Alice, Gordon, Debbie, and Mary, other separatist groups began to gather in Seattle in the early 1970s. A group known as the Gorgons, for example, expanded their suspicion to include socialist lesbians, who, the Gorgons said, should not be privileged to identify themselves as feminists. The socialist analysis that the economic structure was the root of women's problems was not true enough to the feminist belief that the real struggle lay between men and women. The Gorgons even launched guerrilla attacks against other women's collectives. For example, the Gorgons objected when It's About Time, the women's bookstore in the University District, sold books about women that had been written by men. "It upsets us," they wrote to *Out and About*, "to have prick [male-written] anti-lesbian books oppress and invade us in women's places." Similarly, they complained that the women's collective running Red and Black Books should not be selling any books about lesbians to its male leftist customers. "We don't want lesbian lives and politics available to men," the Gorgons protested in another letter to *Out and About.* "Lesbian politics and culture is for lesbians and not to be shared with pricks."

One day, the Gorgons invaded both stores, stripped them of the books in question, and then switched the books—taking the male-written ones about women to Red and Black, while moving the lesbian books to It's About Time.[18]

Many, if not most, gay men in Seattle were at least a little confused by what was happening with the women, unless they themselves subscribed to feminist beliefs. Gay men had no comparable national men's movement to influence. Gay men had borrowed most of their public rhetoric from the black civil rights movement or the black pride movement. Few talked about "choosing" to be gay as a political statement, as lesbians did in the 1970s, or about overthrowing male hierarchies in church or state, or about convincing heterosexual men not to sleep with women as a way of freeing themselves from cultural brainwashing. Male gay activists, at least of the Dorian Society ilk, did not want to change the "power structure" as much as simply persuade the structure to ensure a "civil right": privacy for the bedroom. Also, having been derided as "fags" or "fairies" or "queers," many gay men wanted to be recognized for being as masculine as any heterosexual male. The simple statement "We're the same as any other man" held very different connotations for the men and for women.

Divisions popped up in small and countless ways. At the U.W.'s Experimental College, an informal class on lesbianism—one of the first in the city—charged women two dollars for admission, but men had to pay five dollars. On the mudflats, relations strained. At the old Madison, the Casino, the Garden of Allah, and many other bars, men and women of earlier generations had casually mingled, or so their recollections suggest. By 1973, though, an unnamed writer for a "Lesbian Flash" special edition of *Pandora* in 1973 complained that the lesbian bar, the Silver Slipper, was not only allowing men to be served in the bar, but also encouraging them.

"The question," she wrote, "is why?" She described several nights at the Slipper, contrasting the way it felt when only women were there to how it felt when gay men showed up:

Sunday: The bar was unusually busy for a Sunday night mainly because a woman from Fort Worth was singing tonight. The crowd was all women and everyone really got into her performance. We sang along on some songs and there was a general good feeling amongst the women there. . . .

Thursday: Tonight was drag show night and very depressing. Several gay men came to show off their money and flirt with Misty Dawn who was annoyed that the majority of lesbians talked and laughed throughout the show. There is something degrading about strong women shuffling around to arrange the spotlight for a man mimicking who he thinks we are. He was mainly interested in the kisses and money and jeers of the men in the audience anyway. The majority of lesbians either ignored him or observed without much interest. The poor job of lip singing he did was too much. . . .

Friday: The bar was crowded tonight and the crowd included far too many men. The women at our table were getting more and more angry at two voyeurs staring at the dance floor and came up with a plan of action. One woman accidentally on purpose spilled half a schooner of beer in the lap of both men and was followed soon after by another woman who kicked both men so hard she stumbled to the floor. Great! But they didn't leave. We weren't the only lesbians uncomfortable by the presence of all the men but the management's policy goes something like "We love our brothers as much as our sisters," so much that the bartender is a man.[19]

There were also tensions about the drag styles of older lesbians. "Among the politically oriented lesbian-feminists," Jane Meyerding said, "butch and femme were politically incorrect." Younger lesbians saw no reason to repeat in their own relationships what they took to be the heterosexual idea that one person was masculine and one was feminine. Meyerding added, "We were discarding those mistaken carry-overs from patriarchal culture. . . . It seemed obvious to reject butch-femme roles because they seemed so obviously patriarchal and old-fashioned, and everything we wanted to get away from."

It seemed, she noted, that the community was dividing between what she called the "bar dykes" and the "Coffee Coven dykes."[20]

It was the spring of 1973 when the lesbian chautauquas over new identities reached a climax.

First, at the end of March, the King County Mental Health Board sponsored a two-day forum so social workers could talk with gay men and lesbians. Officially, the American Psychiatric Association still considered homosexuals to be mentally ill, but 1973 would be the last year for that, and, prodded by people like Bob Deisher, King County's mental health system had already begun changing its stance. Most talk at the forum focused on the long-established misunderstandings between the two groups. Gay activist Patrick Haggerty, for example, reviewed other cultures' acceptance of homosexuality as mentally healthy, while a psychiatric nurse named Cheryl Brunner talked of having been fired from a Seattle mental health agency in 1968 for being a lesbian. At one point, Cindy Gipple, of Radical Women, spoke. She was already well known among feminist activists, partly for a blistering attack she had written in 1971 on *Pandora's* more reform-minded feminists, who had endorsed Tim Hill for city council even though Hill had not responded to a NOW questionnaire about his support for women's issues. *Pandora*, Gipple had said then, had "appalled women radicals" by supporting candidates "who are part and parcel of this sexist, militarist, racist and capitalist system." At the forum, she emphasized that more needed to be done to stop the oppression of sexual minorities and that this could be accomplished through socialism.[21]

The arguments about which feminist approach to homosexuality was best had already frayed tempers, and Gipple's comments—although not especially different from anything that had been said in the past—may have triggered an outburst. The night after she spoke, the home of Radical Women at Freeway Hall was spray painted with huge slogans: "Lesbianism for the Lesbians. Straights out of Lesbian Politics. Lesbianism is not a fad. Amazons will win."

By April 17, *Pandora* had joined the attack, with an editorial severely criticizing socialist feminists for trying to disrupt the work of the Feminist Coordinating Council, a group that had been set up earlier to ensure cooperation among all the various types of feminists. "The hassling over politics is beginning to take its toll," Pandora's collective said. "Fewer and fewer people are attending the [coordinating council] meetings. . . . The University YWCA has resigned and several other groups are known to be considering the same step. What happened?"

According to *Pandora*, the catalyst was simple: the tactics and strong rhetoric used by Radical Women. Although the paper also acknowledged that there was a second problem—some women just were not accustomed to hearing other women use such "less-than-feminine tactics to get their point across"—the blame was clearly aimed at the socialists. Incensed, Radical Women replied in the following issue of *Pandora* with a letter that can be read either as a dire prediction or as a warning, both to women in general and to lesbians specifically. Titling the letter "The Politics of Terrorism," the socialists compared those who had painted the slogans to "Hitler's gang of cutthroats" and called them "hysterical and cowardly." "We will not be intimidated," the letter said, "or deterred by any variety of political psychopath—right, left, or center, male or female, minority or white, lesbian or straight."

Even the venerable YWCA did not escape indirect criticism. A May 15, 1973, letter from three Radical Women, including Gipple, grumbled that almost a third of *Pandora*'s coverage of women's activities related to the YWCA, even though there were at least forty organizations that were part of the movement. *Pandora*'s brand of reform and radical feminism, the letter said, had caused the women's newspaper to use "manipulative and destructive tactics" aimed at undermining feminists who held other analyses.

Soon enough, a group of lesbian separatists replied in another letter with equally impassioned rhetoric. "Lesbians in Seattle," the separatists bristled, "have been angry and disgusted at the treatment we have received from Radical Women. . . . Many of us were told to our faces that 'lesbianism is not a political issue.'" Radical Women, the separatists went on, was being "opportunistic" in trying to push its socialist line on gays and lesbians. It was trying to "co-opt" and annex lesbian energy into "straight terms such as the nuclear family and heterosexual monogamy." The separatists declared that the socialists defined lesbians only as oppressed. "It never seems to occur to them that we may also be rejoicing in our love of women." The spray painting of Freeway Hall, the lesbians argued, "was an appropriate political response to the exploitative actions of Radical Women." The letter closed by reasserting each of the slogans that had decorated Freeway Hall.[22]

A few weeks later, on May 21, a second incident highlighted other conflicts, this time between radical lesbians and the NOW brand of reform feminists. One of feminism's founders, Betty Friedan, arrived at the University of Washington for a speech. Her views about lesbians were already well known: Lesbians posed a sexual question, she argued, not a political or civil rights one. They were welcome, but only as women first. To Friedan lesbians were an annex.

Angered by what they saw as the insistence that the only way homosexuals could achieve acceptance was to always join others—such as socialists—in their fight against capitalism, lesbian separatists in 1973 targeted Freeway Hall, the home of Radical Women and the Freedom Socialist Party. *(Freedom Socialist Party Archives)*

On the day of her speech, she took her place at the podium and had barely begun talking when eleven lesbians marched onto the stage with signs reading "traitor" and "sexist." A banner mocked Friedan as "anti-lesbian" as the protesters silently formed a semicircle behind her.

"Get them off!" some in the audience began yelling, according to a report in *Pandora*. Others cheered. One of the lesbians pulled out a small sound system she had buckled around her waist. Another took a microphone. "We do not consider Betty Friedan to be a leader in the women's movement," she began. "We strongly protest Friedan's racism, classism, and anti-lesbianism. She would have us, as lesbians, remain hidden in the closet so that our sexuality could not be an issue. She is under the delusion that lesbians are plotting to take over the movement."

Silenced, Friedan watched.

"As long as lesbians are oppressed because of their sexuality," the protester continued, "lesbianism is an issue that cannot be ignored. We will not hide and we will not be co-opted into taking a lesser stance for fear of alienating men.

"We are lesbians and we are proud. We are the 'lavender menace' Friedan has warned us about."

The women then moved around the podium and claimed the floor in front, according to the *Pandora* account. Finally permitted to speak, Friedan responded icily. "There are enemies of this movement that would like to disrupt it." Gradually, she built from a glare to a shout. "Who's paying you?" the *Pandora* reporter said Friedan demanded. "Who's paying you!"[23]

The marketplace of feminist ideas, which had become so important in helping to rethink lesbian identity, had temporarily become a noisy bazaar.

The changes that happened for Seattle's lesbians in the early 1970s were never solely about political ideologies or consciousness-raising. Del Martin and Phyllis Lyon had been right about their strategy in organizing the Daughters of Bilitis: many lesbians had married in the 1950s or 1960s, had created families, and were not about to meet in bars or even CR groups. Although divorces provided many with a new freedom to explore as single women and to challenge the whole notion of nuclear families, others faced the issue of whether coming out meant losing their existing children—or giving up their hopes of ever having them.

"Many people have never heard of a 'lesbian mother,'" Carol Strong, who had helped establish the Gay Women's Resource Center, wrote in *Pandora* in May 1972.[24] Such individuals, she added, "cannot grasp the concept of a lesbian with children." At a Los Angeles gay women's conference the previous year, Strong noted, no child care had been provided, prompting the lesbian mothers who attended to angrily form a new union. Seattle got its own in 1972, a Gay Mothers' Union that, like so many other feminist groups, began meeting at the University YWCA. Among the most pressing topics: how to stop courts from punishing openly gay mothers by stripping away their children. The notion that lesbians were mentally sick and immoral, and therefore automatically unfit as mothers, had become deeply embedded in the law and was as powerfully frightening a tool as a sodomy prosecution or an involuntary mental commitment.

Strong's story in *Pandora,* for example, told of two women who lived near Seattle raising one of their daughters. To protect the women, Strong referred to them only by pseudonyms. According to Strong's story, a neighbor had claimed the two were "lesbian dopers"; they were arrested for possession of marijuana, and the child was taken by social workers and placed in a foster home rather than with family members. In itself, that might have had to do with the drug charge, but before releasing the child, according to the article, the judge ordered the lesbian lover to move out of the women's home and mandated that the mother receive counseling for her homosexuality. Only when the mother began to tell the social worker that she would find a man to live with was she pronounced "cured."

Since no names were given, it is not possible to verify the *Pandora* account through court records, but the fear that such an intrusion into the family by the courts would occur was certainly a strong presence. An article in *Pandora* commented that the new mothers' group hoped to establish a legal precedent in Washington State that would protect lesbian moms. The chance soon came—but it involved two women who seemed very far in their beliefs from any of the debates about patriarchy that were occurring among other lesbians.

Sandra Schuster and Madeleine Isaacson instead seemed exactly the type of pre-feminist lesbians Martin and Lyon originally had in mind when they started the *Ladder*. Schuster had studied nursing at Stanford, graduating in 1961, joined the navy to help pay her college bills, and then married. She and her husband eventually had four children. Isaacson had also married and given birth to two. At first, Schuster lived with her husband north of San Francisco, slowly growing more alienated.[25]

"I knew there was an emptiness in me, but I didn't know what it was," she would tell the *Advocate* in a later interview. For one thing, her husband did not share her fundamentalist Christian religious beliefs. Schuster prayed for guidance. She told the *Advocate* that one day, in the shower, she thought she heard God say she should move to Seattle to help a friend working in the city as a fundamentalist preacher. At first, she wondered whether she was crazy. A few months later, her husband was transferred to Seattle. Schuster considered it the first miracle.

In April 1970, Schuster was attending an evening service at the friend's church when she saw a woman walking down the aisle with young sons grasping her hands. "I swore that I saw a glow around her head," Schuster said. "I thought, 'Listen girl, you're really sick.'" A few days later, one of Schuster's own sons eagerly dragged her to meet his new Sunday school teacher. It was the same woman—Isaacson. The second miracle.

She, too, had a strained marriage. She, too, had been praying for help. "I remember when we first shook hands," Isaacson would say of that first meeting with Schuster. "My knees got weak. I had this funny feeling all over."

A few camping- and prayer-filled months later, Isaacson confessed her feelings. At first, Schuster resisted by quoting Bible passages. When Isaacson—the Sunday school teacher—was unfazed, Schuster began to reexamine and realized that Biblical condemnations of lust were not condemnations of love. Still, she wanted a more personal sign. She told the *Advocate*, "I said if God will send a prophet, I'll know it's right."

Driving around Lake City one day, the two women stopped on a whim at a Pentecostal church and found a young man from California preaching. In the middle of his service, he suddenly said he felt a great burden from two people in the room and called Schuster and Isaacson forward. "Everything he told us," Isaacson said, "was just what we'd prayed for."

Still, Schuster demanded an even clearer sign before she would agree to act on the feelings that were becoming ever stronger. She told the *Advocate* that she traveled to California to go to her old church, along the way praying, "Lord, are you really sure you know what I've been thinking?" Standing there on the street, by coincidence or design, she found the same young preacher she had met in Seattle. That was finally enough. The third miracle.

Lesbianism through divine revelation. By a patriarchal God sending a sign through a male preacher. That was something the political analyses had certainly not addressed.

Eventually both women divorced, and in 1972 the ex-husbands filed for custody of their children, citing as harmful not only the women's lesbianism but their fundamentalist religious beliefs as well. By then, Schuster and Isaacson had moved into a five-bedroom home in Seattle. Over the dining table for eight hung a wall poster that said, "Hallelujah! Jesus is Lord!" Once their case became known, a *Post-Intelligencer* story tried to capture what seemed to be the oddity of it all. "Lesbianism, motherhood, and religion—like oil and water, they just don't seem to mix," it said. A social worker named Nancy Kaplan and a psychiatrist named S. Harvard Kaufman soon descended on the home.

What they found was a very well adjusted family. Neither woman was attempting to cloak her newly claimed homosexuality. "It's my understanding," Kaplan wrote in her report, "that the danger of homosexuality is indicated by feelings of guilt and self-rejection and a tendency to withdraw from society. I see none of these traits in either Mrs. Schuster or Mrs. Isaacson. Actually, they plan to reach out and help others." The children, all of them under nine, seemed comfortable with their mothers' relationship. If they had questions about it, Kaplan said, they got frank answers from the moms.

"This is a most happy, well organized, creative family," Kaplan wrote.

For his part, psychiatrist Kaufman zeroed in on the worry of whether the children would have the proper role models of gender and sexuality. "The children certainly are getting good physical and emotional care, are being loved and are able to show love in return," he concluded. "They show no identification problems."

Despite the glowing reports, the King County Superior Court judge assigned to the case, James Noe, had his own unusual test. Knowing that both women were deeply religious, he ordered them to reflect on the biblical passage Romans 1, "as it relates to their understanding of the Word of God and its effect on their lifestyle and pattern." The chapter, part of a letter from the Christian apostle Paul to the early church in Rome, included condemnations of those who "lusted" after the flesh more than after God.

The women already knew the passage, but, as Isaacson would tell the *Post-Intelligencer,* "we read it over again to see what he meant." After duly noting all of the letter's references to those who were lustful fornicators, wicked, coveting, malignant, and backbiters of God, Isaacson said she told Schuster, "Sandy, we aren't any of those things!" Schuster added, "God disapproves of lust between people of the same sex or of the opposite sex. But he doesn't disapprove of love."

At least partially content with that response, Judge Noe agreed the women could keep custody of their children. But, he ordered, they would have to break up their new family. Despite all the praise for the home they had created, he instructed the two women to live separately.

It was a victory of sorts, at least for lesbian moms who could demonstrate they knew their Bible and could maintain a respectable household, but it was also a severe intrusion into the two women's ability to create a good home. The weekend the two mothers were breaking up the house and preparing to move, a *Post-Intelligencer* reporter named Susan Paynter visited. The family of eight sat by the fireplace, "Madel[e]ine and Sandy on guitars, the kids banging tambourines and triangles, [singing] 'What color is God's skin? Well, it's red and it's yellow and it's black and it's white, everyone's the same in the good Lord's sight.'" Paynter noted that even Schuster's four-year-old twins knew the words.

The two women were philosophical about the upcoming separation and about having chosen not to hide their homosexuality. Isaacson said, "We just couldn't live a secret schizophrenic life." They were praying that their God would help with another way.

As some lesbians began the fight to keep their children from previous marriages—a Lesbian Mothers' National Defense Fund would be formed in Seattle two years after Noe's decision—others sought to create families in ways that combined from the beginning their identities as lesbians with their identities as mothers. Even while she was harvesting sugarcane in Cuba and counseling draft resisters in Tacoma, Lois Thetford was also planning a family. She became an early volunteer for the new defense fund. "I always knew I wanted to be a mother before I ever knew I was a lesbian," Thetford would say in a later interview.[26] She turned to the same source for help in conceiving a child and creating a family that many lesbians in Seattle eventually would: similarly feminist-minded gay men, some of whom were members of the GLF or the Freedom Socialist Party. Working through networks of friends who knew friends, lesbians found anonymous sperm donors or, as with the arrangement Thetford chose, actively involved gay men as co-parents.

"It was quite a novelty at the time," Thetford said later. She linked with Patrick Haggerty, who had traveled with her as part of the group that had gone to Cuba in 1971. After his return to Seattle, he had written music for an album of gay liberation music called *Lavender Country,* earned a social work degree from the University of Washington, and was assisting the new counseling service for gays and lesbians. Thetford and Haggerty lived in separate political collectives in Seattle, she recalled. "It took about two years," Thetford said, "from the time we decided to have a child until it came to fruition, and we spent that time persuading our collectives that it really was going to be all right, that it wasn't going to be this terrible thing." After she got pregnant, she visited the Silver Slipper once. "People were really shocked . . . like what is she doing here? . . . It was really considered a contradiction in terms."

That was also part of reshaping the identities of homosexuals. Haggerty told an interviewer for the *Advocate* in 1975 that he had no intention of sacrificing his interest in a family because he was gay. That was an old fear used to scare homosexuals in the past, he asserted. "One of the primary social sanctions against gayness is that you have to give up your right to a family. . . . There's that whole stereotype of the gay men who are old and lonely while their peers have seventeen grandkids over on the weekend. I feel like I'm actively participating in eliminating one of the facets of my oppression."[27]

In keeping with their political beliefs, Thetford and Haggerty eschewed the nuclear family and created instead a collective parenting approach that included one of Thetford's former lovers as well as Haggerty's friend from the Gay Liberation Front, Faygele benMiriam (the name that had replaced his old one, John Singer). After a few bumps—including one in which the child frankly told a few of the parents that she loved them but wanted to spend more time with Thetford—they settled to just three parents. Eventually, that also included Thetford's new partner, a woman with whom she would remain for the next twenty-five years.

The effort lesbians were making in Seattle, then, was not just about changing their own invisibility or their own identity. It was also about changing the public nature of the family.

For Sandra Schuster and Madeleine Isaacson, the final victory would come six years after Noe's ruling, in 1978. At first, they and their children found separate houses, struggling with the new heavy financial burden that imposed. Then, one day, in another insight, they realized that living separately did not have to mean living apart. They rented two apartments in the same building across the hallway from each other. The fathers, who by then had remarried, once again sued for custody, claiming the arrangement violated Noe's order.

This time a different superior court judge in Seattle, Norman Ackley, listened for five days as thirty-three witnesses, including eleven psychiatrists and psychologists, mostly reached the same conclusion that Kaplan and Kaufman had. Ackley noted that the testimony pointed to "healthy, happy, normal loving children." He felt particularly reassured, according to a *Seattle Times* report, because a court-appointed psychiatrist did not think the children were at any greater risk for growing up homosexual—the bias that to do so would be bad still apparent in his consideration. The women could keep the children, he ruled. Most important, Ackley decided that since there had been no harm in the children living with both mothers, Noe's previous instruction that they live apart could be lifted.

The fathers appealed. When the case reached the Washington State Supreme Court in 1976, it stalled there for almost two years, time during which the mothers were able to keep their family together but were always under the threat of having it separated. Finally, in 1978, six justices ruled in favor of Schuster and Isaacson keeping custody. The justices took pains, though, to point out that they were not ruling that lesbians could be fit mothers. Instead, the majority decision said that Washington State law presumed stability was the most important factor in determining custody of children, so unless there was a major new reason to shift custody, the court would not do it. Three justices wanted to transfer custody to the fathers.

On the second issue of whether the family could stay together, something quite odd happened. Of the six who had ruled in favor of the mothers' keeping custody, only two agreed with Ackley that the lesbian moms should be able to live together. The other four wanted to split the two lesbians up again. That technically left the majority decision in the power of the three most hostile justices— the ones who wanted to transfer the children to the fathers. But those three issued no opinion whatsoever on this second legal question because, of course, for them the question was irrelevant since they were voting to transfer custody to the fathers anyway. That 2-4-3 split meant there was no majority to overturn Ackley's ruling that the family could stay together.

For Schuster and Isaacson, it looked like another divine intervention.

By the 1990s, after she had been in Seattle for more than two decades, Bryher Herak, who had launched her search to belong by going to the new women's bookstore and the YWCA, had come to think of all the fervent explorations of new lesbian identities as an attempt to produce a new kind of integrity: "to have integrity in our relationships, in our politics, in ourselves." For Herak, the debates were "a really important time."

"Are we going to stay separate? Do we live and act as if we hate men? Do we form separate communities? Are we part of a bigger community?"

Herak would eventually find her own role in Seattle's lesbian community in a way that combined the traditional institutions of the mudflat with the new dialogue about visibility. She turned back to the saloons because in them she saw community centers that unified even more women than the new political groups did. "The bar itself," she said, "has played an important part in the lesbian community because it's been a place where we could be ourselves." In 1984, she would open one herself. But hers would be different, a kind of reflection of the changes that had occurred. It would be on Pike Street on Capitol Hill, rather than on the mudflat. It would combine some of the aspects of a women's coffeehouse, with women's music concerts and women's bands, with the usual aspects of a tavern— pool tables and drink. It would have expansive windows so there was little sense of dreariness or invisibility. Quickly, the Wildrose would become the most popular lesbian bar in the city, for daytime lunches as well as night talks. By the end of the century, it would be able to claim that it was the oldest women's bar on the West Coast.

"My mother says 'I'll never come into your tavern because I don't think there should be women only places,'" Herak said. "I try to explain it's not a women's only place. It's a woman's place, which is different."

As for the name, Wildrose, it was chosen, Herak said, because it reminded her of her favorite Montana flowers and because she thought of it as a symbol about lesbians and the struggle they had had to become visible in Seattle. "It's about our strength," she said. Then she added, "And our orneriness."[28]

# 9
# *Pulpits for Healing*

When a glacier deposited a three-hundred-foot-high load of rocks east of Seattle's Pioneer Square, it shaped three distinct summits out of the debris. These days, the summits have been scraped and the shallow valleys between them paved, so it is easy to pass from one to the other almost without noticing the changes in the terrain. The city's early settlers noticed, however, and they called the summits by three different names and developed each one of them differently. The ups and downs became rhetorical symbols written into the geography, ones that would still be important as Seattle's homosexuals relocated their public community away from Pioneer Square during the 1970s.

Just above the mudflat was the summit named, appropriately, First Hill—since it was the first the settlers encountered as they moved inland. Originally, with its views out over Elliott Bay, it had been home to those wealthy settlers who could afford to move away from the immediate vicinity of the mudflat, but eventually—as the wealthy kept moving farther from downtown—it became the center of the city's hospitals and clinics.

To the north lay the highest of these three summits, one of the locations where the city's wealthy, as well as its increasing numbers of Catholic families, began to move after the 1900s. It was called Capitol Hill. At its peak was Lakeview Cemetery, named for its outlook over Lake Washington. Lakeview was the final home for many of the city's most notable early settlers, such as the Dennys. Here, too, was the city's premiere park, forty acres purchased in 1876 and eventually given over for designing to the famous Olmsted Brothers firm. The Olmsteds fully exploited the Seattle park's stunning views of Elliott Bay and the Olympic Mountains on the western horizon.

At the beginning of its development, the third summit, located to the southeast and called Renton Hill, also showed signs of becoming an exclusive neighborhood. In 1905, the *Seattle Post-Intelligencer* noted that it was "one of the best sections of the city" and that "no other residence section in Seattle has enjoyed the growth of Renton Hill." It had "built up solidly," the value of its real estate doubling within one year. "Grocery stores, meat markets, bakeries, drug stores and even millinery and dry goods stores . . . do a flourishing business . . . not far removed from the streets lined with beautiful homes."[1]

Yet in retrospect, the same story hinted obliquely at something that would prove to be a problem. It tried to describe the boundaries of Renton Hill. What it ended up with was a hefty paragraph of street names that cut a long and irregular swath down the eastern side of the glacial debris ("Thirteenth Avenue from Union Street to the north, . . . East Mercer Street from Fifteenth to Eighteenth Avenues, Eighteenth Avenue from Mercer to Columbia Street, Marion Street from Eighteenth Avenue to Sixteenth Avenue, Marion Street to Union Street, and Union Street from Sixteenth Avenue to Thirteenth Avenue"). Renton Hill simply was not as distinctive a geographic feature as Capitol or First Hill. On topography maps, it is lower and more ridge-like, and its views—across shallow valleys to its more notable sisters and a deeper vale on the east that had been sold to the city's black immigrants— were not nearly as impressive. Eventually, Renton Hill would become an orphan, even its name disappearing from the city's consciousness, so that today residents mostly think of it as just the southern part of Capitol Hill or assign it new names like the "T. T. Minor neighborhood" (after a local elementary school) or the "Squire Park" community (after a pocket-sized green spot).

Still, in its early decades of development, Renton Hill did develop a personality of its own. Russian and Greek as well as Polish Catholics settled there, giving the area a distinctly different feel from the Irish Catholic and Protestant areas on Capitol and First Hills. A Polish Hall formed on Eighteenth Avenue. A Russian Orthodox Church raised its onion domes on Thirteenth. A Greek Orthodox Church moved in a block north. Also, close to one of Renton Hill's flanks was the busy maintenance and storage barn for the Madison Avenue trolley, which ran from downtown over First Hill, up Renton Hill, then down through the city's African American neighborhood, and finally onward to a recreational beach along Lake Washington. The trolley line helped make Renton Hill one of Seattle's few corridors where languages, skin colors, and immigrant religions were almost certain to brush by one another. A Lutheran hospital, which eventually became the Group Health Cooperative hospital, anchored the north, while a Catholic hospital begun by the Sisters of Providence settled on the south end of the hill. The medical institutions on First Hill catered to Seattle's wealthy and upper middle class; those on Renton Hill tended to service a more varied clientele.

By the late 1960s, Renton Hill's housing had quite deteriorated. Because of its location between two hospitals, the housing had begun to be converted to various healing purposes—group homes for the mentally ill, recovery halfway houses for alcoholics, doctors' offices. Not surprisingly, then, it was near the northern edge of Renton Hill that the Dorian Society had been able to afford rent on the first home for its new Seattle Counseling Service, or SCS, on Malden Avenue. That section of Renton Hill would also come to house the most prominent members of the early Gay Liberation Front—Paul Barwick and Faygele benMiriam.

By the early 1970s, Renton Hill would serve as a birthing place for a whole move-

ment of Seattle's homosexuals who were ready to find a public territory in which
to heal their red-light identity.

Whatever the ideological conflicts were between the members of the Dorian Society
and the city's new Gay Liberation Front, Bob Deisher's counseling service on Renton
Hill became an immediate success. Dorian members were happy to provide a tangible service. Gay liberationists were delighted to eventually take over what
amounted to a new community center.

In SCS's first few months in 1969, forty-two clients met with the volunteers that
Deisher had recruited. Some counselors were psychology students from the university, but many others were simply gay volunteers. "We didn't have any money
to hire anyone," Deisher remembered years later, but that did not seem to matter
to the eager gay workers who flocked to the house. Gay volunteers were also the
only solution to the problem that, given the American Psychiatric Association's
policies, any mental health professional who admitted to homosexuality was
admitting to being mentally sick himself. Few were willing to do so.

Andy Johnson, a Dorian member, was one of those longer on enthusiasm than
professional training. He had been kicked out of the army for being gay in 1968,
then had moved to Seattle. At the time, he was studying library science at the
University of Washington. "You have to put it in context," he said in an interview
two decades later. "I was at the university, I was helping to shut down Interstate 5
[in a 1970 antiwar demonstration], and it was suddenly becoming OK to tell somebody you were gay. We used to get all kinds of calls. They'd range from 'where are
the gay bars' to questions about the Society to 'I can't cope with my partner, he or
she is doing this or that.' I had one long phone call from a woman about her partner who had just left her and what was she to do?" Untrained though they were in
the professional means of counseling, Johnson and the others soon figured out
that simply listening was the most important. Nearly all the people who called had
no one else to talk to about being gay. The psychologists and psychiatrists were
still officially defining homosexuality as a mental illness, so if the professionals were
not going to change therapy, gays and lesbians figured they must. With stories like
that of Frances Farmer in the air, they did not trust the psychiatrists anyway.

In SCS's first full year of operation, 1970, the number turning to the counselors
for personal appointments increased sixfold, to 264. More than two thousand
phoned for advice. Taking a lesson from the feminist groups, the counseling service also began weekly group "raps" where homosexuals could create their own
counseling simply by talking to each other and making friendships.[2]

But this led to a built-in tension. Was the counseling service a grassroots organization of enthusiastic gay volunteers, who more and more believed in the rhetoric of gay liberation and gay pride? Or was it a professional mental health
agency—recognized and to be funded by a heterosexually dominated mental health

establishment? The Louisiana-based Erickson Foundation had sent thirty-six hundred dollars in seed money to start the service, but when Deisher asked for twenty-four hundred dollars for its second year of operation, he instead got only nine hundred. Although the Dorian Society had committed to raising contributions, Deisher knew that long-term survival of the service would depend on its gaining certification from the agencies whose very approach to homosexuality was now being challenged by the volunteers.

Certification itself posed tricky questions. It required keeping records on clients, but many gays and lesbians would not seek counseling if it meant leaving their names on records and risking discovery. Certification also required charging professional fees rather than asking for donations. Certification required staying away from political stands on sodomy laws or on police harassment—yet it was the laws and the harassment that the gay volunteers intended to challenge. The purpose was not simply to adjust homosexuals to society, as psychiatry had been attempting. It was also to adjust society to homosexuals.

This view was perhaps stated most succinctly by Patrick Haggerty, the activist who had accompanied Lois Thetford to Cuba and would soon be collectively raising a child with her, as well as working at the counseling service. In his master's thesis in 1972 for a social work degree from the University of Washington, Haggerty argued that "social work sees its gay clients in a mental health context, rather than as people who are being denied basic rights and who are being excluded from the mainstream of society. . . . It is high time that social workers realize that the real issue is that a significant minority of people are being denied basic rights to fair legal treatment, employment, housing, education, military service, and general social acceptance. . . . If the problem is intolerance and oppression of a minority in a larger society, then the social worker must deal with that problem, not the so-called problem of sexual identity."[3]

By 1970, the counseling service and the Dorian Society had severed their connections because of the tension in their missions. Deisher successfully used his clout in the city's medical community to secure forty-five hundred dollars in funding from the King County Mental Health Board. By 1971, as part of the move toward increasing professional respectability, Rae Larson, who was trained in psychology, volunteered to become the service's new director while Deisher assumed the title of executive director. At first, Deisher's clout kept the King County agency happy as well as helped stock the service's own board with community leaders. "It had all this respectability," Larson remembered. "And in many ways, it benefited from the fact that the [community] board never took a very close look because [the volunteer staff] filled up with radicals." One board member, she said, even thought the service "was being founded to help queers convert back to heterosexuality."

Larson began to set up a new, more professional record-keeping system. Written memos and records started to supplement oral conversations. She also deliberately sat a can of gasoline on top of the filing cabinets. She explained, "It was like, you come for our clients' records and we're going to have a fire." Larson felt the conflict between being a social service provider and a political center acutely. "You don't get to do political things if you are a social service organization," she said. "Political action is probably the best mental health medicine for tons of people, but you can't put mental health people there with it."[4]

As some feared, the government funding came with a string attached. For efficiency and accountability, smaller specialized services were told to affiliate with more comprehensive, experienced agencies, which were to act as mentors and auditors. Deisher and Larson decided to link the gay counseling service with the Seattle Mental Health Institute, which had been buying run-down houses on Renton Hill and converting them into halfway homes for alcoholics and the mentally disturbed. In 1973, SCS relocated from Malden into one of the houses its new overseer had purchased on Renton Hill, located at 1720 Sixteenth Avenue. That signaled the changeover from its Dorian connection to its new aspiration to be part of the city's mental health establishment.

By early 1972, the Reverend Robert Sirico had become a darling among Seattle's charismatic ministers. Already an ordained Pentecostal minister though only twenty, he filled city churches and even auditoriums at the Seattle Center. He led other ministers and priests in sessions where they called and sang in spirit-inspired tongues. He performed miracle healings on those who came to him. Seattle's Charismatic Presbytery, an organization of about seventy clergy and laymen, praised him as "a spirit-filled young man whom God has blessed with a marvelous healing ministry," according to a May 1972 *Seattle Post-Intelligencer* article.[5]

It helped that he was handsome in a boyishly fervent way. His hair fell well-tamed and closely cut next to his ears, different from his many tousled hippie contemporaries. His eyebrows could angle either passionately or thoughtfully. His smile and carved chin worked together in a single disarming grin.

But in spring 1972, Sirico announced he was homosexual. He had repressed his feelings, he said, since the age of thirteen. Overnight he went from Pentecostal stardom to exile. "The situation is enough to gag a maggot," a spokesman for the Charismatic Presbytery told the *Post-Intelligencer*.

Neither apologetic nor embarrassed, Sirico immediately applied his fervency to his new cause. "The blessings of the Holy Spirit are being passed onto the homosexual community," he said. "My [Christian] beliefs have not changed. I have a relationship with the Lord that I never knew existed." He refused to repent what was not a sin and instead proclaimed he was "proud and glad that God has made me this way." His intent: to take on the religious establishment much the way SCS was beginning to challenge mental health counselors to look at homosexuality in a new light. He announced that he would immediately begin to build a new congregation in Seattle, one where gays and lesbians could worship without being denounced as sinners.

The amazement among the city's fundamentalists and charismatics was palpable. According to the traditional view, homosexuals could be loved and allowed in congregations so long as they repented and tried either to alter their sexuality or to repress it. There were no churches on Seattle's mudflats—just missions. The wayward could be "ministered to" or, like alcoholics and transients, "understood." But without repentance, there was no acceptance. Yet here was one of the fundamentalists' best and brightest talking about raising a new church of the unrepentant.

At first they tried to fast and pray with Bob Sirico. They wanted, as a spokesman said, to "see him through this sickness." In one especially strained session, twenty Presbytery members urged the young minister to relent and told him it was not too late for the healer to be healed. One even offered to cast out the "homosexual demon" inside him. Sirico angrily threatened to "cast the heterosexual demon out of you."

The letters filled with hate began. Two were reprinted in the *Post-Intelligencer* in August 1972. "You, a minister, are doing a vile and filthy sin in the name of my wonderful Lord," one of his former followers wrote. Even Sirico's past healings were called into question. Perhaps, some suggested, they had been the work of the devil and not of God. "Robert," one writer said, "you should never have started those meetings to let a bunch of us who fully trusted you be dragged down to hell with you. Thanks to the shame you brought to the Whole Body of Christ . . . your image will always follow me to death's door."

"May your followers," one particularly vehement Christian wrote, "be gall to your soul, and God curse and spew you out of His mouth."

Sirico pressed on. He announced that he had met with Los Angeles minister Troy Perry, who four years earlier had founded the Metropolitan Community Church specifically for gays and lesbians. Sirico's new congregation would affiliate with the MCC, and Perry would come for the sanctioning. Then he got a phone call. "Maybe your church will burn down with Perry in it," a voice threatened.

When the *P-I* reporter asked him about the hatred, Sirico just smiled. "I've lived in the same kind of tower they live in," he answered. "Homosexuality is real, and you can't cast it out. And we didn't crawl out of a sewer." Two men in bed together, he continued, was a holy experience—"to hold one another close and confess together, 'Isn't God wonderful?'" Sirico refused to beg for understanding.

First, he needed a place to preach and heal. He found it on Renton Hill. Just a few blocks north of the counseling service's new house on Sixteenth Avenue, Sirico located a Methodist congregation willing to share its building with the new homosexual church Sirico planned to create. The Methodist congregation itself was the result of a split when part of the laity had challenged the hierarchy. The Methodist Protestants who wanted a less powerful clergy had moved away from the Methodist Episcopalians, leaving their old church in downtown Seattle and moving up to Renton Hill. Although the Methodist division had since been healed, the congregation that met in the sandstone church on Renton Hill had adamantly maintained its tradition of telling the clergy what it thought Christianity encompassed, rather than just listening to the ordained professionals. It was the opposite of the Reverend Mark Matthews's approach at the beginning of the century. The congregation was the "force," it was the general. As a result, this particular United Methodist church had set a course different from that of its brethren in the suburbs. It created a food bank for the neighborhood poor. It even invited the patients being released into the neighborhood's new halfway houses into a social center.

The Methodists' decision to accept Sirico's new gay church came at the cost of losing several members, but in August 1972, Troy Perry arrived from Los Angeles to give his official blessing. The *Post-Intelligencer*'s religion editor, Earl Hansen, noted, "This weekend a whole lot of people will dine and worship together in a church and not feel rotten."

Carmelite nuns had arrived on Renton Hill in 1908, more by family accident than by intent. A wealthy Scotsman's daughter had joined the order in 1894, going into seclusion at a Baltimore monastery, but when the Scotsman, Malcolm McDougal, settled in Seattle in the early 1900s, he offered to move the Carmelites to Seattle. Four, including his daughter, came to staff the first Carmelite monastery on the West Coast. McDougal personally saw to the construction of their new home, a two-story red brick building on Eighteenth Avenue. It sat on three-quarters of an acre, surrounded by a garden and small fence to protect the sisters' privacy.

Over the decades, the neighborhood encroached as apartment buildings crept to the enclosure walls. By 1950 the sisters had begun planning to leave; in 1974, they finally did.[6] When the Catholic archbishop sought a new occupant for the vacant monastery, he found two interested persons: a former Catholic priest and a social worker. Both were gay and, like Bob Sirico, both were charismatic and evangelical about healing.

The ex-priest, William DuBay, had been in trouble with the Catholic Church for more than a decade, having asked the Pope to remove the Los Angeles archbishop for failing to provide moral leadership before the Watts riots. That blatant challenge had earned him a suspension. He had then used the time to write a book called *The Human Church* that had only compounded the tension by calling for Catholic clergy to unionize. He had also worked at the Synanon House in Oakland, a private group known for an aggressive, almost militaristic, approach to treating drug addicts. DuBay had found it an oppressive place for homosexuals; in fact, he considered all the treatment centers he had seen to be anti-gay.

In 1970 DuBay left the priesthood to marry Mary Ellen Rochester, the daughter of one of Seattle's most prominent city councilmen. His move gained national publicity in a *McCall's* magazine article in which DuBay agonized about how he had to learn to overcome the way "the church has successfully implanted in its priests an almost crippling inability to carry out a healthy relationship." Seminary had trained him, he wrote, to practice an emotional control that had left him stunted and out of touch with his own feelings.[7]

Almost as proof of that, by 1971 he had discovered his feelings were for men more so than women. In November of that year, he announced to a Unitarian congregation in Seattle that, marriage to Mary Ellen notwithstanding, he was gay. "It took me a long time to accept my homosexuality," he told them. "The surprising thing is that I was able to accept it at all." But "the temporary difficulty of coming out as a homosexual," he told them, "is nothing in comparison with the years of trying to be someone I wasn't."

DuBay separated from Mary Ellen and quickly sought other pulpits. He became a regular columnist for the new national gay newspaper based in California, the *Advocate*. Then he began to organize a Synanon-style group that would address addiction among homosexuals—but in a way that acknowledged the value of homosexuality rather than ignored or demeaned it. In that effort, he was joined by David Baird, a Dorian Society member who had also helped start the *Dorian Columns* newsletter and who had since gone into social work.

They named their group Stonewall, rented a house, and set out to help the gays and lesbians who had been the most tortured by mental health professionals. Clients included drug and alcohol addicts as well as prisoners released from jail. Stonewall became the halfway house for those headed back home from Steilacoom and Walla Walla—the very first gay-run organization in the country for homosexuals on probation or parole.

In an early brochure, Baird and DuBay stated their approach to healing: "The extreme oppression of homosexuals in our society has led many of them into drug addiction, alcoholism, crime, suicide and lives of wasted depression. . . . In contrast to the current legal and clinical approaches which condemn homosexuality as criminal or 'sick,' our approach regards it not only as normal and healthy, but even as restorative and therapeutic, the key to successful rehabilitation."[8]

The key to rehabilitation. Those were the important words. DuBay and Baird asserted that homosexual emotions were actually valuable. Sexual feelings carried a person's ability to love and to bond with others. A Stonewall newsletter described homosexual love as one of "very high intensity, powerful and aglow with great value"—a clear distinction from the self-hating behavior that had gotten the typical Stonewall client in trouble. "His sexuality," DuBay asserted, "is the best thing he has going for him." As such it needed to be a part of any therapy.

Almost immediately after organizing Stonewall in 1971, DuBay and Baird clashed with wardens at Walla Walla. They wanted to start a parole program for gay inmates, but prison authorities refused. Frustrated but determined, DuBay and Baird contacted reporters in May 1972, and the ex-priest charged that gays at the state prison were "simply being warehoused as inferior forms of life. They are treated as problems rather than human beings." He demanded that homosexuals be allowed the same representation on the prisoners' governing council that other minority groups had, so they could participate in decisions about parole, counseling, work assignments, and sentence reductions. He insisted Stonewall be allowed to receive discharged parolees.

The warden claimed he had never heard of Stonewall, but after the *Seattle Times* and the *Advocate* printed the fact that DuBay and Baird's letters had been refused, state officials in Olympia investigated. They eventually, if reluctantly, okayed Stonewall's parole proposal a month later. DuBay and Baird had won their first fight. The following September, the state Department of Social and Health Services certified Stonewall as a center for treating drug addicts. Shortly afterward, the Seattle–King County Drug Commission agreed to award the two fifteen thousand dollars, perhaps the largest allocation of public money to any gay social-service agency in the country at that time. The feisty ex-priest and his fellow social worker were under way, freely using their contacts and their pulpits to create their new vision. In 1974 they moved into the Carmelite monastery, at the same time securing a $120,000 three-year grant from a federal anti-alcoholism agency, the National Institute on Alcohol Abuse and Alcoholism. It was one of the largest grants any federal agency had yet made to gays.

In their therapy, DuBay and Baird adopted a modified Synanon approach using group sessions, a tightly organized structure, and constant supervision. *Advocate* reporter Randy Shilts once described it as an "eclectic blend of reality therapy, gestalt, existential psychology and bio-feedback." They banned alcohol, drugs, and violence and repeatedly emphasized responsibility to the new Stonewall "family." Residents followed an almost evangelical philosophy that reinterpreted the metaphor of the program's name. "I am here," their statement said, "to no longer run and hide behind the stonewalls I have built around myself, which are no refuge, but a barrier between myself and others. Here I am living, changing and growing."

The methods could seem rough to an outsider. For the first month, no contact would be allowed with the outside world. After that, clients couldn't leave the fifty-two-room monastery without permission. Stonewall staffers logged phone calls. Newcomers scrubbed the toilets and floors until they worked up to be "ramrods," supervising other workers. Stonewall became its own sort of monastery.

Most of those who came, Baird told a *Post-Intelligencer* reporter in December 1973, were "desperate, depressed and tired of failure. They need love and care and here they get it." About two years after Stonewall formed, its family of twenty men and women were described as 30 percent hard-core drug addicts, 25 percent chronic alcoholics, 25 percent convicted sex offenders, and 20 percent troubled by other emotional problems. After his 1976 visit to the monastery, Shilts of the *Advocate* described several residents: Merv, for example, who had spent five years in prisons and mental hospitals, masturbating on the psychiatrists' command to heterosexual pornography in an attempt to get him to change his homosexual behavior; Norine, who had been a drug and alcohol addict for thirty-eight of her fifty-four years; and Harry, who had made twenty-two suicide attempts. "I was either put down or ignored in the straight places," Harry told Shilts. "Being here in Stonewall means being alive for me. It's the only choice I have—be here or die."

Sometimes those at Stonewall lay together on a padded floor to angrily beat their hands and feet. It was a way of expressing their rage—not just at themselves, but also at the suffering that had come from constant social isolation. They no longer had to be alone with the pain. "If it weren't for Stonewall," a young resident of the time told the *P-I*, "I'd be lying drunk in some First Avenue gutter."

Instead, he was healing on Renton Hill.

Many of the turn-of-the-century homes on Renton Hill resembled massive square or rectangular containers with an occasional architectural feature—such as a porch or a gable—pasted on. The first one the Dorians rented, on Malden Avenue, was typical, a box with a steeply sloped roof, a porch with three appropriately simple columns, and a double-windowed gable topped by a cornice. It was extraordinarily run-down and groaning for paint. In 1969, when the *Seattle Times* published a story about the Dorians headlined "Seattle's Homosexuals Ask: 'Understand, Don't Generalize,'" a photograph portrayed a man walking up a small set of stairs into the ramshackle house with its unkempt yard. He was pictured from the back and wore a hat and trench coat, so that—in the city's largest newspaper at least—the seediness of the mudflat still seemed to transfer to the new location.[9]

Perhaps it was the interior architecture that was more important than the simple exteriors. Expansive and simple, the rooms seemed able to accommodate the imagination of the occupants. Here's how Charna Klein, who wrote a history of the Seattle Counseling Service, described its second box house quarters, located farther south on Renton Hill on Sixteenth Avenue: "Inside the old, three-story, poorly maintained, purplish-gray house with its dirty white posts, the semi-grandeur of wooden posts and stairwell, stained glass and bay windows, stained carpets and dowdy donated furniture, all merged into an unkempt comfortableness. . . . The walls were bulletined with posters, leaflets and index cards announcing forthcoming and past events, house and job-seekers; all clearly identified a common gay and counter-cultural set of interests."[10]

The experience of arriving into such a home was quite different from the descriptions of that earlier place of gay arrival in Seattle, the Casino. It was a small detail, but here the stairwells ran upward to stained glass and bay windows, rather than downward into an underground.

Next door to the counseling service's box house on Sixteenth Avenue, a third new gay institution opened, also in a box house. On its porch, those who staffed the new Gay Community Center put up a logo that suggested the path they wanted to encourage. It showed three of the symbol for "male," their arrows pointed upward, linked in their circles with three female crosses pointed downward. The number—three of each—was important. Not one of each symbol: gays and lesbians were not alone anymore, pretending to be heterosexual. Not two of each sym-

John Singer, who changed his name to Faygele benMiriam, became a leading spokesman for Seattle's Gay Liberation Front in the early 1970s. He and GLF member Paul Barwick unsuccessfully sought a King County marriage license in 1971. He also helped organize the first Gay Community Center in Seattle as well as a rural gay commune near Port Angeles. He became known for baking lemon bars to support activist causes. *(Geoff Manasse)*

bol: that would be just an imitation of heterosexual coupling. But three of each symbol—a breaking with the heritage of isolation to indicate that a new community was rising, built of men and women, and based more on an extended web of friendships than on monogamous couples.

Seattle's first Gay Community Center had actually opened in September 1971, largely spearheaded by the Gay Liberation Front collective on Malden Avenue—Paul Barwick, Faygele benMiriam, and Robert Perry. Somewhat ironically, they chose an underground basement at 102 Cherry Street, close to Pioneer Square. "That's where the bars were at that time," Barwick said, so even the GLF with its new liberation strategy still felt the need to pay homage to the old traditions. The basement, Barwick recalled, had been a speakeasy during Prohibition. "You had to take steps down to these two big swinging doors and even beyond there, I believe there were more steps down. We wanted to provide a coffeehouse atmosphere, a dance floor where you could interact without alcohol. We had no budget at all. Robert found tabletops, but we needed bases. So he went and bought used automobile wheels from a junkyard, and he welded pipes on them so he could mount the tabletops on these improvised tables. Tacky, tacky, tacky, the whole place was tacky."[11]

By the end of 1971, more than two thousand people had dropped by the new center, and more than four thousand hours of volunteer work had been contributed—an indication of the center's popularity and of how much the city's homosexuals needed it. But a year later, with the building's landlord wanting to jump the monthly rent from $175 to $375, the community center closed. The counseling service's offices up on Renton Hill turned into the drop-in center instead. That quickly became intolerable, so at the counseling service's instigation in 1974, a planning committee began paying $100 a month for another of the rundown box houses owned by the Seattle Mental Health Institute.

During Gay Pride Week in 1974, honoring the fifth anniversary of the Stonewall riots, the new community center opened at 1726 Sixteenth Avenue and quickly came to look much like what Klein had described at SCS. Postings held job and housing notices, a library stocked pamphlets and books about homosexuality, and a pool table in a side room provided an amenity symbolic of the older gay landscape at the bars. The center set up a twenty-four-hour-a-day information and referral phone line and collected clothing to give away to those who needed it. It stored donated food at the front desk and sponsored community feeds during the holidays. A job line started, as did a community newsletter that would eventually replace the old *Dorian Columns* and expand into Seattle's longest-lasting gay publication, the *Seattle Gay News*. The center also launched a gay campground in the Cascade Mountains. Just as the YWCA on the university hillside a few miles away was birthing women's groups, so the Gay Community Center (GCC) became its own midwife.

During its first summer, GCC also found enough money to hire about forty-five gay teenagers. They moved about Renton Hill, working at Sirico's new church, at the counseling service, and at the community center, mowing lawns and painting and repairing the disheveled buildings. "We're talking about kids who had never earned any money before, except by hustling," recalled Jim Arnold, one of GCC's founders and, eventually, one of the two original owners of the *Seattle Gay News*. "We had to have training sessions on how to handle a broom, a mop."[12]

Seattle's homosexuals had begun taking care of one another in a new way.

As it happened, the creation of the four new gay spaces on Renton Hill occurred during a time of nasty neighborhood conflict. Only a few feet of elevation separated what the Renton mound represented—the halfway homes, the food banks for the poor, the evangelical calls for justice—from the wealthier neighborhood on the Capitol Hill summit to the north. Capitol Hill had never really been as much a crossroads as the Renton mound. In the early 1970s, city officials had formed community councils to advise on plans for neighborhood development, but they had ignored the two distinct summits and the two sets of experiences and instead lumped both geographies into a single designation. For the purposes of city planning, the entire zone became "Capitol Hill," represented by a single community council.

Two factions wielded power. The first consisted of north Capitol Hill home-owners who wanted the neighborhood to remain pedestrian-oriented and zoning to protect single-family housing, rather than allowing more multifamily apartments, halfway houses, or community centers. The homeowners controlled the community council. The second faction, consisting of commercial developers, business-men, and some property owners who preferred more commercial uses of the land, wanted to replace the old box houses with apartments, medical clinics, and social service centers. They controlled the Capitol Hill Chamber of Commerce.

Neither of the two groups could be counted on to put much of a priority on gay concerns. Something like a Gay Community Center caused problems for both. To a developer, land was land, and the piece of ground that the GCC—or the coun-seling service or Stonewall—occupied could generate more money than the hun-dred dollars a month GCC paid in the early 1970s. To those who wanted a hill of single-family homes, centers that serviced the needs of gays were not ideal neigh-bors; but on the other hand, at least the box houses themselves were being pre-served. Better that than another parking lot or a modern medical clinic.

In fall 1974, the commercial developers set off a neighborhood feud by trying to solidify their position. Led by Roy Johnson, the president of the Capitol Hill Chamber of Commerce, they put up their own slate of candidates to seize control of the community council, and one told a news reporter for the weekly *Seattle Sun* that they wanted to take the council back from "liberals and food stampers." Sheldon Pritchard, a property broker allied with Johnson, claimed that the coming vote would have enormous consequences for the hill. "This is like the Alamo," he warned forebodingly. And it was—except that it was the developers who were routed. At the community council meeting, 1,008 voted for a slate headed by neighborhood activist Peter Staten, while only 125 voted for the developers' candidates.[13]

A month later, the community council called a public meeting to discuss a request from the Seattle Mental Health Institute (SMHI). Having received one mil-lion dollars in federal construction money, the mental health organization now wanted to tear down the old box houses it had bought and build its own new brick center. The houses occupied by the Gay Community Center and the counseling service would have to go, but SMHI did propose that both stay until construction could begin. However, this would require the extension of a variance from the city's zoning law regulating the use of single-family dwellings.

The request for a variance became the real Alamo for Renton Hill, now becom-ing increasingly known only as south Capitol Hill. The *Seattle Sun* noted, "Residents of South Capitol Hill are an ornery bunch, the few that are left," and the com-munity council's hearing would be the place where "everybody that had a mind to pitched in a piece, and it wasn't sweet." The *Sun* story described the area as a "disintegrating neighborhood" bordered on the north by the "monstrous, rootless Group Health" and on the south by the mental health institute and its group homes, "drug treatment centers, a Gay Community Center, a center for deaf-mutes, for displaced juveniles, for Polish-Americans." One resident commented that the area had "become the garbage pit of the city." Another, though, had posted notices urging all residents to protest "the erection of a caste barrier to protect white middle class North Capitol Hill from you know what!"[14]

About one hundred residents attended the meeting, and most, according to the *Sun,* were "tolerant if not sympathetic" to the gay presence in the neighborhood. Some, however, were overtly hostile. "I hope you get out," one said. Another referred to "that gay outfit." It was Roy Johnson of the Capitol Hill Chamber of Commerce who really laid out the case against the continued presence of the gay groups, especially the Gay Community Center. He urged the council both to let SMHI proceed and to deny the variance, so that the GCC would have to close quickly.

The zoning law, he suggested, should be used to immediately "enforce lawful moral conduct." He particularly objected to the sign the center had posted outside with "several sex symbols"—the one with the logo of male and female signs. "I don't think we need recruiters for this lifestyle among our young," he argued. The *Seattle Sun* noted that "Johnson lists himself as one who would like to 'help' gay people, but laments the fact that these days they don't seem to be 'seeking deliverance from whatever it is that binds them to their lust.'"[15]

Johnson's foes on the council agreed to recommend that SMHI should proceed with its removal of the box houses, although they also expressed the hope that the houses could be moved elsewhere. Then, they added, the city should not allow any other box houses on the territory now being claimed as Capitol Hill to be converted for any other group homes. Eventually, then, the Gay Community Center and the counseling service would lose their houses and would be unable to move into any others on Renton Hill.

Viewing the outcome of the battle, the *Seattle Sun* concluded, "It is an elusive thing, this goal of achieving a more cohesive interurban community. Capitol Hill itself is a monumental paradox, a confusion of identities."[16]

In addition to the assault on its right to exist in a Renton Hill box house, the Seattle Counseling Service faced a second attack during 1974, this one on the way it had chosen to communicate with the people it was helping.

The year had begun with outstanding news: in December 1973, the American Psychiatric Association, which had been under pressure from national gay activists ever since the Stonewall riots, dropped the designation that had caused so much harm for so long. Homosexuals were no longer to be automatically diagnosed as mentally sick. As long as they were not unhappy being homosexual, they were as psychologically normal as anyone else. Only those truly unhappy with their homo-

Gay liberationist and social worker Patrick Haggerty became part of a three-person collective that directed the Seattle Counseling Service, after arguing in his University of Washington master's thesis that counselors needed to link traditional mental health approaches and political activism. Government funders eventually cracked down on SCS as a result. *(Doug Barnes, Freedom Socialist Party)*

sexuality still needed help, the psychiatrists decided. Finally, it seemed, the mental health profession and homosexuals could embark on a new journey. The *Advocate* had trumpeted the news in a huge headline, "Sick No More," and under a caption titled "No Longer Enemies" had shown a leading gay activist shaking hands with the president of the psychiatrists' association.[17]

Six months later, a team of county government investigators arrived at the gay counseling service's box house.

Rae Larson had left as director by then. She had been replaced by the collective style of management so popular with the gays and lesbians who had been influenced by feminism and socialism. Three codirectors formed the collective management team. Each headed a smaller collective composed of staff and volunteers. Policy and administrative decisions were made at weekly meetings where the small collectives gathered into one body. Patrick Haggerty worked as one of the three codirectors, while members of the Gay Liberation Front and the Freedom Socialist Party served as the others. Not surprisingly, they had adopted the approaches to counseling favored by Haggerty in his social work thesis and the coalition-building approaches to political action favored by the socialist feminist strategy. They had taken the counseling service, begun by the Dorian Society as a homophile service, in a new "liberationist" direction.

For example, as part of counseling homosexuals who had been dishonorably discharged from the military, the service had expanded into general draft counseling to help those who were closeted understand the risks involved in either continuing to hide or declaring their homosexuality to avoid the draft. As part of its counseling of young lesbians who had tried to prove themselves heterosexual by getting pregnant, the service had added abortion referrals and taken political stands in favor of expanding access to abortion. In working with men and women who had either lost jobs or feared losing them, staff and volunteers had publicly begun to urge the city to adopt antidiscrimination laws. As part of treating those who had been arrested or threatened by police, SCS volunteers had even started patrolling nearby parks and reporting specific details about the police officers involved.

The new, more activist approach had unsettled not only the county, but even some of the service's own long-time supporters. Deisher, for example, would eventually tell a newspaper that the service had "lost track of its original mission, which was to counsel people."[18]

Little of that—from the administrative practices of collective decision making to the park patrols—fit the traditional professional model of counseling, and so when the government investigating team arrived, headed by a psychiatrist named Irving Berlin, confrontation seemed assured. The counseling service had long argued that it needed unusual approaches to reach homosexuals who had been mistreated by the psychiatric profession, but now, ironically, the APA decision to treat homosexuality as normal rather than "sick" seemed to remove that rationale. One of Berlin's main questions was going to be: Why not fold gay counseling back into the mainstream agencies?

After a visit on May 31, 1974, several months passed, during which Berlin wrote a scant, hostile review. "The Center is simply not doing a good job. They really had no bookkeeping, there was a large staff turnover, and most of the counseling was simply affirmation of sexual identity. The dress, demeanor, etc., of the staff would turn off any middle-class youth or adults and makes their usefulness applicable to a poor and hip culture where these [negative feelings about homosexuality] tend not to be major mental health problems."[19]

To a professional mental health practitioner like Berlin, all that the service did was offer an "affirmation of sexual identity"—an identity that was no longer considered sick. The counseling service volunteers, on the other hand, saw that affirmation as the most important therapy. To Berlin, the focus should have been on middle-class homosexuals who still felt unhappy about their homosexual orientation; to the volunteers, what was important was the unstructured community living room that made no distinctions about respectability or professionalism.

Berlin recommended that the service's funding be entirely eliminated and that the services provided be transferred to other community mental health agencies. He saw no reason to support a separate organization for sexual minorities. In October, the King County Mental Health Board adopted the recommendation, eliminating twenty-four thousand dollars in funding that was paying for rent and utilities at the box house, as well as salaries of two hundred dollars a month for eight staff members.

One counseling service volunteer fumed to a *Seattle Sun* reporter, "Try being gay and walking into Harborview."

For the next three years, the counseling service would wage a back-and-forth battle over the different visions of what type of service should be provided to homosexuals. Supporters of the activist approach packed the board's hearing room when, in November 1974, it finally provided an after-the-fact chance to dispute Berlin's report. They managed to win half the funding back for 1975, but the counseling service gradually began to compromise—although reluctantly. For example, when the mental health board demanded that a traditional organizational chart replace the three-person collective that included socialists like Patrick Haggerty, the SCS board relented and named a single executive director. But it picked as its president Dick Snedigar, a Freedom Socialist Party member himself.

In winter 1976, still fighting, the counseling service responded to yet another cut by appealing to the mental health board's own boss, the King County Council. Felix Reisner, the mental health board's chairman, argued that since homosexuals were no longer considered psychologically disabled, the money should be spent on clients with "severe mental health problems" rather than mere "adjustment problems." Snedigar argued that the cut discriminated against homosexuals. Three King County Council members—Ruby Chow, Mike Lowry, and Paul Barden—disagreed with Snedigar's analysis, but overruled the mental health board anyway and voted to restore $9,721 to the gay counseling service. Still, that represented only part of the money the service had originally been receiving.[20]

Time would be the only healer of the friction. In April 1977, Snedigar resigned, arguing he had made two major contributions: "confronting and even demanding" that the mental health board fund the counseling service, and struggling "to have SCS be an organization of women and men who see feminism as a basis for our working together."

In May, site inspectors complained again about the way Snedigar's staff had been maintaining, or not maintaining, client records—always a touchy subject because of the issue of confidentiality for homosexuals who did not want the government to know their names. The mental health board again voted to end the funding. But over the summer, the SCS appointed a new director, Joyce Owens-Smith, who came from a more traditional counseling background. She held a degree in sociology and was planning to begin graduate studies in social work, and she immediately offered an olive branch. "We're not political. We're a mental health agency," she would say in an interview with the *Seattle Sun* in October 1977. "People here have tended to be very paranoid about being sexual minorities. They've block-aded themselves against the larger mental health community." That, she added, needed to end, so that "we can see both sides."[21]

Immediately, the mental health board responded by rescinding the threat.

That same year, 1977, the counseling service left Renton Hill. At first it did not move far away, just a few blocks down to the corner of Pike Street and Broadway, into the valley that separated Renton Hill from First Hill. But its new location was in a business district on a busy arterial, and its quarters this time were in an office building, not in a home. That, in addition to Owens-Smith's comments, would symbolize its new direction.

For Deisher's Seattle Counseling Service, the activist and outsider approach was ending, and the gay role in the city's conversation about professional mental health counseling was about to become institutionalized.

Stonewall had received its bad news in 1975. When it had moved a year earlier into the old Carmelite monastery on Eighteenth Avenue, its director, David Baird, had known it would need to repair the eighteen thousand square feet of space the nuns had once used. The state had given the program a provisional license until it could do so, but the cost, Baird learned, would be forty thousand dollars.

Stonewall did not have the money to pay for the work itself, and the landlord, the Catholic archdiocese, decided to sell rather than repair.

Baird tried to move, first to an eight-bedroom ranch house on sixty-five acres in Duvall, a tiny farm community near the Cascade mountains. But there, a neigh-bor mounted what she called "Operation Paul Revere" to warn others of the impending arrival of homosexuals. "We and others came out here to raise fami-lies," the *Advocate* reported her saying. "It wasn't so much the drinking and drugs" of the former addicts that bothered her. "It was the criminal element and homo-sexuality. That's a new thing to Mr. and Mrs. America." Baird and others from Stonewall met with the neighbors, but the session turned angry, leading one of the women from Stonewall to write, "What I felt in that room, from those women, those upright Christian ladies of impeccable virtue, was naked hate. . . . I felt loathed." The opponents readied a lawsuit and pressured the ranch house owner not to lease to Stonewall, one housewife saying she would buy a shotgun if Stone-wall came. When the ranch owner backed out of the negotiations, Baird then tried to rent a former nursing home in Poulsbo, a ferry ride west of Seattle. The town Board of Adjustments denied a permit, saying the access road to the site would be inadequate for fire trucks or ambulances. The nursing home's owner, who wanted to sell, dismissed the reasoning since, she said, ambulances had been coming to the nursing home itself for seventeen years. She threatened to sue to overturn the decision, but Baird did not have enough time to wait for the courts to act. He kept looking.[22]

Other bad news flowed in. The state chopped the amount of public assistance money it had been paying to those staying at Stonewall. The provisional license would not be renewed past September 1976. The archdiocese had arranged to sell the monastery to an evangelical Christian youth group that wanted to move in in October. The grant from the federal alcoholism institute would not be renewed, and state matching funds would also be lost. Then, even worse, state officials began to gossip that Stonewall clients were being sexually exploited. An official of the state Office of Alcoholism investigated and reported that the gossip was untrue. "There is no evidence of any of this kind of relationship," he wrote. But, voicing his own anti-gay bias, he added, "Nonetheless, it is a concern of mine that this is happening, knowing gay people as I do." The report was carried in the *Seattle Sun*.[23]

Twenty-one clients were in the program when a beleaguered Baird made the decision to close in July 1976. DuBay had already left by then. Over the five years of its operation, Stonewall had treated some five hundred people. Angrily, Baird told the *Seattle Sun* that he would not try to keep the center operating until it went bankrupt. He explained, "I don't want people to be able to say, 'Look at how irresponsible those faggots are.'"

By September 1976 the old Stonewall was finished, and Baird headed back to government social work.

When the United Methodist congregation on Renton Hill had made its controversial decision in 1972 to allow Robert Sirico's new gay church to share its building, the decision had not gone unnoticed by the rest of the Methodist Church's hierarchy in the Northwest. The Renton Hill pastor Melvin Woodworth conceded to the *Seattle Times* religion editor in 1975 that "there's a desire to have us throw the Metropolitan Community Church out of our building."

Actually, the pressure went beyond that. "There's a more general, and less admitted, move," Woodworth said, "to close our church down" entirely. One of the congregation members added, "We're unpopular with a number of churches because we tend to champion unpopular causes. Minorities are minorities because majorities suppress them one way or another, and our championing of them gets us in trouble."[24]

Woodworth was in a tense situation, caught between the church's conservative evangelical wing and its more liberal, social justice members. He himself was an evangelical, hardly thrilled about homosexuality, and he told the *Times* writer Ray Ruppert that "Homosexuality is not as ideal a state as heterosexuality." But he did not think it a sin. Being heterosexual was just healthier. "That's like saying having two hands is a healthier situation than having one," he added. He also believed that allowing homosexuals to have their own church congregation was a good idea "until we can make the homosexuals welcome in the churches they came from." At least the church was "definitely a step up from the bars and the baths." Woodworth had even gone so far as to propose to the Methodists' Pacific Northwest Conference that openly gay men and women be ordained as ministers and that the church approve gay marriages.

But the decision to allow MCC to meet on Renton Hill had cost members, and by 1975 the United Methodists counted only about forty people for its own Sunday worship service. It was surviving on money contributed from the church hierarchy.

Woodworth brought the schism between the Renton Hill church and other Methodists to a head unintentionally. The old turn-of-the-century building that now housed both the Methodists and MCC needed at least eighty thousand dollars' worth of repairs, but the congregation was able to secure only seven thousand dollars in pledges. After the pastor appointed several congregation members to study the problem, they—in good social activist conscience—recommended that the money could best be raised by cutting one of the church's major expenses: the pastor's own salary. They proposed instead a kind of ministry collective, run by the laity itself and at most visited by a part-time minister to perform baptisms and sacraments. That immediately reignited the old Methodist quarrel that had led to the original split of the church over who should control the spiritual direction of a local congregation: seminary-trained ministers appointed by bishops or senior members of the laity.

As the conflict expanded, enough nasty letters passed back and forth that Woodworth himself eventually suggested that the congregation be scattered to other Methodist churches. The climax came in June 1976, when the Methodists' district superintendent, the Reverend Dr. William Ritchey, sent notice he would recommend to an upcoming general conference that the church congregation be disbanded and the building sold. Then he went to meet with the Renton Hill members.

At first Ritchey tried to offset the tension by smiling broadly and pulling a handful of children's sparklers from a paper bag, and then a firecracker—warning that if the evening got too hot, a spark might set off an explosion. It was his joke, though, that lit the fuse, according to a *Post-Intelligencer* report. "What kind of charade is this?" Ronnie Gilboa, one of the women in the congregation, raged. "Do you think we're a congregation of children? You come in here playing with firecrackers. Who do you think we are? Your patronizing attitude is degrading and absurd!"

A man, shaking and stammering, complained, "You're killing this church . . . You're overstepping your bounds . . . God knows we need some Christianity on this hill!"

Ritchey smiled and tried to deflect to a woman who wanted to speak, but before she could, another woman in the back stood and shouted angrily, "Shame on you for not responding to him."

Faced with such adamant passion, the hierarchy announced a truce a week later, framed in what the *Seattle Times* termed "careful, neutral and, at times, obscure language." The Renton Hill congregation could continue, but it had to pay for at least a half-time pastor. The building would have to be sold. Both the Methodist congregation and the gay MCC would have to find other places to meet.[25]

Just after midnight on a Sunday morning three months earlier—March 28, 1976—Jamie Barton had been upstairs in the Gay Community Center's box house, volunteering on the twenty-four-hour crisis phone line, when a smell of smoke began to softly drift in. Taking a fire extinguisher with him, Barton moved toward the basement where racks of give-away clothes had been stored. A back door had been left unlocked. The arsonist had set the fire easily. Barton tried his best with the extinguisher, but the flames had already spread too rapidly. He fell, overcome by the billowing smoke.

Dick Snedigar was still working next door at the counseling service, and by the time he ran from his office to the center, the smoke had grown so thick that he could not see Barton. He could only hear him coughing. Three times he tried to push into the basement. Three times, the smoke pushed him back.

Finally, helped by a passerby, Snedigar made a fourth run through the smoke. This time, he found Barton and dragged him out of the building. Barton had to be hospitalized overnight. The fire itself was eventually contained in the basement. The center lost about two thousand dollars' worth of uninsured equipment.

A month later, on Friday, April 9, Barton was back, again staffing the late-night crisis phone. At about 2 A.M., a man suddenly burst into the room shouting obscenities about homosexuals. At the same time, a fire blazed across the front of the house, set by a Molotov cocktail. Barton leapt out the back window.

This time, the fire could not be stopped. The Gay Community Center was destroyed.

Three weeks later, the *Seattle Sun* printed a letter attributed only to "Tom J." It said, "I for one am happy that the Gay Center on 16th Avenue burned down. Unfortunately, no gays burned up with it. If they would just pour gasoline over themselves and light it, they could go up like candles too."[26]

The healing days on Renton Hill were ending.

Of the four gay institutions that originally organized on Renton Hill, three still existed twenty-five years later when the century ended: proof that Seattle's gays and lesbians could indeed create their own enduring community institutions. After its cease-fire with the county mental health board, the gay counseling service thrived, even garnering the United Way's blessings and stabilizing both its funding and its approach to counseling. Sirico's Metropolitan Community Church eventually relocated when the Methodist Church finally closed in 1986. Stonewall staff members reorganized into a drop-in, rather than residential, drug and addiction counseling program. Only the Gay Community Center, burned to a shell, eventually disappeared, although even it managed for a few more years in various locations.

The heyday of Renton Hill's influence on gay life in Seattle, and of the gay influence on Renton Hill, passed quickly and was over by 1977. It lasted for only about seven years, far shorter than the decades spent in Pioneer Square. Yet the experience offered an important lesson that would not otherwise have been achieved on the mudflat or at the chautauqua grounds of the University District. The lesson was simply this: To unite the very different types of gays and lesbians who had begun to come out in the early 1970s required communicating a common need for certain healing services, rather than forcing agreement about the causes of homosexual oppression or creating a common joy in the playfulness of dancing and drag. Healing had become an important strategy for constructing a new, more cohesive community that would be able to influence the city's overall civic life.

The underground box theater of John Considine's era had become the above-ground box house of Renton Hill, and a comfortable fireplace hearth had at least temporarily replaced the bar table as a symbolic center point for the new gay and lesbian presence in Seattle. Not surprisingly, then, in the 1990s, when lesbian and gay activists in Seattle formed a new community center targeted specifically at lesbian, gay, and transgendered teenagers, they came home after a decade and a half of absence and chose a spot along Fifteenth Avenue on Renton Hill—in, of course, a rambling old box house with a stairway that led up, rather than down.

# 10

## At the Dance

## A New Leg

*J*uly 14, Bastille Day, 1970. For a Seattle summer, the day had been perfect, eighty-four degrees while the sun was up and sixty-two in the waning dusk. It was just right for the dinner party and parade that Julia and Francois Kissel had planned to celebrate France's national holiday. It would also be a fine evening to mark the rebirth of Pioneer Square with a bit of public street theater.

A few miles away, at a house she was temporarily calling home, an unemployed twenty-three-year-old drifter from Florida named Shelly Bauman had just run out of cigarettes. She decided to drive to the mudflat to buy more. There she spotted the Kissels' parade.

It was another time of change below the Deadline, a name that by now was being forgotten. During the late 1960s, when gays and lesbians had become more publicly visible in Pioneer Square, the city's urban planners had begun debating whether the century-old buildings in the district deserved any future. Some developers wanted the land to be turned into parking lots to serve the government offices on Arthur Denny's knoll to the north. Preservationists countered that a historic district similar to the French Quarter in New Orleans would promote new businesses and draw tourists. Either outcome portended trouble for the ragged set of gay bars and steam baths. Paved or boutiqued, the new mudflat that everyone in power was discussing did not include the continuation of places like the Casino, the Mocambo, or the Atlas Baths.[1]

By 1969, both schools of thought had won a toehold. One side had started tearing buildings down, and the other had begun renovating them. The Kissels were among the renovators. Next door to what had been MacIver Wells's old 614 Tavern, they leased a basement-level workman's bar and grill called the Pittsburgh Lunch. Although the windows were below sidewalk level, customers could look up past sidewalk railings onto a small concrete park built around a totem pole. It was one of the busiest spots on the mudflat, a natural crossroads that had steadily attracted the loggers and sailors who passed it. During the 1940s that had included gay men like Vilma, who frequented the Casino. He remembered the spot during an interview for Don Paulson and Roger Simpson's book, *An Evening at the Garden of Allah.* "The park around the totem pole was the hot cruising place in Seattle," Vilma said. "No matter who you were, it was the place to people watch. Across from the restroom, we used to sit on the railing about the Pittsburgh cafeteria in the basement of the Pioneer Building. They'd ask us not to sit there; I guess they didn't think their customers wanted to look up at a bunch of queens' asses hanging over the edge. Eventually they put spikes on the railings but we sat there anyway."

Under the Kissels, the grill became a grille, a French restaurant by the name of Brasserie Pittsbourg. A new kind of gold rush to the mudflat was about to begin, one quarried from tourists and shoppers, but at the same time, the conversion of the mudflat into parking lots was also moving ahead. Next to the Kissels' restaurant, the city allowed an old triangular-shaped hotel to be destroyed, and in its place came a prow-like multilevel parking lot usually referred to as the "Sinking Ship." Developers also flattened the building half a block away, on Occidental Avenue, where Jake Heimbigner had been operating the Atlas, as well as an adjacent building that had held his Stage Door Tavern. A bit farther south, across Washington Street, they removed another building next to the gay Columbus Tavern and behind the Golden Horseshoe.

By Bastille Day 1970, then, much of what had been the gay landscape of the 1960s had become parking lots, and the heart of the mudflat had been turned into an Occidental Street pedestrian mall.

It was there that Shelly Bauman saw the Kissels' parade.

Dinner had been held earlier atop the Sinking Ship, which had been made festive for the occasion with tables full of French delicacies from the Brasserie Pittsbourg and, for lack of a French band, a Dixieland ensemble. About 11 P.M., the parade swung out from the Sinking Ship southward along the mall, then doubled back on itself for the return. It wasn't much of a parade—a pickup truck carrying the Dixieland band and two French cars. Julia Kissel had also asked Morris Hart, who ran an antique shop in Pioneer Square, to bring along an old fire engine. Hart had long been interested in collecting old fire-fighting equipment and had even named his store, located on First Avenue, the Old Fire House.

Hart had happily agreed to Kissel's request, but, apparently without her knowledge, he had also brought something else. He attached to the rear of his truck an old cannon that had once been used to fire lifelines. He had owned the cannon for about thirteen years, sometimes loading it with black powder and paper confetti to fire during family gatherings on the Fourth of July and New Year's Eve. His own children sometimes dashed in front of the confetti. Later, he would tell a court that the cannon had always fired a harmless shower of paper.

Just before the parade, Hart and his teenage son used a broom handle to pack two ounces of black powder and a wad of shredded paper into the three-foot-long barrel. For safety, Hart kept the lanyard needed to shoot the cannon separate. He did not know whether the Kissels would actually want him to fire the cannon, but he figured that if it seemed appropriate, he would be ready. When he joined the parade, a city policeman waved him into the crowd, either not noticing or simply not choosing to pay attention to the weapon riding behind the truck.

Even in the short distance the parade traveled, Hart's fire truck and cannon quickly became the major attraction. Once the parade turned back, Hart stopped at least once. People lining the mall quickly clambered onto the cannon's barrel. Among them was Shelly Bauman. It was about 11:30 P.M. by then and dark. She would later remember in a court deposition that "there were people all over." Many were speaking French, which Shelly did not understand. Others, she remembered, "were all laughing and saying, 'Come on, get on, get on,'" and so she at first climbed onto the cannon with four or five others, and then, when Hart started driving again, she trailed in the crowd behind, walking ten feet or so away from Julia Kissel.

As the antique truck creaked slowly northward, dozens of people again began climbing onto the cannon, drinking and lighting fireworks as they did. Carol Hart, Morris's wife, and her son noticed the cannon barrel start to wave up and down, as if it were coming loose. It began to point straight into the crowd rather than up into the air. Carol Hart and her son started screaming at people to move away. In the confusion, Bauman believed she saw a man dressed in a blue or gray jacket drop something bright into the cannon barrel. She was staring directly into the bore. She remembered telling a friend she was with that they should move away.

At that moment the cannon fired.

No one has ever been able to adequately explain what happened next. Without its lanyard, the cannon should not have fired at all. More importantly, the confetti inside should not have been hurled outward as a compact paper cannonball. Some speculated that a firecracker had dropped inside and that a spilled beer had wet the confetti so that it compacted under the force of the exploding gunpowder.

Whatever the cause, the result was clear.

Julia Kissel first heard the boom. Then she saw Bauman drop. Kissel ran to her side, grabbed her wrist to check for a pulse, and screamed for an ambulance.

What had begun as a public relations gimmick for the new Pioneer Square would inadvertently launch the next chapter in the history of the mudflat's gay theater.[2]

"Theater," of course, means not only the world of the legitimate stage, but also countless popular forms of communication—vaudeville, movies, singing, even just weekend dancing. At first, during the days of the Casino, the Madison, and the Horseshoe, the gay dance in Seattle was mostly a kind of "internal" communication, performed in refuges and used to seek or solidify friendships. Heterosexuals stayed away or, if they stumbled in by accident or design, were forced out. At the time, there was no public-accommodations clause in the city's civil rights laws that prevented a bar owner from discriminating against patrons on the basis of their sexual orientation—so heterosexuals could be turned away from gay bars just as gays could be excluded from heterosexual ones. But when Seattle's police chief Frank Ramon rolled back from his 1966 proposal to de-license all the gay bars, part of the compromise he and Jake Heimbigner reached included a promise that gay bar owners would stop excluding heterosexuals as long as the straights did not cause trouble. No discrimination, in other words.

The agreement does not seem to have affected many people very quickly. Heterosexuals in Seattle were not demanding to be let into gay dance bars in any great numbers—at least not so long as the gay bars, with their jukeboxes and occasional live drag shows, were simply imitations of straight spaces.

But then came disco.

Shelly Bauman lay on Occidental Street, groping through blood, trying to pull the burning wad out of the left side of her abdomen. A doctor in the crowd, Michael Buckley, quickly came forward. Buckley moved Bauman's hand away, ordering her to leave the smoldering paper in so it could block the blood flow from the ragged wound. Then he jammed his own hand inside her now-gaping intestines and with his fingers clasped shut an artery until an ambulance could speed them to the emergency room at Harborview Medical Center. Buckley's fast maneuvers saved Bauman's life.

Bauman did not know many people in Seattle that night when she was blasted by the cannon. She had been preparing to return to Florida where her parents lived. The only person she knew well was a friend she had met a few weeks before, Joe McGonagle. By then, the co-owner of the Golden Horseshoe was almost thirty. He and several other gay men had rented a house together south of Capitol Hill, and that was where Shelly Bauman had been staying.

McGonagle recalled many years later that Bauman had simply appeared one night at a party. "I don't know how she got there," he told me. "Somebody brought her. Sunday morning she was still there, and she was still there Tuesday morning, and she just stayed."[3]

When McGonagle arrived at the emergency room, Bauman was near death. McGonagle remembered, "She said later that after she had been shot, she reached down and her hand went right through her clothes and she scraped her nails on the sidewalk. She got shot right through." The doctors wanted a release form to operate. McGonagle was not a family member, and Bauman, only partly conscious, was too weak to sign anything. McGonagle said he grabbed a pen, stuck it in her limp hand, and signed her name for her.

With that, doctors rushed her to surgery for the damage to her abdomen. They amputated her left leg and sliced into her pelvic bone. Bauman would be in the hospital undergoing operations and recovery for nine months. When she left, she took up life in a wheelchair.

She also sued—the Kissels for sponsoring the celebration, Morris Hart for bringing the cannon, and the city of Seattle for having police officers who ignored a loaded weapon in a public event. In 1973, she won $330,000 in an out-of-court settlement.

With that, it was time to turn a fantasy into reality.

Before Bastille Day, when Bauman and McGonagle and their other housemates had sat around their living room smoking and talking, one of their rituals had been to fantasize about how much better gay bars in Seattle could be. McGonagle recalled, "We'd be talking, you know, 'God I hate this bar, God I hate that bar. If I had a bar like this, we'd do this or we'd do that.'" The urban renewal of Pioneer Square was eliminating the old ones anyway.

With Shelly's cash, the fantasies suddenly seemed in reach.

McGonagle himself had been out of the gay bar business for several years, and for good reason: the police. Shortly after the scandal about the payoffs broke in 1967, Jake Heimbigner had sold his share of the Golden Horseshoe, turning the bar over to McGonagle and to a new co-owner named Don Jeffers. Like other gay tavern operators who had wearied of the hassles, McGonagle eventually sold his share and moved on before the indictments of police officers started, but in 1971, the year after Shelly was wounded, the county finally appointed a young prosecutor named Doug Jewett to handle the case against certain police officers and their superiors.

McGonagle and others at first conveniently forgot they had made any payoffs; after all, that was a crime itself. As far as they were concerned, continuing the fight with the police to the point of securing prosecutions did not seem worthwhile, particularly since the extortion had ended four years earlier. When Jeffers started talking to the prosecutor, though, McGonagle found himself called to a restaurant next to the county courthouse by the police officers who had once collected from the Horseshoe. McGonagle walked out of one meeting with Jewett and into the other with the cops.

"They bought me a drink," McGonagle said, "and wanted to know what I had said." They seemed pleased he hadn't told Jewett anything. "We have a proposition for you," McGonagle remembers one of the officers saying. "If we give you ten hundred-dollar bills and a non-traceable gun, will you shoot Don Jeffers?"

Stunned, McGonagle stalled. It seemed like such an irony. Here he was taking care of Shelly, who had just gotten out of the hospital, and the police officers wanted him to kill an old bar partner. "I said, 'Well, I'll have to think about that.'"

Once he made it home, he phoned his lawyer. "I thought, holy shit, if they're getting ready to pop people off, this has gone too far." No one needed to end the police payoff system in the same way it had earlier begun—with the shooting in 1901 when John Considine and his brother Tom had been assaulted by police chief William Meredith, and then had shot Meredith dead. McGonagle's lawyer put him in touch with Jewett, and with a guarantee that he would not be prosecuted for paying off the police, McGonagle agreed to join MacIver Wells and Jeffers in testifying against the cops.[4]

Unfortunately, Jewett's case had become hopelessly old. He indicted several officers, but by the time of the trials in 1973—the same year Shelly would win her lawsuit—Jewett would win little. Even those who were sentenced often got off with a light term or probation.

So McGonagle had decided to avoid the gay dance business.

One of his housemates eventually changed his mind. Pat Nesser, whose favorite word for all of his friends—"Mae"—had given McGonagle's household the campy nickname of the "Villa Mae," had once worked as a bartender at the Golden Horseshoe. Now, he had an idea for a new kind of bar—new in Seattle anyway, and certainly new on the mudflat.

"Pat had gone down to California," McGonagle said, "and checked out a couple of their discotheques. And he said to me, 'Mae, there's no discotheque in Seattle. That's the way we should go. But make it splashy.'" McGonagle was skeptical. "Splashy" California-style really did not seem the fashion for low-key, morally schizophrenic Seattle. Fox-trots and even calypsos in the underground and piano bar dancing at the Madison were one thing; Nesser's "splashy" dance was something else. Still, Nesser persisted. He talked to other gay bar owners. McGonagle said they pooh-poohed the idea. Discos had succeeded in New York and Los Angeles with their live music and barely clad go-go dancers in cages, but in Seattle, the closest attempt had been a club called the Trolley that had quickly evaporated.

Nesser would not give up. By 1973, disco itself had entered a second and ultimately more successful phase, eliminating the live bands and relying instead on almost imperceptible fades from one pounding song to another. With Shelly Bauman's money available, Nesser started looking for a location.

Along South Main Street, a few blocks from Madame Peabody's, the Our Home Hotel had long lodged men set on dreams. Built after the Great Seattle Fire leveled Pioneer Square in 1889, the Our Home had first bedded those aimed for the Yukon gold fields and then, during the world wars, those from military ships. Its first floor seems to have always been occupied by a saloon.

In 1973, for eighteen thousand dollars down and seven hundred a month, Shelly Bauman and Pat Nesser bought Our Home and brought to it their new set of dreams. McGonagle found himself joining the venture as a non-owning business manager. With another eight thousand dollars, they and the crew of men from the Villa Mae set about remodeling. Art deco dominated, a style hearkening to a previous time of sexual liberation. Glittering under a chandelier salvaged from an old theater, ersatz palm trees arched over the then-largest dance floor in the city's gay space.

"It was a flashy, flashy place," McGonagle recalled. "Unbelievable."

Bauman, Nesser, and McGonagle named the disco "Shelly's Leg" as a reference to the amputated anatomy that provided their grubstake. For extra effect, the bar's location was always advertised as being "at the foot of Main." In truth, the sexual punster in Nesser preferred other names. "Pat first wanted to call it 'The Great

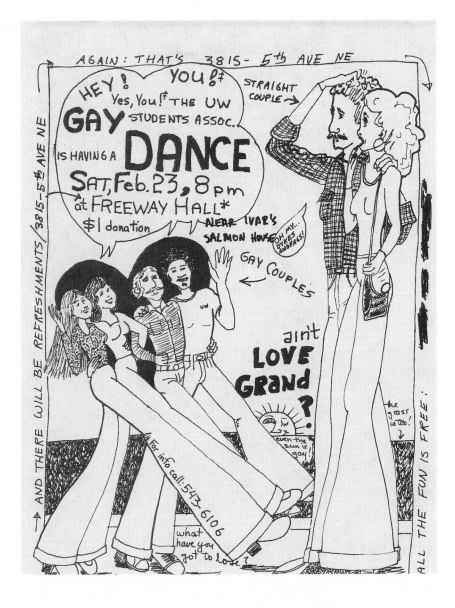

Dance has long played a significant communication role in the lesbian and gay community. In the 1970s, gay liberationists sought areas away from the usual bars to hold their dances, for example making use of the Freedom Socialist Party's Freeway Hall. This 1974 flier from the University of Washington Gay Students Alliance also rhetorically reclaims the anti-gay epithets "dyke" and "fag," words that earlier homosexual activists sometimes sought to avoid. *(Northwest Lesbian and Gay History Museum Project)*

Weekend dances at the Double Header, such as this one in the late 1970s, brought lesbians and gay men together to the tune of a live "oompah" band. *(Geoff Manasse)*

White Swallow,'" Joe McGonagle said. The initial ads for the disco, published in October 1973 before its grand opening, referred to it as "The Organ Grinder." McGonagle said humorless state licensers rejected both names as too sexually suggestive. Of the fifteen names Nesser suggested, the licensers okayed only four he could finally choose from, including "Shelly's Leg."

In a small but important change, Nesser also turned the lighting up. "You could see across the room," McGonagle said, a help to cruising and spotting friends and, perhaps more important, to creating the sense that the gay dance was no longer basement-bound or hidden in dark places. Whether a curse or a blessing, disco was to be the style of music timed to the next step in gay public emergence in Seattle. A new generation would find a new place and a new way to dance in public.

Part of what was new at Shelly's Leg emitted from little boxes with distinctly non-deco names: two Russco Cuemaster turntables, four JBL studio monitor speakers, three phase-linear four-hundred-watt amplifiers (one for reserve as protection against a blowout), a Soundcraftsmen audio-frequency equalizer, and a Lafayette SQ-L 4 channel decoder. All together they added up to a sound system the likes of which no jukebox at the Golden Horseshoe and no piano at the Madison Tavern could hope to imitate. At Shelly's Leg, disc jockeys constantly spinning a hypnotic beat replaced the jukes—and by doing so, also replaced the customers' erratic choices of music. DJ's could segue one song into the beginning of another until the whole dance floor roiled in a communal, undulating, sensual sweat.

Splashy.

As a type of communication and theater, the ballroom dancing of previous decades had epitomized the romance of heterosexual coupling, a concept of romance from which gays and lesbians were excluded. Jukebox rock had moved the couple apart, allowing each individual a new independence of movement, yet the lyrics of rock usually reinforced the same heterosexual romantic ideals. Disco altered the script. Although *Saturday Night Fever* pairing was possible, most who joined the dance simply bumped and ground as they wished. Even partnered, neither person needed to mimic or mirror the other, except by choice and only so long as they wanted. Disco established a different style of theatrical weekend recreation that was particularly appropriate for the time because on floors such as the one at Shelly's Leg, anyone who danced ultimately did so as a member of a group. This was not couple dancing; this was a village celebration. The surrounding sound and disorientations of light drove a common rhythm, banishing the possibility of small talk at surrounding tables. As a ritual enactment that both allowed for individual variations and encouraged group physicality, disco was ideal—a chautauqua of body movements that paralleled the political discourses going on in the University District and the healing work occurring on Renton Hill.

In 1974, The *University of Washington Daily* confirmed that something new was happening at Shelly's. The first paragraph noted, "'Everyone welcome,' say the matchboxes from Shelly's Leg, the gay discotheque that is Seattle's hipper-than-hip place to let the good times roll. And when they say 'everyone welcome,' they mean everybody. Homosexuals, bisexuals, trisexuals, transvestites, transsexuals, pansexuals, and even heterosexuals." The dancers, the *Daily* said, had become a "sexual alphabet soup."

"What draws straights into the gay world of Shelly's is anybody's guess. Some come because of the relaxed atmosphere, others because straights are less uptight these days, some are voyeurs who come to 'look at the queers,' and some just like the good music and the lack of a cover charge. Maybe some who are unsure of their sex identity come to 'check out the other side.'"[5]

It may have been the first time heterosexuals in Seattle acknowledged that there was something they actually enjoyed about the culture being created by the city's newly decloaked gays and lesbians.

A year later, the city's mainstream press also noticed. *Seattle Times* columnist Eric Lacitis described the Leg this way:

On this Wednesday night at Shelly's Leg in Pioneer Square, Seattle's hottest discotheque, Spider is hustling the ladies and doing quite well. He knows the other guys watch him with jealousy as he talks cheek-to-cheek with a woman he met only a few minutes ago.

Spider shrugs. Can he help it if he is so . . . smooth? Spider approaches a young secretary who has come to the disco with a girl friend. "Would you like to . . . dance?" he asks in a low voice.

Of course, the lady answers yes. Four songs later, they are still dancing. By this time, she has nestled in his arms. Watching this scene from a booth at one side of the dance floor is Mike Higgins, the disc jockey whose job is to make sure the recorded music at Shelly's never stops. . . . Unlike many taverns which are full only on weekend nights, this 163-person-capacity disco has a line waiting to get in every night of the week. . . .

Why the success?

"This is a gay disco and those are the ones that are successful," explains Ken Decker, acting manager. "Straight discos don't have the capability or sensibility to put together something like this. We've been crowded the past nine months. Every night about 9:30 P.M. it's like three Greyhound buses full of people descending upon us. The word is just out. This is the place to come and dance."[6]

Two aspects of the Lacitis column are revealing—first, the emphasis on heterosexuals who are now enthusiastically willing to be seen in a gay setting, and second, the focus on dancing as a medium of communication that was uniting two groups previously defined as separate.

For a while the Leg was the favorite gathering spot in Seattle for anyone aged twenty-one to thirty. Every night the bar filled and often passed its legal capacity of 163. "After midnight, it could hold maybe 250," McGonagle said. "Not reasonably

Shelly's Leg in Pioneer Square run by Joe McGonagle, Pat Nesser, and Shelly Bauman became Seattle's first gay disco, so popular with heterosexuals that by 1974 its owners posted a sign to ensure homosexuals would still feel welcome. *(Northwest Lesbian and Gay History Museum Project)*

Disco, like vaudeville and drag before it, became a communication ritual that allowed the city's homosexuals and heterosexuals to mingle. This 1977 flier from the new Union of Sexual Minorities emphasizes the celebration of the new equality. The USM sought to address not only concerns of gays and lesbians, but also the needs of the city's transgendered and bisexual population. *(Northwest Lesbian and Gay History Museum Project)*

comfortable, but you could squeeze in there. And once you got on the dance floor, you might as well forget it. You were on the dance floor for the duration. No way you were going to back off."

Creating the first gay space in the city that also openly welcomed straights was tricky. It was not just a matter of heterosexuals broadening their acceptance of gays. It was also a question of whether homosexuals would patronize bars where their own secrecy was no longer as tightly held, where they might run into a straight coworker who did not know they were gay. Would Seattle's gays really want heterosexuals inside their previously more secluded leisure world?

At the Leg, McGonagle and Nesser approached the issue at least partly by posting a large sign above the bar saying, "Shelly's Leg is a GAY BAR provided for Seattle's gay community and their guests." Nesser did not want to get rid of the straights, "but," McGonagle says, "we wanted to let everybody know that it was a gay bar." The sign became as famous as the disco, appearing in photographs in *Billboard* magazine. It was a noteworthy change from the days when heterosexu-

Ken Decker began the disco migration to Capitol Hill, opening his Brass Door at the corner of Pike Street and Harvard Avenue in 1978. Disco weekends, such as this one at the Door, encouraged a new muscular image for gay men. *(Geoff Manasse)*

als were more likely to flee the gay bars. An accidental cannon shot had turned the gay dance into a common theater. The old hotel really had become Our Home.

The Leg quickly became a legend in Seattle, but it was only two years old when fortune turned on Nesser and McGonagle. Born in an accidental explosion, the Leg began its decline the same way. The two had been preparing for a second anniversary celebration in mid-December 1975, planning to host a benefit for a much-decorated air force sergeant named Leonard Matlovich, who had been discharged because he was gay.

In front of the Leg's doors, the elevated Alaskan Way viaduct straddled a set of Burlington Northern railroad tracks separating Our Home from Puget Sound. Every night, the Leg's patrons lined up and entered the bar directly below the raised freeway.

About 1 A.M. on the rainy Thursday morning of December 4, while more than 150 customers danced inside the Leg, a truck driver was headed south along the freeway with a tanker-trailer he had just filled at the Union Oil Company reservoir along the waterfront. The tanker carried 3,700 gallons of gasoline, and the attached trailer another 4,800 gallons. As the driver accelerated along the freeway, he noticed his truck pulling to the left. He tried to turn, but the truck still pulled. He tried more. The truck instead crashed into the guardrail and careened, unhitching the trailer that then bounced out of control. Helpless to stop the now free-rolling trailer, the driver sped away as quickly as he could to get the rest of the tanker's explosive payload out of range.

It all took only a few seconds. When the trailer reached the crossing above South Main Street, it upended and exploded into a sheet of flame 150 feet long and 60 feet high. The 4,800 gallons of fiery gasoline rained onto a passing freight train and more than 30 automobiles parked in front of the Leg's doors, setting off car fires and a series of additional explosions. Several downtown buildings plunged into darkness as six electrical cables sheered, but the mudflat itself lit up like daylight from the brilliance of the fire.

A man two blocks away, near the corner where Shelly's original leg had been fierily mangled, looked down the street toward the new Leg and later told the *Seattle Times*, "It looked like somebody threw an H-bomb at the place."[7]

Nesser and McGonagle were at the Villa Mae when the phone rang. "I swear we broke every speed limit, and [ran] every red light we went through just to get down there," McGonagle recalled. "We got as far as First Avenue, and by that time, the lights had gone out . . . just completely black." The miracle of the night was that no one was injured, even though the city fire chief would later say that the blaze "had the potential of being as disastrous as any in the city's history."

The Leg's large front windows were blown in, and the DJ's booth and turntables singed. Fortunately, the Burlington Northern boxcars that happened to be beneath the freeway absorbed the brunt of the explosion, soaking up most of the flaming gasoline before it reached the Leg. The boxcars, as it turned out, carried potash and paper products. Created by one flaming wad of paper, Shelly's Leg was ironically saved by another. Everyone inside the disco escaped through a side door.

Still, the damage had been done. After the catastrophic fire, neither the gay nor the straight crowds ever returned to the Leg in quite the same numbers. Instead, they moved on, and so the Leg closed for good in 1977.[8]

For the moment, the legend had ended as quickly as it had begun. But the impact would last. The gay dance was now fully out of the closet in Seattle and not only open to all, but attractive to sizeable numbers of customers who were not homosexual. Where the Leg left off, other imitators would pick up, including the Leg's manager, Ken Decker. Soon enough, he would be opening his own new and splashy disco, the Brass Door. But it would be on Capitol Hill, not on the mudflat.

# 11
## Confronting
## a Police Crackdown

n 1901, Seattle Police Chief William Meredith was forced out of office after several contentious city council hearings in which People's Theater owner John Considine testified he had given one of Meredith's officers five hundred dollars for supposedly "protecting" the box theater. The council's investigating committee reported that the police chief had been paid by numerous operators for "the privilege of being permitted to conduct bunco and 'sure thing' games in the city undisturbed."[1]

Similarly, once MacIver Wells had revealed the gay payoffs, Police Chief Frank Ramon's remaining time on the force would be limited. At first, Mayor Dorm Braman responded by appointing a citizen's investigating committee, which reported in April 1967 that it was unable to confirm the existence of any such payoff system. No one wanted to talk without some benefit of protection. The suspicions and accusations continued to grow, and department morale plunged even more when an outside organization of police chiefs recommended changes in the command structure that no one seemed to like. Although the accusations never touched Ramon himself, eventually it would be reported that Braman had wanted to fire the chief, but each time a crisis of bad publicity intervened, and the mayor did not want to seem to be responding to community criticism. In March 1969, though, Braman resigned as mayor to take a federal post at the Department of Transportation. By autumn, following reports of an attempt to bribe an assistant police chief, the new interim mayor, Floyd Miller, had no such reservations. Ramon was out.[2]

Choosing a replacement became something of a circus when, in early 1970, the U.S. Attorney's office began pursuing indictments, and seventeen witnesses testified that more than sixty-five officers had accepted bribes over the past three decades. No one was sure which officers were likely to be charged. Ramon's top assistant, M. E. "Buzz" Cook, served briefly as chief but was eventually accused of perjury for telling the federal grand jury he had no knowledge of the payoffs. Another officer, Frank Moore, became acting chief, only to step aside because of illness and then to be demoted when he refused to answer the grand jury's questions. Then came two loans from the Oakland police force, Charles Gain and Edward Toothman, the latter of whom set off a small controversy when he supposedly told a *Seattle Times* reporter that the department was "rotten." All four passed through the position during the course of one year.[3]

During that time, the city also acquired a new mayor, Wes Uhlman, a kind of Kennedy Democrat—articulate, attractive, and ambitious. Uhlman had been voted into the state house of representatives at the age of twenty-three as a law student from a district that included the expo grounds around the University of Washington. He had stayed there for a decade and now, in his mid-thirties, was promising to be an urban activist. To get elected, he had smoothly maneuvered among Seattle's sometimes fractious neighborhoods, creating a coalition of Scandinavian fishermen, union workers, educators, and feminists.

For a while, he found himself virtually running the police department as de facto chief. Uhlman was relieved when in late 1970 he finally found the man he thought could replace Ramon—thirty-eight-year-old George Tielsch, who at that time was commanding the police force in Garden Grove, a mostly white middle-class Orange County suburb next to Disneyland. The day of his appointment, Tielsch said he believed in "strong discipline" in police departments, exactly what Uhlman thought he was looking for. A *Post-Intelligencer* reporter later noted that whenever Tielsch appeared on television, he looked "stern, cold and steely-eyed."[4]

By the time Tielsch took over in Seattle, many cops had begun to resent the constant string of bad publicity about the department. They argued they were not to blame for the payoff scandal. Politicians, they said, had been wishy-washy and not forceful enough to clean up Seattle. The schizophrenic compromise that tolerated a red-light district while proclaiming Cotterill-style virtues had tempted them into collecting bribes, they said. Tielsch offered the city and Mayor Uhlman a simple no-nonsense promise: no tolerance for anything the law defined as vice.

At first it looked like a refreshing change. After Tielsch had been in office for only one month, the *Seattle Times* described him as having the "dapper image of a modern corporate executive" who was working hard to "bring together the pieces of a shattered department." But a second story published the same day revealed what would ultimately become Tielsch's destruction. Speaking about gambling, the police chief declared his strong opposition to a plan by then state attorney general Slade Gorton to legalize certain types of petty betting, such as ten-cent bingo for churches and charities. "You would set up the tolerance policy all over again," Tielsch declared. "Who would run such games? You would have to rent the equipment and games. Most people at churches can't act as pit bosses; they don't know how to handle a crap table or deal blackjack. So organized criminal activity could reoccur. And if that comes in, anybody in the Police Department that might be susceptible to persuasion from the criminal element would have that opportunity present again."[5]

It was a moral domino theory, in which ten-cent bingo at a neighborhood church led to organized crime penetration into the police force.

Tielsch quickly became popular with rank-and-file officers by defending the

Seattle Police Chief George Tielsch launched a vice crackdown in the early 1970s that included what lesbian and gay activists condemned as severe harassment. *(Seattle Post-Intelligencer Collection, Museum of History and Industry, Seattle)*

frayed department from its many critics. He denounced the county grand jury investigating the payoffs as a "Spanish inquisition" and pilloried the press for its continuing probes. Wrongdoers on the force, he argued, had been few and were long since fired. He instituted new rules. Cops were not to accept even a cup of coffee for free lest the gesture be misinterpreted. He promoted advanced training programs where he not only lay in the mud at the firing ranges with trainees, but also insisted that his assistants do the same.

A year after his appointment, the *Post-Intelligencer* headlined that Tielsch had become a "hero in the eyes of most policemen." But, the same article noted, "other words which have been used to describe him during his first year on the job here have included 'dictatorial,' 'short-tempered,' 'humorless,' 'peevish,' 'ill-advised,' 'ill-equipped for the job,' 'ready to quit,' [and] 'likely to be fired.'" A reporter jokingly asked the chief who his public relations man was and Tielsch supposedly quipped, "Hitler."[6]

By April 1972, Tielsch began to publicly extend his moral domino theory to sex. When a King County Superior Court judge ruled that two city ordinances banning topless dancing were unconstitutional because dancing could be considered a form of free expression, Tielsch darkly warned that "there is a definite danger this will open the door" to bottomless sex-act performances.[7]

That summer, his vice squad turned its focus to combating sex, particularly along First Avenue, which had become a street filled with heterosexual bars and sexual arcades. It was the street where Wells had once owned the 614 and where the *Seattle Times* reporters had spotted the cops inside the Pacific Tavern. The sex arcades on First offered individual booths where customers could watch films portraying either heterosexual or homosexual acts.

In August 1972, police officers began to raid. According to the arcade owners, the officers would descend without notice, force booth doors open to surprise patrons who were perhaps enjoying themselves a little too much, accost others in the hallways, and sometimes beat them. As they had in the gay bars, police demanded identification from men who simply happened to be in the hallways, threatening to take them to jail for questioning if they refused. Within a few weeks, Tielsch's vice squad had arrested more than 200 people; 157 were charged with lewd conduct and 36 with activities described as "homosexual."

The city attorney would later concede that a few "young patrolmen" had "acted overzealously." When the Western Amusement Company, which owned some of the arcades, sued in federal court in October 1972, U.S. District Judge Morell Sharp agreed. He found that the "over zealousness" had included "excessive numbers of police officers on the premises . . . repeated, unnecessary inspections within a short period of time, [and] requiring persons . . . to identify themselves without the officers having probable cause to arrest such persons."[8]

Not content to fight vice only in downtown, Tielsch's officers soon moved into the emerging gay and lesbian spaces on Renton Hill and in the University District. A complaint to Mayor Uhlman in September 1972 marked the first of what was to become a flood. Richard Andrus, a social worker who counseled gays, wrote that he was "profoundly disturbed as I have become increasingly aware of an (unofficial) change of policy of the police department towards . . . sexual minorities. Not only are the homosexual bars being checked for I.D. far more vigorously than are the heterosexual bars, but some members of the sexual minorities have been arrested in some of the parks without being informed of their rights and by un-uniformed policemen at that. In some instances, no laws were even being violated. Most deplorable of all, some of the language of some of the officers has been atrocious and wholly unexcusable [*sic*]."[9]

Soon came more complaints. Gay men in particular were being accosted by police more often for loitering, jaywalking, or any public displays of affection such as hugging or touching. Some were being arrested, held for a few hours, then released without being booked or charged. Tavern-goers were being checked for identification—up to ten times a night. Patrols were being stepped up in Volunteer Park on the crest of Capitol Hill and in Cowen Park near the University of Washington, both known as areas where gay men went to meet one another. The police argued that the extra patrols were needed to stop sex acts from occurring in the bushes or the restrooms, but often the harassment extended to men simply walking or sitting in the park. Sometimes the harassment became extreme: at Broadway Playfield, a park below Renton Hill, police teargassed a men's room thought to be used for sexual encounters.

By October 1972, gay activists began to fight back. One complaint sent to Uhlman from the Gay Students Association at the university was signed by fourteen gay men: "The harassment and arrest of gay people in Broadway Park beginning 12 September 1972 and the subsequent arrest of members of the Seattle Counseling Service for Homosexuals and the harassment of the Service's offices are actions which indicate need for reform. We understand that the police failed to identify themselves, failed to charge the people they arrested, refused to clarify their rights, and treated them rudely."

Karen West, board chair at what was then still called the Gay Women's Resource Center, also protested the "outrageous" and often "physical assaults."

Heterosexuals joined too. Peter Raible, minister of the University Unitarian Church, sent his own complaint to Uhlman:

> On the night of September 29, from about 10:15 to 11:45 P.M., I was on the sidewalk near [Cowen] park. Beyond whatever unmarked police cars or plainclothesmen which may have been in the area, several police cars were noted. One parked across from the park for over an hour from about 10:30 to 11:30 P.M. At about 11:30 P.M. the car came across the street and one of the police officers therein warned the three individuals of whom I was one in approximately these words:
>
> "We are cracking down on this park. We'll be in here as thick as flies every night, so you'd better be careful. The lieutenant on the shift is really putting the heat on."
>
> I asked the officer if this meant that persons should not be in the park prior to 11 P.M. He replied: "We will be here at all times at night, so you'd better watch out!"
>
> As our mayor, I wonder if you believe that the best use of our police units is to be stationed near our parks for an hour or more when there is so much truly major crime.

Even Dr. Benjamin Spock, passing through town that fall as a presidential candidate for the People's Party, complained to Uhlman that a planned meeting with a dozen gays had fallen through because of fears created by Tielsch's crusade. Spock called the crackdown "illegal and barbaric persecution, quite indefensible from any point of view."

The Feminist Coordinating Council, which represented the multiple women's groups in the University District, condemned Tielsch. One member of the group called him a modern-day Elmer Gantry, "fighting sin . . . and leaving a wake of bloody bodies behind him."

In December 1972, two activists, Chuck Harbaugh at the Seattle Counseling Service and Dan White, co-chair of the university Gay Student Association, called a press conference where they condemned the "harassment, intimidation, and abuse" from the police department and charged Tielsch with having a "personal vendetta" against homosexuals. At the same meeting, an American Civil Liberties Union representative promised help.

To all the complaints, Uhlman responded with a form letter: "An investigation by my office has been completed. . . . There is no crackdown on sexual minorities by the police department. Chief Tielsch agrees with me that police behavior must be highly professional and respectful at all times toward all citizens."[10]

Disappointingly for gay activists, the mayor seemed to have fully cast his lot with the police chief.

In the spring of 1973—the same spring that was so turbulent internally for the city's homosexuals, when lesbians were spray painting Freeway Hall and arguing among themselves—a group of men and women moved onto Denny's knoll in a public political protest for the first time. The picket line in front of police head-quarters that Monday, April 23, was not big or long—only twenty to forty men and women—but it appears to have been the first such organized protest against government by Seattle's gays and lesbians. (The city's first gay pride march would not occur for several more months.) Among those walking the picket line were Bob Sirico from the gay Metropolitan Community Church, Ann Montague from the Feminist Council, and Tim Mayhew of the Seattle Gay Alliance. They demanded a meeting with Tielsch, but were turned away by a lieutenant who said the chief was too busy. Politely, they requested a future appointment and then left.

Sirico reported that the lieutenant phoned the next day to tell him that "Chief Tielsch feels that homosexuals are not a socially recognized minority [so] he feels no need to grant an interview."[11]

The pressure had to be increased.

In a coincidence of timing, the following week a county superior court opened the trial of ten payoff defendants, including Buzz Cook and a ladder of former police captains, inspectors, and officers. That Thursday and Friday, May 3 and 4, pre-Stonewall bar owners from the mudflat gathered in a courtroom to testify about the previous harassment, while on Saturday, post-Stonewall activists from the hillsides took the new struggle against harassment to George Tielsch's own home. There, for four hours, about sixty protestors walked in a residential neighborhood near the University District chanting, singing, and carrying signs that said "I'm a Lesbian and I am beautiful," "It's okay with God," and "Woman Married to Woman and Loving It." Sirico told the press that taking the demonstration to Tielsch's home was intended as both a personal and public rebuke. Reporters who tried to talk to the police chief trapped inside his house got only a stern "no comment" from the intercom system. The demonstration drew even more public notice than the one downtown had. One television station closed its report by commenting, "Some people say that homosexuals are revolting, and, as we have seen today, they are revolting—for their rights."[12]

On Monday, Sirico went to police headquarters for a scheduled talk with one of Tielsch's assistants. The officer refused to meet with him.

Tension continued to build. On May 21 in a letter to Uhlman, ex-priest William DuBay of the Stonewall treatment center added his voice:

> For a couple of weeks now, Reverend Robert Sirico and I, both representing a coalition of gay social services, have been trying to reach you to obtain an appointment without success. The subject at hand, of course, is the continuing harassment of homosexuals, lesbians, and members of other sexual minorities by the Seattle police. . . . We have been working through the proper channels in attempting to get these wrongs corrected. We would hope that the police matters can be taken care of administratively. But if you choose to make a political issue out of this matter, we will be glad to take you on. Seattle boasts not only of a very large and active gay population, but also the mostly highly active one in the country with more than 16 gay organizations and social services as well as several of the more effective organizers and activists of the Gay Liberation Movement.[13]

That summer, Tim Mayhew of the Seattle Gay Alliance reported that vice officers were coaxing gay men into sex and then arresting them, although neither he nor anyone else seems to have compiled reliable numbers. In his notes, preserved at the University of Washington, Mayhew recounted several complaints:

"When about a dozen officers were arresting a number of men in a park for being near a public latrine, the officers taunted the arrested with epithets and remarks such as: 'Faggots! Cocksuckers! With all the pussy running around, this sure is a waste of cock—these guys playing with each other's. Stop that one from smiling at this one—they must be in love!'"

Mayhew continued: "Pantomimes of supposedly homosexual stereotypes were enacted by policemen as they waited to take the prisoners away. When these same prisoners arrived at the police station, the other policemen already there, including clerical personnel, carried on similarly. While the prisoners were waiting in interrogation rooms policemen kept coming to the doors and leering at them. . . . No charges were made."

In another note he said that "A beautiful and quite feminine young woman was stopped on Capitol Hill by two officers. As they frisked her for no stated reason, they said, 'Are you a man or a woman? What you need is a good fuck.' They apparently believed she was a lesbian."

Another incident: An officer stopped a van painted with several slogans, including Gay Power. "As he stood by the window he expressed curiosity about the lifestyle of the three occupants, particularly of the young man in woman's clothing. He then delivered himself of a number of unsolicited opinions and a recommendation: 'What you need is to fuck a good pussy.'"

Still another, according to Mayhew: "A man arrested on suspicion of lewd (homosexual) conduct was handcuffed and put in the back seat of the police car. When one of the officers got into the back seat with him, the officer kneed the prisoner in the belly and crotch."

"Police caught a young man masturbating in the darkness of a pornography theater. As they arrested him and took him out to the car on the street, they would not let him rearrange his clothing to cover his penis. This was on First Avenue, where there were many people to see."

"A woman was arrested on the sidewalk in front of a gay bar. . . . The police later called her employer and told him that she was a lesbian. The woman was fired from her job on the basis of the police report."[14]

In July 1973, the police stubbornly began another vice sweep on First Avenue, this one aimed at the young male prostitutes who had been a special concern of Bob Deisher and of the Seattle Counseling Service. They arrested more than forty— an unprecedented number—with one officer alone apparently making twenty-two of the arrests. Swamped by the number of people turning to it for help, the public defender's office launched its own investigation of the police action and discovered what one of its attorneys, Paul Rogers, called "suspicious incidents which seem to fit into a definite pattern." Rogers told the gay newspaper *The Fountain* that typically in a prostitution arrest additional cops arrived to help the arresting officer in about ten or fifteen minutes, but in the arrests of the young men, assisting officers arrived so quickly "it appears that they are parked around the corner just waiting." Officers, Rogers said, seemed to be inviting gay men into their cars, offering to pay for oral sex, and then, if refused, intensifying their persuasion until the pickups relented. In one case, the attorney said, a youth who had asked to get out of the car was held until he agreed to sex. Then he was arrested. At the time, laws prohibiting police entrapment were not nearly as strong as they would later become.[15]

Police also arrested members of a youth group at Sirico's MCC, and then in October arrested Sirico himself after he left a bar in Pioneer Square. It was about 2 A.M. when the minister saw two vice squad officers arresting two gay youths. Approaching, he shouted he was from MCC. The teens should call him for help, he yelled. Then he crossed the street and stood on the curb with one foot in the road, so that he could copy the license of the police car. Immediately, the cops seized him, handcuffed him, took him to the police holding tank, and booked him into jail. The charge: walking in the road. It was similar to jaywalking, a police spokesman would later explain, although he would concede that normally a person would simply receive a written citation for a ten-dollar fine, not be booked into the jail.

For the next three hours, Sirico sat in the holding tank, repeatedly singing "We

Shall Overcome" until a parishioner bailed him out. When the trial came, the verdict was quick. The judge struck the citation and simply warned Sirico to avoid jaywalking in the future whenever he decided to minister. When Sirico complained that his arrest was yet another example of police vengeance against gays, a Tielsch spokesman answered that the department did not condone any such harassment.[16]

It was just overzealousness.

A few months later, a gay journalism student at the University of Washington, Sam Elwonger, wrote of his own encounter with the police. "I was just walking up First Avenue . . . when I got the signal (a stare, a wave, and a nod) from an orange VW Bug. I got into the car and immediately suspected the man of being a police [officer]. . . . I refused to take the initiative in the conversation, so he started the subtle leading questions—Whatcha doing downtown? Where are you from? Do you have sex with men?" The driver eventually mentioned he had a hotel room and asked Elwonger what he wanted to do. "I played dumb," Elwonger wrote, "and let him make the offer. 'You call the shots, you picked me up.'"

"How about a blow job?" Elwonger said the driver asked as he stopped at the Roosevelt Hotel, adding, "Do you want some money? How do I know you won't run off when we get up to the room? Don't you want ten or fifteen dollars?"

Now, Elwonger knew it was definitely a setup. The law punished those who either offered money or agreed to accept it. He answered instead, "I'm not worried about money, why are you?" When they arrived at the hotel, the floor had been reserved for a jury. A sheriff's guard at first blocked the two, until the man who had picked Elwonger up quickly consulted with the guard and then was admitted. Elwonger wrote, "His cover was so far gone that I had to suppress laughter." Inside the room, the U.W. student decided to stop the game and demanded to see the man's identification. At that point, the officer said he wanted to see Elwonger's because "I'm a Seattle police officer."

"I know," Elwonger said he responded. "I haven't done anything illegal." The officer kicked him out. "I should have made a citizen's arrest," Elwonger wrote, "for he did make me an illegal offer."[17]

Gay men in Seattle were suddenly fighting back.

Within city hall itself, the increased police harassment began to stir concerns over the more fundamental issue of discrimination against homosexuals, particularly with one city council member named Jeanette Williams, who had been elected to begin serving the same year Uhlman had become mayor. She had often been called conservative. Coming from a well-educated family that had settled in Seattle in the early 1900s, Williams could easily appear patrician. Her father had been a doctor and her mother an engineer, and Williams was a musician by training, a prodigy who had entered the University of Washington at age fifteen. That was in the 1930s, and like another powerful woman attending the university, Frances Farmer, Williams was part of the class of pre–World War II women who were challenging stereotypes about their appropriate roles. For a while she pursued a musical career in Los Angeles; by the 1960s, she joined precinct politics trying to help elect John Kennedy president. She eventually became vice chair of the Democratic Central Committee in King County, then surprised everyone by becoming chair—despite stereotypes that a woman could not run the local party. When she decided to run for Seattle City Council, she drew support from the city's labor unions, for whom job relations and job discrimination were always a concern, and in her campaign she urged a social accounting from the city—an annual report on how well its social goals were being met. She was fiscally conservative, but her social goals were those of a reformer.

As a newcomer, Williams had been assigned to chair the council's judiciary and personnel committee, traditionally "a rather dry committee" she would remember later, but she was determined to make it more creative and to use it to address issues about human resources and, inevitably, human rights. At Williams's insistence, the council created a Seattle Women's Commission in 1971, partly because there were few women in anything other than clerical jobs in city government, but also because it was a way to address the overall status of women and discrimination in Seattle. Some of the male council members considered the Women's Commission too feminist; some feminists considered it too milquetoast, but it did provide an avenue into city government for people long stereotyped because of sex or gender—and that would include the city's homosexuals.[18]

An item Williams soon took under review was a city ordinance prohibiting job discrimination. It was another dry task, but with women often passed over in hiring or else paid unequal wages for their work, creating legal wording was a pragmatic change needed in a new era of sexual politics. In May 1973 (the same month protesters picketed Tielsch's home), at an otherwise unremarkable hearing, Williams's committee heard from one of the women at the University YWCA— Karen West, then chairing the Lesbian Resource Center's board. The ordinance, West told the council members, also needed to protect men and women from being fired or discriminated against just because they were gay or lesbian. West then sent Williams a letter reiterating the suggestion.

What is most remarkable in retrospect is how publicly uncontroversial the idea seems to have been within the city council itself. The state sodomy law was still in effect, making a criminal out of anyone who confessed to being actively sexual in any manner other than married intercourse. Tielsch's vice cops were actively harassing gay men and women. Yet the public hearings in Seattle turned up very little heat over the proposal.

Williams liked the notion of granting gays and lesbians some civil rights protection. At least she liked it enough to mention the proposal among amendments to be considered in another hearing a few months later. The Seattle Women's Commission she had created studied the idea, then also voted its support. Other women suggested the ordinance also offer protection against employers who were discriminating against feminists by questioning them about their beliefs or by hiring only married women. In effect, they were asking the city to extend protections against interference in free speech and thought to business hiring and firing. Williams and her committee addressed that by adding a clause banning discrimination by employers on the basis of political beliefs and marital status.

While the amendments were proceeding, Sirico and Ann Montague lobbied Uhlman. Again they got little in the way of public support from the executive. They reported that the mayor actually wanted to maintain job discrimination against homosexuals, at least in the city fire and police departments. Montague claimed Uhlman had told them, "We can't have police hiring homosexuals because they would be subject to blackmail," and they couldn't be in the fire department "because [the men] sleep in the same dormitories together."[19]

Uhlman knew he would be facing a tough re-election that fall. Part of his campaign strategy depended upon drawing credit from the newly reformed image of the police department that George Tielsch had built, and so at that point, Uhlman couldn't afford to offend Tielsch publicly. Uhlman's chief opponent in the 1973 election was to be Liem Tuai, the popular president of the city council who had handily won his most recent election. While Tuai had sometimes sided with liberals on council legislation, he was a conservative Republican who was not going to support job protection for homosexuals.

Clearly, Williams's civil rights amendments were headed into a political imbroglio. If Uhlman weighed the considerations on a ledger sheet—and what politician wouldn't—he would have listed on one side the police and Tuai as strong reasons not to back any law protecting homosexuals. But on the other side, he would have had to note the equally politically powerful Williams and her Seattle Women's Commission. For all the infighting going on among feminist activists, this would be the first year in Seattle when the women's movement was organized enough to impact the mayor's race. Uhlman had to be particularly sensitive to that. After all, his old legislative district encompassed the University District. The newly energetic feminist groups could turn what was beginning to look like a close race.

Throughout the spring and summer of 1973, as the Seattle police continued to harass and arrest gay men, Williams's proposed amendments silently moved through the labyrinth of legal drafting and then into analysis in the city attorney's office. To some observers, they seemed to have vanished from sight, perhaps to be held hostage until after the November election.

Waiting wasn't Williams's style, though. Pragmatic enough to count heads, she knew she had the votes in the council to pass the amendments. The question was what could be negotiated with the mayor to get his signature. June passed, then July, then August. Not until late September did the amendments finally emerge from the city attorney's office as a proposal to the council. Curiously, they had been transformed. They were no longer individual amendments to the old law but a completely rewritten Fair Employment Practices Ordinance. It specified eleven categories prohibiting discrimination. Sexual orientation was one, as were race, religion, political beliefs, age, and sex. Suddenly, the question was no longer one of voting on amendments, but of voting on an entire omnibus law. To vote against gays and lesbians was also to vote against African Americans, women, the elderly, the disabled, and the unmarried.

Eight council members lined up behind Williams. Only council president Tuai cast a vote against the proposed ordinance. Cleverly, he had been isolated. Now it was up to Uhlman.

If signed, the new law would put in place one of the strongest job protection acts for gays and lesbians in the nation. It applied to city government and to all private companies with four or more workers. It covered hiring, promotion, working hours, pay, and firing. Employers could be fined five hundred dollars and taken to court to ensure they changed their practices. And although the city already had a Human Rights Department that investigated instances of racial discrimination, complaints about prejudice against gays and lesbians would instead pass through an Office of Women's Rights where they could be scrutinized more intensely. Not only had Williams designed the law, her interest in more women's representation in city government had created the branch that would enforce it.

But there was one "sleeper"—a bit of wording that looked routine and really quite bland. Nothing in the new law, the clause said, could conflict with the authority of city departments or with civil service requirements. That meant city departments still retained the right to define legitimate job qualifications. Since Washington had not yet repealed its sodomy law, any openly gay man or lesbian could be considered suspect of criminal activity. That might give the police an out. There was another catch. The city police and fire departments participated in the state's Law Enforcement Officer's and Fire Fighter's Retirement System. The regulations governing those pensions said that anyone considered psychologically maladjusted could not join—and in fall 1973, the American Psychiatric Association still listed homosexuality as a mental disorder. Those known to be homosexuals could not join the pension plan, and so they also could not join the city police or fire forces.

Uhlman's concerns had been met. On September 18, 1973, he signed the new ordinance.

During the election, Tielsch and the police stayed quiet about the new law— remarkably quiet considering the chief's moral domino theory. Even Tuai aimed only minor criticisms at it. He had, after all, been outflanked eight to one. Uhlman won his re-election, although by a much narrower margin of about six thousand votes compared with the comfortable margin of forty-three thousand votes he had enjoyed four years earlier.

For the first time, homosexuals were part of the political process at city hall. They had gained mention in a law.

Promptly, a gay activist who would soon join the Freedom Socialist Party became the first to test the law, in a way probably not foreseen by those who had passed it. Sam Deaderick, who had joined the Portland Gay Liberation Front in 1970 and then had moved to Seattle and volunteered for the gay counseling service, took a job as a bell-ringer raising money for the Salvation Army that Christmas season. According to a later news report, he made it clear to some passersby that he was gay, socialist, and an atheist. Someone called the Salvation Army to complain, and Deaderick was quickly told to turn in his bell. Initially, the Office of Women's Rights, which had been assigned to oversee the law, awarded Deaderick back pay and damages on the theory that he had been fired because he was gay. A municipal court judge instead agreed with the Salvation Army that Deaderick had failed to effectively represent the Christian organization. Importantly, the judge dismissed the Salvation Army's argument that the new protection was unconstitutional. The law, he said, was valid.[20]

Throughout the mayoral campaign, Uhlman steadfastly refused to publicly criticize George Tielsch, but behind the scenes the tension had been tightening. Tielsch had especially offended Uhlman by publicly urging the city council to oppose low-stakes bingo games even in churches—something the mayor had favored. It was an egregious faux pas by a subordinate. Compounding the strain, Tielsch then demoted a very popular assistant chief who had been aiding the grand jury investigation of the police. Some of the city's most prominent citizens organized a special dinner in the officer's honor, to Uhlman's severe embarrassment. Then, Tielsch's vice squad decided to raid weekend social gatherings in Chinatown, looking for gambling but instead capturing innocent families. The city's Chinese leaders were outraged. Complaints about police brutality against minorities increased, especially within the African American neighborhoods, and demands began to be made for civilian review boards.

The crime rate was dropping, the payoffs had ended, the police force had a high morale, but Tielsch was a wild card of independent ideology in a city still trained on tolerance.

Uhlman, for one, was not as convinced as the chief that victimless vice crimes needed as much costly attention as the city's cops had assigned them. Tielsch also had his critics within the force, among them a captain named Robert Hanson who had once headed the unit that included the vice squad. Hanson would later say that he disagreed with the chief's "blue nose" approach and that he tired of "seeing our officers running across the stage of the New Paris Theater"—a burlesque house—because "we became part of the act."[21]

Shortly after 1974 began, Uhlman and Tielsch angled toward a confrontation. Uhlman received a confidential letter, later published in the *Post-Intelligencer,* from a well-respected superior court judge named T. Patrick Corbett, advising him that while most of the young, new police officers Tielsch had been hiring were "intelligent, well-balanced and capable," the attitudes and actions of others seemed questionable. "From time to time," the judge wrote, "there seems to be a sudden rise in the number of complaints" about police brutality. "Now," Corbett continued, "is one of those times. I would sincerely appreciate whatever subtle direction you may be able to give to the police that would discourage the unnecessary use of force."[22]

One of the cases that had caused Corbett's concern was that of a young man named Jon Bisha, who had seen two men in street clothes attack a hitchhiker near the University of Washington. Bisha tried to stop the fight, first by calling a 911 police emergency number and then by yelling at the men fighting, but the two assailants were actually plainclothes police officers. They arrested him for interfering and sent him back to police headquarters, where, Bisha claimed, a patrol officer yanked him from the police car and struck his mouth, knocking out two teeth. Presented with the evidence, Corbett ruled Bisha not guilty of the interference charge. The judge was disturbed by the force the police had used against an innocent bystander who thought he was stopping a mugging. An internal police investigation eventually cleared the patrol officer, ruling that Bisha was not credible as a witness, so Tielsch kept the officer on the force. Then the *Seattle Times* learned that the police review board had refused to let Bisha call any witnesses to testify about his credibility and had kept Bisha and his lawyer barred from the hearing room.

Livid, Uhlman demanded that Tielsch fire the officer. The police chief refused, but he also announced on February 26, 1974, that he would resign effective March 31 to become police chief in Santa Monica, California. Publicly, he said he wanted to get away from Seattle's rain and back to where it was sunny. He never made it to March 31. Uhlman issued an ultimatum that he fire the officer, and on a Friday afternoon, March 15, as the mayor prepared to attend the inaugural ball for his second term, Tielsch walked off the job. Moving with lightning speed, within a half-hour Uhlman reached into the ranks to appoint an acting chief—Robert Hanson. The mayor then told reporters that he wanted the police to reduce the emphasis on victimless crimes. A news story in the *Advocate* quoted him as saying "I'm going to be a lot more interested in seeing police officers out on the streets enforcing felony crimes that do have victims rather than wandering around Volunteer Park looking for gays looking for friends."

The head of the vice squad immediately requested reassignment.

The Tielsch crusade was over.

On Renton Hill, Robert Sirico proclaimed, "Who says God doesn't answer the prayers of gay people!"[23]

# 12

# Insiders at City Hall

## The Rhetoric of Privacy

*n*o one would ever have described Charlie Brydon as splashy, and in all likelihood, few would ever have called him "Mae" in that friendly gay lingo of the 1970s. Brydon always seemed to be wearing a conservative sports jacket even when he was not. Perhaps that was suitable for the man who would eventually be recognized, more than any other, for taking Seattle's gays onto Denny's knoll and inside city hall.

As a teen, Brydon had been sent away from his home in New Jersey to be educated in a military prep school in Georgia and then at the Citadel in South Carolina. He dropped his political science studies to join the army during the Vietnam War, serving with the First Cavalry in the central highlands and winning two bronze stars as an intelligence security officer. He had been trained to gather information from well-placed sources and keep communication discreet. Above all, he honored professionalism—nonideological, practical. In a later interview, he would say that during the war he had grown "exasperated with the way career officers responded to the antiwar protests at the time."

"They took it personally. People should have shrugged it off, recognized it for what it was, gone on about their business." He approached politics the same way. "I'm not interested in ideology. Ideology in church, or any ideology. I want to see results. Reforms of the great world problems can come later, but I want to see something happen today."[1]

After Brydon left the army in 1970, he moved to San Francisco but maintained a love affair with a man still serving in the navy. Almost immediately, he began writing letters to the local news media whenever he saw a story about homosexuality he could praise, which meant one that did not emphasize the sexual aspect. To KTVU in Oakland, he sent congratulations for a program that discussed gay liberation in "an intelligent and rational forum" that was "a small but significant step in rending the veil of myth and falsehood." To KQED, he wrote a request that the station cover "the largest minority in the Bay area that remains for the most part ignored or treated superficially" despite its "important contribution to the business, civic and cultural wealth of this region." But, Brydon added, "in fairness . . . the individual homosexual is sometimes his own worst enemy."[2]

In July 1974, he arrived in Seattle to open a branch office for an insurance company. The battle with Police Chief George Tielsch had ended by then. Brydon started attending meetings of the Seattle Gay Alliance, the successor to the Dorian Society, but with his military and insurance background, he contrasted deeply with the mixture of socialists, lesbian feminists, and other grassroots activists then in the SGA. Yet just months after joining, Brydon became the SGA president. That, he once claimed, was because he was the only practical-minded candidate upon whom the various ideological factions could compromise. In 1975, without a great deal of regret from Brydon, the SGA dissolved, the immediate surge of post-Stonewall energy having dissipated.

Of the people he met in Seattle, Brydon did hold high respect for Glen Hunt, a landscape architect who had also been a member of the old Dorian Society. The two decided to begin inviting other gay businessmen to join them at lunches instead of political meetings. Rather than open the lunches to everyone, they compiled an invitation list to ensure an amiable meal, and started calling themselves "Hunt's Mad Hatters." At first they ate in a private dining room at the Mocambo in Pioneer Square, but that location, Brydon recalled, was "pretty dreary," so they transferred to a table at a more upscale restaurant. After several months, Brydon asked the others whether heterosexual visitors from city government could be invited. Some Mad Hatters were reluctant, because that meant a change from purely private socializing. It would force them to be publicly visible as homosexuals to people in power.

"The closet was still the dominant ethic," Brydon said later. "People working downtown—the antithesis of the [gay] stereotype which was popular at that time." Brydon stewed at the reluctance. Finally, ever goal-oriented, he just decided to act.

"Sometimes," he would say a quarter-century later, "progress requires a shove."

City hall in Seattle is unimpressive as architecture; it looks more like a nondescript 1960s hotel than a symbol of civic conversation. Yet whatever its aesthetic failings, it still controls the important rituals of local politics, and homosexuals had to master those rituals if they wanted to be part of the political conversation that had always been controlled by those who operated above the Deadline. Most of those rituals demand discretion. For every public hearing or speech, there were thousands of informal chats, phone calls, quiet meetings, and lunches that shaped public acts of policy making. The knoll, and city hall in particular, were not just pieces of geography or architecture, but a topography of "networks"—and those networks were not made of underground dances, consciousness-raising groups, or pulpits.

Charlie Brydon kept his eye on that different sort of communication, and by doing so he was about to become a new kind of symbol among Seattle's homosexuals: the "downtown gay." Before the 1970s, that term would have referred to those who frequented the bars in Pioneer Square, but with Brydon the geographic metaphor shifted its point of reference to Denny's knoll and came to mean a professional worker, well positioned in business or government, economically comfortable, and, at least by the standards prevalent among the "hill gays," very conservative. The communication ritual favored by this new downtown gay was a business lunch for networking.

Brydon decided to invite Susan Magee, the director of the city's new Office of Women's Rights, which had been given the responsibility for enforcing the recent ordinance banning job discrimination against gays and lesbians. That first conversation between the downtown gays and a city official "struggled along," Brydon remembered, but "towards the end of the hour, she said, 'I'd like to say a few things about what the OWR does and why it might be of interest to you.' She's a very easygoing, pleasant woman, and she made her little presentation. Afterwards, people were saying, 'My, that was interesting. We should do it again.'"

Brydon laughed. "All I needed was that encouragement."

In April, Brydon invited Councilwoman Jeanette Williams, and she too said yes to the invitation. As the social club began to evolve into a more formal network, a mailing list of thirty-six gay men developed. In May 1975, Mayor Uhlman attended. The conversion of the Mad Hatters had begun in earnest.

Despite his initial coolness toward gays and lesbians during the Tielsch years, the mayor's decision to accept Brydon's invitation indicated a warming toward a possible new constituency, particularly if it seemed a little more respectable. Uhlman had his own reasons for reaching out. Even though he had just won re-election in fall 1973, by the summer of 1975 the city's firefighters were planning to launch a recall because of various job disputes. Critical precincts Uhlman needed to carry if he hoped to hang onto his job were on Renton and Capitol Hills.

Brydon sensed the opportunity of the timing. He began to work as he best knew how—as an insider. For Uhlman, he offered to host a fund-raising party, possibly the first that gays in Seattle had openly organized for a city politician. Using the Mad Hatters' list, he succeeded in attracting more than two hundred people and raised one thousand dollars for Uhlman. Perhaps more importantly, in yet another first, after the party was over Brydon took the mayor of Seattle on a tour through the city's gay bars so Uhlman could press the flesh with gay voters. Only nine years had passed since the previous mayor, Dorm Braman, had urged his police chief to harass the bars and "discourage the inflow of these people to Seattle."

It was a stunning public change. By the end of the night, a new alliance had been forged—not only between the city's gays and its mayor, but more personally, between Uhlman and Brydon. When the recall election was held, Uhlman won the critical gay-heavy precincts he needed. Soon enough, he appointed an aide named Tim Hillard to become the first official mayor's liaison to the city's gay community.

By midsummer, almost one hundred gay men were attending each of Brydon's luncheons, and it was clear that a new organization was about to be born—one that would be modeled not after the lesbian or gay social service groups on the hills but after similar constituency lobbies on the knoll.

In October 1975, to avoid what one member called the "tyranny of structure-lessness"—a phrase that at least hints at feelings the downtown gays had about other activist organizations in town—four lunch-goers including Brydon and Pam Weeks, a director of the Lesbian Resource Center, incorporated and adopted bylaws. Asked what the name should be, those who had been attending the lunches chose one that had fallen by the wayside in the liberation aftermath of Stonewall. They appended "group" rather than "society" to the word "Dorian" and adopted similar purposes: to seek respect and to engage in a simple Doric discussion about civil rights for homosexuals. But there were also to be changes from the days of the Dorian Society. This Dorian Group would be committed to a vision reflecting the knoll more than the mudflat, and in subsequent years that would make it more aggressively political than the old society had ever been. It would seek the insider contacts the lunches were creating and would not engage in direct aid to gays and lesbians, as the old society had done by forming the counseling service. Public outreach to schools or churches through speakers' bureaus would be minimized; what was important was insider networking. Where the society's slogan had been "understand us," this new Dorian would try to speak a different phrase: "Get clout."

Pointedly, Brydon's group decided to operate according to *Robert's Rules of Order*.[3]

From the start, the new Dorian Group rhetoric differed from the feminist and socialist analyses that linked the homosexual cause with struggles against sexism, classism, and racism. The Dorians instead adopted a classic, singular civil rights agenda that argued solely against discrimination. Instead of urging new styles of communication that challenged the patriarchy and traditional hierarchies, they adopted the rules by which the patriarchy and hierarchy operated.

"The Dorian Group," Brydon told the *Advocate* in October 1975, "is reaching to a set of people who have never had a gay-identified group before. The gay middle class are non-radical, conservative, establishment people who have never felt represented by any gay organization. Here, they can come to a monthly luncheon like any other luncheon they would have for business. . . . They can come and be with people of the same socio-economic class."

Pam Weeks added that as a lesbian she was an activist, but "I'm not particularly radical. The whole time I was coming out, the only people who I knew were gay were the street people. You're rarely exposed to the gay professional, and this is a comfortable way to get that exposure."

The *Advocate* reporter, Randy Shilts, concluded that Brydon's approach was "the biggest trend to hit the gay movement since Stonewall." In just nine months, Dorian "far and away" had become the Northwest's largest single gay organization, with 250 members. And, Shilts wrote, it was "only getting bigger." Like Pat Nesser, Brydon had tapped into a trend waiting to happen. Of course, it did not hurt his now growing national image that he and David Goodstein, the publisher of the *Advocate,* shared the same view and were becoming friends, and that the *Advocate* itself was now tilting away from its liberationist beginnings toward more middle-class acceptability.

"The real power of the gay community," Brydon told Shilts, "rests with the middle-class group. For a long time, the middle-class gay has felt powerless to change the system. When we start exercising our power, that's when the establishment starts taking civil rights seriously. That's when things get done."

To Goodstein, he would confide in a later letter that "I am disturbed by the low level of understanding and mutual rapport that is pervasive among key people in our movement," a reference to the liberationists.[4]

Brydon's significance may be that he, more than any previous gay male activist, set out to mobilize and appeal to the very group that had been the mainstay of Mark Matthews's and George Cotterill's moralist campaigns in Seattle: not just the homosexual middle class, but the heterosexual middle class. Brydon was not about to apologize for being middle class himself and for working to create public narratives that appealed to middle-class gays, but he also kept his eye on the rhetoric and values that middle-class heterosexuals could understand. He shaped his oratory to awaken the part of gay Seattle that might seldom go to the bars and almost never to a consciousness-raising group. Then he chose symbols and actions that meshed with those held by Seattle's heterosexuals, particularly those who held power. He made it clear that he believed "getting things done" did not mean talking about patriarchy or separatism. It meant making sure middle-class heterosexuals knew and supported gays.

His timing was perfect in that Seattle's most prominent political leaders were ready—after the police scandals, the Tielsch moralism, and the passage of the jobs ordinance—to accord new respect to the city's homosexuals, as long as the homosexuals were of the right kind to join in the political consensus sought at city hall. As one local observer told Shilts, "For straight politicians seeking a way to deal with the homosexual constituency without danger of smear, Brydon's group was a godsend."

Much of Brydon's public rhetoric was cast to calm fears that heterosexuals had about gays. Where other activists angrily denounced police harassment, Brydon instead praised Northwesterners for their heritage of tolerance and progressivism and cajoled them to live up to it. Brydon appealed to an ideal of tolerance that those living in the Northwest enjoyed believing about their section of the country, even when certain facts—the historical treatment of racial minorities and the sweeps of moral crusaders like George Cotterill—suggested Northwesterners had been no more tolerant than those living anywhere else in the nation. Yet repeated often enough as "historical fact" rather than goal, it was exactly the type of shared civic mythology that gays and heterosexuals might together act on.

Brydon also argued that the best common ground between the region's gays and straights could be summed in a single symbol that would appeal to all

Northwesterners: privacy. That became his mantra, as much as the slogans of opposing "sexism" or encouraging "coming out" were the guiding symbols of other activists in Seattle.

As a rhetorical symbol, privacy did fit remarkably well with Seattle's history and ambiance. Seattle, as historian Roger Sale wrote, was "a wonderful city in which to lead a quiet and comfortable private life." Sale added, "The age-old appeal of Seattle" was to "get a job, a house, a family, settle down, move to the suburbs, buy a trailer, have good vacations."[5] That, rather than any message about gender bending or capitalistic evil or socialist reform, was what Brydon and the Dorian Group wanted to tap into: gays and lesbians, they argued, just wanted the same clean-cut middle-class dream. They did not even need to be understood, just left alone and protected from any arbitrary discrimination that resulted from being suddenly visible.

Privacy, not gay liberation. Privacy, not sexual freedom. Privacy. Period.

Seattle's city council had already granted protection against discrimination for the first dream on Sale's list: the job. Now the Dorian Group asked for the second item: the house.

Almost immediately in the meetings with city officials, the Dorians had suggested an amendment to the city's fair housing ordinance to prevent landlords and home sellers from discriminating against gays and lesbians. The issue, of course, was privacy, Brydon argued. Landlords and home sellers had no right to pry into tenants' or buyers' private lives or to base their decisions about renting or selling on what they might presume to know about private love.

While that argument had appeal, it—and the whole concept of privacy—also had a slippery side. The easy counterargument was that owners had a similar privacy right to control the rent or sale of their own property. An earlier city council had already shown a reluctance to regulate such housing discrimination: when the original law preventing race discrimination in both jobs and housing had come up for consideration in the 1960s, a nervous council had split the two, enacting the jobs protection but putting the housing law to a public vote rather than risk taking a stand itself. The law had eventually passed, but only after a passionate crusade by the city's African Americans and its Catholic archbishop.

The proposal to amend the law opened all the old issues. The city apartment owners' association raised the specter of children being molested if landlords were unable to prevent gays from moving in. Homeowners complained they wanted to be able to sell to whomever they chose.

At the end of the summer of 1975, after surviving his recall election partly due to gay votes, Mayor Uhlman announced he would support the amendment. Although the council debate over the proposal was intense, it was also short, lost amid the summer's other issues and the "good vacations" that Sale describes. By a five-to-four vote, the council adopted the amendment. It was a far shakier margin than the council had given to the law protecting gays from discrimination in jobs.[6]

Still, Brydon and the downtown gays celebrated. The Mad Hatters' lunches, the fund-raising party, the new links with the mayor, and the adoption of a new rhetoric had produced a quick insider victory. Seattle was now one of only a handful of cities to protect homosexuals from both job and housing discrimination.

That fall, the Democratic candidate who would soon become the state's governor agreed to come to a Dorian lunch. It was yet another coup for the newly formed group. Dr. Dixy Lee Ray, who had headed the federal Atomic Energy Commission and who was known for her curt and often blunt remarks, answered three questions about gay civil rights:

"The state human rights commission currently doesn't consider gay people a protected minority. If you were governor, would you change that?"

Ray: "I believe that government is so important that it needs to be re-examined to see that all of its parts are functioning in the public interest."

"If you are a candidate for governor, will you support gay civil rights legislation?"

Ray: "I believe in civil rights for all people—regardless."

"As a person who has worked in the federal government for many years, you must know some gay people in high federal positions. What is it like for them? Are they under pressure?"

Ray: "I don't know any. You can't tell by looking at them."

The last answer, according to the *Advocate,* drew applause. It was okay to be discreet.[7]

Any move to become gay insiders talking to heterosexual city hall insiders posed serious questions. Homosexuals as a group had not been part of any public policy making in Seattle before the 1970s. Could homosexuals work as insiders within the city's heterosexual networks of power? Could the city's gays and lesbians imagine having civic leaders and spokespersons much as the African American community did through its church ministers? If so, who would they be? Bar owners and drag queens from Pioneer Square? Ideologists and missionaries from Renton Hill? Feminists from the University District? Or might they arise from the knoll itself, among gays and lesbians who had worked inside the system? If so, would they really know anything about the lives of gays and lesbians who struggled down in Pioneer Square or wept in consciousness-raising groups? And anyway, who would crown particular people as political spokespersons—some group in the gay and lesbian community itself, or the heterosexuals who controlled the city's political and media machinery?

To many gay activists in Seattle, the applause of the Dorians for Dixy Lee Ray was a problem, not a solution. "Privacy" echoed of a closet, and the name of Charlie Brydon quickly became anathema. In 1977, for example, a writer for the *Seattle Gay News* blasted Brydon: "Charlie is one of those middle-class slickers who don't want to acknowledge that they have anything in common with the gays who hang out in parks or the little boys out in front of Penney's [the downtown pickup spot]. He reminds me of those Jews in fascist Italy who thought they had it made because they had connections right up to Mussolini. His military record, the business he's in, his lifestyle are all a denial of what's really at issue in this society. . . . He represents the establishment—the owners, the moneyed people—who often are as conservative and racist and anti-feminist sexist more so than the society at large."

Already, Brydon was no longer a person. He was a symbol.

Downtown gays and lesbians immediately returned the volleys. Ginny Lambert, who was on the Dorian board, responded to one *Gay News* attack by writing, "I am sick and tired of the criticism voiced and written of the 'Middle Class.' The so-called Middle Class is probably paying most of your wages. . . . Try for Gay Rights in any Socialist/Communist nation in the world. I dare you!!"[8]

Three incidents between Brydon and the "hill gays" stand out.

First, in 1975 he invited the new police chief, Robert Hanson, to the Dorian lunch. For once, his timing may have been unfortunate. Gays and lesbians had just claimed a narrow peninsula of land in the University of Washington's arboretum and were using it for occasional nude sunbathing and swimming. The police responded with raids and arrests, overreacting as far as gays were concerned. Even Brydon was upset. "They didn't bother the men," he recalled in a later interview, "but when the women came down and took their tops off, that became a different issue. On some hokey pretext, [the police] went down and they'd come riding across the horizon, sweeping people up. I mean, it was just totally unnecessary."

What he did next confirmed his insider approach. "I went to the mayor and said, 'This is getting nowhere. There needs to be dialogue.' Which is essentially what I had been trying to do, getting dialogues going between city officials and other people in the community."

"So we needed to get the police chief there" to the Dorian lunches.

Gay activists such as Freedom Socialist Party members Dick Snedigar and Sam Deaderick, both working at the gay counseling service, thought differently. They argued for public protests instead. Having dealt with Tielsch, they were skeptical of letting down their guard against Hanson. Rumors circulated that Deaderick would actually lead gay pickets at the lunch, challenging Hanson and denouncing the meeting as a sellout on Brydon's part. If that happened, Brydon knew that no one—especially the members of the Dorian Group—would cross the line.

For help, he turned to a young gay man he had just hired as a receptionist for his insurance business, someone whose politics he had not been aware of at first: Paul Barwick, the same Barwick who was living with Faygele benMiriam at the Gay Liberation Front communal home on Capitol Hill. Barwick, practicing his own brand of discretion, had not told Brydon about his well-publicized attempts in 1971 to marry benMiriam, since all of that had occurred before Brydon had arrived in Seattle. Brydon later confessed he would not have hired Barwick had he known, but for handling the Hanson controversy, Barwick's own connections to the socialist gay activists proved invaluable. Brydon pleaded with him to tell them not to picket. Barwick relayed the message. The answer came back: Open the invitation list and allow the hill activists to sit in on the lunch and ask tough questions about the police raids. Brydon did not trust that, so he proposed another deal. Barwick would record the police chief's talk and the Dorian questions afterwards and give a tape to the hill activists. Brydon promised that the Dorian questions would be tough.

Hanson showed up, and so did the Dorians' biggest crowd yet. "People really packed it," Brydon recalled. "What they had done, stupid police, was that they had impacted the very people who were Dorian Group participants. [These men and women] were largely just working folk that were not political ideologues. The police had interrupted what they considered their innocent recreation" at the arboretum.

Hanson promised changes. Deaderick still complained publicly to the *Advocate* that the Dorians had held a "private audience" with the police chief, had "let him give his usual public relations line," and then had allowed him "to walk out to a standing ovation."[9] But the picketing, if it had actually been planned, had been deflected. Brydon would continue to promote insider lunches.

The second conflict occurred in spring 1976, when a vacancy opened on the Seattle Women's Commission. Gay liberation activists backed the socialist Cindy Gipple, whose comments in 1973 had seemed to trigger the graffiti painting of Freeway Hall by lesbian separatists. Gipple had become a member of the counseling service's board and had been endorsed by many of the gay organizations on the hill as well as by the commission's own nominating committee, but her name had languished for months without action on the desk of the one city council member charged with calling hearings to fill the vacancies, Jeanette Williams. Gossip began that Brydon was lobbying Williams and Uhlman for the spot. The *Seattle Gay News* quoted Brydon as saying he thought Gipple's constituency among gays and lesbians was "not broad enough," a reference to her socialist politics. The dispute became unusually public for three months, even drawing the attention of the city's mainstream press.[10] It did not help the tension between Brydon and the hill gays that during the same months, the Gay Community Center, which had endorsed Gipple, was firebombed. On the one hand, the hill gays were under assault from bigots, and on the other, as far as they were concerned, Brydon was undermining the community with his clout downtown. The *Seattle Sun* published a headline in April 1976 saying, "Gays: Left, Right Square Off," in which the word "right" no longer referred to anti-gay conservatives, but to Brydon himself.

Although Brydon issued a Dorian Group press release denying the accusation that he was blocking Gipple's appointment, the *Seattle Gay News* still went on the attack in an editorial in May 1976 that said Gipple had solicited support from gay and lesbian organizations, while Brydon had "apparently decided to ignore all the existent organizations in the gay community in favor of soliciting support among the political establishment."

It was that question of leadership: If gays and lesbians were claiming more visibility in making city policy, who was selecting their leaders? The activists, or downtown heterosexuals? "We find it impossible to imagine," the *Seattle Gay News* editorial said, "how an individual could possibly hope to morally represent the Gay community without the support of Gay associations."

Williams finally weighed in, saying she thought the commission needed a gay man on it. The rationale was that the commission, through its concern for women—and therefore for lesbians—was the only real entry point at the time into the city bureaucracy where homosexuals could have any say. Other reform feminists on the commission could, presumably, represent lesbians, but gay men, she argued, needed their own voice. Also, Williams said, the commission's nominating committee had violated procedure by submitting only Gipple's name for the post. The logic infuriated the more radical and socialist-minded feminists, prompting one of the commissioners to openly attack Williams for "an insult to the gay community and to Ms. Gipple."

Mayor Uhlman had the final say. To no one's surprise, he finally appointed Charlie Brydon. Enraged, Gipple complained to the *Seattle Gay News* in July 1976 that "Brydon has made it clear he will represent white, middle-class gay professionals, ignoring women, minorities and poor working-class gays." Brydon, for his part, thanked Uhlman in a private letter that echoed some of the old Dorian Society's rhetoric from the days of the Reverend Mineo Katagiri's testimony before the city council in 1966, noting that "gay people have sought an open role in the municipal process in an effort to take responsibility for our own problems." Brydon added, "We seek to demonstrate that gay people are willing, able and responsible participants in the civic life of our home town."[11]

The third major disagreement between Brydon and other gay activists came over demands that the mayor proclaim an official Gay Pride Week. Seattle's annual commemoration of the Stonewall riot had begun with a small observance in 1973. In 1975, activists outside the Dorian Group decided to see if they could capitalize on the mayor's attendance at the Dorian lunch to get him to issue a proclamation of Gay Pride Week as well as to attend a celebration at Seattle Center.

Uhlman was not ready to respond to requests from gay outsiders. He declined, saying he did not believe it was "the proper role for city government to endorse any particular life style, especially in so personal an area as that of sexual preference." He was not hostile, just politic. While he was rejecting one overture, he was simultaneously communicating behind the scenes with Brydon about establishing a small task force that could advise him on gay and lesbian concerns.[12]

By the following year, the battle over the proclamation became more intense. Two different strategies for how to work with city hall were being promoted. Those most concerned with effecting cultural change in definitions of gender and sexuality pushed as outsiders for visible and symbolic actions from the politicians. Those interested in political reform and cooperation with powerful heterosexuals worked behind the scenes and demanded fewer visible gestures of support. The split between hill gays and downtown gays grew more obvious. David Neth, then director of the Gay Community Center, pointed out in a letter that Uhlman had declared such things as "Liver Week," "Salad Week," and "German Shepherd Weekend." In fact, "Gay Pride Week" was the only proclamation Uhlman had refused. "A proclamation from you," Neth wrote, "would help build an increased concept of self-worth among the tens of thousands of our people still living a hidden existence in the Seattle area." Not incidentally, he added, "it would also end . . . the doubts of myself and many others about your commitment to helping our community."

Uhlman again refused. The other proclamations, he explained, didn't involve "matters of public controversy."

Brydon eventually joined the dispute, defending Uhlman in a letter written in June 1976. Many gay people, he argued, did not want or need the government to "tell them they are OK. . . . Personal identity and self-worth are not the government's province to give."

"Further," he added in a sentence that emphasized the symbol he was continuing to test, "we need to recognize that sex and sexuality are essentially privacy matters in our culture and society." There was quite a difference, he said, between declaring a Salad Week and "proclaiming an observance of one form of sexuality or another, especially when the particular sexuality is at issue and anything but a settled matter of general public policy."

It was enough that the mayor and city council addressed the civil rights of gays and lesbians by supporting the jobs and housing ordinances, he added. "Expecting them to orchestrate a brassy fanfare and implying that the mayor is a chicken for not doing so is less than fair."[13]

The move above the Deadline now meant more than activism on the hillsides. Uhlman had become the first mayor of Seattle to find a public representative of the gay community he trusted. And Brydon trusted Uhlman. Some people were beginning to refer to Charlie Brydon as Seattle's new "gay mayor." Others, like Cindy Gipple, were fuming at the mention of his name.

# 13

## At the Capitol

## Limited Conversation

*T*he efforts in the 1970s to make gay and lesbian concerns more public at Seattle's City Hall forced a parallel quest at the statehouse in Olympia. State laws simply did not reflect the new identity homosexuals were creating for themselves. As was true at city hall, the fight in Olympia would be to join the insider conversation so long controlled solely by heterosexuals.

Although the struggle to publicly join the statehouse conversation would have many fronts, the earliest, most important goal would be to eliminate the legal weapon that posed the most danger: the sodomy law that George Cotterill had helped shape in 1909. Its expansive definition of sex acts that were crimes, even when engaged in by consenting adults, endangered jobs and reputations. Even to associate with known homosexuals—by being found in a gay bar or at the counseling service, for example—was to risk guilt by association with individuals assumed to be sex criminals. Also, the ease with which one could be accused of sodomy, and then convicted even without credible testimony, was well known—the case of Keith Rhinehart in the 1960s had demonstrated that. And the details of what had happened to the minister once he had been sent to the state penitentiary at Walla Walla were sufficiently horrifying that even the most publicly out gay liberationist had to keep in mind the power that a prosecutor and a police force would have should they turn truly intolerant.

As gays and lesbians in 1975 geared to find a way to repeal Cotterill's law, the minister's story was part of what they held as a memory.

With his appeal to the state supreme court defeated, Rhinehart had arrived at the prison in Walla Walla on July 10, 1967. In later court documents filed by his attorney, Malcolm Edwards, Rhinehart would say that once there, he was ordered to meet with a Catholic chaplain, but, as a minister himself, Rhinehart protested that he wanted nothing to do with someone else's religion. During the meeting, he called the chaplain "Mr. McCabe" rather than "Father McCabe," and for that, he said, he was ordered into solitary confinement for two days.[1]

On August 6, 1967, he wrote to Edwards that it was "becoming increasingly apparent to me [that] this state through its various agents intends to keep on going past all limits of human decency in its treatment of this case. . . . Since my incarceration, the situation has become more than unendurable. . . . The State is nearly depriving me of my own humanity. I am almost no longer human. . . . And what of my church and those dear people??? My God, will the nightmare of this never stop!"

At the bottom of the typed letter, he penned a postscript that read, "I'm sick. No medicine."

A state prison censor intercepted the letter and refused to send it on to Edwards since, the refusal said, it made "derogatory remarks concerning institutional personnel, the Parole Board, and discusses institutional affairs unrelated to his case."

When two of Rhinehart's friends traveled to Walla Walla in the fall of 1967, they found him physically wasted. "He told us that he hadn't wanted to worry us, but they had been giving him injections of drugs against his will," one said later in an affidavit. "As we watched during the next 15 minutes to half hour, he became incoherent. He perspired. I watched the muscles knot up on his shoulders and I watched his head being drawn steadily backwards just as if he were on the torturous rack used in ancient times. . . . He got tears in his eyes with the pain. He could no longer communicate with us."

Rhinehart sat in solitary confinement for thirty-seven days during his first two years, allowed a light only during meals. Prison officials argued that he was sometimes uncooperative, refusing work assignments. Rhinehart explained that he suffered from asthma and dizzy spells.

Throughout his internment, Rhinehart continued to try to plead by letter with his attorney back in Seattle. Several letters made it; others did not. In one written on February 16, 1968, Rhinehart noted ironically that he had seen several prisoners engaging in sodomy during the weekend showings of movies. Prison officials refused to mail both it and a similar letter, written February 21, that reflected on homosexual relationships at the prison.

On June 30, 1968, Rhinehart wrote, "Please help me. I don't know what to do. I nearly pass out at times. . . . I am very sick and don't know from minute to minute when the next chamber of horrors is going to occur." He added that he had "now witnessed nearly one hundred acts of oral or anal sodomy" among the prisoners, usually during the weekend showings of movies. That also was censored, the prison arguing that it had the right to refuse to forward letters that contained vulgar language or that made complaints.

His attorney, Edwards, filed appeals in the U.S. District Court for Western Washington, trying whatever legal arguments still seemed available: denial of due process, violation of religious freedom, discriminatory enforcement of the sodomy law. He entered the testimony from church members who prowled Seattle's gay bars and described lewd acts that occurred there. Although that seemed a reversal of the Aquarians' support for homosexuals, Edwards was still trying to prove that the Seattle police had selectively singled out Rhinehart.

In April 1968, Edwards lost his argument at the federal district court, but, after an appeal, in March 1969 the U.S. Court of Appeals for the Ninth Circuit ordered a federal trial on two points: whether the sodomy statute had been enforced in a discriminatory manner and whether perjured testimony had been used. The order for the federal trial was a victory in that it at least enabled Rhinehart to be transferred from Walla Walla. He would await the new trial in the King County jail instead.

The state attorney general, Slade Gorton, sent investigators out to find Miller again. They located him in an Oregon jail. Predictably, Miller thought that cooperating could buy him leniency and so, in front of Gorton's men, he once again signed an affidavit—his fifth—swearing that his testimony against Rhinehart had been true. But after federal judge William Gray heard arguments in November 1969, he was skeptical. First, he ordered Rhinehart released without bail; then in April 1970, he ruled that the state had indeed suppressed evidence—the ever-changing testimony of Rhinehart's accuser, James Miller—and he vacated the original conviction. But he did give the county the chance to retry Rhinehart if it wanted to. Still, it looked as if the case might finally be over, and Rhinehart could go free.

Instead, Gorton announced he would appeal Gray's ruling.

For another agonizing year, Rhinehart and his attorney waged their solitary war. Seattle's gay and lesbian community was neither powerful nor public enough to offer much assistance. In March 1971, Gorton won on much the same reasoning that had earlier been used by the state supreme court in ruling against Rhinehart. Several more months of legal jockeying occurred as Rhinehart and his attorney appealed for a U.S. Supreme Court hearing, which was denied in October 1971.

Faced with Rhinehart's imminent re-jailing, Edwards looked again to the original accuser, who was now out of police custody. On November 18, 1971, Miller swore a sixth and final affidavit, saying, "The statement I signed for Stephen C. Way, Assistant Attorney General of the State of Washington and Lee Rickabaugh, Assistant Attorney General of the State of Washington, was false. I was scared and afraid that if I didn't cooperate with them that something bad would happen to me. I wish the police would stop pressuring [me] to sign false statements."

On April 13, 1972, the twisting nightmare finally ended.

Judge Gray, citing the new affidavit, again vacated the original conviction. "This court is of the view," he wrote, "that the 1965 conviction was based on testimony of extremely doubtful credibility and that in light of the entire record as it now stands, the responsible state officials would want to re-evaluate the validity of such a conviction."

It was a declaration that had been obvious from the beginning of the case. King County had a new prosecutor by then, Doug Jewett, and no retrial would be pursued. Nor would the attorney general's office appeal again.

Rhinehart had originally been arrested April 11, 1965. It had taken seven years almost to the day for him to be free again.

The opening for changing Washington's sodomy law would come through a sympathetic heterosexual. The Seattle attorney who agreed to help the Dorian Society incorporate in 1968, Peter Francis, was beginning to eye a run for the state legislature. In June 1968, Francis wrote to the Dorians, saying he had already been talking with the Reverend Mineo Katagiri about his plans and wanted to hear their recommendations about new laws or changes in old ones. His letter added, "I may be way ahead of you philosophically already. More about that when I see you."[2]

Francis, who had graduated from Stanford Law School, was indeed ahead of the Dorians philosophically. A libertarian as much as a liberal, he wanted government out of private lives. He once told a reporter that he sought to curb government's tendency to "force people to do what's best for themselves."[3] He was elected to the state house of representatives and then in 1969 appointed to the state senate to replace Wes Uhlman, once Uhlman became Seattle's mayor. Using the libertarian rhetoric combined with liberal reforms, Francis was often able to recruit conservative legislators to his side while also pleasing the new feminists and gay activists who were part of his Thirty-second District. He saw no reason for police officers to be monitoring bedrooms or worrying about sex crimes that had no victims. He promoted decriminalizing prostitution. Naturally, he fretted about Cotterill's expansive sex laws.

As early as 1962, the American Law Institute had begun encouraging states to eliminate the sodomy penalty, as long as the oral or anal sex occurred in private between consenting adults. The institute argued that the old criminal laws were ineffective at regulating private acts and involved the government in enforcing a religiously based moral code.

At first, the states responded slowly. By 1969, seven years after the recommendation, only Connecticut and Illinois had repealed their sodomy laws. By 1970, at least some legislators in Washington State had concluded that Cotterill's criminal code was also seriously out of date. In addition to the problem with the sodomy punishments, many other misdemeanors and felonies had outgrown their definitions, as had the punishments assigned to them. In 1971, Oregon, Idaho, and Washington all considered the institute's new model penal code eliminating the sodomy penalty, but arrived at different results. In Oregon, a moderate Republican legislator successfully steered the repeal of the sodomy punishment through the legislature and the governor's office. The same happened in Idaho—except that several months after the change, the Mormon Church spearheaded a repeal of the repeal so that Idaho still criminalizes the private sex lives of its citizens.[4]

In Washington State, which also has a powerful Mormon Church, the story became more complex.

The Washington State Bar Association had conducted a study of the state's criminal code in 1967 and had recommended, among many other changes, that the sodomy penalty for consenting adults be repealed. In 1971, when the Washington legislature began to consider significant revisions to the criminal code, including a change to the sodomy law, the proposal failed in the state senate's Judiciary Committee, then controlled by a Democrat who disliked many of the suggestions. Two years later, in 1973, the Democratic leadership put Pete Francis in charge of the senate Judiciary Committee and he quickly introduced a new omnibus bill to revise the entire criminal code, dropping prosecutions for oral or anal sex between adults so long as it was consensual. He successfully guided the bill through a senate vote, but it died in the more conservative house. The omnibus approach included too many changes individually opposed by scatterings of legislators. Among the most controversial reforms was Francis's intention to legalize prostitution.[5]

In 1975, the determined senator decided to try again. Francis still chaired the senate Judiciary Committee, and this time rather than report out a single massive code change as had happened in 1971 and 1973, he split the reforms into six bills and dumped his controversial prostitution proposal. In Senate Bill 2313, which decriminalized victimless sex, Francis proposed the repeal of the sodomy law. He also included a feminist-backed reform that made male customers of prostitutes equally responsible and equally as criminal as the women. Very quietly, behind the scenes, Dorian members encouraged his efforts—but what is more remarkable is how little they seem to have been involved. This was Francis's crusade.

His effort soon ran headfirst into state senator Jack Cunningham, a conservative Republican from Seattle's southern suburbs. Cunningham complained loudly that the proposed sodomy reform would "repeal the Ten Commandments." Then he tried to intimidate those who supported the repeal by asking for their middle initials—he wanted, he said, to be sure their names would be printed correctly in Washington's Catholic newspaper, the *Northwest Progress.* As the bill came to a vote, he and others challenged the prostitution changes. They claimed to be worried that men might be innocently entrapped for agreeing to have sex with a prostitute, even if they had no intention of paying her.[6]

With that kind of rhetoric, Cunningham prevailed in the first critical vote. The victimless crime bill died in the senate, twenty-nine to nineteen. Again, it seemed that sodomy reform, along with all other criminal reform, was dead for another year, but Francis still had a few parliamentary tricks left. With his support, allies on the Judiciary Committee in the house of representatives reverted to the omnibus strategy, putting all six bills into one again, stripping the controversial prostitution section, and sending the rest—including the sodomy reform—back to the senate with house approval.

By then, law enforcement officers, county prosecutors, and the Washington Bar Association were all clamoring for the overdue reforms contained in other sections of the bill. Overall, Francis would tell the *Advocate,* the legislation was a "pro–law enforcement, tough-on-crime bill" that was getting "a lot of support from conservatives." Sodomy reform had been reduced to a few lines repealing Part 6 of Chapter 249. Even those critical lines were buried in a bill now eighty-two pages long.

Cunningham maneuvered. He urged the separation of the few lines about sodomy from the rest of the bill so that those who supported the other criminal reforms could vote yes without repealing the penalty for sodomy. His maneuver produced a twenty-four to twenty-four deadlock. Under the senate's rules, the tie vote meant Cunningham had lost. The senators faced a straight up-or-down vote on the entire omnibus bill.

As he worked to line up support, Francis also maneuvered. He reminded senators that police chiefs around the state wanted the criminal reforms—this year, not next session. On May 30, 1975, he triggered a vote to see how much support he had, but handled it cleverly. According to the legislative rules, senators on the winning side of any vote had the privilege to ask for a revote, while those on the losing side did not. So Francis and a few of his allies voted against their own bill. It lost twenty-six to twenty, with Francis among the twenty-six voting against it. But Francis now had two important pieces of information: how many in that six-vote defeat were senators who would switch back on the recount and which opposition senators he still had to target. He immediately moved for a reconsideration. It was scheduled for several days later—time enough for Francis and his allies to start pressuring reluctant senators.

When the bill came up again, Cunningham tried to turn Francis's technique against him. He urged the senate to refuse the reconsideration and instead to stand by its original vote. It was a maneuver that would have embarrassed Francis by leaving him on record as voting against his own reform. Immediately, a parliamentary argument began over the legitimacy of Cunningham's request. One of Francis's supporters challenged it, but lost a ruling on his point of order. Then debate over the propriety of that ruling started.

As the comments went on and on, a Cunningham supporter at one point demanded that the chair limit each speaker to a single statement. "We will be here forever unless we sooner or later face the issue," he complained. For what would have ordinarily been a routine vote on a decision about procedure, some senators instead demanded a person-by-person roll call. Tension built as the numbers rolled steadily parallel. When the counting was over, twenty-four senators had voted with Cunningham and twenty-four had voted against him. Again, the tie vote meant status quo: that the previous vote to reconsider still stood. Francis had won—but with no margin to spare.

On June 3, 1975, the actual bill moved to the floor. Francis and his switch-voters quickly added an additional eight votes to the original twenty yeas, driving the new criminal code to a twenty-eight to twenty victory. Francis had prevailed, mostly through parliamentary maneuvering. Now, the final decision was up to the governor, a moderate Republican named Dan Evans who had stayed aloof from the entire controversy. On June 30, he signed the bill into law, making no statement about it. A spokesman simply said to the *Advocate* that "the governor was not going to substitute his judgment for that of the legislature—on that matter anyway. He's no fan of victimless crimes."[7]

Unlike the original 1893 sodomy law, which had contained the emergency clause making the penalty effective immediately, the repeal was more leisurely and would not take effect for another year, on July 1, 1976. Still, eighty-two years after it had first been adopted, the major underpinning of a state-sponsored exile for gays and lesbians had finally been dismantled.

In Seattle, gay political activists of all beliefs finally celebrated together. Middle-class advocate Charlie Brydon told the *Advocate* the change was "a major advance for gay people in Washington," while the more socialist-minded Sam Deaderick called it "a really necessary kind of groundwork that gives us some good legal ammunition."

In Seattle especially, legal dominos would begin to fall. The city already prohibited discrimination in job hiring. Now, with the change in state law, openly gay men and women could no longer be presumed to be potential criminals. Thus there was no longer any legal obstacle to prevent openly gay men and women from belonging to the state pension system. And since they could now belong to the state pension system, Mayor Uhlman no longer had a legal reason to refuse them employment in the Seattle police department.

Still, everyone was also cautious. Deaderick warned that the repeal would not necessarily "make the police, landlords, or employers any easier to deal with." Brydon called it "just the first step." And Francis, now the pragmatic as well as idealistic politician, predicted there would soon be a backlash. "The fact that the repeal was passed does not mean that the people of this state or the legislature are that enlightened," he told the *Advocate*. "There's no doubt that people like Cunningham will continue their efforts. And there's a lot of people in churches who really feel they have to express their religious beliefs about society through the law."

Prophetically, he added, "The task of educating the public is just beginning. A great political battle is never over."[8]

For the next eighteen months, the prophecy skirted the edge of becoming reality as the Gay Community Center on Renton Hill was firebombed and as the pressure grew to close the United Methodist congregation that housed Robert Sirico's gay Metropolitan Community Church.

Still, during those eighteen months, there was more good news than bad, so the prophecy was not yet reality.

It was just four weeks after Governor Evans signed the repeal of the sodomy law, for example, that the Seattle City Council expanded the city's Fair Housing

Act by prohibiting landlords and homeowners from discriminating against others because of their sexual orientation.[9]

Then, a few months later, Seattle got its first "celebrity" gay when Dave Kopay, a former University of Washington football player turned professional football star, publicly came out in a story published in the *Washington Star*. Young people, he said, needed to have more role models and to know that homosexuals could succeed in any career, including pro athletics. Seattle's gay activists quickly enlisted him as a kind of poster boy to assist in their arguments for more public acceptance.[10]

Emboldened by success, Charlie Brydon sent a letter to Governor Evans, urging him to issue an executive order prohibiting anti-gay discrimination in state jobs, to create a commission to study other changes in state laws to protect homosexuals, and to review all sodomy convictions and grant paroles to anyone in prison because of consensual homosexual acts. Brydon would find a cordial welcome, invited to meet with members of the governor's staff to discuss the possible commission and assured, in a later response by the governor, that the parole board had investigated and had found "no one incarcerated in Washington prisons on pure charges that would relate to sexual acts between consenting adults."[11]

In April 1976, David Goodstein, the owner of the *Advocate*, arrived in Seattle to honor Brydon's accomplishments, telling Dorian Group members that Seattle had made more progress than almost any other American city in accepting gays. That was due, he said, to the state's liberal attitude and to the professional way in which Brydon and his organization had worked to promote civil rights.[12]

As 1977 opened, then, it appeared a very hopeful year for the gay and lesbian activists who were working for statewide changes.

For one thing, the Washington State Supreme Court had agreed to rule on the case of a Tacoma high school teacher, James Gaylord, who had been fired five years earlier simply because, on his private time, he had joined the old Dorian Society and had driven thirty miles from Tacoma to Seattle to socialize with people like Nick Heer and Martin Gouterman. The facts suggested a clear violation of Gaylord's constitutional rights of free speech and free association. The thirty-four-year-old social studies teacher had never discussed homosexuality in his classes or been public about his sexual orientation. He had not lobbied for or spoken about homosexuality in public. At most, he had responded to a blind ad in the old *Columns* newsletter looking for companionship. Everyone acknowledged he was an outstanding instructor. But on October 24, 1972, a former student told the vice principal at Wilson High School that he thought Gaylord was homosexual, and when the vice principal asked, Gaylord answered honestly and said yes. Outed by the school's administration itself, Gaylord was then fired by the Tacoma School Board on November 21, 1972, because of what the board termed his "immorality" and the effect his now publicly known homosexuality would have on his teaching.

Ironically, just two weeks earlier the board had adopted a district policy promising to eliminate "discrimination, bigotry, abuse and all forms of mistreatment."[13]

Gaylord's lawsuit had been working its way through the courts ever since, and Gaylord himself had had to turn to housecleaning and working part-time jobs to eke out a living on six thousand dollars a year, instead of his twenty-one-thousand-dollar salary.

At the beginning of 1977, the state supreme court seemed to be looking skeptically at the firing. Two years earlier, in 1975, it had reversed a lower court's decision to uphold the firing and had returned the issue for a new trial. When the lower court still supported the firing, the justices had voted to accept Gaylord's appeal once again. That suggested they might overturn the dismissal and perhaps accord some statewide civil rights protections for gay workers.

On a second front, members from Charlie Brydon's new Dorian Group were mobilizing to lobby for an even more positive reference to homosexuals at the statehouse. In 1977, they planned to propose for the first time that the legislature add sexual orientation to the state's antidiscrimination law. That would protect both heterosexuals and homosexuals from arbitrary acts of prejudice—acts such as the one that had cost Gaylord his job. Among a long list of speakers who agreed to testify for the bill was Dave Kopay.

Third and finally, 1977 had also been declared International Women's Year. Regional and national meetings about gender rights and equality were planned throughout the twelve months. Publicity about the meetings was expected to highlight the need to overturn sodomy laws in other states and the need for civil rights laws forbidding anti-gay discrimination.

But then Francis's warning about the long political battle ahead began to come true. Quickly, 1977 became perhaps the bleakest for Seattle's homosexuals since the days of George Cotterill.

The state supreme court delivered the first blow. In a stunning surprise, on January 20 it ruled six to two to uphold Gaylord's dismissal. The court asked, Was Gaylord immoral because he was homosexual? Writing the majority opinion, Justice Charles Horowitz answered yes, citing religious works such as the *Encyclopedia Judaica* and the *New Catholic Encyclopedia*. Horowitz went even further and introduced a dangerous distinction into Washington legal precedent. He distinguished between "overt" and "latent" homosexuals. "Latent," closeted homosexuals willing to seek treatment for their "problem" could be tolerated in government jobs, he said. Had Gaylord remained closeted and sought psychiatric help, Horowitz wrote, "this finding [upholding his firing] would not necessarily apply." However, by joining the Dorian Society, Horowitz said, Gaylord had risked discovery. That made him an "overt" homosexual, and the jobs of overt homosexuals were not to be protected.[14]

Just as the legal and psychiatric exile of homosexuals was beginning to end, Horowitz's opinion offered, in effect, a kind of legal bribe. If homosexuals stayed quiet and sought psychiatric help, the court might protect them from being fired if their sexual orientation happened to be accidentally discovered. But if gays or lesbians did anything "overt" that looked like coming out or socializing with other homosexuals, they lost that protection.

To some observers, that was a blatant trampling of First Amendment rights of free speech and association. Horowitz turned aside all such concerns. He ignored the fact that the state's sodomy law had just been repealed so that gay sex itself was no longer criminal. He ignored the fact that no evidence had been presented that Gaylord had engaged in any illegal sexual behavior. He ignored the American Psychiatric Association's determination that homosexuals were no longer to be considered sick, a determination reached earlier the same year that Gaylord was fired. Whatever its new legal status, he wrote, homosexuality was still immoral, and since Gaylord was not seeking psychiatric help for his immorality, that was sufficient cause for dismissal. "Plaintiff desired no change," Horowitz wrote, "and has sought no psychiatric help because he feels comfortable with his homosexuality. He has made a voluntary choice for which he must be held morally responsible."

The U.S. Supreme Court refused the appeal, leaving the Gaylord decision as the opening shot at keeping homosexuals in Washington in hiding out of fear for their jobs, undoing what Francis had accomplished with his sodomy reform. The decision still stands as state precedent.[15]

For his part, once Judge Charles Horowitz retired, he became one of the major leaders in anti-gay political campaigns in Washington State throughout the 1980s and 1990s.

Suddenly, Horowitz's decision in the Gaylord case made the Dorian Group's effort to secure a statewide law prohibiting job discrimination even more urgent.

Within a few weeks of the Gaylord decision, a committee in the state house of representatives agreed to consider adding the words "sexual orientation" to the state law prohibiting discrimination in jobs, housing, and public accommodations. It was the first time the notion of a state "gay rights bill" achieved official consideration. Appropriately, the house sponsor was a representative from Gaylord's hometown of Tacoma, a moderate Republican named Ted Haley. More than it had with the repeal of the sodomy law, the Dorian Group went into action. Brydon persuaded Mayor Uhlman to testify, as well as Councilwoman Jeanette Williams. In the state senate, Pete Francis announced he would sponsor an identical civil rights bill. In the house, the Social and Health Services Committee scheduled a hearing for March 23, 1977.

In what would be its first time before the legislature, the bill gathered influential endorsers, among them religious groups like the Washington Association of Churches and the Seattle Church Council, as well as the state teachers' federation and, from the eastern part of the state, the Spokane YWCA. The state's three Catholic bishops all endorsed the bill, rebuffing those—like state senator Cunningham and Justice Horowitz—who wanted to cite Catholic moral teachings about homosexuality as a rationale for discrimination in jobs. Dave Kopay appeared too, the *Seattle Gay News* noting that when Kopay spoke to the house committee "there was a noticeable hush in the room."

"Some committee members seemed uneasy and almost embarrassed," the *Gay News* reporter wrote. "For after all, here was a man they themselves had cheered to victory at Husky stadium, a man who served as a role model for their children, now standing before them proudly proclaiming his homosexuality."

Kopay told them, "I am not asking for my rights . . . I am demanding my rights."[16]

Although it had been the state house of representatives that had helped to rescue the sodomy repeal two years earlier, the legislative committee now listened warily. Some worried the change would require affirmative action for homosexuals, forcing quotas on employers. Brydon assured them that was not so. Gays and lesbians, he testified, were already part of the economic system because they were not as readily identifiable as racial minorities. They simply wanted protection for jobs and homes they had already acquired or for which they were qualified. Some legislators talked of passing the bill, but thought school districts should be exempted so homosexual teachers like Gaylord could still be fired. The hearing seemed to go rationally, without much fiery rhetoric about the evils of homosexuality.

Then came a delicate moment—the legislative pause between a hearing and the actual committee vote. It was at that moment that the state's most visible Mormon made his move.

Lloyd Cooney was a recent transplant to Seattle and a fervent convert to Mormonism. He had arrived in the city to preside over one of the church's many properties: the CBS affiliate KIRO-TV. As legislators pondered the civil rights bill, Cooney decided to launch a series of televised editorials. Twice in April he attacked the gay civil rights bill, taking pieces of Horowitz's ruling as his theme.

"If a homosexual does not have the right to teach your children," Cooney said in one editorial, "does he or she have the right to rent your house or work in your company?" Where even Horowitz had restricted his rhetoric to the nexus between the "immorality" of homosexuality and the sensitivity of the particular job of teaching, Cooney joyed in expanding the rhetoric of fear. An overt homosexual could not be a teacher; therefore, according to Cooney, his or her right to work in any company or rent any apartment should also not be protected. If the amendment passed, he warned direly and inaccurately, even small business owners might be forced to hire minimum numbers of homosexuals.

In no time, opposition mail began to rain on Olympia, and quickly, the first attempt to pass a gay civil rights bill was smashed.[17]

In May, gay and lesbian activists received more bad news. President Jimmy Carter had announced he would pick Brock Adams, the congressman from Seattle's Capitol Hill, to be his new secretary of transportation. On the one hand, gay voters on the hill celebrated; Adams was both liberal and sensitive to gay concerns, and now he would be in the president's cabinet. On the other hand, Adams represented an odd district that included not only Capitol Hill, but also suburbs south of Seattle where the voters were very different. They were the ones who had sent Jack Cunningham to the state legislature.

In a special election called to replace Adams, Cunningham himself declared, and with a small turnout and an already established name recognition in the suburbs, he won. Now the congressional representative for the Northwest's largest concentration of gay men and women was also one of its most hostile opponents.

Also in May, encouraged by his role in derailing the bill that would have protected gays from job discrimination statewide, KIRO's Cooney turned his editorial wrath on Seattle's civil rights laws. Unleashing what a *Post-Intelligencer* reporter called "an unprecedented four-in-a-row attack," Cooney began urging voters to overturn the job and housing ordinances and to consider "repealing" the council members who had adopted them. Cooney acknowledged that the station had never before broadcast so many editorials on a single issue, and with a council and mayoral election due in the fall, Cooney's urgings seemed more than idle threat.[18]

In June came worse news. Miami had done what Cooney wanted to do in Seattle. Conservatives led by actress Anita Bryant had wrapped themselves in a religious veil and had repealed Dade County's law protecting gays and lesbians from job discrimination. The popular vote had gone overwhelmingly against homosexuals.

Later that month, Capitol Hill's new congressman, Jack Cunningham, endorsed a conservative protest of the upcoming Seattle Gay Pride celebration. "The promotion of homosexuality," he wrote to the Concerned Christian group that planned to stage the protest, "is yet another example of the erosion of moral standards in the country to the ultimate detriment of family relationships." And on the sunny afternoon of June 30, some 150 Christian protesters, met by about 90 gay counter-demonstrators, turned out on the downtown corner at Fourth Avenue and James Street for what the *Seattle Post-Intelligencer* called "an hour laden with songs, prayers, shouts, band music, hyperbole and some good ol' down home hate." While a Christian loudspeaker proclaimed "This city can be destroyed like Sodom and Gomorrah," the Shriners' Nile Temple band played "Onward Christian Soldiers," met with counter-chants of "Workers, women, minorities, and gays— we want our rights and we want them today."[19]

The attempt to influence the insiders' conversation about political reform had now definitely moved into the public realm.

Then came the Ellensburg rout.

To celebrate International Women's Year, women nationwide had planned state conferences to discuss political goals and to elect delegates to a national meeting in Houston. At each of the state meetings, resolutions supporting gay and lesbian civil rights were being hotly debated. The National Organization for Women was holding to its support, but these meetings were not just tents for NOW supporters. All women were welcome. The meetings were supposed to have been an affirmation of feminism; instead, the conference became the next signal that opponents of homosexuals were mobilizing faster to control the public conversation than gays and lesbians were.

In Washington, the Mormon Church telegraphed a call for members to attend the conference. A public relations spokesman would later describe the effort as low-key compared to what could have been done. "All the Church did on the Ellensburg conference," he explained to a *Seattle Sun* reporter, "was to say, 'This is going to affect you, sisters. We would encourage you to go and take a stand.'" The Mormon women, he said, "were not told how to vote. They were simply told, 'You know our stand on abortion. . . . You know our stand on lesbianism.'" That was enough.[20]

On the opening day of the conference in July, some two thousand Mormon women arrived at the campus of Central Washington University in the small ranch town of Ellensburg two hours east of Seattle. They wore blue and white ribbons so they could identify one another. Surprisingly for a women's conference, they were accompanied by men who appeared to be giving them instructions—at least that is the way it seemed to feminists who staffed the registration tables. The Mormon numbers quickly overwhelmed the conference organizers. Feminist activists arriving later would complain in stories in *Pandora* that they had to stand in line five hours to get their credentials, only to discover no information packets remained. Dorm rooms had been booked and paid for—then left empty, leading some to suspect why and by whom.

"We've been screwed," one conference organizer was quoted in *Pandora* as saying.[21]

In one case, what was to have been a small workshop about lesbian concerns instead drew almost five hundred people, most sporting the blue and white ribbons. After a panel discussed the stereotypes harmful to lesbians, the floor opened to one Mormon comment after another about sickness, perversion, and the need to exterminate homosexuality. Only maneuvering and delaying headed off a Mormon resolution tying homosexuality to pornography and prostitution.

The feminists avoided a complete rout only by staging marches of their own supporters through the campus and negotiating their own sometimes acerbic disagreements about platforms and delegates before votes came to a plenary session. Many concerns the feminists had hoped would produce resolutions were instead sandbagged. For years afterward, Ellensburg was a symbol of the tougher battle that lay ahead.

The Lesbian Resource Center's Kathy Boyle, who chaired the workshop on lesbian concerns, said in *Pandora*, "I still have nightmares about it. That workshop was a war. The only thing missing was the guns."

Then, to cap the whole bad year, Pete Francis announced he would resign as state senator. He told reporters that extra long legislative sessions were making it just too hard for him to support his family and manage his legal business.[22] He was the best supporter that gays and lesbians had so far had in the legislature.

Although few, there were still some hopeful signs for the gay rights quest during 1977.

One was national. In Washington, D.C., Midge Costanza, as a special assistant to President Jimmy Carter, had been given the highest post ever held by a woman in the White House, and she had decided to invite voices seldom heard to come to meetings. In March, she asked gay and lesbian leaders for the first time, and Charlie Brydon was one of fourteen selected to attend. While there would be little immediate national impact—and Costanza herself would become so controversial that she would soon be out of a job—it was certainly the first time that an openly gay activist from Seattle had made it to an official White House meeting. Brydon, the Vietnam vet, urged a reexamination of Pentagon policies that excluded openly gay and lesbian military personnel.[23]

The other positive signs were in the conversation with Seattle's city hall. Brydon managed to secure pledges from Mayor Uhlman and eight of the nine Seattle City Council members to "vigorously oppose" any Anita Bryant–like attempt to repeal Seattle's nondiscrimination laws.[24] At the end of June, to emphasize the point, Uhlman for the first time declared an official Gay Pride Week in Seattle. Nineteen seventy-seven in particular, he said, was a time to recognize efforts "to make this community one which truly does treat all its citizens in a fair and equal manner." Uhlman, who was not running for re-election, had now dropped his earlier hesitations about an endorsement that would be controversial.

In response to Uhlman's proclamation, the Cunningham-supported Christian protesters picketed City Hall and filled Uhlman's mail with warnings that Seattle would meet the fate of Sodom.[25]

Gay Pride Week that year was a turning point for the city's gays and lesbians. From 1973 until 1977, they had commemorated the Stonewall uprising with a mélange of events, no one of them more important than the other. There had been social gatherings, films and plays, the inevitable political workshops. Most had been held inside and had occurred in scattered areas—at the bars still in Pioneer Square, an ethnic hall on Renton Hill, the Seattle Center north of downtown, Volunteer Park atop Capitol Hill, the Radical Women's home in Freeway Hall.

In 1977, with Bryant, Cooney, and Cunningham marching the parapets, gays and lesbians focused the celebration outside and added what became its central feature—a public march along city streets. It was a significant turn in the rhetoric of public visibility, introducing what would become a new summer ritual for gays and lesbians and eventually, as it grew into the city's second-largest celebration, for Seattle as a whole.

About fifteen hundred people joined that first march. Intended or not, it was rich in symbolism, with gays and lesbians following an exodus route out from the center of the mudflat, skirting Denny's knoll by walking up First Avenue, and then arriving at downtown's center, Westlake Mall. Along the way, the crowd passed what had been Mac Wells's old 614 Tavern. Although the timing of the march memorialized a rebellion a continent away, it unconsciously also marked the advances sparked by a locally brewed revolt that had begun the birth of Seattle's own public gay community one decade earlier.

There was another hopeful sign in 1977, but again limited to Seattle. In the fall elections for mayor and city council, the campaign rhetoric—which could indicate how the city's public acceptance of homosexuals was faring—failed to turn ugly.

Uhlman had decided not to run for a third term, and during the summer some of the "downtown" gays, notably Charlie Brydon and the city clerk Wayne Angevine, organized an elections committee to evaluate candidates and to launch the first major drive to register gay and lesbian voters. Cunningham's victory had stung them and shown them the need to organize "get-out-the-vote" efforts. The new group, called the Seattle Municipal Elections Committee or SEAMEC for short, signed about seventeen hundred new voters in time for the primary, more than any other political organization in King County that year. SEAMEC also institutionalized a practice of rating candidates, originally begun by the now faded Seattle Gay Alliance. In a sign of assertiveness, SEAMEC began circulating its evaluations publicly so they could reach all gay and lesbian voters; in earlier years, the old SGA ratings had occasionally been passed secretly to avoid causing trouble for any candidates favorable to gays and lesbians.

In its ratings, SEAMEC reported good news. Only one minor candidate, from the U.S. Labor Party, scored a "0," indicating open hostility to homosexuals. Two city council members running for mayor received a rating of "2," meaning they were "neutral or passively sympathetic," but both of those had also signed the pledge to resist repeal of the antidiscrimination ordinances. The candidates who would eventually move to the general election both earned a "3." Each was considered "a friend, a supporter of gay rights" with some restrictions.

Those restrictions, as it turned out, focused on Uhlman's declaration of Gay Pride Week. Only one candidate supported it—and she was from the Socialist Workers Party and not likely to win. All the major candidates distinguished "not discriminating" against homosexuals from promoting "pride" for homosexuals. Even the candidate who received the highest score of "4" said she thought the Uhlman proclamation "not productive."[26]

Although the hedge about "pride" was useful for politicians, it was frustrating for gays and lesbians who hoped for a more public valuing of different sexual expressions. Still, it had to be counted as progress that in this second citywide election in which gay issues were being openly discussed, even the most hesitant candidates were not talking about ridding the city of "these people," as Mayor Braman's memo a decade earlier had. To honor the special friendship that Uhlman, Brydon, and the gay community had developed, the Dorian Group sponsored a party for the outgoing mayor aboard one of the state's new super ferries, drawing more than eight hundred people.[27]

When the general election was over, a former television newsman named Charles Royer emerged as mayor. Royer was a liberal and a Democrat, cut from the Uhlman cloth. Interestingly, he had worked at KING-TV, which was a rival of Cooney's KIRO and—through corporate links extending all the way back to the 1960s *Seattle* magazine article about Peter Wichern and the Dorian Society—had proven itself more favorable to reporting about the need for civil rights for the city's lesbians and gays. Indeed, during the election campaign, KING-TV had been preparing what would be the city's first major documentary about homosexuals, a thirty-minute special titled "Who Are These People and What Do They Want?" But it had decided to wait until after the election to air the show.

That autumn, during the campaign, Brydon had been growing tired. In a letter to a friend that November, he confided, "The only problem with these things is that I don't get to enjoy them much since I'm so closely involved with the planning and execution. Workaholics like you and I need to find a cure so we can shake the guilt or whatever it is that drives us and get out for some relaxation and enjoyment." Seattle's most visible gay leader was beginning to realize that in fighting to ensure the rights of other homosexuals to their private lives, he was not having much of a private life himself. His relationship with his lover in the navy had ended three years earlier, shortly after he had moved to Seattle. It had been replaced with a network of political friends, but not a close companion. "I ought to get out of this maddeningly demanding gay movement," he wrote to his friend, "and devote more time to myself and to cultivating friends and perhaps even a lover."

To the Dorian board that month, he sent another letter saying he was exhausted "from the battles [mostly with other gay activists] that have been waged to create a viable reformist, middle-of-the-road gay civil rights and public education organization."[28]

Still, Brydon hung on for a few more weeks and, as 1977 drew to its close, he was there at a Dorian Group luncheon when mayor-elect Royer gave a hopeful signal to the city's lesbians and gays. Royer noted that Police Chief Robert Hanson would be retiring, and he promised that when the city selected a new chief, gays and lesbians would be asked—for the first time ever—to assist in the search. Brydon and the Dorians responded with a standing ovation.[29]

The same month, KING finally aired its documentary—well placed on a Friday night during prime time. It was hosted by U.W. football star Kopay who, along with several others, talked of how it felt to be discriminated against and sometimes forced to hide in bars for a social life. Perhaps more importantly, though, in what was then an unusual segment, the show featured a mother and her gay son, Sandy and teenager Greg Kucera. Previous news reports in the city had focused solely on homosexual adults—like Peter Wichern or the anonymous "Jim" interviewed in the U.W. *Daily* in the 1960s—and they had most often been quoted about their fear of coming out to their parents, or about the tension their homosexuality had caused within the family. In the Kuceras' case, Sandy instead spoke at length about how important Greg's decision to be honest had been and about how positively it had affected their relationship. Before he had come out, she said, there had been a great deal of emotional distance and even aggression, at one point causing her to hit him, but once he came out, "our whole relationship relaxed tremendously."

"I now have a part of his life I would not otherwise have," she added. In this segment, then, the show's reporter, Frank Tenczar, and KING presented a young gay man not as someone at odds with family—as had so often been the image— but as someone situated and accepted within a very well adjusted family. Far from causing a problem, his coming out had created closeness. A writer for the *Seattle Gay News* called the documentary "a pioneering effort" and "a tribute to how far gay awareness has come, not only among the historically enlightened Public Affairs crew which put the show together, but among the rarefied air surrounding KING's upper management." Without their approval, he noted, the ten-thousand-dollar budget for shooting the documentary, and its airing during prime time, would not have been possible. "Thanks to KING's courageous and innovative programming decision," he added, that important first step toward understanding gays— and gay understanding—has been taken."

Tenczar would win an Emmy for the program. The younger Kucera, so accepted by his family, would eventually study with noted artist Jacob Lawrence at the University of Washington and then open one of Seattle's leading art galleries, the Greg Kucera Gallery in Pioneer Square. There he would make his name partly by sponsoring some of the city's most controversial shows—of artists such as Robert Mapplethorpe, Sally Mann, and Andres Serrano.[30]

With a new and supportive mayor elected, with the Dorian Group well established, and with one of the city's major television stations willing to present the gay voice, it must have seemed an appropriately safe moment for Seattle's weary "gay mayor" Charlie Brydon to also complete his term and to tend more to his own private life. At the end of 1977, he announced he would no longer serve as president of the Dorian Group. He needed a rest, he said.

At the police department, though, one patrol officer in particular had been growing increasingly angry about the new political clout gays and lesbians seemed to have in Seattle. And about the time Brydon was announcing his retirement, David Estes was determining to put an end to the new gay power Brydon and others had so carefully nurtured.

Estes had joined the Seattle police force six years earlier, in 1971, when he was in his mid-twenties and when George Tielsch was trying to set a new moral direction not only for the police, but also for the whole city. Estes had grown up poor, raised by a father he once said had bootlegged in Georgia. At age seventeen, he dropped out of high school and joined the army, fighting in Vietnam, eventually being discharged at Fort Lewis in Tacoma, and then coming to work in Seattle at the Bon Marché department store as a security guard. Newspaper interviews portray an almost Huck Finn childhood, complete with an absorption in moral wondering and wanderings. In Estes's case, the reflections had resolved themselves firmly in favor of traditional strictures. As a child Estes had moved several times; he once told a reporter that only the local police officers in each new location had taken much notice of him and befriended him. They were the ones who told him to "hang in there." At about the age of twelve, he decided he wanted to be a police officer. Many years later, when he was in his own prowl car one night, the reason he had chosen law enforcement arrived in a kind of Damascene revelation. He would recall later in an interview with the *Seattle Sun* that he had been asking himself, "Why are you here?" The answer that had suddenly arrived as he was driving along Seattle's streets was, "Hey, you stand for the good."

He added, "I made up my mind that from then on I would react the way I perceive is right."[31]

He was assigned to patrols of Pioneer Square and Capitol Hill. In 1973, another police officer took him to one of the porno arcades downtown and then introduced him to the gay bars that still remained on the mudflat. "I was shocked," Estes told the *Sun*. "It was like seeing someone killed in front of you. Then [the other officer] showed me a guy dressed as a beautiful girl, took me around to lesbian and homosexual bars, showed me the various people and lifestyles. It was the first time I really thought about pornography."

Estes's reaction was a bit like the one the young George Cotterill had in 1884 when his tugboat from Tacoma puffed into Elliott Bay, revealing on the one hand a splendid gem of a city and on the other squalor on the mudflat. Seattle's landscape of sexuality did not at all fit with the good that Estes believed he represented or with the Northwest he thought should exist.

A few days after Tielsch quit in March 1974, Estes wrote a letter to the *Post-Intelligencer*. The newspaper gave the letter unusual front-page play and pictured the young patrolman smiling and being hugged around the neck by his two young children. It described him as "resentful of the recent criticism" of the police department, particularly that levied by municipal court judge T. Patrick Corbett, whose note to Mayor Uhlman criticizing the department because of reports of brutality had helped trigger the final confrontation with Tielsch. In the letter, Estes addressed the issue of police raids of the downtown arcades, saying, "What value do these X-rated movies and peep shows really have? These places in reality are little more than parasites that feed on human weakness." He seemed genuinely concerned, wanting to help the people who frequented the shops—although in his own fashion. "Doesn't it make more sense to send individuals to psychiatrists for help rather than 'keeping them off the street' by allowing them to masturbate, engage in oral copulation, and engage in other perverted sex acts while watching a machine. We are copping out on our responsibility toward these individuals when we hide them in a filthy little room with an unfeeling, unthinking machine." He also warned, "There is no assurance they will stay in their dark rooms."[32]

In the nearly four years that had elapsed since the letter, Estes had developed a reputation as a maverick in the department. In December 1976, he had gotten into trouble with Police Chief Hanson while conducting his own independent investigation of what he thought was renewed corruption in the police force. Supposedly, he had relayed alleged payoff information from a prostitute to the U.S. Attorney's office. Also, at a time when some officers felt their regular ammunition was not strong enough to drop a fleeing felon, Estes had been caught carrying more powerful, unauthorized "hot-load" ammunition. Chief Hanson personally demanded he turn over his gun and badge and then suspended him indefinitely. Estes claimed he had been set up. In January, a review board shortened the suspension to thirty days, and Estes returned to work by March 1977.[33]

When Uhlman proclaimed a Gay Pride Week in June of that year, Estes refocused his mission of pursuing what he defined as "the good." "That's what really started the whole thing," he told the Seattle Sun later. "Homosexuals were marching up and down the streets. I saw pictures of it in the paper." Estes stood with four or five other policemen in the locker room one day, talking about Seattle's job ordinance protecting homosexuals, and about how gay rights were "starting to affect the police departments, to get into all walks of society."

He recalled, "The other guys said if I'd write up an initiative, they'd support me." He did not relish the notion of politics, because he knew it included compromise, and "I don't compromise easily. To me, everything is black and white, right or wrong. Either I'm for it, or I'm against it."[34]

The initiative process was the perfect device. With it, Estes could directly repeal Seattle's civil rights ordinance.

"I don't hate homosexuals," he told the Sun. "I'm the first to admit, hey, I've seen homosexuals do some good things." But, he added, gays are "emotionally disturbed." To him, homosexual sex was the same as bestiality, pedophilia, and necrophilia. The solution: psychiatric care. "What we should do," Estes said, "is say this is somewhat of a sickness, and we should start treating it, like we do alcohol."

In January 1978, Estes made his way to the city clerk's counter at City Hall and told the clerk he wanted to start a citizen's initiative. Protecting the job a gay man or woman held was not a civil rights issue, he thought. It was a moral transgression. He wanted a citywide vote to repeal the law. For that he first had to gain enough signatures on a petition whose text had been approved by city officials. He showed city clerk Wayne Angevine a copy of what he wanted to circulate. Point one of his argument asked: "Are you concerned with homosexuals teaching your children?" Point two said, "Are you concerned with homosexuals actively recruiting your children?" Two other questions asked employers whether they were "being forced to hire homosexuals."

Angevine was somewhat taken aback. The city clerk had been in politics for twenty years by then, having been elected at age twenty-three to the state senate as the youngest Washington legislator. He had married, fathered children, and then in the early 1970s as gays asserted more visibility, he had realized and accepted his own sexual orientation. Angevine was gay—a downtown gay. Discreetly, he said nothing to Estes. Professionally, he knew, his job did not "include moralizing over the counter." Instead, he helped the patrolman meet the legal technicalities, and on January 25, 1978, it was a gay man who gave Estes the go-ahead to begin collecting signatures.[35]

With little warning, gays and lesbians in Seattle would suddenly be challenged to find a new rhetorical strategy—one that would work in a contest no longer in the control of political insiders. Charlie Brydon would have no retirement.

## 14

# Initiative Thirteen

## Coming Together, Learning to Persuade

*T*he news that David Estes could begin collecting signatures for the anti-gay initiative arrived the same night in February 1978 that Charlie Brydon's friends had planned a retirement dinner for him. The dinner was to be held at one of the bars that were carving a new gay territory away from the mudflat, Ken Decker's Brass Door located at Pike Street and Harvard Avenue, on Capitol Hill. Harassers had tossed a smoke bomb through the door just a few days earlier, but Decker continued to prepare for Brydon's reception. Pete Francis planned to be there, as did Doug Jewett, the prosecutor who had tried to win the payoff convictions and who had just been elected city attorney. Their presence would be evidence that the civic discourse with gays and lesbians was widening, and Brydon, of course, was getting the credit. Five Everett Community College students even came to thank Brydon for helping them win recognition from school officials for a new gay student alliance at the college.

That night, the dinner went as planned, the usual affair of congratulations, but the gossip among those attending focused as much on the uncertain future as on the achievements of the past. People nervously wondered whether the police officer was going to triumph as easily in Seattle as Anita Bryant had in Florida.

As the dinner ended, Brydon rose to reassure the audience. "This is not going to be a Dade County II," he proclaimed forcefully. "This is Seattle, not Miami."

Then came a surprise from the man who supposedly was retiring; a small group of gay leaders including himself, he told the audience, had already taken matters into hand and was meeting privately to shape a response to the initiative. Few had known about it before that moment.[1]

The crowd applauded. Brydon knew how to get things done. Quickly. Behind the scenes. With insider clout. Two weeks later, Brydon called a press conference to unveil the new organization, Citizens to Retain Fair Employment (CRFE). He was ready to enter the fray again, and he had recruited a steering committee for CRFE that was a testament to just how much support he had been able to build among heterosexuals in Seattle. Among its members were city council members Paul Kraabel, Phyllis Lamphere, and Jeanette Williams; state senators Pete Francis and Jim McDermott; state representatives Bill Burns, Jeff Douthwaite, and Gene Luz; U.W. professors Giovanni Costigan, Pepper Schwartz, and Jennifer James;

Volume 2　Number 14　June 29-July 5, 1977　50 cents

# theWeekly
of Metropolitan Seattle

**The legislature's uninspiring record of retrenchment** page 4

**Can we save the immense parklands of Alaska?** page 10

**Boning up for the Guy Anderson shows** page 13

'Ready when
you are,
Anita'

Charles Brydon,
embattled spokesman
for Seattle's gays
page 8

In 1977, after celebrity Anita Bryant helped overturn a gay civil rights ordinance in Miami, the *Seattle Weekly* personified a similar battle in Seattle as a struggle between Bryant and Charlie Brydon, who had become the city's best-known gay activist. *(Seattle Weekly, Washington State Historical Society, Tacoma)* developer Paul Schell and longtime Seattle jeweler Herb Bridge; activist and Seattle writer Walt Crowley; Secretary of State Bruce Chapman; and a diverse range of gays and lesbians. Cherry Johnson, for example, had volunteered for the Lesbian Resource Center but mostly knew Brydon through her work as secretary for the Dorian Group in 1977. Similarly, William Etnyre had been the group's treasurer. There was a young aide named Cal Anderson working in city council member George Benson's office. He had mostly been active with the Democratic Party. Two men, Lee Trinka and Jerry Reese, represented the city's drag-queen organization. Greg Kucera was the young artist who had been featured in the KING-TV documentary about gays at the end of 1977.

Significantly, the important political committee that would decide campaign strategy was chaired not by a well-known gay activist but by Walt Crowley, who had helped create an underground newspaper, the *Helix,* during the anti-Vietnam years, but who was heterosexual and had played little role in gay politics. A city hall insider would assist him, a lesbian named Shelly Yapp who had earned an economics degree from the University of Washington and was becoming Mayor Royer's deputy director of policy planning. Other political committee members included Tim Hillard, who had been Uhlman's liaison to the gay community; Hugh Spitzer, who was replacing Hillard; Brydon himself; and Pepper Schwartz, the U.W. teacher.[2]

Pointedly missing from both the executive and political committees were the names of any of the most prominent gay activists on Capitol Hill or any of the more radical or socialist feminists—people like Dick Snedigar, Patrick Haggerty, Cindy Gipple, Laurie Morton, Betty Johanna, Jane Meyerding, Faygele benMiriam, or even Jim Arnold or Jim Tully, two supporters of the Gay Community Center who had become the owners of the major gay newspaper in town, the *Seattle Gay News.*

By 1978, there had been years of gay evangelizing and intellectualizing, years of entrepreneuring new groups, and years of small protests against specific troubles, but most communication had been of an "internal" sort, aimed at rallying a new sense of identity and pride among gays and lesbians themselves. It had aimed at making it possible for individuals to come out. Meanwhile, the "external" political persuasion of heterosexuals had primarily been directed at city or state politicians, or to small gatherings in classrooms or churches. When lesbians and gays had won political battles, it had been through the efforts of a few activists who had found heterosexual allies—the early Dorians working with Katagiri and Francis; the city's feminists gaining Jeanette Williams's support for a women's commission; and Brydon working with Uhlman. Gays and lesbians in Seattle had not yet faced the need to persuade a majority of voters to support them, and, as George Cotterill and Mark Matthews had shown at the beginning of the century, the initiative and referendum process could be a thin disguise for a majority telling a minority how to behave socially. What Brydon was about to attempt was a new step, and not everyone agreed Brydon should be the chief choreographer, nor did everyone agree on the rhetoric he would choose. The challenge, then, was twofold: not only to persuade heterosexuals to give gays and lesbians the majority in a popular vote, but also to find a way to come together to do so.

Almost before the microphones were turned off at Brydon's press conference, Wayne Angevine, the city clerk, was being quoted in the *Seattle Gay News* as saying that "Charlie Brydon is putting together an organization to promote Charlie Brydon. He doesn't give a good goddamn about the gay rights movement, and come hell or high water, he's going to divide the gay community if necessary to make himself spokesman."[3]

Within two days, another new group called the Washington Coalition for Sexual Minority Rights held its own press conference. The coalition, discontent with the rhetoric issuing from the Dorian Group, had formed several months earlier as a replacement for the old Seattle Gay Alliance. It was joined at the conference by representatives of the Seattle Counseling Service, the Gay Community Center, NOW, the Feminist Coordinating Council, the Freedom Socialist Party, and Radical Women—all the activist dwellers of the hilltops rather than of the downtown knoll. The coalition first explicitly denounced the Estes initiative. Then it implicitly criticized Charlie Brydon by scheduling its own community meeting to discuss strategies for responding to Estes. Coalition members deliberately contrasted the grassroots way they intended to work against Brydon's intent to form a professional cadre. In March 1978, more than three hundred gay men and women gathered at the Metropolitan Community Church's site on Renton Hill.

By then, Estes had amended his original petition to overturn not just the city's job law protecting gays, but the housing ordinance as well. His initiative had also been assigned a number: thirteen.

At the coalition meeting, Brydon's old nemesis Dick Snedigar, the former director of the counseling service and member of the Freedom Socialist Party, initially urged the audience to remember solidarity. "Whatever views we hold individually or as groups, a united front must be formed," he said. But almost immediately, one of the questions raised was whether the entire campaign should be delegated to Brydon's new organization or whether a separate campaign should be run by the coalition. Overwhelmingly, the audience voted against unifying with Brydon's group.[4]

Before many more weeks had passed, the coalition spawned two political arms to combat Estes. Both would be collectively organized with committees and individual members determining strategy, rather than "leaders" and "campaign directors," the approach of Brydon's Citizens to Retain Fair Employment. One group, called Women Against Thirteen (WAT), would aim at mobilizing those feminists who wanted to work with other women to defeat the initiative rather than having to work with men. WAT's strategy would be to emphasize a little-publicized section of Initiative Thirteen that would strip the city Office of Women's Rights of its power to investigate complaints of discrimination against women. Estes proposed to transfer those powers to the city Human Rights Department. WAT thought women's concerns would be diluted if that happened. The second collective to be formed included both men and women. It would be called the Seattle Committee against Thirteen, or SCAT—an acronym capable of multiple meanings. It too would have its own independent strategy, recruiting as many openly gay volunteers as possible and sending them into neighborhoods to directly challenge heterosexuals to support gay rights.

Brydon cringed. The acronym SCAT he thought "horrendous," and he did not believe that either WAT or SCAT had a message that heterosexual voters would identify with. His group, CRFE, had already commissioned a poll. "We could win," Brydon remembered in a later interview, "if we made [the argument] a right to privacy." Indeed, the survey showed that 95 percent of those polled agreed with the statement "everyone has a fundamental right to privacy." The trick, CRFE figured, was to fit gays' protections against job and housing discrimination into that rhetoric, not to try to make heterosexuals feel more comfortable about homosexuals themselves.[5]

The line between the downtown gays and the hill gays was drawn, and for the next several months, it would be difficult to determine whether the main plot in the fight against Initiative Thirteen was against Estes or against one another.

Seattle was not the sole battleground over gay civil rights in 1978. At the end of March, Anita Bryant's Southern Baptist pastor from Florida, F. William Chapman, arrived in Seattle, making a circuit from Wichita, Kansas, to St. Paul, Minnesota, and to other cities where Bryant's campaign was preparing strikes to repeal similar local ordinances. The Bryant strategy was to build what looked like an unstoppable momentum in cities and then win a statewide vote in California that would signal once and for all that gays should not be protected against discrimination. Eventually, the strategy suggested, even sodomy laws that had been repealed by legislatures could be reinstated by popular vote. That was the ultimate target.[6]

St. Paul would vote April 25; Wichita, May 9; Eugene, May 23. If Estes succeeded in his petition drive, the Seattle vote would come November 7. That would be the same day Californians would consider a statewide initiative authorizing the dismissal of any teacher, gay or straight, who discussed homosexuality in a public setting, whether inside or outside the classroom. By the end of the year, Bryant and her allies calculated, the legal protections that had been slowly granted to gays in a handful of locations could be so soundly repudiated they would not be tried elsewhere.

In every locale, the rhetorical theme would be the same: a focus on religious symbols and on fear. Homosexuals, it would be repeatedly asserted, posed a moral threat to American families, in particular to children. Homosexuals recruited. They engaged in abominable sex acts too disgusting to mention—although they would be etched in glaring detail during campaign speeches. Homosexuals dressed in inappropriate clothing. Homosexuals were unchristian.

In Seattle, most of Estes's supporters on the police force chose to remain in the background. One other officer who did join him in public was Dennis Falk, who also happened to be a member of the ultraconservative John Birch Society. The two police officers soon became codirectors of an organization they named Save Our Moral Ethics, SOME for short. At a press conference with Estes and Falk, the Reverend Chapman asserted that repealing antidiscrimination laws protecting homosexuals was not a matter of civil rights, but of morality. "Legitimate minorities," he said, citing Baptists and Mormons as examples, were groups that had long existed within history. When it came to a homosexual, he said, "history has never given him a place."[7] He ignored the obvious fact: that the two minorities he had cited had also coalesced at a certain point in history and then had had to struggle for their own rights to protection.

The Miami debacle—70 percent to repeal the antidiscrimination law, only 30 percent to uphold—had been laid to several factors, and in every city on the 1978 list, homosexuals and their allies tried desperately to change the narrative terrain. It was said that the campaign in Dade County had lasted only seven weeks, far too short a time to organize and educate the public. The appeals to emotions had not really been countered; experts on sexuality had jetted in to assure voters that homosexuals were not child molesters, but even that was a defensive and intellectual maneuver. To rely on academics to counter deeply metaphoric fears was death in a heated political struggle. It was also said that local gay organizers had not developed deep contacts with heterosexual community leaders. The widespread Cuban neighborhoods had been written off as too hostile and too Catholic. The archbishop had opposed the civil rights law. The media had not understood the civil rights argument.

As the Bryant campaign launched other ballot initiatives, gays and lesbians desperately sought different campaign strategies. "None of the arguments that were advanced by the pro–gay rights side were resonating with the general public," Brydon recalled later.[8] In St. Paul, gays thought the territory would shift. It was a Scandinavian town, much like Seattle, less given to campaigns waged on passion and fear—or so the reasoning went. The Catholic archbishop favored the city's law. Connections were made with heterosexual leaders. The mayor and three past mayors spoke against the repeal. Much of the ammunition Bryant's forces had in Miami appeared to be missing. Yet at the last minute came a barrage of ads featuring the usual themes of molestation and recruitment and once again voters gutted the law.

The public rhetoric of the gay movement simply was not working in places where civil rights could be put to a majority vote. Wichita came next. The result was the same: the majority voted to repeal the civil rights law. In all three cities, gays were able to win about one-third of the vote, but lost the other two-thirds.

Then Eugene. This vote would be of particular interest in Seattle, since it was in another Northwest city. Popular myth held that Oregon was a land of Northwestern tolerance. It had been one of the earliest states to repeal its sodomy law, and Portland had passed a job law protecting homosexuals in 1974, just a few months after Seattle did. The Oregon House of Representatives had come within one vote of adopting a similar statewide protection in 1975. Eugene, a university town, was an emerald magnet. Gay activists there figured a relatively low-key campaign with reasoned media ads about citizens' rights would work. Even the gay opponents seemed gentler in their attacks. But when the vote was counted, once again lesbians and gays lost two to one.

In Seattle, the mood began to turn very grim. "Dade County, St. Paul," Brydon said later, "they had all fallen like bowling pins."[9]

One of the first divisions to occur among Seattle's gays was over how aggressive the campaign should be, particularly while Estes was still gathering signatures during the summer of 1978 to put his initiative on the ballot. Conventional political wisdom held that it was often better not to draw the public's attention to an initiative you opposed. After the May defeat in Eugene, CRFE chose not to issue any news releases or call any press conferences because, Brydon said, he did not want to call unnecessary attention in Seattle to the vote. Then in early June 1978, CRFE issued a position statement saying it believed that "if public awareness of the initiative and the gay-rights issue can be minimized, there is a chance the initiative will fail to qualify for the ballot." In a separate *Seattle Gay News* article written for CRFE's political committee, Walt Crowley likened the anti-gay initiatives to a "strange and insidious social cancer," and said that the "problem in Seattle is to find or generate enough 'antibodies' to destroy the malignancy before it poisons the entire city." Gays and lesbians, he wrote, could be one source of the "antibodies," but to win, more would have to be found among heterosexuals. For the moment, he argued, CRFE's posture was "to avoid inadvertently contributing any momentum to the petition drive by our own actions." Even Brydon's critic Wayne Angevine agreed. He would tell a reporter, "We have to keep a low profile. No billboards, no TV. Don't flaunt the lifestyle. The minute you start smearing it in people's faces, people react negatively."[10]

SCAT and WAT, on the other hand, thought that was a grievously wrong approach. One of the young activists with SCAT was Dennis Raymond, who had moved to Seattle in 1977 after being raised in Detroit and joining the Gay Liberation Front at Wayne State University. Raymond, who would become director of the Gay Community Center, recalled that SCAT used tactics that "only a nimble organization could." "We would send out hordes of people when we found out that the pro-Thirteeners were gathering signatures. You would call people and say, 'It's happening now. Get out to Northgate,' and people would just descend there." While the SCAT and WAT activists could not block individuals from signing the petitions, they could try to dissuade. At times, they were more subversive. Raymond recalled that one activist, Cookie Hunt, often took her two young children, hand in hand, and then pretended to be interested in signing the petitions herself. "She'd act like a dumb housewife [saying] 'Really, I didn't know that. Tell me more.' And [those gathering signatures] were such zealots they would spend all their time trying to convince her"—all the while missing other potential signers.[11]

On June 13, two lesbian activists, Betty Johanna and Jane Meyerding, acted even more aggressively. Imitating a tactic used by anti-Vietnam War protesters, they invaded the SOME office and poured vials of their own blood onto the initiative petitions. The letter they left said: "We are lesbians. We are the people whose lives you want to take away and replace with lives which you have chosen for us. With our blood, we are telling you today that we cannot live without our lives." Both SCAT and CRFE quickly distanced themselves from the blood-pouring, SCAT saying the tactic was not an appropriate way to educate the city, and CRFE adding that acts of violence could not be condoned. Johanna and Meyerding spent eighteen days in jail, charged with destruction of property—but they used the time to order a copy of Del Martin and Phyllis Lyon's book *Lesbian/Woman* from the public library and then passed it on to other women in the jail.[12]

As the late June time for the 1978 gay pride parade in Seattle drew near, unity between the factions of the gay community seemed an unattainable goal. Coming together was not working.

Across the nation, activists had already been debating whether the public parades in honor of the Stonewall riot were doing the gay cause more harm than good since they blended communication themes in ways not often understood by the general public. On the one hand, the parades were political, in the tradition of the civil rights marches of the 1960s. Yet the gay parades were also celebrations of being visible, and as such were carnivals of fun and drag costuming, which made them a mélange of St. Patrick's Day parades mingled with civil rights protests, with a bit of Mardi Gras drag added for vaudeville's sake. The media never could quite explain what the seemingly disjointed images were all about.

In Seattle, a few activists suggested that 1978 would be a good year to skip the march altogether, what with the need to find a political strategy pleasing to heterosexuals. Pictures of parading drag queens just would not help. Two weeks after the vote in Eugene, both the Dorian Group and CRFE dropped from the parade, CRFE declaring that "we believe a gay rights parade in the present political climate involves serious risks." "A parade," the group said, "will be viewed as a provocative gesture by too many otherwise indifferent voters." CRFE members also persuaded the NOW chapter to withdraw its endorsement, and CRFE's campaign manager, feminist Sandra Kraus, defended the decision by saying that CRFE was a "political group" rather than a "gay group." Acting on CRFE's cue, Mayor Royer—whose wife had also become a member of the steering committee—then announced a break with Uhlman's decision of the previous year. The new mayor would not declare a Gay Pride Week. His press office explained, "Such a proclamation in the current atmosphere will damage chances that the city's human rights law will remain intact."

For his part, Brydon suggested a compromise, proposing that the timing of the march be changed. "Would a parade in August"—after the deadline for Estes's petitions had passed—"be a better idea?" he asked. Outraged, the Coalition for Sexual Minority Rights, which had organized the march in 1977, quickly announced it would not appease Estes's anti-gay forces and would, as planned, go ahead on July 1.

At the *Seattle Gay News*, owners Arnold and Tully urged a massive turnout. "No one can free slaves but slaves themselves," they editorialized, "and we, as gays, must be ready to pay our dues for freedom, as members of other minorities have done and continue to do. . . . Let the faint-hearted among us return to the closet and whisper through the keyhole. Let the rest of us march down First Avenue and attack, attack, attack."[13]

The day of the march, about three thousand joined the "attack"—more than ever had before. If nothing else, Estes's moral campaign had mobilized the city's gays and lesbians to be more visible than ever. The question was, in the face of a resolute common foe, had one gay flank deserted while the other had sallied foolishly into the hands of the enemy?

In August, a month after the parade, David Estes dressed in a casual open-necked shirt instead of his Seattle police uniform. Dennis Falk chose a suit and tie rather than his regulation blues. Together, they headed for the city clerk's office where Angevine waited for them. SOME had requested that the city comptroller, E. L. Kidd, also accompany the homosexual city clerk. The organization had gathered more than 27,000 signatures in favor of repealing the ordinance that protected Angevine's job. Only about 17,626 were needed. The *Seattle Times* reported, "As SOME leaders approached the counter, the area was bathed in light from the television cameras and reporters pressed close to hear Angevine's comments. 'What have we here?' Angevine, feigning surprise, said to Falk."

Falk spoke into the microphones that the city's press thrust in front of him. "Initiative Thirteen," he said, "perfects Seattle's human rights laws." Only "legitimate" racial and religious minorities would be protected once the law was stripped of its reference to sexual orientation.[14]

Angevine and Kidd, accompanied by Falk and Estes, then walked the boxes of petitions across the street to the county elections department. There was no doubt the initiative would qualify for the ballot. Estes had easily hurdled his first obstacle.

Outside, gay and lesbian pickets carried signs saying "Save whose moral ethics?" and "Gay rights are equal rights." They delivered a mock counter-initiative, this one from DOME, Demand Obedience to Moral Ethics—pronounced "dumb," the counter-organizers said. Its text said that "No heterosexual male shall be deemed protected by any city ordinance preventing discrimination." The purpose, the organizers explained, was to show what could happen "when one group's religion, philosophy or morals are imposed by law upon the rest of us."[15]

Images are revealing. In political campaigns, entire philosophies have to compress to a single visual kernel, an eye-bite. Among the images that gays and lesbians in Seattle developed for their first major attempt at political persuasion were these:

SCAT adopted a triangle with equal-length sides, poised in tension with its point down and its wide base in the air. SCAT said the symbol echoed the pink triangles that the Nazis once assigned homosexuals to wear inside concentration camps. Inside the triangle, a dark, androgynous figure pressed its right elbow and hand against the walls while its left hand smashed through the imprisoning lines. "It represents liberation," SCAT said. In addition to gays and lesbians, the symbol was meant to appeal to those who might identify with the metaphor of struggle against oppression, be they feminists, labor union workers, or racial and ethnic minorities.[16]

WAT, the women's group, chose the symbol for the female, a circle sitting atop a cross. Inside the circle, the number thirteen carried a slash through it. Of all the logos, it was the most literal rendering of any organization's name, Women Against Thirteen. It was calculated to appeal to feminists.

Brydon's CRFE adopted an outlined keyhole with shadowy figures dressed as spies looking through the hole. CRFE's emphasis was not about struggle or feminism, but about anxiety and privacy. If the forces arrayed against gays were using fear as their chief weapon, then CRFE would employ fear of a different type, warning heterosexuals that the law they were being asked to remove also protected them. "Your privacy is at stake," the CRFE ads said, and sometimes they showed cameras leering into an otherwise peaceful family setting.

By the end of August, it was clear that Seattle's gays and lesbians would present no single unified image or message. Common wisdom suggested disaster.

To win, Estes's group, SOME, counted on carrying voters in North Seattle in heavy numbers. It was in those mostly white suburbs that the evangelical, fundamentalist, and Mormon churches had their strongest bases, and gays, their weakest influence. West Seattle offered a second possible SOME base. It was mostly white and working class and somewhat isolated from the rest of the city. For gays and lesbians, the best hope for voter support would come from the center of the city— the University District, Capitol Hill, Pioneer Square, downtown. Just how much strength gays could count on there would likely be influenced by the position taken by the Catholic archbishop—Capitol Hill was heavily Catholic as well as gay—and by other religious leaders, especially in the African American and Asian American communities just south of the hill.

Feminists and gay socialists had built some connections to those racial and ethnic communities through their interest in combating multiple "isms" and con-

# "But I'm Not Gay..."

How Initiative 13 Could Attack You

If Initiative 13 passes, **anyone** could be fired or evicted solely on the assumption or accusation of being gay. All someone has to do is think or say you are gay. The burden of proof then rests on you, the accused, rather than on the accuser.

You will be vulnerable if:
• You are single, divorced, or live alone
• You share your house or apartment with a friend
• You are not liked, or you speak up too much at work

## Vote No on 13

Paid for by Seattle Committee Against Thirteen, Stuart Leven, Treasurer

In their campaign against Initiative Thirteen in 1978, lesbian and gay activists disagreed over which would be the more effective rhetoric for mobilizing a favorable heterosexual vote. The Seattle Committee Against Thirteen, staffed by many who had been active in feminist and gay liberation groups, emphasized that the initiative was an attack on anyone who might be labeled homosexual. SCAT ads, left, used the word "gay" and showed

an icon of a human breaking out of the pink triangle that that Nazis had forced homosexual prisoners to wear during World War II. Charlie Brydon's Citizens to Retain Fair
Employment avoided the term "gay" and instead more cautiously emphasized that everyone's "privacy" was at stake. *(Northwest Lesbian and Gay History Museum Project)*

structing coalitions. But despite the proliferation of gay clubs and nonprofit organizations that had occurred by 1978, only the white tip of homosexuality in Seattle had visibly emerged to any degree. There was a danger that the racial and ethnic neighborhoods in the Central District and the Rainier Valley crucial to gay victory might split on Initiative Thirteen, particularly if they were convinced homosexuals were not a "legitimate minority" as Falk had begun saying.

Only by holding those central neighborhoods and avoiding too severe a defeat in the northern and western suburbs could gays hope to defeat the initiative.

A small group had already been at work educating members of the Church Council of Greater Seattle, which included representatives of many of Seattle's mainline Protestant and Catholic churches. Three years earlier, in 1975, Robert Sirico's petition for MCC membership in the council had forced a debate on gay and lesbian concerns, especially over the question of civil rights for homosexuals versus the morality of homosexuality. It was resolved by a council insistence that accepting the MCC did not mean it was endorsing homosexuality. Rather, the council simply recognized that the gay group met its definition of being a church and had a right to exist. In the following years, the council had formed a task force to study gay and lesbian concerns and the stances taken by its various member denominations.

When Estes had announced his drive for signatures, adding that he would make a "saturation appeal to the area's churches" to assist by circulating the petitions, the council had already learned enough to respond. It issued a statement saying that although churches were divided over theological issues, such as whether gays could be ordained as clergy, that "should not prevent the church from upholding the basic civil rights of Seattle's gay citizens." The council countered Estes's appeal by instead asking its members to actually forbid the circulation of the petitions in churches. "Let us not perpetuate the fear and hatred which this initiative invokes," it said.[17]

During the weeks of the campaign, the church council and its individual leaders spoke out repeatedly against the initiative. Two days before the vote, they joined a "pray-in" against the initiative that gathered two thousand people into Volunteer Park.

More surprisingly to gay activists, the evangelical Christian churches also remained lukewarm to Estes's appeal. Although the Seattle Association of Evangelicals explicitly rejected the church council's position that gays should not be discriminated against, the group issued a mild statement about Initiative Thirteen, calling on member churches to look to God in making their own decision rather than to the church council—or, for that matter, to Anita Bryant. "We will start with God," the association's president Ray Struthers said, "do our homework and then decide and act accordingly." He added, "For an evangelical, the first point of action is with his or her own shortcomings, not his neighbors'. Thus we need to ask ourselves: Have we abusively discriminated against gays?"[18]

That was far from the kind of attack rhetoric that had been heard in other cities.

Beyond religion, there was the law enforcement angle to be considered. Here too gays had particularly good fortune in Seattle. The reputation of the city police had not yet been fully repaired, and the spy rhetoric being deployed by CRFE tied neatly to yet another police scandal that reminded voters to be skeptical. After Police Chief Tielsch left, the city's newspapers had discovered in 1975 that the department's intelligence squad had built dossiers on prominent, law-abiding Seattle citizens. The intelligence squad had even spied on the U.S. attorney who had begun the federal investigation of the payoffs, Stan Pitkin, perhaps hoping to derail his cleanup—or so Pitkin thought. The *Seattle Times* had noted at the time that "police intelligence focused on the sex lives of prominent citizens and officials with police salting the information away in official files or in 'hip pocket' files kept by individual policemen." Police Chief Hanson had ordered the destruction of 730 files that he thought contained improper information that was, he said, "politically motivated or for intimidation."[19]

Although those particular revelations were old history by the time of Initiative Thirteen, as if on cue there were suddenly timely reminders of the police department's past wayward conduct. A civil lawsuit had been filed by a group calling itself the Coalition Against Government Spying, and during the spring and summer of 1978, the contents of some secret files that still existed began to be released and publicized as part of the discovery process. The *Seattle Times* reported in April that one of the best-known African American activists in the city, Larry Gossett, had been spied on; his file included details on a peaceful protest he had led in front of the newspaper offices. The police had also kept a file on Charlie Royer, the new mayor. Then in June came the news that a police lieutenant had shipped some of the files—thirty-seven hundred information cards with eighteen thousand names on them—to a law enforcement agency in California because he feared that Royer would have them seized or that information in them would be revealed because of the lawsuit. A judge ordered copies retained.[20]

The notion that government needed to be restrained from spying on its citizens fitted nicely with Charlie Brydon's theme of protecting privacy.

In the other cities that had voted, "morality" had always been an argument easily cornered by the anti-gay opponents. In Seattle, gays and lesbians would be able to create doubt about whether their opponents held any real corner on morality. The CRFE symbol of the keyhole captured that doubt.

On Tuesday, August 15, the King County Elections Department validated the number of signatures on Estes and Falk's petitions and sent them back to Angevine. The city council would now have to place the initiative on the November ballot. Four days later, on Saturday, August 19, the campaign took a tragic twist.

Falk was on patrol in the Rainier Valley, one of the ethnic neighborhoods south of Capitol Hill. Suddenly, his radio blurted information about a prowler and possible burglar, described as a twenty-five- to thirty-year-old black man. It was about

7 P.M., and the evening light still lingered when Falk arrived and spotted the suspect running from another officer. Falk sprang from his patrol car, chased the man into a backyard, and then yelled, "Stop or I'll shoot." He pulled his revolver.

Three years earlier, when Senator Pete Francis had relied on police support to reform the state's criminal code, he had left one part of the code undisturbed because the police chiefs had favored it: a state policy stipulating when officers could fire their weapons at suspects. The legislature had reenacted an old section that allowed officers to use deadly force to arrest suspects in many felony cases, such as burglaries, whether or not the officers themselves or other individuals were in any danger. That rule had already created serious frictions in Seattle. Mayor Royer disliked its broadness, so in spring 1978 he had convinced the city council to adopt a more restrictive rule for the city's police force. Officers could fire their guns only if a suspect was actually endangering someone's life or if they were in a "hot pursuit" immediately after the suspect had used a deadly weapon during a crime. The policy, although approved, was not to take effect until November 1. Just as Falk and Estes wanted to repeal the antidiscrimination ordinances, so the police guild, along with city council member Tim Hill, had placed a second initiative on the ballot: Initiative Fifteen, which sought a return to the previous regulation.

That created two flash points for minorities in Seattle: Initiative Thirteen for gays, lesbians, and feminist women worried about the transfer of powers from one city department to another, and Initiative Fifteen for African Americans worried about what sometimes appeared to be all-too-easy shootings of black citizens.

Dennis Falk was about to accidentally meld the two concerns into one.

Although Falk had no way of knowing it, John Alfred Rodney, the black man fleeing from him, was twenty-six years old and retarded. He had already spent five years in a state institution for the mentally retarded, as well as served jail time for burglary convictions. A sentencing report for one of those convictions had noted that Rodney had dropped out of school in the ninth grade and had the potential for only fourth grade skills.

Testimony at a later police inquest, presided over by Seattle District Court Judge Frank Sullivan, would establish that when Rodney entered people's houses that afternoon, he may have had no intention of robbing them. He may have simply not understood that he was supposed to knock before showing up in their hallways. He had apparently been roaming through yards and had entered two homes, then been asked to leave by the residents. One would testify that Rodney had asked to mow her lawn, then left after she said no. Another chased Rodney over a wall after finding him in a backyard. Police officer Ed Marcus had pursued Rodney for about a block on foot when Falk arrived.

After Falk called out, Rodney sprang up and perched momentarily on a board fence separating two backyards. Falk would say later that he warned Rodney four times to stop. He aimed his pistol and then fired. Hit in the heel, Rodney fell to the ground on the other side of the fence, then started running as best as he could.

Falk thought he had missed. He reached the board fence and fired through one of its openings. The second bullet struck Rodney in the back. It killed him.

Immediately, protests began. On the following Wednesday, August 23, sixty demonstrators marched on the police department's headquarters shouting "We want Falk! Put him in jail!" On September 1, the *Seattle Gay News* joined the critics, offering its condolences to the city's black community and then acidly writing in street rhyme, "Officer Falk, the leader of the Seattle bigots, 'kills with no pain like a dog on a chain.'"[21]

It was hardly an auspicious occurrence for one of the two major sponsors of Initiative Thirteen.

On September 9, by a four-to-two vote, the district court inquest jurors ruled that Falk believed a felony had been committed. He had the fleeing suspect in sight. All other reasonable means of apprehension—the requirement of the existing policy—seemed to have been exhausted. Falk had not done anything wrong.

African Americans were outraged. They picketed police headquarters and City Hall, shouting "Try Falk for Murder" and "Justice for John," while ministers, the most powerful leaders in Seattle's black community, denounced the shooting. The city's church council joined a group called Black United Clergy for Action in condemning the inquest decision as "morally unacceptable." Black clergymen demanded continuing courses in human rights for police officers and urged Falk's discharge. The police department announced it would pull him from patrol duty on the streets, a spokesman noting that there were concerns about the officer's personal safety.[22]

At the moment when the campaign was entering its final weeks, the city's gay and African American communities discovered a common ground that included not only theories about minority coalitions, but also a passion for them.

Meanwhile, signals on how the majority of Seattle's citizens might vote on Initiative Thirteen were mixed. A small story in the *Seattle Times,* published in late August just after the Rodney shooting, noted that Brydon's CRFE had released poll results that showed 66 percent of the city would vote to retain the civil rights laws—a two-to-one opposite of the vote that had occurred elsewhere. Optimistic though that sounded, two weeks later the *Seattle Sun* reported that 43 percent of the people CRFE had contacted had refused to answer any questions about gay rights at all, about twice the normal refusal rate for a poll. That cast doubt on how valid the survey was. Also a bit odd was that 40 percent of those who were willing to vote to retain the laws gave no reason for wanting to do so. Only about 14 percent cited a belief in gay civil rights; 17 percent simply said they did not think homosexuals posed any threat. It was hardly an impassioned or solid pro-gay sentiment.[23]

Also, Wayne Angevine, the now well-known gay city clerk, had decided to run for city council, only to be soundly trounced in the September primary. Angevine, in fourth place, had gotten only about forty-five hundred votes; the leader, incumbent Wayne Larkin, received more than twenty-one thousand. Trailing well behind in second place, with about ten thousand votes, was an African American bank executive named Norm Rice, who had taken strong stands in favor of gay rights. Leaders at SOME immediately snickered that the clout and size of Seattle's potential gay vote—which activists had estimated at fifty thousand—had been greatly exaggerated. Even the *Seattle Gay News* was disgusted. "Bend over Seattle gays," it editorialized, "because many should have their posteriors booted."[24]

Still, after the Rodney shooting, it was Estes who felt the pressure to recoup. Being put on the moral defensive was not part of the successful strategy that had enabled Cotterill and the Anti-Saloon League to manipulate Washington's initiative and referendum laws. Nor had any similar situation emerged during the anti-gay campaigns in Miami, St. Paul, or Eugene.

Falk began to lower his public profile as SOME co-chair. After the inquest, an African American named Wayne Perryman briefly emerged as the new SOME spokesman in what appeared to be an attempt to reclaim some moral ground. Perryman began to argue that, as a black, he knew what discrimination really meant, and the repeal of protection for sexual minorities was not discrimination.

As quickly as Perryman appeared, though, he disappeared, resigning and telling the *Seattle Sun* that leaders in the city's black community now felt that any association with SOME meant "that I also support Dennis Falk and his shooting of an unarmed black suspect."[25]

Galvanized by Rodney's death, African American leaders now had their own concerns not only about Initiative Fifteen, but about Thirteen as well. If women were upset that the Estes initiative would weaken the handling of discrimination claims brought by women, African American leaders realized that the city Human Rights Department, which investigated racial discrimination, was already overloaded and would be more burdened by adding discrimination against women to its caseload.

By proposing the repeal of the gay protections and at the same time shuffling the responsibility for who would handle the remaining discrimination complaints, Estes and Falk had erred by attacking three minorities at once—gays, women, and blacks.

Support for keeping the laws continued to accumulate. The city's top political and religious leaders were already on record. In early October, Local 174 of the Teamsters Union, with several thousand members, voted to oppose the initiative, the *Seattle Sun* wryly commenting that the union had not previously been known for its "tolerance of sexual minorities, nor union officials for their liberalism." And KIRO-TV, home to anti-gay commentator Lloyd Cooney, weighed in with a three-part series of news reports on Initiative Thirteen that even Jim Tully and Jim Arnold, the owners and editorialists at the *Seattle Gay News,* praised as "well-considered [and] carefully researched." (Cooney, on the other hand, continued to urge voters to pass the initiative.)[26]

Four weeks before the vote, SOME began to run out of money. Estes and Falk had raised and spent about fifty thousand dollars, one-fifth of it from Anita Bryant's Protect Our Children, and much of the rest from people living outside Seattle. Cash flow problems had become evident in the weeks after John Alfred Rodney was slain. SOME was paying a consultant forty-one hundred dollars a month, but from mid-September until mid-October, Estes and Falk raised only about fifty-six hundred dollars, leaving no money to pay for the last-minute media blitzes about homosexuals molesting children that had worked so well in other cities.

By contrast, the three organizations opposing Initiative Thirteen had gathered forty-five thousand dollars during the same one-month period, mostly from Seattle donors. By the end of the campaign, WAT and SCAT had collected a total of fifty thousand dollars, and CRFE had passed the hundred thousand dollar mark.[27] For a change, thanks to their appeal to very different segments of the voters, the last-minute media barrage belonged to the pro-gay activists. CRFE canvassed swing precincts and hit radio and TV with its keyhole message. SCAT and WAT emphasized person-to-person contact, doorbelling in neighborhoods, posting sentries at major intersections throughout town, raising banners along freeways, and buying ads on the sides of city buses. Their slogan, "Someone you know is gay," emphasized making gays and lesbians visible, rather than making them private.

Suddenly the division in political strategy and organizing began to seem constructive. There could be—indeed, had to be—more than one political dance floor in town. CRFE could organize particular types of people with its appeals. It could raise thousands of dollars at low-key dinner parties. It could avoid using "gay" or "homosexual" in its ads. SCAT and WAT, on the other hand, could hold highly public fund-raising events designed to raise the gay profile—a Halloween dance at the Seattle Aquarium, beer parties at taverns, roller-skating evenings. The money cleared might be minimal, but the excitement generated among potential volunteers was electric. Those volunteers then canvassed neighborhoods all over Seattle.

Perhaps to everyone's surprise, even the messages telegraphed to the larger heterosexual electorate did not have to be precisely the same. What seemed to matter more was that they were assertive rather than defensive and passionate rather than coolly controlled. There was also another hidden card in Seattle. One observer described it this way to the *Seattle Sun:* "One old man in the Pike Place Market said he hadn't decided what he thinks about 'the gays.' Told that a 'no' vote would keep things the way they are, though, he said, 'Well then, I'll vote against it.'"[28]

On the evening of November 7, a typically drizzly night in Seattle, Charlie Brydon's troops gathered inside a cavernous ballroom at the Eagles Hall on Seventh Avenue and Union Street in downtown Seattle to await the results. It was an appropriate place. The Eagles were a fraternal organization that John Considine had helped to create once he had succeeded in vaudeville at the old underground People's Theater.

A few blocks away at Pike Place Market, SCAT and WAT assembled two thou-

Marchers take to the streets to celebrate the victory against Initiative Thirteen, November 1978. *(Doug Barnes, Freedom Socialist Party)*

sand followers in the streets and passed out candles with tiny cup covers to protect the flames from the wind and sprinkle. In North Seattle, about thirty of Estes and Falk's supporters met at a restaurant.

The absentee ballot results came in first. Conventional thinking held they would be the most conservative and anti-gay. But the absentees in West Seattle had voted to oppose the repeal—just by a narrow twenty votes, but it was a hopeful sign. In North Seattle, the absentees refused the initiative by twenty-two votes. After 8 P.M., the tallies started in earnest and the trend soon became clear. In the north Seattle suburbs, the battle had been more pitched than SOME could afford if it hoped to win—49.5 percent for the initiative, 50.5 percent against. In West Seattle, almost the same numbers, Estes and Falk again narrowly losing 48 percent to 52 percent. Along the southern edge of the city, the results grew even bleaker for SOME. The initiative was being defeated there three to two.

Other good news for Seattle's gays and lesbians began arriving. The statewide initiative against homosexual teachers in California was losing. Norm Rice, the supportive black leader, was being elected to the city council. And Mike Lowry, a King County Council member who had always supported funding for the gay counseling service, was unseating Jack Cunningham. By a large margin of some nine thousand votes, Lowry would become Capitol Hill's new congressional representative.

The central city finally turned the night into a SOME rout. Ballard, Wallingford, Queen Anne, and Magnolia voted 64 percent to 36 percent to keep the civil rights laws as they were. On Capitol Hill and in the University District, the count soared to 76 percent in favor of the laws. Only a single precinct out of 163 on Capitol Hill and in the University District voted in Estes's favor—and that by only two votes. Finally, in the heavily racial and ethnic neighborhoods of the Central District, 77 percent voted to keep the laws as they were. Not a single precinct there voted in Estes's favor.

The prohibitionists' strategy of using initiatives and referendums to play on anxieties about morality had stunningly crashed. The final vote was 64,225 for the Estes proposal and 108,124 against it.

That night, the two thousand marchers that WAT and SCAT had assembled paraded across Arthur Denny's knoll and circled the downtown Olympic Hotel where the press had posted its election-night watch. In a sea of twinkling candles, they chanted "Thank you Seattle, thank you Seattle, thank you Seattle." At the Eagles hall, lesbian and gay couples spread across the dance floor. "It was jammed," Brydon remembered. "Jammed to the gills."

The *Seattle Gay News* sang: "We have proven that we can win an electoral battle; we have broken the charge of the bigots."[29] The lesbian and gay role in the city's political conversation had finally been secured.

# 15

# On Broadway

## Creating Markets and Parades

*O*n the November evening in 1978 when Initiative Thirteen was defeated, Jan Denali, the woman who sang with LesBeFriends and worked at the Little Bread collective, walked with the other SCAT and WAT marchers weaving through the drizzle on the streets of downtown Seattle. Denali led a quiet rhythm of victory, singing "Let us be like drops of water, falling on the stone." Like many other gay liberation and lesbian feminists of the 1970s, Denali continued her political work into the 1980s. She too would become one of those lesbians who decided to create a new kind of family, linking with a gay male activist she met during the Initiative Thirteen campaign to birth and parent a child. Denali would play another critical role in 1986, when, in a small replay of the Initiative Thirteen issue, conservatives launched a referendum to overturn a decision by the King County Council to adopt a similar job-protection law for the unincorporated areas around the city. Denali joined a grassroots effort to defeat the referendum before it ever got on the ballot, becoming one of the plaintiffs in a lawsuit that persuaded the court to strike the petitions because of their misleading rhetoric.

In the 1980s, Denali could still be found on the slopes of Renton Hill, but by then she had launched a new brand of gay political work, a kind of evolution from the old experiences at the women's coffeehouse, the Coffee Coven. Here's what she told a passerby one day: "My well-developed palate for coffee was important. What I particularly had to learn was how to operate the equipment. I've become an expert foam maker. You know, you have to foam up the milk."

Denali had opened an espresso cart from which she dispensed lattes, cappuccinos, and mochas—as well as a Postum latte for those avoiding caffeine. "Everyone has their very special way they want their coffee made," she told the *Seattle Gay News*. Denali named her cart "Espress Yourself," and in front of a Thriftway supermarket she joined another aspect of Seattle's gay life: an openly homosexual business entrepreneur operating in a new time and a new marketplace.[1]

In the mid-1970s, a President's Advisory Council on Minority Business Enterprises had observed that power in American society largely results from control over economic resources. Minorities, it had added, needed to claim that power.[2] While the council had in mind spreading economic power to racial and ethnic groups, the maxim also applied to the wave of gays and lesbians now choosing public visibility in Seattle. The defeat of Initiative Thirteen had produced a climax for their political coming out. Although similar electoral battles erupted in subsequent decades—the one over the King County ordinance in the 1980s, for example, and another over a statewide initiative to overturn city civil rights laws in the 1990s—the foundation for visibly engaging in Seattle's political conversation had largely been laid by the end of the 1970s.

A separate, troublesome problem still needed to be dealt with.

While a political crisis could prompt outpourings of volunteer time and money, on a day-to-day basis the city's homosexuals formed only a nascent community with almost no visible economic infrastructure at the end of the 1970s. The business underpinnings were meagerly limited to the gay and lesbian bars and sex businesses that inhabited Pioneer Square and to a small Capitol Hill corridor, also of bars and baths, that had begun to stretch up along Pike and Pine Streets. Agencies like the counseling service, Stonewall, the Gay Community Center, and the Lesbian Resource Center depended on friendly funding from government agencies or supportive heterosexual groups, such as the YWCA. The disappearance of that funding, as a result of either bigotry or budget cutting, often spelled demise. Both the original Stonewall and, eventually, the Gay Community Center, met that fate, and the LRC and the counseling service came quite close when the federal government, under President Reagan, ended a jobs program that had provided salaries for staff members.[3] Although the feminist and radical politics of the 1970s had added a few gay-friendly bookstores and food co-ops to the business network, as a group Seattle's homosexuals were largely without any reliable network of independent wealth.

It was not that homosexuals as individuals necessarily lacked money. Compared with other more impoverished groups, gay men and women sometimes seemed a golden minority, assumed to be free of the financial burden of supporting a family. To some extent, the glitter that others saw came from the prejudice of defining homosexuality as limited to white middle-class males, conveniently ignoring working-class and poverty-stricken gays and lesbians. Yet it was true that being in the closet could protect wallets as well as identities, and that was just the problem. Even if wealth were present among individuals, the money would do little good if it stayed hidden. One academic who had studied economic development in minority communities, Ivan Light, would argue during the 1980s that those groups that fared best developed their own entrepreneurs who felt, he said, "embedded" in supporting the community. Such business owners, he argued, would actively participate in a web where they exchanged information and supported community goals. In turn, the community members would consciously "buy Korean" or "buy Japanese" or "buy gay." Together, the entrepreneurs and the consumers could promote social change through business.[4]

The challenge, then, was to become a public community of commerce as well as a community of dance, social service, and political activism.

Four developments had to occur, each a particular sort of communication. First, there had to be more openly gay and lesbian entrepreneurs ready to engage in their own businesses or professions. That way the term "gay business" could symbolize much more than bars or bathhouses. Second, those entrepreneurs needed structures for sharing information with one another. They needed a kind of Rotary or chamber of commerce. Third, if they were going to return some of the profits to the community, they needed a way to redistribute the money through a clearinghouse that would fund worthwhile projects. Finally, there needed to be a geographic gay business center that most definitely was not tied to the nighttime red-light district. Instead, it needed to be a place where both homosexuals and heterosexuals could feel comfortable shopping either day or night.

Those four networks of communication were valuable economic resources in themselves—perhaps the most critical that a minority could gain.

In the 1980s, gays and lesbians in Seattle—Jan Denali and other activists among them—began to enter the world of commerce in a public manner as never before, either as very visible consumers or as newly out corporate executives and small-business owners. The international business magazine the *Economist* noted the rise of what it called a new "homosexual economy" by 1981. The *Seattle Post-Intelligencer* publicized the increasingly significant role gays and lesbians were playing in business in a small article on its business page in 1984. Three years later, the *Advocate* was trumpeting the "surprising health of gay businesses." Even the *Wall Street Journal* took note of the change by the early 1990s.[5] It was not just the allure of cash, but the appeal of creating another territory in the civic discourse where an imaginative new part of the story of being homosexual could be lived.

That seemed especially true of the small-business owners. "To be an openly gay entrepreneur is to make a political statement in this society," a spokesman for the National Gay and Lesbian Task Force in Washington, D.C., told the *Journal*.

Indeed, to create small shops where customers who were both straight and openly gay or lesbian mingled in the ritual of trading was a way of altering the city's social geography.

In the 1960s, Seattle's dozen or so gay bar and bath owners had formed their own loose network called the Queen City Business Guild. They traded information and gossip, but their numbers were too few and perhaps they were too much in direct competition in a narrow market for the guild to become very influential. MacIver Wells, for one, did not remember the group doing much in its early years—although after Wells left Seattle, the guild became somewhat more active. It supported the creation of the city's Imperial Court of drag queens, which in turn organized drag performances and charity fund raising drives. In the 1970s, it assisted the Gay Community Center in developing a gay campground located in the Cascade mountains and became known for its annual social picnics, one of which—in 1977—attracted an estimated 450 men and women to the Cascade land and gave the new resort, called Triangle Recreation Camp, a huge boost. A grand piano and hundreds of gallons of beer kept the picnickers happy, if a little dazed.[6] But the event was more an extension of the bar than the creation of something new.

In spring 1981, about a dozen gay business owners gathered at a new restaurant called The City, next to Ken Decker's Brass Door Disco at Pike Street and Harvard Avenue. There they planned a new kind of association. Stan Hill, who was then opening a gay-friendly gym called the Body Nautilus just up the street from the disco, described one problem they hoped to solve: "Most gay people, when given the choice, would rather patronize a gay-owned or oriented business, but their knowledge of these businesses is limited." By June, the group had incorporated as the Greater Seattle Business Association, collected $825 in dues from thirty-three charter members, and elected a nine-person board—all men. Its first task was to produce a directory of gay businesses, which it did by the end of the year. That would get the word out to gay consumers.[7]

Although gay and lesbian businesses were spread throughout Seattle, the notion of a business territory would play an important role both in the evolution of the new infrastructure and in its visibility. There were a number of candidates for a new territory, for example the Pike-Pine corridor that had already begun to develop gay bars, the small business district at Fifteenth Avenue and John that separated the Renton and Capitol summits, or the Madison corridor as it crossed Renton Hill. There was also one other: Capitol Hill's main north-south commercial district along Broadway Avenue. What eventually determined the choice was the same clash of interests on Capitol Hill that had marked the demise of gay space on Renton Hill—the battle between urban developers and North Capitol Hill homeowners. Only this time, instead of encouraging the decline of a gay territory, the outcome opened the way for one.

The best way to understand what happened is to first envision Broadway. In 1977, the *Post-Intelligencer* described it as a "Main Street USA" with stores that looked "as though they've been transplanted from some small town."[8] Heading north from Pike Street, a pedestrian would first pass the old Broadway High School, which was being replaced by a campus for Seattle Central Community College. Beyond a car parts shop was a country-corner post office that the federal government hoped to expand into a major distribution center with parking lots and an expansive warehouse. Next came the deteriorating neighborhood movie theater, and, about midway on the walk through the commercial zone, a bowling alley, a pharmacy with an old-fashioned soda counter, and small grocery stores that sometimes delivered to the doorsteps of the neighboring homes. Between Harrison and Republican Streets was one of the monuments of the district, the block-long Broadway Market, built in 1928 as a neighborhood version of the larger Pike Place Market downtown. Farmers and artisans had once sold their wares to city dwellers there, but the market's heyday was definitely past by the 1970s and it had been taken over by the Fred Meyer discount chain. In the next block north, two chain supermarkets, Safeway and QFC, stood on opposite ends of the block, both in rather small buildings with little parking. About three-quarters of a mile north of Pike, where Broadway intersects Roy Street, Doreen DeCaro's Elite Tavern marked the northern edge of the commercial zone. The Elite, still heterosexual at the time, was the epitome of the neighborhood pub, and its owner, Doreen, the epitome of the neighborhood tavern owner. A 1976 article about her in the *Seattle Sun* noted that she knew 98 percent of her regulars by name and that people often dropped by just to show her photographs, comment on her kitchen wallpaper, or, at an occasional wild party, dance with her on the pool table. "You're not dealing in beer," she had told the *Sun*. "You're dealing in people."[9]

Broadway had felt the impact of increased gay visibility almost as soon as Renton Hill started to turn into a public gay space in the early 1970s. A male clothing store called Peter's on Broadway operated from 1966 until 1977, advertising "beautiful clothing for beautiful people." A fashion store called the Gay Bull opened, then vanished. Broadway had also acknowledged gay liberation and feminism at least slightly. For example, an alternative bookstore named the Different Drummer, located across the street from the Broadway Market, added a small section of gay and lesbian books onto its cluttered shelves of political titles—enough to get its clerks harassed by straight teenagers in the neighborhood.

Neighborly though it was in the 1960s and 1970s, Broadway also faced trouble. Some of the small, aging businesses had begun shutting, and crime had begun to rise. The Capitol Hill Chamber of Commerce blamed Broadway's lot sizes—nineteenth-century plats too small to support the kind of automobile-oriented shopping malls then stealing business from the neighborhoods. Some lots ran only ninety feet deep, half the distance between Broadway and the streets paralleling on either side. Behind many of the businesses were houses or small garden apartments, rather than the parking lots that could appease car-oriented shoppers. The answer, the developers figured, lay in expanding the commercial zone so that Broadway businesses could fill in the full two blocks on either side. That way, both Safeway and QFC could build large parking lots. The post office could expand.

The community council dominated by homeowners had other dreams, and, as had happened on Renton Hill, a clash between it and the developers in the local chamber was certain. Broadway, it argued, should remain oriented to pedestrians. Suburban stores with parking lots belonged in the suburbs. At first, the battle looked like a losing one for the homeowners. Thirty-five small businesses had already shut down in the previous two decades. But the council and other ad hoc activist groups soon launched a brisk fight that, at one point in 1970, included leaping in front of bulldozers and, later, temporarily taking over the vacant lot that Safeway wanted for parking and using it as a Berkeley-style People's Park with picnic tables and a huge sandbox.

The homeowners won some skirmishes and lost others. A decade later, in the Elite's block at the north end, most of the storefronts remained. A block south, the grocery chains won, expanding sideways and adding their parking lots. Another block south, the storefronts returned, along with a restored Broadway Market, once again a bazaar of small stores and vending carts. The same storefront pattern continued for the next several blocks—with an occasional drive-in parking lot marking a community council defeat or compromise. But largely the homeowners won, their greatest achievement being to convince the city by the late 1970s to emphasize Broadway as a pedestrian-oriented commercial zone, exempting its businesses from a city requirement for off-street parking. Broadway instead would become what an architecture critic for the *Seattle Times* called an Italian *passeggiata*—a kind of busy public plaza stretched horizontally.[10]

The change occurred rapidly, primarily between 1977 and 1980. Two years after the *Post-Intelligencer* had described Broadway as "Main Street USA," suddenly shops were selling Cuisinart food processors, and restaurants were decorating themselves with hanging ferns. The street began to glitter—in fact, a bit too much for some in the neighborhood. "No one simply walks into the Broadway bars," writer James Thayer noted in the *Seattle Times* in 1980. "They make appearances. Men commonly pause just inside the door—and, like Clark Gable, run a finger along the mustache while scanning the room with amused skepticism. Women plunge into the crowd, heads demurely low, knowing they will be stopped before they rebound off the wall."[11] It was a heterosexual description, of course, because Broadway's first renaissance—or perhaps it would be better called a carnival—was as adamantly heterosexual as it was homosexual.

Some gay and lesbian activists resented the change. Jane Meyerding, for example, had this to say in *Out and About* in March 1978: "The rich white pricks are trying to move lesbians and other poor women and men out of Seattle. . . . Take Monkey Shines on the corner of Broadway and John, which used to be the Congo Room, a restaurant where dykes worked and ate. Since it has become Monkeys, dykes don't work there, most can't afford to eat there, and dykes don't always get seated there." Another group tossed paint at the new restaurants one night, and then left a note saying, "Good Morning Fat Cats: The paint on your establishment is a protest against your rich white intrusion into this poor, multiracial community of Capitol Hill. We are just a few of many pissed off residents who resent having expensive eating places dangled in front of our noses. Food is essential to survival and eating is a human right. By putting this out of reach of the poor and common working folks, you have turned this right into a privilege."[12]

Other gays and lesbians instead helped accelerate the changes. One of the first signs of the new movement onto Broadway by gay entrepreneurs was, perhaps appropriately, the establishment of the district's first neighborhood gay bar. In 1979, Alex Veltri bought the Elite from Doreen DeCaro. Veltri had been bartending and managing at the old gay Columbus Tavern on Washington Street just across from the old Casino. "Broadway was having a tough time," Veltri would tell the *Seattle Gay News* later. "They were thinking it was going to die and the neighborhood would become a ghetto of some kind." Quickly, the Elite began to help change that trend by drawing the gay men who wanted to drink at a neighborhood tavern onto Broadway—and it did it so successfully that Veltri would eventually open an Elite 2 on John Street, a block off Broadway, and an Encore restaurant and bar nearby on Eleventh Avenue. In 1991, he would even receive a Mayor's Small Business Award for his efforts in neighborhood development.[13]

In 1982, Barbara Bailey became one of the first lesbian entrepreneurs on Broadway, opening a new bookstore next to the since-abandoned Different Drummer site. Like the Drummer, her store was well stocked with lesbian and gay titles; unlike the Drummer, it was well lit, modern, smartly attired, and upscale— a bookstore anybody in the neighborhood would be likely to frequent, not just its political activists.[14] Across the street, smaller gay- and lesbian-owned businesses moved into vending carts at a renovated Broadway Market; one, called the Pink Zone, specialized in buttons marked with rainbows—then emerging as the cheerful gay symbol of the 1980s, replacing the older political symbol of the 1970s, the pink triangle that had been worn by gay prisoners in Nazi concentration camps. The Pink Zone would prove so successful it would eventually claim a storefront on Broadway itself. Meanwhile, old-fashioned neighborhood cafes, like a greasy scrambled-egg house called Andy's, mutated into gay-owned urban bistros. Businesses that were not gay-owned knew enough to become gay-sensitive—when a chain bookstore, Crown, opened on the street for a few years, it quickly learned to stock its shelves with gay and lesbian books seldom seen in its suburban outlets. By the end of the 1980s, the new gay commercial zone formed a T-shape, the stores along the north-south Broadway connecting with the gay bars and discos that had relocated into the east-west corridor along Pike and Pine Streets.

Significantly, Broadway never became a Castro Street, where gay outlets seemed to dominate. What happened on Broadway was an integration of styles and sexual sensitivities, a mingling that created a mixed marketplace. Perhaps the difference was just because of numbers—the gay community in Seattle was smaller than that in San Francisco and possibly could not launch a complete takeover of a commercial district. Perhaps too it was timing. Broadway emerged as a gay public space in the 1980s, not the excited Stonewall '70s. More likely, it may just be that no one, least of all Seattle's gay and lesbian entrepreneurs, really wanted the intensity of a Castro in the Northwest. The preferred pattern in Seattle seemed to be one of interweaving.

In 1980, in an article noting the boom of gay businesses on Capitol Hill, a writer for the *Seattle Gay News* carefully noted: "All of the people I talked to made a distinct point of being certain that their business was not to be labeled an exclusively gay establishment. The common feeling was that the gay and straight community could come together . . . to enjoy whatever is available with no overriding concern of one's sexuality."[15]

While the new territory was being claimed, the gay Greater Seattle Business Association continued to grow, providing the necessary organizational communication to "embed" gay business owners in a community wherever their businesses happened to be located—Broadway or not. By the end of its second year, its membership had increased fivefold, to about 150, and it began to seek a more active role. In addition to publishing its annual directory of gay and lesbian businesses, the association assumed some of the Dorian Group's functions, sponsoring monthly luncheons with politicians and other notables and crafting new ideas, such as sponsoring a gay business institute to provide training for new entrepreneurs.

To some in the community, in fact, its visibility was becoming an irritant.

The GSBA clearly was a capitalist entry into the gay world, in a city where trade unionism and socialist feminism had powerful roots among those who were activists. In San Francisco, the Golden Gate Business Association—which had been founded in 1975 and had grown to more than five hundred members by the time Seattle's version was organized—had already become a target of such activists. While buying gay made sense, forming a business association seemed to be pandering to the existing economic order rather than working to change that order.

Could capitalist gay entrepreneurs and socialist gay activists really create a common agenda in Seattle? For a while, the answer seemed to be no.

The flash point came on March 10, 1982, about a year after the founding of the GSBA, when its president, Stan Hill, suddenly announced that the association had decided to organize that summer's gay pride march commemorating the Stonewall riot. If that happened, it would be a symbolic coup—for the association, but against the more political activists.

The public celebrations of the Stonewall anniversary had begun in Seattle in 1973, at first with a small gay music festival at the Russian Center on Renton Hill and a potluck picnic in the arboretum, sponsored by U.W. gay students. The event had grown slowly. In 1974, there had been a rally in a vacant lot next to the counseling service's home on Sixteenth Avenue. Gay socialist activist Patrick Haggerty had sung selections from his album of gay music, *Lavender Country*, and Katherine Bourne, also a socialist activist, had read poetry. That night, at Occidental Park on the mudflat, another rally had been held; socialist feminist Cindy Gipple had played drums to provide music. In 1975 the event expanded, with a gay wedding between two men at a Capitol Hill church, a lesbians-only picnic at Woodland Park, a lawn festival at Volunteer Park, a street dance at Occidental Park, and a rally at Seattle Center. In 1976, more expansion: Radical Women panels, a champagne boogie at Shelly's Leg, a picnic at Volunteer Park, another rally at Seattle Center.

Then, in 1977, the public walks down the city streets had begun, that first one moving from Occidental Park to Westlake Center in the heart of downtown. The *Seattle Post-Intelligencer* headline had called it a "march." One *Seattle Times* article referred to it as a "parade." That difference in terms became the center of the contest between the new gay and lesbian business owners and the political activists.[16]

For the activists, "marching" meant asserting political visibility and demand-

Small rallies in honor of the Stonewall riot began in 1974, but in 1977, lesbians and gays took to Seattle's streets, demanding more civil rights protection. Here, gay liberationists from the Washington Coalition for Sexual Minority Rights, the Union of Sexual Minorities, and Radical Women march along First Avenue from Occidental Park to Westlake. *(Doug Barnes, Freedom Socialist Party)*

ing civil rights. Those who were socialists or feminists also saw it as a way to declare support for a variety of issues, such as the right to an abortion, or to labor organizing, or to economic reforms to help racial and ethnic minorities. The siting of such a march was part of its symbolic communication. Walking downtown signaled a confrontation with the established order, demands on city hall, and visibility to the heterosexual shoppers in the city's retail core.

Other gays and lesbians were more interested in "parading"—celebrating the visibility that had already been won, entertaining, listening to music that was not political, creating floats, and including corporate sponsors such as the beer companies that sold to the gay bars.

When Stan Hill made his declaration in 1982, he seemed to be saying that the businessmen wanted to control what had become the most public of gay and lesbian symbols.

In 1980 the Dorian Group had temporarily seized the organization of the march, announced that the theme would be "Celebration," and then moved it to Broadway—sacrificing, some activists argued, all of the political symbolism that even Dorian stood for. After all, who was there to protest against on Broadway? That first foray into what would become the gay commercial center had been a

By 1980, the lesbian/gay pride "march" had begun to evolve into one of the city's largest public celebrations and "parades." It would move to Capitol Hill. (*Geoff Manasse*)

tentative one. Marchers had assembled at Pine Street and Broadway next to Seattle Central Community College, walked three blocks north—not even making it as far as the Broadway Market—and then had veered away to Twelfth Avenue, finally ending at Volunteer Park north of the commercial district. At the rally that followed, and in the gay press coverage in succeeding weeks, the divisions of opinion about what the march or parade should be surfaced with such a vengeance that the Dorian Group abandoned its organizing role the following year.[17]

For a while, it looked like there might not even be a 1981 march, but five weeks before the usual date, a loose confederation of the more radical activists formed around the name Stonewall '81. They quickly secured a city permit, returned the march downtown, and strengthened its political intent by choosing a route that ran from the federal courthouse to Pioneer Square. Pointedly, the walk that year was called the "Lesbian/Gay Freedom March." This time, the complaints went the other way. One gay man said he was shut out when he tried to carry a "Gays Against Abortion" sign, since the organizers were promoting women's right to abortion. Other gay men and women bedecked a float with American flags to disassociate themselves from the socialists marching at the front of the column. One of the flag float's organizers, Dennis O'Muhundro, was the owner of a gay tavern, Daddy's. He was also a founder of the GSBA.[18]

Hill's announcement in March 1982 was a preemptive strike by the gay business owners, including O'Muhundro. If nothing else, it served notice that the GSBA was willing to flex muscle and tell the political activists what kind of community image the business owners now wanted in the wake of Initiative Thirteen. Not only did the newly visible entrepreneurs intend to take the march away from the old-line activists, they announced a bit of revisionist history as well. The 1982 celebration, Hill said, would not be the Annual Seattle Lesbian/Gay Pride March. Instead, it would be called, "Celebration—The First Northwest Lesbian/Gay Pride Parade." And, Hill added, the parade would occur on Broadway, not in downtown Seattle. The steering committee included O'Muhundro.

Hill rationalized the intervention by saying the GSBA would pick up the tab for the parade, one of its earliest promises of money to be redistributed to the community. But for the first time, he also said, entry forms would be required for those wanting to join, and a charge would be attached—five dollars for nonprofit organizations and ten dollars for businesses.

The political activists were livid. Su Docekal, a longtime socialist feminist and member of the Stonewall Committee (formed from activists who had organized the 1981 march), told the Seattle Gay News that she was "appalled at the sheer arrogance of the GSBA." She called the business operators "self-appointed leaders," denounced their "gall," accused them of trying to delude gays and lesbians into thinking their political struggles were over, and urged others to create something more than a "Mardi Gras parade." It was as bitter a split as had occurred in 1978 when the Dorian Group had failed to endorse the walk because of the pending vote on Initiative Thirteen. For a while, it seemed there might be two separate events—a parade for the business group and a march for the gay activists.

The Stonewall Committee issued a call to an organizing meeting, passing out fliers in the bars that read: "We can have more than just a mardi gras—let's celebrate with outspoken resistance to Reaganomics and the right wing. Lesbian/Gay Pride Week is the time to publicly defend our civil rights and to show solidarity with all the oppressed in our common fight for social justice." When the flier arrived at O'Muhundro's bar, he calmly replied, "It's good to see people getting together to celebrate. They're [the Stonewall Committee] using another means to get people involved who might not otherwise participate." It was a businessman's approach—all customers welcome. But, as his phrasing showed, he still intended the theme to be celebration, not protest.

Stonewall members were less generous. One told the *Seattle Gay News* that what GSBA had done "is an insult to the community. What they want is what is good for business and that can be treacherous for the gay movement."

Despite the feud, those who attended Stonewall's organizing meetings quickly decided that sponsoring a competing march would be even more harmful than agreeing to the business group's plans. The GSBA had outflanked them by moving early, and, after all, the businessmen had the money. The activists instead decided to swallow at least some of their anger and enter a political contingent in the parade. With about fifty people, it was the largest of the groups, its participants marching—not parading—behind a somewhat tongue-in-cheek banner that said, "Celebrate lesbian/gay resistance to the right wing." Even the *Seattle Gay News,* committed though it had been to forceful political activism, surrendered that year and in its headlines continually referred to the event as a "parade" rather than a "march."[19]

That year, for the first time, the parade proceeded the full length of Broadway's commercial district—an affirmation of the emerging importance of the new business zone.

The battle over parade versus march seesawed for two more years until the struggle peaked predictably. Two separate events were held in 1984—a parade on Broadway on Saturday, and a political march beginning in the Central District and moving to Volunteer Park on Sunday. That, finally, seemed to exhaust everyone.

In 1985, a blunt-talking lesbian street activist named Carol Sterling joined a member of the GSBA, Larry Lefler, to co-chair a single event named the Lesbian/Gay Parade March and Freedom Rally. It was a Denny/Maynard–style compromise, as rhetorically cumbersome as navigating the peculiarly angled streets the two original pioneers had platted and joined at the Deadline, but like that skew, worth the trouble if it meant harmony. The walk settled regularly onto Broadway, adding even more heavily to the street's new role as the center of Seattle's gay community. In 1992 the name became even more cumbersome, but more inclusive of the city's various sexual minorities, with a retitling: the Lesbian/Gay/Bisexual/

Transgender Pride Parade/March and Freedom Rally. Many people seemed to give up the old battles and just started calling it the Pride Parade.[20]

By then, everyone from beer companies to floral shops to the police and fire departments had entries, and mayors and politicians, rather than being the targets of the civil rights marches, would be walking in them, just a few spots back from the bare-breasted dykes on motorbikes who always led.

In 1986, the GSBA took another step to solidify the community's economic structure, establishing a new philanthropic organization called the Pride Foundation. The idea was to gather money and estates from lesbians and gays and then redistribute the wealth to the community's nonprofit organizations. One of the foundation's early presidents likened it to a "Gay United Way," saying its intent was to break "the cycle of money made, money spent, and money gone." To ensure that competition for the money would not aggravate the still-existing splits between gay men and women, the foundation decided to target one-third of its gifts to nonprofits serving lesbians, one-third to those for men, and the final third to those helping both.[21]

The idea had been tested in San Francisco, where the local gay business group had created its own philanthropic arm years earlier, but the question was whether the model could actually succeed outside that mecca in a community much smaller and presumably more limited in wealth. It was a bit like Arthur Denny's decision to help create a bank in Seattle rather than continue to rely on financiers outside the little village—even though at the time Seattle had precious little indigenous cash. Like the Dexter Horton Bank, begun more on the reputation of its owners than on the size of its cash reserves, the Pride Foundation started small, mostly by securing a board of directors whose members agreed to pledge free time and $250 a year each. It also spread its money-gathering net by forming an advisory board whose members did not have to commit as much time, but agreed to contribute $1,000 each.

Seattle's gay community had not been entirely without such philanthropy. In the early 1970s, when the first Gay Community Center had folded, some of its organizers had formed Gay Community Social Services, which initially bought land on the Olympic Peninsula for gays wanting a rural retreat. When arsonists burned the retreat, the land was sold and GCSS used the money to catalyze gay theater groups and even a national magazine for rural lesbians and gays called *RFD*. Often, GCSS served as a kind of entrepreneur, allowing other groups to grow under its nonprofit status until they were ready for independence, but GCSS had never taken as aggressive an approach to raising and investing capital as the businessmen starting the Pride Foundation. Also, GCSS had always been linked to the gay liberationists, rather than to the gay business community, which meant it had less access to effective fund-raising.

In retrospect, the Pride Foundation's first grants seem terribly small—about three hundred dollars each to eight organizations in 1987. The Lesbian Resource Center got help to build a wheelchair ramp; the Seattle Counseling Service, money for electrical repairs and a new brochure. Another group used its grant to rent a meeting space. But it was the symbol of gays raising and then distributing money that counted. By 1988, the Pride Foundation's assets climbed dramatically. One of its organizers, Allan Tonning, was an entrepreneur successful at starting and selling a number of small businesses. When he died, he bequeathed one million dollars to the foundation he had helped start, at the time perhaps the largest sum ever left to a gay organization. The same year, the foundation received another hundred thousand dollars from a former city employee who had been largely unknown in the lesbian and gay community. In life, the man had chosen privacy; in death, he wanted to help fight back.

By 1988, the foundation had talked its way into becoming one of the charities recognized by the United Way. Gays and lesbians were now able to designate it on a payroll deduction form. And by 1990, it had contracted with a bank to issue a Pride Foundation MasterCard—the first successful attempt to do so by a lesbian/gay organization. Every credit card purchase meant a few extra pennies or dollars.

The system of tapping into the lesbian and gay community's own wealth and earning power—and then channeling it back to the gay charities that needed the money—had begun to work.

In the early 1990s, the GSBA staged an annual business fair in the Broadway Market, inviting its members to staff booths and talk to passersby about their products and services. One day, a story in the *Seattle Times* reported, a pair of middle-aged women wandered into the fair and began talking to each other. One said quietly to the other, "I didn't realize so many of these people were in business."[22]

That realization that so many publicly out gays and lesbians had become a part of the business world was yet another opening in the civic conversation about homosexual identity. A scholar on city planning, Manuel Castells, once studied the visible gay business structure in San Francisco and reached a conclusion that also applies to Seattle. In gay business districts, he wrote, "We are in a merchant world and in a world of urban freedom."

"We are almost," he added, "in the world of the Renaissance city where political freedom, economic exchange, and cultural innovation, as well as open sexuality, developed together in a self-reinforcing process on the basis of a common space won by citizens struggling for their freedom."[23]

In Seattle, Broadway had become that common space.

# 16
# On Catholic Hill

## The Clash of Dogma and Ministry

*I*n 1978, two factors encouraged Norm DeNeal and Bert Bokern to take what by then seemed a fairly ordinary step: coming out, in public, through a newspaper interview. First, David Estes's campaign to repeal the gay civil rights laws in Seattle had pressured gays and lesbians to become more visible to their neighbors. Second—and for DeNeal and Bokern this would be the more significant factor—waves of change had begun to occur in the Catholic Church, to which both belonged.

DeNeal had studied philosophy and theology at Gonzaga University in eastern Washington, a school operated by the Society of Jesus—the black-robed Jesuits. After graduating, DeNeal had begun volunteering at the Seattle Counseling Service's new home on Capitol Hill, changing his identity from that of a closeted homosexual to that of a very open, articulate gay man. Bokern had discovered his feelings for men in high school and confirmed them during his Peace Corps work. In 1978, both were members of a group in Seattle then six years old, Catholics who had affiliated with a national organization called Dignity whose purpose was both social and religious. Dignity provided a way for gay men and lesbians to meet one another and to share experiences of faith, as well as to seek a more visible role within the religious conversation.

DeNeal and Bokern idealized social justice; their volunteering showed that. As had many other young Catholics in the 1970s, they embraced the revolution that Pope John XXIII's Vatican II conferences of the 1960s had slowly begun to make in the Catholic Church. Now, there was more concern for the poor, more critical reflection on past dogmas, more emphasis on the church working as a community rather than as a hierarchy. In particular, the Jesuits, so often described as the pope's "shock troops" of education, had started to shift their understanding of their own mission—it was no longer so much to teach dogma and to convert others to Catholic doctrine as to minister for changes in unjust political or social institutions.

In March 1978, DeNeal and Bokern agreed to a lengthy interview with the archdiocesan newspaper for western Washington, the *Northwest Progress,* which was ready to publish a series of educational articles about the Catholic Church's stance on homosexuality. That was because the summer before, in 1977, Archbishop

Raymond Hunthausen had made a controversial decision to recognize Mayor Wes Uhlman's proclamation of a Gay Pride Week in Seattle. While Hunthausen had not gone so far as to embrace the phrase "gay pride" himself, he had termed the occasion a "special week to call our attention to the injustices suffered by many homosexuals in our community." The result had been a torrent of dissent from more conservative and anti-gay Catholics, criticism that seemed to throw the *Progress* into the fight to explain precisely what the Catholic Church's post–Vatican II stance was.[1]

At the time, DeNeal was president of Seattle's Dignity chapter.

Half the questions in the *Progress* interview echoed those the *University of Washington Daily* had asked of the anonymous "Jim" twelve years earlier: how DeNeal and Bokern discovered they were gay, what their families thought, what had been the cause of their homosexuality, and, somewhat more voyeuristically, what the gay bar scene in Seattle was like. But the other half moved beyond the usual theme of understanding sexual orientation. More bravely, the *Progress* reporter asked DeNeal and Bokern to comment on the Catholic Church's stance on homosexuality. There was a theological distinction, for example, made in Rome only three years earlier, between "curable" homosexuals and "incurable" homosexuals, with different types of pastoral care to be directed to each. Homosexual orientation itself was not a sin, the church said, just the sex. The difference in the categories was that pastoral ministry for curable homosexuals meant encouraging them to become heterosexuals and holding them responsible if they did not, while incurable homosexuals should be treated respectfully, while being urged toward celibacy.

To the distinction, DeNeal curtly responded, "That's assuming first that there's something to be cured, when there really isn't."

Then he went further, drawing on his experiences as a volunteer counselor. The Catholic Church's approach, he suggested, was actually causing harm. "Some of these people who have been 'cured'—and I've seen them in working two years at Seattle Counseling Service—are grossly bent out of shape. They're scarred beyond proportion. I don't think there's any way . . . the Church can make up for that tremendous destruction."

Bokern agreed. "Why cure something that is beautiful?" he asked.

The reporter pressed them to talk about the church dogma that tolerated "incurable" homosexual orientation but banned actual homosexual sex for everyone regardless of type. DeNeal answered, "My orientation is gay and I engage in activity. I don't think it's valid for the Catholic Church to deny the actualization of a person's feelings, of a person's gift."

Bokern added defiantly, "I don't have to ask anyone's permission to be gay. I don't have to explain myself. I'm not a second-class citizen because I'm gay. Why should I have to quail in front of anyone in order to be who I am?"

In the same series of articles, spread over three weeks, the *Progress* interviewed

Father Kirby Brown, a priest who had agreed to be Dignity Seattle's first chaplain. He too was skeptical of Rome's approach. "You cannot require celibacy of all gay people," he said. "The Church is not realistic."

"If someone comes up to me," Brown continued, "and says 'I have spent two or three years in the bar scene, and now I've found somebody and we've lived together for four months and we're trying to establish a permanent friendship and relationship . . . I'm not going to tell that person, 'Drop it.' . . . People have needs. There's only so much they can do at a point in their life. I will help that person to have a healthy friendship and love relationship and tell them, 'Do what you need for that to grow.'"

Throughout Estes's Initiative Thirteen campaign, the Catholic archdiocese stood with other mainstream churches in Seattle urging that the initiative be defeated and that gay civil rights be protected. But four days after the initiative was defeated, the *Northwest Progress,* the official voice of the archdiocese, finally took a stance against what DeNeal, Bokern, and Brown had said. Dignity, the newspaper editorialized, was refusing to adhere to Catholic doctrine.

"The church must be compassionate in her response to all her people," the editorial warned, "but compassion does not always mean compromise."[2] A public break had begun.

Joining the city's political conversation had been the overriding task of the 1970s, and during that decade many gay and lesbian activists had seemed to avoid direct public conflicts with the city's mainstream Catholic and Protestant churches. Most contact had been pursued privately—through religious allies, such as the Reverend Mineo Katagiri—or had been limited to the promotion of civil rights for homosexuals rather than altering church teachings about the morality of homosexuality. That had been true when securing the Church Council of Greater Seattle's opposition to Initiative Thirteen, for example.

As the 1980s opened, though, confrontations with the mainstream Christian churches in the city edged to the fore. As they created a new self-confidence, gays and lesbians were no longer content to be seen as apostate. In no place would the confrontation be more public or more agonizing than in Seattle's Catholic archdiocese.

The specific challenge facing Dignity was to try to alter two aspects of the Catholic Church: its theological dogma about homosexuality and its pastoral ministry to individual gay men and women. Dogma was controlled in Rome; pastoral ministry, at the local archdiocese. In Seattle, the Dignity chapter also faced another task related to social geography. If by the 1970s Renton and Capitol Hills had become the symbolic new center of the city's gay community, before that time they had been the focus of the city's Catholic community. Catholics and homosexuals had both come to occupy the same square mile, and so how the church hierarchy received gay and lesbian Catholics reverberated more intensely—

or at least more publicly—than the struggles in other religions. The Catholics controlled many institutions on Capitol Hill, and homosexuals now controlled many others.

Historically, the paths of Catholics and twentieth-century gays in Seattle began intertwining as early as the 1800s. French-speaking Catholic missionaries, for example, inserted the word *burdash* into the local Chinook jargon, referring in a derogatory way to the Native American men who cross-dressed or received anal intercourse. The gold rushes heightened the coming connection. At the turn of the century, when Bishop Edward O'Dea decided to move the Northwest diocese from Vancouver, Washington, to Seattle, his way of paying for a new cathedral overlooking Pioneer Square was to rely partly on the wealth being dropped by miners and loggers who were making places like the People's Theater and its teetotaling Catholic owner, John Considine, rich. The chosen place of Catholic settlement: the three interlocked peaks of First Hill, Renton Hill, and Capitol Hill. Largely under O'Dea's guidance, there were soon more Catholic churches, chapels, schools, and hospitals on the hills than there were stations of the cross.[3]

Not only did the Catholics occupy the three peaks and the shallow valleys in between, they competed with one another for control of the territory. The Jesuits alone established not only a university but two churches and a high school. In 1902, O'Dea evicted them from their original downtown parish overlooking Puget Sound and ordered them to move somewhere "beyond Eighteenth Street" so he could build his cathedral on the commanding cliff above Elliott Bay. Miffed, the Jesuits more quickly constructed their Church of the Immaculate Conception, running up a debt of sixty-five thousand dollars, siting it exactly on the eastern edge of Eighteenth and making sure it was the city's biggest, with 950 seats and two 140-foot towers. The church defiantly faced toward downtown rather than toward the neighborhood covered by the new parish.

Not to be outdone, O'Dea then hired the architects who had designed the Cathedral of St. John the Divine in New York City. By 1907, for five hundred thousand dollars, they had crowned the cliff overlooking downtown with a Beaux Arts version of the Italian Renaissance—St. James Cathedral, an immense, buff-colored, cross-shaped building with its own twin towers rising twenty feet higher than the Jesuits'. It seated thirteen hundred. One Catholic historian notes that O'Dea "wanted something immortal, a cathedral to last 'til doomsday, or longer, on a high hill where everyone could see it and say, 'That is the Catholic cathedral.'"[4] The diocese also started its own high school, Bellarmine, even though the Jesuits already had one, and even though not too far away, on another Capitol Hill slope, nuns had built Holy Names Academy, a huge domed high school for girls. The story was the same for hospitals: the Sisters of Providence started one on Renton Hill's south slope, while less than a mile away on First Hill so did the Cabrini nuns.

Even with all the grand monuments, though, Catholics were not entirely welcomed into the Northwest. In the 1920s, making use of the same initiative strategy that had been championed by George Cotterill and the Anti-Saloon League, the Ku Klux Klan in Oregon portrayed Catholics as un-American and won a popular campaign to outlaw all Catholic schools. When in 1924 the Klan launched a similar effort in Washington State, Initiative Forty-nine to ban parochial education, O'Dea and other Catholics convinced newspapers throughout the state to print the names of all those who signed the Klan's petitions—and then, in a tactic even more aggressive than that used by gay and lesbian activists during the Initiative Thirteen campaign in Seattle, they sent neighbors to ask the petition signers to withdraw their names. Soon thousands of embarrassed Protestants were claiming they had been deceived into signing the petitions. On election day, Catholics and their allies also posted supporters at every polling place in the state's major cities. The Klan initiative lost, but the local Catholic hierarchy would remember the lesson about resisting campaigns of intolerance launched as initiatives.[5]

In the 1960s, Catholics and gays in Seattle began to share a few more obvious common interests—the city's original fair housing ordinance, for example, which would eventually be amended in the 1970s to protect gays and lesbians. Passing the original law became the personal crusade of Seattle archbishop Thomas A. Connolly, who began ruling over Catholics in the city in 1948. Connolly had grown up in San Francisco near what was becoming that city's famous gay district, the Castro. In 1963, Seattle mayor Dorm Braman, the same mayor who urged a crackdown on homosexuals, opposed a proposed open housing law and insisted it be submitted to a citywide referendum, hoping it would be defeated. Connolly was enraged that citizens were being asked to vote on other people's moral and civil rights—just what the Klan had asked in the 1920s. From O'Dea's pulpit at St. James Cathedral, he thundered that "prejudice, discrimination and segregation are in absolute conflict with the Word of God." Then he permitted the cathedral to be used as the assembly point for Catholics marching in favor of the law. As one city newspaper put it, Connolly used a "firm but paternal voice" to "set the course for his flock to follow," and eventually the law passed.[6]

Throughout Connolly's reign in Seattle, however, the official Catholic understanding of homosexuality was guided by dogma from the Middle Ages, based on the views of St. Thomas Aquinas, who had argued that all human sex must be linked to procreation to be moral. To St. Thomas, homosexuals did not even exist; they were merely wayward heterosexuals committing immoral acts.

Being nonexistent as far as theology was concerned posed a strategic challenge for gay Catholics; one way around it was suggested in Seattle in December 1967, when leaders of homophile organizations from throughout the West gathered to help launch the new Dorian Society. Among them were representatives from California's Council on Religion and the Homosexual, a group actively organizing to change religious views within various churches. One speaker was the Reverend

Augustine Hartman, a Dominican priest. Hartman, according to the meeting report, "questioned what was the greater sin—a sexual act or keeping Negroes in ghettos or turning away someone coming for help. He said a sexual perversion could not come anywhere near a perversion of the mind. . . . [In] further discussion [he] indicated that the best way to approach Catholics would be by approaching individual priests and Catholic universities and seminaries."[7]

The effort, in other words, would have to advance church by church and priest by priest, with a particular focus on those in charge of local Catholic education. Hartman had predicted the best way into the church's conversation: through its day-to-day pastoral ministry and its classrooms, rather than through demands for change in Thomistic dogma. The key, his words seemed to suggest, was to keep the effort local and to work from the bottom of the church hierarchy up.

By the late 1960s, that effort began in earnest in Seattle, and it would grow more organized once the local Dignity chapter formed in 1972. Even in the 1960s, though, inroads were made as some Catholic priests tried to find a way to blend the theology of St. Thomas with the reality of providing pastoral care to the more vocal homosexual community they were encountering in the streets and in churches. Not surprisingly, the tensions between church doctrine and church ministry first emerged publicly at the city's universities, where priests were ministering to younger, questioning Catholics—like DeNeal and Bokern.

For example, at the University of Washington, there was the Reverend Ambrose Toomey, a Dominican priest at the Catholic student center. He had been interviewed for that first April 1967 series about homosexuality in the *University of Washington Daily* and he told the reporter that homosexuality did not deserve its "illness or defect" label. Toomey focused on love and intimacy, regardless of sexual orientation. "In a homosexual relationship in which physical intimacy is involved," he said, "are we dealing with a commitment of the two involved, a deep love relationship? If not, then it would seem to be using another person for immediate physical gratification, as is sometimes the case in heterosexual relationships. This can only cause deep psychological harm." But what if there was love involved? Toomey left a curious, connotative opening. He did not answer directly, but he recognized the possibility. "The proper environment of sexual intimacy is an integration of love and commitment to another person. Whether this is accomplished in a homosexual union or not, I don't know." Behind the scenes, Toomey was also in contact with Mineo Katagiri. When Katagiri asked his advice on whether to accept his own Unitarian Church's call to set up a street ministry, which would include homosexuals in Seattle, Toomey advised him to do so.[8]

Over on Capitol Hill, at the Jesuit campus of Seattle University, the questions over the church's sexual theology quickly became intense, embroiling the entire university.

For one thing, a group of gay men had moved into a run-down apartment building on James Street, next to the university campus. Doug Wyman, who was one of them, remembers what happened. It was 1964 and Wyman had just been discharged from the U.S. Army for being homosexual. The apartment, which he shared with friends, was, he said, "a great party place, with a sleeping area for whoever happened to come to town." All his roommates were gay—several visibly so since they enjoyed wearing drag.

The Jesuit priests were unhappy, according to Wyman.[9] "They had published somewhere, maybe in their student newspaper, that students shouldn't walk on our side of the street because it would cause some problems. The students picked fights with us and said nasty things when they went by." One day, the students hurled a rock through a window and then stood outside taunting, "Come on out fags, we're going to get you." Wyman recalled, "I had these long curved swords and someone else had a long broadsword so we went after them and chased them."

"A few weeks later the same thing happened, with twenty or thirty students. We went out with a large cleaver and said, 'Hey, you may get us but we'll get one or two of you.' The police suggested we talk with the Seattle U. people, who wanted to talk with our 'leaders.'" Wyman laughed. "We sent Tom Morton who was very straight looking and I think Adrian, who wore big bouffant hairdos, went, and Billy went too—he was very, very visibly gay. And we sent Russell who was black."

Wyman remembers the university officials saying that "they thought we ought to move out."

"We said, we think you ought to stop [your students from] having riots with us."

Eventually, Wyman and the others did move away, but not before airing their complaints to a local community radio station. The radio show got Wyman an invitation from Katagiri to help organize the Dorian Society.

Then, in December 1965, the debate moved even more dramatically onto the Catholic campus. One of the university's two African American professors asserted almost heretically that Thomistic interpretations of natural law could no longer provide a foundation for a modern philosophy of life. In a dense scholarly article that filled almost two pages in the student newspaper, he argued that "phenomenological psychology" and "humanistic existentialism," both arising from individual experience rather than theology, were the "unavoidable foundation stones for any worthwhile operational philosophy."

Natural law, with its emphasis that the only moral sex was sex open to procreation, had always been the foundation for the church's condemnation of homosexuality. The professor's attack, however couched in scholarship, was a direct assault. He announced plans for another article in the paper; even its ponderous title—"In Defense of Responsible Permissiveness toward Sex in the Human Adventure"—made clear the challenge of Catholic teachings about sex. At that point the university president, Jesuit priest John Fitterer, stepped in. Fitterer, often called "Smiling Jack" by the faculty because he was photogenic and slickly articulate with sound bites, was also often a censor of whatever he thought was inappropriate to discuss at a Catholic school. He had already rebuked the professor for the first article; now he went further and ordered the student newspaper not to print the second tract. Immediately, ten professors resigned in protest, arguing violation of academic freedom. One denounced Fitterer and the Jesuits for running a "pastoral ghetto" instead of a university.[10]

Banned from printing a philosophical challenge to church teachings, the student newspaper, the *Spectator,* did manage in May 1966 to publish what may have been its first story about homosexuality itself, cast within a great deal of discussion about morality. The story reveals how Catholics on Capitol Hill were beginning to think about their new neighbors. It was a news report on two speakers sponsored by the campus Christian Activities Program. One was a Jesuit priest, James Royce, then head of the psychology department; the other was Dr. Irving Goldberg, a clinical psychologist. Goldberg challenged the church teaching that homosexuality was a sin; Royce, on the other hand, appears to have been at pains to find an accommodation between Catholic moral teachings and his allegiance to the academic discipline of psychology. Both men reinforced more misconceptions than they dispelled. The paper reported, "The two called homosexuality a disorder of adaptation, the product of arrested development. . . . Dr. Goldberg pointed out the conscious will is lacking in homosexuality and therefore it is not a sin. Fr. Royce maintained that while subjectively this might be so, being homosexual does not remove one from moral responsibility."[11]

Then, in October 1966, the *Spectator* published pictures and stories about an attractive, young, blonde-haired former priest who was coming to campus to discuss "Reform of the Church." The priest had just been defrocked and banned from speaking at several other Catholic campuses, including Notre Dame, Holy Cross, and the Jesuits' own University of San Francisco. Seattle University would be the first Catholic campus to allow him to speak. On October 13, a standing-room-only crowd packed the university's biggest auditorium to listen to William DuBay preach his radical message. Priests, he told the crowd, had to start paying more attention to the needs of people and less attention to rigid Catholic dogma, especially about sex. DuBay, of course, would eventually come out as gay as he worked in the 1970s to establish Stonewall at the old Carmelite monastery just a few blocks away.

After DuBay's talk in 1966, "Smiling Jack" Fitterer issued a statement disavowing any endorsement by the Jesuits or the university.[12]

The conflict in Seattle over Catholic theologies of sex and Catholic ways of ministering to homosexuals had begun in earnest.

For the first three years, from 1972 to 1975, gay Catholics in Seattle's Dignity chapter worked quietly, in apparent harmony with Hartman's suggestion that more progress could be made through individual approaches than through public challenges. Dignity members met in one another's homes; they talked with priests and Catholic educators about their concerns. They maintained a low profile. During those years, the Catholic hierarchy in Seattle had little to say directly or officially about homosexuality, either in dogmatic terms or in terms of actual ministry to individuals. A check with the archdiocese's archivist, for example, turned up no statements from Archbishop Connolly or any of his top advisers.[13] But after 1975, that changed dramatically. That year, two events occurred that began to reshape the relationship between local gay Catholics and the church hierarchy.

The first happened in Rome. Bishops who had attended the Second Vatican Council in the 1960s were still busy producing clarifications. One such paper, entitled a "Declaration on Certain Questions Concerning Sexual Ethics," focused on homosexuality. Finally, Thomas Aquinas's theology began to be modified in the face of modern psychology's insistence that there were indeed different sexual orientations. In the new document, Rome would still argue the Thomist line that some homosexuals were simply heterosexuals making bad choices, but now the church theologians also acknowledged that some were homosexual "because of some kind of innate instinct or a pathological constitution judged to be incurable."

The declaration pointed to a dilemma, but did not solve it. "In the pastoral field," it said, "these [incurable] homosexuals must certainly be treated with understanding and sustained in the hope of overcoming their personal difficulties and their inability to fit into society. Their culpability will be judged with prudence."[14] At the level of the ordinary parish priest attempting to engage in ministry—say, a Kirby Brown in Seattle—the dilemma was how to counsel someone who was no longer morally to blame for his or her sexual acts, but whose sexual acts were still considered disordered.

The second event of 1975 occurred locally, at St. James Cathedral. There, in May, the long reign of Archbishop Connolly ended. Raymond Hunthausen, then the bishop of the diocese of Helena in Montana, moved in.

It was going to be his job to figure out how to actually apply that declaration of sexual ethics to the real gay men and women who were in Dignity.

Dutch Hunthausen, as friends called him, had grown up on the wrong side of the tracks, the poor side of Anaconda, Montana, where an earlier generation of Catholic immigrants, German and Irish, had gone to work the mines. He was plainspoken and even grandfatherly, not at all given to flashy suits, fancy speeches, or pomp. Yet like the Reverend Mark Matthews, Hunthausen would have an enormous impact on Seattle; arguably the two were the city's most important religious leaders during the twentieth century. Both followed a social gospel, promoting programs for the poor and calling attention to injustices. But whereas Matthews excoriated the undesirables with Calvinistic glee and went to great lengths to actively destroy the saloons that he saw as the source of vice, Hunthausen would preach in a different tone. Compassion, he would urge. Always compassion.

In Anaconda, he had fit the definition of the "good little boy," bright and deferential to those in authority, particularly to the Ursuline nuns who had taught him in elementary school. Extremely shy as a child, he never sought the spotlight, but he also respectfully agreed to the nuns' request that he give the welcoming speeches whenever the bishop visited. "It was good for people to push me," he would say in an interview years later. "They saw things that I should be doing even if I didn't see them."[15] By the peak of his career in Seattle, Hunthausen would be known worldwide for his stance against nuclear weapons. He denounced a nearby Trident submarine base as the "Auschwitz of Puget Sound" and refused to pay taxes to support war. Daniel Berrigan, the famous Jesuit, would call him one of the "modern visionaries of our history, a bishop walking toward a new center . . . creating a center of understanding."

Hunthausen felt a passion for social justice. When he arrived in Seattle, he eschewed the fancy archbishop's house where Connolly had lived and chose instead a simple room in the rectory next to St. James. He drove a Volkswagen and sometimes ate lunch at the McDonald's a block away from the cathedral, joining the fast food lines like everyone else.

The major influence upon him had been the Second Vatican Council of the 1960s, which he had attended as a new bishop in Helena. There he listened to the debates that would forever excite and shape him. "Everything that happened there resonated with my own sense and feelings about what church is and what it ought to be," Hunthausen would say. Eagerly, he became part of the new wave of bishops determined to carry out the council's reforms. Little did he know that his greatest test would be finding a way to respond to the calls for justice from his now more visible gay neighbors in Seattle.

In fall 1976, shortly after Hunthausen arrived at St. James, the U.S. bishops issued an official declaration about homosexuality. It said, "Homosexuals, like everyone else, should not suffer from prejudice against their basic human rights. They have a right to respect, friendship and justice. They should have an active role in the Christian community."

Trying to implement that statement would eventually bring Hunthausen into a direct conflict with Rome.

In spring 1977, when Charlie Brydon's Dorian Group launched an effort to amend the Washington State civil rights law so that it would protect homosexuals from discrimination in jobs and public accommodations, the question of whether to support the bill came not only to Hunthausen, but to his fellow bishops sitting in Spokane and Yakima. The discussions among the three were not public, so it is not clear whether the decision was a difficult or a quick one, but in the statement was their resolution of an issue posed, on the one hand, by the 1975 declaration from Rome and, on the other, the 1976 stand by the U.S. bishops. Whatever the church's feeling about the first category of homosexuals (the ones who were really just misbehaving heterosexuals), when it came to making laws, pastoral support for the innate and incurable homosexual required that discrimination be outlawed.

The statement from Hunthausen and his fellow bishops referred to the "terrible impact" of discrimination and called for "all people to cease and desist from discriminatory activity." To discriminate against gays and lesbians, the bishops said, "is not only contrary to sound religious principles but in conflict with protection of basic rights in our American civil life."[16]

It was just a short while later, in July 1977, that Hunthausen endorsed Mayor Wes Uhlman's first declaration of a Gay Pride Week in Seattle, even while delicately sidestepping any direct reference to the words "gay pride." Instead, it was "a special week" to focus on the injustices committed against homosexuals.

Criticisms of the new archbishop's stand began immediately. One letter to the *Northwest Progress* argued that Hunthausen was condoning homosexuality. "Mayor Uhlman didn't just say homosexuals' civil rights should be respected," the letter writer said. "He proclaimed Gay Pride Week! Should we proclaim Murderer's Pride Week? How about Liars' Pride Week? Temper Pride Week? Adulterers' Pride Week?" Other writers flatly refused to accept the fact that Catholic theology about homosexuality had indeed changed. Homosexuals who were public about their sexual orientation, they argued, had no place in Catholic congregations. One Catholic wrote to the *Progress,* "Homosexuals should be legislated out of a civilized society to remove their vile influence."[17]

It was clear that Hunthausen had work to do among his flock, if only to educate them about the 1975 declaration. That, as well as Initiative Thirteen, seemed to be one of the major purposes of the series in the *Progress* in 1978. One of the three articles focused on Dignity; others allowed diocesan theologian Lawrence Reilly to explain the distinctions that Rome and Hunthausen were making. Homosexuality, Reilly said, was an orientation—he called it a "phenomenon" that was "not normal." Homosexual acts, like all sexual acts not aimed at procreation, were a product of original sin and were therefore evil, but homosexual persons were not evil and so they deserved the "same rights to fundamental justice and human respect as anyone else."[18]

Reilly conceded, though, that numerous pastoral questions had been raised by the 1975 declaration and that "the church has not addressed all these specific questions." The sheer length of his list made clear just how many there were:

Are there any circumstances in which homosexual acts can be good? Are there circumstances in which homosexual union can at least be tolerated? Can a homosexual receive the Eucharist? Should a priest give communion to a known homosexual couple? Is the Church someday going to bless homosexual marriages as some ministers and priests have already done? Should Catholics support sexual minority movements? Should Catholics vote to allow homosexuals to teach in the public schools? Should we encourage the hiring of homosexuals in our Catholic schools? Can homosexuality be cured and, if so, should a Catholic homosexual actively seek to be cured? If a homosexual can't be cured, just how is he or she supposed to live? If a homosexual is unable to live a celibate life, should he or she be excluded from receiving the sacraments [which included not only the Eucharist but blessings at death]? Don't we have an obligation to protect our children since homosexuality is believed to be frequently caused by the negative influence of adults on children? Is homosexuality an alternative lifestyle in the Church?

Certainly it was enough to keep both pastoral and dogmatic debates going for a long while.

After the 1975 declaration, members in Seattle's Dignity chapter became bolder. In 1977, they decided to ask whether they could hold their meetings on church property itself. Would any parish be willing to designate one particular monthly Mass at which lesbians and gay men could know they were welcome?

At first, they encountered resistance.

St. Patrick's Church, at the north edge of Capitol Hill, refused them, although it was a gentle refusal, the parish council going so far as to say that homosexuals could join the regular Masses, but a particular Mass aimed at homosexuals would not be scheduled.

Finally, a parish run by the Redemptorist order in downtown Seattle agreed. Father Lyle Konen did his best to make it sound like a casual decision when the *Northwest Progress* reported the event. "I talked it over with a couple of the fathers," he said, "and we couldn't see why not."

"It's not my church" he explained in Vatican II language. "It's the people's church. I'm just the custodian, in the spiritual sense."

"I believe [homosexuals are] children of God, just as anyone else, and that they have a right to be listened to and to be spiritually helped. . . . They have a right to pray and receive the sacraments as well as anybody else."[19]

It was a response born out of pastoral ministry, not out of dogmatic analysis.

Eventually it would be the Jesuits, so busy redefining their own mission to focus more on social justice concerns, who would agree to let Dignity move its Mass to the obvious location, their Capitol Hill church, St. Joseph's, at the corner of Eighteenth Avenue East and Aloha Street. Then, except for the brief public crossfire in the *Progress* in 1978, the issue quieted for a few years. Masses for Dignity members were not different from any other Mass; the core of the ritual was unchangeable and anyone of any sexual orientation could attend. It was simply that at a particular Mass, in this case Sunday evenings, one could expect that homosexuals would be especially welcome and acknowledged, with priests perhaps making a special point to refer to gay and lesbian concerns in their homilies. Dignity members made special banners, Dignity members organized church socials after Mass, Dignity members helped the priests behind the scenes.

Then in the summer of 1983, when a strange new virus began to make its way into Seattle's gay community and raise the visibility of homosexual sex and relationships toward a new peak, the underlying conflict over dogma began fatefully rumbling toward an explosion.

At the beginning of that year, gay political activists from the Dorian Group had again asked the state legislature to amend the state civil rights law to prevent employers from discriminating on the basis of sexual orientation. Once again, the Catholic bishops in Washington State had endorsed the request. And once again, the bill had been defeated.

This time, though, following Archbishop Hunthausen's lead, the bishops in the state decided in June—during the gay pride celebrations—to issue a teaching document called "The Prejudice against Homosexuals and the Ministry of the Church." Filling more than two full pages in the *Progress,* it provided, on the one hand, a detailed reiteration of church doctrine about the evil of homosexual sex, but, on the other, it contained remarkable pastoral statements of appreciation for homosexuals. Among them, for example, was this comment: "A homosexual person may manifest virtues and qualities that are admirable by any standard. In fact, there is some evidence that many homosexuals possess important attributes that are often, unfortunately, lacking in their straight counterparts. Thus, it appears that sensitivity to the needs of persons and the ability to express warm feelings towards both men and women are frequently present in gays. Hence, the church, which considers a person as a whole, can find much good to be praised."[20]

Here, suddenly, was a church document—from bishops, no less—citing homosexuals as role models and actually commending their "important attributes" to heterosexual attention—not to mention adopting the street language referring to heterosexuals as "straight."

The document also attacked attempts to get homosexuals to change their sexual orientation, saying they were not to be blamed for failing to do so.

Also, during the June gay pride events, Hunthausen moved even further in his pastoral role, agreeing for the first time to address the Dorian Group, in a meeting at the downtown Mayflower Park Hotel. Delicately, the title of his speech focused on his favorite topic of "Peace and Disarmament." But at one moment during his speech, the archbishop paused and acknowledged the significance of the occasion. It was the first time in Seattle that someone with such rank in the Catholic Church had met officially and publicly with a gay activist group.

"I hope it's not the last," he quietly told them.[21]

By then, Hunthausen had already made what would become his most controversial decision, one that would bring Rome directly into the changes that were occurring on Catholic Hill.

Throughout the late 1970s and early 1980s, one of Hunthausen's favorite themes was "conversion." By that word, he did not so much mean converting others to Christianity, as missionaries might, but converting an individual away from the convenient values offered by society toward those offered by the gospel. Theologians that he hired for the archdiocese argued that the Christian Church was never meant to be comfortably aligned with the majority, but rather represented a minority people actually living as witnesses to a different set of values. Hunthausen's tone distinctly differed from that of Seattle's other highly charismatic religious leader, Mark Matthews, who in the early twentieth century had instead sought conversions for the purpose of forging a political majority and legislating public policy.

Hunthausen had no grand political strategy for converting people. It was more a matter of slow discernment—figuring out what the appropriate response was to whatever question suddenly presented itself. One night in an interview at the chancery next to St. James, he wryly smiled, "The Spirit doesn't necessarily hit you over the head."[22]

In 1983, local members of Dignity relayed a request to him. The national organization of Dignity had decided to schedule its annual conference in Seattle. The local organizers wondered, Would the archbishop permit St. James Cathedral to be used for a special Mass for those attending the conference?

Hunthausen had not sought out the question, but neither did he shrink from it. Looked at one way, the answer was a simple enough "yes." Masses for special occasions were not that extraordinary. But no one would miss the symbolism of allowing Dignity to transport itself, even once, from the Jesuits' St. Joseph to the archdiocese's St. James.

After pondering, Hunthausen agreed. In an unusual move, the *Northwest Progress* then carried a long interview in which the archbishop explained himself. Catholics, he insisted, must no longer scorn homosexuals. "They must be recognized as full members of the church, integrated into the parish community." That, he acknowledged, "is painfully hard for many of our people to accept." Hunthausen would lead.[23]

On Saturday of Labor Day weekend, more than twelve hundred people, mostly gay and lesbian, moved across the cathedral's balcony with its expansive view of downtown Seattle and went inside to pray. Some forty-five priests, chaplains from the various Dignity chapters around the country, assembled to celebrate what was no ordinary Mass. At the time, Hunthausen himself was in Rome, but he sent a videotape of welcome. "While I am not able to be with you in person," he told the delegates through the video, "I am surely with you in spirit and prayer."

Outside the cathedral about 150 people, including some priests, marched with signs proclaiming: "Remember Sodom and Gomorrah," "Pray for Gays," and "God is not Gay." One priest from Portland condemned the use of the cathedral by homosexuals as "a profanation" and "a sacrilege."[24]

In the *Progress* interview, Hunthausen had said, "I decided that this was a risk that ought to be taken in order to deal with this delicate and highly charged issue in a Christian manner."

Then he had admitted, "I would be naive if I did not acknowledge that the subject is sensitive and volatile."

With that, gay Catholics in Seattle, for all practical purposes, no longer held the title role as the protagonist pushing for changes in the church conversation. Like the rest of the city, they would become observers of a titanic clash over dogma and ministry between Rome and Seattle.

The Vatican moved surprisingly swiftly.

Fewer than eight weeks passed before the Vatican ordered a special investigation, dispatching a well-known conservative on social issues, Archbishop James Hickey of Washington, D.C., to examine, as Hickey obliquely put it, the "criticism regarding pastoral ministry in Seattle." Some tended to assume that the Seattle archbishop's stance on peace and nuclear weapons had caused the Vatican's response, but that was not the case. The catalyst, it would become clear, was the Dignity Mass at St. James. Publicly, Hickey tried to soften the appearance of what was occurring, saying he was coming "not as a grand inquisitor . . . but to support my brother bishop." Yet no one missed the obvious elliptical coding in his communication: that Hunthausen somehow required the "support" of a conservative bishop hand-picked by a conservative pope.[25]

During November 1983, Hickey questioned about seventy critics and supporters. Then he left, and for two years nothing happened, at least in public. Simply leaving the matter unresolved cast doubt on Hunthausen, though, and became an irritating way of discrediting his sympathetic response to gays.

In fall 1985, the Vatican finally acted again.

The first news the public heard was overwhelmingly positive for Hunthausen. A church heavyweight, Rome's ambassador to the United States, Archbishop Pio Laghi, sent a letter in November that bluntly attacked the "exaggerated and mean-spirited criticism" that Hunthausen's opponents had been making and warmly praised the archbishop's "clear evidence of loyalty to the church." There were "areas of concern," Laghi noted, where Hunthausen needed to show "greater vigilance in upholding the church's teaching." One was the ministry to homosexuals. In the letter released to the public, Laghi said no more than that. It seemed the gentlest possible of criticisms.[26]

But what was not publicly known at the time was that six weeks earlier, at the end of September, another powerful Vatican bureaucrat, Cardinal Joseph Ratzinger, had sent a confidential and far blunter letter. He headed the Sacred Congregation for the Doctrine of the Faith, the successor to the church's Inquisition office. In that letter Ratzinger said, "The Archdiocese should withdraw all support from any group which does not unequivocally accept the teaching of the Magisterium concerning the intrinsic evil of homosexual activity. The ill-advised welcome of a pro-homosexual group to your cathedral . . . served to make the Church's position appear to be ambiguous on this delicate but important point. A compassionate ministry to homosexual persons must be developed that has as its clear goal the promotion of a chaste lifestyle."[27]

It was a clear order to expel Dignity, to have no further dealings with the group, and to create a pastoral ministry that would press homosexuals to remain chaste. The fact that Rome had assigned two powerful spokesmen to write the letters indicated the seriousness with which the Vatican viewed the issue.

Two weeks later, Rome suddenly announced that an "auxiliary" bishop named Donald Wuerl would soon be arriving in Seattle to "help" Hunthausen with his duties. That added a new element of mystery to what the public knew. The official guise was that Hunthausen had requested such help with pastoral duties; his previous assistant had retired two years earlier. But even under normal circumstances, Wuerl would have been the oddest of choices. A native of Pittsburgh, the forty-five-year-old priest had never worked in the Northwest and had only been slightly involved in any pastoral ministry whatsoever. Instead, he had worked as a secretary to Pittsburgh's Cardinal John Wright and had followed Wright to the Vatican, where for ten years as a church bureaucrat he had mingled with cardinals and the pope. Then he had returned to Pittsburgh to become a seminary professor. Some who knew him called him a "rock-hard orthodox priest," his doctrinal understandings not yet enhanced by pastoral insights. Also, the Vatican had curiously chosen the title of "auxiliary bishop with special faculties" rather than the more customary "assistant bishop." What could that phrase indicate? local Catholics wondered. Hunthausen's opponents immediately celebrated the appointment.[28]

If there was any doubt about why Wuerl was being sent, it disappeared a month later when Pope John Paul II himself called Wuerl to Rome to be ordained as auxiliary bishop. For the ordination, the pope gave Wuerl one of his own personal miters—the one that the pope had worn on a visit to the Netherlands when liberal Dutch Catholics had booed him.[29]

No one familiar with the Church's sometimes elliptical and metaphorical way of speaking could miss the symbolic message.

After Wuerl arrived, Hunthausen at first tried to maintain harmony. As far as he was concerned, he would later say, Wuerl was just a helper, and officially Hunthausen welcomed him. But personally Wuerl could not have been more different from Hunthausen. The archbishop had come from a small Montana town where he affably, if shyly, knew everyone; Wuerl had grown up on a Pittsburgh hillside isolated from the rest of the city. Sternly gaunt and tall, he was a contrast to Hunthausen's pudginess. He wore finely tailored trench coats and well-polished shoes, causing a *Post-Intelligencer* reporter to write that Wuerl looked as if he had stepped from the pages of *Gentlemen's Quarterly*. The reporter added that, by contrast, Hunthausen looked as if he bought his clothes from REI, a popular outdoors co-op in Seattle. Ignoring Hunthausen's decision to live in a small, ascetic room next to the cathedral, Wuerl suggested the diocese rent a condo in the pricey downtown Watermark Towers for him. The diocese instead sent him its own metaphor, housing him in a small apartment in West Seattle—not at all close to the cathedral. Shortly after he started work, Wuerl ordered a partition erected to separate his office from an open room. The wall quickly became yet another metaphor, a symbol of Wuerl's distance from everyone. Reports had it that during one of his first meetings with priests in Seattle, Wuerl had delivered a fire-and-brimstone speech promising punishment for any "renegades." "It's been all downhill since," a source told the *Post-Intelligencer.*[30]

By summer 1986 Hunthausen and Wuerl had begun to clash over decisions, and it was clear to Hunthausen that the two had very different ideas of the auxiliary bishop's power. Writing to Rome, Hunthausen demanded clarification. When he got it, he was so angry that he refused to keep the information secret. The pope, Hunthausen revealed to the news media in September, had ordered him to surrender "complete and final decision-making power" to Wuerl in several areas of ministry, among them all decisions relating to gays and lesbians. The Vatican's move was astonishing, quickly generating a national swirl of news stories as well as an unprecedented five-hour meeting among priests in the archdiocese—some of whom told of parishioners struggling in tears to try to understand what had happened. A month later, the conflict grew even nastier when the Vatican released a three-and-a-half-page letter detailing its criticisms, among them that Hunthausen needed to avoid "erroneous doctrines" with regard to his empathetic treatment of homosexuals and eliminate "affiliations with groups promoting doctrines contrary to the church's teachings."[31]

Wuerl, then, was not simply Hunthausen's helper; he was a second archbishop sitting in the same archdiocese.

At the end of October, more news from Rome arrived. In what became known instantly as the Halloween letter, Cardinal Ratzinger declared—in a throwback to the church's earlier Thomistic views—that homosexuality was "an intrinsic moral evil" and "an objective disorder." He instructed American bishops to exclude from church property any groups working to protect homosexuals from discrimination and any groups that disagreed with his analysis of church dogma. That meant Dignity.[32]

The group's national leadership responded strongly, insisting that gay Catholics should be able to have committed relationships that included sex. In Seattle, the Dignity chapter was still sponsoring Masses at St. Joseph's with the support of the local Jesuits and the archbishop, but Wuerl held the papal authority to take the next step. Most expected him to move quickly.

Instead, the American bishops acted first. Their national conference had already been scheduled for November 10, and whatever their individual feelings about Hunthausen's stance, the bishops knew that what the Vatican had done by sending in Wuerl was an extraordinary interference in the operation of a local diocese. Yet they could not directly challenge the pope's authority. Concerned, they announced they would allow Hunthausen to present his side at their national meeting. That itself sent a message to Rome.

Once at the meeting, Hunthausen bluntly told his fellow bishops that he considered the situation with Wuerl to be unworkable. He offered to resign and pleaded with them, saying he was "absolutely convinced that the matter of the governance of the church of Seattle needs to be returned to normal as soon as humanly possible, I would even say at once."[33]

It was a dramatic challenge, one that the bishops discussed for an extraordinary five hours in closed sessions.

When the final statement from the conference was issued, on the surface it seemed as if the bishops had sided with the Vatican, saying that the disciplining deserved "our respect and confidence" and that their first allegiance lay with the pope. That was proper, official language. But there was also other curious wording. For example, the bishops said they were "not able to review, much less judge, a case involving a diocesan bishop and the Holy See," language that deferred to the Vatican. Yet, as one analyst wryly noted, they had just spent the better part of three days doing exactly that review. They also offered "any assistance judged helpful and appropriate by the parties involved," virtually treating the pope and Hunthausen as quarrelling spouses. Metaphorically calling the church a family, rather than treating it as a hierarchy governed from Rome, they delicately criticized the way the Vatican had launched a secret investigation that had caused a great deal of hurt: "A family takes steps to see that, in so far as possible, a painful situation does not happen again."

Seemingly deliberate leaks from several bishops also made it very publicly clear that the conference had specifically rejected a previous draft approving of the pope's investigation. Instead, the bishops had substituted language merely acknowledging that the investigation had been pursued in a way consistent with church law. In another subtle message, the bishops pointedly humbled Cardinal Bernard Law of Boston, by rejecting his nomination for eight different national posts in the organization. Law had outspokenly supported the Vatican's seizure of power from Hunthausen.[34]

Slowly, it seemed that Rome began to take heed. The pope was planning to visit the United States the following year; it would not have been in his interest to arrive with such an open, if somewhat coded, conflict occurring with the American church's leadership. It was time to turn down the public heat, and in January 1987, the pope's ambassador to the United States, Pio Laghi, granted a rare interview to a *New York Times* reporter, Joseph Berger. While trying to defend what the Vatican had done and how it had conducted its investigation, he also acknowledged that perhaps the investigation, and the subsequent appointment of Wuerl, could have been handled differently. "I am learning also," he told Berger. Then, in February 1987, came a very terse but significant press release, issued by Laghi through the Americans' National Conference of Catholic Bishops. The pope, he said, had asked that a commission of two American cardinals and one archbishop reinvestigate and "assess the current situation in Seattle." The group consisted of three of the American church's most influential: Cardinal Joseph Bernardin of Chicago,

Cardinal John O'Connor of New York, and Archbishop John Quinn of San Francisco.[35]

Wuerl, meanwhile, bided his time. A week after the announcement about the commission, he visited Rome and met privately with the pope, the *Northwest Progress* noting only that "the Vatican released no details of the meeting and Bishop Wuerl refused to comment on what was discussed." Even as other dioceses began expelling what few remaining Dignity chapters were meeting on church property, Dignity continued its Masses at St. Joseph's. Hunthausen's critics fumed. One, a retired lawyer named William Gaffney, complained to the *Washington Post* in February 1987 that "they [Dignity members] have no right to be there. And I hope they get kicked the hell out of there. I'm pretty hot about this. Some people are going to hell about these teachings [on homosexuality]."[36]

Another month passed, during which the new commission began its inquiries, interviewing past and present bishops in the Pacific Northwest, as well as members of the archdiocesan staff. Then Hunthausen himself met with the commission in Chicago. Reports circulated that he appeared troubled and withdrawn after the meeting; the *National Catholic Register,* a weekly in Los Angeles, suggested that the Vatican and even the commission had pressured him to resign. The chancellor of the archdiocese, Michael Ryan—the number three priest in the local hierarchy after Hunthausen and Wuerl—took the unusual step of issuing a letter to all the archdiocesan priests saying the rumors were untrue. Everyone had become edgy, waiting.[37]

A few more weeks passed, and then it seemed as if Wuerl had finally decided to launch the move against Dignity. On April 23, the *Post-Intelligencer* reported that in a private conversation with Dignity board members, Wuerl had ordered the group to cancel its Mass at St. Joe's. "Wuerl Orders Halt to Sponsored Services," the front-page headline read.

The next day, Wuerl surprised everyone. Through an archdiocesan spokesman, he unequivocally denied the report. Dignity's own directors backed him, saying there had been "absolutely no decision." But a priest who had attended the meeting and requested anonymity stood by the initial report, telling the *Post-Intelligencer,* "We're getting to hardball here. It's not a question of if, but of when and how. That's still up for discussion, as are many things in this archdiocese."[38]

A *Seattle Times* headline a few days later caught the drama. "Last Act of Hunthausen 'Play' Remains Unwritten," it said. One scenario: Hunthausen would resign, Wuerl would be promoted to bishop in his own diocese, and Seattle would get a new archbishop. That was what the *National Catholic Register* had speculated, and it had been right earlier than everyone else in reporting that Wuerl had been given special powers. A second scenario: Hunthausen would get a new "coadjutor bishop" who would eventually succeed him when he retired, and, again, Wuerl would get his own diocese.[39] Everyone went back to waiting.

And Dignity continued sponsoring the weekly Mass.

As it would turn out, Wuerl would never use his special powers. He had been trained to move discreetly as a church bureaucrat, and he was, as many of his critics enjoyed pointing out, an ambitious man hopeful of rising in the hierarchy. The pope had given him a difficult assignment, and what he likely understood—or had been told—was that he did not need to do anything more than be the pope's personal symbol of authority in Seattle. Years later, Wuerl told a reporter for the *Pittsburgh Post-Gazette* that he never used his papal powers in Seattle because he did not want to add more fuel to an already blazing fire. Hunthausen's opponents, he acknowledged, would never forgive him.[40] Wuerl's presence was communication enough, and so, in a paradoxical way, the Seattle archdiocese became the one safe location where it was still okay for Dignity to meet on church property. Wuerl's task was simply to wait for the resolution to be created elsewhere, in this case by the bishops' new blue-ribbon commission.

Among the commission members, Cardinal Bernardin in particular held a reputation for engineering creative compromises that left no one clearly denoted as a winner, but rather left everyone able to maneuver. And that was what was going to be needed to extract both the Seattle church and the Vatican from what had become a far too sensitive crisis.

In May 1987, the commission announced the end of the "play." Hunthausen should get all his powers back, but he should also get a new coadjutor bishop to help him in his duties and replace him when he retired. Unlike Wuerl, the coadjutor would clearly be second in charge. The Vatican had even agreed to a coadjutor with a liberal and pastoral reputation, chosen from Hunthausen's own home state of Montana.

Priests and newspapers quickly hailed the new man, Thomas Murphy. In contrast to Wuerl, whose photos often presented a stern, unsmiling face, Murphy fairly bubbled; one headline even played on his Irish background and dubbed him "Happy" Murphy.

For the American bishops and Hunthausen, "it was a victory," as journalist David Anderson observed. One of several *Post-Intelligencer* headlines read: "American Bishops Pull Off a Victory Ever So Politely." It had been won, Anderson noted, "using classic church political strategy—avoiding confrontation and letting protestations of powerlessness and non-interference speak more powerfully than direct protest." The bishops had "dramatically demonstrated the power of the politics of ecclesiastical ellipsis," and by doing so had won their "significant war of nerves with the Vatican."

As for Wuerl, he went home to Pittsburgh. Nine months later, he became bishop of that city's more than three-quarter million Catholics.[41]

Buried amid the sidebars in the newspapers, though, was the most dangerous development for Seattle's gay and lesbian Catholics. As part of the announcement, the Vatican had released the text of the secret 1985 letter that Cardinal Ratzinger had sent to Hunthausen, ordering him to withdraw all support from groups that did not accept the church's teaching on homosexuality. As long as Wuerl had been in charge of the issue, Hunthausen was not responsible for acting. But now the problem was back in Hunthausen's hands. The commission of bishops had dictated that the Ratzinger letter must be used as the "primary guide for the direction in which the church in Seattle must move." No date was publicly specified, of course—that would have been too direct—but the commission promised to assist Hunthausen "during the course of the next year," suggesting that was the maximum time to make the change.[42]

But Hunthausen was not the only bishop struggling over the issue of Dignity. Perhaps not coincidentally, two members of the commission itself, Cardinal Bernardin and Archbishop Quinn, still had in their own dioceses two of the last Dignity chapters that were meeting on church property.

For a year, Hunthausen continued to allow Dignity to meet at St. Joseph's. Then, when Hunthausen's review was due to end, it was Bernardin who launched a trial balloon. Everyone had expected that Ratzinger's order meant Masses for homosexuals had to end. Bernardin, though, found a compromise possible within Ratzinger's own words. "A compassionate ministry to homosexual persons must be developed," the Vatican cardinal had written, intending that homosexuals be taught to be celibate. In mid-May 1988, Bernardin announced that in Chicago the archdiocese itself would set up a special ministerial office to take over the Dignity Mass for homosexuals—and, very importantly, to keep offering it. One Dignity officer there called the new Bernardin approach "a dynamic model that other bishops can follow."[43]

Hunthausen waited six more weeks. His liaisons contacted the Seattle Dignity chapter. How would they respond to the Bernardin approach? There would not be any real changes made in the Mass, its location at St. Joseph's, or even its time on Sunday evenings. It was just that a new archdiocesan office for gay and lesbian ministry, rather than Dignity, would now officially sponsor the Mass. Hunthausen even promised to underscore his commitment to gays and lesbians in a very special way. This time, he would not just send a video; he himself would go to St. Joseph's to preach the first Mass to be offered under the new sponsorship.

For the Dignity members, the choice felt agonizing. To some, the offer seemed a reasonable face-saving way to let Rome control dogma while local priests pursued the kind of pastoral ministry that seemed appropriate. To others, it felt like a hierarchical demand to return to the closet. Ed Elliott, who had become Seattle Dignity's president, said, "Hunthausen is the best bishop we have in the country" and the most serious about a real ministry to lesbian and gay Catholics. "Many of us feel the best thing we can do now is to continue to have dialogue with the church, so the church can someday show some movement."

Everyone was angry at the Vatican. "Dignity was doing a good job," Elliott argued, and would never have been evicted had it not been for Rome.

The chapter vote split evenly. Dignity would neither endorse the new arch-diocesan gay and lesbian ministry nor set up a separate ritual. "What the decision does," Elliott announced, "is to leave each member of Dignity free to participate or not in the archdiocesan Mass."

On June 30, 1988, Hunthausen ordered St. Joseph's to stop allowing the Dignity chapter any official use of church property and any public sponsorship of a Mass. The date of Dignity's final sponsorship of a Mass was set for July 10.

That Sunday evening, gays, lesbians, and their friends packed the church. Outside, Jim MacKeller, a member of Dignity's board, told TV reporters hope-fully that at least for now the church was officially recognizing the presence of gay and lesbian Catholics. "People come because this is a very spiritual event. We hope we can maintain that and that the church will minister to us in a very loving way." Nani Stewart, another member, also sounded optimistic. Gays on Catholic Hill would still have a special Mass to attend, she said. A third Dignity member, Ken Van Dyke, sounded a caution: "If there was a change toward more hard-line church teaching about homosexuality, then it would be a crisis."

Inside St. Joe's, all the priests who had served the chapter celebrated the Mass. The gay Seattle Men's Chorus pointedly sang "We Are a Family." Dignity's officers ceremoniously returned the keys they had been using to enter the church to set up for Masses. Then, at dusk, priests and Dignity members alike followed the pro-cessional crucifix out the nave and onto the street. The curtain on the years-long struggle had—at least temporarily—fallen.[44]

Two weeks later, on July 24, both Hunthausen and Murphy would attend the first Mass to be sponsored by the archdiocese's new office of gay and lesbian min-istry, to be headed by a priest named Jerry Stanley. Hunthausen delivered the hom-ily. In it, he would say that "from our point of view, the teaching of the church must be the starting point from which we try to understand the experience of gay and lesbian Christians."[45] That stood in contrast to a different form of reasoning: discerning the experience of gay Christians in order to shape church teachings. Unfortunately for homosexuals, Cardinal Ratzinger had now defined the church teachings.

In sixteen years, the Seattle chapter of Dignity had both succeeded and failed. The local ministry to homosexuals had been transformed. Gays and lesbians had become more visible in the social geography of Catholic Hill. Dignity's efforts, along with those occurring in other churches, had shaken the religious conversation in Seattle into at least acknowledging gay and lesbian concerns. But, among the Catholics, Rome had painfully trumped with dogma. The only comfort was that, for the moment, pastoral ministry was out of Wuerl's hands and back in the con-trol of a friendly archbishop.

# 17

# At the Hospital

## A Plague Arrives

*I*n 1959, as MacIver Wells finished his first confrontation with the Seattle police, Arno Motulsky pursued a different battle in the jungles of the Congo. A young medical geneticist working at the University of Washington, Motulsky wondered why some Africans resisted malaria more than others. To find out, he and his team put needles into more than twelve hundred people, drawing blood to test for genetic resistance. In Léopoldville, a Bantu man was tested. Motulsky shipped the blood to the university for analysis, and when his own malaria study was completed, the blood was stored first at the university and then at the Puget Sound Blood Center.

No one would know it for three decades, least of all Motulsky, but the young scientist had just sent evidence of a mysterious new virus to Seattle. In the 1980s, other researchers examining microscopic amounts of the Motulsky collection would designate the Bantu man the earliest documented case of a new infection. His blood showed traces of the human antibodies that even then were struggling against the virus; no one knew whether he had survived, but the chances seemed unlikely. In 1997, other scientists examining Motulsky's samples with more advanced techniques found genetic remnants of the virus itself in the blood.

The samples Motulsky gathered stayed safely quarantined. But when the virus eventually made its way to Seattle a second time—unsealed and unsafely—it would kill more than thirty-five hundred people in the city and its surroundings before the century's end. And it would infect additional thousands. More than three-quarters of the dead would be gay men.[1]

The first news came June 4, 1981, in the *Morbidity and Mortality Weekly Report* from the Centers for Disease Control. A bizarre pneumonia had struck five healthy men in Los Angeles.

At the time, the *Seattle Gay News* was busy noting other developments, not diseases. Charlie Brydon's success against the Initiative Thirteen campaign had propelled him to national prominence and to New York as one of the two directors of the National Gay Task Force, but sharing responsibility with a lesbian director had not worked for Brydon, and the task force itself was being accused of drift in the face of a renewed Christian assault, this one led by the Reverend Jerry Falwell and his organization, the Moral Majority. Falwell perched on the eve of a major triumph—convincing Congress to overturn a repeal of the sodomy law in the District of Columbia. Brydon was resigning and coming home. In Seattle itself, the summer's already warm weather had drawn gay nude sunbathers back to the U.W.'s arboretum, where one police officer had apparently removed his own shirt to walk undetected among the crowd and then had used a walkie-talkie to summon uniformed reinforcements—or so the tales of harassment from the arboretum beach went. On Capitol Hill, a new gay bathhouse prepared to open, the likes of which the city had never seen before. Gone would be the dinginess of the old downtown bathhouses that Jacob Heimbigner and others had operated with the tolerance of the police. Instead, the upscale Club Seattle was installing a thirty-person hot tub, a bunkhouse, workout machines, and what manager Larry Woelich would call an "arena," where, he promised in an interview with the *Gay News,* "anything goes."[2]

For Pride Week that June, the San Francisco Gay Men's Chorus was performing at the Opera House. The hall was packed and new friendships were being made, by day and by night.

In August, the *New York Times* reported forty-one cases of a rare cancer among gay men in New York and California. Club Seattle was planning its grand opening, an extravaganza called "Steam." By the end of the month, doctors throughout the country had counted one hundred diagnoses of either the cancer or the unusual pneumonia, all in homosexual men. Half had already died. A story in the *Seattle Gay News* that month focused on a decision to change the name of the Seattle Clinic for Venereal Health to the Seattle Gay Clinic. It had been created in 1979 to counsel and treat gay men for sexually transmitted diseases. The article made no mention of any new virus.[3]

Few gay men even knew about it. Those who did were mostly beginning to hear from friends in San Francisco or New York.

Seattle would have the bittersweet luxury of fearing the plague before it actually arrived in columns of statistics. It would be known as a "second-wave" city, which meant that it had a little more time to prepare than did San Francisco or New York. But "prepare" did not mean avoiding the initial infections. Those had already occurred. It simply meant time to ready for triage.

On New Year's Day, 1982, the person who sent the letter to the *Seattle Gay News* signed himself "Extremely Concerned." He had heard rumors that a young man in Seattle had been diagnosed with a severe case of cytomegalovirus, or CMV. Although a rather common virus usually carried without problems, sometimes it caused flu-like symptoms—aches, a cough, fever, sore throat. It could also cut a person's ability to fight infections. For some reason, gay men in other cities had begun visiting doctors' offices with high counts of CMV.

"Extremely Concerned" called himself "a sexually active gay man" quite familiar with "bouts of gonorrhea, hepatitis, warts," but the new reports about pneumonias and cancerous purple skin lesions and now cytomegalovirus were bothersome. "I am seriously considering radically altering my lifestyle," he wrote. "What disturbs me the most is the lack of awareness most gay men have of these diseases. . . . Personally, I'm scared monogamous if not celibate. For all our concern about the Moral Majority . . . I would find it extraordinary if we were defeated not by a band of religious zealots, but by our own dynamic sexuality."

That issue of the city's gay newspaper also headlined a long report written by a doctor defining words few gay men in Seattle knew at the time, words that would become much more frightening as the epidemic spread. Pneumocystis carinii. Kaposi's sarcoma. Immunosuppression.[4]

Still, no cases had yet been reported in the city.

Seven more months passed. In July 1982, the strange complex of infections gained its official name: Acquired Immune Deficiency Syndrome. Four months later, on November 12, 1982, the *Seattle Times* discovered that the plague had arrived in the city—indeed, had arrived the previous June just one year after the CDC report, but the health department had not announced it. The first positive diag-. nosis of a case of AIDS had been made in a man who lived in both San Francisco and Seattle, frequently traveling between the two cities. He had developed Kaposi's sarcoma. By the time the announcement was made, he had already left Seattle. His name was never published; he was simply a shadow that had vanished. Dr. Hunter Handsfield, who as director of the health department's sexually transmitted disease program would be taking the lead in responding to the virus, tried to sound reassuring. Although AIDS had arrived in Seattle, he told the *Post-Intelligencer*, it "is not a scourge that's wiping out people on every street corner; the homosexual community has no reason for panic." Headline writers for both newspapers also seemed at pains to comfort their heterosexual audiences. The *Times* headline rather verbosely called AIDS the "deadly disease that mainly affects gay men," while the *Post-Intelligencer* reassuringly titled its story: "Only One Local Case of Gays' Disease Found."[5]

In its issue that week, the *Seattle Gay News* introduced readers to yet another new word: lymphadenopathy. Handsfield already had fifty men with the symptom under study. "The long word," the writer explained, "refers to a swelling of the lymph glands."[6]Suddenly, a lot more men began to suspect they might be sick.

"When I first arrived in Seattle about a year ago," the column writer in the *Gay News* said, "one of my goals was to achieve emotional release, specifically to regain the ability to cry. I finally achieved this release barely four weeks ago." He had visited a doctor in that fall of 1982 to ask why his two lymph nodes were swollen. "As I allowed the tears to flow and the bad feelings to erupt," he wrote, "I became aware of the verbal messages playing themselves over and over in my head. The one that elicited the most woe, the deepest despair was this: 'I don't matter . . . I don't matter.' Would it be too mystical to suggest that acquired immuno-deficiency syndrome is the perfect physical metaphor for 'I don't matter'? After all, why defend a body that doesn't matter?"[7]

The writer did not sign his column. At first, no one who had the disease wanted to be known, lest they be shunned. AIDS had come with its own new closet.

At first, the disease moved very slowly into Seattle. Three months passed before the diagnosis in January 1983 of a second case, a twenty-seven-year-old gay man hospitalized with pneumocystis carinii. The man's illness was a surprise, Handsfield said; he had actually been part of the health department study but had been dismissed because his symptoms had not met the criteria for AIDS. Then, all of a sudden, he grew sicker. Handsfield still projected calm. "Two cases do not make an epidemic," he told the *Post-Intelligencer*. This time the headline writer referred to it as a "mystery gay disease."[8]

The reports of new diagnoses became steadier. Just a week later, in early February 1983, a third diagnosis was made—this time of a heterosexual who claimed to have had no sexual contact with other men, was not a hemophiliac, and said he did not shoot drugs intravenously, the three factors that seemed likeliest to communicate the virus. He even said he had not been out of the city for two years, apparently presuming that one had to travel outside Seattle in order to acquire the virus. The *Times* headline seemed perplexed this time, noting somewhat contradictorily, "Deadly 'Gay Disease' Found in Heterosexual Seattle Man." For its part, the *Post-Intelligencer* felt that the real news, in fact, was that the "Third AIDS Case is Not a Gay Man."[9]

In late March, the first death of a state resident finally occurred—not of a Seattle man as it turned out, but of a thirty-two-year-old Tacoma man who also challenged the stereotype by identifying as heterosexual. Almost at the same time, a thirty-seven-year-old gay man who had had symptoms of the disease for two years died in a Seattle nursing home. Two weeks later, another young man in his thirties died in Seattle from what officials called "wasting syndrome." His lymph glands had swollen; he had rapidly lost weight; he could no longer fight off infections. He claimed to be neither gay nor a drug user. By the end of the month, a fourth man had died, this time of pneumocystis carinii. He had gone to the emergency room at the Virginia Mason Medical Center to try to get a refill for an oxygen bottle a friend had loaned to him.

The *Post-Intelligencer* dutifully described the way one of the four men had died from "a combination of a herpes-like virus and an amoeba-like parasite called 'pneumocystis carinii' that settled in the lungs." The newspaper added, "The organisms that felled him are quite common and usually no problem for people with normal immune systems."[10] It was as if a Hollywood horror film was slowly unfolding. Seattle would be spared the speed of devastation that had occurred in New York, where in the first year there were more than five hundred diagnosed and almost two hundred dead. But for those most likely to be affected, the slow creep carried its own terror.

The virus quickly interrupted whatever other agendas gay activists had. It brought many challenges. Some were global and scientific: unmasking the mystery of the source and its spread, protecting the blood supplies for hospitals, creating a blood screen to see who had been exposed, looking for a vaccine and a cure. Other challenges were very local and could only be addressed city by city, gay community by gay community. Most of these had to do with communication and with the creation of new geographic spaces.

There was, for example, the question of how to help those who had already contracted the disease. Although each of Seattle's major gay organizations—the Dorian Group, the Seattle Counseling Service, Stonewall, the Lesbian Resource Center—might address a piece of the response, none was equipped to fully focus on the crisis and to help the infected cope with the demands of money and medicine.

Too, there was the need to create communications that would head off further infections, to not just educate, but to change the sexual behaviors that spread the virus—once the scientists figured out what those were. There would be that touchy matter of actually communicating about gay sex. In the 1970s, Brydon had avoided that with his rhetoric about privacy; so had SCAT and WAT by talking about gays and lesbians being neighbors. No one publicly talked about what gay men did in bed together, except, of course, the religious extremists who used graphically exaggerated images as part of their strategy for opposing homosexuality. But if gay men were going to stop the disease, they would have to talk explicitly about what to do and not do sexually, and they would have to conduct that talk in public to reach as wide an audience of both closeted and uncloseted men as they could. It was one thing to confront heterosexuals in the 1970s with public talk about civil rights or privacy or even gay pride. It was quite another to suddenly distribute condoms on Capitol Hill carrying explicit pictures of erections and anal intercourse. The sexual boundaries of Seattle's civic conversation would need to be transfigured.

There would also be the quest to reshape the meaning of certain physical spaces and the types of communication carried on there. Pioneer Square had provided the underground refuge for clandestine social meetings; Renton Hill, the pulpits for a new identity; the University District, space for ideological argument; Denny's knoll, insider reforms. Quickly, AIDS would call into question one specific piece of Seattle's established gay territory: the male bathhouses and their role as possible centers for the kind of sex presumed to spread the disease. AIDS would also dramatically introduce gay concerns into the piece of the civic conversation that dealt with medical care for all citizens. The doors of hospitals would have to open. Who would care for someone carrying what seemed an always fatal virus? Who was a "family" member—the parents who might have rejected their gay son, or the ragtag mob of friends and volunteers who maintained twenty-four-hour vigils? Where would there be new asylums for those who would be sick?

And, finally, of course, there would be mourning to be done.

Bobbi Campbell and Tom Richards first met at the Eleven-Eleven Tavern, one of the neighborhood bars for gay men that began to develop away from Pioneer Square during the 1970s. Both were young—in their early twenties—out, gay, sexual, politically active. Richards had come from the Midwest, via Canada while protesting the war in Vietnam. Bobbi Campbell had been born in Tacoma, had attended the University of Washington, and was volunteering at Bob Deisher's Seattle Counseling Service. Like many other young Capitol Hill gay activists in the 1970s, he lived communally with other gay men in the old box houses. Campbell's residence, Richards recalled in a later interview, was known as the "East John Street Gay Men's Collective" and was located at Eighteenth and East John, just at the divide between Capitol Hill and Renton Hill. It was, Richards said, "a notorious and famous house with colorful and smart people"—all of whom would shortly be prematurely dead. Campbell and Richards became lovers, but Campbell soon moved on from Seattle to San Francisco.[11]

In September 1981, Bobbi Campbell hiked along the Big Sur coast and noticed what looked like blood blisters on his feet. At first, he blamed the hike. But when they stayed and grew, he consulted a doctor. The purple spots were Kaposi's sarcoma, and Bobbi Campbell became the sixteenth case of AIDS to be diagnosed in San Francisco. In December 1981, he was visiting Tom Richards in Seattle when a phone call came from a mutual friend in New York, a friend that Campbell had also been sexual with and had grown to dislike. The friend, named Jim, thought he too might have the gay cancer. Richards remembered: "When Jim was on the phone and Bobbi was standing there, I said you two need to stop fighting with each other and talk, because you both have something that is very rare. You are the earliest people in the country to be experiencing this. I got Bobbi on the phone with Jim, and they mended fences and talked. It was shortly thereafter that Jim died, and he died very quickly."

That same month, Bobbi Campbell decided to go public—one of the first persons with AIDS to do so. In a column in San Francisco's gay newspaper, the *Sentinel,* he wrote: "I'm Bobbi Campbell and I have 'gay cancer.' Although I say that, I also want to say I'm the luckiest man in the world." He proclaimed he would become a "KS Poster Boy," not just a victim or a sufferer. "I'm writing," he declared, "because I have a determination to live. You do too—don't you?" From then on, he started wearing a button that said "Survive." He told friends in both Seattle and San Francisco that no one was doing anything. Organize, he kept saying. Organize.

Because of his willingness to be public, Campbell soon became one of the most prominent people with AIDS in the country. He appeared on a brief segment of the *CBS Evening News,* with reporter Barry Peterson telling the nation, "For Bobbi

Campbell, it is a race against time." Campbell also became part of a gay drag group, the Sisters of Perpetual Indulgence, which was beginning to raise money and educate about AIDS. By then he was a registered nurse, so Campbell christened himself Sister Florence Nightmare and helped design one of the earliest AIDS educational pamphlets.

In August 1983, *Newsweek* put his picture on the cover, along with a story about "Sex, Politics and the Impact of AIDS." Campbell tossed his chin upward, looking boyishly defiant. He was only thirty-one. A week later, he came to Seattle for a panel presentation about AIDS, wearing a T-shirt that said "AIDS Poster Boy" and grinning behind wildly oversized black-rimmed glasses. He walked gently because of the swollen lesions on the bottoms of his feet and told the *Seattle Times,* "Just don't call us victims. I looked that word up in the dictionary. It means 'one who is sacrificed.' That admits defeat. I'm still alive."

A year later he was dead.

James Flanigan became the first person with AIDS in Seattle to actually be named by the city's media. He had moved to the city in the mid-1970s from his home in Wisconsin, and in the late 1970s, he had defeated Hodgkin's disease only to suffer by 1981 from the usual symptoms of AIDS. Multiple infections dilated his blood vessels and weakened his lungs. In his final months, he dropped thirty pounds. One friend, George Bakan, who was also chair of a new Seattle AIDS Action Committee, told the *Times* that at the end Flanigan "was just fed up with getting probed and poked by doctors." When he died in August 1983, James Flanigan was thirty-eight.[12]

Lynn Knox found out that same year, 1983. His blood carried the antibodies to the virus. Knox worked as a cosmetologist and, according to friends, loved to be neat, so the unpleasant discord of the disease—especially the incontinence— would bother him greatly. Doggedly, he took a shower every day even when he did not feel well enough to do so. "I've never seen such a fighter," a friend told the *Seattle Times.* "The guy had class." He also had his cockatoo, Tootles, to love. When he died five years later, Lynn Knox would be forty-two. He would leave the cockatoo to a friend.[13]

In October 1983, in a letter to the *Seattle Gay News,* John Aaron had this to say: "Come on you men of Seattle, WAKE UP, get your head out of the sand, stop looking the other way, stop using stupid unrealistic excuses for continuing your incessant promiscuity. All this is going to accomplish . . . is KILL KILL KILL. Does a cock mean so much to you that you DARE to give or take death for it? . . . It is only through LOVE not LUST that we can fight and survive this AIDS period. Why can't we start loving more and fucking less?"[14]

No one knew what to do at first. What to say. How to say it. Whether being gay and sexual really was unhealthy and needed to be stopped. Whether there was some combination of factors that had made gay anal or oral sex suddenly deadly.

At first, no one even knew that condoms could stop the virus. In the absence of even a single confirmed practical recommendation for prevention—save celibacy—rumors and fears abounded. All that a professional counselor writing in the *Seattle Gay News* in 1982 could say to a worried gay man was: Learn what you can about AIDS. Weigh the advantages and disadvantages of certain behaviors, like multiple sexual contacts. Don't waste time worrying. See a doctor if symptoms develop. Help others who already have the infection. Don't panic.[15]

That was it.

But it was hard not to panic. Tom Richards, Bobbi Campbell's friend, recalled, "I was convinced I had it. I couldn't see any way that couldn't be possible. Everyone I knew, who I had an affair with, or had slept with, had all gotten it." Richards even started running up large credit-card debts and neglecting his work, "living like I was going to die in a very short period." Richards would turn out to be unpredictably lucky. The virus was temperamental; he had not contracted it. He had to pay his bills.[16]

For the first three years, from 1982 through 1984, Seattle built while it waited, creating the underpinnings of what would eventually evolve into a multimillion-dollar structured response to the arrival of the virus.

The government's response would be coordinated through the Seattle–King County Health Department, which formed an AIDS Surveillance Group to track the disease, as well as an AIDS Assessment Clinic to provide counseling and, once a blood test was available, determinations of who had been exposed. For their part, gays and lesbians in the city were by now well experienced at organizing new groups, and they quickly heeded Bobbi Campbell's call to do so. They also learned from their own Initiative Thirteen experience, agreeing to disagree when necessary and thereby creating complementary organizations.

Two quickly emerged as dominant, reflecting a division similar to that between the Dorian Group and the SCAT activists during Initiative Thirteen.

The Northwest AIDS Foundation brought together many of the downtown gay insiders—people like Charlie Brydon, attorneys Jack Jones and Tracy Brown, well-known landscape architect David Poot, and Dr. Robert Wood, a gay physician who had begun treating people with AIDS. At first, from 1982 until 1984, the foundation would primarily focus on raising money and helping those already infected work their way through the bureaucratic morass of welfare and disability payments. When necessary, it would even provide cash to people who had lost their jobs. After 1985, it expanded into education campaigns specifically targeted at gay men.

Taking a more grassroots neighbor-to-neighbor approach, activists such as Josh Joshua, working with the Seattle Gay Clinic, launched an appropriately named Chicken Soup Brigade, which quickly emerged as the gay community's Florence Nightingale. Chicken Soup would eventually be staffed by hundreds of volunteers carrying food to the housebound, cleaning their kitchens and their toilets, driving them to doctors, waiting in emergency rooms. The Northwest AIDS Foundation might deal with bureaucracy and with persuading healthy gay men to stay healthy, but Chicken Soup embodied what was quickly going to become the key value needed to meet the epidemic: compassion.

Two other organizations filled gaps by 1984. Shanti/Seattle would train volunteers to understand the emotional stages of dying and then assign them, long-term, to be buddies with individuals and families. The Seattle AIDS Support Group (SASG), which Josh Joshua also helped create, would form a meeting space for people with AIDS, so they could find companionship and talk about their new lives and ways to empower themselves.

Eventually, SASG would find its home in that gay healing space of the early 1970s, Renton Hill, moving into an old box house at Seventeenth Avenue and John Street. It was next to Bobbi Campbell's old corner.

The first challenge was to decide what could be done and what could not—not easy when so little was known about the virus or how, exactly, people contracted it. When a group of gay businessmen held a meeting with Hunter Handsfield in May 1983, one member of the audience angrily accused the man who was in charge of Seattle's response of doing nothing but saying that AIDS could be acquired through sex. According to a *Seattle Times* report, Handsfield shrugged and answered, "You're entirely right. I haven't said much. We don't know why it happens."[17] And no one was sure how to stop it.

In that atmosphere, it was easy to look for any target where it seemed that something—anything—could be done. San Francisco's health department had decided to launch an attack on a piece of gay geography, zeroing in on gay bathhouses and trying to close them. At least, the thinking went, something visible could be done to stop the promiscuous "lifestyle" that physicians were then saying seemed to contribute to what the media was calling "the gay disease." Seattle quickly confronted the same tactical question.

Bathhouses for men had held a place in the city's landscape ever since the 1890s, when several sprang up to serve miners off to the Yukon and Klondike. By the early 1900s, at least seven were listed in a city directory, among them the Marble Baths on Cherry, the Club Baths on Jefferson, and the Hotel Tourist baths on Occidental. They offered a little warm steam to shake off the cold, dirty winters as well as a place to relax and enjoy stories about the fortune ahead or the journey behind. Perhaps the best known had been the Turkish Bath at the Northern Hotel on First Avenue, built by Seattle pioneers Charles Terry and Arthur Denny shortly after the Great Fire of 1889 leveled most of the mudflat. The Northern, constructed in a high Victorian style of red brick and gray stone, had become one of Seattle's major hotels during the Alaskan gold rush and remained so during the early part of the century. Its baths spread through the basement. During World War II, after the Northern's heyday had ended, the steam works became a separate operation, known as the South End Steam Baths. Whatever the mixture of clientele had been before, it now became definitively gay. Like owners of other gay establishments, the South End's operator, Edwin McCleary, took to paying off the police in the 1950s and 1960s to stay in business—up to two hundred dollars a month. The South End would operate for five decades before it closed in the 1990s.

For gay men in Seattle, such places as the South End provided rituals that were both sexual and social. One explanation of their attraction had come in January 1978 before AIDS arrived, when a man whose only name was Stioux talked to the *Seattle Gay News* in exuberant terms about what the baths offered, as well as what the gay sex that some defined as promiscuous provided. Stioux was a spokesman for Dave's Baths in Belltown, which had once been managed by Jacob Heimbigner before Heimbigner bought the Atlas Steam Bath in Pioneer Square. "One of the things I really like about being gay," Stioux said, "is the freedom, which I don't see in the straight community, to express ourselves and play in places like baths, where people are encouraged to do whatever they want to do, within reason, without hurting anyone." Men went to the baths to find not only sex but companions, maybe even their Prince Charming, which he assured the readers happened "often enough." Even when gay men rejected one another's advances, Stioux cheerily noted, they usually very gently removed the hand that had tentatively touched their thigh. No roughness, no rudeness. "How nice, how considerate," he said.[18]

Even after AIDS arrived, the baths held a mystique for gay men. A *Seattle Gay News* writer, T. T. Roth, described the allure in a 1986 story: "There was something about those hallways, their silent promise, that reminded me of barracks, of trusting or needing to trust other men. . . . I met a man some weeks ago. He wasn't obviously attractive [but] our eyes met and there was a kinship."[19] At their best, the baths provided a geography where one could affirm the value of even the briefest of sexual relationships, in a dissent from the cultural belief that the only relationships that truly mattered were those that were long-lasting.

To heterosexuals, the gay baths furnished shadowy sexual intrigue and fear. In 1967, a writer for *Seattle* magazine named Patrick Douglas toured the gay world in Pioneer Square and ventured into Heimbigner's Atlas Steam Bath, located on Occidental Street just behind the Double Header and the Casino. The bath, Douglas wrote, was "the most intriguing item" on his itinerary. He undressed, wrapped a towel around his waist, and walked down a narrow hallway past a three-foot-high replica of Michelangelo's David, all the while listening to the sounds of Rachmaninoff's Second Piano Concerto. He made it as far as the steam room with its three tiers of tiled seats and men hazily visible in the mist. Then he bolted for the outside.[20]

When AIDS struck, Seattle had five gay bathhouses: the South End; Dave's; the Pines, just across the street from the Paramount Theater on Pine Street; the Zodiac Club on Pike Street; and the freshly opened Club Seattle, on Summit Avenue between Pike and Pine. Each projected a particular atmosphere. The South End, having been around for decades, tended to attract the oldest and most sociable crowd, men who had grown comfortable going underground for their gay life. Club Seattle, at the other end of the spectrum, seemed to a *Gay News* writer to be for the gay yuppies, the clean-shaven muscular types who sometimes preferred tease to action. In between was Dave's, "feeling like an old shoe that has been worn a lot," a blue-collar type of bathhouse. The Pines, the *Gay News* writer labeled as the bath for drag queens; the Zodiac for the hairy-chested, sadomasochistically inclined "macho" men.[21]

When the *Seattle Times* published its first major article about the response of the city's gay men to AIDS, it turned to the bathhouses for comment, even illustrating its April 1983 story with a picture taken inside the Zodiac Club. The bath, the *Times* told its readers, "looks like an elderly hotel that has been painted black inside." It was an elderly hotel, the *Times* also noted, with a whirlpool, a weight room, a sauna, and a fantasy room with leather and chains. Standing beneath a huge mural of Superman's ripped muscles, as well as a discreetly smaller painting of a similarly sculpted naked man, the Zodiac's operator, James Brown, confessed that he was beginning to use more germicide and that his customers seemed to be showering more often. But otherwise, he said, they were feeling that the AIDS threat had been sensationalized.[22]

Deciding how to confront the role that bathhouses played in gay life was not only a public health issue, but also the tip of beginning to talk more outwardly in public about the kind of sex gay men were having. For some homosexuals, as well as heterosexuals, the bathhouse became the symbol—rhetorical and geographic—for what had suddenly gone wrong in gay life. In San Francisco, health department director Mervyn Silverman decided that closing the baths was one way to change sexual behavior. In Seattle, the question was whether to do the same. But was it really the public health department's responsibility to force a change in behavior? Or was the more important priority to provide AIDS education, testing, and treatment?

The gay community in Seattle was as divided as that in any other city about what was happening at the baths. In 1983, letters began to appear in the *Seattle Gay News,* criticizing in particular a new ad series from the Zodiac emphasizing photos of naked men. James Brown of the Zodiac angrily responded that some of the writers seemed to prefer pictures of men "dressed as women or in some equally unaggressive, impotent pose." He defiantly promised to keep placing the ads, and praised the *Gay News* for publishing them. David Poot, helping to raise money for the new Northwest AIDS Foundation, would later condemn the baths and those who went. "Bathhouses that are just letting unsafe sexual activity run rampant should be closed down," he told the *Post-Intelligencer.* Paul Kawata, then a board member of the Dorian Group, disagreed; he was concerned about the civil rights of those who wanted to frequent the baths. "Bathhouses don't give people AIDS," he would say. "People give people AIDS."[23]

In the dispute about the gay bathhouses, there was a bit of that old Seattle conflict over the city's red-light zones—the Arthur Dennys meeting up with the Doc Maynards and debating, in this case, what was now respectable for gay men to be doing and what was not, and whether to preserve a small remnant of the public geography where male-male sex could be pursued freely and legally.

Into that fray walked the first, and perhaps most unlikely, of what would become a string of streetwise gay—and lesbian—protagonists combating the virus in Seattle.

Larry Woelich was a burly man who had grown up out in the Missouri countryside in the 1940s and 1950s, a "ridge runner" as he referred to himself in a later interview, "the youngest of eight country hillbillies." "We didn't have running water in our house until I was ten," he would say, "and you went out to the six-shooter outhouse that was twenty feet behind the house, and you wiped your ass with this Sears wish book because toilet paper was a luxury you could not afford."[24] When he was just five years old, Woelich figured out he liked sex with men; very early in his little town of about four thousand people, he was known as the "homo" kid. By high school, the co-captain of the football team would pick him up after dates with the cheerleaders, then "we'd take one of the side roads out in the country and we'd get in the backseat and I'd satisfy him." Once, in 1960, a brother sent him to a psychiatrist. "I had the most wonderful good fortune," Woelich recalled. The psychiatrist did not try to force a change; instead he just warned Woelich that society would treat him like an outcast and what the psychiatrist could do "was to help me accept myself for who I was."

Eventually, Woelich was on the streets, kicked out by his brothers, fending for himself first in St. Louis and later in California. Jobs came and went; so did criminal charges for theft and lewd conduct. Alcohol. Drugs. He finished high school in a California prison and graduated to the Castro just as it was blossoming in the 1960s. Then, back in Missouri in 1970 to care for a father dying of cancer, he went to work for a new national chain of gay bathhouses, the Club Baths. In six months, he became manager of the St. Louis bath. There he would learn a lesson that would prove extremely valuable a decade and a half later in Seattle.

"The health department was harassing us," he said in the interview. "They would come out and say that John Doe was in your baths on such and such a date. He came down with gonorrhea or syphilis. We need to check your records." Then the health department inspectors would go through the lists of men who had checked into the bathhouse that day, ostensibly to track any potential sexual contacts that "John Doe" had had. After several months of visits, Woelich grew impatient. "I said, why don't we try to work out something here? You come here on a weeknight. People will volunteer for smears and blood. You take and run the test, and let's see exactly how many positives, or hot bloods, you get out of here, because I think you're wrong in your presumption. People are using us as a scapegoat and we're not guilty."

Perhaps surprisingly, the health department agreed to the plan.

"It turned out that I was right in that we weren't the cause," Woelich said. "People were getting the gonorrhea and syphilis elsewhere," but rather than be honest, those who had gotten infected were just saying, "I had contact at the baths."

The program worked so well, Woelich began it at other Club Bath outlets once he transferred to Dallas, then became the chain's general manager traveling to several different cities. In Dallas, the police once raided the bathhouse and arrested patrons while Woelich had the health inspectors there. "I asked that the health department be excused," he laughed.

Sent to Seattle to set up a new bathhouse right after Initiative Thirteen failed, Woelich at first had to wait when the financing collapsed, but by April 1981 he was back in charge of the project, and in the summer of 1982, at the most inauspicious time possible, the new Club Seattle opened.

Woelich never believed bathhouses had to be the shadowy, unspoken side of gay life. As much as any other gay business, they could be part of the community's infrastructure. When Stan Hill began promoting the new gay chamber of commerce, the Greater Seattle Business Association, Woelich became one of the founders, serving as the business group's vice president for two years. When the virus hit, he worked with the Northwest AIDS Foundation to search for its first managers; then, he joined the Chicken Soup Brigade as one of its directors, sometimes filling up grocery carts at Costco and conveniently forgetting to charge Chicken Soup for the food.

"We put our heads in the sand, initially, saying [AIDS] wasn't going to happen in Seattle," Woelich remembered. "Then it began to really hit. They began to threaten to close down [the bathhouses]. That's when I really put my nose to the grindstone and really began to kiss butt with the health department. I made changes in the baths, bringing the lights up, closing public areas, being almost monitorial in watching the people."

In late April 1984, Woelich and the operators of Seattle's other bathhouses met privately with Dr. Steve Helgerson, who by then had been placed in charge of the health department's AIDS Surveillance Project. In San Francisco, Silverman's conflict with the baths was already raging. In Seattle, the health department technically had licensing and inspection control over the cleanliness of any hot tubs in the baths, but not over the behavior that was occurring around the hot tubs. However, everyone knew that in a health crisis, extra authority from the city and county governments was available for the asking. Helgerson had been watching what Silverman was trying to do in San Francisco, but he was skeptical, partly because he had seen other health campaigns to change behavior, such as those to reduce smoking, have very limited impact for the amount of money spent. "We have been unsuccessful in changing behavior," he told the *Seattle Gay News*. "People who are intent on having intimate sexual contact are going to do it" whatever the health department says. Better, Helgerson suggested, to focus on the higher priorities. "People with AIDS are not interested in having us regulate their lives," he said.[25]

At the meeting, Woelich argued passionately that the baths could actually be centers for exactly what the health department believed was its priority: getting the word out about what gay men needed to do to avoid contracting AIDS. The issue was not sex, or even promiscuous sex. It was being safer. The baths could be used to distribute condoms. The baths could be used for testing.

A month later, Helgerson and the bath owners met to determine details. Woelich's previous experience and Helgerson's own skepticism fused. The health department, Helgerson agreed, would provide pamphlets and posters for education, even workshops for bathhouse employees and patrons. Bathhouses would circulate the information, a significant step since few bath operators around the country had ever reminded their patrons that anything about sex could be dangerous. At the moment, Helgerson said, the health department could not afford to provide free condoms; bathhouse owners would look for a way to do that.[26]

"People," Woelich recalled later, "thought I was crazy when I started putting condoms in the baths." Soon enough, he was even bringing in porn stars to run AIDS workshops.

"Had you asked me in '73 about gay men using condoms," Woelich said, "I would have laughed in your face, among other things. But in '84 and '85, I saw people changing their attitudes about sex. I was pleased being part of that."

With more money available by the 1990s, the health department would even send workers into the baths to offer free, anonymous testing for AIDS, reaching men unlikely to turn to traditional clinics. The bathhouses, for their part, made customers sign a promise to use condoms if they engaged in oral or anal sex— though the operators left it up to the men themselves to enforce the rule.[27]

In San Francisco, Silverman's approach would generate years of costly court battles, ultimately unsuccessful. Seattle had found a different way: keep the bathhouses part of the city's sexual geography, and make them speakers in the conversation. For his AIDS efforts, Woelich would be given an award from the Greater Seattle Business Association in 1991 and a Northwest AIDS Foundation citizen of the year award in 1993.

This was the tally after the first three years, the period in which it could be said that AIDS arrived in Seattle. In 1982, one person had been diagnosed with AIDS, the man who lived in both Seattle and San Francisco. He died. In 1983, eleven people were diagnosed. They all died. In 1984, sixty were diagnosed. Fifty-seven of them died within a handful of years.

Gradually, gay men who had the disease took the risk of coming out of the AIDS closet and giving a face to the local reporting, much as Peter Wichern had done for local homosexuals in general in 1967. Among those was Carl Orme. In November 1984, Orme discovered that his skin had suddenly begun to erupt in shingles. Each day that winter, he struggled to go to his work as an office manager for the federal government's National Labor Relations Board, but by mid-February, he faced pneumonia and a three-week stay in the hospital. One drug caused a seizure and drove him into intensive care. The diagnosis: AIDS. Orme, a slight and gentle-appearing man with a mustache and an easy smile, eventually managed to go home with the help of his lover, James Finley. Together, they read books on the spirituality of dying. For a year, Orme became a local Bobbi Campbell, one of those with AIDS finally willing to be identified publicly. He addressed gay pride parades, churches, and Congressional hearings and even appeared on KING television. Finley was always with him. He too had been diagnosed with AIDS.

Toward the end, Orme spoke to a group of hospice nurses. "I ask myself," he said, "will the journey be peaceful? Can it be peaceful? Can it be loving, can it be giving, can it be without self-doubt and without beating myself over the head and being hard on myself?"

When he died on September 25, 1986, he was forty-five.

Almost exactly a year later, on September 11, 1987, his partner, James, died. He was thirty-nine.[28]

Despite the frequently heard warnings from Seattle health officials and gay leaders that no one should panic because of the arrival of AIDS, some did anyway.

In fall 1983, for example, an unverified "AIDS alert" list of about ten names of Seattle men believed to be carrying the virus appeared one morning on the seats of police cars, apparently circulated by police officers. About the same time, the police guild's newspaper, the *Guardian,* published an article saying that AIDS could be caught by any contact with mucous membranes, sexual or not, and that any body fluid, whether blood, urine, saliva, semen, or feces, could transmit the disease. Incensed by the list, gay activists demanded an apology; George Bakan of the AIDS Action Committee called it an "affront." The health department's Helgerson also criticized the list as "inappropriate" as well as unverified. The whole incident, Helgerson said, seemed to reflect the "hysteria surrounding AIDS," since police officers taking the reasonable precautions they should with any citizen would have no worry about contracting the virus. Helgerson added that he recognized none of the names as people participating in health department studies. As activists prepared to demonstrate outside the police department, the chief, Patrick Fitzsimons, quickly apologized and ordered an investigation.

In fact, the list was the same as one held by the health department's own employees at Harborview Medical Center. Whether a health worker had violated confidentiality and leaked the document was never clear; the health department quickly denied that any security had been breached just because the hospital had the list.[29]

The health department continuously tried to reassure people that the virus could not be caught casually. Hunter Handsfield, for example, pointed out in 1985 the results of a CDC study that examined 101 family members or housemates of people who had AIDS and who lived with them for more than two years, hugging them, kissing them, sometimes even sharing toothbrushes. None had caught the virus. On the other hand, sometimes the health department's own statistics, or its means of gathering them and discussing their significance, frightened people. The same year Handsfield was being so reassuring, 1985, the department was reporting that one-third of the gay men it had treated for sexually transmitted diseases in its clinics in 1982 and 1983 had been exposed to the virus, and Handsfield told the *Times* that that figure had probably risen to 50 percent during 1984. The lead on the *Times* story promptly emphasized the speculative 50 percent and attributed it to "a new study." That prompted the health department to warn that there was no such thing as "safe sex" for gay men. Even open-mouth kissing was suspect. The problem with the statistic, as even Handsfield acknowledged, was that it reflected only the gay men going to the department's clinics; whether it actually represented all gay men in the city was neither known nor likely, since many were already practicing safer sex techniques and probably not going to the health department for checkups. That particular fact seemed lost in the fears. Even the *Seattle Gay News* headlined that 35 percent of "Seattle gays" had been infected. A month later, in February, when the results from 1984 were finally in and showed that a steady one-third—not 50 percent—of those who had gone to the health department had been exposed, the *Seattle Times* quoted health officials as saying that the statistic "suggested one-third of the gay community may be carrying the germ or have been exposed to it."[30]

Some incidents of fear bordered on the comical. When a trade journal for plumbers printed an article in December 1986 saying that plumbers might contract AIDS from cleaning drains and sewers, a Seattle company refused to go to the Northwest AIDS Foundation offices to unclog a sink, prompting the foundation's president at the time, lawyer Robert Rohan, to angrily complain, "What did they think they were going to do, have sex with the sink?" At Club Seattle, Woelich battled with a deliveryman from Frito-Lay who, after more than three years of making deliveries, suddenly decided to stop servicing the vending machines located inside the bathhouse. He was afraid he might contract AIDS simply by walking in and breathing the air. When the company tried shipping the products by mail, Woelich exploded and filed a complaint with the state Human Rights Commission. He eventually won five hundred dollars and a promise by Frito-Lay to educate its employees about how AIDS could be caught. Elsewhere in the Northwest, the comical bordered on the absurdly insulting. At an Indian guru's compound in Oregon that included six thousand residents, some from Seattle, followers were issued rubber gloves while a spokesman assured the *Seattle Times* that those with AIDS would be treated humanely. They would be isolated, the spokesman said, but if necessary, "they will have a disco or whatever."[31]

The health department was facing its own problems of fear. In 1986, once it had secured a $365,000 grant from the Centers for Disease Control to create a new AIDS Prevention Project to coordinate counseling and testing, it could not find anyone to rent space to the project. One office owner begged off saying that another tenant needed the vacant space being advertised; the space was still vacant two months later. A real estate agent asked whether there was any way to pretend the project was for herpes instead of AIDS. Another agent offered a small space, saying it was probably the only thing she could locate. Still another building owner delayed an answer for more than a month. Others just refused. Out of ten offices the health department thought were suitable, only two owners agreed to rent. Ann Downer, one of the project's health educators, told the *Seattle Times* that the search itself had been a "living lesson" and an example of the "second epidemic of AIDS, the fear."[32]

Even securing enough doctors to treat the disease proved difficult. At first, most gay men saw Dr. Wood or one of two brothers, Tim or Tom Smith. Repeatedly, medical associations and health officials had to call for more doctors to attend workshops and begin treating patients.[33]

Activists began to talk of three epidemics: AIDS, the fear of AIDS, and then underlying it all, a fear of homosexuals, period.

Out on the streets, the fear showed itself in countless little incidents, particularly after the summer of 1985, when Rock Hudson died shortly after announcing that he had AIDS. That was the same year that a blood test to screen for the virus first began to be widely available. Now even those who still appeared healthy started to learn they had been exposed and that the virus was imperceptibly but relentlessly destroying their immune systems.

A gay man with Kaposi's sarcoma told the *Seattle Times* about an incident when he was in a drugstore, wearing sunglasses to mask the chemotherapy he was undergoing. A stranger blurted, "There's AIDS in Seattle. What if I sit next to one of them on the bus!" Another time, two men delivering a sofa overheard him talking about his treatment for AIDS. One dropped the couch and urged his partner to hurriedly leave.

Heterosexuals reported they were no longer eating at restaurants on Capitol Hill, or sharing glasses of water, or nibbling from the same appetizer trays.

At an AIDS hotline the health department had created to answer questions about the disease, calls began to arrive not just about the transmission of the disease but about being fired from jobs or having troubles with supervisors.[34]

Then in September 1985, Jim Wright, a Republican candidate for the chief executive's job in King County, made quarantining people with AIDS the centerpiece of his campaign. Wright, a Port of Seattle commissioner, also said he believed all medical and restaurant workers in the county should be tested for AIDS and fired if they had the virus. He attacked gay men, saying that since they had acquired the disease "through voluntary activities," they, and not Seattle or King County, should "shoulder the economic burden associated with their poor choices." In the primary, he lost. Some suggested gay Democratic voters had crossed over to vote for his opponent, Tim Hill, who eventually won the post in the general election.[35]

In Olympia, gay activists were not as successful. A *Seattle Times* news story noted that in the state's capitol, AIDS was not simply a deadly disease. For Christian conservatives, political reporter Walter Hatch wrote, "AIDS has suddenly become a political weapon, being used to bludgeon gay-rights proposals to death." The Dorian Group, now being led by a new president, Jim Holm, still dutifully tried each year to secure a statewide law to prevent job discrimination, but now encountered the AIDS argument. For example, Ken Steely, the head of the Bill of Rights Legal Foundation, a lobby representing evangelical Christians, told Hatch that if heterosexuals had to hire homosexuals or do business with them, they would be exposed to the virus. Homosexuals, he said, were clearly to blame for the disease, whatever the evidence emerging about heterosexual transmission. "They brought it in," he said, "and they fostered it." Holm complained of an "orchestrated campaign" to exploit fear. The Dorians would succeed at heading off the calls for quarantine and would be able to secure state funding for various AIDS education and treatment programs, but the rest of the civil rights agenda would have to wait.[36]

Whenever Handsfield and other health department officials had to, which seemed repeatedly, they dutifully reiterated their mantra to the politicians: The virus could not be contracted casually. Education, not regulation. Treatment, not punishment.

From 1985 through 1987, when the virus could be said to have settled in, the numbers rose frighteningly—never as bad as the statistics in San Francisco, of course, but still startling percentage increases. In 1985, the number of new cases diagnosed in Seattle and King County passed a landmark: the symbolic 100, or to be exact, 104. The next year, the number almost doubled to 186, then to 274. More than 90 percent of those individuals would be dead within a few years after their diagnosis; only a few would still be living at the turn of the century.

In September 1985, the same month Jim Wright called for a quarantine, Richard Hennigh decided to talk publicly about having AIDS. It wasn't easy; he had grown up in eastern Washington, had married at one point and had a daughter. Also, having been elected "Mr. Leather of Washington" in 1985, Hennigh held a very visible role in that part of gay drag culture emphasizing boots and chains over pumps and beads. Hennigh had interwoven elements of both, becoming known in the local gay bars for the way he juxtaposed street mime and intricate geisha-like fan dances with a uniform that included a leather harness, a black leather cap, and his own muscular, well-haired chest. Sometimes he danced six hours at a time; the audiences loved it. But since 1981, Hennigh had experienced one illness after another: shingles, hepatitis, what his doctor thought was an entrenched sinus infection, and, finally, pneumocystis carinii. Hennigh knew what people would think: leather and AIDS and promiscuity—they went together, didn't they? In an interview with the *Seattle Gay News,* he pointed out that that was false. "I'm the most conservative gay man around," he said. "I can count on my fingers the number of lovers I've had. I wasn't promiscuous. We leather folks get a lot of the blame, and it's just not true." More than four hundred people, including leathermen from across the country, attended a benefit in his honor held at one of the bars, Sparks, where Hennigh had worked.

By the winter of 1987, he weighed less than 120 pounds.

When Richard Hennigh died on April 20, 1987, he was thirty-seven.[37]

If only they knew . . . If only they paid attention . . . If only they changed . . .

Practical as Steve Helgerson's decision had been to avoid frittering the health department's resources trying to regulate the unregulatable in the bathhouses, it still left many questions unanswered: What could be done to change the behaviors in Seattle that were transmitting the disease? Could the number of new infections be cut, even as the old ones were making themselves terrifyingly visible? What, if any, kind of education campaign would work?

At first, as scientists learned more about how the virus moved from person to person, the emphasis became simply getting the information out. Just tell people, the thought went, and their behavior would change. The virus was in the blood, so be careful with blood. Screen the donors. Monitor transfusions. Use caution around other people's bloody noses or open wounds. The virus was in the semen, so avoid semen. Or at least the semen of partners with whom you were not monogamous. When in doubt, abstain from sex.

It was simple, really, especially once scientists confirmed in 1985 that condoms could block the virus. As simple a message as any in a first grade health class. Wash your hands. Brush your teeth. Use a condom. Abstain.

For a while, the new cadre of AIDS educators beginning to form both in Seattle and across the country seemed to believe that the "information model" would be enough. They began coining terms that people could use to easily name, and thus remember, what they were supposed to do or not do, catalogued into lists on brochures or posters. Sometimes it was called "risk reduction," a bureaucratic label that, while accurate, probably appealed to no one, least of all gay men still interested in the adventure or play of sex. In New York and San Francisco, gay activists began promoting a manual called "How to Have Sex in an Epidemic," but they did not have a clear term to refer to this new kind of sex. Bobbi Campbell's group, the Sisters of Perpetual Indulgence, published one of the earliest booklets, referring to "playing fair" and having "fair sex."

Eventually, two different types of information rhetoric emerged, in Seattle as well as the rest of the nation. The first was the government's, which referred to clinical descriptions: penises, semen, anal or oral intercourse, condoms, risk reduction. The mass media was nervous about any explicit sexual descriptions, so it either adopted the government terms or blurred them further, vaguely telling readers and viewers that scientists thought AIDS could be transmitted by "intimate sexual contact," or even sidestepping an explanation altogether.[38] Gay activists, on the other hand, gradually decided that street jargon for sex might be more effective: cocks, cum, fucking, sucking, rubbers, rimming, fisting.

So, there would be two rhetorical campaigns—partly because the government and media terminology never seemed to keep up with all the imaginative ways people could have sex, and all the questions they would have when they found an AIDS educator in a classroom, on the street, or at the baths. If oral intercourse was dangerous, as the government said, who was most at risk, the one giving head or the one getting head? Was the "top" or the "bottom" most likely to transmit the virus? "Bodily fluids" covered a wide range. Was spit as dangerous a bodily fluid as pre-cum? Sometimes the government did not even have words for what people were doing—no easily recognizable clinical terms for "rimming" or "fisting," for example, leading Helgerson to have to blend the language occasionally, as in this comment in the *Seattle Gay News* in 1984 when he was describing problem behaviors: "Receptive anal intercourse involving the exchange of bodily fluids, rimming and fisting are examples of risk factors. . . . Gay males who are sexually active with multiple sex partners and who exchange bodily fluids with them" are most "at risk."[39]

One of the first times that the Seattle media used what would become the most popular slogan occurred when Bobbi Campbell, during his 1983 visit to the city, told the *Times* reporter that he believed people with AIDS could still have "safe sex." Gradually, throughout 1984 and 1985, the term spread until by 1986 it was the dominant way to refer to what the government was still calling "risk reduction strategies."

Quickly, though, AIDS educators found that it was one thing to teach the new rules, and quite another for individuals to actually change behavior. Lovers and new encounters did not necessarily talk beforehand about what kind of sex to have; they just had it. A romantic or lustful silence could enhance the action, especially at the bathhouses. Also, all the rules being propounded by doctors sounded bureaucratic, and everyone knew that no government agency really wanted to promote sex between men.

Were the rules themselves homophobic? Could AIDS educators really be trusted? In an epidemic, could anyone?

David Poot learned his diagnosis not from a doctor but from an insurance company in early 1986. On the advice of his lawyer, he had applied for an extra one hundred thousand dollars in life insurance coverage because he had purchased a new condominium; the insurance company promised that the blood test it wanted would be checked only for signs of the hepatitis Poot had suffered a decade earlier. Instead, the company also tested for the AIDS antibodies, and then denied the policy when Poot tested positive.

Poot was anything but a pushover. At six-and-a-half feet tall, he was built like a basketball star, looked a bit Kennedyesque, and had already created three reputations: professionally as one of the city's leading landscape designers (six Seattle

Symphony Designer Showcase homes to his credit); politically as a creator of the Northwest AIDS Foundation, a member of the governor's Commission on Human Rights, and president of the Greater Seattle Business Association; and socially as a flamboyant and very out gay man who enjoyed wearing a T-shirt that said, "Queen of the Universe." At his well-landscaped home on Capitol Hill, its secluded garden populated by statues and fountains, Poot often staged private receptions for groups like the foundation or for politicians such as California senator Alan Cranston, whose presidential bid he had once helped.

Clearly, the life insurance company had picked on the wrong person. Infuriated, Poot sued. The company ended up not only issuing the policy, but paying a settlement to end the suit.

For Poot, it was an ugly blip in a life that otherwise seemed filled with beauty and grace. As a child in West Seattle, he had early shown an inclination for designing, relocating the plants in his parents' yard and using his allowance money for begonias. He eventually saw his home near Volunteer Park featured in *Architectural Digest* and *Sunset Magazine;* his Hawaiian residence included an acre for unusual tropical plants, sited personally by Poot. At one of the AIDS foundation's awards ceremonies, he showed up with Hawaiian ti leaves, which he told the audience were believed to provide healing and protection. One foundation official remembered that he passed out more than a thousand.

Poot lived for eight years beyond his diagnosis. When he died in April 1994, David Poot was fifty-three.[40]

The same month Poot heard his diagnosis from the insurance company, January 1986, the Northwest AIDS Foundation deployed what would be the first major education campaign in Seattle to combine the staid "information model" of medical advice with Madison Avenue marketing and street activism. Using a federal grant routed through the U.S. Conference of Mayors, the foundation turned to an ad agency and a local gay graphic artist, Lee Sylvester, for ideas that would sell on the street, but, because of the federal funding involved, would not use language as explicit as that being used by gay activists in other cities. The agency decided to capitalize on the notion of "safety" as well as on the idea that many gay men were catching AIDS by leading a "fast lane" life when it came to sex. Combining the two ideas produced the metaphor of highway safety. The foundation put its volunteer coordinator, an affable and talkative man named Carl Wagner, in charge of organizing "safe sex" strike teams that would go onto the streets and into the bars and baths to hand out small, one-inch round, black-and-yellow buttons portraying a road-curve traffic sign with its "S."

Soon enough, the buttons blanketed Capitol Hill, even becoming so popular that at one point, according to a foundation worker, a drag queen made off with several thousand, hoping to turn them into a sequined safe-sex dress. The foundation got them back only by convincing him to make a halter top instead.[41]

Three posters targeted particular subsets of gay men. A picture of a traffic detour sign with wording saying "AIDS is not the end of the road" was intended to reach those who had quit sex all together, panicked at the thought of touching another gay man. A road dip sign with the text "A word about those who won't shift gears for safer sex" was aimed at men still ignoring the warnings. The final poster, the picture of the road curve, read "the gay community takes a turn for the better." That one was for everyone, to emphasize that practicing "safe sex" could produce a better sexual experience, not a worse one.

Wagner's teams also handed out black-and-yellow cards listing the "Rules of the Road." The "safest" sex, the rules said, was mutual masturbation, dry kissing, body rubbing, and unshared sex toys. "Possibly safe" sex included intercourse with condoms, deep kissing, and "external water sports." Unsafe sex was fisting, rimming, oral sex, "water sports, swallowed," and shared sex toys.

But why the buttons, and not just the cards or posters, which, after all, contained the important information? The foundation's first ad in the *Seattle Gay News* explained the reason. "How to talk about such a delicate subject" as safe sex? the ad asked. "Here's how. Let the Safety Pin make your statement. . . . Wear a Safety Pin. You'll find yourself in good company." It was clever. The idea was not only to rivet a new set of rules into gay men's minds, but to amplify an old identification system that some gay men, particularly in bars, had already been using—a code of placing differently colored handkerchiefs in either the left or right back pocket to indicate preferences for the types of sex enjoyed. Now, the foundation hoped, those who intended to practice safe sex could simply wear the pin. No embarrassing negotiations, no "delicate talk" beforehand. And the more pins in a bar or on the street, the greater the peer pressure on all gay men to behave accordingly.[42]

The foundation also hoped to move the conversation past all the "do nots" that had been issuing from the government. "It puts a positive focus on dealing with the issue," Jack Jones, the foundation's president, told the *Seattle Times*. "Before there hasn't been anything positive. We're trying to emphasize a viable option, and our only real option."[43] In the *Seattle Gay News*, the foundation tried to make the campaign even more upbeat, emphasizing that Wagner, the coordinator of the program, was going to have fun with his highway signs. The story, written partially by the foundation itself, joked, "If you're one of those who has the impression that the Northwest AIDS Foundation has tended to be peopled by somewhat stiff types who are happiest with cocktail party chit-chat and yuppie networking . . . go talk to Carl and you'll get over your stereotypes fast. . . . In these somewhat dismal times, it's good to be reminded that laughter is infectious and Carl knows how to turn the energy of anxiety into the release of upbeat talk and action."[44]

The campaign's rhetoric was threefold: to teach the rules, to directly influence changes in interpersonal behavior, and to make the foundation's own messages seem more credible and more personal.

But could success really be measured? A year later, when the "Rules of the Road"

The discovery of the AIDS virus in 1981 presented the city's homosexual community with not only a medical challenge, but also questions about how to discuss sex in education campaigns. The Northwest AIDS Foundation launched its first prevention campaign subtly, with a "Rules of the Road" metaphor urging gay men to use condoms, 1986. *(Geoff Manasse, Northwest AIDS Foundation)*

theme ended, a foundation official told the *Gay News* that he could not point to any statistics proving a certain number of people had avoided AIDS because of the Safety Pins. But, he said, awareness had increased. That would always be the problem for gay AIDS educators—to know, when they saw their friends dying around them, whether their efforts really made any difference. The foundation tried to collect proof at the 1987 gay pride parade, passing around questionnaires. Some 60 percent of the 231 people who responded said they had changed their behavior, and of those, one-third said it was due to safe sex education. That made the educators feel good—except for that other 40 percent, a sizeable number considering that the epidemic was now six years old.[45]

At the start of the "Rules of the Road" campaign, the executive director of the foundation, Bea Kelleigh, had told the *Seattle Times* that only a single measure counted. "If one person does not get sick as a result of the campaign," she said, "it will have paid for itself."

Surprisingly, that was not just a corny sound bite. It was true. The campaign and all the little buttons Wagner was distributing would cost $100,000. Doctors were saying that caring for one person with AIDS was already running up to $150,000.

Michael Gallanger had been a lover with Jack Jones, the attorney who helped create the Northwest AIDS Foundation. Gallanger's other two loves were carpentry—he worked remodeling houses—and his dog, Abigail. After Gallanger became too sick to work, he taught another young man the trade and then gave him his tools. Abigail he fretted about. "He was worried about leaving her," Jones recalled. When he died in December 1986, Michael Gallanger was thirty-three, and Jones inherited Abigail.

Another man with AIDS, Andy Cruz, had moved with his family from Guam to Tacoma when he was three years old. In January 1987, he asked to be let free from a hospital bed so he could go to the Jesuits' St. Joseph's Church on Capitol Hill. He said he wanted to attend a Mass, his first in more than two years. He rolled in in a wheelchair, intravenous tubes and an oxygen tank at his side. He died a month later.[46]

Andy Cruz was just twenty-three.

And the epidemic was just beginning.

# 18
# Becoming Compassion

*a* s some AIDS activists in Seattle developed strategies to change behavior in the hopes of saving those not yet infected, scientists and other activists pursued a different route, setting out to reduce the harm the infections could cause and to treat those who were already infected. Condoms, the researchers pointed out, could never be 100 percent effective even if individuals did use them. They might break. Men might get bored using them. Treatment drugs, vaccines, a cure—those were the things that were really needed. Those, plus spaces to treat the ill and dying.

In summer 1986, the University of Washington was picked to become one of the nation's top AIDS research centers, initially receiving more than seven hundred thousand dollars from the National Institute of Allergy and Infectious Diseases. The U.W.'s project—to find a combination of drugs that could help those who had AIDS continue to live—would be headed by Dr. Lawrence Corey, already nationally known for studying sexually transmitted viruses, and joined by Drs. Hunter Handsfield, Robert Wood, and Ann Collier, all of whom worked both at the Seattle health department and at the university.

In fall 1986, the scientists and doctors began using the multisyllabic word that gay men actually wanted to learn. Azidothymidine. AZT for short. Otherwise spelled as hope.

Burroughs-Wellcome, the company that had developed and was testing the drug, had reported that only one of 145 patients who had been receiving it had died. That compared so favorably to the sixteen who had died among the 137 who had received a placebo that the trials had been discontinued so that the drug could begin to be made available for more widespread testing. The new research center at U.W. would be one of the sites; private physicians would also be able to dispense the drug under certain conditions.

Not everyone with AIDS symptoms could have the drug. At first the test would be limited to those who had recovered from their first case of pneumocystis carinii since the doctors were uncertain whom the drug would help the most, and they did not know how soon after infection the drug would have to be administered to be most effective. AZT also had severe side effects. About one-fourth of those who had taken it had needed blood transfusions to counteract the anemia it caused. Others had suffered rashes and headaches.

Still, those were better than death, and Ann Collier was clearly excited when she talked to the *Seattle Times*. "This is the first thing that has shown promise treating a disease that up until now we thought was untreatable and terminal."[1]

Allen DeShong's path to Seattle had been the familiar one of migration, in his case from Oklahoma to studies for a doctorate in biochemistry at the University of Washington and, in the late 1960s, to Vietnam where he managed an army field hospital. He returned to Seattle to work as a biochemist in laboratories and, eventually, to set up his own consulting firm.

He also fell in love with a younger man named Robert O'Boyle. It was all intensely emotional and even sometimes confusing—O'Boyle in his early twenties, a Long Islander with a solid Catholic upbringing that included training by nuns in elementary school; DeShong more than a decade older, Jewish, Midwestern. Still, they formed a family that included their parents; they both decorated Christmas trees and celebrated Jewish high holy days.

In 1983, DeShong helped create the Northwest AIDS Foundation. Two years later, he noticed that his tongue and the roof of his mouth were coated chalky white. Then the pneumonia came. So did the diagnosis. Afterward, he walked more slowly, ate only snacks or soup. He was always tired.

In November 1986, he became one of the first gay men in Seattle to start taking AZT, which he got under the supervision of Dr. Wood at the U.W. The turnaround was dramatic. He started eating full meals and walking faster. He had energy again. The disease that had been debilitating was now "just a pain in the rear," he told the *Seattle Times*.[2] By 1987 he had become a crusader, visiting middle schools and high schools in Seattle to urge teenagers to avoid the virus and conveying a passion that made them listen. He had ignored the warnings about AIDS, he told them, "parked them in the back of my head."

"This will kill you," he would say. "This will kill you. I am HERE so you will HEAR." In their evaluations of his talks, students would write comments like "he really made us think" and "people really listened" and "he has a lot of courage." The American Red Cross featured his talk in a nationally distributed videotape.

Taking AZT was not easy, though. DeShong's lover, O'Boyle, once wrote that he remembered DeShong "rocking with nausea, talking past AZT's grip on his stomach." DeShong, O'Boyle said, would cry in private whenever he thought about dying, but he would always return to the schools to fight.

Treatment required two approaches: controlling the infection directly was one; providing the bricks-and-mortar space where people with AIDS could find care was the other. While the city's hospitals were the obvious choice for emergencies, at six hundred to eight hundred dollars a day they were simply too expensive for long-term care. Less costly shelter was crucial for those who could no longer afford their own housing or who needed more care than any family member, friend, or volunteer could provide.

On that front, fall 1986 also brought good news for Seattle. The private Robert Wood Johnson Foundation, created by one of the members of the family that had started the Johnson & Johnson company, announced it would make the largest AIDS grant yet in the Northwest, $1.4 million to help local AIDS activists and the health department begin to plan for long-term housing.[3]

One key in selecting Seattle had been the fact that gay activists and government officials were working so closely together, much as they had in defusing the bathhouse controversy. The "big four" of the gay AIDS groups—the Northwest AIDS Foundation, Chicken Soup Brigade, Shanti/Seattle, and the Seattle AIDS Support Group—had all joined to support the health department's application, as had the Capitol Hill hospitals seeing the majority of AIDS patients: Swedish, Harborview, and Group Health. With a small piece of the grant, the AIDS Foundation would hire a housing coordinator, Betsy Lieberman, to plan for all types of nonhospital care, be it small residential homes for three or four patients, larger skilled nursing care facilities, or hospices where people with AIDS could turn for final care. Chicken Soup could help people stay in their homes as long as possible. Shanti and SASG could provide emotional support.

With far less difficulty than that involved in influencing the city's political conversation in the 1970s, or the religious conversation in the Catholic Church in the 1980s, gay activists in Seattle were not only participating in the medical conversation about AIDS—to a large degree, they were the conversation.

Like Allen DeShong, Craig Anderson began his AZT treatments in November 1986. He had been diagnosed the previous year just a week before he was going to buy a house in the Magnolia neighborhood. Anderson loved the small details of life: taking country drives, playing with his dog Casey in the yard, hanging pictures. But he had to surrender the dream of owning his own home. "It's like the twilight zone," he had told the Seattle Times then. Anderson worked as a legal clerk. Quiet and calm, he had agreed to the interview because he said he had a message, especially for those who feared people with the virus. "AIDS is like any other life-threatening illness. If I can be projected as an everyday nice guy who people won't think of as 'AIDS-only' and a threat to them, I'll be happy."[4]

The virus quickly left him frail, suffering from both pneumonia and Kaposi's sarcoma, as well as nausea, fevers, and a swollen face and neck. For a while, he tried fighting with ribavarin and isoprinosine, two drugs he traveled to Tijuana, Mexico, to buy since they were available only in double-blind studies in the United States. Anderson felt too desperate, too sick, to risk receiving a placebo in a blind study. But neither drug had seemed to help.

He took AZT as soon as he could. Within three weeks, though, he developed signs of pneumonia again, and the drug had to be stopped so it would not weaken his body's defenses. By Christmas, with the pneumonia gone but the Kaposi's spreading, his doctor gave him the go-ahead to start AZT again. He used a cane to walk since the cancer covered his calf and the bottom of his foot. He made a New Year's resolution to not worry and to keep peaceful.

By March, the combination of AIDS symptoms and the effects of AZT, including anemia, overwhelmed Anderson. Every four hours, he had to take the pills, even at night when he just wanted to sleep. "It was time," he told a *Post-Intelligencer* reporter, "for me to let go of the hope involved with that drug."

"I just want tomorrow to be comfortable."

When he died in March 1987, only four months after beginning the drug, Craig Anderson was thirty-five.

As treatment began to change, so did the rhetoric being used for education—at least that employed by the city's gay activists. The AIDS Foundation's "Rules of the Road" campaign had moved the goal from simply providing information to actually trying to more directly change sexual behavior. Some activists were not satisfied with how indirect and metaphorical the campaign had had to be in order to not offend funders. With more men dying every month, even with the introduction of AZT, they wanted something bolder.

Enter Malcolm McKay, a blunt-talking forty-six-year-old from Marshall, Texas, who had wandered the world training with gurus, learning tantric sex practices, and teaching a course in human sexuality at Austin Community College. Along the way he had earned a master's degree in educational psychology and completed work at the Advanced Institute of Sexuality. In Marshall, he would remember in a later interview, "The words 'body,' 'sex,' 'fuck,' and other words like that were all weighted equally negative. . . . Everything physical was denied value." He had spent his lifetime trying to escape that restriction and in the fall of 1986, after Carl Wagner talked him into applying for a job as the AIDS Foundation's first health educator, he was determined other gay men would escape too. Ever direct, he once talked on stage about his first orgasm. "Oh my God," he told audience after audience, "I had no idea what I was doing. When I came I clamped my thumb over the end of my dick and ran to the bathroom and shot over everywhere." He'd add, "I remember asking my father how anything that feels so powerful and so strong, how could it be wrong?"[5]

In 1987, after the "Rules of the Road" campaign ended, McKay launched the next education campaign, featuring what he called Hot Sex Workshops. Instead of telling gay men what not to do, he planned to show them what to do—wherever he could assemble an audience. Sometimes it was in a meeting room where men just imagined possibilities; other times it was in a private living room or a bathhouse, where once McKay ended his official presentation, the participants could engage in more than talk. The point, as McKay realized, was not that men failed to understand what to do; they simply were not in the habit of doing it.

As for the images on posters, they too would become more explicit. McKay told the graphic artists to start adding naked flesh. Pornography had taught generations of young men how to have sex. Now, perhaps it could teach them how to expect safe sex. McKay always had to be careful, though, to run the images past what he once called a "smut panel" of citizen advisers. Gradually, the images of torsos, legs, and buttocks would become more and more explicit. He wanted the posters from the Northwest AIDS Foundation to be sexy enough to be on gay men's refrigerator doors and their bedroom walls.

At the workshops, he would have men hold up two fingers and then have a partner unroll a condom on them. "One day, a guy put his mouth on it and unrolled it, and it was just like an orgasm," McKay said during a later interview. From then on, he started teaching men how to do just that.

McKay was following a national pattern, as the earlier "information model" began to be replaced by a new "erotic model"—still based on conveying information, but doing so more unconsciously and more sexually. If gay men were going to practice safe sex, then somebody had better show them what to do, both in images as well as directly and personally. Cute road signs weren't enough. Safe sex had to be hot, and it had to look hot.

"Gay men have worked hard to refine their old behaviors," McKay told the *Seattle Gay News* in the fall of 1986. "Now they need to work hard to change some of those behaviors, and we're going to give them all the help we can."

McKay was far more than just a street activist who wanted the talk to be hot and dirty, though. He also began forming an analysis about how to communicate effectively enough to change sexual behaviors, noticing that the way Seattle's gay men were reacting to AIDS and the need to use condoms resembled the stages of dying that Elisabeth Kübler-Ross had outlined. McKay started training the foundation's volunteers to try to identify the stages, and then move men along to the next higher level. The first stage was denial that there was even a problem. "We'd get that in the older leather community, or among the kids saying that only the older gays got it," McKay recalled. The only thing a volunteer could sometimes do with a man in denial was to wait until one of his own friends got sick. Second, grief and anger: "They had all the information they needed, and they still didn't understand," McKay said. "You don't try to educate them; you just listen to their feelings and hang out with that." One such man poured a bottle of beer over a volunteer's head. A few days later, the man came into the foundation's offices, apologized, and left a three-hundred-dollar donation. Then, bargaining: "Under what circumstances," McKay said, "can I forget about safe sex? If I'm monogamous, can I forget about it? If it's my first date. . . . " Volunteers had to convince bargainers that the virus was not going to negotiate. Fourth, acceptance: gay men would try to get as much information as they could to try

# IN A COMMUNITY AS DIVERSE AS OURS, NO MATTER WHAT YOU'RE INTO...

"When I find myself in a tight spot, I slip into one of these."

"Right after I file my briefs on a risky case, I slip into this."

"Everytime I dive into unsure waters, I get into this first."

"A girl just can't be too carefull these days."

## GET INTO THIS FIRST.

Only Latex condoms used with water-based nonoxyl-9 lubricants can help reduce the risk of getting AIDS from oral and anal sex.

**BE WELL EQUIPPED.**

The Northwest AIDS Foundation

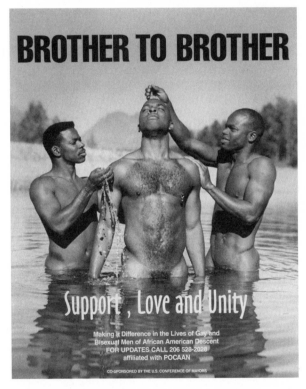

# BROTHER TO BROTHER

## Support, Love and Unity

Making a Difference in the Lives of Gay and
Bisexual Men of African American Descent
FOR UPDATES CALL 206 528-2028
affiliated with POCAAN

CO-SPONSORED BY THE U.S. CONFERENCE OF MAYORS

Condom campaigns became bolder and more erotic by 1987, for the first time show-ing the condom itself as well as more flesh, but gay men were also urged to care for one another. *(Geoff Manasse, Northwest AIDS Foundation and People of Color Against AIDS Network)* to change, and volunteers could finally provide strong encouragement and as much data as they could.

Success was still one more stage away. That, as far as McKay was concerned, depended on much more than information. "Permission for deep behavioral change comes from the unconscious," he said. "You have to be surrounded by it, your friends have to support it, and you have to make an unconscious change." A volunteer reported one day that a sex partner had put on a condom, but then had taken it off as he began to enter. Immediately, the volunteer's body closed tightly. McKay celebrated. The volunteer's body had reacted, not just his mind. Similarly, another volunteer reported a sexual dream in which he had been crossing Broadway and seen "a stud with a condom."

"We were trying to get down to the body," McKay said.[6] Madison Avenue knew how to do that with images of the body, not just words.

Flesh and condoms. That was the important link to make. It took a while for McKay to convince the citizen committees to let the condoms be portrayed, unwrapped, on the posters, but eventually they were there.

Outside the gay community, the Seattle media's willingness to talk more directly about sex and about sexual habits also began to change, at least a little. During the "Rules of the Road" campaign, the AIDS Foundation had created a thirty-second video using the traffic safety metaphor and had sent it to all of the city's television stations to be aired as a public service announcement. In it, five young men ambled along a sidewalk, laughing and talking, and when they reached an intersection, one ignored the traffic light, strolling into the street. His friends quickly pulled him back as the voice-over intoned, "Don't wait for AIDS to hit you head-on. Please be safe." Even the implied connection to male friendship and sex had been too much for four of the city's TV stations. KIRO, KCPQ, KSTW, and KTZZ all rejected the ad, the KTZZ manager explaining his station's decision by saying the spot had gone further than needed to convey information about AIDS. "We're not anti-gay," he told the *Seattle Times*. "We're just anti- that kind of spot that portrays that kind of life." Only KOMO and, of course, KING-TV agreed to broadcast the spot.[7]

By May 1987, KING-TV had readied something more explicit, again breaking ground in discussing a gay-related issue, much as it had in 1977 with its documentary "Who Are These People and What Do They Want?" At the time, national networks still banned advertisements for condoms, so the only way to talk publicly about them was through the service announcements. KING launched a new series of such spots, showing a teenage boy and girl, the boy saying, "I meant to buy a rubber, but it's not easy and it can be embarrassing." The girl said she was worried about AIDS and about becoming pregnant, then asked, "Are you protected?" KING's general manager, Sturges Dorrance, told the newspapers the station did not want to offend its audience, but AIDS was such a problem that "perhaps some shock is in order."[8] It was a tentative start, any possible offense softened by the choice of the target audience—heterosexual teenagers rather than gay men. But it was a start, and KING went even further by combining the introduction of the spots with a documentary on teen sex. One segment showed a sex education teacher, Gordon Dickman, fitting a condom onto a model of an erect penis as high school students watched. Then, to be sure the teens would feel more comfortable with the condoms, Dickman had them practice unrolling the rubbers onto their own fingers. Another segment showed the students negotiating safe sex.

It was some of what McKay was doing in his own Hot Sex workshops, albeit not as erotically. If you wanted people to change, you had to show them and let them practice. But in the mass media, you still could not show gay men doing it, only heterosexuals.

After a few months, Allen DeShong's health worsened again. Still, he kept his rounds at the high schools. One time, he achingly walked into a room of high school newspaper editors to deliberately show them what a person with AIDS looked like when he was not well. "I just wanted you to see who I am," he told them. A different time, he told students at West Seattle High School that he was not afraid of death. "The hardest part," he said, "is standing here looking out at all of you and knowing you're not hearing me."[9]

In October 1987, almost a year after beginning the new drug, Allen DeShong died. He was forty-two.

Within a year, the hope for AZT, which had been so grand, was being tempered by the knowledge that the drug did not always work, and even when it did, the side effects could make life extraordinarily unpleasant. The drug was no cure. The new diagnoses and the dying were continuing and, if anything, they seemed to grow even more public and widespread. Mixed with hope, blame was never far away.

Steven Farmer lived in a paradox. His well-etched jaw, his easy smile, his dark mustache and hair, and his muscled body gave him the Castro Street handsomeness he needed to easily attract men. He even posed nude for gay magazines and for *Playgirl.* But in his twenties, once Farmer had graduated from a high school in the suburbs east of Seattle, he never escaped troubles in his sexual attractions. "I was homophobic," he would later say—as afraid of his own passions for men as others were afraid of gay men in general. He turned to partying and escaping. During the 1980s, his job as a flight attendant, making runs with Alaska Airlines from one West Coast city to another, fitted well with both tactics. So did drinking—so much so that he would eventually have to start attending a drug recovery program. The young male hustlers, sixteen and seventeen years old, also fitted his escapes. Picking them up, Farmer would later concede, seemed less threatening than creating relationships. He also liked to take Polaroid pictures of them naked, storing the pictures in boxes in his closet.[10]

On February 17, 1987, Farmer—who was then thirty—went to downtown

Seattle, where, according to court records, he found a sixteen-year-old named Eric and took him to his apartment. There, Farmer pulled out his camera for photographs, giving the teenager twenty dollars. In late May, Farmer repeated the encounter with another sixteen-year-old named Jim. On May 31, police arrested Farmer when a third teenager, this one seventeen years old and named Robert, told a friend what had happened and the friend reported it.

Over the next seven months, the prosecution's case would unfold in pieces. The police seized photographs from Farmer's apartment, then tracked down one of the other teens. On July 31, the prosecutor charged Farmer with two felony counts of "exploiting a minor" by taking pictures of the two, but since the police had not obtained a proper search warrant, in September a judge eliminated the photographs as evidence. With a weakened case, the prosecutor bargained; on September 11, Farmer agreed to plead guilty to two lesser gross misdemeanor charges of "communicating with minors for immoral purposes" by asking them to remove their clothes. Sentencing was set for three months later, December 18. When the day came, Farmer wept and told the court he was a recovering drug addict who had quit his flight attendant's job when he could not stay sober. Superior Court Judge Herb Stephens sentenced him to two years in the King County jail, then suspended all but two months of the jail sentence provided Farmer continued his Alcoholics Anonymous meetings and had no more unsupervised contact with minors.

Had the case stopped there, it would have been a routine handling of a sex crime. A psychiatrist had told the court that Farmer did not even need sexual deviancy treatment, just counseling for the alcohol binges. Farmer was not considered a sexual predator by the court, nor had he been enough of a threat to anyone to be kept in jail pending his trial. Bail had not even been set; he had been released on his own recognizance. Even after the sentencing, while Farmer's attorney considered an appeal, Judge Stephens set the bail fairly low, at fifteen hundred dollars. Farmer met it that night and was released.[11]

But, with the fears about AIDS, times were not routine. In the three months that had elapsed between Farmer's plea bargain and his sentencing, several twists had combined to ensure that Steven Farmer would soon become a hapless actor in a political and media drama.

First, a Governor's AIDS Task Force, appointed several months earlier to devise a state strategy for responding to the epidemic, had been reviewing questions about quarantining people who had the disease and about when it was appropriate to require mandatory blood testing to see who had been exposed to the virus. On November 23, just three weeks before Steven Farmer was to be sentenced, the task force had concluded that the best way to fight the epidemic was to protect the civil liberties of those who had been exposed so that they would quickly and comfortably seek treatment. Only in very serious cases should health officials be allowed to seek quarantines or try to force blood tests. The one exception, the task force suggested, was that convicted sex offenders should be tested, with or without their consent, so that their victims would know whether exposure had occurred. The group recommended that the legislature adopt a new law that included both the civil liberty protections, as well as the required testing of sex offenders, when it convened the following January.[12]

Second, within the Farmer case itself, there had also been new developments. In October, a deputy prosecutor suddenly asked Farmer's defense attorney whether Farmer had AIDS. The defense attorney, baffled, responded that the question seemed to have nothing to do with the gross misdemeanor charge to which Farmer had pleaded guilty, since neither nudity, nor even photography, could transmit AIDS. On October 22, Farmer unexpectedly received a call from Julie Blacklow, a KING-TV reporter, who told him she was preparing a story about his case. He soon learned she had been talking to his friends in Alcoholics Anonymous. The next day he discovered that one of his friends and one of his ex-lovers had filed affidavits with the prosecutor's office saying that he had told them as early as 1982 that he had tested positive for AIDS—although the blood test for confirming exposure did not exist until 1985. The prosecutor's office had been questioning the two because it suspected they had helped Farmer destroy photographs once he had been arrested.

Suddenly, the reason for the question from the deputy prosecutor and the unexpected call from Blacklow made sense. Somewhere, information and accusations were being leaked.

For Seattle, Steven Farmer was about to become the tragic human face attached to the question of how the government should treat a gay man who did not follow the new safe-sex guidelines. The prosecutor's office had not criminally charged Farmer with actually having sex with the minors, but the minors said he had done so and had sometimes held them against their will. In the popular mind, then, Farmer's crime also included intercourse and possibly rape.

In November, a KING-TV "Top Story" focused on Farmer and, based on the friends' statements, reported that he might have been carrying the AIDS virus when he picked up the male prostitutes. The report included clips of the photos that had been excluded from evidence and quotations that compared Farmer to a loaded gun aimed at unsuspecting teenage males. On November 30, Senior Deputy Prosecutor Rebecca Roe securely directed the Farmer case into the new realm of public opinion and public fears about AIDS, announcing that the prosecutor's office "had reason to believe" that Farmer had tested positive for antibodies to the AIDS virus. While his AIDS status still seemed to have little to do directly with the actual criminal conviction before the court—that of asking minors to take their clothes off and pose for pictures—Roe argued that Farmer's "extensive contacts" with teenagers posed a public threat. He had, after all, pleaded guilty to what, technically, was a sex offense, non-felonious though it might be. Unnamed sources in the prosecutor's office then told the *Post-Intelligencer* they were thinking of even going to the extreme step of subpoenaing Farmer's private medical records from a Bellevue plastic surgeon, even if that meant challenging doctor-patient confidentiality.

The *Post-Intelligencer* put the story on page one and headlined it, "Teen-sex Abuser Is Believed to Have AIDS Virus."[13]

The flame had been lit. The stereotype of a promiscuous gay man preying on the city's children and consciously exposing them to a deadly disease made Farmer a perfect foil for Roe, who was then building a reputation as a no-holds-barred prosecutor of sex-abuse cases. She could make a public example of Farmer and secure a strong symbolic punishment, probably far more easily than if the same circumstances had existed between adults. Yet the teenagers involved were hardly innocent cherubs. They were male hustlers who had had many sexual encounters with other men. And, of course, Farmer was not even being charged with having sex with them or with statutory rape—so to some, Roe's campaign looked like a homophobic, or at least AIDS-phobic, assault.

Three days after Roe's announcement, the *Seattle Post-Intelligencer* editorial board made up its mind: on December 2, it urged the court to force the release of Farmer's medical records, saying that "knowing whether he has AIDS . . . is the overriding public interest."[14]

On December 15, three days before Farmer was to be sentenced, Roe filed new charges against him. She had found out about the third teen he had picked up earlier that year, and that provided a new case. Farmer now faced counts of patronizing a juvenile prostitute (by paying for photographs) and of exploiting a minor (by taking the photographs). Both were felonies. Still, there was no statutory rape charge that involved actual sex—and neither prostitute was charged in the case. At the beginning of 1988, then, Farmer would be appealing the sentence from the gross misdemeanor case and also facing a trial on the new felony charges—all while being portrayed as a deliberate spreader of the AIDS virus.

During February and March, while Farmer awaited trial on the new charges, the state legislature acted on the recommendations from the governor's task force and passed an AIDS Omnibus Bill that declared civil rights protections for anyone who was HIV-positive and restricted forced testing to prostitutes, those convicted of crimes relating to intravenous drug use, and sex offenders. But in a particularly relevant twist for Steven Farmer, the bill limited the required testing to those sex offenders who had been convicted of a crime that included sexual penetration. The charges against Farmer did not include any such accusation. The bill also said that those accused of spreading the virus intentionally had a right to a confidential court hearing so that their medical status would not be widely broadcast. On March 23, Governor Booth Gardner signed the bill into law.[15]

A month later, a jury convicted Farmer on both of the new charges. The normal sentence would have been about two and a half years in jail, maybe even just ninety days for a first-time offender. The superior court judge assigned to the trial, Charles Johnson, scheduled sentencing for a few weeks later. At that point, Roe formally demanded that Farmer be forced to take a blood test to determine whether he had been exposed to the AIDS virus. If Farmer tested positive, her logic went, he should be kept in jail longer—a lot longer. Ten years, Roe said, quadrupling the sentence.

Lesbian and gay activists who supported Farmer exploded. Knowing Farmer's health status was irrelevant, they said, since his conviction was not for any actual sex that could have communicated AIDS. Also, they argued, even if Farmer now tested positive for the virus—in 1988—that did not prove he had been positive when the violations occurred. They also pointed out that no one had ever asked the prostitutes what their AIDS status was, either before or after their encounters with Farmer. Finally, they saw the case in starkly political terms: Roe's boss, King County Prosecutor Norm Maleng, was running for governor that year and using the Farmer case as a ticket for getting there, the activists claimed.[16]

Then, there was also the matter of the new law restricting the categories under which such AIDS testing could be forced—categories which did not include Steven Farmer.

On May 24, Judge Johnson decided that, law or no law, his own judicial power gave him the authority to seek whatever information he needed for sentencing. Farmer, he declared, would have to take the blood test. Incensed, Farmer's attorney, Robert Gombiner, called the order "illegal on its face" and stood in the courtroom yelling and waving a copy of the new AIDS Omnibus Law at the judge. Practically screaming that he would tell Farmer not to comply, he left to file a request for an immediate stay of the order. He was joined this time by a Dorian Group lawyer who argued that court deference to the legislature's restrictions on who could be involuntarily tested was "essential to this state's effective strategy for controlling AIDS." Otherwise, the attorneys argued, "the specter of involuntary testing" could undercut the attempts to stop the spread of the virus.[17]

On May 30, a state appeals court commissioner, William Ellis, cautiously denied the stay. To him, Johnson's order did not seem to contain the "obvious or probable error" that justified an immediate halt to the blood test. The issue could be argued later in an appeal. Two days later, Farmer—still not consenting but also not resisting physically—became the first person in Washington State to be forced to take an AIDS blood test against his will. The fact that such an order had been imposed on a gay man, rather than on any heterosexuals accused of sex abuse, provoked angry activists to call press conferences and stage protests denouncing the prosecutorial action as persecution.[18]

Judge Johnson had promised that the results could be kept secret from everyone but the attorneys and himself to protect Farmer's privacy, and the omnibus law also suggested such information should be confidential. But of course, once the results were available and Roe demanded the longer jail time, it became obvious that Farmer had tested positive for the antibodies to the virus. The *Post-Intelligencer* blazed a four-column headline across its front page: "Sex Offender

Exposed to AIDS" and then followed the next day with an editorial headlined, "Lock Farmer Away." It closed by saying, "He does not deserve to walk free again, ever."[19]

Judge Johnson then tripled Farmer's sentence to seven and a half years in prison. Wiping away tears at his sentencing in early July 1988, Farmer denied he was "the monster" he had been portrayed as.

"I was tried, convicted, and hung in the press," he choked.[20]

Three years later, in a less frantic time, the Washington State Supreme Court would settle Farmer's appeal by ruling that Johnson's order had indeed been illegal. Roe had no compelling reason to have the information about AIDS status that she had demanded.

Even so, the court would still uphold the exceptionally long sentence, basing its decision not on the blood test results but on the testimony from Farmer's two friends, the ones who said he told them he had tested positive.

In July 1991, the state sent Steven Farmer to the Twin Rivers Correctional Center near Monroe to begin serving his sentence of seven and a half years. Rebecca Roe, meanwhile, had been honored in a national magazine article in *Parade,* titled "Women Who Could Be America's Toughest Prosecutors."[21]

Had Farmer been unjustly sentenced because he was a gay man with AIDS? During the 1990s, there was only one similarly publicized case in the state that could provide a comparison involving heterosexuals. Randall Louis Ferguson, a thirty-six-year-old in southwestern Washington, discovered in the late 1980s that he was HIV-positive. Ferguson already had a worse criminal record than Farmer, having been a drug addict convicted of various thefts. Once he discovered he was HIV-positive, he continued to have unprotected sex with what police estimated were more than fifty people. Even when health officials warned him to change his behavior, he refused, supposedly telling one acquaintance that he wanted to "take as many people down" with him as he could. At least five people who had sex with Ferguson died from AIDS, including two of his wives, a male friend, a girlfriend, and a woman who had had a one-night stand with him. In 1995, Clark County convicted him of second-degree assault involving one victim—the statute of limitations had already expired for assault charges involving the others. Ferguson's criminal record and his crime—even involving just the one victim—were far worse than the crime King County had convicted Steven Farmer of, especially since Farmer's conviction was not for sex and no one had died or had been proven to have been infected. Yet, although Ferguson also received what the court called "an exceptional sentence," at ten years it did not seem that much harsher than Steven Farmer's. And Ferguson would be eligible for release for good behavior in just six.[22]

The pace of new AIDS diagnoses in Seattle and King County rose during the late 1980s and early 1990s. In 1988, for example, 352 new diagnoses were made in the city and county. In 1989, that number rose to 460 new AIDS cases, more than a 30 percent jump and well over an average of one new case of AIDS every day. In

1990, 519. In 1991, 563. In 1992, 621. In 1993, 647. Of those cases, more than 1,200 people—or two-thirds—would be dead within about six years. And those were just the diagnoses of full-blown AIDS and did not count the numbers of people newly testing positive for exposure to the HIV virus.[23]

One of those numbers was for James Moore. He was a gay man living on Capitol Hill who believed in magic and took seriously the reports from anthropologists that suggested homosexuals in Native American cultures—the *berdaches* who had been so roundly condemned by Catholic missionaries—had often been shamans. Moore organized a "Lavender Magick" group of pagans to march in Seattle's gay pride parade, studied and taught rituals, and eventually published *Wiggansnatch*, which advertised itself as "a magazine of alternative realities." He also adopted a native-like name, Laughing Otter, after a story he heard about a mountain lion that had stalked a group of otters but had been distracted when one otter sneaked behind him and loudly laughed. Moore saw himself like that, distracting others into humor. His mother would say that when he was young, growing up in Georgia, Moore would sometimes let go of a peal of laughter that "would just make me feel good all over." A friend, John Yohalem, wrote that Moore's laugh was "audible for blocks, unmistakable, irrepressible, scoffing."

Moore could be the romantic, too. When he and his lover, Jim Luthi, hiked to a campground in 1986, Moore had complained about Luthi's slowness, not knowing Luthi would soon die of AIDS—on Moore's own thirty-second birthday. A year later, Moore would write: "While laying in a hammock [at the campground], listening to the sound of the river, I imagined Jim lying next to me. I apologized and I daydreamed that I had gallantly left him in town while I walked my pack to the campground and then came back to get him and to carry his pack for him." Eventually, Moore would commemorate their love with a series of articles in the *Seattle Gay News* titled "In a Time of Falling off and Dying."

Twice, he led all-night rituals for those who had died of AIDS. When his own death approached, he left for a shaman's retreat in eastern Washington, seeking out a house with no electricity or water to engage in sweats and fasting. He had to be rushed back to Harborview. There, he died in October 1988. He was thirty-three.[24]

Carl Wagner was another one of those statistics. He had been one of the Northwest AIDS Foundation's first staff members—the one who had pushed its "Rules of the Road" campaign. He learned he had AIDS in 1988. He would live his final year in a swirl that was sometimes enthusiastic and sometimes angry, prompting a coworker, Mark Dion, to write that knowing Wagner was like encountering an "unending discovery." Wagner gardened, collected tropical fish at home, and fished for food outdoors. He rushed around the city and country on his motorbike, once dragging Dion—who was depressed by the scale of the disease the two of them were trying to fight—away from the AIDS Foundation office and speeding him north to the tulip fields at Mount Vernon. There, pointing at the sweep of colorful blooms, Wagner ordered Dion: "Okay Mark, now look . . . now see." Remember life amid all the death.

Wagner could also fume mightily. Another friend described him as a person whose only tool sometimes was a hammer, and the world was his nail. As his AIDS worsened, he railed at the Northwest AIDS Foundation for not providing enough money and staff for the education projects. He desperately wanted to save lives. In April 1988, his health gone, a very frustrated Wagner quit. When he died in September 1989, he was thirty-two.[25]

Although over three-quarters of the new cases of AIDS were occurring in men who had had sex with other men, by the turn of the decade the disease had certainly widened its claim on others too. One of the most poignant was Claire Cowles, a woman who had become one of the Chicken Soup Brigade's clients. Christine Card, a volunteer who helped her, told the *Seattle Times* that when the two met, "my first thought was, my God, she's so young and so fragile." Cowles, who was only thirty, told Card that while growing up, she had felt vain about her hair and breasts, but by the time the two met, Cowles had lost both. "We began a list of things she wanted to do," Card said, "from eating a peanut butter sandwich with dill pickles and mayo to setting crab pots and eating our catch while watching the sunset."

Card once overheard a friend ask how Cowles had gotten the virus. "She got very quiet. She said, 'There are only two reasons to ask. One is to find out how you get AIDS, and I can't imagine anyone not knowing by now. Two is to fit us into a category. People's compassion changes depending on which division you place them in."

"You should care because we are sick, not because of how we got AIDS."

Cowles had a mission to complete before she died. She had two young children and had to find a place where the younger of them could live once she had died. "She found a loving place where the child would be cared for forever," Card said. "And she made sure they knew as much as possible about her feelings, joys, and thoughts so they can make the child's mother alive when the time comes."

As for the older child, a boy nicknamed "Squeak," there would not need to be a new home to be cared in "forever," because he too had AIDS. When Claire Cowles died in October 1987, she was thirty. Squeak died sixteen days later. He was three.

Card said that Cowles had told Squeak "it wouldn't be very long before they would be flying together and they'd play, and things wouldn't hurt anymore."[26]

As gaps in either the treatment of patients or the education of the still-healthy became apparent, more and more AIDS organizations formed in Seattle, as if by sheer numbers of new groups the epidemic could somehow be controlled. Seattle's black, Asian, and Hispanic communities had not initially been targeted by the Northwest AIDS Foundation, so by 1987 a new group sparked by a lesbian/gay organizing program of the American Friends Service Committee emerged to run education efforts there. The People of Color Against AIDS Network it was called—POCAAN, for short. Similarly, needle exchange programs formed to head off the virus's sweep through the city's intravenous drug users. Heterosexuals who had developed AIDS began a support group. An organization called Rise n' Shine focused on children and teenagers with AIDS. The Babes Network helped women exposed to the virus. Soon, somewhere in the city, there would be a group for virtually every type of person contracting the disease, many of them started or assisted by those suffering the most casualties: gay men.

Beginning in 1988, there would also be a new type of group in the city, one created from what was a growing frustration and anger over the disease. In October, Seattle activists formed a chapter of the AIDS Coalition to Unleash Power—ACT UP—with the intent of forcing confrontations with those they thought were moving too slowly to combat the disease. ACT UP had already been making an impact on the East Coast for two years, holding demonstrations to protest actions—and inaction—by the Reagan-Bush administration and by the U.S. Supreme Court. But, in Seattle, AIDS activists and local government officials were already working so closely together that ACT UP's actions were often aimed elsewhere rather than directed at city or county officials. The first act was to protest the Reagan administration's neglect of AIDS, at a speech in Tacoma being given by then Vice President George Bush. The second was to demonstrate against Safeway stores when the chain refused an issue of a pop music magazine, *Spin,* because it included a condom along with an article about safe sex. The grocery chain would not back down on the magazine, but it did eventually agree to print a safe-sex message and an AIDS hotline telephone number on its grocery bags. Another demonstration in 1990 demanded that the federal government spend more money on AIDS-related programs; although about fifty protestors blocked intersections downtown, city police blocked off traffic and let the rally proceed until it ended three hours later. In 1991, ACT UP did actually target one local group, the University of Washington medical center board, which had voted to bar its HIV-positive hospital workers from performing surgery on patients unless the patients consented. ACT UP member Michael Davidson made his way to the board's lunch table the day after the vote and hopped on it to demand that the policy be rescinded. Instead, the board moved its lunch to another room.

Sometimes, when local government agencies could not move fast enough, ACT UP in Seattle catalyzed. It started a needle exchange for intravenous drug users in 1989, for example, several months before the health department received authorization from politicians to do so; once the political approval came, the health department took over the program, which had already been agreed on. When, a decade after the epidemic started, the Seattle school board pondered whether to make condoms available to high school students, ACT UP members stood on the sidewalks outside the schools in 1991, passing out condoms and explicit safe-sex information until the board voted to begin its own program.[27]

By the late 1980s and early 1990s, activists who had grown angry at the federal government's slow response to AIDS formed a local chapter of ACT UP and began demonstrations. Here, in 1994, the Seattle chapter marches in the lesbian/gay pride parade along Broadway. *(Washington State Historical Society, Tacoma)*

As had gay liberation activists in the 1970s, ACT UP members cultivated coalitions with groups working on other political issues. Perhaps most noteworthy was its help for the United Front Against Fascism, an umbrella organization formed in the 1980s to oppose a very loud and rising white supremacist movement in the Northwest. The UFAF included support from Radical Women and the Freedom Socialist Party. The supremacist movement it opposed was headquartered at a twenty-acre compound near Hayden Lake, Idaho, where the leader, Richard Butler, a former Ku Klux Klansman, had founded the Church of Jesus Christ Christian in the mid-1970s. Better known as the Aryan Nations, Butler's church had taken for its creed a passionate opposition to the government and a pledge to make the Northwest into a whites-only homeland. In the mid-1980s, police imprisoned several of the church's members for a series of murders and bank robberies, and one member, Robert Mathews, was killed in a shoot-out with the FBI north of Seattle on Whidbey Island.

In December 1988, two months after the start of the Seattle chapter of ACT UP, Butler and other Aryan Nations members planned a pilgrimage to Whidbey to memorialize Mathews. Immediately, the UFAF announced a counter-demonstration, and among the four hundred who would bus from Seattle to confront the forty or so Aryan Nations supporters, ACT UP leaders and members ended up being prominently visible in their new trademark "Silence = Death" T-shirts. George Bakan, who had helped organize an early response to AIDS, had by then become editor of the *Seattle Gay News* and had been lending publicity and personal support to both ACT UP and the UFAF. At the rally, Bakan delivered a fiery call for all gays and lesbians to oppose the white supremacist vision of a purified Northwest, and in an editorial a week later the *SGN* urged gays and lesbians to take the "Nazi organizing seriously" and march "to oppose racist murder and violence." "The Lavender Stripe," the *SGN* editorial said, "is wide and powerful in this fight." A few months later, when Butler planned a march in Coeur d'Alene, Idaho, to celebrate Hitler's birthday, Seattle ACT UP members once again visibly joined the hundreds of counter-protesters.

Soon, the city's lesbians and gays would be in the crosshairs of yet another set of utopians intent on cleansing the Northwest of elements they considered sordid. It would be another sideshow to the continuing struggle against AIDS, but a jolting reminder of how strenuously some people still feared and hated homosexuals.[28]

On April 14, 1990, Robert John Winslow, a twenty-nine-year-old former army infantryman who had once been stationed at Fort Lewis in Tacoma, joined two other men at a remote site in a national forest north of Hayden Lake, Idaho. They had with them a section of metal pipe, caps for the pipe ends, gunpowder, a fuse, and, of course, matches. Like Winslow, the two others were members of Butler's Aryan Nations—Procter James Baker, a fifty-seven-year-old mechanic and navy veteran, and Rico Renaldo Valentino, a fifty-three-year-old former wrestler who had once performed in professional rings as the costumed "Masked Avenger." Supposedly, Valentino was now a tax protester being pursued by the Internal Revenue Service, and so he had taken refuge within the church compound.

According to court documents, the three men assembled the pipe bomb, lit it, and watched it explode. Reportedly, Baker then said, "Think what this would do to a room full of people." A month later, Winslow, Valentino, and another member of the church, a thirty-five-year-old named Stephen Nelson, climbed into Valentino's van and headed west toward Capitol Hill. Baker stayed in Idaho. During conversations over the phone and in person, the men had apparently settled on a target: what was then the most popular gay disco in Seattle, Neighbours.

South of Seattle, the three stopped at a hardware store in Federal Way to buy a new six-inch section of metal pipe and caps. Then they drove to a gun shop where they bought a pound of smokeless gunpowder. They put the items in the van where they already carried two yards of cannon fuse, a 12-gauge pump-action shotgun, an electronic stun gun, a .38-caliber revolver, knives, and literature about the Aryan

Nations' promise of a new Northwest. Then they checked into a motel near the Seattle-Tacoma International Airport.

Neighbours' main entry and exit was located in an alleyway between Pike and Pine Streets, just off Broadway. The supremacists, court testimony suggested, planned to place the bomb close to the exit on a Saturday night when the dance floor would be busiest—filled with perhaps five hundred gay men and lesbians. Then one of the supremacists would telephone the bar and warn that a bomb would soon explode. As the dancers crowded the exit to escape, the court documents said, they would unknowingly enter a "kill zone" at the exact time the bomb detonated. In their conversations, the supremacists supposedly suggested to one another that the alleyway would then "resemble a meat grinder."

Saturday, May 12, was to be the chosen night.

At 6 P.M., the three returned to the motel to prepare their attack for a few hours later. But as they emerged from the van, FBI agents suddenly surrounded them and placed two, Winslow and Nelson, under arrest. In Idaho, other agents raided Baker's home and arrested him. All three would ultimately be convicted of conspiring to bomb the gay disco.

The break had come because the fourth man, Rico Valentino, had been working as a paid informant for the bureau. Through wiretaps and recordings that Valentino had been secretly making, the FBI had been listening in all along. An agent had even been fifty yards away when the first bomb had been tested in the forest.

The plot had been foiled, but the enormity of the carnage that had narrowly been avoided stunned not only lesbians and gays, but the city's leadership as well. The mayor, Norm Rice, issued a statement calling the plot "a shocking reminder of the hatred and fear that remain in our society." "Even in Seattle," he added, "where we pride ourselves on our diversity and our commitment to human rights, we are not immune to senseless acts of bigotry."

Eventually, the threat from the supremacists would decline as Butler's church came under increasing pressure from the government and as its appeal lessened. Having been saved from what could have been the second worst tragedy to befall them, gays and lesbians in Seattle returned to struggle against the worst.[29]

Treatment for AIDS demanded new spaces, especially a place where people who needed more than home care could go to die. By the late 1980s, one such hospice had been created in Seattle, a small home called Rosehedge. But, because of the numbers of people who were now dying, a bigger space was needed. Betsy Lieberman, of the Northwest AIDS Foundation, had been at work on that since 1987. First, she looked around the city and county to see whether existing nursing homes had hospice space to handle the ever-increasing numbers of sick. None had enough; they were already 98 percent full. Lieberman also knew that elderly women occupied most of the nursing homes. Those dying from AIDS were young gay men. They not only needed different types of medical care, they needed a different kind of environment.

She assembled the usual committee—in this case, twenty-two people meeting regularly for an early morning breakfast at Swedish Hospital. Within a few months, they had a plan. The hospice should be small, they thought, about thirty-five rooms, to make it feel more like a home than a hospital. The residents—not the "patients," but the "residents"—should have their own rooms and bathrooms. The design should be flexible enough to take into account that one day a resident might feel well enough to move around, fix his own meals, and even garden, while the next he might be bedridden with an array of intravenous tubes. Also, so that the residents were not just isolated and seeing only family and friends, other people should be encouraged to come into the building by including a daytime community space.

By spring 1988, the timing was good. The federal government was ready to partially pay for actual construction, provided three conditions could be met: a detailed enough proposal needed to be written, there had to be proof that private donors could be convinced to support the rest of the construction costs, and a specific location needed to be chosen. Lieberman's planning group incorporated as a nonprofit organization, AIDS Housing of Washington, and Lieberman became executive director. Writing the proposal was the easiest condition to meet. The next step was to get some local seed money for the project. The Northwest AIDS Foundation agreed to put up two thousand dollars, but what was really needed was at least one major financial commitment from another nongovernment source. Without it, the proposal would falter.

At that crucial moment, something unexpected happened, from what must have seemed the unlikeliest of directions. It was June 1988, and Archbishop Raymond Hunthausen was just then reluctantly complying with the Vatican order to oust Dignity from St. Joseph's Church on Capitol Hill. Suddenly, word came that an "anonymous donor" had routed one hundred thousand dollars through the Catholic archdiocese. The money was to be used for the new AIDS hospice.

Neighbors could still be neighbors, however the winds of dogma blew in Rome.[30]


Peter Davis had grown up on Queen Anne Hill doing what every boy did: bicycling in the street and, when he was older, speeding his car around street corners. Few would have expected his eventual vocation, but as a teenager he attended the Jesuits' elite Seattle Preparatory School on Capitol Hill and, in 1963 at age eighteen, entered the novitiate, eventually to become a Jesuit priest. Once ordained, he returned to Queen Anne to say his first Mass at St. Anne's Church in the heart of the middle-class district that George Cotterill had once represented.

In November 1987, while Davis was working in a church in Portland, he received his diagnosis. He would tell the parishioners that he had most likely contracted

AIDS from sex with another man. The church members were stunned. Another Jesuit observed, "He really did throw himself on their mercy and their trust, and it paid off."

Peter Davis would die in December 1988 when he was forty-three. At his eulogy at St. Anne's, a fellow Jesuit priest said, "We slip. We stumble." But, he added, "Peter Davis gave us more of God's spirit in this last year than ever before. As his body shrunk, the spirit of his heart grew more expansive than ever."[31]

Davis would not be the only local Catholic priest affected. Terry Shea, also a Jesuit, taught political science at Seattle University and then became president of the Seattle Preparatory School. Diagnosed as HIV-positive in the 1980s, he would keep his condition confidential from all but a few other Jesuits, until in 1994—while still heading Seattle Prep—he became sick with the full disease. In May 1994, he announced his resignation and his illness, then used the rest of the school year to teach students about the disease. When he died in July 1995, he was fifty-eight.[32]

As the numbers of diagnoses and deaths continued to increase, the demand for money to pay for both education and treatment rocketed. Much of what Seattle spent came from the government, of course, or from the Robert Wood Johnson Foundation, but AIDS activists also developed their own approaches, converting the practical need to raise dollars into community rituals for discussing the disease and its prevention.

After 1987, for example, the final Sunday in September always meant a walkathon sponsored by the Northwest AIDS Foundation, starting at Seattle Center and winding through the city's streets. Eventually, it would be supported by many of Seattle's corporate heavyweights—U.S. West, KING-TV, Microsoft, Nordstrom, Washington Mutual. The first year's walkathon drew three thousand people and raised $250,000. By the 1990s, the QFC supermarket chain was advertising the walk on its grocery bags and raising almost $1.5 million each year. The event became a kind of marketplace for the different types of educational talk being promoted by the health department and the gay activists. Speeches by media celebrities or corporate executives ignored the sexual aspects of the disease and focused instead on the encouragement of a community-wide response. People with AIDS talked about their personal struggles. Off somewhere at a display table, the health department handed out its informational jargon about avoiding the virus, while at another table Malcolm McKay or his successors would pass along fliers about safe, Hot Sex workshops for gay men.[33]

The Chicken Soup Brigade turned to the old fund-raising tactic of churches and granges: bingo games, albeit with additions few heterosexual groups would have risked, such as ball-calling drag queens. Perhaps as important as the money being raised was the fact that on a regular Saturday night schedule, gay men and women sat playing bingo with one another rather than going only to a bar. Heterosexuals who were volunteering for Chicken Soup were there with them too.

Other rituals emerged, ones not aimed at raising money as much as remembering the dead. As early as 1983, a yearly vigil began; by the 1990s, it had become a regular Memorial Day weekend event with candles and altars set in the yard at Seattle Central Community College on Capitol Hill. Pictures of those who had died were shown; names were read, and each year the list lengthened. Most attending were gay friends of those who had died, because gay men would always account for at least three-quarters of the deaths from AIDS in Seattle, but many heterosexual friends and family members came too—yet another public mixing together.

More so than sharing the disco, or being mutually concerned about police corruption, or worrying about violations of privacy, or being included among God's flock, AIDS was producing a common experience for Seattle's homosexuals and heterosexuals to share—an experience of living together through death.

Carol Sterling always talked bluntly, militarily. She had, after all, been in the Women's Army Corps, stationed at Fort Lewis. She had married a career soldier, like herself a nurse. One day, with a bluntness to rival hers, he had pointed out that she was probably a lesbian, and he was right: a lesbian, Catholic mother with two daughters. Not long afterward, she took her youngest daughter to the last gay pride parade to be held in downtown Seattle. She did not think enough people attended. So she eventually chaired the Freedom Day Committee during the arguments about whether the event should be a parade or a march. She wanted everybody involved. In a later interview, she remembered, "I saw huge stripes of the rainbow flag that had been neglected. Where were the businessmen? Where were the people of color? Where are the girls?"[34]

When AIDS struck, her nursing background made it natural for her to be involved. With other lesbians, she helped launch a "Blood Sisters" effort to encourage gay women to donate to blood banks, since gay men were being told not to. "We may have nothing in common [with gay men] except sexual orientation, nothing," she would say in a later interview, "but we can come together and help make a better life for everyone." Soon enough, Sterling was added to the Dorian Group's board—to be a "loud-mouthed girl" she said—and then, in 1987, she assumed command of the Chicken Soup Brigade as its first paid staff member.

Like Larry Woelich at Club Seattle, or Malcolm McKay and Carl Wagner at the AIDS Foundation, or Josh Joshua at the Seattle AIDS Support Group and Chicken Soup itself, Sterling was one of those who put a particularly personal and passionate stamp on the city's fight against AIDS. She inherited a stack of three-by-five index cards with the names of seventeen volunteers. When she left in 1995, Chicken Soup had more than fifty staff, hundreds of volunteers, and a two-million-dollar budget. Like the others, she was more entrepreneurial than managerial. "None of us [who started the AIDS agencies] were fundraisers or managers of social service agencies," she would recall. "We were street-fighters, like me, or medical professionals—but we were able to develop the structure."

Of Chicken Soup's volunteers, she said,

> These were passionate people—and I knew from the moment I walked in the door that these were heroes. They changed people's soiled linens, they offered to wash people's clothing, they would empty kitty litter boxes, and they would go to the market and buy groceries with their own money for somebody they had never met. And they did it with the element of "what if the scientists are wrong? What if I can get this through the air?" But we did it anyway. Some people did it because they knew [AIDS] was coming into their body. People did it because they had a son living in New Jersey who they thought was gay, and it could happen to their son and they lived in Seattle and they couldn't help. People did it because they thought it was never going to happen to them, and they felt relieved, or they felt guilty. But they did it. . . . It was a miracle.

Betsy Lieberman and her new AIDS Housing board knew from the start that the best location for an AIDS hospice would be either on or near Capitol Hill. It made no sense to isolate the majority of those who were dying from AIDS out in the suburbs, even if land was cheaper there. Very quickly the board settled on a site in Madison Valley, just to the east of Renton Hill, where East Madison Street crossed Twenty-eighth Avenue East. A small business district there had begun to dig out of decline, and gay men had begun to renovate houses in the Central District neighborhood that, historically, had been the center of Seattle's black community. The actual site for the hospice held only an abandoned house surrounded by five vacant lots used for parking and trash dumping.

In August 1988, two months after receiving the donation through the archdiocese, AIDS Housing signed an option to buy the land for $450,000. Almost immediately, opposition started, with neighbors threatening a petition drive to keep the hospice out.[35]

They worried in particular about the proposed day program that would put more people with AIDS into what amounted to a community center but would not keep them in the hospice rooms. A letter to city officials explained that "like it or not, most people do not wish to be around ill people often, and here we may be adding the sorts of behavior sometimes associated with AIDS—overt homosexuality, dementia and drug abuse."[36] Some businessmen suggested eliminating the first-floor day center and putting retail stores there instead.

AIDS Housing promised to educate the neighborhood's residents about how AIDS was and was not transmitted—a useful information exercise, but slightly beside the point since the concern was not about transmission but about symbolic geography: about becoming known as the Seattle neighborhood where people with

AIDS went to die, or, perhaps even more dangerously, where people with AIDS went to shop.

The *Seattle Times* would eventually interview one neighbor who said, "We're surrounded by people who have enough money not to have to think about [AIDS] and they don't want to have to deal with this stuff. I was just talking to a customer today who told me he used to go to Broadway all the time, but he won't go there anymore."

Another added, "The first time one of those people comes out of there and takes a stroll down to the corner . . . there's going to be all kinds of disasters."[37]

Despite the opposition, the city approved the permit, but four neighborhood residents filed an appeal, first to a city examiner and then to the city council. At that point, what had been a typical small, neighborhood controversy began to grow uglier. The opponents demanded an environmental impact statement, saying the hospice would create an economic blight. In a separate development, an activist in the surrounding black community told the *Seattle Times* he had seen posters carrying headlines like "Say No to AIDS Prison in Central Area" and illustrations of babies supposedly sitting in front of the hospice playing with hypodermic needles. The hospice itself was drawn as a jail full of tombstones.[38]

In response, gay activists costumed in drag sponsored shopping sprees into the small Madison Street commercial strip, intending to show the businessmen just how overt "homosexual behavior" could be. Others talked of countersuits charging discrimination in public accommodations against people with AIDS.

The Seattle ACT UP chapter became especially demonstrative. About fifty ACT UP demonstrators descended on the downtown office of the attorney representing the opponents, chanting and blowing whistles. ACT UP then discovered that one of the opponents who had filed the challenge sat on the board of the Seattle Art Museum, which at the time was constructing a new museum downtown. To retaliate, several ACT UP members proposed shutting down the museum's construction site with demonstrations, arguing that such action was justified if a museum board member was going to block a building needed by people with AIDS. The threat horrified activists with the mainline AIDS organizations, such as the Northwest AIDS Foundation, who had worked so hard to cultivate support from Seattle's elite.[39]

Lieberman's group, AIDS Housing, tried gentler public relations approaches, sending its board and staff members out at one point to sow wildflowers on the vacant lots in order to beautify the site. But the group also turned to insider pressure by forming a blue-ribbon advisory board headed by one of the city's best-known civic leaders, James Ellis. Among its members, the board counted heavyweights from media and politics and, for the Catholic influence, the Jesuit president of Seattle University. A successful $7.2 million fund-raising campaign also made it clear that city support for the project was more widespread than the

Two women who played key roles in helping the campaign against AIDS were Carol Sterling (above with her family, third from left) and Betsy Lieberman (below). Sterling oversaw the Chicken Soup Brigade, while Lieberman helped create the Bailey-Boushay AIDS hospice. *(Geoff Manasse)*

opposition. Donors included the Boeing Company, Nordstrom, Weyerhaeuser, the Skinner Foundation—and it was not just their money that was important; it was their local prestige. Then the federal government approved a $450,000 grant, specifically including the adult day care program.

ACT UP then scheduled its museum protest for May 30, 1990.

On May 28, the opponents of the AIDS housing project announced they were quitting. The pressure was simply too great.

The AIDS Housing board announced, tactfully, that there had been a "successful conclusion to negotiations." The board would agree to a few architectural requests and a tiny bit of street-side retail space—about fifty square feet, just enough for an outside cash machine. The adult day center would stay.

Wildflowers and hardball had paid off.

Eighteen months later, in January 1992, the new Bailey-Boushay House was ready for dedication, the first of its kind in the United States. It would be named after a gay couple, Thatcher Bailey, who had helped with the fund-raising, and his partner, graphic designer Frank Boushay, who had died from AIDS the year the fund-raising had begun.

The week the hospice was dedicated, doctors in King County diagnosed the area's two thousandth case of AIDS.

Ten years had passed since the first major warning in the *Seattle Gay News*.

Death had become overwhelmingly present in some of Seattle's smaller circles—particularly its arts community.

One statistic was Randall McCarty, one of the city's leading organists. Even after his diagnosis with AIDS, he continued to play every Sunday at St. Paul's Episcopal Church, as well as to offer two monthly concerts with the Early Music Guild, which he had helped create. He loved to pass out copies of obscure musical compositions, and enthusiastically restored an Aeolian organ at the city's Museum of History and Industry. Even his lover was a musical match—a harpsichord builder. Because McCarty and others taking AZT needed regular blood transfusions to offset the drug-caused anemia, musicians in the city organized a benefit concert in 1988 and arranged to have a mobile blood-bank unit present. More than sixty people donated on the spot. When McCarty died in February 1989, he was thirty-seven.[40]

Then there was Robert "Ned" Behnke, an artist who had been born deaf and had turned his disability into a vocation, teaching hearing-impaired students at Seattle's preeminent arts school, Cornish College on Capitol Hill. Behnke came from one of the city's most prominent families, so his diagnosis seemed to affect not only him but also an entire Seattle network. His mother, Sally, was a sister of David "Ned" Skinner, owner of the Skinner Corporation, a partial owner of the Seattle Seahawks football team, and a director of the Boeing Corporation. His father, Robert J. Behnke, worked as vice president for the Skinner Corporation and actively supported many of the city's arts institutions, including the U.W.'s Henry Art

Gallery and the local public television station, KCTS. One brother, John, presided over Fisher Broadcasting, which ran the city's ABC-affiliate, KOMO, while another, Carl, headed the local Pepsi-Cola bottling company. When Ned Behnke died of AIDS in March 1989, he was forty; six months later, his brother Carl would not only support but also help lead the annual AIDS walk, joining KING-TV's news anchor Jean Enerson as the event's cohost. His father created a new holding company named after Ned, R.E.B. Enterprises, to own Sur La Table kitchen stores throughout the region. The family foundation also helped support the Ned Behnke AIDS Leadership Award, given annually by the Northwest AIDS Foundation, and established what would become the prestigious local arts award named the "Neddy"—an unrestricted ten thousand dollars given annually to a Seattle artist.[41]

Like Behnke, another member of Seattle's arts community, Lowell Roddenberry, also taught at Cornish. Although a pianist, his real specialty was teaching young performers what to do with their stage fright. He showed them how to drive the energy and the anxiety directly into the excitement of performing. He became so well known for his approach that he traveled around the country offering seminars, helping, among others, Marni Nixon, the singing voice for Audrey Hepburn in the movie *My Fair Lady* and for Deborah Kerr in *The King and I*. When Roddenberry died in August 1989, Nixon told the *Seattle Times* that the Cornish teacher had "spent his life trying to help people like a guru."

"His death is such a damn waste," she added. Roddenberry was fifty-four.[42]

By the start of 1992, the list of the dead in the arts included dancers Daniel Chick, Robby Huffstetler, and Joe Riley Jr., as well as singers, actors, and theater directors such as Christopher! Caldwell (the exclamation point was deliberate), Chuck Gerra, John Kauffman, Gordon Peone, Rex Rabold, and Roger Ward. Gay arts organizations suffered dramatically—the gay Seattle Men's Chorus, for example, counted twenty-five of its two hundred members dead of AIDS within that first decade of the epidemic, including two of its assistant conductors. The group's main conductor, Dennis Coleman, told the *Seattle Times* that the chorus was holding so many memorial services that he had to just try to keep his focus on the music, especially during the services. "If I get emotional," he said, "the whole chorus loses it. . . . [I] try to make myself angry—angry at the injustice of the disease and of dying when you're so young." Coleman would not always succeed, especially later when he would lose his own partner to the virus.[43]

Some who died, while not artists themselves, helped make art in the city possible. There was Ed Elliott, for example, the gay activist who had been the president of Seattle's Dignity chapter when, in June 1988, it had been forced to leave St. Joseph's Church. Professionally, Elliott worked as an architect for Parsons Brinckerhoff. When he became project director for the design of Seattle's downtown bus tunnel, he insisted it be more than just a tube. "The tunnel," Elliott was said to have told his coworkers, "is an art gallery through which we run buses." If Seattle's mountain- and water-oriented citizens were suddenly to be expected to go underground for transportation, he argued, it had better be an aesthetically pleasing experience. Under his direction, the Westlake Mall station acquired terra cotta; the International District station, stylized origami. When he died in April 1991, Elliott was sixty-one.[44]

With 1992 came even more depletion. Clark Tippet, who had joined the American Ballet Theater in 1972 and had by age twenty-three danced virtually all the major male ballet roles, had come to the Pacific Northwest Ballet. There he had choreographed *Gigue* and *Chrysalis Rising.* He was working on the choreography for a third ballet to be presented by the PNB dancers at the Kennedy Center in Washington, D.C., when he died in February, at the age of thirty-seven. In April, it was Jim Bailey, a marketing director for Seattle Opera, who had been credited with doubling the company's subscription base; the Opera's general director, Speight Jenkins, called him "my right-hand man." Bailey died at age forty-four. In June, it was Michael Schauermann's turn. A popular actor with the Bathhouse Theater Company, he had earlier cared for his own AIDS-stricken partner, Gary Wiggs, a judge and chairman of the state Board of Industrial Appeals. Schauermann was forty-four when he died. In July, one of the city's actors who had been instrumental in creating plays for children, Lee McCormack, died at age thirty-seven. The same month, James Arsenault, who had founded the regional Opera Northwest, died at age forty-four.[45]

The virus continued cutting through the ranks of gay leaders too. Jack Jones had helped create the Northwest AIDS Foundation, had become its president, and had served on the board of the Chicken Soup Brigade. Professionally, he worked as an estate lawyer, and as more young gay men began to plan their wills in the 1980s and early 1990s, they sometimes turned to Jones for help. After Jones's lover, Michael Gallanger, died of AIDS in 1986, Jones inherited and cared for Gallanger's dog, Abigail. But as his own health worsened, it became clear that Abigail would once again be passed along. In January 1991, when Jones died, he was forty-three.

In March 1991, it was Jack Goldman, who owned Goldman's Jewelers in Pike Place Market, had been president of the merchants' association at the market, and had helped start the gay Greater Seattle Business Association and run its annual business fairs. He was forty-one. The same month: Phillip Blumstein, a University of Washington sociology professor who had become nationally known for his human sexuality research. Age: forty-six. In May 1991: Michael Harmon, a cartoonist, comic, and editor who had helped start a newsletter called *Springboard,* which published writings by people with AIDS—sometimes caustic, sometimes hilariously funny. At one point, he designed a T-shirt that said "I lost 85 pounds—Ask me how!" He died at age twenty-eight.

Another activist, Harvey Muggy, had made a life out of gay politics in Seattle, even though he was shy and awkward in public. For years, it seemed you could always run into Muggy sitting at a folding table on Broadway, dutifully registering voters. In the 1970s, he joined the Dorian Society, then the Dorian Group. He helped organize a committee to interview politicians to discover whether they supported gay concerns. After he launched a group for gay Democrats, he became known as Mr. Gay Democrat himself. In 1986, he campaigned for a position as state representative against an incumbent, knowing that he probably would not win but believing, strongly, that the time had come for openly gay political candidates. He even went to night classes to learn public speaking. He lost, but later gay candidates—who were successful—would always acknowledge that Harvey had opened the way. In August 1991, when he died of AIDS, Harvey Muggy was forty-seven.[46]

As the toll kept rising, the fight against AIDS generated a new infrastructure within Seattle's gay and lesbian community that might never have been there otherwise, developing a sense that community life was not just sexual liberation, or projecting a new identity, or even crusading for civil rights. Rather, it meant building the ongoing services and leadership that subsequent generations of gay men and lesbians would need. There seemed to be a new notion of "generations," each with its particular needs. "Coming out," although still important, was no longer the dominant theme it had been since Stonewall. Taking care of the sick was.

Gay activists, for example, worked through a Quaker social justice organization, the American Friends Service Committee, to use a city block grant targeted at youth who were bureaucratically defined as being "at risk" for health and family problems. With the money, they formed a program to focus on gay and lesbian youth, producing both a "safe schools" program that targeted the problems gay teenagers encountered in education and one of the nation's first community centers for gay teens.

At the other end of the age spectrum, the Pride Foundation began to collect and distribute money left by the increasing numbers of gay men who had died. Many had not wanted their estates to return to hostile families or to charities that paid no attention to gay or lesbian concerns. Among the donations was $1.2 million from one of the foundation's creators and its first president, Allan Tonning, an entrepreneurial small businessman. Tonning died just a year after helping set up the foundation, when he was thirty-one.[47]

The virus also changed the leadership roles of gay men and lesbians in the city.

The first impact was that there would no longer be a single male political activist designated Seattle's "gay mayor," as Charlie Brydon had once been. For a while, it had seemed that Jim Holm, the Dorian Group's president from 1982 until 1987, might inherit the title. Holm, a city government employee, worked mightily in insider meeting after insider meeting with city, county, and state officials; everyone agreed he seemed to have a quick mind for both the bureaucratic and the political. But with AIDS now the leading concern, not just civil rights, and with so many new AIDS organizations headed by powerfully public directors and fueled by impassioned missions, Holm watched as the nature of gay leadership shifted during the five years he was Dorian president. He often ended up as supporting actor rather than lead. "The community," he said once in an interview with the *Seattle Times*, "no longer wants one person doing its talking."[48] Holm himself became a member of at least sixteen different gay organizations, eventually leaving Seattle in 1988 to work for a national one—an AIDS organization, of course. As for the Dorian Group itself, it could never inspire thousands to walk or donate money, as the AIDS Foundation could, nor draw hundreds each month to bingo rituals, as Chicken Soup could. Over the years, it would metamorphose through a variety of names, maintaining its role as a political lobby in Olympia, but less and less commanding the symbolic role it had once held.

A second impact was the emergence of powerful women leaders, most especially in the fight against AIDS. Across the city, it was often women—some straight, most lesbian—running the details of the war: Bea Kelleigh directing at the Northwest AIDS Foundation in the mid-1980s. Betsy Lieberman looking for housing. Mary Kay Wright and Jolly Steussy Baker heading the Pride Foundation. Loren Smith and then Arlis Stewart launching the new gay youth program and community center. Carol Sterling assuming direction of the Chicken Soup Brigade from Josh Joshua. And working with Seattle's black, Asian, and Hispanic communities, Catlin Fullwood at POCAAN. Combined, they were in charge of tens of staff members, hundreds of volunteers, and millions of dollars in what was the Seattle gay and lesbian community's biggest campaign of the century.

The third effect on the city's gay leadership was that, finally, other races began to be represented among what until then had largely been a white gay and lesbian leadership in the city. Fullwood, the executive director of POCAAN, was African American; so was the organization's president, Kazas Jones. A forceful Texan who had been an air force officer, Jones also helped found AIDS Housing and, just as important, he was the choir president at one of Seattle's preeminent African American churches, Mount Zion Baptist. In a black community sometimes reluctant to face the presence of gay sons, Jones was a powerfully visible reminder.

At ACT UP, an African American man named Brian Day engineered street actions, including the planned protest against the opponents of the AIDS hospice in the Madison Valley. At the same time, he was working with the Chicken Soup Brigade and with a newly formed Governor's Task Force on AIDS. He gave speeches, he wrote. A picture in the *Seattle Times* showed him with a right finger pointed skyward and a megaphone in his left hand. His friends thought he was blossoming, even though at the same time he was directing his own personal battle against AIDS. In November 1990, when he was thirty, Day lost. From his work in fashion design, he left $110,000 to the Pride Foundation to be used for scholarships for gay men and women of color. He had never finished his university education; he wanted to be sure others did.[49]

Especially as POCAAN strengthened, gay and lesbian leaders from the city's Hispanic and Asian minorities emerged more visibly. With the virus making inroads into all corners of Seattle's very loose network of men who had sex with men, all the niches were developing a voice.

Finally, in 1994, a break came. The number of new AIDS diagnoses actually dropped, from 647 the previous year to 540. The next year, it declined to 502. In 1996, there was another drop, to 407.

Maybe the education programs were working. Maybe new infections were being prevented. Again, hope.

But there was still reason to be concerned. Those were new diagnoses of AIDS, after all. They did not include the number of people testing positive for the virus, nor the number actually living with AIDS and needing treatment, either in clinics or at Bailey-Boushay. Those numbers were more bothersome. In 1996, according to health department statistics, about nineteen hundred people in Seattle and King County had AIDS, compared to fifteen hundred two years before, a 25 percent increase. Upwards of nine thousand had tested positive for the antibodies.

It was still a time of dying.

For the four years since Allen DeShong's death in 1987, his former lover Robert O'Boyle had always kept a picture of Allen nearby. In February 1989, he too had been diagnosed with AIDS. Trained as a journalist at the University of Washington, he began writing a column in the *Seattle Times* about living—and dying—with AIDS. In his first article, he wrote: "I'm having a tough time accepting the view that I'm diseased. Do people worry about eating meals at my table? Am I making parents uncomfortable when I hold their children in my arms? Do people really embrace me less?"

"Will anybody ever touch me or hold me again?"

When he died in January 1992, Robert O'Boyle was thirty-two.[50]

Kazas Jones, the president of POCAAN, "was amazing at his determination to survive," according to his partner Michael Hanrahan. Time and again, Jones looked as if he would succumb to the virus, only to bounce back. Those he worked with stood a bit in awe at his forcefulness—not to mention his practicality. While some were working to ensure that the new Bailey-Boushay House would have an artistic pleasantness to live in, Jones was reminding them that hospital carts could not be wheeled over cobblestones, however elegant the cobblestones. In 1992, Nordstrom gave him a service award for his work to arouse AIDS awareness among the city's racial minorities. When he died in April 1993, "Kaz" Jones was forty-two.[51]

At age six, Kris Anderson had been cast as Prince Charming in a grade school play. Most boys would have been delighted. Kris wasn't. He preferred being Cinderella. At Ballard High School, he joined the chorale, toured the Middle East performing, and then set off for Broadway. In the early 1980s, he returned to Seattle and, along with Lee Richeson, started performing in the "Fabulous Fakes" at the Golden Crown. Whenever Kris Anderson appeared as Crystal Lane, he commanded the stage—nearly seven feet high in his heels, his hair, and his own sapling-thin six-foot four-inch frame. Drag had fallen somewhat out of favor during the 1970s, when gay liberationists were concerned that cross-dressing as women might be seen as anti-feminist and when newer, macho images of gay men were being created. For a while, drag had seemed to be mostly confined to places like the Golden Crown. Perhaps more than anyone else, Kris Anderson brought drag onto Capitol Hill, performing at the new discos that were opening, such as the Brass Connection on Pike Street, or at the new neighborhood bars, like the Encore on Eleventh Avenue. By the 1990s, Crystal Lane was on stage almost every night, most often working to raise money for different AIDS charities, most often singing "New York, New York" and "Over the Rainbow." For a decade, he worked as a member and then empress of Seattle's drag organization, the Imperial Sovereign Court of the Olympic and Rainier Empire. Among Seattle's female impersonators, he was—and continues to be—legendary. George Ray, a KCTS announcer, said of Anderson that "he had a heart as big as all outdoors" and "an indomitable will."

When he died of AIDS in February 1994, Kris Anderson was thirty-three. His memorial service would be held at the Catholic St. James Cathedral.[52]

Something surprising and unpredictable happened during the AIDS epidemic. Throughout most of the century, Seattle's homosexuals had been presented symbolically in the public mind in various negative ways. To people like George Cotterill and Mark Matthews, they had been the city's Unnatural Sex Offenders. For psychiatrists, they evolved into the city's Perverse Citizens and its Mentally Ill Citizens. For city officials of the early 1960s, they were its Promiscuous Citizens, spreading gonorrhea and syphilis. Even after Stonewall, the best that homosexuals could hope for was to become Minority Citizens, deserving of tolerance and civil rights protections.

But with AIDS that seemed to change. For the first time, they became the Compassionate Citizens.

Three types of stories in the city's news media constructed this new symbol.

First, there were the stories about homosexuals caring for one another, supplementing or substituting for traditional family members in tending to the sick. Gay men and lesbians created all-night vigils; gay men and lesbians sewed quilts to remember the names of those who died; gay men tended to their lovers and partners; gay men and lesbians joined Shanti and Chicken Soup; and lesbians ran many of the care-giving organizations. That was reported continually in news stories and obituaries. Jack Jones helped Michael Gallanger. Michael Schauermann cared for Gary Wiggs, and in turn was cared for by his new partner, Kevin Hadley. Neither gay men nor lesbians had ever been portrayed that way before.

Heterosexuals did the same, of course, and that was the second line of news stories: the compassion being called forth from other Seattle citizens by those who were dying. As volunteers for Chicken Soup and Shanti fanned across the city and then began to tell their own stories, it became clear just how deeply those with AIDS were touching the hearts of large numbers of people. In one example in 1987, a Chicken Soup volunteer named Jody Becker wrote in the *Seattle Times* of the simple act of taking one man out to eat at a restaurant after he had been released from the hospital. The man ordered French toast and doused it in butter and syrup to celebrate. But quickly he became too sick to go out again, and Becker shopped for him, made his dinner, and, as she wrote, "listened to his frustrations." His parents had rejected him for being gay, so she became one of his major supports during his final weeks. One day, as he lay on an emergency room gurney, she listened to hours of stories, then decided to escape to play tennis. She made it as far as the parking lot before turning back. When he saw her, he told her, "Go ahead, kid. You've been here long enough." His parents finally showed on the final weekend of his life. "I tried to unpuzzle the emotions," Becker wrote. "Who was I but some stranger who had so self-consciously elected to say 'care'?"[53]

The final line of stories was about the strength of people with AIDS themselves. Early on in Seattle, as elsewhere, headlines and news stories had called them "victims" or "sufferers" or "patients." But as the years went by, and their individual stories began to be told—either while they were living or in the obituaries telling of their deaths—they began to be portrayed as "battlers" and "heroes." Typical was the *Post-Intelligencer* headline on the story about Craig Anderson dying in 1987 despite AZT. "A battler is dead of AIDS," the newspaper reported. The *Seattle Times* headline for Allen DeShong said, "He was committed to letting people know." Other headlines portrayed the same brave struggle. Peter Davis's "calling to the ministry stayed alive." For cartoonist Michael Harmon, his "legacy was candor" and "he always left them laughing." Christopher! Caldwell, an actor, had a "zest for life" represented by that exclamation point he put after his first name. Jim Bailey was "a music lover who directed Seattle Opera's growth." Tracy Brown was "a man of energy." Lee McCormack was said to have "brought high energy to theater and music."

It was not unusual in itself to find laudatory wording in newspaper obituaries. What was unusual was that for the first time in the city's history, the men's homosexuality was being acknowledged even as they were being praised. Partners were being quoted—and recognized as partners. Gay men were being portrayed as mentors offering to their friends and families gifts of insight and wisdom about living and dying that no one—least of all those who in earlier decades would have committed them to prisons or lobotomized them—would ever have imagined.

That change in how the city's gay men were imagined would ultimately be the real legacy that those who died left behind.

Of Seattle actor Robert Cole, the *Seattle Times* said that when he died in 1994, his friends had been gathered around his bed, singing a Bing Crosby tune called "Count Your Blessings."

"When I get weary and I can't sleep," the lyrics went, "I count my blessings instead of sheep."

"Count your blessings," they sang.

On the last note, it was said, Cole had died. He was thirty-four.[54]

# 19
# Cal's Conscience

*I*n the late 1960s, when Cal Anderson was sixteen, he lived in Tukwila, a small working-class town south of Seattle that was dotted with metal foundries and Boeing aircraft hangars. He used to swim in the polluted Duwamish River. Compared to the usual Northwest portrayed on postcards, Tukwila was the wrong side of the tracks, but that gave Cal a passion for change, even as a teenager. When his father, Robert, complained that Tukwila needed more parks for children, if only to keep them out of the river, Cal urged his dad to become a candidate for the local city council. Cal managed the campaign himself. The teen wrote letters to every voter in town, in the end snatching a narrow victory of four votes for his father. The tightness of the contest fueled Cal's almost addictive enjoyment of politics. His mom would later say that he was a fun-loving kid—if fun meant inviting the Young Democrats over for a planning session. Cal's pictures of his teenage years show him at campaign rallies, staffing tables covered with Democratic Party signs.[1]

He had already realized he was gay. Because he thought that his homosexuality would prevent him from ever running for public office, he targeted behind-the-scenes political work instead. "Quite frankly," he said in a later interview, "I thought that being gay did you in."[2] After he graduated from Foster High School in 1966, Cal found a job working as a secretary for Jeanette Williams, then King County chair of the Democratic Party and later the Seattle City Council member who helped add sexual orientation to the city's antidiscrimination laws. Then he was drafted into the army. He decided not to check "yes" next to the question asking whether he was homosexual. He later told a *Seattle Times* reporter, "I thought if I scratched that 'yes,' next day in the paper, there'd be a headline: 'Cal Anderson, Jeanette Williams's secretary, is a fairy.'"[3]

Eventually, he did tell a first sergeant. Instead of being upset, the sergeant ordered him to go back to work, and the army sent him to Vietnam with the Twenty-third Infantry Division. He became a court reporter assigned to gather depositions in combat zones. When the initial investigation of the 1968 My Lai massacre began, Cal got the assignment to be lead court reporter. The quality of his court reporting won him two Bronze Stars. In 1971, the army assigned him as the senior court reporter in the My Lai–related trial of Captain Ernest Medina. That got him one of his four army commendations.[4]

Meanwhile, at nineteen, Cal also found his first male lover among his fellow soldiers. When he returned from the war, he resumed his other love. "Politics," he would say, "is the best way for one person to help a lot of people."[5] For some, that would be a cliché, but Cal seemed to believe it with all the innocent, gee-whiz idealism a kid from the 1960s could muster. He believed it so much that he could make others believe too. Seattle mayor Charles Royer, who would employ him a decade later, once said of Cal that "he's a very sincere guy, almost to the point that you think, gee Cal, are you really that sincere? Are you really that nice?"[6]

Part of his persuasiveness and charm was his appearance. Even when he grew older, Cal stayed short and roundish, like a kid who never lost his baby fat. He always wore suits that looked a size or two too large and oversized black-rimmed glasses that dwarfed his face. He looked like a wide-eyed ten-year-old forever teetering on the edge between the realities of the adult political world and his continually enthusiastic and mischievous boyhood. That's why everyone seemed to call him only by his first name; it seemed odd to ever be too formal with Cal.

In 1988—the same year the state legislature would consider the AIDS Omnibus Bill and Steven Farmer would face a mandatory blood test—Cal achieved his political goal. He became the first openly gay state legislator in the history of Washington State.

His rise in Seattle politics went like this. When he returned from the army, his father had died, so he sought a job instead of going to college. From 1975 until 1983, he worked as an administrative assistant for Seattle City Council member George Benson. Then he became Royer's appointments secretary. He engaged in continuous trench work with the local Democratic Party, and although he served on the steering committee for Citizens to Retain Fair Employment during Initiative Thirteen, he avoided any highly visible role. After being mentored by Harvey Muggy—that longtime gay Democratic activist on Capitol Hill—Cal began to think about actually taking his passion public and running for state political office himself, an inspiration Muggy had given him. Compared to Muggy, Cal had the advantages of being more photogenic and having established insider credentials—and he was not at all shy in public.

The most logical place for a gay representative, of course, would be the Forty-third District that included Capitol Hill. The opportunity came in 1987, when state senator Jim McDermott decided to temporarily leave politics, setting off a domino effect that left the Forty-third's state house seat vacant. Since the vacancy would be filled by appointment, the crucial factor was the recommendation from the party's precinct chairs. From his years of behind-the-scenes work, Cal knew many of them, and when he submitted his name, there was little contest. For the first time, Seattle and Washington had an openly gay state legislator. The fact that he was from a district that, at least in its gathering places and history, remained so symbolically Catholic did not seem to matter at first—eventually, though, it would bedevil him.

The curiosity of having an openly gay legislator was something the news media would always emphasize with Cal, the phrase almost always attached to his name. Overnight it seemed, he had become the new leader of the city's gay and lesbian community, the new Charlie Brydon. Problem was, few people in the city's gay and lesbian community had ever heard of him. As had been true of Brydon, his appointment tapped into all those long-standing tensions between the downtown insiders and hill activists. Even Muggy, who himself had been working within the Democratic Party, told the *Seattle Times* after Cal was appointed that "the only problem that some of us had is that he's not as radical as some of us wanted." Muggy, though, at least allowed that "that's what's going to make him a good representative. He can represent the diversity of our district."[7]

One of Cal's closest political buddies, Ed Murray, remembered his first months as the new "gay spokesman." "Cal was a typical guy, not a very demonstrative guy, controlled in how he came across. I knew him privately to be a person who loved to go out to bars, loved campy humor, and liked having a typical gay guy's time in the 1980s. But you didn't see that face initially. Initially, he tended to be more of a system guy or establishment guy versus a community activist guy."

"At first, there was a dismissal of Cal as a lightweight. Every year he would ask to speak at the gay pride parade, and the organizing committee would vote no, and then they'd finally revote and let him speak. The wealthier part of the gay community would also dismiss him. In those early campaigns, Cal's greatest hurt and his greatest struggles were around being accepted by other gays and lesbians."[8]

Cal's paradox was that his new colleagues in the legislature looked at him as a gay man first of all, while many of his gay constituents saw him mostly as a backroom politico. For example, the AIDS Omnibus Bill posed a serious challenge for him as a freshman legislator. While gay activists liked its civil rights protections for those who were HIV-positive, many disliked the sections allowing even limited mandatory testing and making it a felony to knowingly spread the virus— especially with the Steven Farmer case pending. Faced with the compromises of politics, Anderson chose to vote for the bill and was embarrassed when the American Civil Liberties Union attacked the less desirable sections. Some AIDS activists, mistrustful of the gay legislator in the suit, started periodically trashing his house with graffiti. Others pointed out that in his first session Anderson had little success getting any publicity for the overall gay and lesbian civil rights bill that had been on the community's legislative agenda for a decade. They questioned whether he really could be the gay and lesbian champion they had hoped for.[9]

For his own part, Cal had little interest in pushing only gay-related legislation. Instead, he campaigned for easier voter registration, government reforms, gun control, and daycare insurance. One of his first committee appointments was to the house Government Operations Committee, where he became vice-chair. The first law he proposed was aimed not at gay rights, but at taking away concealed weapon permits of anyone arrested while drunk or using drugs. He managed to have it pass, but only in the typical political fashion of compromise, agreeing to have the weapon taken away for one year instead of the five he had originally sought.

When Cal headed away for a brief vacation after his first session, Murray handed him a copy of Randy Shilts's *The Mayor of Castro Street,* a biography of San Francisco's first openly gay supervisor, Harvey Milk, who had been assassinated ten years earlier, in 1978. Milk had managed to effectively combine the roles of gay spokesman and nuts-and-bolts politician. When Cal returned, he began to adjust his own vision.

According to Murray, "He came back and totally embraced everyone. The leather community, the drag community. Cal the private gay man became the public gay man. He put on a harness at a leather event. He put on his boxer shorts at a bar party."

"As time went on and his legislative skills became apparent, then the gay and lesbian community really adopted him. They grew to love him for what he was able to do."[10]

Having been drafted into the army, Anderson had never made it to college. He always felt a little awkward about that, especially since his Capitol Hill district included so many Jesuit institutions and so much of Seattle's professional class. But his working-class background, his swims in the Duwamish River as a boy, and his father's death from a heart attack at age fifty-two had given him other strengths: an enjoyment of meeting different people on the street and in their living rooms, a willingness to not take himself too seriously, a sense of humorous timing, a desire to get on with the more important things in his life rather than holding grudges. That boyish innocence gradually became charisma.

During his first months as a legislator, Cal kept a weekly diary, some of which was eventually published in the *Seattle Times*—whose editors seemed somewhat taken with the idea of a young gay politician, since within a few months they published two full-page features about him. Here is Cal commenting on his appointment by the precinct chairmen: "It was wonderful. I had the best cheering section! My supporters were so organized! Can you tell I'm excited?" Here he is entering the legislature on his first day: "I walked into the room and looked up in the gallery to get a glance at my mom, Alice Coleman, and Eric [Ishino, his lover], and I thought I might lose it right there. It's really quite exhilarating—not the way 'Gosh, I've got power'—just that you're part of this team, this effort to do some good."

When he took the oath of office for the first time, he remembered, "It was quite overpowering when they lined all of us up to march into the session, taking my seat with my name on it."

January 29, 1988, a few days into the session, he wrote: "This morning I went to the Washington Cattlemen's Association breakfast. A cowboy sits down and says, 'What about this gay legislation?' It turns out he's a gay rancher! He came by my office and said how wonderful it was to have someone in the legislature." Cal learned how to handle the endless round of luncheons and receptions: "What happens is you kind of graze . . . a couple of chicken wings here, a mushroom cap over there. It's changed my eating habits and not for the better. But I'm lucky. I haven't gained weight. In fact, I may have lost a couple of pounds."

What emerges in the diary published in the *Times* is his wonder at being in the legislature. On the final day of the session, when he had to stay overnight at an Olympia hotel and checked in as "Rep. Cal Anderson," he reflected, "It's such a feeling. I still get goose bumps because it's quite an honor."[11]

That feeling would continue, especially as he grew more comfortable in the role. At a later session of the legislature, for example, he used humor to disarm those who felt uncomfortable with his homosexuality—a tactic that had also been used by Harvey Milk. Once he used a double entendre to introduce a resolution to make the apple the "state fruit" of Washington: "Fruits are of vital concern to many of my constituents," he said dryly, then waited for the response. After a moment, the other representatives erupted in laughter. During a Democratic caucus meeting when the party leadership wanted a woman to chair one of the house committees in order to have adequate minority representation, Cal quipped, "Will a sissy do?"[12]

One source of pride was a letter from a constituent that he kept framed in his office at the legislature. It said: "At age eighty-five, I had the traditional social attitude about sexual aberration. I would never have voted for you. But you have been an outstanding representative of my views. I have become a strong supporter of Cal Anderson."[13]

Cal also became a target. One person mailed him a news story about his appointment to the legislature and scribbled on it, "Someday you will pay the Piper! You get your sex in the sewer! I'd like to see all you 'gays' isolated from the human race!" On an "Action-Gram" where Cal solicited messages from constituents, one wrote, "How about a bill mandating prison sentences—unlimited—for all faggots of the 43rd District, including you?! For those unwilling or unable to obey the law, the bill should include severe penalties, including death." Another card said, "Your speeches on T.V. make me sick. . . . Have you considered moving to San Francisco? You'd fit right in there. Drop dead pervert!"[14]

The push for a statewide civil rights law to protect homosexuals from discrimination in jobs and housing had originally begun in the 1977 legislature, eleven years before Cal arrived in Olympia. That first hearing had featured an all-star cast testifying on behalf of the law, including Seattle mayor Wes Uhlman and Seattle council member Jeanette Williams talking about the successful adoption of such a law in Seattle, teacher Jim Gaylord explaining how he had been unjustly fired for simply attending meetings with other gay men, and the gay football star from the University of Washington, Dave Kopay. Thanks partly to the KIRO-TV editorials by Lloyd Cooney, the bill never made it out of the house Social and Health Services Committee.

In 1979, it was reintroduced. Assigned to the house Judiciary Committee that year, it never even received a hearing, despite the impressive victory Seattle's gays and lesbians had just scored in repulsing Initiative Thirteen. In 1981, gay activists tried initiating the bill in the state senate. It died in the Judiciary Committee. Pushing the bill became a ritual of trying to make slight advances, perhaps to win a hearing in one chamber one year, then another the next. In 1983, the house Judiciary Committee actually agreed to a hearing, but then postponed a vote. In 1985, the same. In 1987, the same. The only bright spot in state protection came in 1985 when a Democratic governor, Booth Gardner, issued an executive order prohibiting discrimination against gays and lesbians in state hiring.

When Cal arrived in 1988, he began to steer the process himself. Behind the scenes, he could make the connections that others could not. "What I've always done is to look for common ground," he said in an interview. "If there was a very conservative, homophobic representative who was a Vietnam veteran—and I am a Vietnam veteran—I'd go over to him if there was military legislation going on. I'd say, 'Hey, would you mind if I co-sponsored this with you.' It just drove people crazy. They didn't know what to think." But it broke barriers.

"The biggest thing is just to be there," Cal said. "I provided an example that we're not monsters."[15]

In 1989, he managed to get the bill referred to the house State Government Committee and then, during the second year of the biennial session, through the committee. On February 14, 1990, for the first time ever, the house narrowly passed the bill, fifty-one to forty-seven, but it died in the senate. During the next biennial term of 1991–92, Cal decided to instead push a malicious harassment bill to increase penalties on those accused of committing crimes motivated by bigotry, whether because of race, gender, religion, or sexual orientation. The house eventually passed the bill seventy-seven to twenty-one, but then a state senator from Renton, Leo Thorsness, convinced the senate's Law and Justice Committee to remove the words "sexual orientation" from the legislation. Thorsness argued that while he was a prisoner during the Vietnam war, he believed some of the guards who had tortured him were homosexual. The house refused to concur in the senate's change, and the entire hate crimes bill died.[16]

In the fall of 1992, two crucial factors convinced Cal to try again in the next session for the civil rights protection in jobs and housing, as well as for the hate crimes bill. For the first time in years, Democrats took control of the state house and the senate as well as the governor's office that autumn. One of Governor Mike Lowry's first actions would be to strengthen the executive order that protected state employees from discrimination. Party leaders also promised they were ready to pass a civil rights bill to protect everyone, regardless of sexual orientation. In charge of the critical house State Government Committee, where the Democratic leader planned to assign the bill, would be its prime sponsor, Cal Anderson.

Also that fall, a virulently anti-gay organization in Oregon, the Oregon Citizens' Alliance (OCA), attempted to pass a ballot measure that would have amended that state's constitution to require all government agencies, including the state's schools and libraries, to teach only that homosexuality was "abnormal, wrong, unnatural, and perverse." The constitutional amendment would also have outlawed any civil rights protections based on sexual orientation. The measure had been defeated, but, disturbingly, 43 percent of the state's voters had supported it, and activists in Seattle had begun to anticipate that the OCA's director, Lon Mabon, would export the initiative to Washington State as a way of overturning Seattle's civil rights protections as well as the governor's executive order. It would be Initiative Thirteen written statewide—as well as a repeat of the initiative strategy that the Ku Klux Klan had used in the 1920s, when it attempted to move its anti-Catholic momentum from Oregon into Washington.

As had happened just before David Estes launched his anti-gay initiative in 1978, Charlie Brydon moved quickly to catalyze a response. In October 1992—even before the outcome of the Oregon vote was known—he sent a letter to Seattle lesbian and gay activists announcing that "a group of politically experienced women and men from our community" had already created a new organization called Washington Citizens for Fairness in order to oppose Mabon's expected invasion. The committee included Cal as well as lesbian and gay power brokers from the old Dorian Group and the gay business owners' organization, the GSBA. They had even already chosen a catchy slogan for the anti-Mabon effort: "Hands Off Washington."[17] It was a somewhat hopeful way of trying to seed the idea that the attempts to promote discrimination against homosexuals were alien.

One of the other strategies for doing that, in this year of Democratic control of the government, was to finally pass the civil rights law as well as the malicious harassment bill.

And so, as the 1993 legislative session began, both sides—gay and anti-gay—geared for confrontation.

On January 29, Lon Mabon called a press conference, symbolically situating it in the rotunda of the Capitol in Olympia, and announced that he would indeed press a similar anti-gay initiative in Washington State, barring the inclusion of homosexuals in civil rights laws, prohibiting schools from teaching anything positive about homosexuality, and forbidding the use of tax dollars to support homosexuality—such as through counseling or AIDS education. His new Citizens' Alliance of Washington would be headed by a resident of Vancouver, Washington, named Robert Larimer Jr. "I don't hate anybody," Mabon said, but homosexuals should not have "special rights."

Moments later, at a counter-conference, Charlie Brydon, Seattle mayor Norm Rice, and Governor Lowry denounced the Mabon campaign. Brydon, promoting the "hands off" sound bite, referred to the anti-gay leaders as "carpetbaggers" and added that "today, the OCA has oozed across the Columbia River to plant seeds of intolerance and hatred." Governor Lowry vehemently promised to "drive a wooden stake through the ugly heart of discrimination."[18]

New anti-gay initiatives in 1993 and 1994 forced the formation of a successful state-wide "Hands Off Washington" campaign that drew widespread political support, in this case from Mayor Norm Rice (above, left) and Police Chief Norm Stamper, who joined the lesbian/gay pride march in 1994. Stamper was the first police chief in Seattle to do so. (*Geoff Manasse*)

The initiatives also spawned an activist "Bigot Busters" group. (*Geoff Manasse*)

Coincidentally, that year it had been exactly a century since the Washington legislature had adopted the state's first sodomy law. The rhetoric of "unnatural" and "perverse" that had led to the unquestioned adoption of that law was now, one hundred years later, to have its most intense clash yet with the rhetoric of equal rights for all citizens.

Also by coincidence, Cal Anderson scheduled the hearing on the civil rights bill almost one hundred years to the day after the state senate had adopted the first sodomy law.

On March 2, 1993, the hearing room in a building next to the state Capitol filled quickly, and the crowd spilled over, blocking the hallway outside. One man wearing a fluorescent green badge demanded that a security guard admit him to the room, fuming, "You've got to make room for God." In the hall behind him, others wearing green badges began chanting, "We want in! We want in! We want in!" The outnumbered guard retreated to his walkie-talkie and began calling urgently for help. "I need more security down here," he told someone at the other end.[19]

More and more green badges continued to arrive as the hour for the hearing neared, pouring from church buses from around the state in a protest organized by fundamentalist Christian ministers and Mabon supporters. Just as in 1977 Mormon women had worn blue and white ribbons at the women's conference in Ellensburg and had overwhelmed reform-minded feminists, the protesters at the Capitol wore the badges so that they could identify one another.

One hundred people could fit into the room that Cal had scheduled for the hearing, but by the time the state police responded to the call for help, seven hundred had already overrun the room and blocked the halls. Quickly, tactfully, Cal arranged to move the hearing into an unprecedented location—the house chamber itself. One hundred years after the sodomy bill had passed without public debate, there would finally be a conversation in the statehouse itself about granting equal citizenship to gays and lesbians. Witnesses and spectators poured into the seats normally occupied by legislators and then overflowed into the galleries above.

Cal's chief ally in organizing much of the supportive testimony for the night was Ed Murray, who by then was president of a statewide gay lobbying group called the Privacy Fund, itself a replacement for Brydon's now-defunct Dorian Group. Like Cal, Murray had developed a passion for politics as a young boy. Both had been raised by working-class parents, but Murray had a twist in his background that Cal did not. His family was Irish Catholic, and like many sons in such families, Murray had studied to be a priest. When he was a teenager, his mom had given him a copy of Thomas Merton's *The Seven-Story Mountain,* and, inspired by it, Murray at age nineteen had gone to Belfast to work in community centers teaching children, his real purpose to provide an American shield against bomb attacks.

Together, Cal and Murray had assembled an impressive array of witnesses to speak in favor of the bill. Murray went first with a speech carefully crafted of history. "My grandparents immigrated to this country to escape oppression," he said.

"They settled in Grays Harbor County, logged it, farmed it, and helped build Washington State. They came to this country to ensure that *all* of their children and grandchildren would have an opportunity for a home, a job, and a chance at the American dream."

Merritt Long, the director of the state Human Rights Commission, followed a few minutes later, and provoked the first response from the conservative Christians who dominated the chamber and its galleries. When Long said, "I philosophically support and conceptually agree with the bill," a man with a green badge sitting in a nearby legislator's chair stood, silently raised his Bible, and waved it in the air.

Both Cal and Murray had known that the statehouse would hear from the conservative churches, so they had prepared their own list of church witnesses. Scott Spurling, a rabbi, directly addressed the man with the Bible. "To no one's surprise, purveyors of hate do not distinguish between people of color, Christians, and sexual orientation. My family and my people stood with lesbian and gay people while they put on their pink triangles at Auschwitz and Dachau." David Serkin-Poole, a Jewish cantor, followed Spurling: "Three years ago, my partner and I adopted a child, and then another child. I am very hurt when others use and abuse religious scripture."

Shouts from the gallery began: "Shut up!" "Get out of here, you freak!"

"Homo!" someone shouted.

John Boonstra, executive minister of the Washington Association of Churches, testified next: "We don't speak with one voice as religious communities, but we do unanimously oppose discrimination against anyone."

Shouts: "Sodomy is an offense!"

"When does the next train to Auschwitz leave?"

A mother with a lesbian daughter started to respond: "This wave of intolerance hearkens back to the Salem witch hunts."

The green badges began chanting in unison: "Let the Christians talk, let the Christians talk."

Cal rose. He was short, but he could be imperious when the occasion demanded. He slowly and deliberately crossed his arms. The chanting continued. He simply stood. And finally, after what seemed an interminable time, the chanting stopped.

One of the next speakers would be the lobbyist for the state's Catholic bishops, Ned Dolejsi. Cal was counting on Dolejsi's statement to outweigh the antics of the fundamentalists and to give the bill a secure boost. After all, even with all the years of agonizing debate over dogma versus pastoral ministry to gay Catholics, the Washington bishops had steadfastly supported civil rights legislation ever since it had first been introduced sixteen years earlier.

Cal especially needed the bishops' support that night.

The Catholic Church's declarations on statewide political issues, such as the gay civil rights bill, are crafted by the three prelates in the state: the archbishop in Seattle and the bishops in Spokane and Yakima. To ensure they speak together, the three meet in closed conferences to settle differences on any particular bills. In the 1970s and 1980s, Seattle's gays and lesbians benefited from the fact that two of the three, Hunthausen in Seattle and William Skylstad in Yakima, were appointed by Pope Paul VI and influenced by that pope's broad interpretations of Catholic doctrine. Even the bishop in Spokane, Lawrence Welsh, had been appointed only one month after the selection of Pope John Paul II, before the more conservative pope could have much impact on the selection of the hierarchy.

In 1990, Welsh had retired and Skylstad had relocated to Spokane, leaving the Yakima diocese open. To that central Washington area, populated heavily by Hispanic farm workers and white vineyard owners, John Paul II had sent a theologically conservative priest named Francis George.

A year later, Hunthausen had announced an early retirement. When he had reached his compromise with the Vatican in 1987, he had planned to stay for another ten years, one reason everyone had been comfortable with the idea of a coadjutor bishop being appointed. Such coadjutors usually serve only when bishops are ill or very close to retiring, and since Hunthausen was neither, most figured the coadjutor, Thomas Murphy, was simply a harmless part of the deal. Some priests had even worn buttons saying, "Hunthausen—No more fears, ten more years." But after only three years, Hunthausen had decided to turn his office over to Murphy.

At first, it seemed Murphy would continue Hunthausen's touch. Unlike Donald Wuerl, sent as the pope's personal representative during the troubled Vatican investigation of the Seattle archdiocese, Murphy was a Northwesterner who had developed a reputation much like Hunthausen's when it came to pastoral ministry. The epitome of a gray-haired, bespectacled Irish Catholic bishop, he had a good sense of humor and a willingness to let his friends call him "Gracie" instead of "Your Grace." He hosted pizza parties and, in Montana, when his budget could not support a diocesan weekly newspaper, he had published a monthly newsletter that he wrote, edited, and photographed himself. He seemed flexible and accessible. Typical of the response to Murphy's arrival in Seattle had been the statement from the Reverend Michael Ryan, who, as archdiocesan chancellor and the head priest of St. James Cathedral, was second in visibility in the diocese. He had told the *Seattle Times,* "I think he won our hearts very quickly—I think we saw him as one of us, someone we can walk the road with—happily."[20]

Yet Murphy had not been considered as prophetic and visionary as Hunthausen. He was not one to push the church or to try to "discern"—Hunthausen's favorite word—what God was calling church leaders to do. When he had arrived in Seattle, some priests had even wondered whether Murphy, like Wuerl, had any secret orders from the Vatican or whether Rome was planning other surprises for the archdiocese. One typical comment had been made by the Reverend Jim Moran, of Capitol Hill's St. Patrick's parish. He had told the *Seattle Times* that "I think a lot of people still feel another shoe is to fall, but they don't know who's holding it."[21]

In August 1991, Hunthausen had bid his farewell at St. James Cathedral. In his final speech as archbishop, he had still urged the message he had pressed for years. "Are we a church," he asked, "that includes gays, welcomes the divorced and separated, offers equal opportunity to women? . . . Are our doors sincerely open to the least of our brothers and sisters?"[22]

During the 1991–92 legislative session, the final one over which Hunthausen would set policy for the archdiocese, Cal had opted for pushing the hate crimes bill instead of the job and housing protection bill. He had had Hunthausen's support for that, and if the new conservative bishop in Yakima had objections, Hunthausen and Skylstad had been able to overcome them. For the 1993 session, though, Murphy was setting policy for the archdiocese, and Francis George was more firmly ensconced in Yakima. Not only that, but in July 1992, a new Vatican document on homosexuality had been leaked. In it, Cardinal Joseph Ratzinger repeated his belief that homosexuality was an "objective disorder," but he also went even further and declared that discrimination against gays and lesbians could be just.[23]

That directly contradicted the distinction the Washington State bishops had long made—that whatever one thought of the sinful practice of homosexuality, homosexuals themselves still deserved civil rights.

After Cal silenced the fundamentalist shouts and unfolded his arms, Dolejsi moved to the microphone.

"We find ourselves in an awkward situation this evening," he began.

Cal frowned. It was not the start he expected.

"We might oversimplify serious questions," Dolejsi continued. "We are not in favor of harassment or discrimination. We advocate for those unjustly discriminated against."

Dolejsi was speaking slowly and, it seemed, painfully. "On the face of it, this bill is about prohibiting discrimination."

"But," he added. The conjunction lingered long enough in the air to be noticeable to everyone in the audience. Then, Dolejsi continued solemnly. "Procedurally, we think it might be a mistake. The original drive for civil rights was to protect people because of who they are or what they believe, not because of what they do.

"For a person who is homosexual by orientation only, discrimination is not a problem. But this bill protects whatever their behavior might be."

It was the same old argument that had long been used against gays and lesbians. If they stayed in the closet and did not act on their homosexuality, they would be protected. But if they came out or practiced homosexuality, they would lose the "protection."

Dolejsi was beginning to speak more rapidly, as if in a hurry to get through the unpleasant business. "What would happen to family law? To employment law? We may not want to be hurried into a broader acceptance of homosexuality." Finally,

Dolejsi reached the bottom line. The three Washington State bishops had suddenly and inexplicably opted for ellipsis.

"We cannot support the present legislation," he declared, "but we will not oppose it."

It was a stunning reversal. After a decade and a half of advocating for the bill, the Catholic bishops had declared neutrality.

Only those wearing green badges stood and applauded.[24]

Within hours, Ed Murray was busy trying to arrange a meeting with the archbishop as well as with Dolejsi to find out what had happened. The sudden change had caught both him and Cal off guard. Had Cal miscalculated and not seen the possibility of a switch? Communication between the two major constituencies on Capitol Hill had clearly broken down. Could the church's position be reversed? Did Murphy understand that the bill was the same one the bishops had supported for years?

At first the bishops' new neutrality did not seem to affect the votes. Cal had enough support to move the bill out of the State Government Committee the following day, seven to two , with some legislators even commenting to him that the catcalls on the chamber floor had given them a good demonstration of the kind of prejudice gays and lesbians faced in Washington State. Nine days later, the bill passed the full house by a comfortable fifty-seven to forty-one, and was sent to the senate Law and Justice Committee.

Knowing that Dolejsi would be back to lobby, Murray, Cal, and, for good measure, a gay woman who was a member of one of the archdiocese's most prominent Irish Catholic families, met the archbishop, along with Dolejsi and the archdiocese's press spokesman, John McCoy, on a Saturday night, drinking beer and soda in the mahogany-lined dining room at the archbishop's mansion.

"The discussion went something like this," Murray recalled later. "The archbishop would express a concern or Ned Dolejsi would express a concern—such as about this [bill] leading to marriage. And we'd answer it: The laws governing marriage are different from the laws governing discrimination. The archbishop would act very surprised." Another concern would be expressed about the law forcing churches to hire gays and lesbians. "We explained the law will not affect churches or small businesses. There are various exemptions."

"Every time, the archbishop acted surprised by this new information. Every time that would happen, we would feel closer to an agreement."[25]

To Murray, Seattle's new archbishop seemed ill informed, obviously unable to have shaped the state bishops' conversation about the bill with the same force Hunthausen would have had. The grapevine was already alive with word that it was Bishop George who had actually forced the new stance, taking his cue from the Ratzinger document leaked the previous July. At the time, Pat Roche, a Seattle

Catholic who had been national president of Dignity, had asked Murphy for a clarification, and Murphy had separated the Seattle archdiocese from the document, calling it an internal Vatican memorandum with no force. Murphy had promised Roche at the time that he would continue to "oppose any harassment, prejudice and discrimination against any member of the human family."[26]

Yet at the hearing in Olympia nine months later, all the "serious questions" Dolejsi had been raising seemed to come directly from the new Ratzinger document. So did all the questions being asked at Murphy's dining table.

According to Murray, the discussion lasted for hours and ended with the archbishop wanting more information. Once they had finished, the Privacy Fund board members divided up the research Murphy had requested, especially information on distinguishing between the state's marriage and antidiscrimination laws. The next morning, Murray delivered the package of information to Murphy. "I left it at his doorstep and then sent an official packet in the mail." For him, the discussion had been poignant. "I don't think I was ever happier to be a Catholic and a gay person than that night when we left. It just seemed like we were so close."

But then, nothing changed.

At the state senate, the Catholic line put forward by Dolejsi did not change. Once again, he turned up at a hearing, giving what Murray called "the most unneutral neutral statement I've ever heard." Some initially favorable Catholic senators faltered in the face of the hierarchy's "neutrality." Although the senate Law and Justice Committee eventually passed the bill by a narrow five to four vote, it was then referred to the Ways and Means Committee, ostensibly to determine what the cost of enforcing the new antidiscrimination provision would be. Cal knew immediately that the bill was in trouble, not because the cost of enforcing it would be substantial—there was plenty of indication it would cost little if anything—but because the maneuver seemed a way of stalling. Days passed, seven in all. Nothing happened in the committee itself, the chair, Nita Rinehart, refusing to bring it up for a vote because, she said, she could not find enough support to do so. Several conservative Democrats from rural districts had broken ranks and decided to side with the Republican opponents. Cal tried to persuade the Democratic majority leader in the senate, Marc Gaspard, to pull the bill out of the committee and get it to the senate floor, where he thought he could still win. Gaspard refused.

Murray remembers Cal angrily snarling at him, "Get your Catholic lobbyist out of here. Shut him up!" Years later, Murray would continue to feel that the change in the bishops' stance had been the single most important factor in killing the best chance the bill ever had of becoming law.[27]

By early April, the gay civil rights bill was, once again, dead.

Its companion legislation—the malicious harassment bill—fared better, offering lesbian and gay activists at least one victory, albeit a smaller one. Ironically, the very vociferousness of the opponents to the lesbian/gay civil rights bill seemed to persuade some legislators that hatred of homosexuals was so deep that it justified the need for the hate crimes bill. It passed the house overwhelmingly, eighty-five to twelve, and the senate, twenty-nine to twenty.

For Cal, the civil rights failure was bitter—particularly since the defeat came from his own Democratic colleagues and from the Catholic bishops who had long supported the bill. When he walked onto the floor of the house to concede, he showed none of his usual humor. "I grieve for this loss," he said sadly. "Now I must go around this state and tell lesbians and gay men that they still can't enjoy equal rights or equal justice . . . simply because they are gay."

He looked around the chamber. "I have a dream," he said slowly, "that one day gay men and lesbians will be judged not by their sexual orientation but by their ability to do their job, to contribute to our society."

Then he walked off the floor, looking much older in his suit than he had ever looked before. He told a reporter the defeat had "taken a toll."

"Like having a friend die," he said.[28]

Cal knew his days in the Washington legislature would be brief. Always, he felt his own quests there would have to succeed in a very short time. A deadline stared at him.

As had so many other gay men, Cal had tested positive for the antibodies to the AIDS virus in the 1980s—indeed he had been HIV-positive during his entire time in the legislature. But few people knew. As Cal would say later, he wanted to be known as a legislator, not as an "AIDS poster boy."[29]

The good news for him in 1993 was that he was still healthy—and that Lon Mabon's Citizens' Alliance failed to organize quickly enough to secure signatures for a ballot initiative that autumn. That gave Cal and the other leaders of the Hands Off Washington campaign time to begin to organize statewide. Soon enough, bumper stickers sporting the slogan appeared on cars all across the state, and HOW "citizens coalitions" were organized in about two dozen towns and cities. Importantly, they were in places like Yakima and Spokane as well as in the western part of the state. By early 1994, HOW had twelve paid staff, had raised a half-million dollars, and was preparing to raise three million dollars more.[30]

As it turned out, HOW was going to have to fight two initiatives. Mabon's group, CAW, filed one called The Minority Status and Child Protection Act, repeating its previous demands while also barring homosexuals who got divorced from heterosexual partners from ever securing custody of their children. That would be Initiative 610. A second anti-gay group, the Washington Public Affairs Council, led by a man named Doug Burman, filed what would become Initiative 608, which basically repeated the prohibitions against government granting any antidiscrimination protection to homosexuals and against schools discussing homosexuality positively.

Meanwhile, in Olympia, Cal doggedly introduced the lesbian/gay civil rights bill again, although Gaspard was still signaling he did not want the bill to make it to the senate floor for fear supportive Democratic politicians would be put on the spot in a year of tense confrontation. Still, the bill moved quickly through the house, passing by January 28, and once again through the senate Law and Justice Committee and into the Rules Committee. This time, though, the Catholic bishops dropped even the pretense of neutrality and instead actively opposed the bill. Once five conservative Democrats then declared their opposition, head counts showed that the fate of the bill rested with two moderate Republicans, Shirley Winsley of Fircrest, who had two gay nephews, and John Moyer of Spokane, a physician and member of the governor's AIDS advisory board—and a Catholic with ten children. Both had initially said they favored some sort of antidiscrimination bill, but both had also suggested studying how much discrimination against gays and lesbians was actually occurring. Such a study, of course, posed a chicken-and-egg problem: Since no law protected homosexuals, discrimination usually was not reported, and most of those who had been harmed did not want to broadcast their sexual orientation since there was no law in place to protect them from future discrimination. And the hearings themselves had already generated anecdotal information. Still, despite intense lobbying from both sides—including visits by priests and nuns to Moyer—both senators refused to commit. Without the necessary twenty-five votes to pass the bill on the senate floor, Gaspard again refused to pull it from committee.[31]

Meanwhile, the two anti-gay groups had launched their effort to gain enough signatures to put Initiatives 608 and 610 on the fall 1994 ballot. But in a replay of what had occurred in the Initiative Thirteen campaign in Seattle, they soon found themselves confronted not only by the broad-based and "respectable" coalition that Charlie Brydon had helped catalyze, but by an aggressive grassroots "Bigot Busters" organization that pinpointed their signature gatherers, especially in western Washington, and immediately sent pro-gay activists into the field to talk people out of signing the petitions. When the deadline of July 8 arrived, neither anti-gay initiative had enough signatures to even try to qualify. Each had needed about 182,000 valid signatures from registered voters. Burman's organization had collected about that number of total signatures for I-608, but lacked the usual 15 percent extra "cushion" believed necessary to account for signatures from unregistered voters and for duplications. Mabon's CAW, so effectively labeled as Oregon "outsiders," had collected only about forty thousand for I-610.[32]

Two months later, in September 1994, Cal Anderson learned from his doctors that his immune system had declined enough for him to now be officially considered to have AIDS. Still, he told only his closest friends. He wanted to make one more attempt in his quest to win civil rights protections for lesbians and gays. And, he figured, if the state senate was the block—as it had been for several years in a

State Representative Cal Anderson (left, with his partner Eric Ishino) became the first openly gay legislator in Washington, shown here in the statehouse in 1993, a century after the state passed its first sodomy law. *(Geoff Manasse)*

row—then the state senate was where he would have to go for votes. Bravely—given his health—he declared his candidacy.

That October and November, he campaigned through countless meetings and speeches, always staying optimistic about again introducing a lesbian/gay civil rights bill. Given his popularity in the Forty-third District, there was never any doubt about the election outcome. Cal won an astonishing 81 percent landslide.

But it turned out to be the year of a nationwide—and statewide—Republican sweep. The Democrats lost the state house of representatives and kept their majority in the state senate by only one vote. Cal's hope for a win on the civil rights bill died the same night he was elected to the senate.

A few weeks after taking his new seat, Cal learned he had developed non-Hodgkin's lymphoma, a complication of AIDS. His declining health becoming more visible, he sent each constituent a letter before the news became public. Characteristically, he said he planned to aggressively fight the lymphoma with chemotherapy. By then, though, most of his gay constituents already knew too well the inevitable course of the disease. Those with AIDS had immune systems so weakened already that the chemotherapy would neither cure the lymphoma nor send it into remission for very long.

By the time he died of AIDS in 1995, Anderson had been elected to the state senate and commanded wide respect for his legislative abilities. *(Geoff Manasse)*

Cal's own prognosis at the time: "Who knows? I've known people who've suffered greatly. Naturally I see myself as one of those who will live a long life. I have every intention of beating this. I'm thinking of how I can use this situation as an opportunity to educate."

Governor Lowry issued a statement honoring him. "Senator Anderson will continue to fight for fairness and individual liberty as he has always done," it said.[33]

Others took the chance to send hate messages. One person cut out a photograph that had appeared in the *Seattle Times,* showing Cal now bald from the chemotherapy, and wrote, "Pervert. Walking corpse. AIDS poster girl!" Another sent a letter saying, "Why don't you admit the mistake you made in sticking your cock into the assholes of other 'gays.' Your AIDS is your reward. It's not a mystery. One and one make two. You determined your own fate."[34]

To ensure that the Democrats could have their one-vote majority on crucial issues, Cal repeatedly made painful drives to Olympia. He maintained his sense of humor. Bald, he arrived late for a legislative meeting one day and joked, "I couldn't do a thing with my hair." He grew short of breath, drinking water constantly to wet his mouth and lips. At age forty-six, he took to walking with a cane. In June, he skipped an appearance as grand marshal of Seattle's gay pride parade because of blood clots in his legs and lungs.

He began planning for the inevitable.

Ed Murray remembered: "Cal and I were discussing his funeral. He said, 'What should I do?' And I said, 'It'll probably be a big thing.'" Murray suggested he plan the funeral at St. Mark's, the Episcopalian cathedral on Capitol Hill.

Cal had another idea.

"He said instead," Murray recalled, "'I really would like to have it at St. James.'"[35]

Cal was not Catholic, and certainly after the 1993 betrayal by the Catholic bishops, he was not a friend of the local church hierarchy. But Cal's mother had converted to Catholicism a few years earlier and had even traveled to Rome, where she had a photo taken with the pope. Many of Cal's constituents were Catholic, of course, and they, Murray knew, "really liked him."

Even so, Murray was momentarily incredulous that the state's most symbolic gay leader would ask that his funeral be held in the spiritual center of the archdiocese that had caused his most significant defeat. Cal's own gay constituents would likely be furious. And who knew how the Catholic hierarchy would react. When the bishops helped scuttle the civil rights bill, they had triggered a public feud on Capitol Hill. Several priests and nuns who had been working in the gay and lesbian ministry publicly denounced their own archbishop's action and then quit the ministry, saying it was hypocritical for the church to pretend to compassionately minister to gays and lesbians while working against gay civil rights in Olympia. Even Father Michael Ryan, the head priest at St. James Cathedral who had welcomed Murphy's arrival in Seattle, had professed disagreement on the issue with the new archbishop.

Still, when drag performer Kris Anderson—Crystal Lane—had died of AIDS a year earlier, he too had requested and received a Catholic funeral at St. James. His had been presided over by the Reverend David Jaeger, one of the priests working in the gay and lesbian ministry. Jaeger had pointedly used the occasion to note that if gays were sinners, so was the Catholic Church.

If a drag queen could be buried from St. James, why not the state's leading gay politician?

Murray remembered answering Cal. "I said, 'Well, maybe you could have it there.' But I was thinking to myself, 'My God, I'm setting this guy up to be hurt. This is the Catholic cathedral.'"

Like an innocent boy, Cal said, "Could you ask?"

Hesitantly, Murray phoned the Reverend Jerry Stanley, the priest who had been in charge of the archdiocese's gay and lesbian ministry. Stanley had been one of those who publicly disagreed with Murphy's retreat on civil rights.

Stanley agreed to call Mike Ryan, the cathedral's pastor. It did not take long to get the answer back, and it was yes. Stanley also told a surprised Murray that Ryan would like to preside at the funeral himself.

In late July, Cal granted what was to be one of his last interviews—perhaps appropriately to a student from the Jesuits' Seattle University, Jill Bateman. He had grown gaunt and tired, except when he talked of his parallel loves: for his partner, Eric Ishino, and for the state legislature. Once again, his favorite quotation turned up:

"Politics is the best way for one person to help a lot of people."

"I really see that," he added. "My being the first openly gay member of the legislature really opened some eyes. They've got to see that we care about education, transportation, all the issues." Among his proudest accomplishments, he said, were the more technical pieces of legislation that had helped widen participation in elections by making it possible for anyone to request an absentee ballot or to register to vote while renewing a driver's license.

"It's fun to have been in the battle and been able to get things done."

His message? Bateman asked.

"Continue on with the effort . . . We'll get it. We'll get it."[36]

On Friday, August 4, 1995, Cal Anderson died at the age of forty-seven. Two nights later, more than six hundred men and women walked silently along Broadway, their hands cupped around candles against a brisk August wind.

In the days that followed, even Cal's political opponents would acknowledge his impact. One of his most strident critics had been a conservative Republican newspaper columnist in Seattle named John Carlson. But after Cal's death, Carlson crafted perhaps the best eulogy. Writing in the *Seattle Times,* he told those in his own party to "approach politics the way Cal Anderson did" if they wanted to gain respect.

"This would seem surprising advice," Carlson wrote. "Anderson was a liberal Democrat from Seattle's most liberal district. His most cherished political goal in his eight and a half years in the Legislature was a gay rights bill that I oppose. But his short time in political office . . . was guided by qualities and a sense of character that are timeless in defining the virtuous public servant."

"Anderson," Carlson continued, "entered public life believing in something bigger than himself. His work carried a mission statement that was backed up with a clear political agenda aimed at something more meaningful than his own career. . . . Anderson was honest. As a former lobbyist told me, 'He voted on what he ran on and ran on how he voted.' No wonder why he was viewed as one of the top half-dozen lawmakers in the Legislature. . . . Being on the opposite side of many issues, I could argue that society is better served if it resists most of Anderson's liberal political views. But I can argue at least as persuasively that American society—all of us—are better off for his being here. Much better."[37]

Similarly, the *Times* lauded Anderson's career in politics, and stories noted that in a poll of legislators, his colleagues had ranked him as one of their most effective.[38] The gifts of an openly gay man were being acknowledged—openly.

When the day for the funeral arrived, more than two thousand people completely filled the seats and the aisles of the cathedral that had become such a symbol of the gay struggle to win public acceptance in Seattle. The crowd flowed outward onto the plaza overlooking the mudflat. It would virtually be a state funeral, Cal's body lying under the dome, his own most personal attempt to advance the conversation between Capitol Hill's two dominant cultures made dramatically clear.

The governor and the leaders of the legislature arrived and sat to one side of the casket. It had been draped with an American flag in honor of Cal's service in Vietnam and with a red ribbon for those who had died of AIDS. Family and friends sat to another side. Behind Ed Murray was William Sullivan, the Jesuit president of Seattle University, surrounded by a crowd of priests. All the top hierarchy of the archdiocese were present—except the archbishop. The *Seattle Gay News* reported that only Anderson could have inspired such diverse mourning. "Legislators, judges and local officials sat near leathermen." When the drag queens of the Sisters of Perpetual Indulgence entered wearing their full habits and winged white nun's caps, the newspaper reported, one person said "Now it really is divine."[39]

Father Ryan rose to the pulpit. Not everyone buried from the cathedral had his eulogy spoken by the cathedral's head. Once again, the symbolism was clear. What could not be said through dogma could be done through ministry.

Ryan talked about visiting Cal in the hospital. Like so many others in Seattle who had learned from those who died of AIDS, Ryan said that "before long, I felt like I was visiting a dear friend. Cal opened his life to me, as he did to so many."

"I am better for it."

Ryan compared Cal Anderson to John F. Kennedy, saying that both men had "great stature and great substance." "Cal believed that all people counted," Ryan continued, "the little as much as the great, the marginalized as well as the mainstream." That, he said, was as every Christian should. Then, pointedly, he reminded everyone that one day, Cal's dream would come true: Gays and lesbians would indeed have equal civil rights.

"It is a hero we have come to celebrate and remember today," he added. "With uncommon courage and uncompromising honesty, Cal Anderson made his mark on our city, our state, our country and our conscience."

"Most importantly, our conscience."[40]

# *Epilogue*

## On the Hill

*a*t the start of the summer of 1993, a century after the enactment of Washington's first sodomy law, the state governor, Mike Lowry, traveled to Seattle for what would be a historic purpose. On June 27, he became the first governor to address the annual lesbian and gay pride rally. In his speech, Lowry warned that "if one person's civil rights are being abused, then everyone's civil rights are endangered." He again called for the passage of a statewide law to protect homosexuals in their rights to jobs and housing. Somewhere between sixty thousand and seventy-five thousand people attended that pride rally, making it one of Seattle's largest public events.

What may be most remarkable—in a positive sense—is how casually the city's newspapers reported the affair. Both the *Times* and the *Post-Intelligencer* noted Lowry's speech in their routine coverage of the pride rally, but neither paid it particular heed or treated it as especially significant news. One might say that the newspapers gave the occasion almost as little attention as they had given to the passage of the sodomy law in 1893, when homosexuals were exiled from the civic conversation. Within the different city cultures of their times, neither event must have seemed particularly extraordinary to the editors. The *Post-Intelligencer* went so far as to note that Lowry's speech, along with the appearance of numerous other politicians, "underscored the fact that the gay community . . . is considered by many, including Lowry, to be part of the mainstream."[1]

The same day, a lanky, bespectacled Seattle police officer named Rob Boling chose one of the most dramatic ways he knew to come out, rolling his police car into the parade and joining the marchers. For blocks, thousands cheered him. The following year, for the first time ever, the Seattle police chief—Norm Stamper at the time—would join too.[2]

In a century, then, much had changed in Seattle's civic discourse about politics, religion, and culture—and especially about who in the conversation was a valued speaker. It seems too easily metaphoric that in one hundred years, lesbians and gays had moved the center of their public speech from the city's lowest point on the mudflat to atop Capitol Hill. Yet the fact is undeniable. From generation to generation, the specific challenges had changed, but always the urge had been the same—to find a place to truly feel valued and at home. To a great extent, the quest had succeeded.

Individuals who had been most involved moved on, of course.

After they had helped break the police blackmail scams in the 1960s, MacIver Wells and John Chadwick sold their bars and moved to Camano Island north of Seattle for a quieter life, free of police payoffs. Chadwick died at age seventy in 1994; Mac, at age seventy-nine in 2000. They are buried on the island under a shared headstone, engraved with roses and a Canadian maple leaf.

Those who had created the Dorian Society and the Seattle Counseling Service, such as Nick Heer, Martin Gouterman, and Bob Deisher, concentrated on teaching at the University of Washington. The Reverend Mineo Katagiri, after helping to launch the Dorians, became one of the founders of Seattle's Northwest Harvest food bank, then left for a job in New York City in 1970. He eventually moved to San Francisco.

Similarly, some of those in the initial wave of Seattle's gay liberationists—Robert Sirico, Paul Barwick, William DuBay, and Bobbi Campbell—headed to California or to the East Coast. Sirico, for example, became director of the Los Angeles Gay Community Services Center in July 1975, and helped that gay counseling service make the transition from grassroots activism to professional service. Others, such as David Baird, Jane Meyerding, Faygele benMiriam, Lois Thetford, Sam Deaderick, Tim Mayhew, Patrick Haggerty, and Jan Denali, stayed in the Northwest. BenMiriam fought and won a lawsuit against the federal government opposing discrimination in the civil service. He died of a brain tumor in 2001. Deaderick, who had so often challenged Charlie Brydon's middle-class approach to politics and had been the first to test Seattle's gay rights law with his Salvation Army bell-ringing, continued supporting the Freedom Socialist Party through his writings, particularly his small booklet *Gay Resistance: The Hidden History*. He died of a heart attack in 1991. Sometimes the activists gradually lowered their profile in gay politics and focused on other causes. Lois Thetford, who had gone to Cuba to cut sugarcane, promoted community health care in Seattle, helping to create the Fremont Women's Clinic and the Forty-fifth Street Clinic. In spring 2001, she received one of the *Seattle Post-Intelligencer*'s Jefferson Awards for citywide leadership. Her partner, Jean Rietschel, became Seattle's presiding municipal court judge; her daughter, raised by the collective of parents that included Patrick Haggerty and benMiriam, was in college at the end of the century. Meanwhile, some of the other women who helped create the first consciousness-raising groups, the lesbian newsletter *Out and About,* and the Lesbian Resource Center went on to organize lesbian and gay youth and to help preserve the city's gay history by promoting museum exhibits.

Charlie Brydon periodically vanished from the city's gay politics, only to reemerge again and again as an organizer of this or that effort to oppose yet another anti-gay initiative—always remaining the true insider working behind the scenes.

In one irony the Reverend Mark Matthews and George Cotterill would almost assuredly not have appreciated, Brydon eventually secured a gubernatorial appointment to the agency charged with overseeing the state's saloons—the Washington State Liquor Control Board. Another city hall insider, Shelly Yapp, who had co-chaired the political committee for Brydon's Citizens to Retain Fair Employment during Initiative Thirteen, became a deputy mayor in the late 1980s and then received a gubernatorial appointment to the University of Washington Board of Regents.

Socialist activist Dick Snedigar made headlines a different way in the 1980s and 1990s. Snedigar, who had directed the gay counseling service and had often clashed with Brydon's approach to gay politics, offered to help the Freedom Socialist Party find a new home when Seattle restaurateur Ivar Haglund bought the building housing Freeway Hall in 1978. Snedigar contributed $22,500 to a relocation fund, but later he demanded the money back and in a lawsuit asked for copies of the party's membership lists, contributors' names, and minutes. The case quickly became a civil rights cause célèbre over the right of a political association to keep its records private; the case lasted for eight years before the Washington State Supreme Court finally established a strong legal rule protecting the group's privacy rights. Snedigar lost.

Many key organizers during the AIDS epidemic—those who survived—dropped out of activism, exhausted. Carol Sterling stepped down from running the Chicken Soup Brigade, worn by the death of so many friends. Catlin Fullwood of POCAAN left for New York City to teach gay and lesbian youth. Larry Woelich, tired of running bathhouses, turned instead to cleaning houses and condominiums. Malcolm McKay left his education post at the Northwest AIDS Foundation to teach sexuality classes, as well as host an Internet gay radio show. Of the early organizers of the major gay AIDS agencies, only Betsy Lieberman continued working at the end of the century, still helping to find housing for people with AIDS.[3]

Steven Farmer, who had been given a seven-and-a-half-year sentence in prison, never lived long enough to serve it. He spent almost two years at the Twin Rivers Correctional Facility near Olympia, then—ill from AIDS—received conditional clemency in 1994 from Governor Mike Lowry so he could live in a Tacoma hospice rather than die in jail. But the scapegoating was not over. Although Farmer was too sick to solicit anyone, the Tacoma police still issued a warning that a sexual predator was in the neighborhood and made his address public, leading to an outcry that forced state corrections secretary Charles Riveland to defend Farmer's release. "The mystery of AIDS," Riveland said, "it frightens people." Although Riveland pointed out that Farmer had never committed any subsequent offenses after his initial arrest and never fit the state's legal definition of a sexual predator, the *Tacoma News-Tribune,* in particular, continued to refer to him as such. And Rebecca Roe, the King County prosecutor who had fought Farmer, still adamantly insisted he should die in jail, not in a hospice. In September 1995, Farmer did finally die, at age thirty-nine. The family kept his funeral secret to avoid another media circus. Farmer's was perhaps the only local AIDS death in which no accomplishments were noted. The headline on the *Seattle Times* obituary said: "Sex Offender's Death Linked to AIDS."[4]

As some lesbian and gay leaders moved on, others moved in, replacing the earlier activists and newsmakers. Cal Anderson's old mantle as the only openly gay representative in the state legislature passed to his friend Ed Murray. Two lesbians, Sherry Harris and Tina Podlodowski, were elected to the Seattle City Council, but in what perhaps was a sign of the enormous changes in visibility that had occurred, the city news media only seldom noted that either Harris or Podlodowski was homosexual. By the time Podlodowski joined the city council in the mid-1990s, for example, the media more often referred to her as a retired Microsoft millionaire than as a lesbian, and neither ever emerged as the symbolic political leader of the Seattle lesbian and gay community in the way that Cal Anderson had.[5]

Within each major segment of the civic conversation and civic landscape—be it the theater of life, the politics of governance, the economic network, the life of worship represented in the churches, or the compassion hoped for in illness—the presence of lesbians and gays in the city continued to deepen throughout the end of the century.

In the world of dance and theater, for example, Rick Rankin, working as a waiter and a singer, created a gay and lesbian theater festival in 1984 at a small venue on Capitol Hill, then parlayed the success into his own company, Alice B. Theatre. The idea was to produce stories that reflected the lives of gays and lesbians, stories that mainstream theater in Seattle was still overlooking. The focus was not a limit, Rankin would say; it was a way to understand the fullness of human experiences through a different set of eyes. He wanted an audience that would be one-third lesbian, one-third gay, and one-third straight, and he not only thought he achieved it, but he doubled its size every year. By the 1990s, Alice B. drew major arts funding from the state, from the national business community's Corporate Council for the Arts, and from the National Endowment for the Arts. Alice B. Theatre would survive for a decade until Rankin decided to pursue his own writing.[6]

Gays and lesbians also launched choruses that crossed the arts divide, drawing audiences both heterosexual and homosexual as well as funding from established corporate sources. The Seattle Men's Chorus, begun in 1979, achieved the most success. At first it tried to avoid being publicized as a "gay" chorus, its executive director explaining that the chorus wanted to avoid any "adverse effect" and first prove to the city that its gay citizens "can do well along any line." It was just a matter of timing, he said—one reason, apparently, that "gay" had been left out of the name. Gradually, through the 1980s and 1990s, the chorus began risking productions sung by members dressed in drag and then also used songs to introduce straight audiences to the emotions that gay men felt when they lost their lovers to AIDS. From a first sold-out concert at a small theater in the city's Museum of History and Industry, the chorus attracted a total of more than thirty thousand subscribers by the end of the century, taped programs for television, and commissioned its own works by major composers. The director of the chorus, Dennis Coleman, actively worked in the late 1990s with the Seattle Symphony to help design the city's new Benaroya Hall, making sure it would be suitable for its two major occupants: the symphony and the gay men's chorus.[7]

In politics, new issues moved to the fore as gays became accustomed to the ritual of fighting, usually successfully, the initiatives and referendums designed to reverse gains made through the insider route of executive orders, city councils, and the legislature. After repulsing the assault by the Oregon Citizens' Alliance in the mid-1990s, lesbian and gay leaders of the Hands Off Washington group even tried to use the moralists' weapon themselves, launching a statewide initiative to outlaw job discrimination based on sexual orientation. Some would say it was a drastic mistake, undermining the activists' own previous argument that the civil rights of any minority should never be subject to a popular vote. Even Cal Anderson had passionately opposed the idea when it had first surfaced in 1994. And he turned out to be right. HOW's Initiative 677 gathered the necessary 230,000 signatures to make the November 1997 ballot, but then crashed in a 60 percent landslide defeat—despite polls that had indicated most voters in the state thought job discrimination against gays and lesbians should be outlawed. The defeats on both sides created at least a temporary détente in the use of initiatives that neither seemed able to win.[8]

Sometimes the victories in politics aimed to fill small gaps and went almost unnoticed, such as that to convince the Seattle City Council to strengthen the job antidiscrimination law that had been the target of Initiative Thirteen. The original law had only allowed for complaints, investigations, and reinstatements to be handled administratively through city offices. In 1999, the city council changed that to allow direct lawsuits in the courts by those who believed they had been discriminated against. Few noticed.[9]

Other times, political battles over the recognition of lesbian and gay families became pitched, with debates about whether gays and lesbians should be allowed to adopt, to be given the same employment benefits as heterosexuals, or to marry. The University of Washington, for example, came under attack from eighteen Republican state representatives in 1997 after it okayed health and housing benefits for the partners of lesbian and gay students. They accused the university of codifying "amorality," but the university stuck to its policy. Similarly, by the late 1990s Seattle had strengthened its own domestic partnership ordinance to require any companies undertaking significant contract work for the city to include same-sex relationships in their own benefit programs. That provoked grumbles, but no successful repeal attempt. Conservatives were more successful at the state level when it came to banning any attempts to recognize lesbian or gay relationships as marriages. Although some other states—notably Hawaii and Vermont—inched in that direction by the turn of the century, in 1998 Washington's legislators passed a bill banning gay marriages. Governor Gary Locke vetoed it, but was almost immediately overridden.[10]

With Puget Sound the site of numerous military bases, and Seattle a comfortable fortress of gay visibility, battles over homosexual inclusion in the military services became routine by the end of the 1990s, as navy sailors and army soldiers sued and sometimes won. Most prominent were the fights of army sergeant Perry Watkins, discharged after years of honorable service even though he had always been honest about his homosexuality, and Margarethe Cammermeyer, the chief nurse of the Washington Army National Guard and the highest-ranking officer to be discharged because of her sexual orientation. Cammermeyer's quest even became the subject of a 1995 television movie, "Serving in Silence," which was funded by Barbra Streisand and starred Glenn Close as the lesbian heroine. Both Watkins and Cammermeyer eventually won their lawsuits before retiring from the military.[11]

In Seattle's religious conversation, gays and lesbians steadily transformed the dialogue about pastoral ministry—the practical and local application of dogma—even if the struggle against church doctrines always proved more difficult. At the University Friends Meeting, for example, Quakers struggled for years about whether to recognize homosexual relationships. At first, respecting traditional doctrines but also wanting to accommodate new discernments, they settled on the term "celebration of commitment" to recognize gay and lesbian couples. But after more years of continued argument, they reconciled the rhetoric by allowing couples themselves to choose whatever term they wished. Not too far away from the Friends' meeting house, the Woodland Park United Methodist Church struggled with its hierarchy over the role of two lesbian and gay pastors when first the Reverend Karen Dammann, a lesbian, applied in early 2001 for a position, and then the Reverend Mark Williams, already hired, also came out. The local congregation stood behind the pastors, but the denomination's hierarchy insisted on upholding a ban against homosexual ministers who were not celibate. In mid-2002, however, investigative committees of the Methodists' Pacific Northwest conference decided they had no way of proving that the ministers were sexually active without prying into their private lives in an unseemly way.[12]

Seattle's Catholics, meanwhile, continued to agonize, unable to find a suitable accommodation between the Vatican's interpretation of dogma and the insights arising from the local ministry in the city. Archbishop Thomas Murphy, who had retreated from supporting gay civil rights legislation, would die prematurely, to be replaced in late 1997 by yet another bishop from Montana, Alexander Brunett, who was known as one of the pope's delegates to international ecumenical conferences. Brunett refused to characterize himself as either a conservative or a liberal, but by March 2001, the *Seattle Times* would be reporting that many other church leaders and city politicians considered him both more conservative than either Murphy or Hunthausen and far more confrontational. On gay issues, he would at first be offhand, commenting at his initial news conference in October 1997 that he supported the gay-launched statewide initiative to ban job discrimination and adding that if same-sex marriage were proposed, he would "have to see the legislation" to decide a stance. But when the press misinterpreted his marriage comment as a possible softening of the Catholic dogmatic stance, Brunett quickly backed away from the implication.[13]

The Sunday evening Mass at St. Joseph's continued to be aimed at gays and lesbians, but because the issue of sponsorship grew into so deep a wound once Murphy retreated from the civil rights law, the language had to change again. A Denny-Maynard style compromise—accept the sudden jolt in the streets and don't talk about it—finally seemed the only answer. As one priest who participated in the archdiocese's ministry said, "We started off saying 'This Mass is sponsored by God'. . . . We [also] coined a new phrase, that the Mass is sponsored by the gay and lesbian community to which we all belong."

"We're all trying to use language to keep it going," the priest had said in 1994.[14]

For years, Dignity members continued to help, just not as officially—patiently waiting for some sort of change. Then, in September 2001, the chapter members gave up. They voted to start their own prayer service at a United Methodist Church, completely disassociating themselves from the archdiocesan gay/lesbian ministry. The compromise created by Cardinal Bernardin and Archbishop Hunthausen seemed to have finally collapsed, at least at St. Joseph's Church. A Dignity spokesman, Leo Egashira, told the *Seattle Gay News,* "It is hypocritical and demeaning that the Archdiocese of Seattle can, on the one hand, claim to have an effective ministry to [gays and lesbians], while on the other hand, refuse to support laws giving us equal rights to jobs and housing. How can the church possibly minister to gays and lesbians in a credible and effective manner when it refuses to support our basic human rights?"[15]

As for Bishop George, the conservative Yakima prelate who seemed to represent the views of Rome more than Hunthausen or Bernardin had, the pope would eventually give him the cardinal's red hat in Chicago that had been worn by Bernardin. Although it had taken years, the other shoe that had been expected to fall after Hunthausen's settlement with the Vatican had indeed seemed to land.

The city's Episcopalians, on the other hand, opened the new century by selecting Robert Taylor as an openly gay dean to lead St. Mark's, their major cathedral on Capitol Hill. Taylor, who was from South Africa, drew the internationally famous bishop Desmond Tutu to Seattle for his installation. Compared to what was happening in other Christian denominations, his ascendance seemed smooth and charmed.

In the city's health care conversation, concerns about AIDS continued to dominate, at least among gay men. Between 1982 and the start of 2000, more than fifty-seven hundred cases of AIDS had been diagnosed in Seattle and surrounding King County; more than thirty-four hundred of those individuals had died, and more than three-quarters were men who had contracted the virus from having sex with other men. But as the dual approaches of activist and scientist began to succeed after 1993, AIDS began to fade from the intensity it had once commanded. Multiple combinations of drugs made living with the virus more routine; obituaries in the *Seattle Gay News,* which had sometimes filled two pages each week, became occasional oddities again. After 1993, the new cases found each year in King County dropped from the peak of 647 to fewer than 100 per year at the turn of the century. AIDS looked manageable—so much so that AIDS organizations had to scramble for money from donors. In September 1999, the annual AIDS walk drew only half as many people as it had in 1995, and raised a third less money.[16] Partly because of financial concerns, the Northwest AIDS Foundation and Chicken Soup Brigade would be forced to merge into a single organization, newly named the Lifelong AIDS Alliance.

AIDS activists worried that gay men would turn smug and give up condoms, so the education strategy again shifted as a third model absorbed the previous two. After 1995, the information model and the erotic model were packaged into an attempt to build gay men's friendships with one another, with activists arguing that low self-esteem and lack of friendships often caused men to risk unsafe sex. In Seattle, a former health department employee named John Leonard pioneered the model by forming a new organization called Gay City and sponsoring a variety of social activities, such as gay town meetings laced with sexy come-ons and talk-show formats, summer retreats at mountain campgrounds, book reading groups, and game days at Volunteer Park. As in past events, free condoms were omnipresent, but now they were part of a new gay social scene rather than intrusions into the old one. By 2000, Gay City claimed to have more than five thousand men participating in its programs each year.

The cautionary signs that AIDS might re-attack still disturbed, though. In March 2001, Bob Wood and other city health officials warned that gonorrhea, syphilis, and chlamydia among Seattle's gay men had all rebounded, in some cases back to the rates that existed in 1982. Gay men caught the other infections the same way as AIDS; the other diseases simply showed themselves faster. Jim Holm, who had headed the Dorian Group in the 1980s and had left to work as an AIDS activist in Washington, D.C., returned to Seattle and to the news, this time as a chair of the Seattle HIV/AIDS Council, a coordinating group, and promised to try to "craft new messages." Derick Myricks-Harris, a manager at the People of Color Against AIDS Network, added, "People have started to believe that there's no need to protect themselves."[17]

In June 2001, exactly twenty years after the first reports of the virus, the Centers for Disease Control reported that nationwide the rates of infection were once again rising among young gay men. Seattle was one of the cities studied; the rate of new cases had risen for the first time since 1992.

The pause in combating the epidemic seemed to be ending.

And finally, what of the city's social geography—in particular, the location where the city's homosexuals had first learned to meet and to publicly speak? By the turn of the century, one of the last remaining gay establishments on the mudflat, the South End Steam Baths on First Avenue, finally closed. Its landmark sign over the underground space was saved by volunteers and eventually taken to the city's Museum of History and Industry.

At the corner at Washington Street and Second Avenue, however, the Double Header persisted, still claiming the title of being the city's oldest continuously operating gay bar. The staircase leading into the underground was still there too. Although the Casino itself had long since closed and been abandoned, its marquee remained. Madame Peabody's children had found glittering new dance floors, but the underground was now under new management, operating as the Catwalk Club. On a web page, the Catwalk advertised itself as a place to listen to raucous industrial or gloomier gothic music. An ad showed a profile of a kneeling, highly bosomed woman, nude but for a leather collar and corset, her hands bound to a rope behind her. The web page advised that on Saturday nights, patrons should "dress impressively"—which the *Seattle Times* at one point said meant "to lose the baseball cap and leave the jeans at home." Sometimes, the bar scheduled all-women's nights or "boyz 4 boyz" nights. In 1996, the state liquor control board had temporarily suspended its liquor license because of reports of lewd conduct, including accusations that a man had masturbated or pretended to do so on stage, while a woman had gone "crying and protesting" to a back space known as the "spanking room." The bar owners blamed the problem on a personality conflict with a liquor board investigator, who had apparently suggested the Casino be turned into an ordinary sports bar. Eventually, the Catwalk got its license back—without turning to more customary sports.[18]

It all sounded like a comfortable old tale. John Considine's theater of the people still challenged Seattle's stories of sex and respectability.

To return to Martin Heidegger's philosophical question: What does it mean to dwell, to construct a sense of belonging out of images of exile?

Is it possible for gays and lesbians, for example, so long in hiding and so diverse in race, class, and politics, to really construct a sense that they belong within a heterosexual landscape such as Seattle's?

It seems that an answer could justifiably be yes, simply based on the increasing tolerance among heterosexuals that the city's gays and lesbians have experienced. Over the course of a few decades, they became able to win elections, to influence policies, and to participate in all the important fragments of the civic conversation.

But dwelling also requires more than just tolerance constructed from insisted-upon conversations. Dwelling is also about the ability to construct and tell one's own stories, regardless of acceptance by others—and in that, Seattle's homosexuals also succeeded. Through oral history projects, newspapers, and simple conversations among friends, they had found ways to talk from generation to generation, be it by Robert's Rules of Order or in consciousness-raising groups. Dwelling, after all, is the ability to pass a stairway leading down into the underground or up to an old box house or into a cathedral overlooking a mudflat, and to know more stories about those stairways than you could ever tell in a single book like this—however long.

And to keep adding new ones.

# NOTES

PROLOGUE

1. For the criminal case against John Collins, see King County Superior Court Criminal Appearance Dockets, book 5, case 1195 (1895). The dialogue from this case that is presented in the text is taken from the court testimony. For discussions of Seattle's history of moral conflict, see, among many sources, Norman Clark, *The Dry Years: Prohibition and Social Change in Washington* (Seattle: University of Washington Press, 1988), especially chapters 1–8; Murray Morgan, *Skid Road: An Informal Portrait of Seattle* (New York: Viking Press, 1960); Roger Sale, *Seattle: Past to Present* (Seattle: University of Washington Press, 1976); William Spiedel, *Sons of the Profits* (Seattle: Nettle Creek Publishing, 1967); and "Let Us Show You Pioneer Square," (Seattle: Seattle Convention and Visitors Bureau, 1976).

2. For examples of sexual diversity in Native American tribes, see Walter Williams, *The Spirit and the Flesh: Sexual Diversity in American Indian Culture* (Boston: Beacon Press, 1992), chapter 8 generally and 153–54 and 159–60 particularly. Three dictionaries of Chinook list the word *burdash* and indicate that it was adopted into the jargon from French, although all three, interestingly, translate the word to mean "hermaphrodite" rather than the usual French reference to men who cross-dressed as women and were believed to be the recipients of anal sex. It seems unlikely that true biological hermaphrodites would have been numerous enough in the Northwest to be named within a sparse trade jargon; more likely, the translators had not yet come upon the modern words "homosexual" or "transgendered" and felt it indiscreet to describe the sexual behavior *burdash*es were believed to engage in. See John Gill, *Gill's Dictionary of the Chinook Jargon* (Portland, Oreg.: J. K. Gill, 1909; reprinted in 1989 by the Muckleshoot Indian Tribe and White River Valley Historical Society), 24; George C. Shaw, *The Chinook Jargon and How to Use It* (Seattle: Rainier Printing Company, 1909), 34; and Edward H. Thomas, *Chinook: A History and Dictionary* (Portland, Oreg.: Binfords and Mort, 1935; 3rd ed. 1970), 58. The story of Sarah Yesler's friendship with Eliza Hurd is detailed in Linda Peavy and Ursula Smith, *Women in Waiting in the Western Movement* (Norman: University of Oklahoma Press, 1994), especially 160–62.

3. Clark, *The Dry Years*, xi.

4. Walter Bruggemann, *The Land: Place As Gift, Promise, and Challenge in Biblical Faith* (Philadelphia: Fortress Press, 1977), 187.

5. Martin Heidegger, "Building Dwelling Thinking," in *Basic Writings from Being and Time to The Task of Thinking,* ed. David Farrell Krell (New York: Harper and Row, 1977).

I / THE LAW

1. For background on sodomy laws generally, see Wayne and Alice Bartee, *Litigating Morality: American Legal Thought and Its English Roots* (New York: Praeger, 1992); Laurence Friedman, *A History of American Law* (New York: Simon and Schuster, 1985); Robert C. Bensing, "A Comparative Study of American Sex Statutes," *Journal of Criminal Law* 42 (1951): 57–72; and Karl Bowman and Bernice Engle, "A Psychiatric Evaluation of Laws of Homosexuality," *Temple Law Quarterly* 29 (1956): 273–326. Quote from Bowman and Engle is on p. 275; quote from Bartee is on p. 40.

2. To track the evolution of Washington's penalties for "offenses against morality and decency," it is useful to compare sections of the state penal code for 1873 and 1881 (prior to the passage of the sodomy law) and for 1893, 1902, and 1909. For the passage of the laws, see *Journal of the House* (1893): 333, 335, 565; *Journal of the Senate* (1893): 443, 458, 627; *Journal of the Senate* (1909): 464, 632; and *Journal of the House* (1909): 585.

3. Carlos Schwantes, *The Pacific Northwest: An Interpretive History* (Lincoln: University of Nebraska Press, 1989), 221.

4. "Two People in Bed: It Is Not a Healthy Way to Sleep," *Seattle Press-Times,* Feb. 10, 1893, 3.

5. The records of early sodomy cases are in the microfilm archives of the King County Superior Court and are indexed in the Criminal Appearances Dockets, located at the King County Archives. Cases mentioned in this chapter are Charles Wesley and Eddie Kalberg, book 4, case 854 (1895); J. P. MacKendray and Oscar Brunson, book 5, case 1173 (1895); Andrew Cleary, book 11, case 3104 (1904); Pat Morrow and Alfred Franseen, book 12, case 3230 (1904); Philip McGuire and Herbert Carpenter, book 3, case 3718 (1906); Thomas Longbottom and Albert Jenner, book 14, case 3851 (1907); A. Mor and Robert Timmons, book 18, case 5277 (1910); Frederick Evans and Dan Paxman, book 18, cases 5056 and 5303 (1910) and book 19, case 5329 (1910); Charles Morrhauser and Ora Spriggs, book 19, case 5521 (1910); and Harry Douglass and Russell Spitler, book 19, case 5540 (1910).

6. King County Superior Court Criminal Appearances Docket, book 5, case 1173 (1895).

7. Theodore Winthrop, *Canoe and Saddle* (1862; reprint, Portland, Oreg.: Binfords and Mort: 1956), especially 18, 82.

8. Roger Sale, *Seattle: Past to Present* (Seattle: University of Washington Press, 1976), 87. Additional information about Cotterill in this chapter comes from the collection of his personal papers and diaries at the University of Washington Libraries, Seattle.

9. George Cotterill Papers, Special Collections, University of Washington Libraries, Seattle.

10. Murray Morgan, *Skid Road: An Informal Portrait of Seattle* (New York: Viking Press, 1960), 116–47, details the role of John Considine and the People's Theater. Additional information about Considine can be found in Richard Berner, *Seattle 1900–1920: From Boomtown, Urban Turbulence, to Restoration* (Seattle: Charles Press, 1991), especially 35–36, and

Eugene Elliott, *A History of Variety-Vaudeville in Seattle: From the Beginning to 1914* (Seattle: University of Washington Press, 1944), 25–44.

11. Morgan, *Skid Road*, 116–17.

12. "Where Music and Vaudeville Flourish in Dog Days," *Seattle Post-Intelligencer*, July 30, 1899, 10.

13. Berner, *Seattle 1900–1920*, 9.

14. For information on Mark Matthews, see the Mark Matthews Papers, Special Collections, University of Washington Libraries, Seattle; and Dale Soden, *The Reverend Mark Matthews: An Activist in the Progressive Era* (Seattle: University of Washington Press, 2001). The quoted sermons are from Matthews, *Sermonettes*, in the Mark Matthews Papers, particularly "Seattle's Unemployed Church Forces," 1906, and "Coffee or Coffin Houses—Which?" 1907.

15. For a sprinkling of the comments about the city's tenderloin problem, as well as about Matthews and the evangelist Wilbur Chapman, see "The Removal of the Tenderloin," *Seattle Times* illustrated section, May 11, 1902, 1–8; "Church People in Big Parade," *Seattle Times*, Apr. 18, 1905, 1; "Children on Parade," *Seattle Post-Intelligencer*, Apr. 19, 1905, 1; and "Matthews, the Boss," *Seattle Times*, May 28, 1911, 2.

16. Useful newspaper articles about Cotterill include an untitled cover article, *Seattle Mail and Herald*, Jan. 23, 1904, 1; untitled article, *Seattle Mail and Herald*, Feb. 13, 1904, 3; "Election Aftermath," *Seattle Mail and Herald*, Nov. 10, 1906, 3; untitled article, *Patriarch*, Sept. 28, 1907, 1; "George Cotterill and Co., Moralists," *Patriarch*, Nov. 2, 1907, 4; "George Cotterill—The Characterless," *Patriarch*, March 6, 1909, 1; "The Triumph of Rascality," *Patriarch*, Nov. 26, 1910, 1; "Ex-Mayor Cotterill, 92, Dies," *Seattle Times*, Oct. 14, 1958, 39; "Just Cogitating: G. F. Cotterill Was Leader in Temperance Movement," *Seattle Times Magazine*, June 19, 1960, 6. Norman Clark's *The Dry Years* considers Cotterill's and Matthews's roles, in chapters 5–7 particularly.

17. The collection of Vaseline jars is mentioned, for example, in the cases against Pat Morrow and against Thomas Tassus, King County Superior Court Criminal Appearances Docket, book 12, case 3230 (1904) and book 22, case 6398 (1912), respectively.

18. Lowell S. Hawley and Ralph B. Potts, *Counsel for the Damned* (New York: J. B. Lippincott, 1953), 66.

19. King County Superior Court Criminal Appearances Docket, book 12, case 3230 (1904). Besides the case of Alfred Franseen, two other early-twentieth-century cases involved "children" who were likely teenagers rather than preteens. In a case against Nicholas Davlopsolus, book 15, case 4147 (1908), Davlopsolus was accused of having sex with John Blakey, a "male child" whom the prosecutor asked to either post a two-hundred-dollar bond or be committed to jail. Not much is recorded about Blakey other than that he apparently did not live in Washington State and had no permanent abode. Given the prosecutor's concern that he would leave town, it can be surmised that Blakey was also not intent on pressing charges against Davlopsolus and was not a preteen. Davlopsolus was found not guilty. In another case, involving R. E. Hurzman, book 15, no. 4232 (1908), the teen witness Jim Whitehead apparently did leave town before he could be committed to the jail, so the prosecutor had to drop the case.

20. King County Superior Court Criminal Appearances Docket, book 3, case 3718 (1906).

21. King County Superior Court Criminal Appearances Docket, book 14, case 3851 (1907).

22. Sale, *Seattle: Past to Present*, 106–7.

23. *Journal of the Washington Senate* (1909): 464, 632; *Journal of the Washington House* (1909): 585.

24. The *Sermonettes* file in the Mark Matthews Papers, Special Collections, University of Washington Libraries, Seattle, contains the vice committee's May 1910 report.

25. King County Superior Court Criminal Appearances Docket, book 18, case 5277 (1910).

26. King County Superior Court Criminal Appearances Docket, book 18, cases 5056 and 5303 (1910) and book 19, case 5329 (1910).

27. King County Superior Court Criminal Appearances Docket, book 19, case 5540 (1910).

28. King County Superior Court Criminal Appearances Docket, book 19, case 5521 (1910). Only a very few early cases of heterosexual or oral sodomy were prosecuted. Besides the Morrhauser case mentioned, William Cogswell, book 20, case 5842 (1911) was accused of knowing a woman "by the mouth and tongue." The charge against Cogswell was dismissed. Where heavy sentences occurred for oral sex, either force or a female preteen may have been involved, although the docket records are often not specific about the details or the age of the victim. See, for example, cases involving John Schencke, book 22, case 6314 (1912), sentence of five to ten years; Adam Mayer, book 22, case 6516 (1913), sentence of eighteen months to ten years; and Avery Houston, book 24, case 6866 (1914), sentence of two to five years.

29. Letter to Seattle Police Chief Claude Bannick, March 14, 1914, George Cotterill Papers, Special Collections, University of Washington Libraries, Seattle.

30. The incidents at Walla Walla are mentioned in John McCoy, *Concrete Mama: Prison Profiles from Walla Walla* (Columbia: University of Missouri Press, 1981), 4–5.

## 2 / MENTAL HEALTH

1. The most thorough books available on Frances Farmer's life are William Arnold, *Shadowland* (New York: McGraw-Hill, 1978), and Farmer's autobiography, *Will There Really Be a Morning* (New York: Dell Books, 1972). Additional published information about Farmer comes from newspaper and magazine accounts. Many of these are most easily accessible in Special Collections, University of Washington Libraries, Seattle, or, in 2001, at a website dedicated to Frances Farmer, http://www.geocities.com/~themistyone. The website collection contains unpaginated articles from the following movie magazines: *Modern Screen*, Dec. 1957; *Movie Mirror*, uncertain month 1937; *On the QT*, uncertain month 1957; *Screen Album*, summer 1937. The actress's obituaries can be found in the *Seattle Post-Intelligencer*, Aug. 3, 1970, A5; and the *Seattle Times*, Aug. 3, 1970, D16. Fictional accounts

of her life are contained in the Brooksfilm 1983 movie *Frances* and in an Orion Television drama "Will There Really Be a Morning." The Seattle lesbian newsletter *Out and About* published a two-part series about Farmer, written by Cookie Hunt, in June 1979, 11, and Sept. 1979, 17.

2. There are many sources available on the psychiatric profession's classification of homosexuality. See, for example, Thomas Szasz, *The Manufacture of Madness* (New York: Harper and Row, 1970), chapter 13 especially, and John-Manuel Andriote, "Shrinking Opposition," *Percent Magazine*, (fall 1993): 61. An example of psychiatric treatment for homosexuality is discussed in Samuel Hadden, "Newer Treatment Techniques for Homosexuality," *Archives of Environmental Health* 13 (Sept. 1966): 284.

3. King County Superior Court Criminal Appearances Docket, book 18, cases 5056 and 5303 (1910).

4. Register of Inmates, Western State Hospital, Washington State Archives, Olympia. Specific case references mentioned are: George Kincaid, 10305; Albert Kohlmorgan, 10938; Fred Schlig, 10397; Carl Sundling, 10902; and Annie Walton, 11421.

5. Lillian Faderman, *Odd Girls and Twilight Lovers* (New York: Columbia University Press, 1991), 109.

6. Sophie Rosenstein, Larrae Haydon, and Wilbur Sparrow, *Modern Acting: A Manual* (New York: Samuel French, 1936), 3.

7. Virginia Boren, "Enthusiastic Audience Witnesses 'Alien Corn,'" *Seattle Times,* Dec. 13, 1934, 9.

8. For information about The Group Theater, see Howard Taubman, *The Making of American Theater* (New York: Coward-McCann, 1967), chapter 21.

9. Frances Farmer, "Why I Am Going to Russia," *Seattle Times,* March 29, 1935, 2.

10. "Frances Farmer, U.W. Girl, Gets Ingenue Lead in Movies," *Seattle Times,* Jan. 10, 1936, 15.

11. Walter Freeman's views on lobotomy are explained in a book he coauthored with James Watt, *Psychosurgery in the Treatment of Mental Disorders and Intractable Pain* (Springfield, Ill.: Charles C. Thomas, 1950), as well as in several articles, among them: "Transorbital Lobotomy," *American Journal of Psychiatry* 105 (Apr. 1949): 734; "Level of Achievement after Lobotomy: A Study of One Thousand Cases," *American Journal of Psychiatry* 110 (1953): 269–76; "Lobotomy in Limbo?" *American Journal of Psychiatry* 128, no. 10–11 (Apr. 1972): 1315; and "Sexual Behavior and Fertility after Frontal Lobotomy," *Journal of Biological Psychiatry* 6, no. 1 (Feb. 1973): 100. Additional information on Freeman comes from Mary Ellen Ford, "A History of Lobotomy in the United States," *The Pharos* (summer 1987): 7–16; Laurence Weinberger, "Lobotomy: A Personal Memoir," *The Pharos* (spring 1988): 17–18; and Don Jackson, "A Clockwork Orange: It's Not Fiction," *Advocate,* May 10, 1972, 12.

12. Lucille Cohen, "New Brain Surgery Used on 9 Patients, *Seattle Post-Intelligencer,* July 8, 1949, 3. See also "Surgery Aid in Insanity Told," *Seattle Times,* Oct. 15, 1948, 8.

13. From the preface to the second edition of Freeman and Watt, *Psychosurgery in the Treatment of Mental Disorders and Intractable Pain* (1950), x, xv.

14. For general information about conditions at Western State Hospital, a variety of periodicals and annual reports were used, including the Seventh, Ninth, Tenth, and Thirteenth Biennial Reports of Western State Hospital (covering a period from 1932 to 1946), and a Report to the Legislature on "Mental Institutions in the State of Washington," Jan. 1948. Newspaper articles about Western State included an early *Tacoma Times* series published on front pages March 18–20, 1920, with headlines such as "Brutality is Described by Eyewitness," "A Naked Idol of Barbarity," and "Inmates Victims of Gross Neglect." Other sources included a *Seattle Times* series examining conditions at Western State Hospital, published Feb. 27–March 1, 1947; another *Times* series on treatments at Washington mental hospitals, Apr. 26–30, 1953; and a three-part *Times* series on shock treatment development at Northern State Hospital, Nov. 13–15, 1955. Other references can be found in the *Seattle Weekly*, Nov. 15, 1978, 10; *Seattle Times*, Nov. 3, 1979, A1, Aug. 24, 1980, A28, Feb. 15, 1982, C2, and Jan. 9, 1989, A1. See also a *Post-Intelligencer* special report on "What's Wrong with Washington's Mental Health System," including an article on hydrotherapy and electroshock, published Aug. 29, 1985, section C.

15. See Freeman and Watt, *Psychosurgery in the Treatment of Mental Disorders and Intractable Pain* (1950), 132, 346; and Freeman, "Sexual Behavior and Fertility after Frontal Lobotomy," 97–104.

16. Case 465 is discussed in Freeman and Watt, *Psychosurgery in the Treatment of Mental Disorders and Intractable Pain,* (1950), 142; and Freeman, "Sexual Behavior and Fertility after Frontal Lobotomy," 100.

17. Western State Hospital Records, Oct. 1946–June 1954, Washington State Archives, Olympia. Although the ledgers are dated from Oct. 1946, they also contain a typewritten note stapled to an entry page that states that between July 3, 1942, and June 12, 1953, 252 lobotomies were performed at the hospital.

18. Charles Jones and James Shanklin, "Transorbital Lobotomy," *Northwest Medicine* 47, no. 6 (June 1948): 421–27. In the same volume are reports on Vancouver General Hospital's use of prefrontal leucotomy in Canada.

19. Personal communication from David Farmer, June 2001.

20. A taped excerpt from the program, "Mysteries and Scandals," broadcast in fall 1998, could be found in 2001 at http://www.geocities.com/~themistyone/related_audio.htm

21. "Memories of a Street Dyke," the oral history interview with Jackie Cachero, was published in *Out and About* in Apr. 1979, 13; May 1979, 13; June 1979, 13; Aug. 1979, 15; Sept. 1979, 13; and Oct. 1979, 11. The interviewers were Karen Strawhat, Janet Lewis, Jane Meyerding, and Betty Johanna.

### 3 / NEW SALOONS AND VAUDEVILLE

1. Clark, *The Dry Years,* 54.

2. *Polk's Seattle City Directory,* 1928–1940.

3. Don Paulson and Roger Simpson, *An Evening at the Garden of Allah* (New York: Columbia University Press, 1996), 22–28.

4. Schwantes, *The Pacific Northwest*, chapter 16 generally, and Richard Berner, *Seattle Transformed, World War II to Cold War* (Seattle: Charles Press, 1999), 68–79.

5. All material from Rose Bohanan comes from an interview by Ruth Pettis and Lisa Cohen, Northwest Lesbian and Gay History Museum Project, May 1998.

6. Esther Newton, *Mother Camp: Female Impersonators in America* (Englewood Cliffs, N.J.: Prentice Hall, 1972), 100–4.

7. See the *Seattle Post-Intelligencer*, "Stuart—The Male Patti," Feb. 27, 1898, 14–15; and "With the Players," March 6, 1898, 14–15; in the *Seattle Times*, "Amusements," Feb. 26, 1898, 5, and March 2, 1898, 5.

8. King County Superior Court Criminal Appearances Docket, book 18, cases 5056 and 5303 (1910) and book 19, case 5329 (1910).

9. Advertisements for the People's Theater listing acts can be found weekly in the *Seattle Post-Intelligencer*, beginning Feb. 1, 1898. The ad for *Damon and Pythias* appeared Feb. 21, 1898.

10. "Vaudeville: A Sketch" and "Vaudeville in the Northwest," *Washington Magazine*, Sept. 1906, 1.

11. Albert McLean Jr., *American Vaudeville As Ritual* (Lexington: University of Kentucky Press, 1965), especially chapters 1 and 2. See also, generally, Charles and Louise Samuels, *Once upon a Stage: The Merry World of Vaudeville* (New York: Dodd and Mead, 1974).

12. The summary of information about the Garden of Allah comes from an unpublished interview with Skippy LaRue by Emilie Hafner, the Seattle University Community and Communication Project, May 1995, as well as from Paulson and Simpson, *An Evening at the Garden of Allah*.

13. Interview with Rose Bohanan, Northwest Lesbian and Gay History Museum Project, May 1998.

14. Interview with Elaine Burnell, Northwest Lesbian and Gay History Museum Project, March 1995.

15. Shirley Maser, in Paulson and Simpson, *An Evening at the Garden of Allah*, 60–64.

16. Pat Freeman, in Paulson and Simpson, *An Evening at the Garden of Allah*, 64–68.

### 4 / STIRRINGS OF RESISTANCE

1. All material in this book attributed to MacIver Wells and John Chadwick comes from a personal interview conducted by the author in June 1992. A subsequent interview with Wells by Ruth Pettis of the Northwest Lesbian and Gay History Museum Project occurred in Dec. 1997.

2. In 1955 another young Canadian national, twenty-one-year-old Clive Michael Boutilier, entered the United States. Four years later, he was arrested for sodomy, but the charge was dismissed. In 1963 he applied for U.S. citizenship and admitted the previous charge to the naturalization examiner. When the government demanded to know his full sexual history, Boutilier conceded that he had had regular homosexual experiences, as well as a few heterosexual ones. He was then excluded when a Public Health Service examiner deemed him "afflicted with" a "psychopathic personality." On Boutilier's appeal, the

Supreme Court ruled in 1967 that "the legislative history of the [1952 Immigration and Naturalization] Act indicates beyond a shadow of a doubt that Congress intended the phrase 'psychopathic personality' to include homosexuals." *Boutilier v. Immigration and Naturalization Service,* U.S. Supreme Court, 387 U.S. 118 (1967).

3. Extensive newspaper material on the Seattle police payoff system is available from *Seattle Post-Intelligencer* and *Seattle Times* coverage after 1967. For an overview, see William Chambliss, *On the Take* (Bloomington: Indiana University Press, 1978). However, neither the newspapers nor Chambliss extensively report the involvement of gay business owners in challenging the system.

4. The specifics on payoffs by gay bar owners come from affidavits filed in the federal case of *U.S. v. M. E. Cook,* U.S. District Court for Western Washington, no. 51944 (1970).

5. This affidavit was filed as part of the case of *Keith M. Rhinehart v. B. J. Rhay,* U.S. District Court for Western Washington, civil no. 8447 (1969), and *Keith M. Rhinehart v. B. J. Rhay et al.,* civil no. 8448 (1969).

6. *Madison Tavern Inc. and James G. Watson dba Blue Note v. H. J. Lawrence and City of Seattle,* King County Superior Court, no. 527-660 (Oct. 9, 1958).

### 5 / IS DANCE THE ENEMY?

1. Interview with Margaret King, Alice B. Theatre Oral History Project, 1992, Special Collections, University of Washington Libraries.

2. All material attributed to Joe McGonagle is from a personal interview by the author, May 1992.

3. For background on dance as a communication process that builds a sense of ritual, particularly for minority groups that do not have access to other forms of mass media communication, see, for example, Curt Sachs, *World History of the Dance* (London: George Allen and Unwin, 1938) and Judith Lynne Hanna, *To Dance Is Human: A Theory of Nonverbal Communication* (Austin: University of Texas Press, 1979).

4. Quotations about dance at the Casino come from affidavits filed in support of Keith Rhinehart. His case is discussed more extensively and cited in the next chapter.

5. Interview with Stephen Blair, Alice B. Theatre Oral History Project, 1992, Special Collections, University of Washington Libraries.

6. Interview with Tamara Turner, Alice B. Theatre Oral History Project, 1992, Special Collections, University of Washington Libraries.

7. "Memories of a Street Dyke," *Out and About,* Apr.–Oct. 1979.

### 6 / CROSSING OVER

1. Author's personal interviews with Joe McGonagle, May 1992, and MacIver Wells and John Chadwick, June 1992.

2. From prosecution memos filed in *U.S. v. M. E. Cook,* U.S. District Court for Western Washington, no. 51944 (1970).

3. Records of the prosecution against Keith Rhinehart come from the U.S. National Archives for the Pacific Northwest Region, King County Superior Court, and the U.S. District Court for Western Washington. See *Keith M. Rhinehart v. B. J. Rhay*, U.S. District Court for Western Washington, civil no. 8447 (1969); *Keith M. Rhinehart v. B. J. Rhay et al.*, U.S. District Court for Western Washington, civil no. 8448 (1969). Arrest reports, parole reports, and affidavits from Rhinehart's accuser, James Gary Miller, are available as exhibits in the file of case 8447. Details are also available from Rhinehart's appeal to the Ninth U.S. Circuit Court of Appeals, *Rhinehart v. Rhay*, 440 F. 2d 718 (1971). See also Ed Jackson, "Seattle Group Tries to Free 'Innocent' Man, Overturn Sex Laws," *Advocate*, Nov. 1969, 5. Information about the mid-1960s membership and locations of the Aquarian Foundation, as well as its position on the privacy of sexual relations, is included in a statement filed by Rhinehart's attorney in the U.S. District Court, civil no. 8447. The state supreme court decision in the case can be found at *State of Washington v. Rhinehart*, 70 Wn. 2d 649. For the marriage of two gay men at the Aquarian Church, see "Seattle Psychic Church's Founder Marries Two Men," *Advocate*, June 6, 1973, 9. Rhinehart's Aquarian Foundation is located at 315 15th Avenue East on Capitol Hill.

4. In a later civil suit, the officer, William Allmon, would explain that a statement attributed to him that Miller was "known to hustle homosexuals" should have read that Miller was "known to allow himself to be hustled" by homosexuals. *Keith M. Rhinehart v. B. J. Rhay*, U.S. District Court for Western Washington, civil no. 8447 (1969).

5. John Wilson, "Seattle Homosexual Problem Reported to Be 'Out of Hand,'" *Seattle Times*, Sept. 21, 1966, 48.

6. A partial list was published in an article by Patrick Douglas, "Sin, Seattle Style," *Seattle*, Aug. 1967, 27–32. A more complete listing can be found in Deputy Police Chief C. A. Rouse, intra-department communication to F. C. Ramon, Chief of Police, Sept. 22, 1966, Seattle Mayors' Papers, Special Collections, University of Washington Libraries. The businesses listed as either off-limits or under investigation because of "homosexual patronage" were the Atlas Steam Baths, Busy Bee Cocktail Lounge, Cafe Club, Double Header, Gallery (MacIver Wells's 614), Golden Goose Submarine Room, Golden Horseshoe Tavern, Madison Tavern, Mocambo Cocktail Lounge, Pike Street Tavern, 611 Tavern, South End Steam Baths, Spag's Tavern, and the Stage Door Tavern. The Casino Club was listed as under investigation for homosexual activity, but for unstated reasons the Armed Forces board recommended that it be dropped from observation.

7. John and Marshall Wilson, "Homosexual Club: Police Made Mistake, Says License Head," *Seattle Times*, Sept. 22, 1966, 9.

8. F. C. Ramon, intra-department communication to Mayor J. D. Braman, Sept. 27, 1966, Seattle Mayors' Papers, Special Collections, University of Washington Libraries.

9. J. D. Braman, letter to Police Chief Frank Ramon, Sept. 28, 1966, Seattle Mayors' Papers, Special Collections, University of Washington Libraries.

10. Deputy Police Chief C. A. Rouse, intra-department communication to F. C. Ramon, Chief of Police, Sept. 22, 1966, Seattle Mayors' Papers, Special Collections, University of Washington Libraries.

11. Douglas Willix, "Standards Studied for Deviate Cabarets," *Seattle Times,* Nov. 29, 1966, 48.

12. Mineo Katagiri, letter to Mayor J. D. Braman, Dec. 1, 1966, Seattle Mayors' Papers, Special Collections, University of Washington Libraries. A "Memorandum of Authorities" arguing the case for the gay bars was submitted to the council by the attorney Richard Kane and can be found in the Charles Harbaugh Papers, Special Collections, University of Washington Libraries.

13. E. L. McAllascer, memo on the Gallery, Dec. 5, 1966, originally an exhibit in the case of *State v. Carroll et al.,* King County Superior Court, no. 57842 (1971).

14. Author's personal interview with MacIver Wells, June 1992.

15. See, in particular, the following *Seattle Times* articles, all written by John Wilson and Marshall Wilson: "Ramon Probes Report Some On-Duty Policemen Play Poker in Tavern," Jan. 13, 1967, 1; "Surveillance Like a Keystone Cop Comedy," Jan. 13, 1967, 9; "Tavern Operators Describe Payoffs," Jan. 16, 1967, 4; and the article in which MacIver Wells is quoted anonymously, "$30-a-month payoff grew to $370, Says Club Operator," Jan. 17, 1967, 19.

16. *State v. Rhinehart,* Washington State Supreme Court, 70 Wn. 2d 649 (1967).

17. See pp. 390–96 in particular, Reporter's Transcript of Proceedings before Judge William Gray, *Rhinehart v. B. J. Rhay,* U.S. District Court for Western Washington, civil no. 8447 (1969).

## 7 / ROBERT'S RULES AND GAY LIBERATION

1. John Eccles Papers, Special Collections, University of Washington Libraries.

2. Dorian Society members Nicholas Heer, Martin Gouterman, Sheldon Daniels, Andrew Johnson, Michael Ramey, and Doug Wyman were interviewed by the author and by David Doss, of the Seattle University Community and Communication Project, Nov. 1994. For Dorian Society minutes and other documents, see the Tim Mayhew Papers, Special Collections, University of Washington Libraries, and David Doss, "Becoming Visible: The Dorian Society of Seattle and the Emergence of Seattle's Gay Community" (undergraduate research paper, Seattle University, 1994). See also "Seattle Welcomes West-Con with Open Arms—Really," *Advocate,* Jan. 1968, 3.

3. Gouterman interview, Seattle University Community and Communication Project, Nov. 1994.

4. Wyman interview, Seattle University Community and Communication Project, Nov. 1994.

5. See *University of Washington Daily* stories by Bob Hinz: "Homosexuality More Prevalent," Apr. 25, 1967, 4; "Homosexuality a Sickness, Not a Sin, Say Ministers," Apr. 26, 1967, 8; "Lawyers Desire Tolerance of Homosexual Acts," Apr. 27, 1967, 6; "My Personality Seems Permeated by Homosexuality," Apr. 28, 1967, 8; and "Most Don't Really Want to Change," May 2, 1967, 3.

6. Bill Sieverling, "It's a Gay, Gay World," *Seattle Post-Intelligencer, Northwest Today,* Apr. 30, 1967, 14.

7. Patrick Douglas, "Sin, Seattle Style," *Seattle,* Aug. 1967, 27.

8. Ruth Wolf, "The Homosexual in Seattle," *Seattle,* Nov. 1967, 35.

9. Peter Bunzel, "A Post-Mortem while the Body is Still Warm," *Seattle,* Dec. 1970, 22.

10. Heer interview, Seattle University Community and Communication Project, Nov. 1994.

11. A copy of Ken Hoole's letter is contained in the Tim Mayhew Papers, Special Collections, University of Washington Libraries.

12. *Gaylord v. Tacoma School District,* Washington State Supreme Court, 88 Wn. 2d 286 (1977). For a discussion of the case, see, for example, Kent Hansen, "Gaylord v. Tacoma School District No. 10: Homosexuality Held Immoral for Purposes of Teacher Discharge," *Willamette Law Journal* 14 (1977): 101.

13. A copy of questions from the Portland State University students is contained in the Tim Mayhew Papers, Special Collections, University of Washington Libraries.

14. Heer, Gouterman, Wyman, and Daniels interviews, Seattle University Community and Communication Project, Nov. 1994.

15. For accounts of Dr. Robert Deisher's views and activities, see "Troubled Teens—Growing Problem," *Seattle Post-Intelligencer,* Oct. 14, 1979, C5; Robert Deisher, "The Young Male Prostitute," *Pediatrics* 43 (June 1969): 936; and Deisher, "Young Male Prostitutes: The Physician's Role in Social Rehabilitation," *Journal of the American Medical Association* 212 (June 1970): 1661. Other material comes from an interview with Deisher by Ruth Pettis and Jeannie Galloway of the Northwest Lesbian and Gay History Museum Project, Aug. 1999.

16. Interview with Paul Barwick by Ruth Pettis, Northwest Lesbian and Gay History Museum Project, Jan. 2000.

17. Interview with Faygele benMiriam/John Singer by Jill Bateman, Seattle University Community and Communication Project, June 1995. Additional material about Singer is drawn from an interview by Ruth Pettis, Northwest Lesbian and Gay History Museum Project, Jan. 2000, as well as from multiple conversations with Singer conducted by the author between 1995 and 2000.

18. "Two Men Refused License to Marry," *Seattle Post-Intelligencer,* Sept. 21, 1971, A14; "Gay Groups Back License Seekers," *Seattle Post-Intelligencer,* Sept. 26, 1971, E4; and "Non-believers Seek License to Wed," *Advocate,* Nov. 10, 1971, 12.

19. For news accounts, see, for example, Sasha Yasinin, "Gay Marriage Test Due in Washington State Courts," *Advocate,* Jan. 16, 1974, 14, and "Wedding Licenses are Not for Gays," *Advocate,* July 3, 1974, 10.

20. "Gays Arrested at Roller Rink," *Northwest Fountain,* May 1972, 3; "Hand-holding Gets Pair Busted at Roller Rink," *Advocate,* May 10, 1972, 10.

### 8 / CHAUTAUQUAS OF FEMINISM AND LESBIANISM

1. Interview with Bryher Herak by Marianne Onsrud of the Seattle University Community and Communication Project, Dec. 1994. Interview with Jane Meyerding by Ruth Pettis of the Northwest Lesbian and Gay History Museum Project, Feb. 1997.

2. John D'Emilio, *Sexual Politics, Sexual Communities: The Making of a Homosexual Minority in the United States, 1940–1970* (Chicago: University of Chicago Press, 1983); Del Martin and Phyllis Lyon, *Lesbian/Woman* (San Francisco: Glide Publications, 1972).

3. Susan Paynter, "After 20 Years, Cause Comes of Age," *Seattle Post-Intelligencer,* Apr. 6, 1973, A12.

4. For details on the planning of the Alaska-Yukon-Pacific Exposition, see, for example, Nard Jones, *Seattle* (New York: Doubleday, 1972). Background on women's roles at the exposition, and on the YWCA, can be found in Mildred T. Andrews, *Washington Women as Pathbreakers* (Dubuque, Iowa: Kendall Hall, 1989).

5. Paul Anderson, "University Y.W.: It Sure Isn't Like It Used to Be," *Seattle Times,* March 29, 1972, C1. Other information about the YWCA's transformation can be found in "U District Y.W. 'Alive and Kicking,'" *Seattle Post-Intelligencer,* March 6, 1971, 4; Susan Paynter, "YWCA Gets Involved 'Because We Must,'" *Seattle Post-Intelligencer,* March 11, 1971, 15; Joanne Hooker, "Banishment of an Institution," *Seattle Post-Intelligencer,* Nov. 23, 1980, D3; "U.W. Branch of Y.W. Praised by Magazine," *Seattle Times,* Feb. 26, 1975, D2; and Jane Cartwright, "Rent Increase Threatens Women's Groups," *Seattle Times,* Nov. 11, 1980, C2.

6. Rachel daSilva, "First Gay Women's Meeting," *Pandora,* Dec. 1, 1970, 2.

7. "Gay Women's Alliance," *Pandora,* Dec. 14, 1970, 2.

8. Susan Paynter, "Lesbianism: A New Center Will Help Gay Women," *Seattle Post-Intelligencer,* Oct. 3, 1971, C1.

9. Anderson, "University Y.W.: It Sure Isn't Like It Used to Be," *Seattle Times,* March 29, 1972, C1; Kathleen Fury, "Can the YWCA Really Swing?" *Redbook,* March 1975, 59.

10. Diane Winslow, "We Dare to Be Honest," *Pandora,* Nov. 1976, 6.

11. Betty Johanna, "Open Letter to Washington Coalition for Sexual Minority Rights," *Out and About,* May 1978, 10. See also Johanna's letter to the editor in *Seattle Gay News,* Apr. 14, 1978, 9.

12. Gwen (no last name given), "C. C. Grains: Sharing the Changes," *Out and About,* Apr. 1978, 12.

13. Interview with Lois Thetford by Jody Doherty and David Huddleston, Northwest Lesbian and Gay History Museum Project, June 1995. See also Regina Hackett, "Lois Thetford: Commitment to Community Health," *Seattle Post-Intelligencer,* Apr. 9, 2001, A7.

14. Interview with Jan Denali by Karina Luboff, Northwest Lesbian and Gay History Museum Project, March 1998.

15. For specific references to the relationship between Seattle's lesbians and the National Organization for Women, see, for example, Barbara Love, "NOW It Is," *Advocate,* March 28, 1973, 3; and several noteworthy articles in *Pandora* such as Meredith Stannard, "Lesbians Protest at Friedan Speech," May 29, 1973, 4; "The Politics of Lesbian Separation: An Open Letter to Radical Women," May 29, 1973, 6; and Colleen Patrick, "Friedan Unresponsive to Movement," June 25, 1973, 4.

16. Background on the socialist relationship to homosexuals, as well as a radical analy-

sis of gay history from the time of the Greeks, can be found in an eight-part series by Sam Deaderick, Robert Crisman, and Tamara Turner, originally published in the *Freedom Socialist* newspaper in fall 1978 to fall 1980. See especially "The SWP and Gays: The Boys on the Bandwagon." The series was reprinted as Deaderick and Turner, *Gay Resistance: The Hidden History* (Seattle: Red Letter Press, 1997). See also Laurie Morton, "The Feminist Movement and the Gay Movement: How Are They Related?" speech to the Bicentennial Conference on Gays and the Federal Government, Washington, D.C., Oct. 12, 1975, issued as a booklet by Radical Women, 1975. For an overview of the first ten years of the history of Radical Women, see Sarah McCoy, "Ten Years of Strife: The Politics of Principle," *Seattle Sun*, Feb. 1, 1978, 1.

17. For writings by Alice, Gordon, Debbie, and Mary, see *For Lesbians Only: A Separatist Anthology*, ed. Sarah Lucia Hoagland and Julia Penelope (London: Onlywomen, 1988), 31–44, 304–9, 379–94.

18. For writings by the Gorgons, see Hoagland and Penelope, *For Lesbians Only*, 394–98. For the Gorgons' raid on Red and Black Books and It's About Time, see "The Switch," *Out and About*, Feb. 1978, 5; and "Open Letter to the Gorgons," *Out and About*, March 1978, 16.

19. "Does the Slipper Still Fit?" "Lesbian Flash" edition, *Pandora*, Dec. 11, 1973, 7. A similar sentiment about gay men was expressed in a later letter to the *Seattle Gay News*, in which a woman complained that on the Slipper's ninth anniversary, "I could not help feeling angry and resentful at the presence of men—males were on the dance floor, they were seated around several tables, and campaign posters for the court [of Seattle] were plastered on the walls." She continued: "I don't expect anyone (male or female) who has never experienced a women's space to truly understand my point, but the difference in women when we are in an all-female environment is striking. It is one place where we are truly free. So men, stay away, don't invade our space." Ren Miller, the Slipper's owner, argued against such an approach and noted that some women viewed the men's presence as "a means to get to know one's gay brothers." See *Seattle Gay News*, Feb. 17, 1978, 12, and March 3, 1978, 5.

20. Meyerding interview, Northwest Lesbian and Gay History Museum Project, Feb. 1997.

21. Cindy Gipple's criticism was printed in *Pandora*, Nov. 30, 1971, 6. See also Susan Paynter, "Message from a Sexual Minority," *Seattle Post-Intelligencer*, Apr. 1, 1971, D6.

22. See the following in *Pandora*: "Political Hassles Hurt F.C.C.," Apr. 17, 1973, 4; "Vandalism of Freeway Hall Denounced," May 1, 1973, 6; "Letters to Pandora: Feminist Coordinating Council," May 15, 1973, 6; "Letters," May 29, 1973, 6.

23. Meredith Stannard, "Lesbians Protest at Friedan Speech," *Pandora*, May 29, 1973, 4.

24. Carol Strong, "Lesbian Mothers: Victims," *Pandora*, May 16, 1972, 7.

25. Sources for the custody case involving Sandra Schuster and Madeleine Isaacson, as well as other lesbian mothers, are: "Gay Mothers' Group Formed," *Pandora*, Feb. 8, 1972, 2; Susan Paynter, "Lesbian Mothers: Their Lives and Fears," *Seattle Post-Intelligencer*, June 11, 1972, D1; "A Small Victory for Lesbian Mothers," *Pandora*, Oct. 17, 1972, 5; "Gay Mothers

Win Children But Lose Each Other," *Advocate,* Jan. 17, 1973, 10; Susan Paynter, "The Lord and Lesbians, Strange Mix for Half-Victory in Court," *Seattle Post-Intelligencer,* Feb. 18, 1973, D1; Susan Paynter, "Loving the Lord, the Kids, Each Other," *Seattle Post-Intelligencer,* Feb. 19, 1973, A15; "Lesbian Couple to Keep Custody of Six Children," *Seattle Times,* Sept. 4, 1974, A11; Kirie Pedersen, "Lesbian Mothers Win Right to Live Together," *Pandora,* Oct. 1, 1974, 9; "National Defense Fund Planned," *Pandora,* Oct. 1, 1974, 9; Randy Shilts, "Sandy and Madeleine," *Advocate,* Oct. 22, 1975, 26; Katie Robinson, "Lesbian Mothers in Child Custody Dispute," *Pandora,* Jan. 1, 1976, 5; "Two Lesbians Win Child Custody Fight," *Seattle Post-Intelligencer,* Oct. 5, 1978, 1; "Two Lesbian Mothers Win in Court," *Seattle Times,* Oct. 5, 1978, A18; Roger Winters, "Sandy and Madeleine: 'We Won It All,'" *Seattle Gay News,* Oct. 13, 1978, 1; Susan Paynter and Bruce Sherman, "KIRO Cancels Show on Lesbian Mothers," *Seattle Post-Intelligencer,* Nov. 29, 1978, A1. See also the court records for *James Earl Schuster v. Sandra Lee Schuster* and *Jerry Floyd Isaacson v. Madeleine Cecil Isaacson,* King County Superior Court, D-36867 (1974), and Washington State Supreme Court, 90 Wash. 2d 626, 585 P. 2d 130.

26. Thetford interview, Northwest Lesbian and Gay History Museum Project, June 1995.

27. "Planned Parenthood," *Advocate,* Oct. 22, 1975, 30.

28. Herak interview, Seattle University Community and Communication Project, Dec. 1994.

### 9 / PULPITS FOR HEALING

1. "Renton Hill Has Had Large Growth," *Seattle Post-Intelligencer,* Nov. 26, 1905, 14.

2. Information on the Seattle Counseling Service comes from an interview with Andrew Johnson by the author and David Doss of the Seattle University Community and Communication Project in Nov. 1994; interviews with Robert Deisher and Rae Larson by Ruth Pettis and Jeannie Galloway of the Northwest Lesbian and Gay History Museum Project in Aug. 1999; Charna Klein, *Counseling Our Own: The Lesbian/Gay Subculture Meets the Mental Health System* (Seattle: Publication Services, 1986); and the Tim Mayhew Papers, Special Collections, University of Washington Libraries.

3. For background on the activists' philosophy and the conflict over funding, see Klein, *Counseling Our Own,* chapter 6, as well as Patrick Haggerty, "The Oppression of the American Male Homosexual: A View by a Homosexual Social Worker," M.S.W. thesis, University of Washington School of Social Work, 1972, chapter 8 particularly.

4. Larson interview, Northwest Lesbian and Gay History Museum Project, Aug. 1999.

5. This quote and those that follow are from Earl Hansen, "Not Much Rejoicing in Plans for a Gay Church," *Seattle Post-Intelligencer,* May 13, 1972, A8. For periodical coverage of the Reverend Robert Sirico, see "Pastor to Perform Homosexual Marriages," *Seattle Times,* May 11, 1972, A7; Ray Ruppert, "Seattle Churches Grapple with Role of Homosexuals," *Seattle Times,* June 17, 1972, A11; "Young Revivalist Minister Starting MCC in Seattle," *Advocate,* June 21, 1972, 33; "Rebuttal Offered on Homosexuality," *Seattle Times,* June 24, 1972, A10; "MCC/Seattle Squares Off with Newspaper Over Ad," *Advocate,* July 5, 1972, 12; Charles

Brown, "Church for Homosexuals to Get Charter," *Seattle Times*, Aug. 5, 1972, B5; Earl Hansen, "Gay Church: Bodyguards to Keep It Gay," *Seattle Post-Intelligencer*, Aug. 5, 1972, A8; "Evangelist's Seattle MCC Already 'In'," *Advocate*, Aug. 30, 1972, 2.

6. For background on the Carmelite monastery, see, for example, "New Carmelite Monastery Planned Here," *Seattle Times*, Oct. 20, 1958, 2; Lane Smith, "Monastery a Powerhouse of Prayer," *Seattle Times*, Dec. 6, 1958, 4; Jerolyn Ann Nentl, "Monastery Marks 75th Anniversary," *The Northwest Progress*, Dec. 8, 1983, 12.

7. For background on William DuBay, see Earl Hansen, "Former Priest Critical of Church Roles," *Seattle Post-Intelligencer*, Aug. 2, 1970, 34; William H. DuBay, "The Fragile Marriage of an Ex-Priest," *McCall's*, Sept. 1970, 70; Ray Ruppert, "Transition: Celibate Priest to Husband," *Seattle Times*, Sept. 12, 1970, A10; William H. DuBay, "Gays Should Avoid Condemning All Religion," *Advocate*, Dec. 22, 1971, 27; William H. DuBay, "Gay 'Seekers' are Free to Find Own Answers to Life," *Advocate*, Jan. 3, 1973, 37; William H. DuBay, "Gay Sex Slandered!" *Advocate*, March 27, 1974, 37; Emmett Watson, "A Native Son: When You Talk Seattle, You Have to Talk Al Rochester," *Seattle Times*, Nov. 27, 1983, C1.

8. For information about the founding and philosophy of the Stonewall community, see Marjorie Jones, "A 'Realistic' Center for Homosexuals," *Seattle Times*, Jan. 5, 1972, B2; William H. DuBay, "Seattle's Experience: Steps to a Halfway House," *Advocate*, March 15, 1972, 29; "Prison Officials Accused of Bias Against 'Gay' Inmates," *Seattle Times*, May 20, 1972, A12; "Stonewall Prison Program Wins Approval from State," *Advocate*, Aug. 30, 1972, 16; "Stonewall OK'd by State," *Seattle Times*, Sept. 12, 1972, A9; "Stonewall Center May Get $10,500," *Advocate*, Dec. 6, 1972, 2; "Minneapolis Branch for Stonewall," *Advocate*, Feb. 14, 1973, 14; "Halfway House," *Northwest Fountain*, Aug. 1973, 3; Sasha Yasinin, "Rustic Retreat Acquired by Gay Halfway House," *Advocate*, Aug. 29, 1973, 2; Diana Montgomery, "Stonewall: Gay Is Good and Caring Is Everything," *Seattle Post-Intelligencer*, Dec. 9, 1973, C1; Sasha Lewis, "Center in Seattle Gets $120,000," *Advocate*, Nov. 6, 1974, 3; Randy Shilts, "Way Out: Stonewall Therapy," *Advocate*, June 30, 1976, 23. For a statement of Stonewall's philosophy, see, "The Gays: Who Are We? Where Do We Come From? What Are We For?" *Stonewall Report*, Sept. 1975. See also the Charles Harbaugh Papers, Special Collections, University of Washington Libraries. Harbaugh worked briefly for Stonewall.

9. Paul Henderson, "Seattle's Homosexuals Ask: 'Understand, Don't Generalize,'" *Seattle Times*, Dec. 9, 1969, 60.

10. Klein, *Counseling Our Own*, 1986.

11. Interviews with Paul Barwick and Faygele benMiriam by Ruth Pettis of the Northwest Lesbian and Gay History Museum Project, Jan. 2000. Volunteers from both the old Dorian Society and the Gay Women's Alliance helped staff the first community center, and it even managed to secure a cabaret license from the city—despite the reluctance of some Seattle City Council members. See "Seattle Gay Community Tries Unity," *Advocate*, Sept. 15, 1971, 2; "Gay Alliance Dance Hall Recommended," *Seattle Times*, Oct. 19, 1971, D1; "Seattle Center Shut; New Location Sought," *Advocate*, Nov. 8, 1972, 19; Katherine Grant-Bourne, "Gay and Lesbian Pride—A History," *Seattle Gay News*, June 27, 1986, 25. Once the first center closed, several activists formed a new organization called Gay

Community Social Services, which then began funding new cultural projects, such as a rural gay collective on the Olympic Peninsula and, when arsonists burned that down, a national rural gay magazine called *RFD*.

12. Grant-Bourne, "Gay and Lesbian Pride—A History," 25.

13. See *Seattle Sun* stories by Bruce Olson: "Land Owners Grab for Hill Power," Sept. 25, 1974, 1; "Activists Sweep Community Council Elections," Oct. 2, 1974, 1.

14. Susan Chadwick, "Battle of the Notices," *Seattle Sun*, Nov. 13, 1974, 3.

15. "Use Zoning to Enforce Morals, Says Chamber of Commerce President," *Seattle Sun*, Nov. 27, 1974, 3.

16. "Scrapbook," *Seattle Sun*, Nov. 27, 1974, 1.

17. "Sick No More," *Advocate*, Jan. 16, 1974, 1. See also David Aiken, "Gays Leave Psychiatric 'Sick' List," *Advocate*, Jan. 2, 1974, 1.

18. "Counselors for Gays Regain County Funds," *Seattle Sun*, Oct. 26, 1977, 3.

19. Bruce Olson, "'Dress, Demeanor' of Gay Counseling Causes Fund Cut," *Seattle Sun*, Oct. 30, 1974, 3; Joan Moritz, "Counseling Center May Lose Funding," *Pandora*, Nov. 1974, 4.

20. Lou Corsaletti, "Fund Cut May Be Restored to Gay Counseling Service," *Seattle Times*, Feb. 11, 1976, A9.

21. Steve Mettner, "Snedigar Leaves SCSSM," *Seattle Gay News*, Apr. 1977, 6; "Counselors for Gays Regain County Funds," *Seattle Sun*, Oct. 26, 1977, 3.

22. Marjorie Jones, "Program for Homosexuals Finding No Welcome Mat in Small Towns," *Seattle Times*, Sept. 24, 1975, G5; "Stonewall R.F.D.," *Stonewall Report*, Sept. 1975, 1; Randy Shilts, "Homophobia Backfired When Stonewall Went House-Hunting," *Advocate*, Nov. 5, 1975, 17.

23. Robert Myerson, "Stonewall to Close," *Seattle Sun*, Aug. 18, 1976, 5; "Stonewall Center to Close in Fall," *Seattle Times*, July 29, 1976, D1; "Stonewall Decides to Close," *Advocate*, Sept. 8, 1976, 11; Hilda Bryant, "New Tenant at Old Monastery," *Seattle Post-Intelligencer*, Oct. 1, 1976, A11. See also Charles Harbaugh Papers, Special Collections, University of Washington Libraries.

24. Ray Ruppert, "Capitol Hill Pastor Caught in Conflict over Homosexuals," *Seattle Times*, March 8, 1975, A10.

25. Earl Hansen, "A Showdown in an Old Sanctuary," *Seattle Post-Intelligencer*, June 5, 1976, A11. See also Ray Ruppert, "Methodists May Close Unorthodox Capitol Hill Church," *Seattle Times*, May 24, 1976, A6; Ray Ruppert, "Century's Fight: Laity v. Clergy in Capitol Hill Church," *Seattle Times*, June 5, 1976, A4; Ray Ruppert, "Church, Congregation Compromise on Issues," *Seattle Times*, June 11, 1976, B5; "Conference Marks Turning Point," *Advocate*, July 28, 1976, 20.

26. "Arsonist Hits Gay Center," *Seattle Gay News*, Apr. 1976, 11; "Arson Fire Damages Gay Community Center," *Seattle Sun*, March 31, 1976, 5; "Gay Center Destroyed After Second Fire Set," *Seattle Sun*, Apr. 14, 1976, 3; "Arson Fire," *Seattle Sun*, Apr. 21, 1976, 2; "Hate Mail," *Seattle Sun*, Apr. 28, 1976, 2; Robert Mayerson and Lenore Norrgard, "Gay Leaders Blame Courts and Jackson for Backlash," *Seattle Sun*, May 12, 1976, 7.

## 10 / AT THE DANCE

1. On Pioneer Square's restoration, see, for example, Kristi Farley, *A Primer: Preservation in Seattle* (Seattle: City of Seattle, 1977). See also Victor Steinbrueck, *Architectural and Historical Survey of Pioneer Square* (Seattle: City of Seattle, 1969); Department of Community Development, "Pioneer Square Profile: An Update on Redevelopment," (Seattle: City of Seattle, 1979); James Halpin, "Square Dance," *Seattle Weekly,* June 17, 1992, 25.

2. For details on the Bastille Day celebration, see *Shelly Ann Bauman v. Morris Hart, Pioneer Square Association, et al.,* King County Superior Court, civil no. 726096 (1971), and the news reports on the accident: "Woman, 23, Hurt by Blast from Cannon," *Seattle Times,* July 15, 1970, A5; "Woman Badly Hurt," *Seattle Post-Intelligencer,* July 15, 1970, 4; Jim Sass, "Shelly's Leg," *Vector,* Aug. 1974, 33.

3. Author's interview with Joe McGonagle, May 1992.

4. Author's interview with Joe McGonagle, May 1992. See also the affidavit of Joe McGonagle, *State v. Carroll et al.,* King County Superior Court, criminal no. 57842 (1971).

5. Mike Mowrer, "Shelly's Leg: Dancing in a Sexual Twilight Zone," *University of Washington Daily,* July 25, 1974, 12.

6. Eric Lacitis, "Shelly's Leg Draws All Kinds to Dance," *Seattle Times,* Aug. 31, 1975, E4. See also Bruce Buls, "Disco Madness," *Seattle Post-Intelligencer Northwest Magazine,* Apr. 25, 1976, 7.

7. Charles Brown, "Viaduct Fire Destroys 17 Cars," *Seattle Times,* Dec. 4, 1975, 1. See also Martin Works, "Viaduct Fire Sparks Action," *Seattle Post-Intelligencer,* Dec. 5, 1975, A8. For a while, it seemed as if the Our Home Hotel would be torn down. Instead, it was eventually restored. See Dick Clever, "Crumbling 90-Year-Old Hotel May be Doomed," *Seattle Times,* March 15, 1985, A1; Maude Scott, "Tricky Rehab Begins at Our Home Hotel," *Seattle Daily Journal of Commerce,* Sept. 15, 1986, 1.

8. After the fire damaged Shelly's Leg, two other gay-oriented discos quickly replaced it in popularity. The Dancing Machine was located in Seattle's Fremont neighborhood several miles north of downtown, while the Boren Street Disco moved into an old heavily timbered building below Capitol Hill, in what is called the Regrade area. For the decline of Shelly's Leg, see "Where Have the Crowds Gone?" *Seattle Gay News,* March 1977, 11. Pat Nesser died in 1991. Joe McGonagle wrote a tribute: "We will all miss you, Patty Mae. The light came on when I met you. It shined bright over the years. You were a shining example of what we wanted life to be. You taught me to be the best person I could be. . . . We laughed, cried, bitched and complained and got so close with each other I felt I became of age. I'll miss you Patty, God how I'll miss you." *Seattle Gay News,* July 12, 1991, 4.

## 11 / CONFRONTING A POLICE CRACKDOWN

1. Murray Morgan, *Skid Road: An Informal Portrait of Seattle* (New York: Viking Press, 1960), 137–39.

2. David Suffia and Jerry Bergsman, "Ramon to Retire November 6," *Seattle Times,* Oct. 8, 1969, 1, 39; David Suffia, "Ramon Termed Good Cop," *Seattle Times,* Oct. 10, 1969, 6; "Police Chiefs Come and Police Chiefs Go," *Seattle Post-Intelligencer,* Nov. 25, 1972, A3.

3. In the *Seattle Times,* see Dee Norton and Lou Corsaletti, "30-Year History of Police Payoffs Unfolding," June 28, 1970, A8; "Police Are Competent Despite Difficulties, Says Acting Chief," Aug. 28, 1970, A7; "Tielsch: New Chief Stresses Discipline, Education," Sept. 3, 1970, B9.

4. In the *Seattle Times,* see David Suffia, "Tielsch Appointed Seattle Police Chief," Sept. 3, 1970, A1; Don Tewkesbury, "Chief Tielsch: Outspoken-Hero to Most Policemen," Aug. 15, 1971, 19.

5. In the *Seattle Times,* see Lou Corsaletti, "Tielsch Is Neat, Business-Like Man," and David Suffia, "Race Issues, Gambling Get Main Attention," Oct. 18, 1970, E7; also "Tolerance Ruled Out by Tielsch," Sept. 24, 1970, C6.

6. In the *Seattle Times,* see Don Tewkesbury, "Chief Tielsch: Outspoken-Hero to Most Policemen," Aug. 15, 1971, 19. See also John Wilson, "Tielsch Had a 'Muddy' Beginning as Chief," *Seattle Times,* Dec. 13, 1972, C6.

7. "Topless Decision May Lead to Bottomless, Says Tielsch," *Seattle Times,* Apr. 6, 1972, D15. That same year, the U.S. Supreme Court ruled in *California v. LaRue,* 409 U.S. 109 (1972), that topless dancing was indeed entitled to some First Amendment protection.

8. *Western Amusement Company v. City of Seattle et al.,* U.S. District Court, Western Division of Washington, civil no. 655-72C2 (Oct. 1972). Statistics on arrests in the arcades come from a Defendant's Brief in Opposition to a Petition for a Temporary Restraining Order, dated Oct. 20, 1972. See also George Arthur, "ACLU to Help Seattle Gays Counter Arrests," *Advocate,* Jan. 17, 1973, 16.

9. Letter from Richard Andrus to Mayor Wes Uhlman, Sept. 26, 1972, Seattle Mayors' Papers, Special Collections, University of Washington Libraries.

10. For protest letters written to Mayor Uhlman about the police crackdown, see the Seattle Mayors' Papers, Special Collections, University of Washington Libraries, particularly box 61, which contains letters from Dr. Benjamin Spock, Sept. 19, 1972; the Reverend Peter Raible, Oct. 2 1972; the U.W. Gay Students Association, Oct. 4, 1972; and Karen West, Nov. 10, 1972. See also John Bell, "Homosexuals Charge Harassment," *Seattle Times,* Dec. 6, 1972, E18; George Arthur, "ACLU to Help Seattle Gays Counter Arrests," *Advocate,* Jan. 17, 1973, 16.

11. "Pickets Charge Police Harassment," *Seattle Times,* Apr. 24, 1973, E5; letter from Robert Sirico to Mayor Wes Uhlman, May 25, 1973, Seattle Mayors' Papers, Special Collections, University of Washington Libraries; "Police Beating of Gay Woman Triggers Protests in Seattle," *Advocate,* June 6, 1973, 10.

12. "Police Beating of Gay Woman Triggers Protests in Seattle," *Advocate,* June 6, 1973, 10. See also, "'Gay' Pickets Pay a Call on Chief Tielsch," *Seattle Times,* May 6, 1973, D11.

13. Letter from William DuBay to Mayor Wes Uhlman, May 21, 1973, Seattle Mayors' Papers, Special Collections, University of Washington Libraries.

14. Tim Mayhew Papers, Special Collections, University of Washington Libraries.

15. "Police Up Arrests," *The Fountain*, Aug. 1973, 1; "Seattle Public Defender–ACLU–SGA Fight Entrapment," *The Fountain*, Sept. 1973, 2; Sasha Yasinin, "Male Prostitution Charges Soar in Seattle," *Advocate*, Sept. 12, 1973, 8.

16. "Gay Liberation Leader Calls Arrest Police Harassment," *Seattle Times*, Oct. 19, 1973, B5; "MCC Pastor Is Arrested in Seattle," *Advocate*, Nov. 7, 1973, 3; "Sirico Let Off with Warning on Jaywalking Charge," *Advocate*, Nov. 21, 1973, 16.

17. Sam Elwonger, "The Vice Squad—Never Say Yes," *The Gay Pub*, Feb. 1974, 3.

18. For background on Jeanette Williams and the revision of Seattle's civil rights ordinances, see a video interview with the councilwoman by Donald A. Schmechel, Seattle Public Library oral history collection. For the creation of the Women's Commission, and feminist controversy surrounding it, see "Council Unit Approves Commission," *Seattle Times*, Apr. 7, 1971, D1, and the following articles in *Pandora*: "Seattle Women's Division," Jan. 11, 1971, 1; "City Commission Lacks Knowledge, Commitment," Oct. 19, 1971, 5; "Lackluster Commission Needs Push," Dec. 14, 1971, 3; "Aliesan Quits City Commission," May 2, 1972, 4; "Commission Leaves Questions Unanswered," June 13, 1972, 2.

19. Ann Montague, "Gay Action Caused Seattle Law," *Advocate*, Nov. 7, 1973, 36. For additional background on the adoption of the ordinances, from a gay perspective, see William DuBay, "Seattle Mayor Admits Prejudice," *Advocate*, July 4, 1973, 19; Tim Mayhew, "Seattle Protects Gay Jobs," *Fountain*, Oct. 1973, 1; "New Seattle Law Protects Gay Jobs," *Advocate*, Oct. 10, 1973, 1; Sasha Yasinin, "Seattle Rights Law: Seldom Has So Little Produced So Much," *Advocate*, Oct. 24, 1973, 2; "Seattle Rights Law Belatedly Becomes Political Issue," *Advocate*, Nov. 7, 1973, 21.

20. "Ruling on Ordinance," *Advocate*, Nov. 5, 1975, 15.

21. George Foster, "A 'Policeman's Policeman' Stars," *Seattle Post-Intelligencer*, March 21, 1974, A15.

22. Dick Clever, "Why Uhlman Stepped into Police Breach," *Seattle Times*, March 21, 1974, A15. See also Ross Anderson, "Incident 4-1/2 Months Ago Led to Resignation by Tielsch," *Seattle Times*, March 16, 1974, A3.

23. On Tielsch's final days in office, see "Tielsch to Resign, Take California Job," *Seattle Times*, Feb. 27, 1974, A1; "New Chief from Ranks—Larkin," *Seattle Times*, Feb. 27, 1974, A15; Sam Sperry, "Mayor Considers Civilian Chief," *Seattle Times*, Feb. 28, 1974, A1; Dave Birkland and Sam Sperry, "Hanson Is Acting Chief As Tielsch Walks Out," *Seattle Times*, March 16, 1974, A1; "Anti-Gay Police Chief Hired in Santa Monica," *Advocate*, Apr. 10, 1974, 3; "Mayor Shackles Million-Dollar Vice Squad," *Advocate*, Apr. 24, 1974, 3.

## 12 / INSIDERS AT CITY HALL

1. Quoted material from Charlie Brydon in this chapter comes from interviews conducted by Larry Knopp and Mikala Woodward, Northwest Lesbian and Gay History Museum Project, June 2000; and from Eric Marcus, *Making History: The Struggle for Gay and Lesbian Equal Rights, 1945–1990* (New York: HarperCollins, 1992).

2. Charlie Brydon, letter to KTVU-TV, Oakland, Aug. 4, 1970, and letter to KQED-

TV, San Francisco, Feb. 5, 1971, Charlie Brydon Papers, Washington State Historical Society Archives, Tacoma.

3. For accounts of the start of the Dorian Group, see Randy Shilts, "Future of Gay Rights? The Emerging Middle Class," *Advocate,* Oct. 22, 1975, 10; Bob Kus, "History of TDG," *Seattle Gay News,* Oct. 1977, 22; interviews with Glen Hunt, Alice B. Theatre Oral History Project, Nov. 1991, Special Collections, University of Washington Libraries; and interviews with Charlie Brydon, Northwest Lesbian and Gay History Museum Project, June 2000.

4. Charlie Brydon, letter to David Goodstein, Sept. 15, 1977, Charlie Brydon Papers, Washington State Historical Society Archives, Tacoma.

5. Sale, *Seattle: Past to Present,* 85, 147.

6. Randy Shilts, "Seattle Adds More Rights," *Advocate,* Sept. 10, 1975, 6.

7. "Questioning Dr. Ray," *Advocate,* Oct. 22, 1975, 11.

8. "A Team Player He Is Not," *Seattle Gay News,* June 1977, 7. The editorial was also quoted in Roger Downey, "Ready When You Are, Anita," *Seattle Weekly,* June 29, 1977, 8. Virginia Lambert's reply was printed in the letters to the editor, *Seattle Gay News,* July/Aug. 1977, 7.

9. Randy Shilts, "Future of Gay Rights? The Emerging Middle Class," *Advocate,* Oct. 22, 1975, 10.

10. For coverage of the Gipple-Brydon dispute, see Sam Deaderick, "Unfair Politics," *Seattle Gay News,* Apr. 1976, 2, and "Editorial," 14; Lenore Norrgard, "Gays: Left, Right Square Off," *Seattle Sun,* Apr. 28, 1976, 5; Mike Kenney, "Gays on Women's Commission," *Seattle Gay News,* May 1976, 2; "Rights Panel Replacing Its Nominee?" *Seattle Times,* May 12, 1976, F5; Patricia Foote, "Gay Nominees Included on Commission Slate," *Seattle Times,* May 18, 1976, D1; Mike Kenney, "C. F. Brydon Named to Women's Commission," *Seattle Gay News,* July 1976, 4; "Gay Rep Seated on Women's Panel," *Seattle Sun,* Aug. 4, 1976, 3.

11. Cindy Gipple's response was included in Mike Kenney, "C. F. Brydon Named to Women's Commission," *Seattle Gay News,* July 1976, 4. For Brydon's letter to Uhlman, written July 14, 1976, see the Seattle Mayors' Papers, Special Collections, University of Washington Libraries.

12. For background on the debate about Mayor Uhlman's endorsement of the gay pride parade, see letters from Gavin Dillard of the Union of Sexual Minorities to Wes Uhlman, and Uhlman's reply, June 6 and 18, 1975; the exchange of letters between Uhlman, Charlie Brydon, and Jack Anderson on May 21 and 22 and June 25, 1975; the letters between David Neth and Wes Uhlman, June 10 and 17, 1976; and a letter from Uhlman to James Tochia, June 17, 1976, all in the Seattle Mayors' Papers, Special Collections, University of Washington Libraries. See also David Neth, "Open Letter to Mayor Uhlman," *Seattle Gay News,* June 1976, 3; "Your Emerging Sense of Pride," *Seattle Gay News,* July 1976, 2.

13. Seattle Mayors' Papers, Special Collections, University of Washington Libraries.

## 13 / AT THE CAPITOL

1. Information in this chapter about the treatment of Keith Rhinehart and the eventual dismissal of his conviction comes from documents filed in *Keith M. Rhinehart v.*

*B. J. Rhay*, U.S. District Court for Western Washington, civil no. 8447 (1969), and *Keith M. Rhinehart v. B. J. Rhay et al.*, U.S. District Court for Western Washington, civil no. 8448 (1969).

2. Letter from Peter Francis to Michael Ramey, June 27, 1968, Tim Mayhew Papers, Special Collections, University of Washington Libraries.

3. Bob Liff, "A Good Guy Resigns," *Seattle Sun*, Nov. 23, 1977, 1.

4. See, for example, "Sex Reform: Adult Consent Law Adopted; Nation's Third," *Advocate*, June 9, 1971, 1; "Oregon Reform Bill Sent to Governor," *Advocate*, June 23, 1971, 1; "Major Sex Reform Measure Signed into Law for Oregon," *Advocate*, Aug. 14, 1971, 1.

5. In the *Advocate*, see "Washington State Mulls Reform," Jan. 6, 1971, 1; "New Code Logjammed in Washington State Senate," June 23, 1971, 5; Arthur Evans, "Washington Reforms Pass Senate Panel; Success Predicted," Apr. 11, 1973, 3.

6. For background on the repeal of the sodomy law, see *Journal of the Washington Senate* (1975): 748–50, 2138–39; and Randy Shilts, "Sodomy Repeal Signed by Washington Governor," *Advocate*, July 30, 1975, 5.

7. Shilts, "Sodomy Repeal Signed by Washington Governor," 5.

8. Ibid.

9. Randy Shilts, "Seattle Adds More Rights," *Advocate*, Sept. 10, 1975, 6.

10. On Dave Kopay's coming out, see, for example, Robert McQueen and David Rothenberg "Interview," *Advocate*, March 10, 1976, 18; Kirk Smith, "An All-American Story Jumbled," *Seattle Post-Intelligencer*, May 1, 1976, A4.

11. Letter from Charlie Brydon to Governor Dan Evans, Jan. 29, 1976; letter from Charlie Brydon to William C. Jacobs, June 19, 1976; letter from Governor Dan Evans to Charlie Brydon, June 16, 1976, all in Seattle Mayors' Papers, Special Collections, University of Washington Libraries.

12. Marjorie Jones, "Editor Cites Progress of Gay People in Seattle," *Seattle Times*, Apr. 14, 1976, A11.

13. Jack Hopkins, "A Test Case in Tacoma," *Seattle Post-Intelligencer*, Sept. 25, 1977, A14.

14. *Gaylord v. Tacoma School District No. 10*, Washington State Supreme Court, 88 Wn. 2d 286, 559 P. 2d 1340. For earlier proceedings, see *Gaylord v. Tacoma School District No. 10*, Washington State Supreme Court, 85 Wn. 2d 348, 535 P. 2d 804.

15. For additional information on Gaylord, see, for example, Kent Hansen, "Gaylord v. Tacoma School District No. 10: Homosexuality Held Immoral for Purposes of Teacher Discharge," *Willamette Law Journal* 14 (1977): 101–14. News reports include Hal Nelson, "SGN Talks with Jim Gaylord," *Seattle Gay News*, March 1977, 4; "ACLU Takes Gaylord Case to Supreme Court," *Seattle Gay News*, July/Aug. 1977, 3.

16. "Kopay, Uhlman Push Rights Bill," *Seattle Gay News*, Apr. 1977, 1.

17. "Gay Rights Bill Stalled" and "Gays Picket KIRO," *Seattle Gay News*, May 1977, 1, 3.

18. Susan Paynter, "KIRO Wires on Fire Over Gay Editorials," *Seattle Post-Intelligencer*, May 18, 1977, B3. See also "Pickets Protest KIRO Attack on Gay Rights," *Seattle Post-Intelligencer*, May 20, 1977, A8; "Battle of KIRO," *Seattle Gay News*, June 1977, 1; "KIRO Editorials Get Heated Response," *Seattle Sun*, Aug. 31, 1977, 3. For a later story on Lloyd

Cooney, see Emmett Watson, "Lloyd Cooney: A Free Spirit Beneath a Stuffed Shirt," *Seattle Times,* Dec. 20, 1992, D2.

19. Joel Connolly, "Evangelicals to Demonstrate," *Seattle Post-Intelligencer,* June 30, 1977, A3; Joseph Guppy, "Anti-Gay Demonstration Leads to Noisy Debate," *Seattle Times,* July 1, 1977, A14; Kirk Smith, "'Love' at 4th and James," *Seattle Post-Intelligencer,* July 1, 1977, A1.

20. Carol Ostrom, "Behind Mormon Power," *Seattle Sun,* Sept. 21, 1977, 1.

21. For background on the International Women's Year battle, see Diane Clark, Kathleen Foley, Donna Kanter, and Colleen Patrick, "In the Face of Opposition—Unity Is Born," *Pandora,* Aug. 1977, 1; Sarah McCoy, "Feminists Try to Unify," *Seattle Sun,* Aug. 31, 1977, 1; "Ellensburg—Victory or Defeat for Feminism," *Pandora,* Sept. 1977, 2; "Victory or Defeat for Feminism?" *Seattle Gay News,* Sept. 1977, 6.

22. Alex MacLeod, "Francis to Resign As State Senator," *Seattle Times,* Nov. 22, 1977, B1; Bob Liff, "A Good Guy Resigns," *Seattle Sun,* Nov. 23, 1977, 1.

23. For Charlie Brydon's involvement in the White House meeting, see the Charlie Brydon Papers, Washington State Historical Society Archives, Tacoma, and Karen West, "Seattle Gay Leader Praises Carter for Policy Changes," *Seattle Post-Intelligencer,* Sept. 9, 1977, A6.

24. One council member, Tim Hill, refused the pledge. "I don't see lumping gay rights together with well-established rights of racial minorities and women," he said. He also promised that if the ordinances came before the council, he would vote to repeal the sections protecting homosexuals. See Steve Johnston, "Mayor and Council Back Gay Rights," *Seattle Post-Intelligencer,* June 9, 1977, A8. Years later, however, as chief executive of King County, Tim Hill would sign a similar county ordinance into law, protecting gay and lesbian jobs in areas outside Seattle.

25. For the 1977 debate about Gay Pride Week, see the copies of many letters to the mayor in the Seattle Mayors' Papers, Special Collections, University of Washington Libraries. Relevant news reports include: Steve Johnston, "Mayor and Council Back Gay Rights," *Seattle Post-Intelligencer,* June 9, 1977, A8; "'Gay Pride' March Set Saturday," *Seattle Times,* June 19, 1977, A22; Charles Dunsire, "Uhlman Provokes Protests," *Seattle Post-Intelligencer,* June 30, 1977, A3; Robert Mayerson, "Gay Voters Brandish Ballots," *Seattle Sun,* Sept. 14, 1977, 14.

26. On the establishment of the Seattle Municipal Elections Committee, see, for example, "SEAMEC Leads in Voter Registration," *Seattle Gay News,* Sept. 1977, 3; Mayerson, "Gay Voters Brandish Ballots," 14; "Lloyd Cooney Roast Nets $2000 for SEAMEC" and "SEAMEC Endorses," *Seattle Gay News,* Oct. 1977, 1, 3; "Gay Group Flexes Muscle," *Seattle Sun,* Nov. 12, 1977, 3.

27. Kent Stevenson, "A Nautical Night," *Seattle Gay News,* Dec. 1977, 8.

28. See Dorian Group Board minutes, July 23, 1977; and letters from Charlie Brydon to "Michael," the Dorian board, George Gosselin, and Mort Schwab, dated, respectively, Nov. 8, 1977; Nov. 30, 1977; Dec. 14, 1977; and Dec. 30, 1977, in the Charlie Brydon Papers, Washington State Historical Society Archives, Tacoma.

29. Mike Wyne, "Gays Will Have Part in Police-Chief Selection, Says Royer," *Seattle*

*Times,* Dec. 13, 1977, A14. See also "Royer Talk Sets Off Anti-Gay Caller," *Seattle Sun,* Dec. 21, 1977, 3.

30. Frank Tenczar, "Who Are These People and What Do They Want?" KING-TV, Dec. 2, 1977. See also Bill Alpert, "KING's Gay Special Tops," *Seattle Gay News,* Dec. 1977, 17. For background on Greg Kucera and his gallery, see, for example, *Seattle Times* articles by Deloris Tarzan Ament, "Gallery's Success Is His Masterpiece," Oct. 24, 1984, F7; and "Kucera's Secret: 'I Know How to Sell Things,'" Oct. 28, 1993, E4; as well as a *Seattle Post-Intelligencer* article by Regina Hackett, "Greg Kucera: The Seattle Art Dealer and Gallery Owner Is Best Known for Two Passions: Love of Art and Love of Controversy," Apr. 29, 1996, C1. Frank Tenczar eventually died of AIDS at age forty-five. At the time, he was working as a reporter in New Jersey. See "Ex-Seattle TV Reporter Dies," *Seattle Times,* Nov. 24, 1988, H7.

31. Doug Honig, "David Estes, Sodomy and the Family," *Seattle Sun,* Apr. 2, 1980, 7.

32. Stan Nast and Paul Boyd, "What Is Brutality? Police Officer Asks," *Seattle Post-Intelligencer,* March 24, 1974, A1.

33. See Dave Birkland, "Probing Policeman Suspended" and "Police Chief Denies He is 'Out to Get' Suspended Officer," *Seattle Times,* Dec. 15, 1976, A1, A7; Dee Norton, "Hot Loads: Gun Enthusiast Tells How" and Dave Birkland, "Suspended Officer Carried Forbidden Ammo, Say Tests," *Seattle Times,* Dec. 16, 1976, A6; Dave Birkland, "Review Panel Member Named," *Seattle Times,* Dec. 18, 1976, A5; "Disciplinary Hearing on Policeman Continues," *Seattle Times,* Dec. 28, 1976, A11; "Officer Suspended for Month," *Seattle Times,* Jan. 10, 1977, A6; "Suspended Officer Returns," *Seattle Times,* March 9, 1977, D4.

34. Doug Honig, "David Estes, Sodomy and the Family," *Seattle Sun,* Apr. 2, 1980, 7.

35. For background on Wayne Angevine and David Estes's filing of Initiative Thirteen, see, for example, Bob Kus, "Gays in Action," *Seattle Gay News,* Dec. 1977, 18; Martin Works, "Gay Rights Target of Drive," *Seattle Post-Intelligencer,* Jan. 23, 1978, A4; Ross Anderson and Dave Birkland, "Police Officer Begins Gay Rights Repeal Drive," *Seattle Times,* Jan. 26, 1978, A14; Ross Anderson, "Gay City Clerk Steps into the Middle," *Seattle Times,* Feb. 5, 1978, A14.

### 14 / INITIATIVE THIRTEEN

1. Roger Winters, "TDG Honors Brydon at Brass Door," *Seattle Gay News,* Feb. 3, 1978, 18. See also, in the same issue, Orv Johnson, "The Estes Petition Threat," 6.

2. Early correspondence of Citizens to Retain Fair Employment, along with notes from early political committee meetings, can be found in the Charlie Brydon Papers, Washington State Historical Society Archives, Tacoma.

3. Orv Johnson, "An Answer to Estes," *Seattle Gay News,* Feb. 17, 1978, 6. See also a letter to the editor critical of Wayne Angevine's attack on Charlie Brydon written by Mike Ramey, *Seattle Gay News,* March 3, 1978, 5.

4. Joel Connolly, "Gays Meet to Map Strategy," *Seattle Post-Intelligencer,* March 20, 1978, B1; Orv Johnson, "Gays Meet to Fight Initiative 13," *Seattle Gay News,* March 31, 1978, 1.

5. Interview with Charlie Brydon by Mikala Woodward and Larry Knopp, Northwest Lesbian and Gay History Museum Project, June 2000. For the poll results, see the Charlie Brydon Papers, Washington State Historical Society Archives, Tacoma.

6. Anita Bryant's campaign generated a great deal of magazine and newspaper publicity. Among the relevant local and gay press articles about the start of the Bryant campaign see "Money for Miami," *Seattle Gay News,* June 1977, 3; Steve Johnston, "Mayor and City Council Back Gay Rights," *Seattle Post-Intelligencer,* June 9, 1977, A8; John Hinterberger, "Anita Bryant Strikes Out with Seattle Gay Groups," *Seattle Times,* June 11, 1977, A11; Roger Downey, "Ready When You Are, Anita," *Seattle Weekly,* June 29, 1977, 8; "After Miami, What's Next?" *Seattle Gay News,* July/Aug. 1977, 19; Joe Baker, "Miami," *Advocate,* July 13, 1977, 6; Lee Solomon, "Lessons from Losing," *Advocate,* Aug. 24, 1977, 7; Orv Johnson, "Dade County—Lessons for Seattle," *Seattle Gay News,* May 26, 1978, 7.

7. Ray Ruppert, "Preacher Visits Seattle to Advise Campaigners Against Gay Rights," *Seattle Times,* March 31, 1978, D16; Ray Ruppert, "Rival Groups Fire Opening Volleys," *Seattle Times,* Apr. 2, 1978, C15; "Anti-Gay Drive Finally Comes Out," *Seattle Sun,* Apr. 5, 1978, 3.

8. Brydon interview, Northwest Lesbian and Gay History Museum Project, June 2000.

9. Ibid. For other local reaction, see Hilda Bryant, "Seattle Reaction to Gay Rights Repeal in St. Paul," *Seattle Post-Intelligencer,* Apr. 27, 1978, A5; "Anti-Gay Vote Hit by Foe of Initiative 13," *Seattle Times,* May 24, 1978, B12; "Once Again, We Lose Our Rights," *Seattle Gay News,* May 26, 1978, 1; Ross Anderson, "Gays Reassess Initiative Strategy," *Seattle Times,* May 28, 1978, B4.

10. See Walt Crowley, "A Point of View: Citizens to Retain Fair Employment," *Seattle Gay News,* June 9, 1978, 4; Ross Anderson, "Gays Reassess Initiative Strategy," *Seattle Times,* May 28, 1978, B4. See also Charlie Brydon Papers, Washington State Historical Society Archives, Tacoma, for CRFE's position statement.

11. Interview with Dennis Raymond by Larry Knopp and Charles Fuchs, Northwest Lesbian and Gay History Museum Project, May 2000.

12. For the original letter by Betty Johanna and Jane Meyerding, see "So Many Lives Have Been Lost," *Out and About,* July 1978, 15. See also Orv Johnson, "Lesbian Blood Protests 13," *Seattle Gay News,* June 23, 1978, 1, and "Trial Set for Two Accused of Splattering Blood in Office," *Seattle Times,* June 17, 1978, E6. An angry criticism of the Johanna/ Meyerding action written by Roger Winters, who was working with the Dorian Group, can be found in the letters to the editor, *Seattle Gay News,* July 7, 1978, 9.

13. For the 1978 gay pride parade dispute, see in *Seattle Gay News,* June 9, 1978: Debra Dragovich, "Some Groups Ignore Pride Parade," 1; Walt Crowley, "A Point of View: Citizens to Retain Fair Employment," 4; "Citizens Against Parade," 6; the editorial "Gays v. Gays," 7; and a report from the Washington Coalition for Sexual Minority Rights, 11. See also "Anti-13 Groups in Rift on March," *Seattle Sun,* June 21, 1978, 3. For additional coverage see *Seattle Gay News,* June 23, 1978: Jerry Bock, "March Endorsed by Majority," 1; "Rights Week Lacks Royer's Support," 3; and the editorial "March!" 7. For coverage of the march itself, see Jack Broom, "Gays to March Downtown Saturday," *Seattle Times,* June 27, 1978, B10; John O'Ryan,

"3,000 in March for Gay Rights," *Seattle Post-Intelligencer,* July 2, 1978, D10; Timothy Egan, "Gay-Rights Backers March in Downtown," *Seattle Times,* July 2, 1978, F18; Debra Dragovich and Jim Arnold, "4,000 Gays March in Seattle," *Seattle Gay News,* July 7, 1978, 1.

14. Jack Broom, "Initiative 13 Backers, Foes Vie for Attention As Petitions Are Filed," *Seattle Times,* Aug. 8, 1973, A10.

15. Jim Arnold and Steve Mettzner, "SOME Hands in Signatures," *Seattle Gay News,* Aug. 4, 1978, 1.

16. See report by Washington Coalition for Sexual Minority Rights, *Seattle Gay News,* May 12, 1978, 6.

17. Ray Ruppert, "Church Council Hits Anti-Gay Move," *Seattle Times,* March 16, 1978, G1. For the earlier acceptance of MCC by the Church Council, see Ray Ruppert, "Church Council Accepts Faction with Gay Membership," *Seattle Times,* June 11, 1975, A16.

18. Ray Ruppert, "Evangelical Group Takes Stand on Gay Rights," *Seattle Times,* March 30, 1978, A9.

19. Sam Sperry, "Meets Held on Scope of Probe," *Seattle Times,* Dec. 19, 1975, A6; David Suffia and Dee Norton, "Police Probe of Pitkin Disclosed," and "Many Files Politically Motivated, Says Hanson," *Seattle Times,* Dec. 23, 1975, A1; David Suffia and Dee Norton, "Tielsch Levels Blast at Hanson, 'Politics,'" *Seattle Times,* Dec. 24, 1975, A1; David Suffia and Dee Norton, "Bayley Favors U.S. Probe into Police Intelligence Files" and "Pitkin Disclosure Triggers Varied Reaction," *Seattle Times,* Dec. 25, 1975, A1, A17.

20. See, for example, "Police File on Black Leader Released," *Seattle Times,* Apr. 17, 1978, A14; Larry Brown, "Judge to Ban Transfer of Disputed Police Files," *Seattle Times,* June 5, 1978, A1; Larry Brown, "Officer Won't Be Held in Contempt," and "Police Misled Council on Intelligence Access, Says Anti-Spying Group," *Seattle Times,* June 7, 1978, C3.

21. For news reports on the John Rodney shooting, see, for example, "Fleeing Man Shot, Killed by Officer," *Seattle Post-Intelligencer,* Aug. 20, 1978, A1; "Stricter Firearms Policy Called For," and "Slain Man's Relatives Charge Police Cover-up," *Seattle Times,* Aug. 22, 1978, A14; "Demonstrators March on Police Headquarters" and "Mental Problems in Victim's Past," *Seattle Times,* Aug. 23, 1978, A10; "SPD and ERA" and John Carl, "Shot in the Back," *Seattle Gay News,* Sept. 1, 1978, 3; Jack Broom, "Inquest Opens into Police Shooting," *Seattle Times,* Sept. 7, 1978, A1; S. L. Sanger, "Police-shooting Inquest Stirs a Demonstration," *Seattle Post-Intelligencer,* Sept. 8, 1978, A1; Wendy Walker and Jack Broom, "Suspect Warned Four Times, Says Falk," *Seattle Times,* Sept. 8, 1978, C10; Jack Broom, "Four Say They Heard Shots, No Warning," *Seattle Times,* Sept. 9, 1978, A3; Jack Broom, "Jury Clears Officer in Shooting," *Seattle Times,* Sept. 10, 1978, A1.

22. Dave Birkland, "Officer Falk Taken Off Patrol Duty Indefinitely," *Seattle Times,* Sept. 12, 1978, A1. See also Wayne Jacobi, "Falk Won't Face Criminal Charges," *Seattle Post-Intelligencer,* Sept. 12, 1978, A1; Marcia Friedman, "Falk Is Removed from Street Duty," *Seattle Post-Intelligencer,* Sept. 13, 1978, A1; Ray Ruppert, "Church Council Calls for Inquiry of 'Morally Unacceptable' Shooting," *Seattle Times,* Sept. 14, 1978, B3; Ross Cunningham, "John Rodney, Larry Ward," *Seattle Times,* Sept. 15, 1978, A12.

23. "Poll Shows 66% Support, Says Gay-Rights Group," *Seattle Times,* Aug. 29, 1978,

A14; Erin Van Bronkhorst, "How 13 Can Win: Don't Mention It," *Seattle Sun,* Sept. 13, 1978, 6; CRFE records in the Charlie Brydon Papers, Washington State Historical Society Archives, Tacoma.

24. Robert Mayerson, "Angevine Defeat—An Omen?" and "SGN Agrees," *Seattle Gay News,* Sept. 29, 1978, 2, 3.

25. "SOME Changes Tactics to Gain Support," *Seattle Gay News,* Sept. 29, 1978, 7; Robert Mayerson, "Anti-Gay Campaign Leaders Revealed," *Seattle Sun,* Oct. 4, 1978, 1. See also a letter to the editor by Wayne Perryman, *Seattle Sun,* Oct. 24, 1978, 6.

26. "Teamsters Swat Initiative 13," *Seattle Sun,* Oct. 18, 1978, 3; "Editorial," *Seattle Gay News,* Oct. 27, 1978, 3; "Citizens to Retain Fair Employment Report," *Seattle Gay News,* Oct. 27, 1978, 9.

27. For financial figures, see Robert Mayerson articles, "This is It, Folks," *Seattle Gay News,* Oct. 27, 1978, 1; "We Won!" *Seattle Gay News,* Nov. 10, 1978, 1; and "Saving the Queen City's Honor," *Seattle Sun,* Nov. 15, 1978, 1.

28. Robert Mayerson, "Saving the Queen City's Honor," *Seattle Sun,* Nov. 15, 1978, 1.

29. For the post-election coverage, see Neil Modie, "Homosexuals Celebrate the Rejection of Initiative 13," *Seattle Post-Intelligencer,* Nov. 8, 1978, A4; Neil Modie, "Gays Gain Political Clout with Defeat of Initiative 13," *Seattle Post-Intelligencer,* Nov. 9, 1978, A16; Robert Mayerson, "We Won!" "Thank You, Seattle," and "Gay Rights Wins in California," *Seattle Gay News,* Nov. 10, 1978, 1, 2; Robert Mayerson, "Saving the Queen City's Honor," and Michelle Celarier, "Facing Fear in the Voting Booth," *Seattle Sun,* Nov. 15, 1978, 1, 5; Jeanne Cordova, "Gay Rights Victories—Enemies Can Be a Blessing," *Seattle Gay News,* Nov. 24, 1978, 9.

## 15 / ON BROADWAY

1. Katherine Grant-Bourne, "Espresso Yourself with Community Activist and Friend: Jan Denali," *Seattle Gay News,* March 18, 1988, 16. See also interview with Jan Denali by Karina Luboff, Northwest Lesbian and Gay History Museum Project, March 1998.

2. Samuel I. Doctors and A. S. Huff, *Minority Enterprise and the President's Council* (Cambridge, Mass.: Ballinger, 1973).

3. The difficulty for Seattle gay organizations in relying on federal funding is noted in Karen Frank, "Is the End of CETA the End of Gay Agencies," *Seattle Gay News,* June 5, 1981, 1, which points out that all four then-existent lesbian/gay agencies were in financial difficulties because of government cutbacks. The four were the Seattle Counseling Service, the Lesbian Resource Center, the Gay Community Center, and Stonewall's successor, the Chemical Dependency Program. GCC never did recover and folded in August 1981.

4. Ivan Light, "Ethnicity and Business Enterprise," in *Making It in America: The Role of Ethnicity in Business Enterprise, Education, and Work Choices,* ed. M. M. Stolarik and Murray Friedman (Lewisburg, Pa.: Bucknell University Press, 1986), especially 13ff.

5. See "The Homosexual Economy," *Economist,* Jan. 23, 1982, 71; Evelyn Iritani, "Gays Play Significant Role in Business, Leader Says," *Seattle Post-Intelligencer,* May 18, 1984, B6;

"The Surprising Health of Gay Businesses," *Advocate*, March 3, 1987, 43; David Jefferson, "Leaving the Corporate Closet," *Wall Street Journal*, Nov. 22, 1991, A8; Barbara Marsh, "More Gay Women Are Starting Own Businesses," *Wall Street Journal*, July 1, 1992, B2.

6. "QCBG Helps Index," *Seattle Gay News*, May 1976, 7; "QCBG Annual Picnic Succeeds in Sun," *Seattle Gay News*, Sept. 1977, 16.

7. Ed Estes, "Business Group Organizes," *Seattle Gay News*, May 8, 1981, 1; "Local Guide Released by GSBA," *Seattle Gay News*, Dec. 31, 1981, 4; Lynn Tilden, "GSBA Network of Vision," *Seattle Gay News*, Jan. 29, 1983, 25. See also "Capitol Hill Booms with Gay Business," *Seattle Gay News*, Feb. 15, 1980, 10.

8. Susan Phinney, "Broadway's for Shoppers," *Seattle Post-Intelligencer*, May 15, 1977, C1.

9. Robert Mayerson, "Regulars at Elite: There for Doreen," *Seattle Sun*, Apr. 28, 1976, 7.

10. For a sampling of the controversies and accomplishments in Broadway's redevelopment from the early 1970s to the early 1980s, see, for example, "Capitol Hill Residents Erect 'Public' Park on Site of Parking Lot," *Seattle Times*, July 20, 1970, B8; Stephen Dunphy, "Another Skirmish in City's Land-Use War," *Seattle Times*, Oct. 1, 1971, E7; "Architect Resketches QFC Plan," *Seattle Sun*, Sept. 11, 1974, 8; Bruce Olson, "Landowners Grab for Hill Power," *Seattle Sun*, Sept. 25, 1974, 1; Bruce Olson, "Activists Sweep Hill Elections," *Seattle Sun*, Oct. 2, 1974, 1; Brandt Morgan, "Sparring Between Community, Developers Changes Broadway," *Seattle Sun*, Jan. 8, 1975, 3; Patrick Douglas, "Booming Broadway," *Seattle Weekly*, July 20, 1977, 15; Lara Ringneth, "Henry's: Bigtime Comes to the Hill," *Seattle Weekly*, July 20, 1977, 18; Patrick McDonald, "Seattle's Broadway Has Plenty of Bright Lights," *Seattle Times, Tempo*, Nov. 7, 1980, 3; Jane Hadley, "City Denies Parking Lot for Safeway," *Seattle Post-Intelligencer*, July 26, 1981, E1; Don Duncan, "Jackhammers Tap Out Broadway Lullaby," *Seattle Times*, Sept. 22, 1981, C1; Susan Biskeborn, "So Long, Broadway," *Seattle Weekly*, Sept. 29, 1982, 6; Rae Tufts, "Broadway Parade Is Seattle's Version of Italian 'Passeggiata,'" *Seattle Times*, Nov. 20, 1983, D18; Norman Johnston, "Teamwork by Merchants, City and Planners Rebuilt Broadway," *Seattle Times*, Dec. 18, 1983, D20.

11. James Thayer, "Seattle's Lullaby of Broadway," *Seattle Times*, Nov. 23, 1980, F1.

12. Examples of the criticisms of Broadway's changes can be found in Jane Meyerding, "Lesbians and Welfare," *Out and About*, March 1978, 3; and Riotsong, "Good Morning, Fat Cats," *Out and About*, Apr. 1978, 3.

13. For information on Alex Veltri and his ownership of the Elite, see, for example, "New Places, New Faces," *Seattle Gay News*, Sept. 28, 1979, 12; "New Encore Won't Crowd Out Elite, Says Energetic Owner," *Seattle Gay News*, Aug. 15, 1986, 12; "Encore Restaurant Gets Mayor's Award," *Seattle Gay News*, Aug. 7, 1987, 6; "Elite Tavern Throws Party to Celebrate 9th Anniversary," *Seattle Gay News*, May 13, 1988, 1; Tom Flint, "Elite Tavern Celebrates History," *Seattle Gay News*, May 5, 1989, 12; "Alex Veltri Receives Small Business Award," *Seattle Gay News*, May 10, 1991, 1.

14. For information on Barbara Bailey, see "Community Activists Barbara Bailey and Michael Coy Share Some Insights," *Seattle Gay News*, Apr. 15, 1988, 14; and Carole Paulson, "Equal Treatment Helps Make Any Business Successful," *Greater Seattle Business Guide*, 1991–92, 18.

15. "Capitol Hill Booms with Gay Business," *Seattle Gay News*, Feb. 15, 1980, 10.

16. For two early overviews of the gay pride parade versus march controversy as it unfolded nationally, see Christopher Stone and David Brill, "Gay Pride: Circus, Serious?" *Advocate*, July 30, 1975, 17, and Vito Russo, "The Shift in Emphasis Deserves Scrutiny," *Seattle Gay News*, July 13, 1984, 8. Early reports on Seattle's gay pride march include "Seattle Pride Activities Late," *Advocate*, July 18, 1973, 6; Rick Anderson, "A Gay Celebration," *Seattle Post-Intelligencer*, June 25, 1975, A11; "Gay Pride Week '76," *Seattle Gay News*, June 1976, 4; John Deardurff, "Gay Pride Week—Success or Failure?" *Seattle Gay News*, July 1976, 7; "March for Our Civil Rights," *Seattle Gay News*, June 1977, 1; Karen West, "Gays Plan Rights March," *Seattle Post-Intelligencer*, June 23, 1977, B4; "Parade to Begin Gay Pride Week," *Seattle Times*, June 23, 1977, B7; "Church Will Oppose Gay Pride Week," *Seattle Times*, June 24, 1977, A11; Ross Anderson, "Public Not Too Proud of Gay Pride Week," *Seattle Times*, June 23, 1977, A9; "Gays Rally for Their Rights," *Seattle Times*, June 26, 1977, A14; Dan Seligman, "2,000 Join Seattle Gay Rights March," *Seattle Post-Intelligencer*, June 26, 1977, A3; "Gay Pride March a Success!" *Seattle Gay News*, July/Aug. 1977, 1.

17. For coverage of the 1980 event, see Bruce Stores, "Lesbian-Gay Pride 1980," *Seattle Gay News*, June 20, 1980, 1; "Gay Politics: Left or Right?," Dave Haining, "'Celebration' or Harangue?," and "Celebration: We Are Everywhere," all in *Seattle Gay News*, July 3, 1980, 2, 3; "'Sticks and Stones' Bruise Gay Movement," *Seattle Gay News*, Aug. 1, 1980, 2; Karen Frank, "Rally Full of Lost Opportunities," and "Open Letter Calls for Reassessment," *Seattle Gay News*, Aug. 15, 1980, 2; "Editorial," *Seattle Gay News*, Nov. 20, 1980, 2; and a letter announcing that Dorian would not repeat its organization of the march, *Seattle Gay News*, Apr. 24, 1981, 2.

18. For the 1981 gay pride event, see "March Planned by Stonewall '81 Committee," *Seattle Gay News*, June 19, 1981, 2; Karen Frank, "Marching: Sheer Pleasure!" and L. Mas Makei, "March Needs Freedom of Expression," *Seattle Gay News*, July 3, 1981, 2; Tony Lind, "Mercedes Benz—The Truth," *Seattle Gay News*, July 17, 1981, 16.

19. For the conflict over the GSBA's takeover of the gay pride event, see Robin Evans, "Lesbian/Gay Pride Week Plans Spark Praise and Dispute at Meeting," *Seattle Gay News*, March 12, 1982, 1; Sue Docekal, "Parade or March?" *Seattle Gay News*, March 26, 1982, 4; "Militant Coalition Is Planned for Parade," *Seattle Gay News*, Apr. 23, 1982, 3; Robin Evans, "Pride Week Plans Include Parade, Dance, Seminar," *Seattle Gay News*, May 7, 1982, 3; "Pride Week—82," *Seattle Gay News*, June 18, 1982, 1; and Robin Evans, "Good Spirits Reign at Parade," *Seattle Gay News*, July 2, 1982, 1.

20. See, for example, Caitlin Sullivan, "FDC Adopts Human Rights Theme for Parade/March," *Seattle Gay News*, Apr. 12, 1985, 1; Katherine Grant-Bourne, "Mass Unified Parade/March Planned for June 30th," *Seattle Gay News*, May 31, 1985, 6; "Record Turnout Shows Strength Through Unity and Pride," *Seattle Gay News*, July 5, 1985, 1; Tom Flint, "Town Meeting Struggles over New Pride March Name," *Seattle Gay News*, Apr. 24, 1992, 1; and various letters to the editor commenting on the name change, *Seattle Gay News*, Apr. 3, 10, 17, and 24, 1992, 4, and May 1, 1992, 4.

21. Early *Seattle Gay News* stories that help track the steady expansion of the Pride

Foundation include the following articles by Chris Dziewiontkoski: "Pride Foundation Prepares for First Fundraising Cycle," June 12, 1987, 13, "Pride Foundation Announces $2,500 to 8 Organizations," June 26, 1987, 8, "Two Large Bequests Benefit Pride Foundation," and "Jerry Giesert Leaves His Estate to the Pride Foundation," March 18, 1988, 10; the following by Shani Dirzhud-Rashid: "Interview with Danette Leonhardi, President of Pride Foundation," July 8, 1988, 7, and "Sign Up Now for Your Payroll Charity Deductions," Nov. 4, 1988, 8; the following by Casey Hannan: "Pride Foundation Announces Grants," Apr. 28, 1989, 1, "Pride Foundation Announces Grants and Awards," Sept. 8, 1989, 1, and "Pride Foundation Receives Grants from National Sources," Jan. 12, 1990, 10; Matt Nagle, "Flash Your Plastic with Pride," May 11, 1990, 1; George Bakan, "Flash Your Mastercard with the Pride Foundation," Dec. 7, 1990, 1.

22. Daryl Strickland, "Marketing in the Gay Community," *Seattle Times,* June 27, 1991, B1.

23. Manuel Castells, *The City and the Grassroots: A Cross-Cultural Theory of Urban Social Movements* (Berkeley: University of California Press, 1983), especially 162–63.

### 16 / ON CATHOLIC HILL

1. The 1978 *Northwest Progress* series contained these articles: "Homosexuality: Church Actions Mixed," and Tom Miller and Barb Collins, "Dignity's Goal Is Church Acceptance," March 3, 1978, 12; Barb Collins and Tom Miller, "Counseling the Homosexual," "Dignity Members Talk about Themselves, Their Church," and "Homosexual Teacher Chose Celibate Life," March 10, 1978, 12; and Lawrence Reilly, "Homosexuality: A Theologian's View," and "Fathers Brown, Reilly Discuss Series Issues," March 17, 1978, 8. In addition, letters to the editor commenting on the series were published March 17, 1978, 5; and March 24, 1978, 5.

2. "Dignity: A Point of Concern," *Northwest Progress,* Nov. 10, 1978, 4. See also letters to the editor the following week, Nov. 17, 1978, 5.

3. For the history of Catholics in Seattle, see particularly Wilfred P. Schoenberg, S.J., *A History of the Catholic Church in the Pacific Northwest, 1743–1983* (Washington, D.C.: The Pastoral Press, 1987), and John McCorkle, "Saga of a Century," *Northwest Progress,* Sept. 8, 1950, 9.

4. Schoenberg, *A History of the Catholic Church in the Pacific Northwest,* discusses what he calls Bishop O'Dea's "dreams of grandeur" at 420–21 and 447–49.

5. "History in Headlines—The Progress Years," *Northwest Progress,* Sept. 8, 1950, 25.

6. For Archbishop Connolly, including his open housing stance, see, for example, Robert Heilman, "'Tac' Connolly—The Slender Athlete Who Became Archbishop," *Seattle Times,* Feb. 14, 1960, 5; "Ignorance and Fear—Not Bigotry and Prejudice" and "Archbishop Calls for Total Commitment on Racial Justice," *Northwest Progress,* March 6, 1964, A1, B1; James Gandrau, "Worth Raising," from the *Program for the Silver Episcopal Jubilee of The Most. Rev. Thomas Connolly,* Aug. 26, 1964, 3; Ray Ruppert, "Archbishop Connolly Marks 20th Year of Changing Seattle," *Seattle Times,* Apr. 27, 1968, 2; Ray Ruppert, "A Rare Interview with the 'First Among Equals,'" *Seattle Times,* Jan. 19, 1975, B1; Ray Ruppert, "The

Connolly Years—An Assessment," *Seattle Times Magazine,* May 18, 1975, 8; Robert Heilman, "'Tac'—The Private Thomas A. Connolly," *Seattle Times Magazine,* May 18, 1975, 10; Bill Dodds, "Leader in the Northwest for 30 Years," *Northwest Progress,* Jan. 12, 1979, 8; Carol Ostrom, "Bishop Connolly Dies; Led Church for 25 Years," *Seattle Times,* Apr. 19, 1991, 1.

7. See "Minutes of the Western Regional Conference of Homophile Organizations, Dec. 1–3, 1967," copy in the Tim Mayhew Papers, Special Collections, University of Washington Libraries. See also William Beardemphl, "Seattle Hosts Western Regional Conference," *Vector,* Jan. 1968, 13.

8. Bob Hinz, "Homosexuality a Sickness, Not a Sin, Say Ministers," *University of Washington Daily,* Apr. 26, 1967, 8. For the Reverend Katagiri's encouragement by Reverend Toomey, see Ray Ruppert, "Rev. Katagiri Quietly Treats City Sore Spots," *Seattle Times,* May 28, 1969, 33.

9. Interview with Doug Wyman by the author and David Doss, Seattle University Community and Communication Project, Nov. 1994.

10. Walt Crowley, *Seattle University: A Century of Jesuit Education* (Seattle: Seattle University, 1991), especially chapter 9.

11. Michael Bucher, "Panel Considers Homosexuality," *Seattle University Spectator,* May 25, 1966, 2.

12. For coverage of William DuBay's visit in the *Seattle University Spectator,* see Richard Houser, "Defrocked Priest to Speak on S.U. Campus Thursday," Oct. 12, 1966, 1; Emmett Lane, "'Management' Slows Progress in Church" and "President's Statement," Oct. 14, 1966, 1, 8.

13. Personal communication from Christine Taylor, archivist, Archdiocese of Seattle, Apr. 14, 1993.

14. The "Declaration on Certain Questions Concerning Sexual Ethics" is discussed in Lawrence Reilly, "Homosexuality: A Theologian's View," *Northwest Progress,* March 17, 1978, 8.

15. Gary Atkins, "The Bishop and the Bomb," *Seattle Times Pacific Magazine,* June 20, 1982, 6. For additional background on Hunthausen, see, for example, Ray Ruppert, "New Archbishop Is Offspring of Vatican II," *Seattle Times,* May 18, 1975, A16; Jerry Dooley, "A Man for this Season," *Northwest Progress,* June 9, 1983, 9; Cynthia Wilson and Rebecca Boren, "The Peace Bishop," in *Washingtonians: A Biographical Portrait of the State,* ed. David Brewster and David Buerge (Seattle: Sasquatch Books: 1989), 469.

16. "Archbishop's Statement," *Northwest Progress,* July 1, 1977, 5.

17. Ibid.; letters to the editor, *Northwest Progress,* July 8, 15, 1977, 5.

18. Lawrence Reilly, "Homosexuality: A Theologian's View," *Northwest Progress,* March 17, 1978, 8.

19. Barb Collins and Tom Miller, "Counseling the Homosexual," *Northwest Progress,* March 10, 1978, 12.

20. "The Prejudice against Homosexuals and the Ministry of the Church," *Northwest Progress,* June 16, 1983, 10. See also "Hearing on Discrimination against Homosexuals,"

*Northwest Progress*, March 10, 1983, 5; Jerry Filteau, "Church View of Homosexuals Highlighted," *Northwest Progress*, June 9, 1983, 2.

21. "Hunthausen at Dorian," *Seattle Gay News*, July 1, 1983, 3.

22. Author's interview with Raymond Hunthausen, May 1982.

23. "Archbishop Addresses Issue of Homosexuality," *Northwest Progress*, Sept. 1, 1983, 6.

24. Bill Dodds, "Dignity Convenes Amid Protest, Welcome," *Northwest Progress*, Sept. 8, 1983, 6. See also, in the same issue, James Eblen, "Homosexuality and the Old Testament," 7, and Peter Chirico, "The Archbishop's Reception of Dignity," 12. Eblen, a church theologian, also wrote on "Homosexuality and the New Testament" on Sept. 15, 1983, 6.

25. For initial reports on the investigation, see, for example, Carol Ostrom, "Vatican to Investigate Archbishop Hunthausen," *Seattle Times*, Oct. 27, 1983, A1; "A Letter from Archbishop Hunthausen," *Northwest Progress*, Oct. 27, 1983, 5; Carol Ostrom, "Vatican Official: Visit Aimed at Fact-finding," *Seattle Times*, Oct. 29, 1983, A8; Carol Ostrom, "Local Groups Reaffirm Support for Hunthausen's Social Views," *Seattle Times*, Nov. 2, 1983, G2; "Vatican Investigation Begins This Week," Erich Michels, "Archdiocesan Leaders React to Investigation," and Mary Ann Walsh, "Vatican Official Discusses Visitation Process," *Northwest Progress*, Nov. 3, 1983, 9, 10, 12; Carol Ostrom, "Vatican Representative Holds Court with Friends, Foes of Hunthausen," and Carol Ostrom, "Is Probe a Blessing in Disguise?" *Seattle Times*, Nov. 5, 1983, A9, A13; John McCoy, "A Top Critic of Hunthausen Tells What He Told the Vatican's Man," *Seattle Post-Intelligencer*, Nov. 8, 1983, A12; Bill Dodds, "Archbishop Hickey Concludes Visit, 'Gains Insight into Range of Viewpoints,'" *Northwest Progress*, Nov. 10, 1983, 9.

26. For reports on Pio Laghi's letter, see Carol Ostrom, "Vatican Report Praises, Cautions Archbishop; Calls Critics Strident," *Seattle Times*, Nov. 27, 1985, A1; "Vatican Finds Scant Basis for Criticism of Bishop," *Washington Post*, Nov. 28, 1985, A8. For a profile of Cardinal Ratzinger and his role in disciplining Hunthausen, see Russell Chandler, "Ratzinger: Point Man for Vatican," *Los Angeles Times*, Nov. 7, 1986, A1.

27. The text of Cardinal Ratzinger's letter was released by the Vatican two years later. See "Vatican Releases Cardinal Ratzinger Letter," *Northwest Progress*, May 28, 1987, 5.

28. Carol Ostrom, "New Auxiliary Bishop Called 'Rock-Hard Orthodox Priest,'" *Seattle Times*, Dec. 4, 1985, B1; Carol Ostrom, "New Auxiliary Archbishop Makes a Deft Press Debut," *Seattle Times*, Feb. 1, 1986, A6.

29. The miter is mentioned in Ann Rodgers-Melnick, "The Bishop Moves Ahead Self-Disciplined, Driven and Ascetic," *Pittsburgh Post-Gazette*, March 24, 1996, A1.

30. Mary Rothschild, "Bishop in a Bind: Complaints Greet Wuerl's Every Act," *Seattle Post-Intelligencer*, Apr. 30, 1987, A1.

31. See, for example, Russell Chandler, "Seattle Archbishop Stripped of Authority," *Los Angeles Times*, Sept. 5, 1986, A13; Marjorie Hyer, "Vatican Clips Wings of Seattle Bishop," *Washington Post*, Sept. 6, 1986, A3; Carol Ostrom, "Restore Hunthausen's Power, Priests Ask," *Seattle Times*, Sept. 13, 1986, A10; Carol Ostrom, "Archbishop to Be Forced Out, Says Writer," *Seattle Times*, Sept. 13, 1966, A10; Marjorie Hyer, "The Vatican and Dissent:

Crackdown in America Increasingly Evident," *Washington Post,* Sept. 15, 1986, A1; Carol Ostrom, "Rome Says It's Punishing Hunthausen," *Seattle Times,* Sept. 17, 1986, B1; Marjorie Hyer, "Vatican Defends Prelate's Punishment," *Washington Post,* Oct. 28, 1986, A3; Carol Ostrom, "Vatican Letter Criticizes Hunthausen," *Seattle Times,* Oct. 28, 1986, B1. For a feature on Hunthausen's local critics, see Joe Mooney, "Chill Breeze Buffets Archbishop and Catholic Church," *Seattle Post-Intelligencer,* Oct. 12, 1986, F1.

32. For reports on the Ratzinger Halloween letter, see, for example, Don Schanche, "Vatican Warning Seen against Liberal Sexuality," *Los Angeles Times,* Oct. 31, 1986, A10; Russell Chandler, "Ratzinger: Point Man for the Vatican," *Los Angeles Times,* Nov. 7, 1986, A1.

33. Carol Ostrom, "Pope's Letter to Bishops: A Truce or a Warning?" *Seattle Times,* Nov. 11, 1986, A1; "U.S. Bishops Back Vatican Curbing of Liberal Prelate but Allow Him to Give His Views," Russell Chandler, "Bishops Hear from Disciplined Seattle Prelate," and Bill McAllister, "'Peace Bishop' Is Outspoken Liberal," *Los Angeles Times,* Nov. 12, 1986, A1, A3; Carol Ostrom, "Hunthausen Offers to Step Down," *Seattle Times,* Nov. 12, 1986, A1. The text of Hunthausen's statement to the bishops was published in the *Seattle Post-Intelligencer,* Nov, 13, 1986, A4.

34. For analyses of the bishops' conference, see Russell Chandler, "Bishops Avoid Dispute, Cite Allegiance to Pope," *Los Angeles Times,* Nov. 13, 1986, A1; Marcia Friedman, "Hunthausen Backers Here Disappointed," *Seattle Post-Intelligencer,* Nov. 13, 1986, A5; "Vatican May Be Wrongly Assessing Bishops' Stance," *Seattle Times,* Nov. 14, 1986, E1; Mark Stein, "Hunthausen Gets a Warm Welcome, Future Uncertain," *Los Angeles Times,* Nov. 15, 1986, A1; Carol Ostrom, "Many Catholics Find They're a Long Way from Rome," *Seattle Times,* Nov. 16, 1986, A12.

35. See Joseph Berger, "Vatican and Seattle: A New View," republished in the *Seattle Times,* Jan. 30, 1987, A1; Marjorie Hyer, "Seattle Archdiocese Copes with Turmoil," *Washington Post,* Feb. 2, 1987, A4; "Pronuncio Says U.S. Catholics Want Candor, Vatican Prefers Privacy," *Northwest Progress,* Feb. 5, 1987, 2; "Disciplining of U.S. Bishop to Be Reviewed," *Los Angeles Times,* Feb. 10, 1987, A4; "Vatican Forms Commission to Review Seattle Situation," *Northwest Progress,* Feb. 12, 1987, 2.

36. "Bishop Wuerl Meets with Pope at Vatican," *Northwest Progress,* Feb. 19, 1987, 5; Marjorie Hyer, "Seattle Archdiocese Copes with Turmoil, *Washington Post,* Feb. 2, 1987, A4.

37. "Vatican's Special Commission Meets with Local Catholic Leaders," *Northwest Progress,* March 12, 1987, 3; Carol Ostrom, "Is the Vatican Forcing Hunthausen to Resign?" *Seattle Times,* Apr. 15, 1967, A1; Carol Ostrom, "Plan to Remove Hunthausen Is Denied," *Seattle Times,* Apr. 16, 1987, C2. The *National Catholic Register* report, which the archdiocese denied, was published April 19, 1987, and is mentioned in Ostrom, "Plan to Remove Hunthausen Is Denied."

38. Mary Rothschild, "Mass by Gays Is Canceled," *Seattle Post-Intelligencer,* Apr. 23, 1987, A1; Mary Rothschild, "Wuerl Denies He Ruled Out Gay Masses," *Seattle Post-Intelligencer,* Apr. 24, 1987, A1.

39. Carol Ostrom, "Last Act of Hunthausen 'Play' Remains Unwritten," *Seattle Times,* Apr. 26, 1987, B1.

40. Ann Rodgers-Melnick, "The Bishop Moves Ahead Self-Disciplined, Driven and Ascetic," *Pittsburgh Post-Gazette,* March 24, 1996, A1.

41. For reports on the restoration of Hunthausen's powers, see, for example, Mary Rothschild, "Hunthausen Gets Back His Powers," *Seattle Post-Intelligencer,* May 27, 1987, A1; Carol Ostrom, "Hunthausen Welcomes 'A Friend,'" *Seattle Times,* May 28, 1987, C1; Mary Rothschild, "A Return to Total Control," and David Anderson, "American Bishops Pull Off a Victory Ever So Politely," *Seattle Post-Intelligencer,* May 29, 1987, A1, A4; Caroline Young, "'Happy' Murphy Piled with Praise," *Seattle Post-Intelligencer,* May 28, 1987, A5; Cindy Wooden, "Vatican Restores Archbishop's Faculties," *Northwest Progress,* May 28, 1987, 1; Carol Ostrom, "Coadjutor's Good Humor Allays Catholics' Concerns," *Seattle Times,* May 30, 1987, A10. For the text of the commission's report, see *Northwest Progress,* May 28, 1987, 3.

Ironically, after he was appointed bishop of Pittsburgh, Wuerl had his own run-in with the Vatican over two issues: meeting with married priests and removing a priest for alleged child molestation. When he was ordered to reinstate the man, Wuerl refused. The Vatican eventually backed down. Intriguingly, Wuerl also allowed the Pittsburgh chapter of Dignity to continue to meet informally on church property until 1996, almost eight years longer than Hunthausen would. Wuerl tried to convince the members to renounce their stance against celibacy and, since they would not, permitted use of church property by Courage, a rival gay Catholic organization that promoted celibacy. For additional information on Wuerl after he left Seattle, see, for example, Marjorie Hyer, "Wuerl to Be New Pittsburgh Bishop," *Washington Post,* Feb. 13, 1988, D18; Pat Bartos, "Bishop Wuerl Installed in Pittsburgh," *Northwest Progress,* March 31, 1988, 21; and the following articles by Ann Rodgers-Melnick in the *Pittsburgh Post-Gazette:* "Vatican Clears Priest, Wuerl Rejects Verdict," March 21, 1993, A1; "Diocese Pushes Gay Chastity," Nov. 1, 1993, B1; "Diocese to Gays: No More Masses," Jan. 30, 1996, D1; "Ousted Gays to Maintain Catholic Pursuit," Jan. 31, 1996, B3; "The Bishop Moves Ahead: Self-Disciplined, Driven and Ascetic," March 24, 1996, A1; and "Speculation about Bishop's Next Move," March 24, 1996, A15.

42. For the text of the Ratzinger letter, see *Northwest Progress,* May 28, 1987, 5.

43. "Chicago Archdiocese Assumes Sponsorship of Weekly Dignity Mass," *Northwest Progress,* May 26, 1988, 2.

44. For Dignity's expulsion from St. Joseph's, see Carol Ostrom, "Church Taking Over Gay Mass," *Seattle Times,* June 30, 1988, C1; Carol Ostrom, "Church Says It Won't Greatly Alter Gay Mass," *Seattle Times,* July 1, 1988, E2; Jim MacKellar, "Dignity Seattle to Hold Exodus Mass Sunday," *Seattle Gay News,* July 8, 1988, 1; Larry Werner, "Dignity's Last Mass for Gays and Lesbians Is in 'Spirit of Unity,'" *Seattle Post-Intelligencer,* July 11, 1988, B1; Cathy Gruilkshank, "Dignity Has Let Down Lesbian/Gay Catholics by Cooperating," *Seattle Gay News,* July 15, 1988, 5; Jim Mackeller, "Dignity Holds Final Mass at St. Joe's, Pledges to Continue Ministry," *Seattle Gay News,* July 15, 1988, 11; Seattle Dignity's *Weekly Bulletin,* July 19, 1988.

45. For Hunthausen's appearance, see Tom Flint, "Archbishop Addresses Dignity on Catholic Ministry," *Seattle Gay News,* Aug. 5, 1988, 1.

1. Statistics on AIDS in Seattle come from the *Quarterly Reports* and *Annual Reports* of the Seattle–King County Public Health Department. For Arno Motulsky's work, see: Lawrence Altman, "Study of H.I.V. Family Tree Pushes Back Origins," *New York Times,* Feb. 4, 1998, A16; Lawrence Altman, "AIDS Virus Originated around 1930," *New York Times,* Feb. 2, 2000, A15; and "How AIDS, Once Benign, Evolved into a Menace," *Seattle Post-Intelligencer,* June 9, 2000, A1.

2. See, for example, the following articles in the *Seattle Gay News:* Ed Estes, "Rapes in the Streets, Police in the Bushes," and "New Steam Bath Opening in Seattle," June 5, 1981, 2, 5; Larry Bush, "NGTF Reorganizes, Brydon Resigns," June 12, 1981, 3.

3. Lawrence Altman, "Rare Cancer Seen in 41 Homosexuals," *New York Times,* July 3, 1981, A1; advertisement for "Steam" and untitled article on the Seattle Gay Clinic, *Seattle Gay News,* Aug. 28, 1981, 5, 8.

4. "Cause of 'Gay Cancer' Unclear," and "Scared Celibate," *Seattle Gay News,* Jan. 1, 1982, 1.

5. Warren King, "Deadly Disease That Mainly Affects Gay Men Surfaces in Seattle," *Seattle Times,* Nov. 12, 1982, A1; John Hessburg, "Only One Local Case of Gays' Disease Found," *Seattle Post-Intelligencer,* Nov. 13, 1982, C1.

6. Robin Evans, "AIDS Case Is Diagnosed in Seattle," *Seattle Gay News,* Nov. 19, 1982, 1.

7. Anonymous author, "A Healing Journey: One Man's Response to AIDS," *Seattle Gay News,* Nov. 19, 1982, 3.

8. Kerry Webster, "Mystery Gay Disease Fells Second Victim," *Seattle Post-Intelligencer,* Feb. 1, 1983, A1.

9. Warren King, "Deadly 'Gay Disease' Found In Heterosexual Seattle Man," *Seattle Times,* Feb. 3, 1983, A1; "Third AIDS Case Is Not a Gay Man," *Seattle Post-Intelligencer,* Feb. 4, 1983, A4.

10. For reports in April, see Warren King, "Tacoman Is First State AIDS Fatality," *Seattle Times,* Apr. 15, 1983, B1; John Hessburg, "Tacoma Man Is First State Resident to Die from AIDS," *Seattle Post-Intelligencer,* Apr. 16, 1983, A5; Warren King, "Rapid Increase of AIDS Reported in Seattle-Tacoma Area," *Seattle Times,* Apr. 19, 1983, A9; "AIDS Kills Three in Seattle Area in Three Months," *Seattle Post-Intelligencer,* Apr. 20, 1983, A3; "Mystery Disease Takes 4th Victim," *Seattle Times,* Apr. 23, 1983, A12; "4th State Man Dies of AIDS," *Seattle Post-Intelligencer,* Apr. 23, 1983, C1.

11. Information on Bobbi Campbell comes from George Bakan, untitled article, *Seattle Gay News,* Aug. 5, 1983, 1; Suzanne Harris, "AIDS Patients Need Not Live in Bubble," *Seattle Times,* Aug. 7, 1983, D3; "Gay America: Sex, Politics and the Impact of AIDS," *Newsweek,* Aug. 8, 1983, 30; Randy Shilts, *And the Band Played On* (New York: St. Martin's, 1987), especially 107–8, 123, 171–73, 200, 215; Michael Callen and Dan Turner, "A History of the People With AIDS Self-Empowerment Movement," *Body Positive,* Dec. 1997, http://www.the body.com/bp/dec97/hist.html; and an interview with Tom Richards by Charlie Fuchs and Larry Knopp of the Northwest Lesbian and Gay History Museum Project, July 2000.

12. Ron Endersby, "Fifth Seattle Death," and "In Memoriam," *Seattle Gay News*, Aug. 19, 1983, 1, 2; Don Tewkesbury, "AIDS Suspected in Death of Capitol Hill Man," *Seattle Post-Intelligencer*, Aug. 20, 1983, C1; Warren King, "Sixth Washington State Man Dies of Complications from AIDS," *Seattle Times*, Aug. 20, 1983, A6.

13. Carey Quan Gelernter et al., "The AIDS Quilt: Stitches in Time," *Seattle Times*, July 17, 1988, K1.

14. Letter from John Aaron, *Seattle Gay News*, Oct. 14, 1983, 2.

15. Jack Anderson, "To Stop the Panic Is the First Step to Deal with AIDS," *Seattle Gay News*, Dec. 3, 1982, 5.

16. Richards interview, Northwest Lesbian and Gay History Museum Project, July 2000.

17. Warren King, "Gay Community 'Galvanized' against Threat of AIDS," *Seattle Times*, May 25, 1983, D1.

18. Orv Johnson, "The Baths—A Sexual Playground?" *Seattle Gay News*, Jan. 20, 1978, 16.

19. T.T. Roth, "The Love of Comrades at the Baths," *Seattle Gay News*, Nov. 21, 1986, 16.

20. Patrick Douglas, "Sin, Seattle Style," *Seattle*, Aug. 1967, 27.

21. Joel Vincent, "Reader Spotlights Seattle Bathhouses," *Seattle Gay News*, May 3, 1985, 12. See also Aubrey Sparks, "My Night at the Baths," *Seattle Gay News*, Apr. 19, 1985, 24.

22. Elizabeth Rhodes, "Seattle's Gay Community Deals with Threat of AIDS," *Seattle Times*, Apr. 26, 1983, D1.

23. Rita Hibbard, "Gay Baths: The Debate in Seattle," *Seattle Post-Intelligencer*, Nov. 14, 1985, A1. For the letter from James Brown and other staff members of the Zodiac, see *Seattle Gay News*, July 22, 1983, 2, and Aug. 5, 1983, 2. The controversy arose again in January 1985, when the Zodiac published an advertising photo of a naked man crawling into a television set with the caption, "Sometimes Magic Is the Only Thing That Is Real." See *Seattle Gay News*, Jan. 4, 1985, 17; Jan. 11, 1985, 2; and Jan. 18, 1985, 2.

24. Interview with Larry Woelich by Larry Knopp and Pat Freeman of the Northwest Lesbian and Gay History Museum Project, January 2001.

25. Steve Foiles, "Health Dept. and Bath Owners Meet," *Seattle Gay News*, May 4, 1984, 1. Information on the San Francisco debate can be found in Randy Shilts, *And the Band Played On* (New York: St. Martin's, 1987) 153–55, 259–60, 315–18, 430–99; as well as "Silverman Resigns," and "San Francisco Demands List of Bathhouse Customers," *Seattle Gay News*, Dec. 21, 1984, 1, 8; and Michael Helquist, "S.F. Bathhouses: Silverman to Get Last Word," *Seattle Gay News*, Dec. 28, 1984, 1.

26. "Cooperation the Key in Health/Bath Meeting," *Seattle Gay News*, June 1, 1984, 1.

27. For later developments, see Caitlin Sullivan, "AIDS Hysteria: House Votes to Close Down Public Bathhouses," *Seattle Gay News*, Oct. 4, 1985, 1; Keith Hughes, "Bar Owners Meet to Discuss Bath House Vote and Safe Sex," *Seattle Gay News*, Oct. 11, 1985, 1; "Editorial: Bathhouse Closure Not Answer," *Seattle Gay News*, Nov. 8, 1985, 3; Alan Reade, "Everybody's Talking about the New Seattle Bathhouse Policy," *Seattle Gay News*, Jan. 29, 1988, 8.

28. For information on Carl Orme, see Katherine Grant-Bourne, "Carl Orme to

Represent Seattle in D.C. for Day of Accounting," *Seattle Gay News,* Sept. 13, 1985, 1; Caitlin Sullivan, "Orme, First Seattle PWA to Go to Washington D.C. to Lobby Congress," *Seattle Gay News,* Nov. 1, 1985, 1; Carl Orme, "Carl Orme Reflects on AIDS," *Seattle Gay News,* Apr. 11, 1986, 20; Katherine Grant-Bourne, "Carl Orme, Beloved Member of the Family," *Seattle Gay News,* Oct. 3, 1986, 8; untitled obituary for James Finley, *Seattle Gay News,* Oct. 2, 1987, 4; Carey Quan Gelernter et al., "The AIDS Quilt: Stitches in Time," *Seattle Times,* July 17, 1988, K1.

29. Warren King, "Unverified List of AIDS Sufferers Reported Circulating among Police," *Seattle Times,* Sept. 27, 1983, A1; George Foster, "Mysterious AIDS List Appears in Police Cars," *Seattle Post-Intelligencer,* Sept. 28, 1983, D1; Warren King, "'AIDS Alert' List Sparks Demand for Apology from Police Chief," *Seattle Times,* Sept. 28, 1983, A1; "Medical Workers May Have Drawn up AIDS Victim List," *Seattle Post-Intelligencer,* Sept. 29, 1983, A11; "Harborview Has Same List of Purported AIDS Victims As Police," *Seattle Post-Intelligencer,* Sept. 30, 1983, A5.

30. Warren King, "Gay Men Warned on AIDS Danger," *Seattle Times,* Jan. 13, 1985, A1; Warren King, "Test Shows Many Exposed to AIDS," *Seattle Times,* Feb. 27, 1985, D2. See also George Bakan, "New AIDS Infection Data Prompt Guideline Discussion," Michael Helquist, "Condoms Block AIDS?" and "Healthy Sex" advertisement, *Seattle Gay News,* Jan. 4, 1985, 1, 8, 13; Warren King, "AIDS/Health Experts Gathering to Discuss Deadly Virus," *Seattle Times,* Jan. 11, 1985, B1; George Bakan, "AIDS Virus Infection 35% in Seattle Gays," *Seattle Gay News,* Jan. 11, 1985, 1.

31. For the plumbing incident, see Warren King, "AIDS Support Group Says Firm Is Biased," *Seattle Times,* Apr. 6, 1987, B1; Chuck Morris, "Plumbing Company Refuses Service Call to Northwest AIDS Foundation," *Seattle Gay News,* Apr. 10, 1987, 1. For the bath-house incident, see Keith Hughes, "Bathhouse Owner Files Complaint with State Human Rights Commission," *Seattle Gay News,* Nov. 22, 1985, 5; "Female Wrestler, Gay Bath Owner Get Settlements from Human Rights Commission," *Seattle Gay News,* June 27, 1986, 6. For the disco comment, see Warren King, "Fear of AIDS Creates On-the-Job Troubles," *Seattle Times,* Aug. 22, 1985, A1.

32. Warren King, "Landlords Closed Doors to AIDS Program," *Seattle Times,* June 19, 1986, A1.

33. Warren King, "Doctors Asked to Treat More AIDS Patients," *Seattle Times,* March 20, 1986, D1; Warren King, "Doctors Respond to Appeal on AIDS," *Seattle Times,* May 7, 1987, E3; Warren King, "Wanted: More Doctors For AIDS Patients," *Seattle Times,* Sept. 18, 1987, E1.

34. Among the stories about AIDS fears published after Rock Hudson's announcement are Pete McConnell, "Backlash Hurts Even the Gays Who Are Healthy," *Seattle Post-Intelligencer,* Aug. 23, 1985, A1; Warren King, "Fear of AIDS Creates On-the-Job Troubles," *Seattle Times,* Aug. 22, 1985, A1; Katherine Grant-Bourne, "AIDS Fear Causes Loss of Jobs for Local Folk," *Seattle Gay News,* Aug. 23, 1985, 1; Warren King, "AIDS Facts: Deadly Disease Isn't Spread by Casual Contact," *Seattle Times,* Sept. 3, 1985, D1; Paul Andrews, "An Epidemic of Fear," *Seattle Times,* Sept. 19, 1985, F1.

35. For coverage of Jim Wright's call for a quarantine, see, for example, Mike Merritt, "Wright Favors AIDS Quarantine," originally published in the *Bellevue Journal-American,* republished in *Seattle Gay News,* Sept. 6, 1985, 1; Walter Hatch, "AIDS Infects Political Field: Gay Rights under Fire," *Seattle Times,* Sept. 9, 1985, B1; Doug Underwood, "County Executive Candidate Wants Food Workers Tested for AIDS," *Seattle Times,* Sept. 12, 1985, B7; Caitlin Sullivan, "Wright Comes under Fire for AIDS Quarantine Campaign," *Seattle Gay News,* Sept. 13, 1985, 1; Warren King, "Health Officials Stress Limits of AIDS Danger," *Seattle Times,* Sept. 20, 1985, D2; Caitlin Sullivan, "Gay/Lesbian Seattle Meet the Press on Jim Wright Quarantine Issue," and Katherine Grant-Bourne, "How Gay/Lesbian Seattle Swayed This Year's Low-Turnout Primary," *Seattle Gay News,* Sept. 20, 1985, 1, 4; Sylvia Nogaki, "Jim Wright: Where Now?" *Seattle Times,* Oct. 3, 1985, E1.

36. Walter Hatch, "AIDS Infects Political Field: Gay Rights under Fire," *Seattle Times,* Sept. 9, 1985, B1.

37. For information on Richard Hennigh, see "Recognition Past Due for Fan Dancers," *Seattle Gay News,* Dec. 14, 1984, 17; "Mr. Leather of Washington: His Involvement with AIDS," *Seattle Gay News,* Sept. 27, 1985, 1; Keith Hughes, "400 People Turn Out for Richard Hennigh Benefit at Sparks," *Seattle Gay News,* Oct. 11, 1985, 1; Chuck Harbaugh and Marc Sauer, "Richard Hennigh," *Seattle Gay News,* Apr. 24, 1987, 1.

38. For examples of how the transmission of AIDS was described, see Warren King, "Tacoman Is First State AIDS Fatality," *Seattle Times,* Apr. 15, 1983, B1; John Hessburg, "Tacoma Man Is First State Resident to Die from AIDS," *Seattle Post-Intelligencer,* Apr. 16, 1983, A5.

39. Steve Foiles, "Health Dept. and Bath Owners Meet," *Seattle Gay News,* May 4, 1984, 1.

40. For information on David Poot, see Kurt Weischedel, "He Sold His VW for $500 and Dug into Yards," *Seattle Gay News,* Jan. 4, 1985, 4; Warren King, "Man Unknowingly Tested for AIDS," *Seattle Times,* June 17, 1987, D1; Warren King, "Suit over AIDS Test Settled," *Seattle Times,* Aug. 16, 1989, C1; Carole Beers, "W. David Poot, AIDS Activist and Noted Seattle Designer," *Seattle Times,* Apr. 9, 1994, B8.

41. Author's interview with Malcom McKay, Apr. 2001. See also "Education Campaign Hits Streets with Message of 'Please Be Safe,'" *Seattle Gay News,* Jan. 17, 1986, 1.

42. The first Safety Pin advertisements appeared in *Seattle Gay News,* Jan. 24, 1986, 3. The strategy was explained in the author's interview with Malcolm McKay, Apr. 2001.

43. Warren King, "Safety Campaign Aims at AIDS Risk," *Seattle Times,* Jan. 23, 1986, D2.

44. "Education Campaign Hits Streets with Message of 'Please Be Safe,'" *Seattle Gay News,* Jan. 17, 1986, 1.

45. Chris Dziewiontkoski, "'Rules of the Road' 1986 Campaign Winds Down, Broader Scope for '87," *Seattle Gay News,* Jan. 2, 1987, 1; William Freeberg, "Safe Sex Education Has Led to Strong Changes in Behavior," *Seattle Gay News,* Aug. 7, 1987, 1.

46. On Michael Gallanger and Andy Cruz, see Carey Quan Gelernter et al., "The AIDS Quilt: Stitches in Time," *Seattle Times,* July 17, 1988, K1.

18 / BECOMING COMPASSION

1. Dean Katz, "New AIDS Drug Buoys Hopes Here," *Seattle Times,* Sept. 21, 1986, D1; Warren King, "A Ray of Hope," *Seattle Times,* Oct. 21, 1986, D1; Rita Hibbard, "AIDS: Reason to Hope," *Seattle Post-Intelligencer,* Nov. 15, 1986, A1. For the University of Washington's role in the drug tests, see, for example, Warren King, "UW Chosen for Major AIDS Research Role," *Seattle Times,* June 30, 1986, A1; Warren King, "Target: AIDS," *Seattle Times,* Aug. 24, 1986, E1.

2. Warren King, "New Drug for AIDS Finally in Use," *Seattle Times,* Dec. 11, 1986, D1. For other information about Allen DeShong and his partner Robert O'Boyle, see Warren King, "He Was Committed to Letting People Know," *Seattle Times,* Oct. 11, 1987, A1; Carey Quan Gelernter et al., "The AIDS Quilt: Stitches in Time," *Seattle Times,* July 17, 1988, K1; and these columns by Robert O'Boyle in the *Seattle Times:* "Symptoms Left Nagging Premonition of Illness," Oct. 7, 1990, K1; "Robert's Home and Eager to Write Again," Nov. 4, 1990, K5; "Life and Death Look a Lot Different Now," Oct. 27, 1991, K3; "Visit to AIDS Quilt Has Deeper Meaning the Second Time," Nov. 24, 1991, K9.

3. Warren King, "County Gets $1.4 Million AIDS Grant," *Seattle Times,* Oct. 22, 1986, A8.

4. Elizabeth Rhodes, "The Burden of AIDS," *Seattle Times,* Nov. 17, 1985, K1. For other stories about Anderson, see those by Rita Hibbard in the *Seattle Post-Intelligencer:* "AIDS: Reason to Hope," Nov. 15, 1986, A1; "Seattle AIDS Patient Is Taken off Experimental Drug," Nov. 19, 1986, D1; "AIDS Patient Able to Resume Taking New Drug," Jan. 3, 1987, D1; "AIDS Patient Stops Experimental Drug," Feb. 24, 1987, D1; "A Battler Is Dead of AIDS," March 12, 1987, A1. See also Carey Quan Gelernter et al., "The AIDS Quilt: Stitches in Time," *Seattle Times,* July 17, 1988, K1.

5. Interview with Malcolm McKay by Alice B. Theatre Oral History Project, May 1992. Other information on McKay and the education strategy he pursued comes from the author's interview with him, Apr. 2001, and from Chris Dziewiontkoski, "Meet Malcolm McKay," *Seattle Gay News,* Oct. 10, 1986, 6.

6. McKay's use of Elisabeth Kübler-Ross's stages was described during the author's interview with him, Apr. 2001.

7. Warren King, "Some Stations Refuse to Show Ad about AIDS," *Seattle Times,* Oct. 17, 1986, C1. See also Warren King, "AIDS Group Produces TV Spot to Promote Safe Sex," *Seattle Times,* Sept. 7, 1986, B9; George Bakan, "TV Stations Refuse to Air NWAF Public Service Safe Sex Spots," *Seattle Gay News,* Oct. 17, 1986, 1; Thomas Harshbarger, "Royer Writes TV Stations on Their Refusal to Air AIDS Spot," *Seattle Gay News,* Nov. 21, 1986, 5.

8. See these stories by Marsha King in the *Seattle Times:* "TV Spot Talks AIDS, Condoms in Frank Terms," May 30, 1987, A1; "Sex Goes Public," June 4, 1987, G1.

9. Warren King, "He Was Committed to Letting People Know," *Seattle Times,* Oct. 11, 1987, A1.

10. Information on Steven Farmer comes from a variety of sources, including the author's interview with him, May 1988; *State of Washington v. Steven George Farmer,* Washington

State Supreme Court, 116 Wn. 2d 414, 805 P. 2d 200 (1991), and numerous news articles. The most important are indicated in subsequent notes. For a chronology of the case, see "Sentence Upheld: Farmer to Go to Prison," *Seattle Gay News,* Feb. 22, 1991, 1. For an overview, see Gary Atkins, "Steven Farmer: Media Case Plays Supporting Actor in State's Drama of Making New AIDS Policy," *Dorian Group Newsletter,* June 1988, 2.

11. Julie Emery, "Seattle Man to Serve Two Months for Sex Acts with Teen-Age Boys," *Seattle Times,* Dec. 19, 1987, A18.

12. Warren King, "State Panel Rejects Forced AIDS Test for All but One Group," *Seattle Times,* Nov. 24, 1987, A1; "State Panel's AIDS Proposals," *Seattle Post-Intelligencer,* Nov. 27, 1987, A14.

13. See the following stories by Steve Miletich and Rita Hibbard in the *Seattle Post-Intelligencer:* "Teen-sex Abuser Is Believed to Have AIDS Virus," Dec. 1, 1987, A1; "Strict Controls Placed on Sex Offender," Dec. 5, 1987, A1.

14. "Records Needed in Sex-Abuse Case," *Seattle Post-Intelligencer,* Dec. 2, 1987, A6. See also Rita Hibbard, "AIDS and Liberty: New Questions," *Seattle Post-Intelligencer,* Dec. 2, 1987, B1. Farmer's defense attorney, Robert Gombiner, attempted to have a gag order put on the prosecution to keep it from making statements about Farmer's medical condition. A judge rejected the request. See Julie Emery, "Defendant in Sexual Abuse Case Seeks Gag Order for Prosecutors," *Seattle Times,* Dec. 17, 1987, F2; Julie Emery, "Gag Order on AIDS Rejected in Sex Case," *Seattle Times,* Dec. 30, 1987, H3.

15. See Alan Reade and ShaniBear Woman, "AIDS Omnibus Bill Discussed," *Seattle Gay News,* March 4, 1988, 1; Mike McNamara, "Lawmakers Break Stalemate; Pass Omnibus Bill," *Seattle Gay News,* March 11, 1988, 1; Gary Atkins, "The Good, the Bad, and the Political," *Dorian Group Newsletter,* Apr. 1988, 2; Chris Dziewiontkoski, "Omnibus Bill Not That Ominous, Say AIDS Lobbyists," *Seattle Gay News,* Apr. 15, 1988, 7.

16. For an overview, see Gary Atkins, "Steven Farmer: Media Case Plays Supporting Actor in State's Drama of Making New AIDS Policy," *Dorian Group Newsletter,* June 1988, 2; Marsha King, "Does AIDS Issue Have Relevance in Farmer Case?" *Seattle Times,* June 5, 1988, D1; Tom Paulson, "Mandatory AIDS Testing Raises a Host of Fears," *Seattle Post-Intelligencer,* July 15, 1988, E1. Casey Hannan published a three-part interview with Farmer in the *Seattle Gay News:* "Justice and the Media: The Steven Farmer Case," June 1, 1988, 1; "Farmer: His First-Hand Impression of His Trial," June 10, 1988, 1; "Steven Farmer: Up Against the System and the Media," June 17, 1988, 10. The June 17, 1988, issue of *Seattle Gay News* contains numerous letters about the case, as well as a story on a protest: Shani Dirzhud-Rashid, "Stonewall Organizes Protest," 1. Deputy Prosecutor Michael Hogan responded to the criticisms raised by gay activists in an article published in *Seattle Gay News,* Aug. 26, 1988, 1.

17. Julie Emery, "Judge Orders Man Tested for AIDS Virus," *Seattle Times,* May 24, 1988, A1; Casey Hannan, "Court Orders Mandatory HIV Test for Steven Farmer," *Seattle Gay News,* May 27, 1988, 1; Gary Atkins, "Steven Farmer: Media Case Plays Supporting Actor in State's Drama of Making New AIDS Policy," *Dorian Group Newsletter,* June 1988, 2.

18. Steve Miletich, "Sex Offender Steven Farmer Submits to AIDS Blood Test—Under

Protest," *Seattle Post-Intelligencer,* June 2, 1988, B1; Terry Tang, "Forcing an AIDS Test in an Ugly Case," *Seattle Weekly,* June 22, 1988, 19.

19. In the *Seattle Post-Intelligencer,* see Jack Hopkins, "Sex Offender Exposed to AIDS," June 28, 1988, A1; and "Lock Farmer Away," June 29, 1988, A10. Also see Julie Emery, "Farmer Loses AIDS Test Battle," *Seattle Times,* June 28, 1988, B1; Casey Hannan, "Court Breaks Confidentiality During Hearing," *Seattle Gay News,* July 1, 1988, 1; Casey Hannan, "Farmer Sentenced under Protest," *Seattle Gay News,* July 8, 1988, 1.

20. Jack Hopkins, "Sex Offender with AIDS Virus Gets a 7-1/2 Year Term in Prison," *Seattle Post-Intelligencer,* July 2, 1988, A1.

21. Sherrye Henry, "Women Who Could Be America's Toughest Prosecutors," *Parade,* Feb. 26, 1989, 4. For additional developments, see Casey Hannan, "Steven Farmer Approved for Home Detention," *Seattle Gay News,* June 2, 1989, 1; Tom Flint, "State Supreme Court to Hear Farmer Case February 20," *Seattle Gay News,* Feb. 16, 1990, 1; "Sentence Upheld: Farmer to Go to Prison," *Seattle Gay News,* Feb. 21, 1991, 1; Tom Flint, "Community Activists Join Farmer at Press Conference," and "Eve of a Prison Term: Steven Farmer Speaks Out," *Seattle Gay News,* March 1, 1991, 1; Robert O'Boyle, "The Man behind the News Stories," *Seattle Times,* June 2, 1991, K6; Matt Nagle, "Steve Farmer Goes to Prison," *Seattle Gay News,* July 12, 1991, 1; Tom Flint, "Farmer Imprisoned amidst Protest and Grief," *Seattle Gay News,* July 19, 1991, 1; Tom Flint, "Witness Admits Perjury in Steven Farmer Testimony," *Seattle Gay News,* March 13, 1992, 1; J. R. Stone, "Letters Pour in to Free Farmer, but Governor's Hands Are Tied," *Seattle Gay News,* Nov. 20, 1992, 8; Dave Birkland, "Sex Offender's Death Linked to AIDS," *Seattle Times,* Sept. 30, 1995, B10.

22. For the Randall Ferguson case, see, for example, the following stories by Bruce Westfall in the Vancouver, Wa., *Columbian:* "AIDS Carrier 'Dangerous,'" May 17, 1995, 1; "Ferguson Denies Keeping AIDS Secret," Sept. 26, 1996, 1; "Ferguson Case Hinged on Months of Work by Camas Detective," and "Contrite Ferguson Expects to Die in Prison," Sept. 29, 1996, 1; "Prosecutors to Recommend Ten Years for Ferguson," Oct. 16, 1996, 1; "Ferguson Appeals AIDS Assault Conviction," May 6, 1998, 1.

23. Statistics on AIDS in Seattle come from the Seattle–King County Public Health Department, *Quarterly Reports* and *Annual Reports.*

24. For information on James Moore, see, for example, the following *Seattle Gay News* articles: Thomas Leland (a pseudonym for Moore), "Grieving—A Personal Story," July 17, 1987, 10; Laughing Otter, "Women, Men, Straight and Queer Attend AIDS Ritual," Dec. 18, 1987, 16; Laughing Otter, "The Vigil Was Like the Long Dance: A Transformation," June 3, 1988, 30; John Yohalem, "In Memoriam: James Leland Moore," Oct. 21, 1988, 18.

25. For information on Carl Wagner, see, for example, Eric Pryne, "AIDS Group Biased, Says Ex-Worker with AIDS," *Seattle Times,* Sept. 10, 1988, A12; and the following *Seattle Gay News* stories: Casey Hannan, "Wagner Files Claim of Discrimination against NWAF," Nov. 4, 1988, 16; Casey Hannan, "Carl Wagner/NWAF Dispute: Current Developments," Nov. 18, 1988, 9; Mark Dion, "In Memoriam: Carl Wagner," Sept. 22, 1989, 10.

26. For information on Claire Cowles, see Carey Quan Gelernter et al., "The AIDS Quilt: Stitches in Time," *Seattle Times,* July 17, 1988, K1.

27. For information about the Seattle ACT UP chapter, see the Tom Flint Papers, Washington State Historical Society Archives, Tacoma, which contain both news clippings and organization press releases. See also *Seattle Gay News* articles such as Tom Flint, "AIDS Coalition to Unleash Power Demonstrates at Bush Rally," Oct. 28, 1988, 1; George Bakan, "ACT UP! Seattle Plans Protest of Safeway Ban of Spin Magazine," Nov. 4, 1988, 1; George Bakan, "ACT UP! Pickets Saturday; Progress Reported in Ongoing Safeway Controversy," Nov. 11, 1988, 1; George Bakan, "ACT UP! Seattle Proclaims Safeway Victory," Nov. 18, 1988, 1; Shani Dirzhud-Rashid, "Safeway Grocery Bags to Have AIDS Hotline Number Soon," March 31, 1989, 6; Tom Flint, "Adults Don't Show Up for Confrontation in Volunteer Park," Aug. 10, 1990, 2; Tom Flint, "Condoms for Teens Comes to Final Vote," Dec. 6, 1991, 1; "Outstepping Goodloe: ACT UP Files First," Jan. 10, 1992, 5; Tom Flint, "ACT UP Disrupts Goodloe Meeting, Meets with Force," Jan. 24, 1992, 1; Tom Flint, "Seattle High School Condom Plan Delayed," Dec. 4, 1992, 9; Tom Flint, "Condom Plan Moves Closer to Approval by School Board," Dec. 18, 1992, 17. See also Warren King, "Anti-AIDS Protesters Arrested in Traffic," *Seattle Times,* Dec. 3, 1990, E1.

28. For reports on the lesbian and gay involvement against the white supremacist movement, see, for example, the following *Seattle Gay News* stories: Casey Hannan, "Lesbian/Gay Activist Groups to Protest Neo-Nazi Memorial Service," Dec. 9, 1988, 1; Tom Flint, "Neo-Nazi Protest Success: Gay/Lesbian Community in Force," and "Editorial: Reflections on the Rise of the New Right," Dec. 16, 1988, 1, 2; and Tom Flint, "200 Gather to Participate in Anti-Fascist March," Dec. 23, 1988, 1.

29. For news reports on the bomb plot, see the following *Seattle Times* stories: Walter Hatch, "Neo-Nazi Plot Aimed at Gay Bar, FBI Says," May 15, 1990, A1; "Aryan Nations Chief Disputes Bomb Charges," May 16, 1990, G2; "Grand Jury Indicts Three in Bomb Plot," May 17, 1990, B7; Richard Seven, "Three Suspects in Bomb Plot Will Be Tried in Idaho," May 18, 1990, B3; Quane Kenyon, "Trial Set to Begin in Alleged Bombing," Oct. 3, 1990 (first edition), F3; "Bomb Plot Blamed on FBI Informant," Oct. 3, 1990 (final edition), H4; "Defendant's Van Held Bomb Parts, Jurors Told," Oct. 6, 1990, A7; Cliff Hadley, "Racist Leader to Testify in Trial," Oct. 13, 1990, A14; "Idaho Man Denies Role in Bomb Plot," Oct. 17, 1990, G2; "Defendant in Bomb-Plot Case Denies Conspiracy," Oct. 18, 1990, E1; "Three Convicted in Capitol Hill Disco Plot," Oct. 19, 1990, E1. See also, in the *Seattle Gay News:* Tom Flint, "First on the List: Neo-Nazis Attack Gay Community"; Matt Nagle, "Community Responds to Neo-Nazi Mass Murder Scheme," and Tom Flint, "A Child's Garden of Neo-Nazis," May 18, 1990, 1, 4; Matt Nagle, "Boise Trial under Way," Oct. 12, 1990, 17; Matt Nagle, "White Supremacists Guilty; Local Activists Respond," Oct. 26, 1990, 1; and Matt Nagle, "Aryan Bomb-Plotters Sentenced—Too Lenient?" Jan. 18, 1991, 3.

30. For the early development of AIDS housing, see "Seattle/King County Health Department Receives $1.4 Million AIDS Grant," *Seattle Gay News,* Oct. 24, 1986, 1; Warren King, "County Plans Homes for AIDS Patients," *Seattle Times,* June 23, 1987, A1; William

Gough and Warren King, "Millions Raised for AIDS Facility," *Seattle Times*, Oct. 5, 1989, C3; "Bailey-Boushay House: A Report to the Community," *AIDS Housing of Washington* newsletter, Jan. 13, 1992.

31. For information on Peter Davis, see, for example, "Portland Priest from Seattle Diagnosed As Having AIDS," *Northwest Progress*, Dec. 10, 1987, 14; Vince Stricherz, "AIDS-Stricken Priest Served until the End," *Seattle Times*, Dec. 29, 1988, C1; "Memorial for Priest to Be Held Friday," *Seattle Times*, Jan. 7, 1989, C14; Don Duncan, "A Joyful Eulogy, but No Excuses," *Seattle Times*, Jan. 14, 1989, A1.

32. For information about Terry Shea, see Constantine Angelos, "Rev. Terry Shea, Jesuit Educator and 'Man of Vision,'" *Seattle Times*, July 18, 1995, B6; and Kelly McBride, "Jesuit Priest, Educator Dies," *Spokesman Review*, July 19, 1995, B1.

33. For information about the first AIDS Walk, see Chuck Martin, "All Walks of Life, a NW AIDS Foundation Walkathon Sept. 27," *Seattle Gay News*, July 17, 1987, 6; Richard Seven, "AIDS Fighters Come from All Walks of Life," *Seattle Times*, Sept. 28, 1987, C3; Chuck Martin, "Walkathon Raises $3,000 to Fight AIDS," *Seattle Gay News*, Oct. 2, 1987, 1. For walks in the early 1990s, see, for example, these *Seattle Gay News* articles: Tom Flint, "NWAF AIDS Walkathon Tops $900,000," Oct. 5, 1990, 1; Tom Flint, "Walkathon Generates over $1.1 Million to Fight AIDS," Sept. 27, 1991, 1; J. R. Stone, "AIDS Walk Brings out All Walks of Life and Surpasses Goal," Sept. 25, 1992, 1; J. R. Stone, "After Walk: Where Does NWAF Money Go?" Oct. 16, 1992, 5.

34. Comments from Carol Sterling come from an interview by Jill Bateman of the Seattle University Community and Communication Project, July 1995.

35. See two stories by Casey Hannan in the *Seattle Gay News:* "AIDS Facility, Planned for Madison, Faces Opposition," Oct. 28, 1988, 1; and "AIDS Housing of Washington Holds Meeting about Concerns," Nov. 4, 1988, 19; also, Matt Nagle, "AIDS Housing of Washington Receives $3.2 Million," *Seattle Gay News*, Oct. 20, 1989, 1.

36. Quoted in Carol Ostrom, "AIDS Hospice Siting in Madison Valley Draws Opposition," *Seattle Times*, March 21, 1990, B1.

37. Ibid.

38. Ibid.

39. For the ACT UP chapter's involvement in the AIDS home controversy, see ACT UP correspondence and files in the Tom Flint Collection, Washington State Historical Society Archives, Tacoma; as well as these articles in *Seattle Gay News*: Tom Flint, "ACT UP/Seattle Says: Roger Leed Shame! Shame!" March 23, 1990, 1; "Lawsuit to Stop AIDS Housing Project Dropped," and "A Victory for PWAs," June 1, 1990, 1, 20; "AIDS Housing of Washington Scores Victory," June 15, 1990, 4.

40. "Organist Randall Jay McCarty Dies," *Seattle Times*, Feb. 13, 1989, D8.

41. For information on the Behnke family background, see "Who Runs Seattle," *Seattle Times*, Apr. 12, 1987, C11. See also "Robert 'Ned' Behnke Dies," *Seattle Times*, March 26, 1989, B8; Tom Flint, "7,000 People from All Walks of Life '89 Raise over $580,000," *Seattle Gay News*, Sept. 29, 1989, 1; Carole Beers, ""Robert J. Behnke, Active in Arts," *Seattle Times*, Dec. 9, 1999, B6; Judi Hunt, "Robert J. Behnke, Avid Supporter of KCTS and Arts," *Seattle*

*Post-Intelligencer,* Dec. 10, 1999, C15; "AIDS Foundation Announces Winner of Annual Awards," *Seattle Times,* May 18, 1994, B3; Regina Hackett, "First 'Neddy' Award Honors Painter Michael Spafford," *Seattle Post-Intelligencer,* June 12, 1996, D5.

42. Melinda Bargreen, "Lowell Roddenberry, Pianist, Expert on Avoiding Stage Fright," *Seattle Times,* Aug. 5, 1989, C8.

43. The *Seattle Times* published a partial list of the city's arts deaths from AIDS in 1991. See Ferdinand DeLeon, "Losses in Our Creative Community Affect Seattle and the World," and Janine Gressel, "Tragic Impact of AIDS Is Felt Locally, Nationally," Oct. 6, 1991, L1, L4; Ferdinand DeLeon, "Former Cast Members Face Personal Tragedy," Oct. 7, 1991, C1.

44. Ross Anderson, "Ed Elliott, Man Who Insisted Art Belonged Beneath the Streets," *Seattle Times,* Apr. 25, 1991, D8.

45. See these *Seattle Times* obituaries: Carole Beers, "Clark Tippet, Ballet Dancer, Award-Winning Choreographer," Feb. 1, 1992, C8; Melinda Bargreen, "Jim Bailey, 44, A Music Lover Who Directed Seattle Opera's Growth," Apr. 25, 1992, B10; Richard Seven, "Michael Schauermann: Actor, Therapist on Partners' AIDS Issues," June 20, 1992, B10; Leonard Fleming, "Lee James McCormack Brought High Energy to Theater and Music," July 8, 1992, D9; Penelope Carrington, "James Bradley Arsenault, Founder of Bainbridge's Opera Northwest," July 11, 1992, A10.

46. See these *Seattle Times* obituaries: Chuck Taylor, "Jack Jones," Jan. 16, 1991, F5; Nancy Montgomery, "Jack Goldman, 41, Jewelry Store Owner," March 9, 1991, B6; "Passages," March 17, 1991, A11; Robert O'Boyle, "Michael Harmon: His Legacy Was Candor," May 5, 1991, K3; Ross Anderson, "Harvey Muggy, Gay Leader Who Used Political Power," Aug. 17, 1991, B6.

47. See Chris Dziewiontkoski, "Pride Foundation Receives $1 Million," *Seattle Gay News,* Feb. 12, 1988, 1.

48. Richard Seven, "Leaving Holm," *Seattle Times,* Apr. 29, 1988, C1; also Chris Dziewiontkoski, "Jim Holm Accepts NAN Position; Goes to Washington," *Seattle Gay News,* Apr. 22, 1988, 1.

49. Diedtra Henderson, "Endowment Fund for Gay Men of Color Is Activist's Legacy," *Seattle Times,* Apr. 1, 1993, D3; also, in *Seattle Gay News,* see Chuck Martin, "Police Attention Both Racist and Homophobic, Says Store Owner," Feb. 20, 1987, 16; and "A Tribute to Brian Matthew Day," Dec. 7, 1990, 17.

50. Robert O'Boyle's columns appeared weekly in the *Seattle Times,* beginning June 17, 1990; his final column appeared Dec. 29, 1991. For his obituary in the *Times,* see Terry Tazioli and Warren King, "Award-Winning Columnist Gave AIDS a Tough Fight," Jan. 7, 1992, F1.

51. Kay Kusumoto, "Kazas Jones Lived Life As Example of How to Keep Living with AIDS," *Seattle Times,* Apr. 6, 1993, F8. See also "In Memoriam: Kazas Jones," *Seattle Gay News,* Apr. 9, 1993, 16.

52. For background on Kris Anderson (Crystal Lane), see these *Seattle Gay News* stories: Chris Dziewiontkoski, "Crystal Lane: I'll Be Back!" Oct. 31, 1986, 28; Tom Flint, "Seattle Entertainment Icon: Crystal Lane," Sept. 13, 1991, 25; and numerous articles and letters to

the editor, March 4, 1994. See also Carole Beers, "Kristopher Anderson's Shows Were Anything but a Drag," *Seattle Times*, Feb. 26, 1994, B10.

53. Jody Becker, "A Touch of Dignity," *Seattle Times*, Dec. 23, 1987, C1. Other stories focused on families caring for their dying. For one example, see Larry Brown, "An AIDS Patient and His Family Tell about Coping with Crisis," *Seattle Times*, July 23, 1987, D1.

54. Mary Pols, "Actor Robert Cole Maintained a Flair for the Dramatic Right up to the End," *Seattle Times*, Feb. 1, 1994, B6.

## 19 / CAL'S CONSCIENCE

1. Sources for general background in this chapter include the author's personal discussions with and observations of Cal Anderson, 1992–95; Cal Anderson Papers, Washington State Historical Society Archives, Tacoma; author's interviews with Ed Murray, May 1996 and Oct. 2001; an interview with Cal Anderson by Jill Bateman of the Seattle University Community and Communication Project, July 1995; and numerous news articles as indicated in subsequent footnotes. The photographs of Cal as a teenager working for the Democratic Party were on display at a Paramount Theater reception following his memorial service in 1995.

2. Anderson interview, Seattle University Community and Communication Project, July 1995.

3. Elizabeth Rhodes, "A New Face in the House," *Seattle Times*, Jan. 10, 1988, K1.

4. For Anderson's military career, see Mindy Chambers, "Openly Gay Lawmaker Is Bronze Star Winner," *Daily Olympian*, Feb. 4, 1993, A2.

5. Anderson interview, Seattle University Community and Communication Project, July 1995.

6. Elizabeth Rhodes, "A New Face in the House," *Seattle Times*, Jan. 10, 1988, K1.

7. Ibid.

8. Author's interview with Ed Murray, May 1996.

9. See, for example, the following articles in *Seattle Gay News:* Mike McNamara, "Lawmakers Break Stalemate; Pass Omnibus Bill," March 11, 1988, 1; ShaniBear Woman, "AIDS Omnibus Bill 'Irrational and Illogical,'" March 18, 1988, 6; Chris Dziewiontkoski, "Gov. Gardner Signs AIDS Omnibus Bill" and Chuck Martin, "Representative Cal Anderson Talks about His First Year in Olympia," March 25, 1988, 1, 8. Anderson's home was also vandalized by AIDS activists in 1993. See Tom Flint, "Cal Anderson's Home Vandalized," *Seattle Gay News*, March 5, 1993, 7.

10. Author's interview with Ed Murray, May 1996.

11. Elizabeth Rhodes, "Freshman Diary," *Seattle Times*, March 11, 1988, D1.

12. For Anderson's humor, see *Seattle Times* articles by Carole Beers et al., "Cal Anderson, Legislator, Dies," Aug. 5, 1995, A1; and Jim Simon, "Anderson Used His Life to Educate," Aug. 6, 1995, B1.

13. Quoted in Kery Murakami, "Anderson Makes His Fight with AIDS a Public One," *Seattle Times*, Feb. 14, 1995, A1.

14. Cal Anderson Papers, Washington State Historical Society Archives, Tacoma.

15. Anderson interview, Seattle University Community and Communication Project, July 1995.

16. A chronology of the gay/lesbian civil rights bill, prepared for Anderson, can be found in the Cal Anderson Papers, Washington State Historical Society Archives, Tacoma. For Thorsness's change to the hate crimes bill in 1992, see Tom Flint, "Hate Crimes Bill Goes to Senate, without Those Words," *Seattle Gay News*, March 6, 1992, 1.

17. Letter to the author from Charlie Brydon, Oct. 28, 1992. Author's personal files.

18. "Oregon Anti-Gay Group Fires First Shots Here," *Everett Herald*, Jan. 30, 1993, B4.

19. The description of the March 2, 1993, hearing is based on the author's personal observations. For news coverage, see, for example, Kathy George, "Crowd Packs Hearing for Gay Rights Bill," *Seattle Post-Intelligencer*, March 3, 1993, A1; Pat Matuska, "Gay-Rights Hearing Is Packed with Emotions," *Seattle Times*, March 3, 1993, B1; Mindy Chambers, "Gay Rights Heats Up," *Daily Olympian*, March 3, 1993, A1; David Postman, "Angry Exchange on Gay Rights," *Tacoma News-Tribune*, March 3, 1993, B1; Tom Flint, "Hearings on Civil Rights Bill Packed," *Seattle Gay News*, March 5, 1993, 1; Kathryn Robinson, "Gay Rights Showdown," *Seattle Weekly*, March 31, 1993, 27.

20. Carol Ostrom, "Coadjutor's Good Humor Allays Catholics' Concerns," *Seattle Times*, May 30, 1987, A10.

21. Ibid.

22. Carol Ostrom, "Hunthausen Steps down at Warm Farewell," *Seattle Times*, Aug. 13, 1991, A1. See also these articles by Ostrom in the *Seattle Times:* "A Change of Leadership for Catholics," June 19, 1991, D1; "At Heart, He's a Pastoral Priest," *Seattle Times*, June 22, 1991, A16.

23. Tom Flint, "Vatican Demands Opposition to Gay/Lesbian Rights," *Seattle Gay News*, July 24, 1992, 1.

24. Author's observation of the hearing, March 2, 1993.

25. Author's interview with Ed Murray, May 1996. See also Joni Balter, "Gay Power Brokers: Money, Stature and Savvy Give Leaders More Clout," *Seattle Times*, Aug. 1, 1993, A1.

26. See *Seattle Times* stories by Bill Dietrich, "Vatican's Stance Dismays Seattle's Homosexuals," July 19, 1992, B3; Lee Moriwaki, "Ex-Leader of Catholic Gays Applauds Support," July 21, 1992, B4; "Rally Protests Document from Vatican on Gays," July 27, 1992, E2; Lee Moriwaki, "Area's New Archbishop Quiets Some Criticism," Aug. 24, 1992, B2.

27. Author's interviews with Ed Murray, May 1996 and Oct. 2001.

28. Jim Simon, "Bill's Death a Bitter Loss for Gay Legislator," *Seattle Times*, Apr. 18, 1993, B1.

29. See *Seattle Times* articles by Jonathan Martin, "Anderson Ponders Whether to Resign," May 10, 1995, B1; and Carole Beers et al., "Cal Anderson, Legislator, Dies," Aug. 5, 1995, A1.

30. For a review of the HOW campaign, see David Rayside, "American Exceptionalism in Sexual Diversity Politics: A Washington State Case Study," paper presented to the American Political Science Association, Aug.–Sept. 2000.

31. On the 1994 attempt to pass the civil rights bill and the Catholic lobbying against it, see articles by Tom Flint in the *Seattle Gay News:* "Gay/Lesbian Civil Rights Bill Moves Steadily Forward," Feb. 4, 1994, 1; "Gay/Lesbian Civil Rights Bill Grinds through Senate Hearing," Feb. 18, 1994, 1; "Lesbian/Gay Catholics Furious with Bishops over SHB 1443 Opposition Letter to State Senators," Feb. 25, 1994, 1; "Civil Rights Bill Passes/Fails," March 4, 1994, 1; "Gay/Lesbian Catholics Pray for Bishops' Change of Heart," March 18, 1994, 8; and the *Seattle Gay News* editorial, "We'll Be Back," March 11, 1994, 1. See also *Seattle Post-Intelligencer* articles by Michael Paulson, "Gay Rights Bill Goes to Senate," Jan. 29, 1994, B1; "Two Senators Control Fate of Gay Rights Bill," March 1, 1994, B1; and "Gay Rights Bill on Verge of Another Defeat," March 4, 1994, A1; as well as *Seattle Times* articles by Jim Simon, "Bishops Fight Bill Protecting Gay Rights," Feb. 22, 1994, A1; "Battle Lines Blur over Gay Rights Bill as Supporters Work to Win Senate Backing," Feb. 27, 1994, A1; "Gay Rights Bill Dies in Senate with No Vote," March 5, 1994, A1.

32. Tom Flint, "Initiatives 608/610 Go Down in Defeat," *Seattle Gay News,* July 15, 1994, 1.

33. See *Seattle Times* articles by David Postman and Dee Norton, "State Sen. Cal Anderson Says He Has AIDS," Feb. 13, 1995, A1; and Kery Murakami, "Anderson Makes His Fight with AIDS Public," Feb. 14, 1995, A1. See also James Burke, "Cal Anderson Goes Public with Fight against AIDS," *Seattle Gay News,* Feb. 17, 1995, 1.

34. Cal Anderson Papers, Washington State Historical Society Archives, Tacoma.

35. Author's interview with Ed Murray, May 1996.

36. Anderson interview, Seattle University Community and Communication Project, July 1995.

37. John Carlson, "Republicans Should Also Appreciate Cal Anderson," *Seattle Times,* Aug. 8, 1995, B4.

38. See *Seattle Times* articles by Jim Simon, "Anderson Used His Life to Educate," Aug. 6, 1995, B1; and "Cal Anderson's Legacy to his City and the State," Aug. 7, 1995, B4.

39. James Burke, "Thousands Mourn Anderson," *Seattle Gay News,* Aug. 11, 1995, 1.

40. Author's personal observation of Anderson funeral, Aug. 10, 1995. See also David Ammons, "A Final Tribute to Cal Anderson," *Seattle Times,* Aug. 11, 1995, B4.

## EPILOGUE

1. For coverage of the 1993 lesbian/gay pride parade, see Paul Shukovsky, "Marchers Turn up Gay Solidarity," *Seattle Post-Intelligencer,* June 28, 1993, B1; Susan Gilmore, "Pride in Numbers: Gays March in Seattle," *Seattle Times,* June 28, 1993, B1; and "Rain on Parade Doesn't Dampen the Pride," *Seattle Gay News,* July 2, 1993, 1.

2. Rob Boling was interviewed by Tom Flint of the *Seattle Gay News* in "Gay Police Officer Drives down Broadway and Comes Out," July 2, 1993, 1. Chief Norm Stamper's decision to join drew front-page coverage in the *Seattle Post-Intelligencer.* See "A March for Pride" and Arthur Gorlick, "Jammin' Broadway," *Seattle Post-Intelligencer,* June 27, 1994, A1, B1;

and Alex Tizin, "Less Skin and More Politics at Seattle Gay-Pride Parade," *Seattle Times,* June 27, 1994, B1.

3. Information about the people mentioned in this section comes from the author's personal knowledge and from published articles. For Mineo Katagiri, see "Katagiri Quits Post for N.Y. Church Job," *Seattle Times,* Apr. 15, 1970, B8; and Don Fair, "A Food Bank Founder Sees 'Seeds for Revolution' in the Growth of Poverty," *Seattle Post-Intelligencer,* Apr. 23, 1986, A3. For Robert Sirico, see Randy Shilts, "Will the Gay Community Services Center Survive?" *Advocate,* May 19, 1976, 10. Many articles were published about Faygele benMiriam over the course of two decades; for an overview see "Grand Marshal—Faygele benMiriam," *Seattle Gay News* Pride Week Program, June 21, 1991, 14. For Lois Thetford's Jefferson Award, see Regina Hackett, "Lois Thetford: Commitment to Community Health," *Seattle Post-Intelligencer,* Apr. 9, 2001, A7. For Shelly Yapp's background, see http://www.washington.edu/regents/yapp.html. Sam Deaderick's obituary can be found in *Seattle Gay News,* Feb. 15, 1991, 3. Dick Snedigar's fight with the Freedom Socialist Party is documented in Susan McDonald, *They Refused to Name Names: The Freeway Hall Case Victory* (Seattle: Red Letter Press, 1995).

4. For Steven Farmer's later years, see in the *Seattle Gay News* J. R. Stone, "Letters Pour in to Free Farmer, but Governor's Hands Are Tied," Nov. 20, 1992, 8; "Rest in Peace: Steven Farmer Dies in Tacoma," Oct. 6, 1995, 1; and Bruce Caszatt, "Steven George Farmer," Oct. 13, 1995, 16. See also Peyton Whitely, "Lowry Grants Clemency to Inmate Who Has AIDS," *Seattle Times,* Jan. 5, 1994, B2; Kathy George, "Steven Farmer, Dying of AIDS, Is Granted Clemency," *Seattle Post-Intelligencer,* Jan. 5, 1994, A1; Kathy George, "Sex-Predator Warning Sent on Farmer," *Seattle Post-Intelligencer,* Jan. 6, 1994, B1; Kathy George, "Farmer Outcry Noted, Public Misled, Says Correction Official," *Seattle Post-Intelligencer,* Jan. 8, 1994, A1; "Fears over Farmer's Transfer to a Hospice," *Seattle Times,* Jan. 15, 1994, A15; Anthony Albert, "Freed Sex Predator Dies of AIDS," *Tacoma News-Tribune,* Sept. 29, 1995, B2; Dave Birkland, "Sex Offender's Death Linked to AIDS," *Seattle Times,* Sept. 30, 1995, B10; Debra Harrell, "Steven Farmer, Central Figure in Case on HIV Testing, Dies," *Seattle Post-Intelligencer,* Sept. 30, 1995, B2; and Patrick O'Callahan, "Steven Farmer Didn't Deserve His Friends," *Tacoma News-Tribune,* Oct. 19, 1995, A10.

5. In one story, for example, Tina Podlodowski was first referred to as "a former Microsoft executive making her first try at public office." A paragraph later, she was referred to as "a newcomer, a woman, and a lesbian." That was the only mention of her sexual orientation in the story. Subsequent references repeated the "former Microsoft executive" identification. See Scott Sunde, "Wineberry, Podlodowski Vie for Popular 'Outsider' Role," *Seattle Post-Intelligencer,* Sept. 21, 1995, A10. Similarly, in endorsing her, the *Seattle Times* first referred to Podlodowski as a "former Microsoft executive and political newcomer." Her sexual orientation was only implied in a much later reference to her service as "past president of the Pride Foundation, a funding source for gay and lesbian organizations." See "Tina Podlodowski for Seattle City Council," Oct. 23, 1995, B4.

6. For Rick Rankin's early involvement in gay theater in Seattle, see, for example, Alan

Neff, "Gay and Lesbian Theatre Festival for Pride Week," *Seattle Gay News,* June 15, 1984, 13; also "Alice B. Theatre—It's Not a Place, It's a State of Mind," *Seattle Gay News* Pride Week Program, June 21, 1991, 30.

7. For the start of the Seattle Men's Chorus, see in the *Seattle Gay News* Bruce Stores, "Men's Chorus Prepares for Appearance," Apr. 25, 1980, 15; and the letter from the chorus's executive director, C. David George, "Chorus Leader Explains," May 23, 1980, 4; also, Andre Rolff, "Men's Chorus Steals Audience Hearts in Smash Debut," June 20, 1980, 13.

8. For a review of Initiative 677 and the collapse of Hands Off Washington, see David Rayside, "American Exceptionalism in Sexual Diversity Politics: A Washington State Case Study," paper presented to the American Political Science Association, Aug.–Sept. 2000.

9. For the change to the Seattle ordinance, see Tom Brune, "New Seattle Ordinance Lets Gays Sue for Job Bias," *Seattle Times,* Feb. 19, 1999, A1.

10. For an overview of the debates about lesbian and gay family relationships, see Rayside, "American Exceptionalism in Sexual Diversity Politics: A Washington State Case Study."

11. The struggles by Perry Watkins and Margarethe Cammermeyer were extensively documented. For overviews, see Gary Atkins, "I'm Not Trying to Be a Hero," *Seattle Weekly,* March 8,1989, 1; and Linda Keene, "The Colonel Fights Back," *Seattle Times Pacific Magazine,* Jan. 3, 1993, 10.

12. For the debate at the Woodland Park United Methodist Church, see *Seattle Times* stories by Marsha King: "Gay Pastor Seeks Seattle Post," Apr. 7, 2001, A1; "Gay Clergywoman Puts Methodist Law to Test," June 15, 2001, A1; "Gay Pastor's Declaration Startles Church Meeting," June 16, 2001, B1; "Church Debates Pastor's Future," June 20, 2001, B1; and "Religions Divided over Gays in Clergy," July 1, 2001, B1; as well as Eli Sanders, "Methodist Clergy Create Activist Alliance," *Seattle Times,* July 28, 2001, B1; Sara Green and Janet Tu, "A Show of Support for Gay Pastors," *Seattle Times,* Oct. 31, 2001, B2; Janet Tu, "Gay Minister Won't Lose Post As Pastor," *Seattle Times,* May 31, 2002, A1; Sheila Lalwani, "Gay Pastor Won't Face Methodist Trial," *Seattle Times,* July 26, 2002, B1.

13. On the appointment of Archbishop Brunett, see the *Seattle Times* articles by Sally Macdonald, "Western Washington Catholics Get a New Archbishop," Oct. 28, 1997, A1; "New Archbishop Gets a Lesson in Seattle's Media," Nov. 1, 1997, A12; "Archbishop a Healer, Here and Abroad," May 20, 2000, A1.

14. Interview with the Reverend Gerald Stanley by LaShawna Lako and Christina Richards, Seattle University Community and Communication Project, Oct. 1994.

15. "Gay Catholic Group, Dignity/Seattle, to Leave St. Joseph's Catholic Church after 21 Years," *Seattle Gay News,* Oct. 5, 2001, 2.

16. On the declining support, see, for example, Alex Tizon, "As AIDS Deaths Drop, So Does Support for Walk," *Seattle Times,* Sept. 22, 2000, A1.

17. See the *Seattle Times* articles by Warren King, "Syphilis Increase among Gays Points to Unsafe Sex Practices," Sept. 10, 1989, B1; and "Some Gays Say They're Burned out on Safe Sex," Sept. 26, 1999, A1. See also Neil Modie, "Sexual Diseases Are up Sharply in Seattle," *Seattle Post-Intelligencer,* March 21, 2001, B1; news release from the Seattle/King County Public Health Department, March 22, 2001; Tom Paulson, "State AIDS Cases Rise for the

First Time since 1993," *Seattle Post-Intelligencer,* May 16, 2001, B1; and Marlene Cimons, "AIDS Infections Rising among Young Gay Men," *Seattle Times,* June 1, 2001, A1.

18. See Diedtra Henderson, "Catwalk Nightclub Attempting to Get Liquor License Back," *Seattle Times,* May 28, 1996, B2; Florangela Davila, "Hemp Fest—A Learning Experience?" *Seattle Times,* Aug. 24, 1997, B1; Pam Sitt, "Hip-Hot: There's More than Puff to the Hip-Hop Scene," *Seattle Times,* Dec. 6, 2001, E1; and advertisement for Catwalk Club, Apr. 23, 2001, http://www.catwalkclub.net/sat.htm.

# SOURCES

INTERVIEWS

1. The following oral history interviews were part of the Seattle University Community and Communication Project, conducted under my supervision from 1994 until 1997: Cal Anderson, Faygele benMiriam, Jennifer Burton, Laura Byrne, Corey Clemons, Ric Cohen, John Coker, Catherine Crossan, Jason Crowley, Sheldon Daniels, Vinh Do, Sam Elwonger, Patty Ferris, Mark Finley, Charles Fite, Thomas Gamble, Gerald Garret, Maura Geary, Mitchell Gonzales, Martin Gouterman, Nicholas Heer, Jeff Henness, Bryher Herak, David Hoffman, Edward Janos, Andrew Johnson, David Johnson, Jeanne Johnston, Matthew Kangas, Greg Kucera, Skippy LaRue, Ross and Luis Lopton, Rick Mangin, Michael Martin, Isidor Martinez, John McCoy, Rose Mesec, Jeffrey Mitchell, Ruby Montana, Diane Moore, Matt Nagle, Evelyn Nichols, Rita Okura, Don Paulson, Rick Peterson, Michael Ramey, Mark Richards, Rev. Gerald Stanley, Karen Swannek, Carol Sterling, Cynthia Taylor, Scott Taylor, William Wassmer, Kathy Wheeler, Doug Wyman, Ashleigh Sandy Yati. Some interviews were quoted directly in the text. Others were used for context. Individuals were interviewed for their knowledge of relevant city or lesbian/gay history; therefore, no presumption should be made about their sexual orientation from their inclusion in the project. The videotapes and indices are currently housed as part of the author's lesbian/gay history collection and in the future, may be relocated to the Seattle University and University of Washington libraries.

2. The following interviews were conducted by the author between 1992 and 2001: John Chadwick, Joe McGonagle, Ed Murray, Rick Rankin, MacIver Wells. In addition, numerous informal conversations were held with individuals not named here. Also, interviews with Archbishop Raymond Hunthausen were conducted in 1982.

3. The following oral history interviews were part of the Alice B. Theatre Oral History Project in 1992: Stephen Blair, Nola Blanes, Robert Carter, Kay Engel, Glen Hunt, Margaret King, Malcolm McKay, Robert Riopelle, Hurdie Styles, Tamara Turner. Some interviews were quoted directly in the text. Others were used for context. Individuals were interviewed for their knowledge of relevant city or lesbian/gay history; therefore, no presumption should be made about their sexual orientation from their inclusion in the project. Some names are deleted for purposes of confidentiality. The audiotapes are currently housed at the University of Washington Libraries.

4. The following oral history interviews were conducted for the Northwest Lesbian and Gay History Museum Project: Reverend Thomas Anastasi, Larry Anderson, Doug Barnes, Paul Barwick, Faygele benMiriam, Rose Bohanan, Marsha Botzer, Charlie Brydon, Elaine Burnell, Robert Carter, Leigh Champlain, Armand Dalmage, Jerry DeGrieck, Jan Denali, Bob Deisher, Christopher Durant, Pam Flodine, Ward Folsom, Sandra Fosshage, Pat Freeman, Richard Gates, Dawn Griffin, Martin Gouterman, Mel Habel, Rev. Gwen Hall, Jan Harnish, Leslie Harnish, Nick Heer, John Hoy, Tasceaie Jennings, Harold Johnson, Selma Kannel, Nancy King, Linda Knighton, Bill Kramer, Rae Larson, Skippy LaRue, Ann Manley, Gail McDougall, Joe McGonagle, Paul McPherson, Jane Meyerding, Lenore Norrgard, Michele Nota, Dale Peters, Vernell Pratt, Mike Ramey, Dennis Raymond, John Reed, Greg Redfox, Bill Regan, Irene Reynolds, Tom Richards, Sunny Rivera, Dorothy Rockwell, Ken Sanchez, John Sheets, Chris Smith, Margaret Sorrel, Marvin Sterling, Beth Strayer, Greg Swales, Lois Thetford, Lynn Tritsch, Janice Van Cleve, Lynn Waddington, MacIver Wells, George Whitaker, Roger Winters, Larry Woelich. Some interviews were quoted directly in the text. Others were used for context. Individuals were interviewed for their knowledge of relevant city or lesbian/gay history; therefore, no presumption should be made about their sexual orientation from their inclusion. Some names are deleted for purposes of confidentiality. The audiotapes and transcripts are currently housed with the NLGHMP and in the future may be relocated to the University of Washington libraries.

## MANUSCRIPTS

Cal Anderson Papers, Washington State Historical Society
Charlie Brydon Papers, Washington State Historical Society
George Cotterill Papers, University of Washington Libraries, MSCUA
John Eccles Papers, University of Washington Libraries, MSCUA
Tom Flint Papers, Washington State Historical Society
Charles Harbaugh Papers, University of Washington Libraries, MSCUA
Mark Matthews Papers, University of Washington Libraries, MSCUA
Tim Mayhew Papers, University of Washington Libraries, MSCUA
Northwest AIDS Foundation Papers, Washington State Historical Society
Seattle Mayors' Papers, University of Washington Libraries, MSCUA

## GOVERNMENT DOCUMENTS

King County Superior Court. Criminal Appearance Dockets, 1893–1914.
King County Superior Court. *Shelly Ann Bauman v. Morris Hart, Pioneer Square Association, et al.*, Civil No. 726096, 1971.
King County Superior Court. *Madison Tavern Inc. and James G. Watson dba Blue Note v. H. J. Lawrence and City of Seattle,* No. 527-660, 1958.
King County Superior Court. *James Earl Schuster v. Sandra Lee Schuster* and *Jerry Floyd Isaacson v. Madeleine Cecil Isaacson,* D-36867, 1974.

King County Superior Court. *State v. Carroll et al.*, Criminal No. 57842, 1971.

Seattle–King County Public Health Department. *Quarterly Reports* and *Annual Reports,* 1990–99.

U.S. District Court for Western Washington. *Keith M. Rhinehart v. B. J. Rhay,* Civil No. 8447, 1969, and *Keith M. Rhinehart v. B. J. Rhay et al.,* Civil No. 8448, 1969.

U.S. District Court for Western Washington. *U.S. v. M. E. Cook,* No. 51944, 1970.

U.S. District Court for Western Washington. *Western Amusement Company v. City of Seattle et al.,* Civil No. 655-72C2, 1972.

U.S. Ninth Circuit Court of Appeals. *Rhinehart v. Rhay,* 440 F. 2d 718, 1971.

U.S. Supreme Court. *Boutilier v. Immigration and Naturalization Service,* 387 U.S. 118, 1967.

U.S. Supreme Court. *California v. LaRue,* 409 U.S. 109, 1972.

Washington State House of Representatives. *Journal of the House,* 1893, 1909.

Washington State Senate. *Journal of the Senate,* 1893, 1909.

Washington State Supreme Court. *James Earl Schuster v. Sandra Lee Schuster,* and *Jerry Floyd Isaacson v. Madeleine Cecil Isaacson,* 90 Wn. 2d 626, 1978.

Washington State Supreme Court. *State of Washington v. Rhinehart,* 70 Wn. 2d 649, 1967.

Washington State Supreme Court. *Gaylord v. Tacoma School District,* 88 Wn. 2d 286, 1977.

Western State Hospital. Seventh, Ninth, Tenth, and Thirteenth Biennial Reports, 1932–46.

Western State Hospital. Untitled Record of Lobotomies, October 1946–June 1954.

Western State Hospital. Register of Inmates.

Western State Hospital. Report to the Legislature on "Mental Institutions in the State of Washington," January 1948.

## BOOKS AND ARTICLES

Andrews, Mildred T. *Washington Women As Pathbreakers.* Dubuque, Iowa: Kendall Hall, 1989.

Arnold, William. *Shadowland.* New York: McGraw-Hill, 1978.

Bartee, Wayne and Alice. *Litigating Morality: American Legal Thought and Its English Roots.* New York: Praeger, 1992.

Bensing, Robert C. "A Comparative Study of American Sex Statutes." *Journal of Criminal Law* 42 (1951): 57–72.

Berner, Richard. *Seattle 1900–1920: From Boomtown, Urban Turbulence, to Restoration.* Seattle: Charles Press, 1991.

———. *Seattle, 1921–1940: From Boom to Bust.* Seattle: Charles Press, 1992.

———. *Seattle Transformed, World War II to Cold War.* Seattle: Charles Press, 1999.

Bowman, Karl, and Bernice Engle. "A Psychiatric Evaluation of Laws of Homosexuality." *Temple Law Quarterly* 29 (1956): 273–326.

Bruggemann, Walter. *The Land: Place As Gift, Promise, and Challenge in Biblical Faith.* Philadelphia: Fortress Press, 1977.

Castells, Manuel. *The City and the Grassroots: A Cross-Cultural Theory of Urban Social Movements.* Berkeley: University of California Press, 1983.

Chambliss, William. *On the Take.* Bloomington: Indiana University Press, 1978.

Clark, Norman. *The Dry Years: Prohibition and Social Change in Washington.* Seattle: University of Washington Press, 1988.

Crowley, Walt. *Seattle University: A Century of Jesuit Education.* Seattle: Seattle University, 1991.

Deaderick, Sam, and Tamara Turner. *Gay Resistance: The Hidden History.* Seattle: Red Letter Press, 1997.

Deisher, Robert. "The Young Male Prostitute." *Pediatrics* 43 (June 1969): 936.

———. "Young Male Prostitutes: The Physician's Role in Social Rehabilitation." *Journal of the American Medical Association* 212 (June 1970): 1661.

D'Emilio, John. *Sexual Politics, Sexual Communities: The Making of a Homosexual Minority in the United States, 1940–1970.* Chicago: University of Chicago Press, 1983.

Doctors, Samuel I., and A. S. Huff. *Minority Enterprise and the President's Council.* Cambridge, Mass.: Ballinger, 1973.

Doss, David. "Becoming Visible: The Dorian Society of Seattle and the Emergence of Seattle's Gay Community." Undergraduate research paper, Seattle University, 1994.

Elliott, Eugene. *A History of Variety-Vaudeville in Seattle: From the Beginning to 1914.* Seattle: University of Washington Press, 1944.

Faderman, Lillian. *Odd Girls and Twilight Lovers.* New York: Columbia University Press, 1991.

Farley, Kristi. *A Primer: Preservation in Seattle.* Seattle: City of Seattle, 1977.

Farmer, Frances. *Will There Really Be a Morning.* New York: Dell Books, 1972.

Ford, Mary Ellen. "A History of Lobotomy in the United States." *The Pharos* (Summer 1987): 7–16.

Freeman, Walter, and James Watt. *Psychosurgery in the Treatment of Mental Disorders and Intractable Pain.* Springfield, Ill.: Charles C. Thomas, 1950.

———. "Transorbital Lobotomy." *American Journal of Psychiatry* 105 (April 1949): 734.

———."Level of Achievement after Lobotomy: A Study of One Thousand Cases." *American Journal of Psychiatry* 110 (1953): 269–76.

———. "Lobotomy in Limbo?" *American Journal of Psychiatry* 128 (April 1972): 1315.

———. "Sexual Behavior and Fertility after Frontal Lobotomy." *Journal of Biological Psychiatry* 6, no. 1 (February 1973): 100.

Friedman, Laurence. *A History of American Law.* New York: Simon and Schuster, 1985.

Gill, John. *Gill's Dictionary of the Chinook Jargon.* Portland, Oreg.: J. K. Gill Company, 1909, reprinted in 1989 by the Muckleshoot Indian Tribe and White River Valley Historical Society.

Hadden, Samuel. "Newer Treatment Techniques for Homosexuality." *Archives of Environmental Health* 13 (September 1966): 284.

Haggerty, Patrick. "The Oppression of the American Male Homosexual: A View by a Homosexual Social Worker." M.S.W. thesis, University of Washington School of Social Work, 1972.

Hanna, Judith Lynne. *To Dance Is Human: A Theory of Nonverbal Communication.* Austin: University of Texas Press, 1979.

Hansen, Kent. "Gaylord v. Tacoma School District No. 10: Homosexuality Held Immoral for Purposes of Teacher Discharge," *Willamette Law Journal* 14 (1977): 101–14.

Hawley, Lowell S., and Ralph B. Potts. *Counsel for the Damned.* New York: J. B. Lippincott, 1953.

Hoagland, Sarah Lucia, and Julia Penelope, eds. *For Lesbians Only: A Separatist Anthology.* London: Onlywomen, 1988.

Jones, Charles, and James Shanklin. "Transorbital Lobotomy." *Northwest Medicine* 47, no. 6 (June 1948): 421–27.

Jones, Nard. *Seattle.* New York: Doubleday, 1972.

Klein, Charna. *Counseling Our Own: The Lesbian/Gay Subculture Meets the Mental Health System.* Seattle: Publication Services, 1986.

Light, Ivan. "Ethnicity and Business Enterprise." In *Making It in America: The Role of Ethnicity in Business Enterprise, Education, and Work Choices.* M. M. Stolarik and Murray Friedman, eds. Lewisburg, Penn.: Bucknell University Press, 1986.

Marcus, Eric. *Making History: The Struggle for Gay and Lesbian Equal Rights, 1945–1990.* New York: HarperCollins, 1992.

Martin, Del, and Phyllis Lyon, *Lesbian/Woman.* San Francisco: Glide Publications, 1972.

McLean, Albert Jr. *American Vaudeville As Ritual.* Lexington: University of Kentucky Press, 1965.

Morgan, Murray. *Skid Road: An Informal Portrait of Seattle.* New York: Viking Press, 1960.

Newton, Esther. *Mother Camp: Female Impersonators in America.* Englewood Cliffs, N.J.: Prentice Hall, 1972.

Paulson, Don, and Roger Simpson. *An Evening at the Garden of Allah.* New York: Columbia University Press, 1996.

Peavy, Linda, and Ursula Smith. *Women in Waiting in the Western Movement.* Norman: University of Oklahoma Press, 1994.

Rayside, David. "American Exceptionalism in Sexual Diversity Politics: A Washington State Case Study." Paper presented to the American Political Science Association, August–September 2000.

Rosenstein, Sophie, Larrae Haydon, and Wilbur Sparrow. *Modern Acting: A Manual.* New York: Samuel French, 1936.

Sachs, Curt. *World History of the Dance.* London: George Allen and Unwin, 1938.

Sale, Roger. *Seattle: Past to Present.* Seattle: University of Washington Press, 1976.

Samuels, Charles and Louise. *Once upon a Stage: The Merry World of Vaudeville.* New York: Dodd and Mead, 1974.

Schoenberg, Wilfred P. *A History of the Catholic Church in the Pacific Northwest, 1743–1983.* Washington, D.C.: The Pastoral Press, 1987.

Schwantes, Carlos. *The Pacific Northwest: An Interpretive History.* Lincoln: University of Nebraska Press, 1989.

Seattle Convention and Visitors Bureau. "Let Us Show You Pioneer Square." Seattle: Seattle Convention and Visitors Bureau, 1976.

Shaw, George C. *The Chinook Jargon and How to Use It.* Seattle: Rainier Printing Company, 1909.

Shilts, Randy. *And the Band Played On.* New York: St. Martin's, 1987.

Soden, Dale. *The Reverend Mark Matthews: An Activist in the Progressive Era.* Seattle: University of Washington Press, 2001.

Spiedel, William. *Sons of the Profits.* Seattle: Nettle Creek Publishing, 1967.

Steinbrueck, Victor. *Architectural and Historical Survey of Pioneer Square.* Seattle: City of Seattle, 1969.

Szasz, Thomas. *The Manufacture of Madness.* New York: Harper and Row, 1970.

Taubman, Howard. *The Making of American Theater.* New York: Coward-McCann, 1967.

Thomas, Edward H. *Chinook: A History and Dictionary.* Portland, Oreg.: Binfords and Mort, 1935. Third ed., 1970.

Weinberger, Laurence. "Lobotomy: A Personal Memoir." *The Pharos* (Spring 1988): 17–18.

Williams, Walter. *The Spirit and the Flesh: Sexual Diversity in American Indian Culture.* Boston: Beacon Press, 1992.

Winthrop, Theodore. *Canoe and Saddle.* Portland, Oreg.: Binfords and Mort, 1956. Originally published by Ticknor and Fields, 1862.

# INDEX

psychiatric treatment of homosexuality, 35–37, 69, 108, 170–71. *See also* American Psychiatric Association; Cachero, Jackie; Farmer, Frances; Freeman, Walter; Seattle Counseling Service for Sexual Minorities; Western State Hospital

Quakers, 378
Queen City Business Guild, 84, 260–61
Quinn, John, 290, 292

Radical Women: begun, 142–43; Freeway Hall painting, 147–48; mentioned, 231, 241, 265, 334
Raible, Peter, 197
Ramey, Michael, 113
Ramon, Frank, 89–94, 99, 181, 193
Rankin, Rick, 376
Ratcliffe, Jean, 45, 50
Ratzinger, Joseph, 286–87, 291–92, 363–64
Ray, Dixy Lee, 214
Raye, Robin, 64
Raymond, Dennis, 244–45
Red and Black Bookstore, 140, 145
Reese, Jerry, 240
Reid, Frank, 62
Rhinehart, Keith: and Aquarian Church, 85–86; arrested, 87–88; testimony to Seattle City Council, 96–97; trial proceedings, 95–96, 102–3; at Walla Walla penitentiary, 218–220; wins appeal, 220–21
Rice, Norm, 254, 256, 336, 358
Richards, Tom, 299, 301
Rietschel, Jean, 374
Rinehart, Nita, 365
Rise n' Shine, 333
Ritchey, William, 176
Riveland, Charles, 375
Robert Wood Johnson Foundation,

320, 338. *See also* AIDS: financing of response to
Roche, Pat, 364
Roddenberry, Lowell, 344
Rodney, John A., 252–53
Roe, Rebecca, 327–30, 375. *See also* Farmer, Steven
Rohan, Robert, 309
Romano, Albert, 71
Rosehedge House, 336. *See also* AIDS: housing people with
Rosenstein, Sophie, 39
Royce, James, 279
Royer, Charles, 233, 245–46, 251–52, 353
Ryan, Michael, 290, 362, 370–72

St. James Cathedral, 275, 285, 349, 362–63, 370–72
St. Joseph's Church, 283, 290, 293, 317, 379
saloons: opposition to, 28, 32, 55; value to gays/lesbians, 55–56, 58–59
Salvation Army, 205
Sappho's, 84
Save Our Moral Ethics (SOME), 243, 245–47
Schauermann, Michael, 345, 349
Schell, Paul, 240
Schuster, Sandra, 151–55
Schwartz, Pepper, 238, 240
Schwiesow, Anne, 133, 137
Seattle AIDS Support Group, 302, 320, 339
Seattle City Council: adoption of antidiscrimination ordinances, 202–5, 209, 212, 224–25, 376–77; licensing gay establishments, 96–99
Seattle Committee Against Thirteen (SCAT): created, 242; fundraising of, 255; mentioned, 258, 374; strategy of, 244–45, 247, 255; victory of, 255, 257. *See also* Initiative Thirteen
Seattle Counseling Service for Sexual Minorities: early success, 158–61;